Rights-Based Constitutional Review

STUDIES IN COMPARATIVE LAW AND LEGAL CULTURE

In today's shrinking world it's important to extend our horizons and increase our knowledge of other people's laws. This series publishes in-depth volumes covering various aspects of private and public law in diverse legal traditions. Additionally, it seeks to encourage improved techniques and methods of comparative legal research, including the use of interdisciplinary studies. Individual volumes may deal with the law and culture not merely of well-known and frequently studied countries, but also with lesser-known, mixed, religious, and plural systems of the world. The focus ranges from important aspects of legal history, culture, and institutions to local experience and evolving legal trends.

Titles in the series include:

Order from Transfer
Comparative Constitutional Design and Legal Culture
Edited by Günter Frankenberg

Corruption and Conflicts of Interest
A Comparative Law Approach
Edited by Jean-Bernard Auby, Emmanuel Breen and Thomas Perroud

Legal Innovations in Asia
Judicial Lawmaking and the Influence of Comparative Law
Edited by John O. Haley and Toshiko Takenaka

Rights-Based Constitutional Review
Constitutional Courts in a Changing Landscape
Edited by John Bell and Marie-Luce Paris

Rights-Based Constitutional Review

Constitutional Courts in a Changing Landscape

Edited by

John Bell

Professor of Law, University of Cambridge, UK

Marie-Luce Paris

Lecturer in Law, University College Dublin, Ireland

STUDIES IN COMPARATIVE LAW AND LEGAL CULTURE

Edward Elgar PUBLISHING

Cheltenham, UK • Northampton, MA, USA

Published by
Edward Elgar Publishing Limited
The Lypiatts
15 Lansdown Road
Cheltenham
Glos GL50 2JA
UK

Edward Elgar Publishing, Inc.
William Pratt House
9 Dewey Court
Northampton
Massachusetts 01060
USA

A catalogue record for this book
is available from the British Library

Library of Congress Control Number: 2015957871

This book is available electronically in the **Elgar**online
Law subject collection
DOI 10.4337/9781784717612

MIX
Paper from responsible sources
FSC® C013604

ISBN 978 1 78471 760 5 (cased)
ISBN 978 1 78471 761 2 (eBook)

Typeset by Columns Design XML Ltd, Reading
Printed and bound by CPI Group (UK) Ltd, Croydon, CR0 4YY

Contents

Contributors

John Bell is Professor of Law at the University of Cambridge. He teaches and researches in comparative law in Europe, particularly in French law. His recent publications include *European Legal Development: The Case of Tort* (with David Ibbetson, 2012). Previous publications have included *Judiciaries within Europe* (2006), and books on French constitutional and administrative law. He has also written on comparative law methodology and on the liability of public authorities. He is editor of the *Cambridge Law Journal.*

Eoin Carolan is Senior Lecturer in Law at University College Dublin Sutherland School of Law with research interests in constitutional law, administrative law and comparative public law. He has authored or co-authored a number of publications, including *The Right to Privacy: A Doctrinal and Comparative Analysis* (2008), *The Irish Constitution: Governance and Values* (2008), *The New Separation of Powers: A Theory for the Modern State* (2009), *Media Law in Ireland* (2010), and *The Constitution of Ireland: Perspectives and Prospects* (2012). His work on *The New Separation of Powers* was shortlisted for the Society of Legal Scholars' Peter Birks Prize in 2010, and won the Kevin Boyle Prize for Outstanding Legal Scholarship in 2011.

Chintan Chandrachud is a PhD Candidate at Sidney Sussex College, University of Cambridge and Chairperson of the Cambridge Pro Bono Project. He holds a BCL and MPhil from the University of Oxford and an LLB from the Government Law College, Mumbai. His recent publications include: 'Declarations of Unconstitutionality in India and the UK: Comparing the Space for Political Response' (*Georgia Journal of International and Comparative Law*, 2015); 'Interpretation' (Choudhry et al, *The Oxford Handbook on Indian Constitutional Law*, 2015); 'Reconfiguring the Discourse on Political Responses to Declarations of Incompatibility' (2014); 'International Humanitarian Law in Indian Courts: Application, Misapplication and Non-application' (Jinks et al, *Applying International Humanitarian Law in Judicial and Quasi Judicial Bodies*, 2014).

Aileen Kavanagh is Associate Professor of Law and Fellow of St Edmund Hall at the University of Oxford. She has written widely on questions concerning human rights, constitutional law and constitutional theory. Her book *Constitutional Review under the UK Human Rights 1998* (2009) was shortlisted for the Peter Birks Prize for Outstanding Legal Scholarship.

Cliona Kelly is Lecturer in Law at University College Dublin Sutherland School of Law, having previously taught at Cardiff University and National University of Ireland Galway. She completed her PhD as an Irish Research Council Scholar in 2006. Since then she has developed her research reputation in contract law and has worked with the Irish Law Reform Commission and as a member of the *Common Core of European Private Law* project hosted by the University of Trento. She was invited to join the Irish Government's Advisory Group on a new Consumer Rights Bill. Her research interests also include the process of incorporation of the European Convention on Human Rights in Ireland and the impact of Europe on national legal regimes and she is the co-author of *European Convention on Human Rights Act: Operation, Impact and Analysis* (with Fiona de Londras, 2010).

Juha Lavapuro is Professor of Law at the Faculty of Law of the University of Turku. He teaches and researches constitutional law and theory, in particular questions regarding constitutional review and the domestic status of international human rights. Recent publications include several law review articles, book chapters as well as an award-winning monograph on new constitutional review in Finland (2010). He is an expert member of the multidisciplinary research network FRANET of the European Union Agency for Fundamental Rights, member of the National Discrimination Tribunal of Finland, and a repeatedly heard constitutional law expert of the Constitutional Law Committee of the Finnish Parliament.

Tuomas Ojanen is Professor of Constitutional Law at the University of Helsinki and part-time Professor at the European University Institute in Florence within the SURVEILLE project. He is also Chair of the Non-Discrimination and Equality Tribunal of Finland and Director of the LOSS Research Consortium (LOSS: Laws of Surveillance and Security: Constitutional Limits, Legislative Discourses and Transnational Influences) funded by the Academy of Finland. He is regularly heard as an expert by the Constitutional Law Committee of the Finnish Parliament. His main areas of research and expertise include Finnish constitutional law, international human rights law and constitutional law of the European Union. His recent publications include several articles on various human rights issues in counter-terrorism activities, privacy and data protection, and the impact of European integration on Finnish constitutional law and legal order in general.

Marie-Luce Paris is Lecturer in Law at University College Dublin Sutherland School of Law. She is a graduate from Université Paris II Panthéon-Assas (France). She is also a qualified barrister-at-law from the *Ecole D'Avocats Du Barreau De La Cour D'Appel De Paris*. Her research interests are in European human rights law, European Union law and comparative law. She has widely published in these fields in, among others, the *Yearbook of European Law*, the *German Law Journal*, the *Irish Journal of European Law*, the *Irish Jurist* and the *Revue Internationale De Droit Comparé*. Her recent publications include law review articles and book chapters on issues of comparative constitutional law. She has also an interest in legal education. She has held research visiting positions at the University of California, Davis School of Law and the Australian National University Centre for European Studies, and worked for the European Commission as a TAIEX expert in EU institutional and constitutional law. She is currently the Academic Director of International Cooperation.

Paolo Passaglia is Associate Professor of Public Comparative Law at the University of Pisa and Coordinator of the Comparative Law Area of the Studies and Research Department of the Italian Constitutional Court. He has written books on the formal invalidity of legislative acts in Italy and France (L'invalidità procedurale dell'atto legislativo. Le esperienze italiana e francese a confronto, Torino, Giappichelli, 2002, XII–653), the French constitutional tradition (La Costituzione dinamica. Quinta Repubblica e tradizione costituzionale francese, Torino, Giappichelli, 2008, XI–313), interactions between the legislator and the Constitutional Court in Italy (Le juge constitutionnel et le législateur. L'expérience italienne, 2011), and the abolition of the death penalty in a comparative perspective (L'abolition de la peine de mort. Une étude comparée, 2012). He has also written several articles on different fields of constitutional and comparative law: his main articles deal with the French and Canadian systems of constitutional justice, the entry into force of enacted law, the organization of the French Constitutional Council and the Italian Constitutional Court, the Canadian Senate, the EU Parliament, the interactions between the Italian State and Regions, the interactions between the Italian Constitutional Court and European supranational courts, the right to access

Internet in comparative law, the impact of the judgments of Constitutional and Supreme Courts in Western countries, the use of comparative law by courts, and voting secrecy.

Agustín Ruiz Robledo is Professor of Constitutional Law at the University of Granada. He is the author of more than 100 publications in this field, including books on the Spanish constitutional system and books and articles on the federal state, the most recent of which is 'The Spanish Constitution in the Turmoil of the Global Financial Crisis' (in Xenophon Contiades, *Constitutions in the Global Financial Crisis: A Comparative Analysis*, 2013). He has combined his teaching work with other legal activities; he was a supplementary Magistrate in the Provincial High Court of Granada (1988–91), and has been Director of the Analysis Advisory Council of the Presidency of the Andalusian Parliament (1996–2004). He has taken part in a considerable number of national and international conferences, speaking on his special topics, especially in the constituent assemblies of Bolivia and Nepal. In addition, he is a regular contributor to the radio and the newspaper El País.

Michel Rosenfeld is University Professor of Law and Comparative Democracy and Justice Sydney L Robins Professor of Human Rights at the Benjamin N Cardozo School of Law of Yeshiva University in New York City. He is also Director of the Cardozo Program on Global and Comparative Legal Theory. He was the President of the International Association of Constitutional Law (1999–2004) and the founding Editor-in-Chief of the *International Journal of Constitutional Law* (2001–14). His recent publications include: *The Identity of the Constitutional Subject: Selfhood, Citizenship, Culture and Community* (2010); *Law, Justice, Democracy and the Clash of Cultures: A Pluralist Account* (2011); *The Oxford Handbook of Comparative Constitutional Law* (co-edited with András Sajó, 2012); and *Constitutional Secularism in an Age of Religious Revival* (co-edited with Susanna Mancini, 2014). He has lectured worldwide and held the Chaim Perelman Chair in Legal Philosophy at the Free University in Brussels in 2011; The Distinguished Fulbright-Tocqueville Chair at the University of Paris I (Panthéon-Sorbonne) in 2013; and was a Leverhulme Visiting Professor at the University of London, Birkbeck College of Law in 2014.

Martin Scheinin is Professor of International Law and Human Rights and the Dean of Graduate Studies at the European University Institute in Florence. His scholarship ranges from Finnish and comparative constitutional law to international human rights law and public international law. In 1993–98, he was Professor of Constitutional Law at the University of Helsinki where he also received his doctorate in 1991. He participated in the drafting of the fundamental rights chapter in the Finnish Constitution as one of the secretaries of the drafting commission in 1989–92. In 1998–2008, he was Professor of Constitutional and International Law and Director of the Institute for Human Rights at Åbo Akademi University in Turku, Finland. In 1997–2004 he was a member of the UN Human Rights Committee, the treaty body acting under the Covenant on Civil and Political Rights. In 2005, he was appointed as the first UN Special Rapporteur on human rights and counter-terrorism, a position of trust he held until July 2011. In his academic work he has also dealt with issues related to human rights and counter-terrorism, including, in 2012–15, as the leader of the EU-funded research project SURVEILLE that assessed surveillance technologies from the perspectives of effectiveness, efficiency, ethics and fundamental rights. He served three terms on the Executive Committee of the International Association of Constitutional Law, including in 2010–14 as President of the Association.

James Stellios is Associate Professor of Law at the Australian National University College of Law and Director of the Centre for International and Public Law. His primary research interest is constitutional law, particularly the operation of the federal judicial system in Australia. He has written extensively on the constitutional obstacles to the effective operation of statutory human rights models in Australia. He is the author of a leading book on the federal judicial system: *The Federal Judicature: Chapter III of the Constitution* (2010). He is also the author of the sixth edition of Professor Leslie Zines's classic work, *The High Court and the Constitution* (2015) and is co-author of *The Constitution of the Commonwealth of Australia: History, Principle and Interpretation* (with Nicholas Aroney, Peter Gerangelos and Sarah Murray, 2015). He is also a practicing barrister at the New South Wales Bar and has appeared in a number of constitutional cases.

Renáta Uitz is Professor of Law and Chair of the Comparative Constitutional Law Programme at the Department of Legal Studies, Central European University, Budapest. At the centre of her research interests are theories and practices of good government in and after transition to democracy, questions of personal autonomy and equality, including religious liberty and LGBT rights. She is the author of *Constitutions, Courts and History* (2004) and *Freedom of Religion in European Constitutional and International Case Law* (2007). More recently, she edited *Arguments that Work: Strategies, Contexts and Limits in Constitutional Law* (2013); *Religion in the Public Square: Perspectives on Secularism* (2014); *Freedom and Its Enemies: The Tragedy of Liberty* (2015).

Marc Verdussen is Professor of Constitutional Law at the University of Louvain (UCL). He teaches constitutional law, comparative constitutional law and constitutional justice. He is a member of the Research Center on State and Constitution (CRECO), which is a branch of the Institute for Interdisciplinary Research in Legal Sciences of UCL (Institute JUR-I). He is also Senior Adviser to the President of UCL and President of the Research Ethics Commission of UCL. He actively works with several public law research centres around the world. He was visiting scholar at the Law School of the University of Berkeley and invited professor at the University of Ottawa, at the University of Szeged, at the University of Liège, at the University of Aix-Marseille and at the University of Lille. On many occasions, he has been in charge of scientific reports and lectures for international conferences and meetings. He was regularly an expert before the Belgian Federal Parliament and for governmental departments. He is the author and editor of numerous publications. He is sub-editor of the *Revue Belge De Droit Constitutionnel* and member of the Editorial Board of several scientific journals, in Belgium, Canada, Greece and Spain.

Matthew Zagor is Associate Professor of Law at the Australian National University College of Law and Adjunct Fellow at the ANU Centre for European Studies. He teaches and writes in the areas of international refugee and human rights law, comparative constitutional law, judicial rhetoric, and public law theory, and is senior co-editor of the Federal Law Review. From 2010–11, he directed the law programme at the ANU Centre for European Studies as its inaugural Deputy Director. He has also held visiting fellowships at the London School of Economics' Centre for Human Rights and Society, and the University of Grenoble's Centre for International Security and European Cooperation (CESICE). Prior to joining academia, he worked as a refugee and human rights advocate for international NGOs, a legal aid solicitor representing asylum seekers, a senior legal officer at the Attorney-General's Department's Native Title Division, and a member on the Migration Review Tribunal/Refugee Review Tribunal. He remains involved in law reform initiatives at the domestic and international levels, currently sitting on the National Committee of Australian Lawyers for Human Rights, the ACT International Humanitarian Law Committee of Australian Red Cross, and the Australian Chapter of the Cluster Munitions Coalition.

Preface and acknowledgements

GENESIS OF THE BOOK

'Rights-Based Constitutional Review' is based on the contributions originally presented at the Annual Seminar of the Society of Legal Scholars (SLS) held in Dublin in July 2013, organized by Marie-Luce Paris. The SLS is the oldest and largest society in the field of legal scholarship in the United Kingdom and Ireland. Its aim is to advance legal research and legal education. The strength of the SLS, which covers all areas of law, allows for the organization and funding of ambitious projects, often of comparative nature. The theme of the Seminar naturally emerged from the observation of the significant developments that several legal systems have experienced in seeking to adapt review mechanisms to a better constitutional protection of rights. These developments have taken different forms – whether as acts of incorporation of the European Convention on Human Rights (ECHR) in, for example, the UK with the Human Rights Act 1998 or Ireland with the European Convention on Human Rights Act 2003, or as incorporation of bills of rights in a non-European context such as, for example, the 2004 Australian Capital Territory Human Rights Act and the 2006 Victoria Charter of Human Rights and Responsibilities in Australia; these developments have also taken the form of constitutional revisions enhancing systems of constitutional review in, for example, Belgium and France with increased review powers vested in the Belgium's Constitutional Court and the French Constitutional Council. The idea of furthering the discussion on the evergreen topic of constitutional review of legislation driven by the protection of fundamental rights was well received. Invited contributors and participants embraced the idea of joining an increasing body of events and publications in this particular field of comparative legal studies. The organizer of the SLS Seminar (and second author of these lines) has a special interest in the study of several of these legal systems. The British legal system was the object of her doctoral thesis dealing with the implementation of the ECHR in the UK; the Irish legal system was the topic of her dissertation presented at the Academy of

European Public Law and is part of her ongoing research; research on the Australian legal system was undertaken during her fellowship at the ANU Centre for European Studies of the Australian National University; her current research projects are about French constitutional law, and constitutional review in particular.

The Seminar was organized on the basis of targeted invitations to leading scholars in constitutional law and/or international and European human rights law. The Seminar led to inspiring and provocative discussions. Contributors then returned to their comparative studies with insightful feedback from their peers and participants. They were invited to finalize their chapters on the basis of a common template divided into two main parts, namely the evolution of rights-based constitutional review and the endurance of rights-based constitutional review – although some contributors departed from this structure. The common issue examined is how the existing system of constitutional review has evolved, from an institutional, procedural and substantial point of view, in its efforts to increase the efficiency of the politico-legal system of rights protection. The issue indeed deserves continuing analysis – even from the dominant perspective of liberal-western constitutionalism – in light of the challenges posed to the development of constitutional justice in the domestic and international context. An interesting feature of the chapters is the way in which the 'civil law/common law' distinction does not capture the main differences in approach to the protection of fundamental rights. Whatever may be true of the heartlands of private law, fundamental rights (and especially their constitutional protection) respond to traditions and contemporary imperatives which are more complex and diverse than anything captured by the common law/civil law distinction.

ACKNOWLEDGEMENTS

Bringing a wide range of experts together, not only from Ireland, the UK and continental Europe, but also from the US and Australia, to examine such a vivid topic is no mean feat. We are immensely grateful to the SLS for providing the very generous funding and support which made the realization of this project possible at the 2013 edition of their Annual Seminar. We particularly thank the SLS Research Sub-Committee for their sponsorship award. This was the first time that the SLS Annual Seminar had been held outside the UK. Thanks also go to the UCD Constitutional Studies Group for their complementary sponsorship and particularly to Eoin Carolan for his continuing support as Academic

Director of the Group. We also warmly thank all the participants, particularly Professor David Feldman, Professor Christopher McCrudden and Professor Hector McQueen, for their enthusiasm and challenging questions which contributed to a much lively debate on many issues. Our appreciations also go to colleagues in the UCD Sutherland School of Law, in particular Professor Colin Scott, Professor Imelda Maher, Suzanne Egan, and John O'Dowd for the various ways in which they supported the event.

The book itself is the culmination of considerable efforts and our first appreciations go to the contributors who have brought so much work and sharpness in their analysis, and contributed with their reciprocated comments to improve the chapters of fellow contributors. We are particularly grateful to Professor Michel Rosenfeld for accepting the invitation to deliver the keynote speech on the US system of rights-based review and whose thought-provoking piece on US exceptionalism features as the first country study.

We would like to express our sincere thanks to the publishing team at Edward Elgar Publishing, in particular to John-Paul McDonald, Iram Satti and Victoria Litherland for their patience, support and precious advice along the process.

John Bell and Marie-Luce Paris
Cambridge, Dublin, July 2015

Journal abbreviations

Adel L Rev	Adelaide Law Review (Australia)
AJ Admin L	Australian Journal of Administrative Law (Australia)
AJIL	American Journal of International Law (US)
ALJ	Australian Law Journal (Australia)
Am J Comp L	American Journal of Comparative Law (US)
Am L Rev	American Law Review (US)
Aust Bar Rev	Australian Bar Review (Australia)
Canberra Bull Pub Admin	Canberra Bulletin of Public Administration (Australia)
Cardozo L Rev	Cardozo Law Review (US)
CLJ	Cambridge Law Journal (UK)
CLP	Current Legal Problems (UK)
CML Rev	Common Market Law Review (EU)
Common Law World Rev	Common Law World Review (Common Law)
Con Law Pol Rev	Constitutional Law and Policy Review (Australia)
Deakin LR	Deakin Law Review (Australia)
Duke J Comp & Intl L	Duke Journal of Comparative and International Law (US)
DULJ	Dublin University Law Journal (Ireland)
EHRLR	European Human Rights Law Review (UK)
ELJ	European Law Journal (EU)
EPL	European Public Law (EU)
EUConst	European Constitutional Law Review (EU)
FL Rev	Federal Law Review (Australia)
Georgia J of Intl & Comp L	Georgia Journal of International and Comparative Law (US)

Harv L Rev	Harvard Law Review (US)
HRLJ	Human Rights Law Journal (Germany)
HRLR	Human Rights Law Review (UK)
ICLQ	International and Comparative Law Quarterly (UK)
Ind LJ	Indiana Law Journal (US)
Intl J Cons L	International Journal of Constitutional Law (US)
JR	Judicial Review (UK)
KCLJ	King's College Law Journal (UK)
LQR	Law Quarterly Review (UK)
LS	Legal Studies (US)
Mich L Rev	Michigan Law Review (US)
MLR	The Modern Law Review (UK)
MULR	Melbourne University Law Review (Australia)
OJLS	Oxford Journal of Legal Studies (UK)
Osgoode Hall LJ	Osgoode Hall Law Journal (Canada)
PL	Public Law (UK)
PLR	Public Law Review (Australia)
Res Jud	Res Judicatae (Australia)
Stat LR	Statute Law Review (UK)
Sup Ct L Rev	Supreme Court Law Review (Canada)
Syd LR	Sydney Law Review (Australia)
Temp Pol & Civ Rts L Rev	Temple Political and Civil Rights Law Review (US)
Touro L Rev	Touro Law Review (US)
UNSWLJ	University of New South Wales Law Journal (Australia)
U Tas LR	University of Tasmania Law Review (Australia)
UTLJ	University of Toronto Law Journal (Canada)
Wake Forest L Rev	Wake Forest Law Review (US)
Yale LJ	Yale Law Journal (US)
YEL	Yearbook of European Law (EU)

Setting the scene: elements of constitutional theory and methodology of the research

Marie-Luce Paris

1. FOCUS OF THE STUDY

This book examines the broad issue of constitutional review in the context of rights litigation. The topic has proved to be of continuous academic, legal, political and societal significance not only because of the prominence acquired by constitutional review but also because of the continuing changes which subject its operation to new parameters in a number of legal systems. The growth of constitutional review of legislation driven by the protection of fundamental rights has indeed been, and continues to be, at the heart of comparative legal analysis.[1] This is particularly salient in light of recent developments seeking to adapt review mechanisms to better constitutional protection of rights. These developments, which have occurred in several countries, have taken different forms – whether as acts of incorporation of the European Convention on Human Rights (ECHR) such as, for example, the enactment of the Human Rights Act 1998 in the United Kingdom (HRA) or the enactment of the European Convention on Human Rights Act 2003 (ECHR Act) in Ireland, or as incorporation of bills of rights in a non-European context such as, for example, the 2004 Australian Capital

---

[1] See, among other comparative works, Gerhard Van der Schyff, *Judicial Review of Legislation: A Comparative Study of the United Kingdom, the Netherlands and South Africa* (Ius Gentium 2010); Allan R Brewer-Carías, *Constitutional Courts as Positive Legislators: A Comparative Law Study* (CUP 2011), Maartje de Visser, *Constitutional Review in Europe: A Comparative Analysis* (Hart 2013); Wojciech Sadurski, *Rights Before Courts: A Study of Constitutional Courts in Postcommunist States of Central and Eastern Europe* (Springer 2014); Laurence Gay (ed.), *La Question Prioritaire de Constitutionnalité: Approche de Droit Comparé* (Bruylant 2014).

Territory Human Rights Act and the 2006 Victoria Charter of Human Rights and Responsibilities in Australia; these developments have also taken the form of constitutional revisions enhancing review systems such as, for example, the introduction in 2003 of new review powers vested in the Belgian Constitutional Court, and in 2008 of those new powers of review of promulgated laws vested in the French Constitutional Council.

The approach taken in this volume is multi-jurisdictional and allows authors of the ten different legal systems represented to present an in-depth analysis of major issues and recent developments in rights-based constitutional review while engaging with general theories of constitutionalism. In its treatment of the national situation, each contribution addresses issues of constitutional design relating to the relevant model of constitutional review as well as issues of constitutional adjudication that pertain to the role of the constitutional court. This collection of country studies aims at increasing knowledge of the laws of these jurisdictions, through elements of legal history, institutional features and evolving legal trends. It also puts in perspective constitutional review practices of well-known and frequently studied countries with lesser-studied countries. In that sense this book addresses a gap in the literature by focusing on one of the most challenging role of constitutional courts and its evolution in recent years in a selection of typical and atypical common law and civil law countries. The collection thus naturally finds its place within the Studies in Comparative Law and Legal Culture Series. In order to help the reader orientate herself throughout the book, the next paragraphs will further explain the themes developed, as well as the methodological approach adopted.

1.1 Prominence of Constitutional Review: A Constitutional 'Acquis'?

There is certainly a triumph of constitutional review which is 'now generally accepted as an essential or desirable feature of a liberal constitutional democracy' and has become a 'global phenomenon'.[2] This widespread device can be shortly defined as the power of a court to determine the constitutionality of legislation enacted by Parliament, as a

[2] See Albert HY Chen and Miguel Poiares Maduro, 'The Judiciary and Constitutional Review' in Mark Tushnet, Thomas Fleiner and Cheryl Saunders, *Routledge Handbook of Constitutional Law* (Routledge 2013) 100–101; Mark Tushnet, *Advanced Introduction to Comparative Constitutional Law* (Edward Elgar Publishing 2014) 41. See also C Neal Tate, 'Why the Expansion of of Judicial Power?' in C Neal Tate and others (eds), *The Global Expansion of Judicial Power* (New York UP 1995) 27.

means to check and limit the exercise of power by those in charge. Usually known as judicial review in the United States, it is also referred to, in the context civil law jurisdictions, as judicial control of constitutionality. On a comparative global scale, it appears that this point of terminology has been settled and most comparative constitutional law scholars now use indifferently constitutional review when referring to the US, European (including British) or other legal systems's practice.[3]

At core an intrument of efficacy,[4] constitutional review requires the setting up of an institution – a constitutional court[5] – or rather this particular role performed by the constitutional court materializes the effectiveness of the normative constitution, that is the fact that the rules contained in the Constitution are put into practice and that the whole political system works properly. A powerful constitutional court would typically have three main functions and, in addition to ensuring the normative force of the Constitution, it would be entrusted with the task of resolving conflicts between the state and territorial powers, and guaranteeing the fundamental rights of citizens. This deliberate choice of institutional design – the US system differing in that respect – with a constitutional court facing the other branches of political power, has gone with a great deal of debate primarily aimed at justifying the idea of constitutional review. Two arguments typically justify the right for judges to declare laws unconstitutional: one is that it guarantees the supremacy

---

[3] Tushnet (n 2) 40.

[4] According to the explanation given by Kokott and Kaspar, 'constitutional efficacy' describes and measures if methods used to secure constitutional rights and rules – that is the set of control mechanisms, such as constitutional review, which limit the arbitrary discretion of those in power, especially when it comes to guarantee civil liberties – are successful. They contrast it with 'constitutional efficiency' which is usually used to describe how smoothly government is able to function. See Julianne Kokott and Martin Kaspar 'Ensuring Constitutional Efficacy' in Michel Rosenfeld and András Sajó, *The Oxford Handbook on Comparative Constitutional Law* (OUP 2012) 796 and 805. See also Stone Sweet who refers to 'constitutional effectiveness' meaning that 'important constitutional disputes that arise in the polity are litigated, that the constitutional court seeks to resolve these disputes through defensible reasons, and that those governed by the constitutional law accept the court's case law as authoritative' (Alec Stone Sweet, 'The Politics of Constitutional Review in France and Europe' (2007) 5 *Intl J Cons* L 69, 76).

[5] In these developments, the term 'constitutional court' is used to refer to both Kelsenian type of courts (including atypical ones such as the French Constitutional Council) and supreme courts entrusted with constitutional competence, whether in a system of decentralized review such as the one in place in the US, or in an atypical system such as the one in Ireland.

of the constitution, and the other is that 'it provides a check on the lawmaker for the protection of minorities'.[6] It is not the place here to rehearse the historical roots of the establishment of constitutional review, nor the different features – abstract or concrete, ex ante or ex post – of its structure.[7] Suffice it to refer here to a schematic sequence of the different dimensions that have arisen as regards the establishment and practice of constitutional review. The first dimension is an existential one relating to the justification of the establishment of constitutional review – whether to have it or not – translated into the debate of whether to maintain the tenet of parliamentary sovereignty or to embrace judicial review of legislation as a constitutional principle; in other words, a debate about political constitutionalism versus legal constitutionalism. A second dimension involves a structural issue about the form of constitutional review – whether to use existing courts or not – as illustrated by the alternative between the US model and the European model of constitutional review, which both emerged as the result of very specific institutional and political circumstances with the former being the result of an early judicial move and the latter the product of conscious political design at a later stage. The third dimension is linked to the practice of constitutional review and revolves, in most contemporary Western liberal democracies which experience a well-developed system of constitutional justice, around the role of the constitutional court and its modus operandi (and modus vivendi) with the other parts of the institutional setup, namely the other domestic political powers, including ordinary courts, and international supranational courts – this is where we are at and is the main object of our reflection.

These dimensions, schematically presented here, deconstruct the underlying ever-debated question of the justification and legitimacy of constitutional review of legislation which has pervaded the theoretical discourse on the matter.[8] Phrased as the 'countermajoritarian difficulty' (mainly in the Anglo-American discourse), the main criticism directed at judicial review of legislation in general posits that the judiciary acts antidemocratically when, by way of review of legislative (or executive) acts, it substitutes its own policy preferences for those of the elected branches, and supercedes the more legitimate representative legislature in

---

[6] Aalt Willem Heringa and Philipp Kiiver, *An Introduction to Comparative Constitutional Law* (3rd edn, Intersentia 2009) 12.

[7] See Rosenfeld and Sajó (n 4); and Tushnet and others (n 2).

[8] See, among others, Jeremy Waldron, 'The Core of the Case Against Judicial Review' (2006) 115 *Yale LJ* 1346; Michel Troper, 'The Logic of Justification of Judicial Review' (2003) 1 *Intl J Cons* L 99.

determining and protecting constitutional rights. Country studies show the extent to which this criticism is addressed in the respective jurisdictions.

To conclude on this, the prominence of constitutional review in contemporary constitutionalism is arguably making the device appear as an 'acquis'. However, further reflection is needed on the many challenges that still transform its structure and operation even in stable democratic systems such as those selected in this collection.

1.2 Constitutional Design and Models of Constitutional Review

The two well-known models of constitutional review are the American model of decentralized review by ordinary courts, and the continental European model of centralized review by a specialized constitutional court. The US model emerged in the nineteenth century from the *Madison v Marbury* case[9] entailing several distinctive features, notably the diffusion of constitutional review through the judicial system performed by ordinary courts, and the triggering of constitutional review by a range of litigants. The alternative model is the result of a deliberate institutional choice based on Hans Kelsen's theory developed in the twentieth century. Conceived as a structure to resolve conflicts of power between the different authorities established under the constitution – and hence originally not concerned with the protection of human rights – constitutional review is, according to Kelsenian orthodoxy, envisaged as a special task concentrated in a centralized court placed outside the traditional structure of the judicial branch, and to which judicial access is limited. For reasons of deep political, judicial and cultural differences with the US, most Western European countries with a civil law system were unable, or reluctant, to adopt the American model.[10] So, while most of the civil law countries adopted the Kelsenian model, the US model was adopted by mostly common law countries.

This is obviously a very schematic comparative brush. If constitutional review can be regarded, as any other constitutional item, as a constitutional commodity,[11] the export of a particular model to other jurisdictions

---

9 *Marbury v Madison* 5 US 137 (1803) 178.

10 These reasons lie mainly in the approach to the separation of powers, the role of the judicial precedent, the authority and place of the ordinary civil law courts and the mentality of their judges. See Allan R Brewer-Carías, *Judicial Review in Comparative Law* (CUP 1989) 128–31.

11 Günter Frankenberg, *Order from Transfer: Comparative Constitutional Design and Legal Culture* (Edward Elgar Publishing 2013) 1.

does not, and cannot, mean its perfect replication. The design of a particular system of constitutional review did not indeed equate with a mere 'transplant' of one of the chosen models – US American or Kelsenian European. Most often, the original pattern was adapted to the particular jurisdiction inspired by it in light of its own contextual background. Not all countries have designed a working system of constitutional review for the same reasons, at the same time and at the same pace – some have not at all at present.[12] For instance, the Netherlands and New Zealand (not represented in this collection) are still committed to a system of parliamentary supremacy in the sense that the last word about an unconstitutional law belongs to Parliament and not the courts. It is correct though that some form of judicial review of legislation has been adopted in traditionally reluctant jurisdictions, such as New Zealand, which put in place a system akin to that of constitutional review with the adoption of its 1990 Bill of Rights – similarly to what the UK did with the HRA, but contrary to Australia, which has retained the traditional tenet of parliamentary sovereignty despite the adoption of sub-federal bills of rights. The Netherlands now seems to be the one country in Europe to lack a formal mechanism of constitutional review. Article 120 of its Constitution states that '[c]ourts shall not review the constitutionality of acts of Parliament and treaties [as opposed to other acts of public authorities]'.[13] The design of constitutional review is never a clear-cut choice though between an all judicially-based review system and a politically-based one. Most countries, while having in place a constitutional review system by courts, allow some kind of review of legislation by the legislature in the form of, for example, parliamentary committees with a review remit on constitutional rights matters such as

---

[12] According to Comella, 25 out of 27 (at the time of writing) EU member states possess some form of constitutional review. See Victor Ferreres Comella, *Constitutional Courts and Domestic Values: A European Perspective* (Yale UP 2009) 154. The Netherlands and the UK are counted as the exceptions in that book since they do not have a formal mechanism of constitutional review. Of these EU states, 21 have opted for exclusive centralized review, while there is a diffused constitutional review system on the American model in Denmark, Finland, Sweden and Switzerland. In 18 of these countries, this is ensured by a separate constitutional court, whereas in Ireland, Cyprus and Estonia, this is fulfilled by a supreme court.

[13] See Gerhard Van der Schyff and Anne Meuwese, 'Dutch Constitutional Law in a Globalizing World' (2013) 9 *Utrecht Law Review* 1. See also Juha Lavapuro, Tuomas Ojanen and Martin Scheinin in Chapter 5 of this collection on the example of Finland which retains a prohibition of judicial review.

the UK House of Lords Constitution Committee and the Joint Committee on Human Rights, or the Finnish Constitutional Law Committee.

In terms of the reasons for establishing constitutional review, most of the systems which associated it with the establishment of a constitutional court emerged as devices to democratize post-authoritarian regimes (for example, Germany, Spain and Italy), or to legitimize a newly independent regime (for example, Ireland) – but not all. France and Belgium offer examples of atypical reasons not linked to a country's dramatic transition: the French Constitutional Council was established for reasons of powers' supervision as a means to regulate the relationships between the government and Parliament, and primarily entrusted with the task of preventive review, whereas the Belgium Court of Arbitration – as it then was – was established in order to resolve conflicts linked to the country's federalization process. All too aware of the Anglo-Eurocentric approach adopted here, it remains clear that these observations refer to Western liberal democracies mainly. Countries currently under an authoritarian regime and a dominant party system, such as China for instance, have not yet developed a fully-fledged system of constitutional review, or have a much more limited understanding of it, despite growing scholarly interest in the field. Constitutional review is, in any case, not really supported by what appears to be, in the Chinese example, a perfunctory political inclination on the matter.[14]

Also, the adoption of a model of constitutional review does not necessarily follow the most obvious model attached to one particular legal family – that a common law jurisdiction would follow the US model, and that a civil law jurisdiction would follow the Kelsenian model. The absence of necessary connection between one model of constitutional review of legislation and one particular legal tradition is long acknowledged. As a matter of fact, 'the major variants of constitutional review – centralized or diffuse, abstract or concrete – [are] compatible with both civil and common law traditions'.[15] For example, some Latin America countries of civil law heritage adopted the US model, with more or less success. In any case, US constitutional review is hardly typical; it indeed follows from the exceptionalism of its design,

---

[14] See, for example, Xueyang Chen, 'Institutional Developments, Academic Debates and Legal Practices on the Constitutional Review in China : 2000–2013' (2014) 9 *Frontiers of Law in China* 636 ; Wang Wei, 'La Mise en Œuvre d'un Contrôle de Constitutionnalité en Chine' (2014) 98 *Revue Française de Droit Constitutionnel* 413.

[15] Brewer-Carías cited in Mark Tushnet, 'Introduction' in Tushnet and others (n 2) 1.

that is the US conception of the separation of powers, the limitation of the powers of the federal judiciary to the adjudication of concrete cases (or 'cases or controveries' cases), the rigidity of the constitutional amendment provision, and the particular approach to fundamental rights – that the US system stands apart not only from civil law countries but also from other common law countries.[16] Besides, in-depth historical analysis reveals much disagreement in a number of jurisdictions about the adoption of one model over the other, and when one was chosen, it was often with significant adaptations resulting in the adoption of a mixed system. This is the case in Italy, for example, where political parties looked at both the European and US models and then favoured a system which was not a straightforward version of the Kelsenian type but a hybrid version between a centralized and decentralized system.[17] This is also the case in common law countries such as Ireland which opted for a mixed system of judicial review of legislation drawing from a variety of comparative sources not limited to the US and British Westminster traditions.[18] The rooting of a structure of constitutional review is indeed a complex process of 'legal acculturation' which requires adaptation of many elements of not only legal but also political and socio-legal nature. As Kelsen put it at the time, '[i]t is impossible ... to propose a uniform solution for all possible constitutions: constitutional review will have to be organized according to the specific characteristics of each of them'.[19] There are thus many variants of constitutional review structures, arguably as many as legal systems, each one having adapted one or the other main theoretical model to its own constitutional environment.

The fact that most contemporary constitutions provide for constitutional review, whether designed to confer the power to a specialized court or to a generalist court, does not entail that it is effectively exercised. A working system of rights-based constitutional review means that it guarantees effectively individual rights within a particular constitutional context. However, this context has become increasinlgy intricate for constitutional courts especially due to the development of international and supranational human rights norms and courts. As Tushnet puts it, 'changes in understanding about how constitutional review could contribute to a well-functioning government, began to reshape courts that

---

16 See Michel Rosenfeld in Chapter 1.

17 See Paolo Passaglia in Chapter 6.

18 See Eoin Carolan in Chapter 3.1.

19 Louis Favoreu citing Hans Kelsen in Louis Favoreu, 'Constitutional Review in Europe' in Louis Henkin and Albert J Rosenthal, *Constitutionalism and Rights* (Columbia UP 1989) 46, 51.

initially were designed on the US or Kelsenian models'.[20] What has generally been observed is that, instead of settled systems which would seemingly have matured since the establishment of constitutional review, new issues have appeared carrying further challenges for constitutional courts. In other words, and stating the obvious, if constitutional review arguably stands as an 'acquis' of Western constitutionalism, rights-based constitutional adjudication has further tested its efficacy forcing its evolution and challenging its endurance, even in stable democracies, thereby revealing the fascinating dynamic nature of constitutional structures.

1.3 Constitutional Adjudication and Changing Landscape

The establishment of constitutional review is, by definition, disruptive. It alters the traditional balance of powers between the constitutional court and Parliament – which is exactly the point since it seeks to curtail the power of the legislature – and has also an impact on the relations within the ordinary judicial branch. Constitutional review of legislation being 'an inherently political activity ... however judicial in form',[21] the constitutional court is expected to resolve policy disputes by interpreting constitutional rules, whether by supplementing them or by updating them, and by setting out possibly further fundamental rules and principles governing the polity. In terms of the effect on the domestic judiciary, the issue primarily concerns Kelsenian systems since the constitutional court is an 'add-on' to the existing institutional setup which already comprises supreme courts in civil and/or administrative matters. The disturbing effect comes from procedures such as incidental review and constitutional complaints which invite the constitutional court to participate 'in the adjudication of individual cases by ordinary jurisdictions, either by resolving preliminary questions of the constitutionality of statutes or by reviewing the constitutionality of final judicial decisions'.[22]

The role of constitutional courts has been further transformed by the growing significance and enforceability of fundamental rights. Originally concerned with 'primarily issues of government structure', the focus of constitutional review has indeed shifted to concerns 'about violations of

---

[20] Tushnet (n 2) 51.

[21] Stone Sweet (n 4) 69, 83. See also Hans Kelsen, 'La Garantie Juridictionnelle de la Constitution' (1928) 44 Revue du Droit Public 197.

[22] Lech Garlicki, 'Constitutional Courts versus Supreme Courts' (2007) 5 *Intl J Cons L* 44, 46.

fundamental individual rights'[23] since, in almost all systems, 'constitutional texts referring to fundamental rights give the judiciary the vast opportunity to take moral considerations into account in deciding cases with significant political implications'.[24]

This transformation stemmed from changes of a substantive normative nature and politico-institutional nature. On a substantive level, the proliferation of constitutional adjudication is very much linked to an increasing variety of rights being enforced at constitutional level, even more so with the emergence of a 'third generation of rights' arguably further testing the connection between those rights and structures of constitutional review.[25] At the institutional level, pressure exerted on the constitutional courts has affected the way these courts face the political and judicial (domestic and supranational) powers. First, since constitutional courts perform an essentially politico-legal function, which has led them to develop in some cases highly intrusive styles of adjudication in rights-based litigation, their relationship with the legislature has been marked by issues such as the politicization of the courts' membership or the influence of politics on their decisions, all of these having contributed, to an extent, to strain a review system supposedly perfectly designed at its inception. The politicization of membership is in fact about a perversion of the Kelsenian model: the process for appointing constitutional court's judges must have significant political input according to Kelsenian orthodoxy; but the problem lies when there is too much of it, as has been the case, for example, of the Spanish Constitutional Court where the selection of constitutional judges results more from politically-driven negotiations between majority political parties than from a rigorous process aimed at screening the actual competence of the candidates.[26] Regarding the influence of politics on constitutional courts' decisions, it can happen that constitutional rulings are overriden by a series of amendments by the constituent power as has recently been the case with the Hungarian Constitutional Court, for example.[27] These examples again vividly illustrate the rapport de force between these courts and the political branch. These observations mostly apply to constitutional courts of the Kelsenian type which were originally

[23] Tushnet (n 2) 51. See Paolo Passaglia in Chapter 6 on Italy as a counterexample in this respect, since its Constitutional Court has changed from a 'Court of rights' into a 'Court of conflicts'.

[24] Tushnet and others (n 2) 16.

[25] Tushnet (n 2) 67.

[26] See Agustín Robledo in Chapter 7.

[27] See Renáta Uitz in Chapter 10.

entrusted with much power, legitimacy and aura, but whose sophisticated institutional setting has come under pressure when these courts have encountered resistance on sensitive issues in rights litigation. The US system sets an interesting contrast but one which also shows the extent of politicization of constitutional issues even though the structure of constitutional review was precisely to avoid it by 'confining constitutional adjudication to judicial application of a particular body of law to particular facts'.[28] As for the relationships of constitutional courts with domestic supreme courts, it is characterized by their 'systemic tension'[29] arising from the interference of constitutional courts with the ordinary judicial process, on the one hand, and the degree of empowerment procured to the judiciary by the development of constitutional review – a development called 'constitutionalization of the legal order'[30] – on the other hand.

Secondly, the influence of international human rights instruments, supranational and transnational courts, notably well-developed in the European context under the authoritative jurisprudential activity of the Court of Justice of the European Union (CJEU) and the European Court of Human Rights (ECtHR), has instilled a new dynamic to the practice of constitutional review leading to the recognition of pluralistic forms thereof. The adoption of bills of rights, or more generally human rights-related legislation, in several common law countries such as the UK, Ireland and, in a more limited way, Australia, was a move – often more politically than legally motivated – to mark their commitment to, and compliance with, international human rights standards. A rethink of constitutional review structures ensued. In those particular jurisdictions, it forced the adaptation of the parliamentary model which has been theorized under the concept of 'dialogic review' – or otherwise labelled 'weak-form constitutional review' or 'new Commonwealth model of judicial review'[31] – seeking to describe a structure of rights protection which accommodates protection through rights adjudication, and protection through parliamentary sovereignty as a core constitutional principle. Under this transformed model, generally characterized by a statutory bill of rights, a weak form of judicial review with interpretive and declaratory elements, leaves the final decision-making power on rights issues to the political branch of government.

---

[28] See Michel Rosenfeld in Chapter 1.
[29] Garlicki (n 22) 44, 63.
[30] Stone Sweet (n 4) 69, 90.
[31] Tushnet (n 2) 57, citing Hogg and Bushell, Tushnet and Gardbaum.

In the European context (including non-Kelsenian settings such as those in the UK and Ireland), the influence of European law has entailed the necessity for national constitutional courts to engage in a dialogue with those external courts. This dialogue has not only reinforced the commitment of constitutional courts towards a high and consistent level of rights protection but has also enhanced, in most cases, their legitimacy as the ultimate guarantor and interpreter of the domestic constitution. In this regard, constitutional courts of various jurisdictions, in particular in France, Italy and Belgium, have had to assert themselves vis-à-vis not only the European courts but also vis-à-vis the ordinary courts in their own system, which have notably been empowered by a practice of decentralized review when applying EU law. All this has had an impact on how constitutional courts have approached their role in rights-based litigation. The question to be explored then is to make sense of the impact of these changes on the structure and practice of constitutional review in the selected jurisdictions.

1.4 Adaptability and Endurance of Constitutional Review

In an era of inflated constitutionalism and global phenomenon of constitutional review, it is paradoxically difficult to identify an encompassing analytical framework of all the changes undergone by a variety of well-known constitutional review systems. The present study, through the identification of divergences and common trends, seeks to provide a basis to identify such a framework and hence join the rich scholarly discussion on the development of pluralist constitutional review in global comparative constitutionalism.

Two interesting analytical concepts are those of adaptability and endurance. The notion of adaptability refers here to the ability of the constitutional court, in a given legal system, to adapt its role in an efficient way to the above-described process of change.[32] The notion also aids to capture the endurance of a constitutional review system, that is its ability to transform and work well on the long run – in other words, how a renewed practice of constitutional review is able 'to catalyse legal

[32] On a more general level, the related concept of constitutional (in)flexibility is evoked by Elaine Mak to describe, by reference to the overall constitutional framework, 'the relative openess of the constitutional framework of a specific legal system as regards the expression of normative change'. See Elaine Mak, *Judicial Decision-Making in A Globalised World: A Comparative Analysis of the Changing Practices of Western Highest Courts* (Hart 2013) 18 ff.

development in a changed society'.[33] Referring to these two concepts means that the analysis of the structure and practice of constitutional review is a 'work in progress' where straightforward yet core questions must constantly be asked such as: What is a constitutional right? What is the role of a constitutional court? What is its legitimacy vis-à-vis the political power? Is that desirable the court increases its jurisdiction and power via an enhanced constitutional review? Overall, the analysis poses significant questions about the democratic process and about the 'relative merits of [judicial and political authorities] in the pursuit of constitutional goals'[34] which most contributors allude to in their respective chapter. What can be hypothesized at this stage is that a satisfactory degree of adaptibility and endurance of rights-based constitutional review would be inferred if the system responds well to changes and ensures the continuing legitimacy of its constitutional court, as well as a healthy dialogue with the other powers, or 'good faith' attitude[35] or 'constitutional loyalty'[36] among all constitutional actors.

Whatever the design and practice of constitutional review, the constitutional legal order will respond with variants to the core question of the proper role of constitutional courts 'in shaping political and social life'.[37] The ten country studies reflect the diversity in the way constitutional courts cope with these relevant changes and how this has affected the original model of review. Yet, discernible common trends can be identified which confirm what has been observed in previous studies – with the 'thicker' commonality being identified, as expected, as regards European jurisdictions. Chen and Maduro indeed rightly point to 'an increased degree of convergence in Europe with regard to the forms of constitutional judicial review and the roles attributed to constitutional courts'.[38] Signs of convergence can be seen in three respects.

First, constitutional legal systems arguably tend to move towards a more complete system of review as is the case, for example, of the French system which was relatively recently enhanced by the addition of ex post review to its traditional ex ante review operated by the Constitutional Council. From another angle, the acts of incorporation of the ECHR in the UK and Ireland were supposed to complete and supplement, and not replace, the existing systems in these juridisdictions,

---

33 Ibid., 20.
34 Chen and Maduro (n 2) 107.
35 Tushnet (n 2) 60.
36 See Agustín Robledo in Chapter 7, p 301.
37 Chen and Maduro (n 2) 103.
38 Ibid., 102.

namely the protection founded on common law rights and principles (including the principle of legality) in the UK, and the one based on constitutionally protected rights in Ireland. This 'completeness' of the review system is, however, not necessarily a guarantee of efficiency in the long term. A sophisticated system of review such as the one established with a powerful constitutional court in Spain or, for the last wave of constitutional courts, Hungary–both plagued by politically-related issues–shows that other factors may deeply affect a well-designed structure of review and even challenge the role and raison d'être of the constitutional court.

Secondly, another discernable trend, alluded to above, is the spread of a decentralized form of review in the European context whereby all courts, including the highest, in EU member states have the power to review the validity of national laws against EU law and, if appropriate, set aside those laws which are contrary to EU law. What has been identified in this regard by previous studies, and explored in some of this collection, is a relevance of the American model of review for European jurisdictions, denoting a convergence, 'albeit slower and more limited, between the European and American models of constitutional review.[39] The other European law-related form of review has developed via the taking into account of ECHR-based rights whereby domestic ordinary courts can review national law under a separate review of conventionality, that is conformity of domestic law with ECHR obligations as is, for example, the case in France. The empowerment of domestic courts via a European law-based review has pushed towards a 'dichotomization' of the review. In many respects, this has represented a multi-faceted challenge for the domestic constitutional courts which have, in some cases, become marginalized as in Italy, or arguably 'subordinated' as in Belgium, but which, in other cases such as in France have managed to enhance the constitutionally-based review system to give the constitutional court a new centrality and relevance.

Thirdly, a common denominator in all country studies is the pervading theme of dialogue and collaboration between branches of powers – judicial and political – in the context of rights-based constitutional review. Analyses on the topic are traditionally phrased into a discourse of the 'last word' or 'final say'. In other words, where does supremacy lie? 'with the legislature, as political constitutionalists desire, or with the

[39] See, for example, Leonard Besselink, 'The Proliferation of Constitutional Law and Constitutional Adjudication, or How American Judicial Review Came to Europe After All' (2013) 9 *Utrecht Law Review* 19; Chen and Maduro (n 2) 102.

judiciary, as legal constitutionalists wish'?[40] As explained above, constitutional courts necessarily face the nexus between the efficient protection of individual rights and the respect of political democracy. The selected country studies provide updated insights about where each jurisdiction stands in terms of legal and political constitutionalism, with a number of authors referring to the theoretical distinction between strong judicial review (with decreased legislative or parliamentary authority) and weak judicial review (with strong parliamentary authority). Some authors go beyond the distinction such as Carolan on Ireland who develops an argument about 'collaborative constitutionalism', or the authors on Finland who refer to 'a peculiar example of intermediate constitutionalism'. It must be pointed out that this discourse of the 'last word' – as pertaining to the political branch of government in a weak review system, or to the judicial branch in a strong review system – appears somewhat less relevant in continental European literature. As a matter of fact, the discourse on the 'last word' has concerned less a conflict as between the political and judicial branches of government than a conflict between courts, that is which, from the constitutional court or the European courts, is the final arbitrator in the protection of rights. This is exemplified by the telling title of the Belgium contribution about the 'subordination of the Constitutional Court to the European Court on Human Rights'.[41] The present collection goes further than the 'last word' discourse and delves into the notion of collaborative constitutionalism. The debate has indeed matured in the sense that issues faced by constitutional courts in rights litigation now call for reconciliation (between rights and democracy) and not competition, for relationship and not confrontation. This collaboration between constitutional actors takes place at different levels. First, there is the collaboration within the judiciary, between the constitutional court and ordinary courts – or how the 'battle of courts' has eased off in, for example, France between the Constitutional Council and the Court of Cassation (supreme ordinary

---

[40] Richard Bellamy, 'Political Constitutionalism and the Human Rights Act' (2011) 9 *Intl J Cons L* 86, 89. See also WF Murphy, 'Who Shall Interpret? The Quest for the Ultimate Constitutional Interpreter' (1986) *Review of Politics* 48. See Mark Tushnet, *Taking the Constitution Away from the Courts* (Princeton UP 1999); Waldron (n 8). Political constitutionalism claims that government power and law-making is and should be legitimized through Parliament, whereas legal constitutionalism holds courts as the crucial branch of power to create conditions under which public power is limited by respecting articulated constitutional principles and legally enforceable rights.

[41] See Marc Verdussen in Chapter 9.

court) as regards ex post form of constitutional review; secondly, there is the collaboration between the constitutional judge and the legislative and executive branches of power – or how a change of political culture and mentality can be expected, for example, in Ireland in order to advance the operation of the ECHR Act; thirdly, there is the collaboration between the constitutional judge and the European judge – or how constitutional courts in France and Belgium, for example, have been 'okayed' by the CJEU regarding their priority rule in constitutional review, or how constitutional courts have started to make references for preliminary rulings to the CJEU.[42]

In any event, systems of rights-based constitutional review are at a stage where further changes are needed to consolidate their relationships with the other branches of power for the good working of the democratic process and the stability of the domestic regime especially in the face of crisis and challenges. This is so whether we are in the presence of established courts facing legitimacy challenges such as in, for example, the US or Spain, or established systems experiencing transformative practice of constitutional review such as in, for example, France or Ireland, or in the presence of relatively new courts reaching the next maturity phase such as, for example, the Constitutional Court in Hungary, or the Supreme Court in the UK. It is hoped that the present collection will provide a heightened understanding of the responses to these topical issues, including on the regulating role of the constitutional courts,[43] and hereby contribute to generalist works or specific studies in the field.

2. METHODOLOGY

Comparative legal studies are crucial for the twenty-first century lawyer, not only from the perspective of the law researcher, but also from the perspective of the law practitioner and judge. The area of constitutional law is no exception and comparative constitutionalism scholarship is

---

[42] Regarding this last collaboration, what is at stake is the sustainability of a European model of rights adjudication which arguably requires further changes, especiallly structural, from the national supreme courts. See Rt Hon Lady Justice Arden, 'Peaceful or Problematic? The Relationship Between National Supreme Courts and Supranational Courts in Europe' (2010) 29 *YEL* 3.

[43] The reflection about the coordinating role of the constitutional courts is also engaged in the context of contemporary authoritarian regimes. See, for example, Eric C Ip, 'The Democratic Foundations of Judicial Review under Authoritarianism: Theory and Evidence from Hong Kong' (2014) 12 *Intl J Cons L* 330.

thriving, including on the specific topic of constitutional review. The distinctive structure of the present collection is the result of methodological choices. These are reflected in the outline of the book which is divided into two main parts. A first part groups jurisdictions which possess a bill of rights, whether resulting from an incremental constitutional development of rights protection such as the US, or resulting from an act of incorporation of an international human rights treaty such as, in mainly common law countries, the UK, Ireland and Australia, as well as in the interesting cross-legal family example of Finland – this set of countries therefore puts the uniqueness of the US experience in perspective when compared with the variants of the adaptation of the parliamentary model. A second part groups a variety of civil law countries' experiences in Europe as relevant instantiations of the evolution of the Kelsenian model. The final part consists of the concluding chapter which brings a comparative analysis of the issues posed in the preceding chapters.

2.1 Methodological Choices

By bringing together a critical mass of common law and civil law countries, the collection is not a 'least different study', nor a 'most different study'.[44] The ten countries were selected because of, in the case of most, their long tradition in the area of constitutional review, and because of, in the case of all, the significant changes which have occurred in these jurisdictions in recent years. Three points regarding the structure and methodology of the book deserve explanations to allay possible criticism. First, the choice of Western liberal democracies might reinforce the impression of adhering to the dominant perspective of an 'Anglo-Eurocentric constitutionalism',[45] hereby implying that there is no inclination to incorporate other legal systems. This is of course incorrect. The approach taken here is rather to offer country studies written by domestic experts with a view to sharing knowledge and starting collaborations with other scholars worldwide. It is also important to acknowledge that Western liberal oriented studies are still of significant comparative interest to other (non-Western) systems which are in the process of reflecting on, or introducing, enhanced constitutional review practice by reference to so-called dominant models.[46]

---

[44] Tushnet (n 2) 6.

[45] Frankenberg (n 11) 2.

[46] We mentioned above the case of China. There are other examples. See, for a general comparative study, Rosalind Dixon and Tom Ginsburg, *Comparative*

Secondly, the almost perfect split between common law and civil law countries might be regarded as defeating the purpose of a trans-legal families comparison, especially since we have acknowledged that forms of constitutional review do not necessarily follow the common law/civil law division; besides, legal families are not homogeneous as is evident from the US and Finnish examples. The intention is rather to break the line between well-known and frequently studied jurisdictions, such as the US, the UK, or France, and less well-known, often smaller, jurisdictions, such as Finland, Belgium or Ireland. Thirdly, Ireland and Australia both contain two sub-chapters. As explained below, the sub-chapters do not overlap in content. Ireland was the jurisdiction 'à l'honneur' on the occasion of the tenth year anniversary of the ECHR Act adopted in 2003 as the host of the Society of Legal Scholars Seminar where the contributions were originally presented. Australia presents quite a complex constitutional system within the parliamentary model and, having two reputed scholars providing engaging analyses from different and complementary angles, appears as a judicious choice.

2.2 Outline of Country Studies

Country studies help isolate specific reasons for the distinctive treatment of rights-based constitutional review, but also point to some 'close-to-universal' requirements in the area.[47] Each chapter is structured along two parts, namely the evolution of the system of constitutional review, on the one hand, and the practice and endurance of constitutional review, on the other hand. The first part provides an examination of the general constitutional setup, including the origins of the system of constitutional review as well as its main transformations. The second part aims at exploring specific issues in rights-based litigation by reference to key cases, as well as the relationship between the constitutional court with the other branches of power. Both parts allow each author to engage with constitutional theory. Most chapters follow the two-fold analytical framework; others depart, but refer in substance to the same key issues.

Part I presents country studies in the US, the UK, Ireland, Australia and Finland. The US legal system, from where the first model of constitutional review originally emerged, typically finds its place as the

---

Constitutional Law in Asia (Edward Elgar Publishing 2014) and, for a specific study on Taiwan, Brian Christopher Jones, 'Assessing The Constitutionality of Legislation: Constitutional Review in Taiwan's Legislative Yuan' (2015) 23 *Asia Pacific Law Review*.

[47] Tushnet (n 2) 6.

first country study. The American system is, however, atypical in this group of mostly (except for Finland) common law countries. In Chapter 1 ('A comparativist critique of US judicial review of fundamental rights cases: exceptionalisms, paradoxes and contradictions'), Michel Rosenfeld offers a critical account of US rights-based constitutional adjudication by emphasizing its exceptional features as well as its paradoxes. US exceptionalism resides in a number of traits which are the Supreme Court's unique challenge posed by the need to interpret an eighteenth century bill of rights for a contemporary society, the controversy over originalism, the tendency to convert all important divisive political issues into constitutional ones, and the enormous powers of the Supreme Court in fashioning and shaping fundamental rights aided by the extreme rigidity of the US Constitution's amendment provision. In terms of paradoxes, one is 'the politicization of constitutional law as an inextricable consequence of the systematic constitutionalization of divisive political issues' such as abortion, assisted suicide, gay marriage, death penalty, etc. The author illustrates these traits with some of the most significant rulings of the Supreme Court, including the recent cases on same sex marriage in *Hollingsworthy v Perry* and *United States v Windsor* as 'vivid example[s] of conjunction between ordinary politics and judicial politics'. He argues that these features render the comparison with constitutional courts and other highest courts in most other common law and civil law countries barely relevant. However, he also suggests that the US example may yield some worthy comparative insights if issues are approached at a higher level of abstraction, in particular when these issues relate to the nature and scope of fundamental rights to be safeguarded through adjudication in constitutional democracies.

Chapter 2 by Chintan Chandrachud and Aileen Kavanagh ('Rights-based constitutional review in the UK: from form to function') introduces the UK rights-based constitutional review system. In its form, the HRA was designed to preserve parliamentary sovereignty while ensuring that rights would receive robust protection. The model – labelled under different appellations including 'the third wave bill of rights', 'the new Commonwealth model', 'the parliamentary model', 'the dialogue model' and 'weak-form review' – grants the courts the power to review legislation for compliance with incorporated Convention rights but not the power to strike down primary legislation, thereby leaving to Parliament the last word on how to uphold rights. However, a detailed analysis of the design (or form) and operation (or function) of the HRA shows that constitutional design is not necessarily determinative of how a system of judicial review works in practice. The authors argue indeed that, under the HRA, Parliament does not seem to have the final say but that, in many cases, the courts have had 'normative finality' on questions of rights thanks to the strength of the interpretive obligation and the fact that declarations of incompatiblity are complied with in almost every case. In other words, '[c]onstitutional practice suggests that Parliament accepts a constitutional division of responsibilities whereby the courts determine whether a right has been violated, whereas Parliament has the role of devising a remedy for such violation if such is found'. So, the practice of the HRA has revealed that judicial powers granted to courts have proved to be stronger than originally envisaged, hereby displaying an arguably relevant rapprochement between the British approach under the HRA and a US-style of strong judicial review.

Ireland is the object of Chapter 3 subdivided into two sub-chapters. While Eoin Carolan's contribution presents a critical account of the affiliation of the Irish experience with models of rights-based review, Cliona Kelly's focus is on the derangement of the Irish system by the adoption of the ECHR Act. First, Carolan's chapter ('Leaving behind the Commonwealth model of rights review: Ireland as an example of collaborative constitutionalism') sets out the historical and theoretical context of rights-based review in the Irish legal system referring to the most authoritative sources in common law constitutionalism. Rather than embracing Gardbaum's new Commonwealth model of constitutionalism, Carolan contends that this model does not quite well describe the Irish situation. To support this claim, the author provides a comprehensive account of structural barriers to judicial supremacy by examining interpretative and susbtantive constitutional principles of Irish law, as well as other factors in the political-judicial interaction between the legislative and judiciary. The value of his argument lies in the alternative model of collaborative constitutionalism that he proposes. Between the American model of so-called 'strong form' of judicial review and the new Commonwealth model of parliamentary-judicial dialogue, the Irish experience reflects a possible third way which 'eshew the exaggerated images of institutional conflict that the language of judicial or parliamentary supremacy tends to evoke'. Coined as 'a collaborative model of constitutionalism', Carolan explains that this alternative would rest more on accountability of the different branches of power than their 'dialogue' which arguably still entails a 'final say'.

Secondly, Cliona Kelly's chapter ('A tale of two rights-based reviews or how the European Convention on Human Rights Act 2003 has impacted on the Irish model of review') focuses on the derangement of the model of rights-based review brought about by the adoption of the ECHR Act which incorporates the ECHR into Irish law. The examination of the relationship between the ECHR and the Constitution shows how the Irish version of Gardbaum's new Commonwealth model operates against the matrix of a written constitution with strong judicial review. This reveals the picture of a multi-layered and complex system of rights review divided into two sets of rights, namely constitutional rights, which are subject to strong constitutional review, on the one hand, and Convention rights, which are to be primarily enforced by the legislature supported by a form of dialogic review, on the other hand. Kelly argues that, while the minimalist approach of the ECHR Act 'is unlikely to represent a challenge to the dominant constitutional paradigm of strong judicial review', more could have been done in terms of design and judicial application of the ECHR Act to encourage a culture of rights awareness, including within parliamentary processes.

Both chapters show that rights-based constitutional review in the Irish system is the object of interesting theoretical attempts to categorize it within the broader debate on new Commonwealth constitutionalism. The introduction of the ECHR Act has not made the task more obvious – quite the opposite. While the ECHR Act has the potential to raise significant challenges regarding tenets and commitments in constitutional governance and litigation, further conditions of legal and political culture are needed in order for certain features, especially the interpretative and declaration of incompatibility powers, to be significant.

Australia is the object of Chapter 4 and also includes two-sub-chapters. First, James Stellios ('Australian constitutionalism and the UK-style dialogue model of human rights protection') discusses the attraction exerted at federal and state level by the British dialogue model of human rights protection for the Australian legal order. The constitutional framework for the exercise of judicial power was not contemplated as presenting obstacles when two jurisdictions, namely the Australia Capital Territory and Victoria, adopted bills of rights modelled on the UK-style dialogue. However, Stellios examines to what extent the decision of the High Court in *Momcilovic* has seemingly frustrated the operation of such a dialogue model by relying on separation of judicial power principles without much reflection about their theoretical underpinnings and 'certainly without any regard to liberty protecting understandings'. The thrust of the argument is that Australian constitutionalism does not allow a wider role for the judiciary in the protection of rights. The judiciary acts in a limited fashion and by applying conventional interpretive assumptions about legislatures and by not intruding into rights – and this has little prospect of changing in the absence of a constitutional amendment.

Complementing the analysis of the Australian legal system, the focus of Matthew Zagor's chapter ('Adventures in the grey zone: constitutionalism, rights and the review of executive power in the migration context') is on the relationship between the executive and the judiciary in the context of the protection of rights by public authorities in administrative decision-making. Indeed, in the absence of a bill of rights at federal level, 'human rights claims have found a home in administrative law'. Zagor contrasts:

> the notorious rights reluctance of the Australian political system and its culture of deference and trust in the executive with the architecture of administrative justice that has developed over the past three decades, as well as the contentious role played by 'legalism' as both a shield and a sword in the juridical arsenal for scrutinizing executive conduct.

Zagor draws on Dyzhenhaus' metaphore of legal 'grey holes' to describe how an impression of legality is created by legislative and judicial endorsement of strategies which exclude 'more elevated and openly political forms of rights review' of executive conduct. This judicial response to deferential government arguments is explored through the examination of key cases – *Tampa*; *Al-Kateb*; *Plaintiff S157*; and *Plaintiffs M61 and M70* – in which the judiciary have considered the source and breadth of the control exercised by the executive power in a migration context.

Both chapters relate to theoretical elements of constitutionalism and offer interesting insights into competing forms thereof. A common trend here is about the degree of unease and uncertainty about the role of the Australian judiciary when it comes to rights protection.

Chapter 5 on Finland ('Intermediate constitutional review in Finland: promising in theory, problematic in practice') offers the interesting perspective of a Nordic system. Although its legal culture is based on the civil law tradition, the Finnish system arguably lends itself to relevant parallels with the new Commonwealth model of constitutionalism. The authors Juha Lavapuro, Tuomas Ojanen and Martin Scheinin explain the developments – most notably of Finland joining the EU and the Strasbourg system as well as other domestic constitutional reforms – which resulted in a shift from a centralized and legislative-based constitutionalism to an institutionally pluralist and predominantly rights-based paradigm. However, they also argue that this shift has fallen short of materializing into a fully-fledged constitutionalism. In this regard, the Finnish system stands as a 'peculiar example of intermediate constitutionalism'. It is indeed characterized by a tension between old doctrines and institutions emphasizing the legislative supremacy of Parliament – with an intact principle of prohibition of judicial review of legislation – and a new paradigm underlining the importance of rights and the role of courts. Taking the analysis further, the authors question the extent to which the Finnish system offers a genuine 'third' alternative of constitutional review since the transformation of the system has resulted in institutional confusion and tensions – with the main constitutional actors missing a clear understanding of their constitutional role – rather than led to a meaningful constitutional dialogue between the courts and the legislature.

Part II deals with specific experiences of constitutional courts in Europe and examines the evolution of the Kelsenian model of review in Italy, Spain, France, Belgium and Hungary. In Chapter 6 on Italy (The Italian system of constitutional review: a Kelsenian model moving towards a decentralized model?'), Paolo Passaglia offers a critical account of the legal and political trends that have transformed the system of constitutional review. Essentially established as an adaptation of the Kelsenian type of court, the role of the Italian Constitutional Court has changed so dramatically over the past 20 years that, Passaglia argues, it might be necessary to look at the system from a different point of view. The political and social context, but also the influence of European integration, are the main factors of this transformed practice in rights-based constitutional litigation. The former explains the circumstances under which the Constitutional Court's main function has changed from traditionally being the protector of individual rights to currently acting as the arbiter of an increasing number of disputes. These disputes concern not only the allocation of powers between the central state and local authorities, but also the very exercise of power in terms of conflicts between the political class and the judiciary. As regards the latter European-related factor, the increasing role of the CJEU in particular, through the preliminary ruling procedure at the expense of the reference procedure before the Constitutional Court, has had the effect of putting an end to the monopoly of the Constitutional Court in its interaction with ordinary courts. The ensuing marginalization of the Constitutional Court has arguably accentuated the hybridity of Italian constitutionalism in which, following a transitioning pattern between centralized and decentalized form of review, the court has to share its constitutional responsibility with other courts (ordinary and European), as well as weave its way through political constraints, without having apparently established a structured dialogue with these actors. This prompts to suggest that maybe new competences should be given to the constitutional court.

Spain is the object of Chapter 7 ('The Spanish experience of rights-based review or how constitutional case law has been more principled than legislation in defence of fundamental rights'). Spanish constitutional review derives from the Kelsenian model which saw the establishment of a powerful Constitutional Court endowed with wide-ranging powers aimed at ensuring the normative force of the Constitution, the adjudication of conflicts between territorial powers of the state, and the guarantee of the fundamental rights of the citizens. Agustín Robledo explores the causes and effects of the somehow degeneration of this seemingly perfect model of constitutionalism. A range of anomalies have indeed affected the work of the Constitutional Court in recent years such as the politization of the appointment process of constitutional judges or the issue of delays in constitutional justice. This last issue is due to a growing number of claims being referred on the basis of the appeal for constitutional protection; this is compounded by the complex institutional setup of the Spanish state, in particular as regards the rising number of politically-motivated constitutional claims from local government. The Spanish experience seems to suggest that, however ideal a system might be when established, the endurance of the constitutional review system is dependent on a variety of parameters others than those related to its design. Robledo argues in particular that technical solutions – such as the abandonment of constitutional remedies (for example, the appeal of unconstitutionality) or even, in the most extreme case, the demise of the Constitutional Court – do not appear as reasonable options in order to restore a fully working constitutionalism. The way forward rather lies in a change of political culture 'meaning that political parties should internalize constitutional mandates and act with *constitutional loyalty*'.

In Chapter 8 on France ('The French system of rights-based review: from exceptionalism to parochial constitutionalism'), Marie-Luce Paris provides a clear analysis of the French system of review, recently transformed by the addition of ex post review to the competence of the Constitutional Council under the Priority Preliminary Ruling on the Issue of Constitutionality. The argument is made that this reform brings rights-based constitutional review towards more completeness in line with the dominant model of constitutionalism. However, a focus on domestic concerns as regards the design and operation of ex post review reinforces the impression of exceptionalism. The further transformation of the Constitutional Council into a fully-fledged constitutional court, and the development of an appeased and meaningful relationship with other constitutional actors, have indeed occurred within the very specific parameters of the French context. Relevant comparisons with other constitutional systems of the Kelsenian type, notably the Belgian one, as well as reference to the wider theoretical debate on constitutionalism, about a weak form of review in particular, assist in understanding the far-reaching effects of the enhanced form of review, and how French constitutionalism is still marked by parochial considerations in this respect.

Chapter 9 is on Belgium ('The Belgium experience of rights-based review: has the Constitutional Court become a body subordinated to the European Court of Human Rights'). Having established a fully-fledged Constitutional Court on the Kelsenian model, Belgium has witnessed a progressive extension of the jurisdiction of its Court to include fundamental rights as enshrined in the Constitution, though not comprising those guaranteed under international treaties and conventions. In this context, Marc Verdussen analyzes the ways in which the Constitutional Court has sought to adapt to the influence of international and European norms by elaborating on two specific interpretative judicial methods in rights-based litigation, namely the 'combination method' and the 'reconciliation method'. The other focus of the analysis is on the articulation of the different review mechanisms in the Belgian legal system, featuring a dichotomy between centralized constitutional review operated by the Constitutional Court against rights protected under the Constitution, and a decentralized form of review operated by ordinary courts against mainly rights guaranteed under the ECHR. The Belgium example vividly illustrates the adaptability of the Constitutional Court and its responsiveness to external standards, but also the difficulties it faces in determining its primary role – whether the protection of rights or the protection of the operation of the federation – as it has arguably become involved in a relationship of quasi-subordination with the ECtHR.

The last country study offers the perspective of a post-communist Central Eastern European jurisdiction. In Chapter 10 ('The illusion of a constitution in Europe: the Hungarian Constitutional Court after the Fifth Amendment of the Fundamental Law'), Renáta Uitz offers a critical account of the position of the Hungarian Constitutional Court. While it used to be 'among the most internationally respected courts for the quality of its jurisprudence [especially concerning fundamental rights] and for its contribution to transition to democracy' and entrusted with a 'formidable constitutional review forum', the Court is currently 'best known as the victim of perpetual constitutional amendments'. The author's argument revolves around the crucial issue of the 'vulnerability of the Constitutional Court' and shows that, due to jurisprudential and political factors, the Court has been entangled in an increasingly uncomfortable position, stuck between a not-so-prone-to-constitutional-dialogue government and the imperatives stemming from Hungary's European and international obligations. Overall, dialogue among constitutional actors is difficult as attested by the numerous constitutional amendments which have overruled the Court to prevent its interference in matters of political significance for the government.

Part III on 'Comparative law and fundamental rights' forms the concluding chapter. Referring to Gardbaum's hypothesis, John Bell agrees that there is a degree of convergence between the legal systems studied in that they all tend towards 'a common enterprise of constitutional liberalism which makes use of the institution of rights to advance democracy'. However, he also agrees that there are divergences given the differences in institutional mechanisms – primarily of judicial review of legislation – and rights protected. Adopting a comparative approach, he argues that this 'tension between general movements of ideas and values and local issues, which permeates the comparison of different systems of public law', has to be seen in two perspectives: the institutional and processual one, on the one hand, and the normative one, on the other hand. The former puts the focus on the state officials who have to implement rights (and not just on the constitutional courts which have the final word in interpreting them). The latter perspective revolves around the constitution viewed as 'a work in progress' document. The supreme norm makes each constitutional legal order distinct from one another. This distinctiveness, argues Bell, is also the result of the place of the constitution within a wider conversation which seeks to embrace the constitution's specific past, its current specific local social needs as well as its connection with external standards such as supranational instruments and courts protecting fundamental rights.

PART I

Bill of rights and acts of incorporation: US exceptionalism and adaptation of the parliamentary model

1. The United States of America

A comparativist critique of US judicial review of fundamental rights cases: exceptionalisms, paradoxes and contradictions

Michel Rosenfeld

1.1 INTRODUCTION

US constitutional adjudication is exceptional and in certain ways paradoxical. American judicial exceptionalism is widely recognized and mainly linked to the US Supreme Court's (USSCt) unique challenge posed by the need to interpret an eighteenth century bill of rights for a contemporary society; the controversy over originalism; the tendency to convert all important divisive political issues into constitutional ones; and the enormous powers of the USSCt in fashioning and shaping fundamental rights aided by the extreme rigidity of the US Constitution's amendment provision.[1] The paradoxes surrounding US constitutional adjudication, on the other hand, do not as readily come to the fore. These paradoxes are nonetheless numerous, and to cite but one, include the politicization of constitutional law as an inextricable consequence of the systematic constitutionalization of divisive political issues.[2] To better appreciate this latter paradox, it is useful to draw a brief comparison between the USSCt and specialized civil law constitutional adjudicatory bodies, such as the German Constitutional Court (GCC) and the French Constitutional Council (FCC). For over 200 years, the US Constitution has been treated as law and constitutional rights as legal rights.[3] In

[1] See US Constitution 1787, art V.

[2] See below 1.2.2 Key extrinsic factors bearing on the distinctiveness of US constitutional adjudication.

[3] See *Marbury* v *Madison* 5 US 137 (1803).

comparison, the GCC applies constitutional standards to private party transactions,[4] thus directly entering the realm traditionally left to legislative policymaking;[5] and the FCC was squarely set up as a political body.[6] Accordingly, the USSCt would seem much less political than its two European counterparts, both in terms of its institutional setting and of its adjudicative mission. Nevertheless, within the past several decades, the USSCt has had greater legitimacy problems for being overly political than either the GCC or the FCC.[7] More generally, as will become apparent in the course of the analysis below, both American exceptionalism and the paradoxes associated to it are complex, multifaceted and overdetermined.

To better appreciate the exceptionalism and paradoxes involved, US constitutional adjudication must be placed in the context of the legal tradition from which it emerges and understood in relation to the particular conception of fundamental rights that is predominant in the US. Accordingly, the first part of this chapter lays out the institutional context in which USSCt constitutional adjudication is embedded. The second part outlines the American conception of rights and the US Constitution's basic scheme for the protection for fundamental rights. Finally, the third part concentrates on some of the most controversial USSCt decisions in fundamental rights cases, including some of the most recent ones, with special emphasis on institutional implications and on conflicts among proponents of more expansive views of rights and those of more restrictive views. Ultimately, as we shall see, both US exceptionalism and the paradoxes it generates are based on a combination of institutional and contextual factors as well as on a series of dichotomies and contradictions. Given all this, one might expect a great deal of disillusion regarding the predicament of US constitutional adjudication.

---

[4] Jörg Fedtke, '*Drittwirkung* in Germany' in Jörg Fedtke and Dawn Oliver (eds), *Human Rights and the Private Sphere: A Comparative Study* (Routledge 2007) 144.

[5] This is done through deployment of the 'third party effect' or *Drittwirkung*. *See* Norman Dorsen et al., *Comparative Constitutionalism: Cases and Materials* (Thomson/West, 2nd edn, 2010) 896. See also Bernhard Schlink, 'German Constitutional Culture in Transition' in Michel Rosenfeld (ed.), *Constitutionalism, Identity, Difference and Legitimacy: Theoretical Perspectives* (Duke University Press 1994) 197 (criticizing GCC for engaging in policymaking).

[6] Alec Stone Sweet, *The Birth of Judicial Politics in France* (OUP 1992) 48.

[7] Michel Rosenfeld, 'Constitutional Adjudication in Europe and the United States: Paradoxes and Contrasts' (2004) 2 *Intl J Cons L* 633, 652 (nothing equivalent in France or Germany to the US 'countermajoritarian' difficulty).

Surprisingly, for the most part, it is not American exceptionalism as such or the paradoxes it fosters in and of themselves that bear the brunt of discontent. Instead, as will become apparent in the course of the following analysis, most frustrations and criticisms come from within antagonistic positions within exceptionalism – for example, originalists versus adaptionists – and within the contrasting poles giving rise to the contradictions and dichotomies that shape the actual paradoxes at play.

1.2 US CONSTITUTIONAL ADJUDICATION IN ITS INSTITUTIONAL AND HISTORICAL CONTEXT

For both intrinsic and extrinsic reasons, the USSCt differs in significant respects from highest courts engaging in constitutional adjudication in both civil law and common law countries. The intrinsic reasons in question stem from differences in constitutional design and from contrasts in legal approach and judicial culture. The extrinsic reasons are, for their part, contextual in nature as they relate primarily to issues arising in the ongoing relationship between constitutional adjudication and political as well as societal factors, that relationship being mediated by the dynamic imprints of the relevant polity's constitutional identity.[8]

1.2.1 Intrinsic Reasons for the Distinctiveness of US Constitutional Adjudication

Four principal features of constitutional design set the USSCt apart from other constitutional adjudicatory institutions. Moreover, the differences at stake are most obvious in comparison to constitutional courts in civil law countries, but they are also important in comparison to supreme or high courts in other common law countries. The four features involved include: the US Constitution's separation of powers provisions that make the federal judiciary one of the three separate and coequal branches of the US Government, the other two being the legislative branch entrusted to the US Congress and the executive branch headed by the US President;[9] the limitation of the powers of the federal judiciary to the adjudication of 'cases or controversies',[10] thereby precluding ex ante or

---

[8] See generally, Michel Rosenfeld, *The Identity of the Constitutional Subject: Selfhood, Citizenship, Culture and Community* (Routledge 2010).

[9] See US Constitution 1787, arts I, II, and III.

[10] Ibid., art III, s 2, cl 1.

abstract review[11] as well as advisory opinions;[12] the rigidity of the constitutional amendment provision,[13] thus effectively precluding adoption of any proposed amendment that does not command virtual consensus resulting in a lack of significant political opposition; and the particular constitutional formulation of the fundamental rights to which it affords protection and which are for the most part specified in the US Constitution's Bill of Rights and Fourteenth Amendment.

Not only is the US the paramount model for decentralized constitutional review as nearly every state and federal court throughout the country is empowered to adjudicate constitutional rights claims, but it also stands out by virtue of its embedding judicial review within a 'checks and balances' framework. The federal judiciary headed by the USSCt is thus an independent and coequal branch of the federal government that is meant to check and counterbalance the powers of the US President and those of the legislative branch comprised of the US House of Representatives and the US Senate. Moreover, the overall scheme of 'checks and balances' put forth by the US Constitution is one designed to foster competition among several distinct units of democracy in order to minimize what the country's founders perceived as a particularly pernicious evil of unrestrained democratic government, namely 'the tyranny of the majority'.[14] The constitutionally set divisions among units of democracy within the US operate both vertically and horizontally: vertically, through American federalism, each of the country's 50 states constitutes a unit of democracy with its own executive, legislative and judicial branch;[15] and horizontally, through the accountability to different electorates respectively, by the US President, the US House of Representatives, and the US Senate,[16] and even indirectly the

---

[11] Wojciech Sadurski, 'Constitutional Review in Europe and in the United States: Influences, Paradoxes, and Convergence' (2011) Sydney Law Research Paper 11/15, 10 <http://ssrn.com/abstract=1754209> accessed 31 March 2015.

[12] Ibid., 11.

[13] Ibid., 17.

[14] See James Madison, *The Federalist Papers* (1788) N 10.

[15] See US Constitution 1787, art IV, cl 4 ('The United States shall guarantee to every State in this Union a Republican form of government …').

[16] The President is elected upon obtaining a majority in the Electoral College which depends on voting in each individual state and upon according each state a number of electors in the Electoral College based on that state's population. To become a Senator, a candidate must win a statewide election whereas to become a Representative in the US House of Representatives, a candidate must win a district wide election within a state. Thus, for example, if a state is in part urban and in part rural, a Senator would be accountable to both

USSCt to the extent that the President nominates and the Senate confirms USSCt justices by majority vote. As federal judges are appointed for life, however, the federal judiciary ultimately provides an antimajoritarian check on its coequal branches of the federal government whenever they decide that a federally enacted law or an executive order or decree is unconstitutional. At the same time, the federal judiciary also administers an antimajoritarian check upon individual state majorities whenever it strikes down a state law that it adjudges incompatible with the US Constitution.

Because the US Constitution is very difficult to amend – to be adopted, an amendment must garner a two-thirds vote in each of the two houses of the US Congress plus a positive vote in three-quarters of the state legislatures[17] – the combination of the first and the third of the four constitutional features listed above sets USSCt constitutional adjudication as an 'unchecked check' on all majoritarian units encompassed within the US constitutional design.[18] This, in turn, gives rise to the 'counter-majoritarian difficulty', which, if left uncontained and unmitigated, arguably would risk transforming the basic commitment to democracy and majoritarianism inscribed in the US Constitution with few textually based antimajoritarian exceptions[19] – albeit in the context of a plurality of majoritarian political and institutional units – into a judicial dictatorship.[20] In as much as USSCt decisions on constitutional fundamental rights questions can only be overruled by the USSCt itself, but remain, as a *matter of fact*, beyond repeal or modification by any other institution or

these constituencies whereas a Representative with an urban or a rural district would only be accountable to one of the two.

[17] As one state is unicameral and the others are bicameral, there are 99 state legislative bodies. Accordingly, a negative vote by 13 of the 99 state legislative bodies on a proposed amendment would be sufficient to assure its defeat.

[18] In contrast to the USSCt's constitutional adjudications which are pretty much de facto immune from review or overturning by any other governmental institution or electoral process, that court's decisions in cases that do not involve the US Constitution do not amount to an unchecked check. Thus, for example, the US Congress enacted the Civil Rights Act of 1991 in part to overcome USSCt's statutory interpretations with which it disagreed. See Civil Rights Act 1991, Pub L No 102-166, paras 2(2), 3(3) (explicitly repudiating the USSCt's interpretation in *Wards Cove Packing Co, Inc* v *Atonio* 490 US 642 (1989)).

[19] The principal such antimajoritarian constitutional prescriptions emanate from the Bill of Rights, which is made up of the first ten amendments to the 1787 Constitution and was adopted in 1791.

[20] See, for example, Robert H Bork, *The Tempting of America: The Political Seduction of the Law* (Free Press 1990).

democratic process within the US, the power of US judges is unlike that of other major constitutional democracies. Indeed, in Canada, constitutional adjudication does not give rise to any 'unchecked check' as most Supreme Court fundamental rights constitutional decisions are subject to a legislative override.[21] Similarly, although clearly established as the authoritative interpreters of their respective constitutions, neither the GCC nor the FCC has the final word to the extent that the USSCt does, as the French and German Constitutions are much more easily amended than their US counterpart.[22]

The 'countermajoritarian difficulty' and the 'unchecked checker' problem issuing from the exercise of USSCt constitutional review powers may seem to be significantly compensated by the limitations on the powers of the federal judiciary contained in the second of the four features of constitutional design mentioned above. These limitations revolve principally around the 'case or controversy' requirement[23] whereby federal courts cannot choose the constitutional issues they address, but must depend on the generation of legal proceedings by parties who can appeal to a legally cognizable 'injury in fact' caused by application of an unconstitutional law or some other unconstitutional official conduct.[24] The 'case or controversy' requirement precludes ex ante or abstract review as well the issuance of advisory opinions.[25] Arguably, these limitations added to the above mentioned firm commitment to treat the US Constitution as law makes constitutional adjudication much like statutory or private law common law adjudication and thus clearly distinguishable from the clearly political ex ante abstract review such as that practiced by the FCC, often based on a demand by 60 members of Parliament who had voted against a law just adopted by a majority of that body's members.[26] In the latter case, the constitutional adjudicator seems directly thrust into the political fray and is unconstrained by any concrete facts; in the case of the US, in contrast, the judge has to address the particular facts before her and apply the law of

---

[21] See Canada Constitution Act 1982, s 33.

[22] See Rosenfeld, 'Constitutional Adjudication in Europe and the United States' (n 7) 654–65, n 80. Germany does have unamendable constitutional provisions, but otherwise the German Basic Law is easier to amend than the US Constitution. See German Basic Law 1949, art 79.

[23] US Constitution 1787, art III, s 2.

[24] See *Lujan* v *Defenders of Wildlife* 504 US 555 (1992).

[25] Sadurski (n 11).

[26] George A Bermann and Etienne Picard, *Introduction to French Law* (Kluwer Law International 2008) 31–2.

the constitution as she would any other law to provide a judicial resolution to the case before her. In short, by confining constitutional adjudication to judicial application of a particular body of law to particular facts, the US Constitution is presumably designed to prevent over politicization of constitutional review, thus affording plausible means of confining the USSCt 'countermajoritarian' and 'unchecked checker' problems within reasonably manageable fairly narrow bounds.[27]

Upon further consideration, however, the 'case or controversy' requirement has not constrained the USSCt sufficiently to satisfactorily manage, let alone overcome, the 'countermajoritarian' and 'unchecked checkers' problems. The reasons for this may be multiple and complex, but two factors stand out. The first of these involves a blunting of the particularizing and concretizing meant to be secured by the 'case or controversy' requirement; the second, revolves around the common law grounded practice of judicial interpretation which has traditionally given judges broad lawmaking powers in constructing and developing common law legal doctrines and norms as well great interpretive latitude in dealing with statutes.

Unlike all other federal courts which lack much choice in the cases or controversies which they must adjudicate, the USSCt has had virtually complete freedom since 1988[28] to choose a handful among the thousands of petitions for review submitted to it every year. In recent times, the USSCt has accepted in the order of 75 out of 10 000 yearly petitions.[29] In view of this, the USSCt is pretty much free to choose which constitutional cases and issues it wishes to adjudicate and this undermines the analogy to the common law judge who has no choice, but to adjudicate the tort or contract dispute that an aggrieved private party decides to

---

[27] Strictly speaking, to the extent that judicial review of the constitution can be cast as a distinct legal, as opposed to a political, function – for example, the First Amendment to the US Constitution protects the 'free exercise of religion' and therefore a judge would have to find, as a matter of straightforward legal interpretation, a law authorizing Christian prayer and penalizing Muslim prayer to have been unconstitutionally applied to a Muslim who sues to invalidate a fine imposed on him for having uttered a prayer according to the dictates of Islam – USSCt constitutional adjudication would be 'checked' by the Constitution itself aided by generally accepted canons of professional judicial conduct.

[28] See Supreme Court Case Selections Act 1988, 28 USC para. 1257 (enacted 27 June 1988), an Act of the US Congress that eliminated appeals as of right to the USSCt from lower state court decisions.

[29] Editorial, 'The Best Lawyers Money Can Buy' *New York Times* (New York, 25 December 2014) <http://www.nytimes.com/2014/12/26/opinion/the-best-lawyers-money-can-buy.html?_r=0> accessed 31 March 2015.

bring before her.[30] Compounding this, moreover, is the prominent role of nongovernmental organizations and civil rights groups in fostering and financing constitutional litigation.[31] Again, unlike in the case of the individual who unexpectedly finds himself embroiled in a tort or contract dispute, the typical civil rights nongovernmental organization is likely to search for attractive individual challengers of presumably unconstitutional legislation and to direct, coordinate and finance the subsequent constitutional litigation.[32]

The second factor that stacks up against depoliticization of the judiciary through the 'case or controversy' requirement is the tradition and practice of common law adjudication.[33] The common law is judge made law. Common law judges adjudicate legal disputes brought before them and, in the absence of precedents, are free to set the law which will determine the outcome of the dispute before them. For example, if the downstream neighbor of an upstream landowner sues the latter claiming damages resulting from dumping waste in the river that flows through both of the properties involved, the judge will 'make law' upon deciding that there is liability for damages (or that there is not), under the specific circumstances of the case. Moreover, once the latter judge's decision is made, other judges confronted with similar disputes in the future would be obligated to treat the first judge's decision as precedent, but would still have a great deal of discretion in determining whether the precedent in question is controlling or distinguishable in terms of the case before them. To expand on the preceding example, is the upstream neighbor who dumps waste in the river liable only if he knew that the waste in question was toxic or regardless of such knowledge (assuming that the defendant in the first case was clearly aware that what he was dumping was toxic)?

---

[30] Although the USSCt's freedom to choose constitutional cases for adjudication is in principle virtually unlimited, in practice the Court has been mindful to secure uniformity throughout the country on important constitutional questions. Accordingly, when lower courts are divided over important constitutional questions, including those pertaining to fundamental rights, the USSCt is more likely than not to accept for review a pertinent case that would allow it to promote constitutional uniformity throughout the country.

[31] See Nancy Winemiller Basinger, 'Charities in Court: The Advocacy Efforts of Charitable Nonprofit Organizations in the Judicial Venue: When? How? And How Much?' (DPhil thesis, University of Georgia 2003).

[32] Ibid.

[33] For a more extended discussion of this point, see Rosenfeld, 'Constitutional Adjudication in Europe and the United States' (n 7) 648–9.

Common law legal rules can be overridden by statutes, and not only have statutes to a large extent replaced common law judicial law making in the US, but the country's written constitution is, formally at least, much more like a statute than like an evolving juridical norm extracted from a string of relevant precedents. In spite of this, however, judicial interpretation in the US remains open-ended, leaving much room for common law-like judicial lawmaking. This is due principally to two cumulative factors: first, many key fundamental rights constitutional provisions, such as 'Due Process', 'Equal Protection' or the prohibition against 'Cruel and Unusual Punishments', are articulated at a very high level of generality, making for a broad array of plausible interpretatively driven concretizations that are often likely to divide the citizenry. For example, does equal protection protect or prohibit affirmative action resulting in preferential treatment in favor of historically discriminated against minorities?[34] To this vastly open-ended constitutional articulation of key fundamental rights, one must add a second factor that operates to expand and magnify the consequences associated with the first factor. This second factor is the widespread judicial use of the open-ended characteristic common law interpretive approaches when confronting issues of statutory law. Thus, for instance, in a five-to-four decision, the USSCt interpreted an employment statute that prohibited discrimination against any individual on account of his/her race as being consistent with preferential treatment in the hiring of traditionally discriminated against racial minority employment candidates.[35] In short, not only are many key statutory texts like US constitutional provisions akin in terms of generality to broad principles and standards that serve as guideposts in common law adjudication, but judicial interpretation in the US, whether statutory or constitutional, looms as still deeply anchored in the moorings of typical common law blending of judicial interpretation and law making.

The fourth and final feature of constitutional design identified above concerns the conception and formulation of fundamental rights included in the US Constitution. The original 1787 US Constitution contained very few individual rights provisions. Indeed, the latter were by and large

---

[34] See, for example, *City of Richmond* v *Croson* 488 US 469 (1989) (contrast between USSCt's majority's conclusion that preferential treatment for racial minorities in heavily segregated construction industry is unconstitutional and Court's minority's assertion that such preferences are constitutional as a means to eradicate the present effects of past racial discrimination).

[35] See *United Steelworkers* v *Weber* 443 US 193 (1979).

limited to protection against ex post facto laws,[36] against state impairment of contracts,[37] and against curtailing or suspending the right of habeas corpus, except in cases of insurrection or invasion.[38] The reasons for this dearth of fundamental rights were basically twofold: from an institutional standpoint, the federal government was meant to be one of 'limited and enumerated' powers,[39] thus leaving most dealings between government and individuals in the hands of the federated states; from the standpoint of the dominant American political philosophy during the times of the country's founding generation, on the other hand, fundamental individual rights were understood in Lockean terms as natural, inalienable and pre-political, being thus essentially negative rights that required government non-intervention and non-interference.[40] In other words, unlike in the Continental European tradition, in which fundamental rights are perceived as essentially positive and as requiring active state intervention to secure their enjoyment by the citizenry, for the American constitution-making generation (and for subsequent generations to a large extent) such rights were best conceived as pre-given, and government's proper role in relation to them, as strict confinement to a hands-off policy.

In spite of the strong Lockean underpinnings of the dominant conception of American fundamental rights, the founding generation was divided over whether a constitutional bill of rights would enhance or erode enjoyment of the natural rights to which each individual was thought to be entitled.[41] Pursuant to a compromise reached among the 1787 constituents, the US Bill of Rights was adopted in 1791. Although judicial interpretation of the latter will be more extensively discussed in the second part below, two general points deserve brief mention here. First, the rights enshrined in the US Bill of Rights are overwhelmingly negative in nature. Thus, for example, the First Amendment provides that 'Congress shall make no law respecting an establishment of religion, or prohibiting the free exercise thereof; or abridging the freedom of speech or of the press …'.[42] And second, the USSCt made it clear early on that

---

36 US Constitution 1787, art I, s 9, cl 3.

37 Ibid., art I, s 10, cl 1.

38 Ibid., art I, s 9, cl 2.

39 See James Madison, *The Federalist Papers* (1788) N 45: The Alleged Danger From the Powers of the Union to the State Governments Considered.

40 Ibid., N 10.

41 See Richard Beeman, *Plain, Honest Men: The Making of the American Constitution* (Random House 2009) 341–3.

42 US Constitution 1787, Am I (1791).

the Bill of Rights was applicable against the federal government but not against the states.[43] Only much later, after the US Civil War and the adoption of the Fourteenth Amendment in 1868, did the protections of the US Bill of Rights became gradually nationalized and made applicable to the states.[44] At present, by far most, but not all, of the rights protected in the US Bill of Rights have been adjudged applicable against the states.[45] Moreover, in addition to US Bill of Rights, the Fourteenth Amendment – which through its Equal Protection clause first introduced constitutional equality in the US – currently provides an additional source of fundamental rights protection under the US Constitution.[46]

1.2.2 Key Extrinsic Factors Bearing on the Distinctiveness of US Constitutional Adjudication

Not only has the constitution been primarily cast as law in the US, in contrast to other polities, such as France, which have envisioned their constitution as being essentially political in nature, but also for Americans the constitution plays a key central role that has no equivalent anywhere else.[47] Indeed, in the US the constitution figures prominently in the very construction of the nation and in the elaboration of its national identity. Whereas in the France of the 1789 Revolution, the state and a well defined, though not fully consolidated, nation preceded the constitution, in the US the 1787 Constitution launched the state and anchored a future nation whose contours and identity would take several generations to cement.[48] To put it differently, whereas in most polities, the constitution builds upon a nation, its history and a distinct national identity, in the US it is the nation and national identity that have been framed by the constitution. In 1787, the present US Constitution was crafted in the

---

[43] See *Barron* v *Baltimore* 32 US 243 (1833).

[44] See Richard E Labunski, *James Madison and the Struggle for the Bill of Rights* (OUP 2006) 259.

[45] See Bill of Rights Institute, 'Fourteenth Amendment: Incorporation (1868)' <http://billofrightsinstitute.org/educate/educator-resources/landmark-cases/incorporation/> accessed 31 March 2015.

[46] All the post-civil war amendments, which include the Thirteenth (1865) which prohibits slavery and the Fifteenth (1870) which grants the franchise to African-American males, secure additional fundamental rights, but for purposes of examining issues pertaining to judicial interpretation, the Fourteenth far overshadows the other two.

[47] See Rosenfeld, *The Identity of the Constitutional Subject* (n 8) 73, 293, n 2.

[48] Ibid., 158–63.

name of a 'We the People' who would not cohere into the present American nation for more than a century as it first had to abolish slavery and to absorb various massive future waves of immigrants. The US motto *E Pluribus Unum* and the associated metaphor of the American 'melting pot'[49] depend for any meaningful degree of realization on convergence around the US Constitution and the values and vision it projects.

Every nation-state with a working constitution projects a particular national identity that is distinct from its constitutional identity.[50] Moreover, both of these kinds of identity are, to use Benedict Anderson's characterization, imagined.[51] Though they remain distinct from one another, national identities and constitutional identities are intertwined and overlapping.[52] In most cases, national identity can be conceived independently from the constitution or constitutional identity. For example, it is not difficult to imagine France or Germany as projecting a rich and varied national identity based on history, culture and common destiny without reference to their respective constitutions. In stark contrast, without reference to the US Constitution, it is difficult to envisage a plausible national identity for the US. This does not mean that national and constitutional identities do not remain distinct in the case of the US – for example, some of US policies and actions in pursuit of the post 9/11, 2001 'war on terror' may be integrated within the country's self-image as a nation while defying the US's constitutional self-perception as the foremost defender of human rights. But the inseparability of the US's national and constitutional identities underscores both that the constitution plays a central role in the preoccupations of the citizenry and that it has an important and ubiquitous role in carving out the nation's evolving self-image.

The centrality of the constitution as law coupled with the close intertwining of national and constitutional identity has a crucial impact on the role and place of constitutional adjudication in the US. As often noted, '[n]early all of the most controversial issues in American politics ... end up before the [USSCt]',[53] where they await final and authoritative resolution by judges appointed for life and hence presumably above

---

[49] See Will Kymlicka, *Multicultural Citizenship* (OUP 2001) 14.

[50] See Rosenfeld, *The Identity of the Constitutional Subject* (n 8) 11–12.

[51] See Benedict Anderson, *Imagined Communities: Reflections on the Origin and Spread of Nationalism* (Verso 1991).

[52] See Rosenfeld, *The Identity of the Constitutional Subject* (n 8) 11–12.

[53] Jeffrey Rosen, 'The Court and Democracy' *(The Supreme Court,* December 2006*)* <http://www.pbs.org/wnet/supremecourt/democracy/history.html> accessed 31 March 2015.

the fray of politics and of its continuous give and take. Accordingly, Americans have a tendency to constitutionalize politics. Ideally, such constitutionalization would remove the most important and potentially most divisive issues, such as abortion, affirmative action, the clash between secularism and religion, gay marriage, assisted suicide, the death penalty, and many others, from the political arena. In practice, however, throughout US history, the constitutionalization of politics has seemingly inevitably gone hand in hand with the politicization of the constitution – or, more precisely of the constitution as law. In short, political disputes tend to become constitutional issues and, as such, questions of (constitutional) law. But that, in turn, seemingly inevitably politicizes constitutional adjudication. What remains an open question at this point – which will be addressed in the course of what follows – is: Does the judicial politics associated with constitutional interpretation somehow ultimately rise above politics, amount to just one more iteration of ordinary politics, or does it represent an altogether different kind or dimension of sui generis politics, largely confined to the realm of constitutional adjudication?

1.3 FUNDAMENTAL RIGHTS AS THEY EMERGE THROUGH JUDICIAL INTERPRETATION OF THE US CONSTITUTION

The combination of conceiving constitutionally enshrined fundamental rights as negative rights and of likening them to pre-political, innate and inalienable Lockean natural rights opens the way to casting their judicial interpretation and application as plausibly rising above all politics. Indeed, if free speech requires maintaining a state hands-off policy, and if every reasonable and responsible person is supposed to agree on the contours of the inalienable pre-political right to free speech, then all judges ought to be able to resolve free speech cases without any recourse to politics. Moreover, consistent with this, US constitutional adjudication in the context of a Lockean conception of rights would bear one crucial analogy to the Kelsenian vision of the apolitical constitutional judge operating within the ambit of the civil law. Both American fundamental rights adjudication and Continental European constitutional review could function in ways that would altogether sever them from politics: in the former case, by striking down laws that trampled on pre-political rights with rationally discoverable content; in the latter, by confining constitutional adjudication to process-based questions – for example, was the parliamentary law being challenged adopted by the constitutionally requisite majority?[54] In short, in both cases, the judicial actor would function as an apolitical negative legislator: in the Kelsenian European context by confining the constitutional judge to a policing process; in the Lockean American context, by charging judges with striking down unwarranted state abridgments of rationally ascertainable pre- and extra-political rights.

Just as the Kelsenian metaphor of the negative legislator does not extend to the civil law constitutional adjudicator who is called upon to strike down legislation that contravenes constitutionally protected fundamental rights, so too the Lockean ideal embodied in natural rights collapses when confronted with the realities of fundamental rights adjudication. There is, however, one major difference between the judge as negative legislator and the judge as natural rights protector. Framing the constitutional adjudication function in terms of negative adjudication seems entirely plausible so long as the judicial review involved is limited to constitutional process based determinations. In contrast, natural rights-based adjudication seems wholly implausible *in principle* to the extent that the rights encompassed within natural law, such as liberty and property, constitute what philosophers have labeled 'essentially contested concepts'.[55] In other words, all may agree that liberty and property are fundamental rights but there are bound to be inevitable disagreements concerning their precise meaning and concrete reach. Accordingly, judicial interpretations of such fundamental rights are bound to differ with the consequence that they will inevitably loom as contestable and that their legitimacy will in many cases become contested.[56]

The contradiction between the assumed transparency of pre-political natural rights and the inevitable discretion that judges enjoy when interpreting them in their constitutional incarnation exacerbates the 'countermajoritarian' difficulty and the 'unchecked checker' problem outlined above. The constitutional adjudicator speaks in the name of all, but decides in agreement with the values of some and against those of

---

[54] Hans Kelsen, *Introduction to the Problems of Legal Theory* (OUP 1992).

[55] Michel Rosenfeld, 'Constitutional Identity' in Michel Rosenfeld and András Sajó (eds), *The Oxford Handbook of Comparative Constitutional Law* (OUP 2012) 756.

[56] A salient example is provided by *Roe* v *Wade,* the 1973 USSCt abortion decision, the legitimacy of which has now been contested for over 40 years. See, for example, Sydney Lupkin, 'Abortion 40 Years after Roe v. Wade' *ABC News* (18 January 2013) <http://abcnews.go.com/Health/roe-wade-abortion-america-40-years/story?id=18242770> accessed 31 March 2015.

others. Fundamental rights controversies are taken to judges to rise above politics, but end up mired in other controversies. Are the latter reducible to mere politics? Or do they become caught in something else, such as moral disagreement or some different order of politics exclusively related to judicial craft and ideology?

On the premise that natural rights are discoverable to all who are sensible and who rely on reason, they presumably need no listing – or, at least, no exhaustive listing – in the written constitution. On the other hand, however, to the extent that natural rights inevitably turn out to be essentially contested in practice, not listing them or listing them in the most general and abstract terms within the text of the constitution only exacerbates their indeterminacy and their seemingly inexhaustible pliability to the interpretive whims of their judicial interpreters. A prime example of this is furnished by the Ninth Amendment to the US Constitution, which is part of the 1791 US Bill of Rights, and which provides: 'The enumeration in the Constitution, of certain rights, shall not be construed to deny or disparage others retained by the people.' This Amendment has been invoked to provide judicial recognition to an unenumerated broad constitutional right to privacy that extends to the freedom to use contraceptives,[57] to have an abortion,[58] and to engage in consensual adult homosexual sex.[59] Moreover, to underscore the seemingly unlimited plasticity of the Ninth Amendment, it bears emphasizing that its invocations have prompted strong dissents with altogether radically different interpretations. Thus, the dissenting justices in *Griswold* accused their colleagues in the majority of using 'natural justice' to fashion fundamental rights according their own subjective predilections and interpreted the Ninth Amendment as protecting the federated states from 'federal invasion'.[60] Consistent with the latter view, far from granting additional unenumerated rights, the Ninth Amendment ought to be understood as protecting federated state legislative majorities from any national constitutional constraints issued from any federal constitutional fundamental right that is not explicitly inscribed in the text of the US Constitution.

---

[57] See *Griswold* v *Connecticut* 381 US 479 (1965) (Goldberg J, concurring).

[58] See *Roe* v *Wade* 410 US 113 (1973).

[59] See *Lawrence* v *Texas* 539 US 558 (2003), a six-to-three decision overruling *Bowers* v *Hardwick* 478 US 186 (1986), a five-to-four decision holding that the right to privacy does not bar a state from criminalizing consensual adult homosexual sex and providing for punishment of up to 20 years in prison.

[60] *Griswold* (n 57) (Black J, dissenting).

The interpretive rift between the majority and dissenting justices in *Griswold* was not limited to the Ninth Amendment, but it also extended to the Due Process clause of the Fourteenth Amendment, which provides that no state 'shall deprive any person of life, liberty or property, without due process of law'. As a matter of fact, some of the majority justices interpreted the Due Process clause as guaranteeing substantive rights, including privacy,[61] whereas the dissenters interpreted it in purely procedural terms and linked its use by their colleagues in the majority to the latter's reference to the Ninth Amendment. In the dissenters' view, both of these amendments were being invoked in vain by the majority to create a 'natural justice' cover to mask their giving expression to their subjective preference.[62] In short, just as in the case of the open-ended Ninth Amendment, the very broadly stated Due Process clause emerges in *Griswold* as being susceptible of diametrically opposed judicial interpretations.

To recapitulate: both in terms of their specification and their interpretation, US constitutionally protected fundamental rights emerge in the context of a series of dichotomies that give rise to a seemingly insurmountable sequence of paradoxes and contradictions. The principal dichotomies at stake include: law versus politics; natural rights (or their contemporary progeny[63]) versus positivism; common law versus statutes (with the Constitution formally resembling a statute but acquiring determinate content much like any other common law subject matter, such as contracts or torts); predictability versus fairness in the struggle to conform to the dictates of the rule of law; substance versus procedure; originalism versus adaptation to meet generational needs; and majoritarianism versus countermajoritarianism – or, more precisely, protection of clearly defined uncontestable countermajoritarian rights, such as judicial protection against legislative interference with free political speech, versus contestable such protection unwarrantedly leading to judicial expansion, or downright invention, of clearly contestable antimajoritarian rights.

Navigating these various dichotomies is certainly a daunting task which is somewhat rendered more manageable on many occasions due to intrinsic or extrinsic factors that happen to reduce the number of

---

[61] Ibid., (Harlan J, concurring).

[62] Ibid., (Black J, dissenting).

[63] Ronald Dworkin's conception of fundamental rights under the US Constitution may be regarded as a contemporary version of a natural rights perspective. See Ronald Dworkin, *Taking Rights Seriously* (Harvard University Press 1977).

operative dichotomies at play. Where there is large societal agreement or indifference about a matter, dichotomies involved in constitutional adjudication may vanish beneath the surface or remain dormant. For example, whereas whether racial apartheid was permitted or prohibited under the Equal Protection clause was a highly disputed matter for over a half century,[64] it is no longer an issue and the dichotomies that animated the heated controversy that ended over 50 years ago have now completely receded. Indeed, even Justice Scalia, the fiercest champion of originalism, which requires judicial interpretation of the Constitution to be confined to the meaning it had or could have had for the generation of the framers, is unequivocally against racial apartheid, and hence in conflict with the views that prevailed in 1868 when the Equal Protection clause was adopted.[65] There may also be intrinsic factors in given cases that blunt or render key dichotomies inoperative. It is not difficult to imagine cases where matters of substance and procedure merge, such as in the exclusion of African-Americans from juries, or where originalists and adaptionists concur as certain relevant standards have not changed over the centuries. Thus, both in 1791, when the US Bill of Rights was adopted, and up to the present, a virtually unanimous consensus has prevailed concerning the proposition that the Free Speech clause of the First Amendment extends to political speech that is critical of existing domestic government policy.[66]

In order to better focus on the major practical and legitimacy related issues surrounding US judicial constitutional adjudication, the following summary and selective review of some of the USSCt's most notorious, and in many instances, most criticized decisions will focus on cases that exacerbate rather than smoothly manage or minimize those among the above listed dichotomies that emerge as pertinent under the unique set of circumstances involved. Doing so will highlight the tensions and fault lines characteristic of US constitutional adjudication. However, in so doing, one should not lose sight that the overall level of acceptance and legitimacy of the USSCt in the US depends on placing it in its full

---

[64] Compare *Plessy* v *Ferguson* 163 US 537 (1896) (racial apartheid held constitutional so long as 'separate but equal' accommodations provided for blacks and whites) with *Brown* v *Board of Education* 347 US 483 (1954) (racial segregation in public education held unconstitutional).

[65] Ronald Turner, 'Was "Separate but Equal" Constitutional?: Borkian Originalism and Brown' (1999) 4 *Temp Pol & Civ Rts L Rev* 229.

[66] See, for example, Robert Bork, 'Neutral Principles and Some First Amendment Problems' (1971) 47 *Ind LJ* 1.

context which comprises cases that are little controversial alongside cases that are so contested as to divide the American citizenry over generations.[67]

In the broadest terms, the USSCt's greatest challenge in constitutional adjudication is to reconcile an eighteenth century bill of rights with the constitutional challenges and aspirations of the twenty-first century. Some of the most salient dichotomies, such as that between natural rights/law versus positivism, trace back to the beginning of the USSCt's trajectory and have evolved without resolution through the centuries. Thus, already in 1798, in one of its earliest decisions, *Calder v Bull,*[68] the USSCt justices were divided, with Justice Chase placing natural law/rights above the Constitution and Justice Iredell adopting the positivist standpoint and declaring that there is no higher law than the Constitution. Iredell's views prevailed, but the dichotomy has since been displaced rather than resolved. The US Constitution has been accepted as the highest law, but both the unenumerated and the broadly articulated fundamental rights that it has slated for protection have been interpreted in natural rights fashion by some and in positivistic terms by others as the above discussed rift between the majority justices and the dissenters in the 1965 *Griswold* decision attests to.[69]

The dichotomy between substance and procedure in the context of fundamental rights cases was first faced squarely by the USSCt in its infamous 1857 *Dred Scott* decision.[70] Pairing down a complex set of circumstances to its essentials, Dred Scott was a slave who was brought by his master from the southern state of the latter to a federal territory. Pursuant to a federal statute, Dred Scott became emancipated upon entering federal territory. Subsequent to that emancipation, however, Dred Scott returned to the state where he had been a slave and ownership over him was reclaimed on the grounds that his emancipation had violated the slave owner's property rights under the Due Process clause of the Fifth Amendment.[71] Had the USSCt interpreted the Due Process clause in purely procedural terms, it would have had to uphold the emancipation on the grounds that the federal emancipation statute at

---

[67] One such case already mentioned is *Roe* v *Wade* (1973).

[68] 3 US 386 (1798).

[69] Griswold (n 60–62 and accompanying text).

[70] See *Dred Scott* v *Sanford* 60 US 393 (1857).

[71] The Due Process clause of the Fifth Amendment applies against the federal government whereas that of the Fourteenth Amendment affords protection against the several states.

stake had satisfied all the relevant process based constitutional requirements and that all valid federal laws prevail over inconsistent state laws by virtue of US Constitution's Supremacy clause.[72] The Court chose, however, to interpret the Due Process clause in substantive terms and to hold the federal emancipation law unconstitutional for depriving the slave owner of his private property though the latter had done nothing to justify interference with his lawfully acquired and used property. The Due Process clause protects liberty rights as well property rights, and one might have thought accordingly, that once the USSCt had decided to opt for a substantive approach over a procedural one, it could have pitted the emancipated former slave's liberty interest against his former owner's property right – and perhaps even have ruled that in the case at hand the liberty interest involved prevailed over the property interest invoked against it. That latter option was nonetheless precluded by the USSCt's holding that members of the slave race were neither persons nor citizens under the US Constitution. Using what may be characterized as an originalist argument, the USSCt stressed that the Constitution's framers believed that the slave race was 'so far inferior, that they had no rights which the white man was bound to respect'.[73] Besides being shameful, scandalous, morally repugnant and downright destructive to the extent that it might have helped precipitate the US Civil War, *Dred Scott* dramatically exemplifies the actual convergence of several dichotomies besides the one between substance and process. These include the one between originalism and adaptionism, the one between politics and judicial philosophy, and the one between natural rights (for example, property) and positivism. Moreover, these dichotomies play an interrelated role in the context of the case and raise as many questions as they answer. For example, there is a clear political cleavage (as well as a moral one) between the slave owning state concerned in the case and the federal government. Also superimposed upon that latter dichotomy is the one regarding judicial philosophy. And, given that the originalist interpretive stance that prevailed seemed perfectly aligned in terms of consequences with the politics of slave owning, should questions of judicial philosophy be regarded as proxies for, or subordinated to, politics or as independent though sometimes convergent?

There are two additional factors that contribute to the shaping of American exceptionalism in constitutional adjudication: the first derives from the US conception of fundamental rights as negative and Lockean

---

72 US Constitution 1787, art VI, cl 2.
73 *Dred Scott* (n 70) 407.

in nature; the second, from the use of federalism based claims as substitutes for, or complements to, fundamental rights ones. As already pointed out, Lockean negative rights evoke a government hands-off or no trespass vision and are accordingly articulated in absolutist terms. This is in sharp contrast with more recent iterations of fundamental rights protections. Thus, for example, the Canadian 1982 Charter provides that rights it protects are subject to 'such reasonable limits prescribed by law as can be demonstrably justified in a free and democratic society'.[74] Similarly, the European Convention on Human Rights stipulates limitations concerning most of the rights it protects. Freedom of religion rights, for example, 'are subject to such limitations as are prescribed by law and are necessary in a democratic society in the interests of public safety, for the protection of public order, health or morals, or for the protection of the rights or freedoms of others'.[75] These limitation clauses provide interpretive guidance, give backing to the judicial use of the proportionality standard in constitutional adjudication, and suggest judicial balancing of competing rights claims. Operating in the absence of any such limiting clause coupled with the predominance of Lockean negative rights, in contrast, affords the US constitutional adjudicator with greater interpretive latitude and has arguably resulted in the nearly complete absence of recourse to proportionality in American constitutional adjudication.[76] Furthermore, American constitutional jurisprudence is remarkable for its lack of tools or of consideration of competing constitutional fundamental rights claims. This is well illustrated in cases in which constitutional interests of different members of the same family come into conflict. In *Troxel* v *Granville,*[77] the USSCt adjudicated a conflict over grandparent visitation rights where the mother of the child opposed visitation by the parents of the deceased father from whom she had become widowed. A state law that the mother challenged as unconstitutional provided for grandparent visitation rights. Whereas the USSCt could have cast the controversy in terms of a clash among the respective constitutional privacy rights of the mother, the grandparents and the child, it resolved the case by pitting the constitutional right of the mother

[74] Canadian Charter of Rights 1982, s 1.

[75] Convention for the Protection of Human Rights and Fundamental Freedoms 1950, art 9.

[76] See, for example, Michel Rosenfeld, 'Judicial Balancing in Times of Stress: Comparing the American, British and Israeli Approaches to the War on Terror' (2006) 27 *Cardozo L Rev* 2083.

[77] 530 US 57 (2000).

against the state interest advanced in the grandparent visitation legislation. Unsurprisingly, the USSCt held that the mother's constitutional right prevailed over the conflicting state interest. One can of course imagine a different result if the grandparents' interest had been cast as constitutional rather than as statutory and if the child's constitutional interest in an ongoing relationship with his closest paternal blood relatives had been factored in.

The last factor relating to American exceptionalism in constitutional adjudication that bears mentioning here is that concerning the use of federalism considerations to expand or limit the scope of fundamental rights. As already noted, before the US Civil War, the US Bill of Rights was adjudged solely applicable against the federal government and only with the adoption of the post Civil War amendments[78] did fundamental rights gradually became applicable against the federated states as well.[79] Shortly after the adoption of the post Civil War amendments, the USSCt interpreted them very narrowly and reasoned explicitly in its 1873 *Slaughter-House Cases*[80] decision that to do otherwise would lead to undue interference with the sovereignty rights of the federated states.[81] Although fundamental federal constitutional rights have become since applicable against the states almost in their entirety, claims of 'state rights' have been historically interposed against expansive interpretations of fundamental rights. The 'states rights' appellation is a misnomer as, strictly speaking, it is a matter of 'state powers' whenever the USSCt is urged to interpret a fundamental right narrowly lest it sanction federal trampling on state sovereignty. Be that as it may, the use of 'state rights' rhetoric allows masking racist, sexist or homophobic positions, for example, in the guise of seeking protection for the integrity of the sub national democratic units enshrined in the Constitution.[82]

---

[78] The Thirteenth Amendment was adopted in 1865, the Fourteenth in 1868, and the Fifteenth in 1870.

[79] See above (n 43–45 and accompanying text).

[80] 83 US 36 (1873).

[81] Ibid., 121–3.

[82] See the discussion of the *Hollingsworth* and *Windsor* cases below (n 108–117 and accompanying text). In principle, federalism based initiatives can be shaped to enhance fundamental rights protection as well as to constrain it. Significantly, in recent times, as the USSCt has embraced more restrictive interpretations of certain fundamental rights, certain states have proceeded to afford more expansive protection of the rights in question within their own borders in reliance on their own subnational constitution. See, for example, Lina R Carbuccia, 'New York's Grant of Greater Fifth Amendment Rights to Sexual Predators in SOMTA Proceedings' (2012) 28 *Touro L Rev* 857.

1.4 USSCT CONSTITUTIONAL ADJUDICATION IN HIGHLY CONTROVERSIAL FUNDAMENTAL RIGHTS CASES: RESTRICTIVE VERSUS EXPANSIVE APPROACHES

As it is of course impossible to deal adequately with even a highly select list of the USSCt's most controversial fundamental rights cases within the scope of the present undertaking, only brief reference will be made to some key cases in order to set the stage for the discussion of the two recent same-sex marriage cases that will be examined in greater detail. The focus on these two 2013 cases seems well justified for a number of reasons: the two cases were five-to-four decisions, with the justices splitting in different configurations; same-sex marriage issues fit within the *Griswold* line of cases involving unenumerated rights and substantive due process; the US politics concerning homosexual rights and the popular acceptability of same-sex marriage have been evolving at a very rapid pace; sexual orientation issues have risen at the forefront of the heated US controversy over citation to foreign authorities – particularly, European ones – in constitutional adjudication; and the two cases involved squarely raise controversial issues relating to the proper interplay between fundamental rights, separation of powers and federalism.

1.4.1 Key Cases in Delimiting the Most Salient Controversies in US Constitutional Adjudication

The two most important cases that have framed the US constitutional treatment of race relations after the emancipation from slavery and the embrace of constitutional equality through adoption of the Equal Protection clause are *Plessy* v *Ferguson* (1896)[83] and *Brown* v *Board of Education* (1954).[84] In *Plessy,* the USSCt adopted the 'separate but equal' standard thus casting apartheid as consistent with constitutional equality. To reach this result, the USSCt conceived constitutional equality among the races to extend to civil and political rights, but not to social rights that would call for racial integration of railroad cars and of other public facilities. Only Justice Harlan dissented and penned the famous dictum that 'the Constitution is color blind'.[85] To the contemporary reader, the decision in *Plessy* seems heavily influenced by racist mores

[83] 163 US 537 (1896).
[84] 347 US 483 (1954).
[85] *Plessy* (n 83) 559.

according to which mingling between the races emerges as socially undesirable if not downright unacceptable. More than half a century later in a unanimous decision, the USSCt held in *Brown* that racial segregation in public schools was unconstitutional, thus launching a veritable constitutional revolution. *Brown* not only struck down laws that mandated school segregation, but also decreed that those state agents responsible for segregation undertake full desegregation of the schools under their jurisdiction – a process that led to a large volume of litigation over four decades and that has not yet come to full fruition.[86] In contrast to *Plessy*, *Brown* went squarely against the mores of the states that mandated segregation and prompted some dramatic resistance against integration that required federal marshals to forcefully impose racial integration against obstructing state officials.[87] *Brown* can be read as imposing morals over mores and as having fairness trump predictability in terms of rule of law concerns. Moreover, it has been suggested that the holding in *Brown* was to a significant degree influenced by US foreign relations concerns as glaring images of racial segregation tainted US's claims to be a champion of freedom and human rights in the context of the battle of ideologies prevalent during the Cold War.[88]

The ongoing bitter political divisiveness unleashed by the USSCt's decision in *Roe* v *Wade* is ubiquitous, but one key aspect of the decision requires further brief mention as it bears particularly salient interpretive consequences. *Roe* would have been inescapably controversial as it recognized an unenumerated right to abortion, a subject over which Americans have been passionately divided. But even under these circumstances, the *Roe* decision might have been much less inflammatory had the USSCt strictly adhered to the constraints imposed by the 'case or controversy' requirements. In *Roe*, a woman who wanted to have an abortion challenged a Texas law that criminalized all abortions except those undertaken to save the life of the mother. The USSCt could have simply struck down the Texas law, and specified that as the right to an abortion is constitutionally protected, the state would have to advance a compelling interest for any limitation it sought to impose on the exercise of that right. That may have been enough for the plaintiff in *Roe* to obtain relief and for further specifications of the right involved to await further state legislation and future cases raising specific objections to the latter.

---

[86] See The Editors of Black Issues in Higher Education, *The Unfinished Agenda of Brown v. Board of Education* (J Wiley and Sons 2004).

[87] See James T Patterson, *Brown v. Board of Education: A Civil Rights Milestone and Its Troubled Legacy* (OUP 2001) 107.

[88] Ibid., 2.

Instead of that, however, the USSCt acted pretty much as a legislator, dividing pregnancy into three trimesters and the granting a woman an unrestricted right to abortion in the first trimester, authorizing limited state restrictions in the second trimester and allowing for all state restrictions save when the mother's life or health is endangered in the third semester. Whereas the contrast between strict adherence to the 'case or controversy' constraint and the broad lawmaking approach in *Roe* is dramatic, the tension between tailoring constitutional adjudication to particular facts and fashioning it so as to provide greater guidance and unity within the decentralized US system of constitutional review is an inescapable one. And although more general decisions going clearly beyond the facts at hand will in most cases seem more political, there is much to be said for the need for USSCt constitutional adjudication relating to fundamental rights to provide meaningful unity throughout the country and sufficient guidance to judges and other official actors charged with interpreting and protecting fundamental rights.

The line between judicial philosophy and ordinary politics may often be difficult to draw, but seems conceptually sound. A judge may be an originalist or devoted to a restrictive interpretation of fundamental rights, or else one who believes in reconciling constitutional interpretation with the morals and the mores of the present generation and taking an adaptive and expansive approach to fundamental rights and yet adjudicate without regard for the political consequences or impact of her decision. For example, a judge may have a restrictive view of fundamental rights and of federal as opposed to state powers, but that would commit her to constitutionally upholding politically conservative policies, such as bans on abortion as well as politically progressive ones, such as legalization of assisted suicide.

Two of the most controversial recent USSCt decisions, *Bush* v *Gore* (2000)[89] and *Citizens United* v *Federal Election Commission* (2010)[90] may at first appear to belie the distinction between judicial philosophy and politics, but upon further examination provide an excellent illustration of the proposition that the distinction in question is conceptually sound and yet at the same time difficult to maintain in practice. Both decisions undoubtedly had a profound political impact: *Bush* v *Gore* practically handed the contested 2000 US presidential election to George W Bush, and that by a five-to-four decision in which all the justices in

---

[89] 531 US 98 (2000).
[90] 558 US 310 (2010).

the majority happened to have been nominated by Republican presidents;[91] and *Citizens United,* which was also a five-to-four decision, struck down a federal law that limited corporate contributions in support of political candidates through television commercials and other means on the grounds that such law violated free speech rights, thus giving corporate interests virtually unrestrained power to disproportionately influence the outcome of elections. The judicial handing over the 2000 election to Bush and the USSCt's equating of money to speech have been widely criticized and have cast the Court in a particularly bad light.[92] Nevertheless, the two cases are clearly distinguishable along the judicial philosophy versus politics divide.

In *Bush* v *Gore,* the five justices who handed the presidency to Bush departed from their restrictive judicial philosophy which had hitherto led them to strike down an unusually high number of immensely popular federal laws – including the prohibition of possession of guns in schools[93] and the law tackling violence against women on a nationwide basis[94] – in order to deviate from one of the firmest and longest standing pillars of US federalism honored consistently by restrictive and expansive judicial interpreters alike. Indeed, it is a mainstay of American federalism that the highest state court is the authoritative interpreter of that state's law and that federal judges are bound to conform to such highest state court's interpretation when considering the (federal) constitutionality of any such law. In spite of this, however, five USSCt justices in fact handed the election to Bush by ordering an end to the recount of Florida voting ballots which had been imposed by the Florida Supreme Court based on its interpretation of Florida's election law. In order to reach the result they did, these justices had to substitute their own interpretation of the relevant Florida law for that of that state's highest court. And this is precisely what the USSCt majority did. Furthermore, there was yet another glaring anomaly in the USSCt decision which was not outcome

---

[91] For an extended account and critique of the USSCt's *Bush* v *Gore* decision, see Michel Rosenfeld, '*Bush v. Gore*: Three Strikes for the Constitution, the Court and Democracy, But There is Always Next Season' in Arthur Jacobson and Michel Rosenfeld (eds), *The Longest Night: Polemics and Perspectives on Election 2000* (University of California Press 2002) 111. The discussion that follows is largely based on the account provided in the just cited work.

[92] See, for example, Adam Liptak, 'Supreme Court Gets a Rare Rebuke, in Front of a Nation' *New York Times* (New York, 28 January 2010) <http://www.nytimes.com/2010/01/29/us/politics/29scotus.html> accessed 31 March 2015.

[93] *United States* v *Lopez* 514 US 549 (1995).

[94] *United States* v *Morrison* 529 US 598 (2000).

determinative,[95] but which figures as strong evidence of politics taking over standard judicial practice. Indeed, the USSCt majority held that the disparity in the means of recounting votes accepted by the Florida Supreme Court violated the equal protection rights of Florida voters, but specified that its decision on this issue should not be construed as a judicial precedent in the context of future elections. Arguably, for a responsible judge, serious consideration that present decisions will serve as future precedents provides a significant buffer against fashioning judicial results solely geared to the politics of the moment. If the equal protection holding in *Bush* v *Gore* were to become a precedent for future presidential elections, it would have to require a complete overhaul of the way in which Americans vote. In 2000, in Florida alone, there were 67 electoral districts with a variety of different ways of recording and counting votes leading to citizens in different districts having measurably different probabilities that their vote would be properly counted.

The equating of speech and money in *Citizens United* is also consistent with an elitist brand of American conservative politics that promotes corporate interests and that abhors state policies that have a redistributive effect. Unlike in the *Bush* v *Gore* instance, however, judicial philosophy and ideology standing alone afford a plausible justification to the holding in *Citizens United.* Two related factors account for this latter proposition. The first of these is American exceptionalism in the context of free speech jurisprudence. Not only, as noted above, does the US Bill of Rights enshrine free speech rights that are articulated in absolute terms, but also US protection of such rights has been much more extensive than those promoted by most other constitutional democracies.[96] The second factor, in turn, derives from the Lockean tradition in the conception of fundamental rights. For Locke himself, natural rights were conceived as flowing from a broad conception of property that weaves together individual dominion over his or her person, thoughts, conscience, beliefs

---

[95] Even if the methods of vote recount accepted by the Florida Supreme Court were unconstitutional, the USSCt could have prescribed federally acceptable standards which would have allowed Florida to restart the recount from scratch and still meet all the pertinent deadlines for formally submitting the results of the recount to the US Congress which has the constitutional task of providing final certification of the outcome of presidential elections. See US Constitution 1787, Twelfth Amendment.

[96] See Michel Rosenfeld, 'Hate Speech in Comparative Perspective: A Comparative Analysis' (2003) 24 *Cardozo L Rev* 1523.

and possessions.[97] Viewed accordingly, keeping in mind the metaphor of the individual as sovereign over his land, his crops and his pursuit of happiness within his own delimited space, it seems perfectly logical to regard one's money and one's ideas as inextricably linked. To be sure, for many this Lockean scenario cannot be credibly transplanted from its eighteenth century pre-industrial original setting to the contemporary world dominated by multinational corporations controlling wealth and resources that far exceed those of many nation-states. Be that as it may, the dispute between the Lockean speech absolutists and those seeking to achieve a proportionate balance between free speech and the integrity of the democratic process can be construed as tracking the conflict between originalists and adaptionists and that between the respective proponents of conflicting philosophies of fundamental rights. In sum, even if in practice it is impossible to determine whether politics shapes judicial philosophy or vice versa, in theory it remains possible to cast the two as distinct.

1.4.2 The USSCt 2013 Same-sex Marriage Cases: Judicial Resolution or Political Deferral?

The US political and constitutional landscape regarding homosexual rights, sexual orientation discrimination, and same-sex marriage has recently evolved at a very rapid rate. In 1986, the USSCt determined in a five to four decision in *Bowers* v *Hardwick*[98] that punishment of up to 20 years in prison for engaging in consensual adult homosexual sex did not violate the constitutional privacy right recognized in *Griswold. Bowers* was overruled six to three in the 2003 *Lawrence* v *Texas*[99] case which specified that privacy rights encompassed homosexual as well as hetero-sexual consensual adult sex. In between these two decisions, in 1996 in *Romer* v *Evans,*[100] the USSCt struck down on equal protection grounds, a state constitutional amendment specifically authorizing discrimination based on sexual orientation in relation to dealings not involving sexual relationships.[101] At around the same time, same-sex marriage came

---

[97] John Locke, *Second Treatise of Government* (first published 1689, Simon and Brown, 3rd edn, 2012) ch 5.

[98] 478 US 186 (1986).

[99] 539 US 558 (2003).

[100] 517 US 620 (1996).

[101] The state involved was Colorado where homosexual sex was legally permissible at the time of the adoption of the challenged state constitutional amendment. See *Romer* (n 100) 635.

suddenly upon the national legal and political scene following the 1993 decision by the Supreme Court of Hawaii, which decreed that its state constitution's own Equal Protection clause made it unconstitutional not to extend the right to marry to same-sex couples in *Baehr* v *Lewin.*[102] Following that decision, fear set in that Hawaii would soon legalize same-sex marriage and that homosexuals would travel en masse there, get married and then return to their states of residence demanding that their marriages be recognized under the Supremacy clause of the US Constitution the same way as heterosexual marriages have been all along.[103] To prevent this, the US Congress enacted the Defense of Marriage Act (DOMA) in 1996.[104] Among other things, DOMA allowed states not to recognize same-sex marriages performed under the law of sister states and excluded lawful same-sex married couples from federal benefits available to their heterosexual counterparts. In the end, Hawaii did not legalize same-sex marriage in the aftermath of *Baehr*, but Massachusetts did so after its highest court ruled the same way under its own state constitution in *Goodridge* v *Department of Public Health*[105] decided in 2003. Since then, several states have followed suit and, by the time the USSCt squarely considered the constitutionality of same-sex marriage, 36 states and the District of Columbia provided for same-sex marriage.[106]

In 2015 the USSCt decided by a five to four vote that same-sex marriage was constitutionally protected under the Due Process and Equal Protection clauses of the US Constitution's Fourteenth Amendment,[107] but a bare two years earlier in two same-sex marriage cases before it the Court deliberately avoided doing so. Although the importance of these two 2013 cases decision discussed below is now significantly eclipsed by the *Obergefell* decision, they nonetheless fully retain their worth as

102 74 Haw 530 (1993).

103 US Constitution 1787, art VI, cl 2. In the US eligibility and qualifications for marriage are a matter of state as opposed to federal law. Moreover states deviate somewhat from one another in the criteria they set. Nevertheless, all states have to accept the validity of a heterosexual marriage concluded in a sister state under criteria that the former state does not accept as a basis for marriage under its own requirements. For example, a state may not allow first cousins to marry, but must recognize a marriage among first cousins legally entered into in a sister state with no equivalent ban.

104 Pub L 104–199, 110 Stat 2419, enacted 21 September 1996, 1 USC para 7 and 28 USC para 1738C.

105 798 NE 2nd 941 (Mass 2003).

106 See <http://www.freedomtomarry.org/states/> accessed on 31 March 2015.

107 *Obergefell* v *Hodges,* 135 S. Ct. 2584 (2015).

illustrative of an unusually high number of interpretive and institutional dichotomies and paradoxes.

The two cases in question were decided on the same day. The first of these, *Hollingsworth* v *Perry*[108] dealt with a rather messy state of affairs relating to same-sex marriage in California. In 2008, the California Supreme Court ruled as had its Hawaii and Massachusetts counterparts as mentioned above. In California, however, the decision was followed several months later by adoption pursuant to a state referendum, known as Proposition 8, of a constitutional amendment that explicitly limited legal marriage to unions between a man and a woman.[109] Subsequently, the California Supreme Court upheld the above amendment as constitutional and California same-sex couples wishing to marry sued the California Governor and Attorney General in federal court alleging that the California amendment violated the federal Due Process clause and Equal Protection clause. The California executive officials named as defendants in the suit (who were charged with implementation and enforcement of state laws) refused to defend the lawsuit though they enforced the challenged law within the state. Under these circumstances, the proponents of Proposition 8 were allowed to intervene to defend the attacked law. Both the federal trial court and appeals court found the California law unconstitutional, and the trial court issued an injunction prohibiting state officials from enforcing the ban against marrying same-sex couples.[110]

While the appeal was pending before the USSCt, the situation in California was quite awkward. Several thousand same-sex marriages had been performed within the state during the interval between the 2008 California Supreme Court decision and the referendum on Proposition 8. This left matters unsettled not only among heterosexual and homosexual couples wishing to marry, but also among some of the latter who were already legally married within the state and others who might henceforth be prohibited from doing likewise. Finally, even those who had managed to obtain a same-sex marriage during the short period when California offered that alternative were facing a great uncertainty. Indeed, if the USSCt reversed the lower federal courts decisions, would the existing same-sex married couples be treated differently than their heterosexual counterparts? Would the former not be able to avail themselves of future benefits readily available to the latter?

---

108 570 U.S. ___, 133 S Ct 2652 (2013).
109 Ibid., 2659.
110 Ibid., 2660–63.

A definitive USSCt decision on the merits would have resolved these uncertainties or at least stabilized expectations and allowed for greater harmonization throughout the US. The USSCt refused to address the merits of the case, however, on the grounds that the proponents of Proposition 8 did not have a legally sufficient adversarial stance to meet the 'case or controversy' requirement. Did the USSCt engage in sound jurisprudence or did it buckle under out of political concerns? From a practical standpoint, the USSCt made the decision of the federal trial court overturning California's ban on same-sex marriage final as it barred any appeal by the Proposition 8 proponents. Consistent with this, the trial court decision became de facto the final word for the State of California. Hence, while staying away from the merits, the USSCt in effect enshrined same-sex marriage as a constitutional right in California and thus rendered moot the uncertainties and concerns listed above.

One might conclude that the result in *Hollingsworth* amounted to a brilliant display of judicial craftsmanship with fortunate political side effects were it not for the USSCt's decision the same day in *United States* v *Windsor.*[111] *Windsor* was a challenge against DOMA's prohibition against federal benefits available to opposite sex married individuals being also made available to their same-sex counterparts in a state that had legalized same-sex marriage. The Obama administration in *Windsor* took the same position as had the California Governor's administration in *Hollingsworth*: it enforced DOMA, but refused to defend its constitutionality in court.[112] Unlike in *Hollingsworth,* a different line up of five justices held that the unwilling executive branch could be properly replaced for 'case or controversy' purposes by a (legislative branch) group made up of members of the US House of Representatives. Accordingly, the lower federal courts' holding that the challenged DOMA provision was unconstitutional was upheld on the merits by the USSCt. Interestingly, the USSCt Chief Justice who wrote the Court's opinion in *Hollingsworth* dissented in *Windsor,* but three justices joined the majority in both cases.[113]

DOMA defined marriage for all federal purposes to be exclusively between a man and a woman, thus in fact excluding lawfully married same-sex couples from the benefits provided by more than 1000 federal laws.[114] In *Windsor,* the plaintiff had become the heir of her deceased same-sex spouse with whom she had resided in New York, a state where

---

[111] 570 U.S. ____, 133 S Ct 2675 (2013).
[112] Ibid., 2683–4.
[113] These were justices Breyer, Ginsburg and Kagan.
[114] *Windsor* (n 111) 2694–5.

same-sex marriage is lawful. Federal tax law does not impose any tax on any property left to one's surviving spouse. In the case of heterosexual marriage, state law determines whether a couple is lawfully married and therefore whether the federal tax exemption is applicable. In the case of Ms Windsor, however, whereas New York recognized her marriage as valid under its laws, DOMA deprived her of any exemption and she had to pay over $360 000 in estate taxes for which she sought a refund.[115]

On the merits, the USSCt held, based on well-settled, federalism-based jurisprudence, that since it is up to the states to determine the criteria for lawful marriages within their own boundaries, DOMA's recognition of some valid New York marriages to the exclusion of others was in violation of federal constitutional liberty and equality rights.[116] Thus, in *Windsor*, as it had in *Hollingsworth*, the USSCt avoided addressing the question of whether the federal constitution should be understood as protecting a right to same-sex marriage. Beyond that, and although the circumstances and posture of the two cases are different, the upshot is that the USSCt silence on the merits in *Hollingsworth* results in the federal district (trial) court in that case having had the thus far final word to the effect that at least as far as California is concerned, the federal constitution guarantees a right to same-sex marriage that overrides that state's prohibition of the latter under its laws – much like nearly a half a century earlier the USSCt invalidated on similar grounds Virginia's ban on interracial marriage.[117] In sharp contrast, in *Windsor*, the USSCt deferred to state's law on marriage and invalidated a federal law based on a combination of federalism and federal liberty and equality grounds. All this left the question of the constitutional status of same-sex marriage in a jurisprudential limbo, as it now turns out, for a two-year period.

Same-sex marriage, like abortion, is part of the culture wars that have long divided the US polity. Remarkably, the USSCt has been as cautious in the context of the former as it has been (perhaps unwittingly) intrepid in that of the latter. There is, however, one dramatic difference between the two. Opposition to same-sex marriage has greatly shrunk in the nearly two decades since DOMA was enacted.[118] The split over abortion, on the other hand, seems to have remained fairly steady, both in terms of

---

[115] Ibid., 2683.

[116] Ibid., 2695.

[117] See *Loving* v *Virginia* 388 US 1 (1967).

[118] See, for example, Gallup Poll, 'Americans Favor Rights for Gays, Lesbians to Inherit, Adopt' (17 December 2012) <http://www.gallup.com/poll/159272/americans-favor-rights-gays-lesbians-inherit-adopt.aspx.> accessed 31 March 2015.

numbers and of vehemence in the four decades since *Roe* v *Wade*.[119] In spite of this important difference, as the above discussion of the 2013 cases clearly indicates, it is difficult to disentangle the politics from the genuine constitutional issues involved and from the need to achieve a uniform judicial resolution of the latter. The two 2013 cases also plainly demonstrate that for all the USSCt did to avoid deciding the constitutional status of same-sex marriage, it in effect did so only in part thus accelerating the inevitable, now enshrined in the bitterly divided decision announced in *Obergefell*.

1.5 CONCLUSION

Constitutional review of fundamental rights in the US proves to be a complex and unique mix that weaves together different kinds of politics and conceptions of rights that can be regarded as rising above politics – either in some Lockean pre- or extra-political sense or else in that they ought be cast ideally as rising above existing political divisions. As the ultimate constitutional adjudicator, the USSCt is exceptional and operates in a sui generis way that sets it apart from constitutional courts and other highest courts in most other civil law and common law jurisdictions. Moreover, the exceptionalism in question results from a confluence of factors that include: constitutional architecture; a legal tradition framed by an apparently seamless mutual adaptation between common law methodology and a written constitution; a strong constitutional identity that tends to transform most major contentious political issues into constitutional ones; a particularly strong ideological commitment to interpreting fundamental rights as nearly exclusively negative rights; and a very special institutional positioning of the USSCt that has developed over time and that now provides it with a privileged vantage point in terms of checks and balances and of the interplay between rule of law and politics.

As the above discussion regarding the USSCt highlights, one can maintain consistently a theoretical distinction between ordinary politics, judicial politics and constitutional jurisprudence based on an ideologically coherent conception of fundamental rights. Indeed, the USSCt's two 2013 same-sex marriage cases provide a vivid example of a conjunction between ordinary politics and judicial politics: the former made manifest by the concerted avoidance of a decision on the merits;

---

119 *Roe* v *Wade* (n 58).

and the latter, by the concentration on the intricacies of the 'case or controversy' constraints. Ironically, to the extent that *Bush* v *Gore* figures as a purely political outlier, it highlights how other cases, politically divisive though they may end up being – such as *Roe* v *Wade* or *Citizens United* – do contain a separable jurisprudential dimension steeped in a distinct conception of fundamental rights. The main problem from the standpoint of the USSCt's legitimacy as the ultimate constitutional adjudicator stems from practical difficulties in sorting out what ought to emerge as theoretically distinct in a large number of cases. Moreover, these practical difficulties do not only result from conflation of ordinary politics, judicial politics and constitutional jurisprudence. But also, these difficulties are to a significant extent the product of divisions within each of these domains. Transforming politically divisive issues into constitutional ones does not, in most cases, purge these of the ordinary political passions with which they have become identified. At the same time, judges are often divided over judicial politics and, given the clashes between restrictive and expansive interpretations of fundamental rights, over the proper meaning and scope of constitutionally enshrined fundamental rights. Under these circumstances, fluctuations in the perceived legitimacy of the USSCt adjudication depends on the interrelation between a complex set of factors. Success seems most likely when the various factors are better aligned or when the constitutional jurisprudence and rule of law dimensions of a decision appear to be more discernibly detached from politics.

By casting a comparatist's glance on US constitutional adjudication, one can place in sharper focus the many intricate and intertwined ways in which the latter is exceptional as well as the various paradoxes to which it gives rise. Switching directions, can a comparatist draw any lessons from the US case that may be useful in considering constitutional adjudication in other jurisdictions? At first, the answer would clearly seem to be in the negative. If we add up originalism, Lockean negative rights and the role of US federalism in fundamental rights adjudication, nothing comparable comes to mind in connection with other jurisdictions with developed practices of constitutional adjudication. On further reflection, however, and after attempting to set comparisons at the most appropriate levels of abstraction, the US example may well yield some worthy insights to comparativists examining constitutional adjudication in other jurisdictions. As it is impossible to properly support this latter claim within the scope of the present chapter, suffice it for now to mention a couple of possibilities that would warrant further exploration. The most obvious possibility, approached at a relatively high level of abstraction, concerns the nature and scope of fundamental rights to be safeguarded through adjudication in constitutional democracies. Abortion, assisted suicide and same-sex marriage, among others, raise similar issues and lead to similar debates in a large number of Western constitutional democracies. Moreover, in a large number of such democracies, there are controversies regarding whether, or to what extent, judges rather than legislators ought to have the last word. Even if institutional differences render comparison unfruitful at some levels of abstraction, the larger question of whether, for example, assisted suicide ought to be constitutionally guaranteed (based on some implied or explicit general privacy right) or left to democratic majorities poses similar challenges for judges in the US and in several other jurisdictions. A second possibility for fruitful comparison concerns the level of abstraction at which fundamental rights constitutional issues are, or ought to be, addressed by constitutional adjudicators. Institutionally, with its concrete ex post 'case or controversy' requirements, the US seems at one end of the constitutional adjudication spectrum where a civil law country, like France that once relied exclusively – and now in part – on abstract ex ante review would be at the other end of the same spectrum. A close comparison of US cases such as *Roe* v *Wade* and civil law court cases – such as the GCC abortion decisions – is likely to reveal a great deal of congruence in how the constitutional adjudicator tackles the issues before her and how she handles the arguments and proposed resolutions concerning the contested constitutional question subject to her decision. In sum, US exceptionalism poses numerous challenges to the comparativist, but provided a proper balance is struck between similarities and differences, there seems to be ample room for US constitutional adjudication to prove illustrative and illuminating in the context of other jurisdictions.

2. The United Kingdom

Rights-based constitutional review in the UK: from form to function

Chintan Chandrachud and Aileen Kavanagh

2.1 INTRODUCTION

In traditional British constitutional thought, rights-based constitutional review on the American model was considered anathema. After all, one of the fundamental principles of the UK Constitution is parliamentary sovereignty. According to this principle, Parliament has a legally unlimited power to make whatever law it wishes. Moreover, Acts of Parliament cannot be overruled by any other institution, including the courts. Therefore, it seemed to follow straightforwardly that no court could strike down an Act of Parliament for non-compliance with rights-guarantees. Nor could they even review primary legislation to test for such compliance.[1]

In 1998, this traditional position changed. Under the Human Rights Act 1998 (HRA or 1998 Act), the UK courts were given the power to assess whether legislation was compatible with the rights enumerated in the European Convention on Human Rights 1950 (ECHR or Convention). Crucially, the 1998 Act stopped short of giving the courts the power to strike down legislation which was found to be incompatible with Convention rights. Instead, the courts were given the power to either interpret legislation compatibly with Convention rights, or, where this was not possible, to issue a declaration of incompatibility – a declaration which had no impact on the validity of the legislation. It was then up to Parliament to consider whether it would amend the legislation or not.

[1] Anthony Lester, 'Fundamental Rights in the United Kingdom: The Law and the British Constitution' (1976) 125 *U Pennsylvania L Rev* 337ff.

The scheme of the HRA was widely viewed as an ingenious way of preserving parliamentary sovereignty, while ensuring that rights would receive robust protection. As a matter of constitutional design, the HRA's model of rights protection – a strong interpretive obligation coupled with a non-binding declaration of incompatibility – was described as 'the third wave bill of rights',[2] 'the new Commonwealth model',[3] 'the parliamentary model',[4] the 'hybrid approach',[5] 'the dialogue model'[6] and 'weak-form review'.[7] It seemed to steer a middle course between pure parliamentary sovereignty on the one hand, and US style constitutional review on the other hand. Whichever label is used, the key feature of the UK's model is that while the courts have powers to review legislation for compliance with rights, they are not empowered to invalidate or strike down primary legislation. Nor can they compel the legislature to change the law if it is found to violate Convention rights. The distinctive lynchpin of the British approach was that it seemed to give Parliament, rather than the courts, the last word on how to uphold rights in the UK legal system.[8]

The question posed in this chapter is: has the HRA succeeded in steering a successful middle course between parliamentary sovereignty, on the one hand, and US-style constitutional review on the other hand? Crucially, does the UK Parliament have the last word on human rights

---

[2] Francesca Klug, 'The Human Rights Act – A "Third Way" or "Third Wave" Bill of Rights' (2001) *EHRLR* 361.

[3] Stephen Gardbaum, 'The New Commonwealth Model of Constitutionalism' (2001) 49 *Am J Comp L* 707.

[4] Janet L Hiebert, 'Parliamentary Bills of Rights: An Alternative Model?' (2006) 69 *MLR* 7; Janet L Hiebert, 'New Constitutional Ideas: Can New Parliamentary Models Resist Judicial Dominance When Interpreting Rights?' (2004) 82 *Texas L Rev* 1963.

[5] Jeffrey Goldsworthy, 'Homogenising Constitutions' (2003) 23 *OJLS* 483.

[6] Alison Young, *Parliamentary Sovereignty and the Human Rights Act 1998* (Hart 2009); Francesca Klug, 'Judicial Deference under the Human Rights Act 1998' [2003] PL 125, 130.

[7] Mark Tushnet, *Weak Courts, Strong Rights: Judicial Review and Social Welfare Rights in Comparative Constitutional Law* (Princeton UP 2009); though for an argument that this idea does not aptly capture the key features of the UK HRA 1998, see Aileen Kavanagh, 'What's so Weak about Weak-Form Review? The Example of the UK Human Rights Act 1998' (2015) 13 *Intl J Cons L* 1040–48.

[8] Klug (n 6) 130; Gardbaum (n 3) 709. For Parliament's options once a declaration of incompatibility has been made, see Chintan Chandrachud, 'Reconfiguring the Discourse on Political Responses to Declarations of Incompatibility' [2014] PL 624, 625.

questions, as originally hoped and promised? Supporters of the HRA presented a picture of an emboldened Parliament and a chastened court. But has this been borne out in practice? Our argument is that judicial powers have proved to be stronger under the 1998 Act than many commentators originally envisaged; and Parliament has been slow to seize the 'last word' on rights-issues, despite the non-binding status of the judicial declarations of incompatibility. Constitutional practice suggests that Parliament does not seize the last word very often – either because it does not want to have the last word, or feels unable to assert its views against judicial decisions. That is not to say that Parliament has had no role to play in protecting rights. On the contrary, there has been an increase in parliamentary scrutiny on human rights issues, largely due to the impressive work of the parliamentary Joint Committee on Human Rights (JCHR).[9] There is some evidence that human rights concerns are being mainstreamed in the UK's legislative process. Nonetheless, once the courts have declared legislation to be incompatible with Convention rights, Parliament has generally followed the courts, rather than defied them. In so doing, it seems that Parliament is willing to leave the last word to the courts.

2.2 EVOLUTION OF THE MODEL OF CONSTITUTIONAL REVIEW

2.2.1 General Constitutional Setup

In most modern democracies, revolutions or independence movements have produced periods of constitutional formation, resulting in codified constitutions. But unlike with other democratic nations from across the world, political scientists and constitutional scholars have struggled to pin down a single definitive constitutional moment in the history of the UK. The Constitution of the UK has thus remained uncodified, and has developed through incremental evolution rather than radical revolution.[10]

---

[9] See Murray Hunt, 'The Impact of the Human Rights Act on the Legislature: A Diminution of Democracy or a New Voice for Parliament' (2010) *EHRLR* 601ff; Aileen Kavanagh, 'The Joint Committee on Human Rights: A Hybrid Breed of Constitutional Watchdog' in Murray Hunt, Hayley Hooper and Paul Yowell (eds), *Parliaments and Human Rights: Redressing the Democratic Deficit* (Hart 2015).

[10] As Bell notes, 'a narrative of overt rupture is rendered impossible outside of a formal codification process'. See Christine Bell, 'Constitutional Transitions:

Although many parts of the Constitution are written somewhere – whether in statutes, judgments or executive codes – the UK does not have any single canonical text resembling those enacted in Italy, Germany or Japan following the Second World War. Further, in the absence of a written document, conventions (for instance, that the Monarch should not withhold Royal Assent to legislation enacted by Parliament, or that the Prime Minister should be the leader of the party that commands an absolute majority in the House of Commons, the Lower House of Parliament) play a significant role in the UK's constitutional landscape.[11]

Since the seventeenth century, parliamentary sovereignty, or the notion that anything that the Queen in Parliament enacts is law, has been a fundamental and distinctive principle of the constitution. The principle of parliamentary sovereignty had three important implications. First, Parliament enjoyed 'unlimited legislative authority',[12] which meant that there would be no legal restrictions on its ability to enact legislation on any subject. Any fetters on Parliament's lawmaking power could only be imposed through the political process. Second, courts in the UK could not strike down or disapply primary legislation on the basis that it breached fundamental rights or human rights. Third, Parliament could not entrench legislation binding on its successors, because that would effectively limit the sovereignty of future Parliaments.

2.2.2 Original Model of Constitutional Review

The principle of parliamentary sovereignty meant that no court could be empowered to nullify or set aside primary legislation. It also implied that there was no scope for courts to explicitly review primary legislation on rights-based grounds and no specialized tribunal to decide constitutional disputes. Nonetheless, this is not to say that the courts had absolutely no means of protecting rights when adjudicating disputes prior to the enactment of the HRA. In particular, even in traditional common law adjudication and ordinary statutory interpretation, the UK courts have relied on presumptions of statutory interpretation in order to uphold rights. The most well-known presumption is called 'the principle of legality'. This principle requires that:

The Peculiarities of the British Constitution and the Politics of Comparison' [2014] PL 446, 457.

[11] Vernon Bogdanor, *The New British Constitution* (Hart 2009) 16.

[12] AV Dicey, *Introduction to the Study of the Law of the Constitution* (6th edn, Macmillan 1902) 39.

> general words [in a statute] … should not be read as authorising the doing of acts which adversely affect the basic principles on which the law of the United Kingdom is based in the absence of clear words authorising such acts.[13]

Thus, it is now 'a familiar principle of statutory interpretation'[14] that 'fundamental rights cannot be taken away by a generally or ambiguously expressed provision in a statute'.[15] As one judge of the UK Supreme Court put it: 'The courts will (…) decline to hold that Parliament interfered with fundamental rights unless it has made its intentions crystal clear.'[16] This is 'a presumption of general application operating as a constitutional principle'[17] which can only be rebutted by express words or necessary implication.[18] Thus, if Parliament sought to override fundamental rights, it would have to do so using clear, unequivocal language and then pay the political price for it. Even before the enactment of the HRA, Murray Hunt argued that reliance on this presumption of statutory interpretation marked the move from a 'sovereignty-derived system of rules to a more rights-based constitutionalism'.[19] Indeed, a former judge of the UK Supreme Court opined that by relying on presumptions like these, 'the UK courts apply principles of constitutionality little different from those which exist in countries where the power of the legislature is expressly limited by a constitutional document'.[20] However, the key point about the principle of legality was that it could only take effect if legislation was open to a rights-consistent interpretation by reason of

---

[13] *Jackson v Attorney General* [2005] UKHL 56 [28], [29] (Lord Bingham); *R v Secretary of State for the Home Department, ex parte Pierson* [1998] AC 539, 575 (Lord Browne-Wilkinson); see further Philip Sales, 'A Comparison of the Principle of Legality and Section 3 of the Human Rights Act 1998' (2009) 125 LQR 598.

[14] *Axa General Insurance Ltd v The Lord Advocate* [2011] UKSC 46, [151].

[15] *Bank Mellat v HM Treasury (No 1)* (2013) 3 WLR 201 [55].

[16] *Jackson* (n 13) [159].

[17] *R v Secretary of State for the Home Department, ex parte Simms* [2000] 2 AC 115, 130.

[18] *Bank Mellat* (n 15) [55].

[19] Murray Hunt, *Using Human Rights Law in English Courts* (Hart 1997) 130.

[20] *Simms* (n 17); *Pierson* (n 13).

textual ambiguity or vagueness. Parliament still had the power to override rights if it expressed itself in statutory language which was sufficiently clear.[21]

In the course of the twentieth century, increasing pressure was placed on the orthodox principle of parliamentary sovereignty. In 1972, Parliament enacted the European Communities Act 1972, giving Community law primacy over existing and future domestic law.[22] How do the UK courts give priority to Community – now EU – law? There are two ways. The first is by 'conforming interpretation', such that UK laws are interpreted in conformity with EU law wherever this is possible. As a judge of the UK Supreme Court commented extra-judicially: 'it is amazing how much can be done in this way.'[23] However, if such an interpretation is not possible, the House of Lords decided in the landmark *Factortame* litigation that the courts could, for the first time, disapply statutes that were inconsistent with Community law.[24] According to Lord Bridge, 'it was the duty of a UK court, when delivering final judgment, to override any rule of national law found to be in conflict with any directly enforceable rule of Community law'.[25]

The UK's membership of another transnational legal regime – the Council of Europe – has also had a profound impact on the orthodox notion of parliamentary sovereignty. The Council of Europe drafted the ECHR, a treaty for the protection of primarily civil and political rights in member states. The European Court of Human Rights in Strasbourg (ECtHR or Strasbourg Court) hears applications concerning claims that member states have breached rights under the ECHR. The UK ratified the

---

[21] On the principle of legality, see Michael Fordham, 'Common Law Rights' (2011) 16 *JR* 14; Aileen Kavanagh, *Constitutional Review under the UK Human Rights Act* (CUP 2009) 99, 103, 296, 302.

[22] Many have argued that the UK's membership of the European Community did not detract from the ultimate sovereignty of Westminster Parliament, which remains free to repeal the European Communities Act 1972. See HWR Wade, 'Sovereignty – Revolution or Evolution' [1996] *LQR* 568; Mark Elliott, *The Constitutional Foundations of Judicial Review* (Hart 2001) 83.

[23] Baroness Hale, 'The Supreme Court in the United Kingdom Constitution' (The Bryce Lecture 2015, Oxford, 5 February 2015) 12 <https://www.supremecourt.uk/docs/speech-150205.pdf> accessed 22 April 2015.

[24] *R v Secretary of State for Transport, ex parte Factortame Ltd (No 2)* [1990] 1 AC 603. This judgment fuelled vigorous academic debate about whether the ultimate legal rules of the constitution had changed. See Wade (n 22); John Laws, 'Law and Democracy' [1995] PL 72; TRS Allan, 'Parliamentary Sovereignty: Law, Politics, and Revolution' (1997) 113 *LQR* 443.

[25] *Factortame* (n 24).

ECHR in 1951 and accepted the right of individual petition to the ECtHR in 1966, falling under an international obligation to bring its domestic law, including primary legislation, into compliance with judgments of the Strasbourg Court.[26] Although parliamentary sovereignty is formally preserved since the Westminster Parliament is not bound to obey the Strasbourg Court under domestic norms, refusing to do so constitutes a breach of treaty obligations. These developments resulted in courts becoming increasingly receptive to the idea of constitutional review of primary legislation – an issue that was, until not long ago, treated as off-limits in constitutional discourse. UK courts' jurisdiction to disapply legislation inconsistent with EU law resembled the kind of hard-edged constitutional review seen in many jurisdictions with codified constitutions.

2.2.3 Transformation of Model

As the discussion above shows, the UK was undergoing significant constitutional transition towards the close of the twentieth century. Major constitutional reforms were on the agenda following the victory, after 18 years of Conservative Party rule, of the Labour Party in the general elections of 1997. The New Labour Government carried through many of the promises of its election manifesto, including: changing the composition of the House of Lords, devolving lawmaking authority from Westminster Parliament to Scotland and Wales, enacting freedom of information legislation and strengthening regional government in England. So profound were the changes brought in by New Labour that some commentators referred to the reformed constitutional landscape as a new constitution.[27] Among the most important constitutional changes brought in by the Labour Party was the enactment of the HRA which was intended to give special legal effect to the ECHR.[28]

---

[26] A Committee of Ministers, comprising the foreign ministers of each member state, monitors compliance with the judgments of the Strasbourg Court.

[27] Bogdanor (n 11). Others, however, disagree on the basis that this assessment overestimates the extent of constitutional change under New Labour and underestimates the extent of constitutional change under previous governments. See, for example, Colin Turpin and Adam Tomkins, *British Government and the Constitution* (7th edn, CUP 2012) 36.

[28] Historically, the Labour Party had opposed a bill of rights on democratic grounds and the poor record of courts in protecting civil liberties against

Until 1998, no domestic statute in the UK incorporated or gave legal effect to rights under the ECHR. This meant that litigants were unable to enforce their Convention rights in the domestic courts. They were faced with heavy expenses and considerable delays in making claims to the Strasbourg Court.[29] The HRA, which sought to transform rights available to British citizens under the ECHR into 'British rights',[30] was considered the antidote to this problem. Significant as the 1998 Act was, it did not replace the rights and principles (including the principle of legality) established under the common law.[31] Rather, the HRA was intended to supplement them, and there were many matters on which the common law accorded greater protection to individual rights than the HRA.

When the HRA was being enacted, a key concern across party lines was to find a way of allowing judges to enforce human rights standards while preserving the notion of parliamentary sovereignty.[32] There was no political appetite for giving the courts an American-style strike-down power. As the then Lord Chancellor observed: 'I doubt that consent to the Human Rights Act could have been achieved if it gave the judiciary the right to strike down Acts of Parliament in whole or in part.'[33] The challenge was to find a way of protecting rights, while ensuring that Parliament would ultimately have the 'final say' in determining what the law should be.[34] The drafters sought to achieve this with a novel

executive encroachment (Francesca Klug and others, *A British Bill of Rights* (IPPR 1996) vi).

[29] Until 1998, individuals did not have direct access to the Strasbourg Court. They had to first apply to the European Commission on Human Rights, which would launch a case in the Strasbourg Court on behalf of the individual. The Commission was abolished by Protocol 11 to the ECHR, which entered into force in 1998.

[30] *Rights Brought Home: The Human Rights Bill* (Cm 3782, 1997) [1.14].

[31] Fordham (n 21).

[32] Klug, 'Judicial Deference under the Human Rights Act 1998' (n 6); Fransesca Klug, 'A Bill of Rights – Do We Need One or Do We Already Have One?' [2007] PL 701, 703; Kavanagh, *Constitutional Review under the UK Human Rights Act* (n 21) 310–13.

[33] Lord D Irvine, *Human Rights, Constitutional Law and the Development of the English Legal System* (Hart 2003) 98; Lord A Lester, 'The Magnetism of the Human Rights Act 1998' (2002) 33 *Victoria U of Wellington L Rev* 58; David Feldman, 'The Human Rights Act 1998 and Constitutional Principles' (1999) 19 LS 165, 169.

[34] Klug, 'Judicial Deference under the Human Rights Act 1998' (n 6) 126.

'compromise solution'[35] which they embedded into the HRA's structure and design.

The HRA contains three mechanisms designed to enhance the protection of human rights in primary legislation. The first two are powers given to the courts; the third is a mechanism oriented towards 'parliamentary procedure'. The powers given to the courts are interlinked. The first is an interpretive duty contained in section 3 which reads: 'so far as it is possible to do so, primary legislation and subordinate legislation must be read and given effect in a way which is compatible with the Convention rights.'[36] However, if a court decides that a rights-consistent interpretation is not possible, this triggers the second judicial mechanism for protecting rights, namely, the power to issue a 'declaration of incompatibility' under section 4. Crucially, this declaration 'does not affect the validity, continuing operation or enforcement of the provision in respect of which it is given';[37] and is not binding on the parties to the proceedings in which it is made.[38] It has no automatic legal effect, aside from trigerring a ministerial power to amend the statute by executive order if it is considered necessary to do so.[39]

The HRA was not just aimed at the courts. Section 6 places a duty on all public authorities to ensure that their decisions and actions are compatible with Convention rights.[40] However, in a bid to protect the formal supremacy of Parliament, the HRA insulated Parliament from the general duty contained in section 6. Thus, under the terms of the 1998 Act, Parliament does not act as a public authority when it enacts legislation[41] and public authorities (including the courts) do not act unlawfully when they enforce a statute that cannot be rendered compatible with the Convention by interpretation.[42] However, section 19

---

35 Feldman, 'The Human Rights Act 1998 and Constitutional Principles' (n 33) 169; *R (Chester) v Secretary of State for Justice* [2013] 3 WLR 1076 (SC) [120] (Lord Sumption).

36 Human Rights Act 1998, s 3(1).

37 Ibid., s 4(6)(a).

38 Ibid., s 4(6)(b).

39 Ibid., s 10.

40 Ibid., s 6.

41 Ibid., s 6(3). See further, Jan Van Zyl Smit, 'Statute Law: Interpretation and Declarations of Incompatibility' in David Hoffman (ed.), *The Impact of the UK Human Rights Act on Private Law* (CUP 2011).

42 Ibid., s 6(2); *Wilson v First County Trust Ltd* [2003] UKHL 40 [25].

provides that, when introducing legislation into Parliament,[43] the Minister in charge of a bill must make:

> a) a statement to the effect that in his view the provisions of the Bill are compatible with the Convention rights ("a statement of compatibility"); or b) make a statement to the effect that although he is unable to make a statement of compatibility the government nevertheless wishes the House to proceed with the Bill.

This provision incorporates legislative rights review into the HRA – requiring mandatory review by the political branches before draft legislation is enacted into law.[44]

Section 19 of the HRA specifically allows the government to proceed with legislation even when it believes that it may violate Convention rights. But it obliges the government to make such an intention explicit during the passage of the bill through Parliament.[45] Although there is no legal obligation on a proposing Minister to give reasons for the section 19 statement or even to initiate parliamentary debate on the issue,[46] a practice has now developed whereby the government provides a memorandum outlining its reasons for its views on compatibility.[47] Ministers almost always make a positive statement of compatibility.[48]

Another major constitutional reform (albeit one which was quite haphazardly realized)[49] under New Labour was the replacement, through the Constitutional Reform Act 2005, of the six-centuries old judicial functions of the House of Lords with a new Supreme Court for the UK. In October 2009, the UK Supreme Court took over the judicial functions of the House, becoming the final court of appeal on matters of English

---

[43] This statement must be made before the second reading of the bill. See ibid., s 19(1).

[44] Stephen Gardbaum, *The New Commonwealth Model of Constitutionalism: Theory and Practice* (CUP 2013) 30–31.

[45] Kavanagh, *Constitutional Review under the UK Human Rights Act* (n 21) 12.

[46] See Kavanagh, 'The Joint Committee on Human Rights' (n 9); Murray Hunt, 'Reshaping Constitutionalism' in John Morison, Kieran McEvoy and Gordon Anthony (eds), *Judges, Transition and Human Rights* (OUP 2007) 473.

[47] Communications Bill 2002–03 HL Bill [41].

[48] A negative 'statement of incompatibility' has only been made on one single occasion (in relation to the Communications Bill 2003), and that statute was subsequently held by the UK Supreme Court to be compatible with Convention rights. See Communications Bill 2002–03 HL Bill [41].

[49] Mark Elliott and Robert Thomas, *Public Law* (2nd edn, OUP 2014) 28.

and Welsh law, Northern Ireland law and Scottish civil law.[50] The Supreme Court sits not within Parliament, but in a separate building on the western side of Parliament Square.[51] Judgments of the 12 justices, who usually sit in panels of five, seven or nine, take the form of opinions rather than parliamentary speeches. The Lord Chancellor could no longer sit on the UK's highest court and his role as head of the judiciary of England and Wales was transferred to the Lord Chief Justice. In another break from past practice, Supreme Court justices would no longer have seats in the Upper House of Parliament (the House of Lords).[52]

Like the Appellate Committee of the House of Lords, the Supreme Court was not a constitutional court in the Kelsenian sense. As the second President of the Court, Lord Neuberger, put it, '[t]he Supreme Court is not a special constitutional court, but it generally limits the appeals it considers to those that raise points of general public importance'.[53] The UK Supreme Court only carries out concrete – not abstract – review and it is not restricted to deciding constitutional issues. In general, the courts in the UK are considered to have a 'constitutionally subordinate role'[54] to Parliament – and this is why they are not given the power to invalidate primary legislation.

Part of the difficulty of conceiving of the Supreme Court as a constitutional court is that in the absence of a codified constitution, there is no formal distinction between 'constitutional' statutes and 'ordinary' statutes,[55] although some judges[56] and scholars[57] have propounded substantive distinctions between them. However, a House of Commons

---

[50] See further Aileen Kavanagh, 'From Appellate Committee to Supreme Court: Independence, Activism and Transparency' in James Lee (ed.), *From House of Lords to Supreme Court: Judges, Jurists and the Process of Judging* (Hart 2011).

[51] On the possible impact of this symbolic locational shift on the Supreme Court's functioning, see Kate Malleson, 'The Evolving Role of the Supreme Court' [2011] PL 754, 765.

[52] Existing Law Lords appointed to the Supreme Court were disqualified from sitting or voting in the House of Lords while holding judicial office.

[53] *Bank Mellat* (n 15) [60].

[54] Anthony Lester, 'English Judges as Law-Makers' [1993] PL 269, 271.

[55] Sophie Turenne, 'Constitutional Adjudication and Appointments to the UK Supreme Court' in Simon Shetreet and Christopher Forsyth (eds), *The Culture of Judicial Independence: Rule of Law and World Peace* (Martinus Nijhoff 2012) 397.

[56] *Thoburn v Sunderland City Council* [2002] EWHC 195 (Admin).

[57] David Feldman, 'The Nature and Significance of "Constitutional" Legislation' (2013) *LQR* 343.

Select Committee concluded that the UK would not need a separate constitutional court *even if* a codified constitution were to be adopted.[58]

Nonetheless, the final years of the House of Lords and the early years of the UK Supreme Court reflect a dramatic increase in the proportion of human rights and public law cases on the judicial docket.[59] Therefore, much of the UK Supreme Court's time is spent deciding issues of constitutional importance. The HRA and the devolution legislation was a major contributor to this shift. Speaking extrajudicially, Lord Neuberger said that the 1998 Act and devolution legislation gave the courts 'their first taste of what it is to be a constitutional court'.[60] Other judges have also spoken of their constitutional – or at least 'quasi-constitutional' – role as a result of the growth of judicial review, the HRA, EU law and devolution to the regions.[61]

2.3 PRACTICE AND ENDURANCE OF CONSTITUTIONAL REVIEW

2.3.1 Specific Issues in Recent Case Law

A. Interpretation under section 3 of the HRA

The crucial question surrounding section 3 of the HRA is how far judges can go when interpreting legislation compatibly with Convention rights.[62] The terms of section 3 do not provide much guidance, stating simply that courts should adopt a Convention-compatible reading 'so far as it is

---

[58] House of Commons Political and Constitutional Reform Committee, 'Constitutional Role of the Judiciary if there were a Codified Constitution' (14 May 2014) ch 5.

[59] Alan Paterson, *Final Judgment: The Last Law Lords and the Supreme Court* (Hart 2013) 17. Paterson's research indicates, for example, that from 1970–72, public law and human rights cases comprised 13 per cent of the House of Lords' docket. In contrast, the corresponding figures for 2006–08 and 2009–13 were 39 per cent and 40 per cent respectively.

[60] Lord Neuberger, 'The Supreme Court: Is the House of Lords "Losing Part of Itself?"' The Young Legal Group of the British Friends of the Hebrew University (2 December 2009) cited in Turenne (n 55); Hale (n 23).

[61] Lord Neuberger, 'The UK Constitutional Settlement and the UK Supreme Court' (Legal Wales Conference, 10 October 2014) <https://www.supremecourt.uk/docs/speech-141010.pdf> accessed 10 April 2015.

[62] This meaning of 'possible' in s 3(1) HRA 1998 was one of the major preoccupations of the initial scholarship on the 1998 Act. See Kavanagh, *Constitutional Review under the UK Human Rights Act* (n 21) 25–9.

possible to do so'. One option might have been to interpret section 3 to mean that judges should choose a Convention-compatible interpretation when statutes were ambiguous – as stated earlier, courts had already begun reading statutory provisions in the light of Convention rights before the HRA had been enacted. On this approach, section 3 would only have codified existing practice. But the UK courts chose not to interpret it in this restrictive way.[63] From the earliest cases, they took their cue from the White Paper which preceded the enactment of the HRA, which stated that the purpose of section 3 was '*to go far beyond the present rule* which enables the courts to take the Convention into account in resolving any ambiguity in a legislative provision'.[64] The courts have settled on an expansive understanding of section 3 which allows them to alter the interpretation of otherwise unambiguous statutory provisions.

Let us examine how this occurs. When a litigant brings a case under the HRA claiming that primary legislation violates Convention rights, the courts adopt a two-stage approach to the interpretive obligation.[65] The first step is to establish whether the legislation, as ordinarily understood, violates Convention rights. If it does not, that is the end of the matter. However, if the courts believe that there is a prima facie infringement of Convention rights, then the courts go on to see whether it is nonetheless possible to find a rights-consistent interpretation under section 3(1) of the HRA which could remove or 'cure' the apparent incompatibility. At this second stage, the courts have held that section 3 allows them 'to adopt an interpretation which linguistically may appear strained. The techniques to be used will include the reading down of express language in a statute but also the implication of provisions'.[66]

The leading case on interpretation under section 3(1) of the HRA is the House of Lords' decision in *Ghaidan v Mendoza*.[67] This case concerned the rights of a surviving same sex partner of a tenant to a statutory tenancy under the Rent Act 1977. The 1977 Act granted a right of succession to the 'surviving spouse' of a tenant, where 'spouse' was defined as 'a person who was living with the original tenant as his or her

---

63 *Rights Brought Home* (n 30) [2.7].

64 Ibid.

65 See further, Kavanagh, *Constitutional Review under the UK Human Rights Act* (n 21) 23–4; Conor Gearty, 'Reconciling Parliamentary Democracy and Human Rights' (2002) 118 *LQR* 248.

66 *R v A* [2002] 1 AC 45 (HL) [44].

67 [2004] 2 AC 557 (HL).

wife or husband'.[68] The question was whether this provision applied to same sex partners. The House of Lords held that, as ordinarily understood, the Rent Act 1977 did not apply to same sex couples and therefore clearly violated Mr Mendoza's Convention rights.[69] The next question was whether this apparent or prima facie infringement could be eliminated by adopting a section 3(1) interpretation. By a majority of 4:1, the House of Lords held that it could. How was this achieved? The House of Lords held that while the language of the Rent Act 1977 seemed to preclude same sex couples, the 'social policy' underlying the 1977 Act was to give secure tenancies to couples who were in a stable and loving relationship and this policy could be applied equally to same sex couples. In this way, the courts used section 3 to read the Rent Act 1977 compatibly with Convention rights, thus removing its potentially discriminatory effect on same sex couples.[70]

All judges agreed that the interpretive obligation in section 3(1) of the HRA was 'of an unusual and far-reaching character'[71] and was not confined to resolving ambiguities in the legislation being interpreted in favour of a Convention-compatible meaning.[72] Giving the leading judgment, Lord Nicholls clarified that:

> ... even if, construed according to the ordinary principles of interpretation, the meaning of the legislation admits of no doubt, section 3 may nonetheless require the legislation to be given a different meaning ... in the ordinary course the interpretation of legislation involves seeking the intention reasonably to be attributed to Parliament in using the language in question. Section 3 may require the court to depart from the legislative intention, that is, depart from the intention of the Parliament which enacted the legislation ...[73]

What interpretive tools could the courts use to make legislation compliant with Convention rights? Lord Nicholls offered some guidance:

> Section 3 enables language to be interpreted restrictively or expansively. But section 3 goes further than this. It is also apt to require a court to *read in words* which change the meaning of the enacted legislation, so as to make it Convention-compliant. In other words, the intention of Parliament in enacting section 3 was that, to an extent bounded only by what is 'possible', a court

[68] Rent Act 1977, Sch 1, para. 2(1).
[69] [2004] 2 AC 557 (HL) [24].
[70] Ibid., [35].
[71] Ibid., [30].
[72] Ibid., [29]–[30] (Lord Nicholls), [44] (Lord Steyn), [119] (Lord Rodger), [67] (Lord Millett).
[73] Ibid., [29].

> can *modify the meaning, and hence the effect,* of primary and secondary legislation.[74] (emphasis supplied)

Although this expansive approach to the interpretive obligation is not without its academic critics,[75] it has been fully endorsed in subsequent cases and is now well-settled in the jurisprudence. There is now 'no room for doubt'[76] that the interpretative obligation under section 3 of the HRA is 'a very strong and far-reaching one, and may require the court to depart from the legislative intention of Parliament'.[77]

Using section 3 of the HRA, the courts have adopted bold and creative interpretations. There have been a number of cases where the courts have used section 3 to 'read down' provisions which clearly imposed a legal burden of proof on the defendant, to mean that the defendant was only obliged to discharge an evidential burden of proof.[78] In *R (Hammond) v Home Secretary*,[79] the House of Lords treated a statutory provision that a life prisoners' tariff 'is to be determined by a single judge of the High Court *without an oral hearing*' as giving the judge a discretion *to require an oral hearing* where fairness required it in order to render it compatible with the right to a fair trial.[80] In the most controversial case decided in the early days of the HRA,[81] the House of Lords held that a rape-shield provision enacted by Parliament just the previous year,[82] which severely curbed judicial discretion to admit sexual history evidence of the complainant in rape trials, violated the accused's right to a fair trial. Although the relevant statutory provision was extremely detailed and clearly excluded the admissibility of such evidence,[83] the court read an

---

[74] Ibid., [32].

[75] Timothy Endicott, *Administrative Law* (2nd edn, OUP 2011) 79. See also, Van Zyl Smit (n 41); Danny Nicol, 'Law and Politics After the Human Rights Act' [2006] PL 722.

[76] *Sheldrake v Director of Public Prosecutions* [2005] 1 AC 264 (HL) [28] (Lord Bingham).

[77] Ibid.

[78] See, for example, *R v Lambert* [2002] 2 AC 545 (HL). In this case, the Court read the words 'to prove' under section 28(2) of the Misuse of Drugs Act 1971, to mean 'to give sufficient evidence'.

[79] [2005] UKHL 69.

[80] Criminal Justice Act 2003, Sch 22, para. 11(1).

[81] For an analysis of this and other early cases, see Kavanagh, *Constitutional Review under the UK Human Rights Act* (n 21) ch 2. See also Aileen Kavanagh, 'Unlocking the Human Rights Act: the "Radical" Approach to Section 3(1) Revisited' [2005] *EHRLR* 260.

[82] Youth Justice and Criminal Evidence Act 1999.

[83] Ibid., s 41.

entire subsection into the 1999 Act in order to give judges the discretion to decide whether such evidence was 'so relevant to the issue of consent that to exclude it would endanger the fairness of the trial under Article 6 of the Convention'.[84] Though 'linguistically strained', this implication of provisions was deemed permissible under section 3(1) of the HRA.[85]

Therefore, it is clear that the interpretive power under section 3 is a far-reaching one, enabling courts to modify statutory language in compliance with Convention rights. In a sense, the absence of a strike-down power under the 1998 Act is compensated by the strong interpretive obligation. When judges rectify a statute by way of interpretation, they effectively engage in a form of judicial amendment,[86] thus curing the rights-violation with immediate effect.[87] Judicial rectification of statutory terms involves some displacement of the will of Parliament, since it entails the replacement of clear statutory language in favour of rights-compatible language chosen by the court. And in most cases, this displacement is effectively final because Parliament bears a burden of legislative inertia if it wishes to override a section 3 interpretation.[88] In fact, in the years since the HRA has been enacted, Parliament has never overcome that inertia threshold to enact legislation that counters or modifies a section 3 interpretation.[89] In the vast majority of cases, Parliament has simply not responded to section 3 interpretations in any way.[90] Therefore, at least in relation to rights-issues decided using section

---

84 The full 'test of admissibility' which was read into s 41 of the 1999 Act is set out at [46]; see also Kavanagh, *Constitutional Review under the UK Human Rights Act* (n 21) 21.

85 For another (more recent) case of 'reading in', see *R v Waya* [2012] UKSC 51.

86 Philip Sales and Richard Ekins, 'Rights-Consistent Interpretation and the Human Rights Act 1998' (2011) 127 *LQR* 217, 230–31.

87 Frederick Schauer, 'Ashwander Revisited' [1995] *Sup Ct Rev* 71, 94–5.

88 For discussion of the different burdens of inertia between sections 3 and 4 of the HRA, see Christine Bateup, 'Reassessing the Dialogic Possibilities of Weak Form Bills of Rights' (2009) 32 *Hastings Intl & Comp L Rev* 529, 569; Sujit Choudhry, 'The Commonwealth Constitutional Model or Models?' (2013) 11 *Intl J Cons L* 1094, 1099; Tsvi Kahana, 'Understanding the Notwithstanding Mechanism' (2002) 52 *UTLJ* 221, 250–51; Chandrachud, 'Reconfiguring the Discourse' (n 8) 634.

89 Christopher Crawford points out that the Scottish Parliament implicitly rejected a section 3 reading by the Sheriff Court in one case. However, this was most likely done unknowingly. See Christopher Crawford, 'Dialogue and Rights-Compatible Interpretations under Section 3 of the Human Rights Act 1998' (2014) 25 *King's Law Journal* 34, 40.

90 Ibid., 41.

3, the courts have the last word on the implications of Convention rights for statutory meaning – and Parliament has not sought to override those judicial determinations in any way.

B. The interplay between sections 3 and 4 of the HRA

The previous section revealed the effects of section 3 of the HRA on primary legislation. Let us now turn to the declaration of incompatibility. The declaration of incompatibility is inextricably linked with the interpretive mandate under section 3. This is because the courts can only issue a declaration 'if construction cannot resolve the incompatibility'.[91] Therefore, section 4 effectively begins where section 3 ends. How do the courts decide that the limits of section 3 have been reached? The HRA does not specify what those limits are and, therefore, it was up to the courts to articulate the grounds on which it would decide that a rights-consistent interpretation was not possible and that a declaration of incompatibility was a more appropriate solution.

In *Ghaidan,* the House of Lords outlined two main limits. The first is that 'the courts should not adopt a meaning inconsistent with a fundamental feature of the legislation'. The second is that the courts should not make decisions for which they are not equipped. 'There may be several ways of making a provision Convention-compliant, and the choice may involve issues calling the legislative deliberation'.[92] These limits indicate that even when it is possible for the courts to read down or read in words to statutes using section 3(1) of the HRA, they must not go against 'the entire substance'[93] of the legislation being construed.[94] Where a rights-consistent interpretation would cause too much discordance within the legislative scheme or require comprehensive legal reform, then the courts will tend to issue a declaration of incompatibility, leaving it to Parliament to remedy the rights-violation.[95] In other words, the courts have to make an evaluation of which institution – the court or Parliament – is best placed to remedy the rights-violation.

---

[91] *R (Morris) v Westminster City Council* [2005] EWCA Civ 1184 (CA) [56] (Sedley LJ); *Wilson v First County Trust* [2003] UKHL 40 [14].

[92] *Ghaidan v Godin-Mendoza* [2004] UKHL 30 [33].

[93] Ibid., [111] (Lord Rodger).

[94] Ibid., [33] (Lord Nicholls).

[95] See further, Kavanagh, *Constitutional Review under the UK Human Rights Act* (n 21) 270–74, 279–82.

In general, the courts have 'declined to try to formulate precise rules'[96] on when the limits of section 3 of the HRA have been reached, but they have expressed confidence that, in practice, such cases will be 'fairly easy to identify'.[97] *Bellinger v Bellinger*[98] provides a good illustration of the grounds on which the UK courts may decide to issue a declaration of incompatibility, rather than rectify the rights-violation using section 3. Mrs Bellinger was a post-operative male to female transsexual who argued that the Matrimonial Causes Act 1973, which only allowed a 'male' and 'female' to marry (with gender determined at birth) violated her right to a family life and was discriminatory. The House of Lords agreed that, as ordinarily understood, the 1973 Act violated Mrs Bellinger's Convention rights. Although they could have easily read in words to include transsexuals in the 1973 Act,[99] thus remedying the rights-violation with immediate effect, they declined to do so. Opting for a declaration of incompatibility, they explained that giving 'male' and 'female' an extended meaning:

> … raises issues whose solution calls for extensive inquiry and the widest public consultation and discussion … . The issues are altogether ill-suited for determination by courts and court procedures. They are pre-eminently a matter for Parliament.[100]

This was an issue 'calling for comprehensive legislative reform and not piecemeal judicial development'.[101] The House of Lords also recognized that an interpretive solution under section 3(1) of the HRA would have produced collateral consequences in many contexts, including 'housing and residential security of tenure, social security benefits, citizenship and

---

96 *Ghaidan* (n 92) [50]; *Sheldrake* (n 76) [28]; *R v Waya* [2012] UKSC 51 [14].

97 *Ghaidan* (n 92) [50].

98 [2003] 2 AC 467 (HL).

99 Bateup (n 88); Kavanagh, *Constitutional Review under the UK Human Rights Act* (n 21) 120; Gavin Phillipson, 'Deference, Discretion, and Democracy in the Human Rights Act Era' (2007) 60 CLP 40; Tom Hickman, *Public Law After the Human Rights Act* (Hart 2010) 92.

100 *Bellinger v Bellinger* [2003] 2 AC 467 (HL) [37].

101 *Chief Constable of West Yorkshire Police v A* [2005] 1 AC 51 (HL) [12]; Kavanagh, *Constitutional Review under the UK Human Rights Act* (n 21) 137–42.

immigration, taxation, pensions, inheritance, life insurance policies, criminal law (bigamy)'.[102] Therefore, a declaration of incompatibility was considered the most appropriate solution.

A number of points can be made about this interplay between sections 3 and 4 of the HRA. The first is that the choice between judicial rectification of an incompatible law under section 3 and the declaration of incompatibility mechanism under section 4 is a context-dependent one, heavily influenced by remedial concerns, including a judicial assessment of whether remedial action would be better coming from the courts or the legislature.[103] If the courts believe that they can remedy the rights-violation by way of interpretation of section 3 (thus doing justice to the individual litigant) without causing undue discordance in the legislative scheme under scrutiny or causing any other negative side effects, then they will opt for a section 3 interpretation. However, if root-and-branch reform of the whole area is required and the courts believe that they have insufficient legitimacy to rectify the problem, then they will tend to opt for section 4.[104]

Second, the UK courts have enunciated a general principle that section 3 of the HRA will be treated as the *primary* remedial measure under the 1998 Act, with declarations of incompatibility only used as a last resort.[105] This is now a settled principle in the case law.[106] As the Supreme Court has held on numerous occasions: 'section 3(1) is the *primary remedy* and resort to making a declaration of incompatibility *must always be an exceptional course*' (emphasis supplied).[107] One of the key reasons for this principle is that only a section 3 interpretation can give the individual litigant an immediate remedy. Thus, the fact that the declaration of incompatibility has no immediate legal effect, can create

---

[102] *Bellinger* (n 100) [42].

[103] See further, Jan Van Zyl Smit, 'Looking Up From Reading Down' (unpublished manuscript, on file with author); Kavanagh, *Constitutional Review under the UK Human Rights Act* (n 21) 123.

[104] Rosalind Dixon has argued that this remedial dimension skews the case law such that the courts will always tend to go for a s 3 interpretation in criminal and civil cases, but will feel freer to issue a declaration of incompatibility in 'pure public law cases' where the remedial concerns are not so strong or immediate (Rosalind Dixon, 'A Minimalist Charter of Rights for Australia: The U.K. or Canada as a Model?' (2009) 37 *FL Rev* 335). See also Fergal Davis and David Mead, 'Declarations of Incompatibility, Dialogue and the Criminal Law' (2014) 43 *Common Law World Rev* 62.

[105] *Ghaidan* (n 92) [46].

[106] *Sheldrake* (n 76) [28]; *R v Waya* (n 96) [14].

[107] *R v A* [2002] 1 AC 45 (HL) [44] (Lord Steyn).

strong incentives for British courts to adopt bolder more creative statutory interpretations than would generally be the case in systems where the courts have the power to invalidate legislation.[108] Ironically, it is precisely the remedial weakness of the declaration of incompatibility which leads the courts to interpret legislation in creative ways. And, as we have seen, when the courts do this, Parliament has allowed the courts to have the last word.

2.3.2 The Declaration of Incompatibility

We now turn to examine the nature and impact of the declaration of incompatibility. At the outset, it is useful to note that courts have refused to make hypothetical declarations of incompatibility, in the absence of identifiable victims whose rights have been affected in some way.[109] Further, as we saw earlier, a key feature of the declaration of incompatibility is that it is not binding on the parties and offers litigants no remedy. That is certainly a weakness of the declaratory mechanism and a reason why most litigants will prefer a section 3 interpretation. But although the declaration of incompatibility is not legally binding on the government or legislature, it is not as weak as may at first appear for a number of reasons.

First, there is the crucial international law dimension in the scheme of the HRA, which must not be overlooked.[110] If a British court issues a declaration of incompatibility which the government and/or Parliament fail to remedy, the aggrieved litigant is likely to bring an application to the Strasbourg Court. There, the applicant will argue that his or her Convention rights have been violated (as confirmed by the highest domestic courts) and that the UK Government has nonetheless failed to remedy the violation. In this situation, it is highly likely that the Strasbourg Court will find a rights violation,[111] whereupon the UK

---

[108] Kavanagh, *Constitutional Review under the UK Human Rights Act* (n 21) 132. For the view that heavy reliance on s 3 of the HRA is often a reaction to the relative weakness of section 4, see further Robert Wintemute, 'The Human Rights Act's First Five Years: Too Strong, Too Weak or Just Right?' (2006) 17 *KCLJ* 209, 215.

[109] *R (Rusbridger) v Attorney General* [2004] 1 AC 357; Chintan Chandrachud, 'Declarations of Unconstitutionality in India and the UK: Comparing the Space for Political Response' (2015) 43 *Georgia J of Intl & Comp L* 309.

[110] See further Kavanagh, *Constitutional Review under the UK Human Rights Act* (n 21) 284; Sales and Ekins (n 86) 228ff.

[111] On the reasons for this, see Kavanagh, *Constitutional Review under the UK Human Rights Act* (n 21) 284, 286–7.

Government is placed under an international law obligation to change the law in light of this judgment.[112] The risk of suffering significant political embarrassment if it were to lose a case in Strasbourg creates a strong incentive to comply with a declaration – all the more so, since it was partly to avoid such embarrassment that the British Parliament adopted the HRA in the first place.[113] Therefore, the UK Government has a lot to lose and potentially very little to gain by defying a declaration. Although the declaration of incompatibility is often portrayed as a purely political mechanism, it also has significant legal repercussions, since it is a means by which the courts can alert Parliament to a binding obligation in international law.[114]

The possibility of a ruling against the government from Strasbourg is compounded by the fact that section 2 of the HRA requires British courts to 'take into account' decisions of the Strasbourg Court when deciding cases in respect of Convention rights. In other words, Strasbourg jurisprudence is a 'mandatory relevant consideration'[115] which courts are obliged to consider when deciding whether or not to make a declaration of incompatibility. Courts have developed the 'mirror principle' approach to Strasbourg jurisprudence, which requires them to follow 'clear and constant' jurisprudence of that Court,[116] unless it arrived at a conclusion that was fundamentally at odds with the British Constitution. This principle sometimes compels British judges to follow Strasbourg jurisprudence which they seriously disagree with. This is best demonstrated through Lord Rodger's succinct opinion in a case before the House of Lords, where he said: '[e]ven though we are dealing with rights under a

---

[112] Kavanagh, ibid. 284; Lord A Lester, 'The Art of the Possible – Interpreting Statutes under the Human Rights Act' [1998] *EHRLR* 663, 668, 671; Mark Elliott, 'Parliamentary Sovereignty and the New Constitutional Order: Legislative Freedom, Political Reality and Convention' (2002) 22 *LS* 340, 348; Helen Fenwick, *Civil Liberties and Human Rights* (Routledge 2007) 190, 199–204.

[113] Kavanagh, ibid. 3; Michael Perry, 'Protecting Human Rights in a Democracy: What Role for Courts?' (2003) 38 *Wake Forest L Rev* 635, 671.

[114] *R (Animal Defenders International) v Culture Secretary* [2008] UKHL 15 [53] (Baroness Hale); *R (Countryside Alliance) v Attorney General* [2007] UKHL 52 [113] (Baroness Hale); Aruna Sathanapally, *Beyond Disagreement: Open Remedies in Human Rights Adjudication* (OUP 2012) 77; *R (Morris) v Westminster City Council* [2005] EWCA Civ 1184 (CA) [56] (Sedley LJ).

[115] Sir Phillip Sales, 'Strasbourg Jurisprudence and the Human Rights Act: A Response to Lord Irvine' [2012] PL 253, 257.

[116] *R (Alconbury Developments) v Secretary of State* [2003] 2 AC 295 [26] (Lord Slynn). See also *R (Ullah) v Special Adjudicator* [2004] UKHL 26; *R (Al-Skeini) v Secretary of State for Defence* [2008] 1 AC 153.

United Kingdom statute, in reality, we have no choice: *Argentoratum locutum, iudicium finitum* – Strasbourg has spoken, the case is closed.'[117] Thus, declarations of incompatibility made by British courts are likely to be based on Strasbourg jurisprudence – stacking the odds further in favour of Strasbourg deciding along the lines of the domestic court.

Second, when the Human Rights Bill was being introduced in Parliament, many members of the government stated in parliamentary debate that there would be a strong expectation that government would comply with the declarations. Thus, the then Lord Chancellor stated that 'we expect that the government and Parliament will in all cases almost certainly be prompted to change the law following a declaration of incompatibility'.[118] This expectation, described by some commentators as a 'constitutional expectation',[119] that the government/Parliament will remedy the rights-violation following a declaration of incompatibility,[120] has been generally borne out in practice. Since the enactment of the HRA, there have been 20 final declarations of incompatibility and in almost every single case, the government/Parliament has responded in some way to remedy the rights-violation.[121]

It is true that compliance has sometimes been minimal and begrudging, and in recent times has been accompanied by excoriating political rhetoric about the problems of court rulings (particularly those of the Strasbourg Court) on Convention rights.[122] Moreover, there has been considerable delay in implementing declarations.[123] However, despite

---

[117] *Secretary of State for the Home Department v AF (No 3)* [2009] UKHL 28 [98].

[118] Cited in *Burden v UK* (2006) 21 BHRC 640 [22].

[119] Jeffrey Jowell and Jonathan Cooper, 'Introduction' in Jeffrey Jowell and Jonathan Cooper (eds), *Delivering Rights: How the Human Rights Act is Working* (Hart 2003) 3.

[120] Kavanagh, *Constitutional Review under the UK Human Rights Act* (n 21); Timothy Endicott, *Administrative Law* (2nd edn, OUP 2011) 82–3.

[121] UK Ministry of Justice, 'Report to the Joint Committee on Human Rights on the Government's Response to Human Rights Judgments' (October 2013) 44; Chandrachud, 'Reconfiguring the Discourse' (n 8) 625.

[122] See the political rhetoric following the Strasbourg Court's decision in *Hirst v UK* [2005] ECHR 681.

[123] On the problem of delays, see Jeff King, 'Parliament's Role Following s4 Declarations of Incompatibility' in Murray Hunt (ed.), *Parliaments and Human Rights: Redressing the Democratic Deficit* (Hart 2015); Van Zyl Smit (n 41) 74–6; Merris Amos, 'Problems with the Human Rights Act and How to Remedy Them: Is a Bill of Rights the Answer?' (2009) 72 *MLR* 883, 893; Joint Committee on Human Rights, 'Monitoring the Government's Response to Court

these factors, we have a near perfect rate of compliance with declarations of incompatibility since the HRA was enacted.[124] As Jeff King observed following a broad-ranging analysis of all the parliamentary debates following judicial declarations of incompatibility: 'the general trend is one of workaday acceptance of the domestic court's judgment and the need to respond to it.'[125] Parliament and the government look upon their role as fashioning the remedy for a rights-violation, rather than deciding whether to comply with a declaration of incompatibility to begin with.[126]

Thus, one could say that while the courts have effectively the last word on *whether* legislation complies with rights, Parliament has the last word on *how* the judicially declared rights-violation should be remedied. Parliament and the government certainly have some leeway to decide how exactly to respond to a declaration of incompatibility. However, even here, courts have sometimes given suggestions as to how declarations of incompatibility should be complied with from time to time.[127] For instance, in *Thompson*,[128] statutory provisions that imposed unreviewable notification requirements on certain classes of sexual offenders under the Sexual Offences Act 2003 were at issue before the Supreme Court. While making a declaration of incompatibility, Lord Phillips clarified that Parliament could impose an 'appropriately high threshold for review' to avoid opening the floodgates to review applications.[129] He further stated that Parliament could make it difficult to secure a review through controls such as the time at which an application can first be made, the general frequency at which applications can be made, and what applicants need to prove for notification requirements to be varied or discharged. The incompatibility was later addressed through a remedial order[130] which incorporated the Court's suggestions of imposing a high threshold for review for those subjected to indefinite notification requirements under the Sexual Offences Act 2003. Such judicial suggestions are not binding, but they have nonetheless been followed by Parliament in some cases.

Judgments Finding Breaches of Human Rights' (2007) HC 728, [110]–[111] (2007) HL 128.

124 Alison L Young, 'Is Dialogue Working under the Human Rights Act 1998?' [2011] PL 773, 779.

125 King (n 123) 176.

126 Chandrachud, 'Reconfiguring the Discourse' (n 8) 636.

127 Ibid., 627.

128 *R (Thompson) v SSHD* [2011] 1 AC 331.

129 Ibid., [57].

130 Sexual Offences Act 2003 (Remedial Order) 2012.

The only possible exception to the general trend of responding positively to declarations of incompatibility is a declaration of incompatibility concerning a ban on prisoner voting where the government has delayed almost ten years in implementing any legislative change.[131] Not only has there been defiant political rhetoric to the effect that the UK Government will refuse to give prisoners the right to vote – despite numerous Strasbourg rulings – there was also a debate in Parliament where the vast majority of elected members of Parliament supported a motion that prisoners should not be given the right to vote.[132] Nonetheless, a parliamentary Select Committee on Prisoner Voting recommended that the government should implement the ruling in a minimal way, by giving the vote to prisoners who are incarcerated for two years or less.[133] It still remains to be seen whether the government will implement the Strasbourg (and now domestic) ruling to some degree. It is worth noting that the prisoner voting issues is highly unusual since there is cross-party support for the view that prisoners should not be allowed to vote, and virtually no electoral cost to taking such a stance. If this is the threshold at which Parliament is prepared to seize the last word, then it is a high threshold indeed – one which will only be met in truly exceptional circumstances.

In general, the high rate of compliance with declarations of incompatibility is partly explained by the broader political repercussions which ensue when a declaration of incompatibility is issued. Not only is there the problem of adverse publicity attracted by a judicial ruling declaring that legislation violates rights, these rulings are often seized upon by opposition members of Parliament to galvanize opposition to the government's policy within Parliament.[134] Furthermore, declarations are often relied on by the parliamentary JCHR to raise the profile of the human rights violation and to strengthen the political pressure on the government to remedy the rights-violation, both within and outside

---

[131] CRG Murray, 'A Perfect Storm: Parliament and Prisoner Disenfranchisement' (2012) *Parliamentary Affairs* 1, 3.

[132] For discussion, see Ed Bates, 'Analysing the Prisoner Voting Saga and the British Challenge to Strasbourg' (2014) *HRLR* 1.

[133] See Joint Committee on the Draft Voter Eligibility (Prisoners) Bill 2013–14 (16 December 2014) HL 103, HC 924 <http://www.publications.parliament.uk/pa/jt201314/jtselect/jtdraftvoting/103/103.pdf> accessed 22 April 2015.

[134] Sathanapally (n 114).

Parliament.[135] All told, the political repercussions of resisting a judicial finding of a rights violation, combined with the legal repercussions in the (highly likely) event of an adverse finding from the Strasbourg Court, set against the backdrop of the traditional comity between Parliament and the courts and the general respect for court decisions, means that a declaration of incompatibility can have a much stronger practical force than its legally non-binding status might suggest.[136]

The near perfect rate of compliance with declarations of incompatibility has led some scholars to suggest that a constitutional convention may be developing whereby Parliament is under a constitutional obligation to comply with them.[137] Although it may be premature to state with confidence that such a convention has clearly formed, much of the evidence is pointing in that direction.[138] The Strasbourg Court, tasked with determining whether the declaration of incompatibility is an effective domestic remedy for the purposes of article 35 of the ECHR, adopted a similar position.[139] It observed that although there was no legal obligation to address declarations of incompatibility, it was possible that in the future, evidence of a 'long-standing and established practice' of giving effect to declarations of incompatibility 'might be sufficient to persuade [it] … of the effectiveness of the procedure'.[140] However, the crystallization of a constitutional convention that all declarations of incompatibility will be complied with, may be difficult to discern, especially given that once a declaration of incompatibility is made, the burden of legislative inertia lies on the body that makes the declaration, that is the court, and not on the body to whom the declaration is addressed, that is Parliament.[141]

---

135 Following *F (A Child) v Secretary of State for the Home Department* [2010] UKSC 17 (which held that requiring people who were on the Sex Offenders Register to notify the police for the rest of their lives was incompatible with the right to a private life under article 8 of the ECHR), the Prime Minister David Cameron said: 'I am appalled by the Supreme Court ruling. We will take the minimal possible approach to this ruling' (HC Deb 16 February 2011, vol 523, col 955).

136 Kavanagh, 'What's so Weak about Weak-Form Review?'(n 7).

137 Kavanagh, *Constitutional Review under the UK Human Rights Act* (n 21), 289, 488; Adrian Vermeule, 'The Atrophy of Constitutional Powers' (2012) 3 OJLS 421; King (n 123) 182–6.

138 King (n 123) 186.

139 *Burden v United Kingdom* (2007) 44 EHRR 51.

140 Ibid., [39].

141 Chandrachud, 'Reconfiguring the Discourse' (n 8) 639–40.

Nonetheless, the strength of the various pressures to comply with a declaration has led some leading commentators on the 1998 Act to suggest that although the UK courts are not empowered to strike down legislation, they are 'effectively doing so indirectly, given that government would almost certainly want to change the law'.[142] Although in theory hortatory, in practice, a declaration of incompatibility resembles 'a de facto judicial power to procure the amendment of legislation which unlawfully qualifies fundamental rights' akin to a strike-down power.[143] Lord Hoffmann has suggested (albeit extra-curially) that the difference between a judicial strike-down power and the declaration of incompatibility is merely a 'technical distinction', because 'if the courts make a declaration of incompatibility, the political pressure upon the government and Parliament to bring the law into line will be hard to resist'.[144] Certainly, if the declarations of incompatibility are complied with in almost every case, then they have a similar effect as a strike-down power in terms of ultimately securing prospective legislative change in line with judicial pronouncements on what rights require.[145] Again, this raises questions about whether the UK model is as different from US-style constitutional review as is often claimed.

Of course, the main difference between the declaration of incompatibility and the strike-down power lies in the fact that the declaration of incompatibility has no immediate impact on the legislation and gives no instant benefit to the litigants. As we have seen, this difference is not without significance. It can incentivize the courts to adopt a rights-consistent interpretation (even when that strains the language of the statute) out of a traditional judicial concern to achieve corrective justice.[146] Conversely, it may incentivize relying upon a non binding declaration of incompatibility over a rights-consistent interpretation in cases where tampering with the statutory scheme produces collateral consequences which the court wishes to avoid. It may also disincentivize

---

[142] KD Ewing, 'The Human Rights Act and Parliamentary Democracy' (1999) 62 *MLR* 79, 92; Lester, 'The Art of the Possible' (n 112) 668; Fenwick (n 112) 190, 199ff.

[143] Elliott, 'Parliamentary Sovereignty and the New Constitutional Order'(n 112) 349; Lester, 'The Art of the Possible' (n 112) 672; Ewing (n 142) 92; Sales and Ekins (n 86) 230.

[144] Lord Hoffmann, 'Human Rights and the House of Lords' (1999) 62(2) *MLR* 159, 160.

[145] Kavanagh, *Constitutional Review under the UK Human Rights Act* (n 21).

[146] Dixon (n 104) 346; Sujit Choudhry and Kent Roach, 'Putting the Past Behind Us? Prospective Judicial and Legislative Constitutional Remedies' (2003) 21 *Sup Ct L Rev* 205.

potential litigants from bringing human rights challenges at all in those cases where the rights-violation is embedded in a fundamental feature of the legislative framework, thus precluding a section 3 interpretation.[147]

The UK Supreme Court's decision in *Nicklinson*[148] provides us with a unique glimpse into the judges' understanding of declarations of incompatibility. The question before the nine-member panel in that case was whether the English law criminalizing assisted suicide[149] violated the right to privacy under article 8 of the ECHR, and whether a Code published by the Director of Public Prosecutions,[150] on the prosecution of those who assisted suicide, was lawful. The Supreme Court held that this legislation did not violate Convention rights. However, three of the judges (Lords Neuberger, Mance and Wilson) opined that even if the law was incompatible with Convention rights and could not be given a rights-compliant interpretation, no declaration of incompatibility should be issued. Lord Neuberger justified this position on the basis that the matter required anxious consideration by Parliament, and was due to be debated by it soon.[151] It seems that the judges refrained from issuing a declaration of incompatibility in this case in order to allow Parliament as much room for manœuvre as possible in devising legislation on assisted suicide. Although the issue was not addressed directly, this may go to show that courts perceive the declaration of incompatibility as placing some pressure on Parliament to comply with the declaration.[152] Even though a declaration of incompatibility has no automatic legal effect on the incompatible legislation, it does trigger a ministerial power to amend

---

[147] However, in some cases, litigants have taken recourse to s 4 of the HRA as the first line of remedy in the knowledge that the statutory provisions could clearly not be interpreted consistent with Convention rights under s 3. Examples are: *McR's Application for Judicial Review* [2002] NIQB 58; *R (M) v Secretary of State for Health* [2003] EWHC 1094 (Admin); *R (Nasseri) v Secretary of State for the Home Department* [2008] 2 WLR 523; *R (T) v Chief Constable of Greater Manchester Police* [2012] EWHC 147 (Admin).

[148] *R (Nicklinson) v Ministry of Justice* [2014] UKSC 38.

[149] Suicide Act 1961, s 2(1).

[150] Policy for Prosecutors in respect of Cases of Encouraging or Assisting Suicide 2010.

[151] *Nicklinson* (n 148) [116]. On the caution of courts when dealing with issues that have recently been, or are about to be, debated in Parliament, see Aileen Kavanagh, 'Proportionality and Parliamentary Debates: Exploring Some Forbidden Territory' (2014) 34(3) *OJLS* 443.

[152] On the space available to Parliament following a declaration of incompatibility, see Chandrachud, 'Reconfiguring the Discourse' (n 8).

such legislation.[153] This places the Minister in the position of having to explain (politically) why the power has, or more importantly, *has not*, been invoked.

There is one other interesting feature of the political practice following declarations of incompatibility which follows on from this point. This is that many leading politicians and journalists in the UK describe the decisions relying on the declaration of incompatibility as binding or as having the effect of 'overturning' or 'striking down' primary legislation.[154] Even in relation to the most controversial declarations of incompatibility, the language used in parliamentary debates suggested that many government MPs (that is not just opposition MPs) treat the declarations as if they have the effect or invalidating the legislation or legally requiring its amendment. Thus, in the parliamentary debates following many declarations of incompatibility, the declaration of incompatibility issued there is treated by MPs as 'an authoritative finding, not merely as opinion or advice'.[155] Even when MPs express considerable frustration with declaration of incompatibility, they sometimes suggest that their hands are tied by it.[156] This phenomenon of treating the declaration of incompatibility as having binding legal effect akin to a strike-down power requires more empirical and theoretical analysis.

One explanation for the phenomenon is suggested by Jan Van Zyl Smit and others, namely, that it is a crude form of political buck-passing which allows Ministers to avoid the blame for unpopular decisions while directing public criticism towards the courts.[157] A less cynical explanation is also possible. It may simply be that in countries where the courts are held in high esteem and there is a relatively strong belief in the importance of protecting rights and the rule of law, all judgments by the highest courts (whether declaratory or not) will effectively be treated as authoritative or at the very least highly persuasive and worthy of respect

---

153 Human Rights Act 1998, s 10.

154 Sathanapally (n 114) 154.

155 Ibid., 192.

156 Ibid., 168.

157 Van Zyl Smit (n 41); Fergal Davis, 'The Human Rights Act and Juridification: Saving Democracy from Law', (2010) 30(2) *Politics* 91, 92–3; Ran Hirschl, 'How Consequential is the Commonwealth Constitutional Model?' (2013) 11 *Intl J Cons L* 1086, 1089. See also Mark Graber, 'The Nonmajoritarian Difficulty: Legislative Deference to the Judiciary' (1993) 7 *Studies in American Political Development* 35.

in most cases.[158] If this is true, then the novel design mechanisms associated most prominently with the 'third wave bill of rights' are unlikely to fulfill their promise of giving the legislature 'the last word' on questions concerning rights – at least in the sense of enabling elected representatives to disagree regularly and overtly with a high-profile court ruling concerning rights.[159] Constitutional practice suggests that Parliament accepts a constitutional division of responsibilities whereby the courts determine whether a right has been violated, whereas Parliament has the role of devising a remedy for such violation if such is found. Rather than seizing the last word from the courts as many scholars hoped and predicted, Parliament generally acquiesces in court rulings about whether rights have been violated.

2.4 CONCLUSION

There is no doubt that when the HRA was being drafted, a conscious effort was made to ensure that judges would not have the power to strike down primary legislation and that Parliament would be free to take its own view of what rights required and even to enact legislation which seemed to violate Convention rights, if it so wished.[160] However, when we examine the detail of how the 1998 Act works in practice, a somewhat different picture emerges. For one thing, there is the enormous strength of the interpretive duty as a way of giving (immediate) legal effect to Convention rights in primary legislation. Moreover, not only are declarations of incompatibility used as a last resort in cases concerning rights, they are complied with in almost every case. Furthermore, when we turn to examine the practice surrounding section 19 of the HRA, it transpires that although the government is entitled to introduce legislation which it believes to contravene Convention rights, it has only done so in one instance. In general, all legislative proposals introduced by the government are accompanied by a 'Statement of Compatibility', rather than a statement to the effect that although the Minister is unable to make

---

[158] For an analysis of the strategic incentives motivating political respect for judicial rulings, see Bateup (n 88).

[159] See Chandrachud, 'Declarations of Unconstitutionality in India and the UK' (n 109) (arguing that the political space available for responses to declarations of incompatibility in the UK is very similar to that available for responses to exercises of the 'strike-down' power in India).

[160] Lester (n 112) 663.

a statement of compatibility, the government 'nevertheless wishes the House to proceed with the Bill'.[161]

So, when we look at how the mechanisms of rights-based constitutional review actually work in the UK, we can see that they are much stronger than they might at first appear. Certainly, as a matter of constitutional design, the UK HRA seems to be structured so as to give the legislature the possibility of having 'the last word'. However, in practice, court rulings have been treated as authoritative and binding on the other branches and have tended to prevail. The legislature has not been keen to rely on the mechanisms available to it under the HRA to defy, overrule or ignore court decisions. In reality, the emerging constitutional practice under the 1998 Act reveals that, in many cases, the courts have 'normative finality' on questions of rights[162] in much the same way as they do under US-style constitutional review, despite the lack of a formal power to strike down legislation.[163]

This only goes to prove the adage of well-seasoned comparative constitutional lawyers that constitutional function does not always follow constitutional form. We should not expect that constitutional design will be determinative of how a system of rights-based judicial review will work in practice.[164] The possibility of variation between systems with similar design is borne out by the fact that the adoption of similar design-features to the UK HRA in two Australian states (Victoria and the Australian Capital Territory) have produced quite different constitutional practices than that which we have experienced in the UK.[165] Here we see that the background constitutional culture has an enormous influence on the implementation of human rights in particular countries.

Nevertheless, even though the level of engagement with rights at the post-legislative stage is not as meaningful as one might have expected, Parliament is increasingly deliberating about rights at the pre-legislative stage. By scrutinizing bills on rights-based parameters, the JCHR – a

---

[161] See Communications Bill 2002–03, HL Bill.

[162] Tushnet (n 7) 3.

[163] Kavanagh, 'What's so Weak about Weak-Form Review?' (n 7).

[164] See Sathanapally (n 114) 223 ('DOIs [declarations of incompatibility] in the UK provide one example of the fact that innovations in constitutional design may not necessarily translate to different *practice* or different *behaviours* in the ways one might expect').

[165] See Adrienne Stone, 'Constitutional Orthodoxy in the United Kingdom and Australia: The Deepening Divide' (2014) *MULR* 836. For an analysis of rights-based constitutional review in Australia, see James Stellios and Matthew Zagor in Chapter 4.

permanent select committee of both Houses of Parliament – has pressed Parliament to engage in political or legislative rights review,[166] as some scholars describe it. It is hard to objectively measure the performance of the JCHR, since the influence of parliamentary committees tends to be subtle and silently exercised.[167] Overall, it seems that although the JCHR's success in persuading Parliament to carry out amendments to draft legislation has been limited, it has performed a valuable role in fostering a culture of human rights in government.[168] The real manifestation of the third wave bill of rights, then, may not be in parliamentary engagement with declarations of incompatibility, but rather, with parliamentary deliberation about rights more generally. The UK Parliament may not be rushing to seize the last word, but it seems to be internalizing human rights norms when issuing the first word, that is when enacting primary legislation which may engage human rights concerns.

As a final point, it bears mentioning that as an unentrenched statute, the existential threat to the HRA has never been too distant. After increasing dissatisfaction with judicial decisions and the influence of the Strasbourg Court on domestic decision-making, the HRA has been a soft target within political circles. The Conservative Party has often advocated the repeal of the 1998 Act, and its possible replacement with a home-grown bill of rights.[169] But even if the HRA were to be repealed, many commentators argue that common law principles would continue to provide robust protection for individual rights and liberties in the UK.[170] Whether the common law can step into the void left by the HRA – or perhaps even go beyond it – are matters that, for now, remain in the realm of speculation.

---

[166] Gardbaum, *The New Commonwealth Model of Constitutionalism* (n 44) 25; Janet Hiebert and James Kelly, *Parliamentary Bills of Rights: The Experiences of New Zealand and the United Kingdom* (CUP 2015) 3. See also Jack Simson Caird, 'Parliamentary Constitutional Review: Ten Years of the House of Lords Select Committee on the Constitution' [2012] PL 4.

[167] Kavanagh, 'The Joint Committee on Human Rights' (n 9) 131.

[168] Janet Hiebert, 'Parliament and the Human Rights Act: Can the JCHR help facilitate a Culture of Rights?' (2006) 4 *Intl J Cons L* 1. See also David Feldman, 'Can and Should Parliament Protect Human Rights?' (2004) 10 *EPL* 635, 651.

[169] David Barrett, 'Tory manifesto will promise to scrap Labour's Human Rights Act, says Theresa May' *The Telegraph* (London, 30 September 2013); Mark Elliott, 'Repealing the Human Rights Act: What Might Lie Ahead?' (*Public Law for Everyone*, 30 September 2013) <http://publiclawforeveryone.com/2013/09/30/repealing-the-human-rights-act-what-might-lie-ahead/> accessed 22 April 2015.

[170] Fordham (n 21) 20.

3. Ireland

Eoin Carolan and Cliona Kelly

3.1 LEAVING BEHIND THE COMMONWEALTH MODEL OF RIGHTS REVIEW: IRELAND AS AN EXAMPLE OF COLLABORATIVE CONSTITUTIONALISM

Eoin Carolan

3.1.1 Introduction

> We have – and it is hardly necessary for me to say it – had rather too much in the last 25 years of constitutional law and constitutional lawyers. For 25 years, we have arid futile and unending discussions as to the nature and character of our constitutional position and our constitutional and international relations with Great Britain, with the other members of the Commonwealth of Nations … . I do not care what the position is going to be from a constitutional point of view, provided we know definitely where we stand. I can understand the position, constitutionally and internationally, of this country being a member, a full, recognised, decent member of the British Commonwealth of Nations. I can understand a decent declaration of a republic. But I cannot understand the indecency which is being perpetrated on this country by this Bill. I do not know into what political pigeon-hole we are going to be put when this Bill is law, but whether we are in the Commonwealth of Nations, whether we are a republic, or whether we are neither one thing nor the other – a State unknown hitherto in political theory – I want at least that it should be definite … .[1]

[1] An Taoiseach, John A Costello, debating The Republic of Ireland Bill 1948, quoting from an earlier debate on The Executive Authority (External Relations) Act 1936 (Dáil Éireann Debates 24 November 1948, vol 113).

Comparative classifications have always presented problems for Irish constitutional law. Lacking a definitive moment of independent statehood, Ireland lingered in its early years in the half-light of external association, somewhere between subject, dominion, and sovereign.

This ambiguity influenced domestic constitutional design. While the objective was to 'swe[ep] away all the old dead wood of British constitutional theory that lay or appeared to lie in the path of constitutional progress', this was complicated by the shifting international realpolitik over the extent of Commonwealth (and Irish) autonomy from Westminster. Ireland's constitutional history between 1922 and 1948 is accordingly a tale of gradual evolution punctuated by intermittent moments of major constitutional change.

This encouraged a peripatetic approach to constitutional borrowing which – for the modern comparative scholar – presents both problems and opportunities. Traditionally, Ireland has been regarded as an early attempt at marrying American style judicial review with the Westminster system of cabinet government. It has more recently been revealed that the drafters of the 1937 Constitution in fact drew on a more diverse and eclectic range of sources. New historical research has demonstrated that the drafters looked to constitutional systems, particularly those of European contemporaries, with the result that:

> [a]s the draft Constitution headed towards its first publication and restricted circulation on March 1937, it now reflected legal thinking and influences from a variety of sources including the Weimar Constitution (1919), the Polish Constitution (1921), the Austrian Constitution (1934), the Portuguese Constitution (1933) and Papal Encyclicals, as well, of course, as constitutional law and theory drawn from the US and British traditions.[2]

While Costello's concern about Ireland as 'a State unknown hitherto in political theory' goes too far, this mutable diversity of influences means that the domestic regime that ultimately resulted can be difficult to situate within familiar typologies of rights-based review. Yet this may, in itself, raise questions about the utility and scope of such typologies. Ireland does not conform to the prescriptions of either political or legal constitutionalists. Yet, neither can it be said to follow the emergent 'third way' of comparative constitutional design: the so-called Commonwealth model. Is Ireland an institutional outlier, neither one thing nor the other? Or is Ireland an illustrative – and far from unique – riposte to the

[2] Gerard Hogan, *The Origins of the Irish Constitution 1928–1941* (Royal Irish Academy 2012) 279.

monolithic assumptions of much macro-constitutional comparativism? This chapter argues for the latter – and further makes the case for an alternative model of rights-based review. Just as the Costello Government found clarity only with Ireland's departure from the Commonwealth, so – it is contended – should comparative scholarship leave behind the Commonwealth model of rights-based review.

3.1.2 The Parliamentary Model Adapted?

There are many aspects of Ireland's legal system that seem, in part, to ape the system originally inherited from Westminster. These include the continued application of common law principles, the ongoing influence of English legal authorities and, of course, the structure of the legislature (the Oireachtas) itself, especially with regard to the familiar Bagehotian 'near fusion' of executive and legislative branches.

However, there are a number of features of Ireland's constitutional regime that would place it outside the parliamentary model of rights-based review as it is appears to be currently conceived. Most notably, the superior courts are invested with an express constitutional power to strike down an Act of the Oireachtas where it is deemed to be repugnant to the constitution.[3] Similarly, they are also entitled to invalidate administrative or executive conduct where it is adjudged to be unconstitutional.

For advocates of what have variously been described as systems of parliamentary bills of rights,[4] or common law or Commonwealth constitutionalism,[5] the existence and exercise of this power would place Ireland firmly in the judicial supremacist sphere. The power of the courts to authoritatively annul the expressed view of Parliament is ostensibly incompatible with what is claimed to constitute an intermediate model between legislative and judicial supremacy. Janet Hiebert has described this emergent category as:

> [a]n alternative or hybrid blend of political and juridical forms of constitutionalism [which] emphasises the ability of parliament to disagree with judicial interpretation of rights as a distinguishing feature of this new model.[6]

---

[3] Irish Constitution 1937, arts 15 and 34.

[4] Janet L Hiebert, 'Parliamentary Bills of Rights: An Alternative Model?' (2006) 69 *MLR* 7.

[5] Stephen Gardbaum, *The New Commonwealth Model of Constitutionalism: Theory and Practice* (CUP 2013).

[6] Hiebert (n 4) 9.

Stephen Gardbaum's more prescriptive enumeration of the core *indicia* of his model would similarly situate Ireland outside his common law or Commonwealth model.

> For me, the essential and defining features of the new Commonwealth model as a general, innovative and distinctive model of constitutionalism are threefold: (1) a legalised bill or charter of rights; (2) some form of enhanced judicial power to enforce these rights by assessing legislation (as well as other governmental acts) for consistency with them that goes beyond traditional presumptions and ordinary modes of statutory interpretation; and (3*) most distinctively, notwithstanding this judicial role, a formal legislative power to have the final word on what the law of the land is by ordinary majority vote*[7] (emphasis added).

According to this model, Ireland, as a system which denies the Oireachtas the formal power to reverse the ruling of a court by ordinary majority vote (and in which one of the courts' seminal early rulings, in fact, invalidated legislation for the precise reason that it sought to effectively determine the outcome of court proceedings)[8] must be classified as one based on judicial supremacy.

Yet, a closer analysis of the Irish system raises doubts about the accuracy of the supremacist diagnosis and, thus, about the tripartite typology as a whole. Although the Irish courts retain and periodically exercise the power to invalidate legislation, there are several structural features of the Irish system which belie Gardbaum's automatic equation of judicial supremacy with the absence of a parliamentary override. It is contended, on the contrary, that the Irish experience demonstrates that the supremacist dichotomy at the heart of this analysis rests on a caricatured and abridged account of both the practicalities and potentialities of the legislative-judicial relationship.

3.1.3 Judicial Supremacy in Ireland?

For Gardbaum, judicial supremacy is problematic for the degree of power and authority it confers on courts in the resolution of inherently contestable rights-based issues:

> Judicial supremacy, with its associated tendency toward exclusivity and monologue in rights reasoning is especially problematic in the inevitable real

---

[7] Stephen Gardbaum, 'Reassessing the New Commonwealth Model of Constitutionalism' (2010) 8 *Intl J Cons L* 167, 169.

[8] *Buckley v AG* [1950] IR 67.

> world context of reasonable disagreement – among judges, between courts and legislatures, and among citizens – regarding the meaning, scope, application and permissible limits on the relatively abstract text of a bill of rights.[9]

Gardbaum is undoubtedly correct that there must be scope in any functioning democratic system for legitimate disagreement about the precise content or consequences of a fundamental rights guarantee. Furthermore, it is also correct that a declaration that a legislative instrument is unconstitutional and thereby void does represent a definitive resolution of that particular, and usually contestable, controversy. However, it does not follow from the mere presence of such a remedy that the constitutional system in question is therefore one of judicial supremacy. To so conclude is to overlook the many ways in which a system which includes 'American-style' powers of judicial review can also acknowledge and permit legitimate value contestation between political and legal organs. It is questionable whether a single form of remedy can serve as a reliable proxy for the relative power or influence of different institutions. Rather, as the Irish experiences suggests, this relationship may be influenced by a variety of other structural factors which a more comprehensive account of rights-based review models ought to take into account.

A. Structural barriers to supremacy

One of the suggested attractions of the 'new' model of rights-based review is that it takes seriously the position of political institutions like the legislature on contested rights issues. This is also a feature frequently highlighted by those who favour metaphors[10] of 'dialogue' or 'deference' in describing the interaction between the courts and other (usually legislative) branches. Yet, it should not necessarily be assumed that a system which retains the option of striking down legislation will also tend to take little or no account of the legislative position on contestable controversies that are, in principle, capable of being framed in terms of individual rights. On the contrary, the legal process provides a range of

---

[9] Gardbaum, 'Reassessing the New Commonwealth Model' (n 7) 173.

[10] This is deliberately intended to suggest that these models often seem to involve either a simplified guide or an ex post facto rationalization of how such a relationship *could* (or perhaps even *should*) work rather than an account of how they actually operate. On this theme, see Peter Hogg, Alison Bushell Thornton and Wade Wright, 'Charter Dialogue Revisited – or Much Ado about Metaphors' (2007) 45 *Osgoode Hall LJ* 1; Gardbaum, 'Reassessing the New Commonwealth Model' (n 7) 181.

opportunities – both procedural and substantive – for weight to be given to the preferences of the legislature over those of the courts.[11]

For example, a litigant who wishes to challenge an Act of the Oireachtas in Ireland faces a number of evidential or procedural obstacles to success. These serve, in effect, to reduce the likelihood that a court will invalidate an Act of the Oireachtas. They accordingly operate as barriers to the judicially-supremacist outcome in respect of which Gardbaum, among other critics of 'judicial supremacy' have such concerns. In this regard, it is noteworthy that these structural barriers have been justified and explained as a tangible manifestation of the respect which the courts owe to the considered position of the Oireachtas. They are explained in more detail below. However, in the context of the criticism made above about the blunt equation of a strike-down power with a system of judicial supremacy, the important point to note is that the practical (and intended) implications of these measures is that the courts will typically issues a declaration of unconstitutionality only as a remedy of last resort.

(i) Determination on non-constitutional grounds The first relevant principle adopted and applied by the Irish courts is that they will deal with an issue of constitutionality only if it is strictly necessary to resolve the controversy between the parties. As Henchy J summarized the approach in *The State (Woods) v AG*, 'a court should not enter upon the question of constitutionality unless it is necessary for the determination of the case before it'.[12] As Murray CJ's formulation of the principle in *Carmody v Minister for Justice, Equality and Law Reform* emphasises, this means that the court should only examine a challenge to an Act of the Oireachtas as a last resort:

> The question involving any validity of a statute or a section thereof should be postponed until consideration has been given to any other question of law the

---

[11] Cultural factors may obviously also influence how such a system operates. For example, Ireland's 1922 Constitution conferred similar rights of judicial review upon the courts. However, these were never used to strike down legislation, a reticence which is typically attributed to the residual influence of Diceyan notions of parliamentary supremacy on both bench and bar. See, for example, Ronan Keane, 'Across the Cherokee Frontier of Irish Constitutional Jurisprudence: The *Sinn Féin Funds* Case: Buckley v Attorney General (1950)' in Eoin O'Dell (ed.), *Leading Cases of the Twentieth Century* (Round Hall Sweet & Maxwell 2000) 185, 188; Donal Coffey, 'The Judiciary of the Irish Free State' (2011) 33 *DULJ* 61.

[12] [1969] IR 385, 400.

> resolution of which could determine the issues between the parties. If a decision on such questions of law does determine such issues then, in principle, it is not necessary for the court to address the constitutional question.[13]

The principle is a flexible one which is generally, but not rigidly[14] applied. Nonetheless, the very existence of the principle serves as a clear – and much endorsed – imprecation to a court that it should exercise forbearance when confronted with proceedings that raise, in part, a constitutional issue.

(ii) The presumption of constitutionality The presumption of constitutionality is another principle of long-established application which, both in intention and in impact, reflects a judicial acknowledgment of the necessity for inter-branch respect and restraint. Hanna J's decision in *Pigs Marketing Board v Donnelly*[15] – which, it must be noted, suggests a degree of discomfort with the judicial review powers provided by the then 'new' Constitution – contains one of the earliest articulations of the principle:

> When the Court has to consider the constitutionality of a law it must, in the first place, be accepted as an axiom that a law passed by the Oireachtas, the elected representatives of the people, is presumed to be constitutional unless and until the contrary is clearly established … . The question of peace, order and good government of the State in reference to legislation is primarily a matter for the Oireachtas, and the application of the phrase would seem to be more a guide than a positive law … . It seems to me to be a vague phrase, a kind of political shibboleth, the meaning and application of which has changed and will continue to change from one generation to another.[16]

This reticence towards impugning legislation by reference to the open-textured language of the constitution persisted for several years. However, the Supreme Court's decision in 1950 to invalidate the legislative provisions at issue in *Buckley v AG* signalled a new willingness on the part of the courts to employ the full range of remedies conferred on them by the 1937 text. Yet, the Supreme Court retained the presumption

---

[13] [2010] 1 IR 635, 649.

[14] See, for example, *John Grace Fried Chicken Ltd v Catering JLC* [2011] 3 IR 211.

[15] [1939] IR 413.

[16] [1939] IR 413, 417–18.

identified by Hanna J in *Donnelly* in a manner which, again, suggested a judicial view of the power to invalidate legislation as a remedy of last resort:

> Where a particular law is not expressly prohibited and it is sought to establish that it is repugnant to the Constitution by reason of some implied prohibition or repugnancy, it has already been laid down in this Court that such repugnancy must be clearly established. Such a principle, in our opinion, springs from, and is necessitated by, that respect which one great organ of the State owes to another.[17]

The retention of this now 'universally applied'[18] presumption of constitutionality has a number of practical consequences for constitutional litigation in Ireland. The presumption has given rise to a number of ancillary principles (discussed below), all of which provide a degree of protection for Acts of the Oireachtas. At its most basic, the presumption places the onus of proof on the party calling the constitutionality of an Act into question.

> Where a law is not expressly prohibited and it is sought to establish that it is repugnant to the Constitution by reason of some implied prohibition or repugnancy, such repugnancy must be clearly established. There is thus in such cases a presumption in favour of the constitutionality of an Act of the Oireachtas, which is said to arise from that respect which one great organ of State owes to another. The onus in such cases thus lies on those challenging the validity of an Act to rebut that presumption and to establish clearly any repugnancy.[19]

This consistent placing of the legal and evidential burden on the party alleging unconstitutionality[20] may seem a relatively minor matter. However, it may in practice have a practical influence on both the conduct and outcome of constitutional litigation.

The presumption establishes a persistent procedural bias in favour of the legislative status quo. The proceedings operate as an examination of the evidence and arguments of the challenger – first by his or her opponents and then by the court – rather than as a search for objective constitutional value. If the evidence and arguments offered are weak, poorly researched or directed to other issues, a legislative provision

---

17 [1950] IR 67, 80.

18 *Curtin v Dáil Eireann* [2006] 2 IR, 556, 620.

19 *O'Donovan v AG* [1961] 1 IR 114, 125, citing *Buckley v AG* [1950] IR 67.

20 Which does not apply to pre-1937 legislation.

which might have been adjudged unconstitutional will remain intact. As Walsh J explained it in *State (Quinn) v Ryan*:

> Acts of the Oireachtas are, as I have already stated, presumed to be valid and not repugnant to the Constitution under which they were enacted. If, therefore, an Act or a section of an Act is unsuccessfully challenged as to its validity, the rejection of that challenge is not what gives validity to the Act. The Act continued to enjoy its original presumption of validity. A challenge to an Act based on a particular ground or upon several particular grounds does not ordinarily, if ever, involve an examination of every possible ground of invalidity and the decision of a Court in rejecting the challenge is a decision that the presumption of validity has not been displaced by any of the grounds advanced in support of the challenge.[21]

In addition, the presumption may also have some effect on the substantive content of any proceedings. As described below, the presumption provides logical support for a number of related ancillary principles, all of which tend to militate against a declaration of unconstitutionality.

More generally, it might also be speculated that the existence and everyday invocation of so many principles of legislative preservation may, in itself, encourage a residual judicial reluctance to issue such an order, even where it might, in principle, be supported by the law. Hogan J's description of a potential declaration of unconstitutionality in *G v District Judge Murphy*[22] as 'a Samson-like collapsing of the legislative pillars which gave rise to the unconstitutionality in the first instance', with its allusive evocation of the mutually destructive exercise of official duty, is illustrative of such concerns.

(iii) Double construction rule One of the most commonly invoked principles in Irish constitutional litigation is the so-called 'double construction' rule. This was first set out by the Supreme Court in *McDonald v Bord na gCon* as follows:

> [O]ne practical effect of this presumption is that if in respect of any provision or provisions of the Act two or more constructions are reasonably open, one of which is constitutional and the other or others are unconstitutional, it must be presumed that the Oireachtas intended only the constitutional construction and a Court called upon to adjudicate upon the constitutionality of the statutory provision should uphold the constitutional construction. It is only

---

21 [1965] IR 70.
22 [2011] IEHC 445.

> when there is no construction reasonably open which is not repugnant to the Constitution that the provision should be held to be repugnant.[23]

This rule – which is not dissimilar in its operation to the interpretive obligation laid down by section 3 of the Human Rights Act 1998 (HRA)[24] – minimizes the potential for a finding of unconstitutionality. As with the previous principles, this is a self-imposed principle of judicial restraint which acknowledges the necessity to refrain from any undue interference with the agreed position of the Oireachtas. Similarly, it again renders the finding of unconstitutionality a remedy of last resort.

In addition, however, it also provides in practice the sort of opportunity for political-judicial interaction that advocates tend to associate with the Commonwealth model of rights-based review. It is not uncommon for the Attorney General in defending a challenge to the constitutionality of legislation to place considerable emphasis on the double construction rule. This is usually done as a fallback position but can, on occasions, be presented as the Attorney General's primary defence. In formulating an argument on the basis of the double construction rule, it is necessary for the relevant parties to consider what interpretations are reasonable, and what interpretations would accord with the policy objectives and interests which underlie the legislation.[25] This, in many respects, fulfils a similar function to the post-ruling political response to which the dialogical or Commonwealth models attach such emphasis.

While judicial restraint gave rise to the double-construction rule, it also – as with section 3 of the HRA – imposes certain limits on its use. As Walsh J explained in *East Donegal Co-op v AG*, the court should not adopt an interpretation which strains the limits of language or credulity. Judicial forbearance in the face of one particular outcome cannot become judicial creativity in favour of a plainly unanticipated alternative:

> [I]nterpretation or construction of an Act or any provision thereof in conformity with the Constitution cannot be pushed to the point where the interpretation would result in the substitution of the legislative provision by another

[23] [1965] 1 IR 217, 239.

[24] As discussed in Chapter 3.2 of this collection, Ireland's European Convention on Human Rights Act 2003 also contains an interpretive obligation but its influence has arguably been more limited. See, in particular, *McD v L* [2009] IESC 81.

[25] This raises an obvious question concerning the right of the Attorney General, as a member of the executive, to urge (or refrain from urging) particular interpretations of the legislature's wishes, but that it outside the scope of this chapter.

> provision with a different context, as that would be to usurp the functions of the Oireachtas. In seeking to reach an interpretation or construction in accordance with the Constitution, a statutory provision which is clear and unambiguous cannot be given an opposite meaning.[26]

(iv) Presumption of constitutional conduct Walsh J proceeded in the next section of his decision in *East Donegal Co-op* to identify a related presumption of constitutional conduct 'that the Oireachtas intended that proceedings, procedures, discretions and adjudications which are permitted, provided for, or prescribed by an Act of the Oireachtas are to be conducted in accordance with the principles of constitutional justice'.[27] This presumption has had a significant impact both on the conduct of bodies invested with statutory powers but also on the conduct of constitutional litigation involving a challenge to such statutory powers. In its breadth, this presumption is similar to the related constitutional concepts of constitutional justice and the right to fair procedures in that it imposes general obligations on administrative bodies that go beyond those specified by the Oireachtas (or, indeed, by the relevant minister or executive agency). As a judicially-created command to the other branches, this could be presented as an example of the sort of imbalance of institutional power which Gardbaum or others associate with 'judicial supremacy'. However, it should also be borne in mind that the practical consequence of this presumption is that the courts can, in many instances, resolve the dispute by invalidating the administrative act at issue rather than the legislation as a whole. That this was an expected consequence of the presumption is clear from Walsh J's observation in *State (Quinn) v Ryan* that:

> In the exercise of powers conferred by an Act of the Oireachtas, any act inconsistent with the provisions of the Constitution is probably ultra vires the statute unless expressly authorised by the statute or authorised by necessary implication because it may be presumed until the contrary be clearly shown that the Oireachtas did not intend to give legislative authority for acts inconsistent with the Constitution to which the Oireachtas itself is subject.[28]

The presumption thus serves an important practical purpose in preserving the rights of the affected individual while reducing the potential for direct legislative-judicial conflict. It is, of course, open to the Oireachtas to clarify that the conduct in question was, in fact, what it had expected and

---

[26] [1970] 1 IR 317, 341.
[27] Ibid.
[28] *State (Quinn) v Ryan* (n 21) 130.

mandated to occur. In that case, the courts would then be required to assess the constitutionality of the regime itself. However, the presumption of constitutional conduct ensures that it is only in such clear cases of value contestation that this judicial scrutiny and potential override will occur. This, once again, serves to substantially narrow the scope for a clearly 'supremacist' judicial response.

(v) Substantive principles applicable for review In addition to the essentially interpretive principles set out above, it is obviously also possible for judicial restraint to manifest itself in the form of the substantive principles applied by the courts when dealing with constitutional challenges. There are many substantive principles of Irish constitutional law which, arguably, demonstrate judicial deference towards the actions or opinions of the Oireachtas and executive.[29] Decisions on the separation of powers,[30] the right to equality,[31] the constitutionality of taxation statutes,[32] and so on, can all be characterized as specific examples of judicial restraint rather than supremacy. However, these decisions may also reflect textual or jurisprudential considerations specific to a discrete right or doctrine. For the purposes of this chapter, it is more relevant to have regard to those substantive doctrines that bespeak a more general judicial respect for the position of the Oireachtas.

In Ireland, perhaps the most notable of these is the threshold applied by the courts to constitutional challenges involving the striking of a balance between competing rights. The most widely cited formulation is that set out by the Supreme Court in *Tuohy v Courtney*:

> The Court is satisfied that in a challenge to the constitutional validity of any statute in the enactment of which the Oireachtas has been engaged in such a balancing function, the role of the courts is not to impose their view of the correct or desirable balance in substitution for the view of the legislature as displayed in their legislation but rather to determine from an objective stance whether the balance contained in the impugned legislation is so contrary to reason and fairness as to constitute an unjust attack on some individual's constitutional rights.[33]

---

[29] For a more detailed discussion of deference in Irish constitutional law, see Brian Foley, *Deference and the Presumption of Constitutionality* (IPA 2009).

[30] *Sinnott v Minister for Education* [2001] 2 IR 545; *TD v Minister for Education* [2001] 4 IR 259.

[31] *D v Ireland* [2012] IESC 10.

[32] *Madigan v AG* [1986] ILRM 136.

[33] [1994] 3 IR 1, 47.

The test bears obvious resemblances to the deferential approach involved in the classic *Wednesbury* formula. Of course, this principle is only one factor in the courts' assessment of the merits of a constitutional challenge. The role of the *Tuohy* test should not be overstated. In particular, Irish law has yet to clarify the precise relationship between the *Tuohy* formulation and the Canadian-imported proportionality test identified in *Heaney v Ireland*.[34] At the same time, the *Tuohy* test had been frequently cited, especially in situations concerning a potential conflict between constitutional rights. This was well illustrated by the *Re Abortion Information Bill* decision concerning rights which the constitution expressly describes as of equal value.[35] What this illustrates is that there is scope for courts operating under a so-called supremacist system to allow space for legitimate disagreement over fundamental values.

Indeed, there is no necessity for such tolerance to be confined to cases of countervailing rights. The courts have also acknowledged (albeit on occasions in a manner that is closer to judicial submission than respect) the first-order primacy of the Oireachtas in its assessment of public interest or social policy.

> States have, for centuries, wrestled with questions of great sensitivity concerning the appropriate age to set, whether to differentiate between males of different ages, or to differentiate on grounds of difference in age between the persons, not to mention the more recent liberation of same-sex activities from the stigma of criminality.
>
> Decisions on matters of such social sensitivity and difficulty are in essence a matter for the legislature. Courts should be deferential to the legislative view on such matters of social policy.[36]

(vi) Doctrine of severability Finally, the Irish courts have also elaborated a doctrine of severability which holds that the court may limit the invalidity of a statutory regime or provision to that portion of it which is, strictly speaking repugnant to the constitution. Unlike the principles outlined above, this applies after the court has determined that the actions of the Oireachtas were, in some respects, contrary to the constitution. Nonetheless, it is appropriate for it to be considered here as an a priori constraint on the exercise of the strike-down power because of the

---

[34] [1994] 3 IR 593.

[35] [1995] 1 IR 1, 45. In a similar vein, *Tuohy* was applied by the Court to assess the balance struck between the rights of employers and employees in *Re Article 26 and the Employment Equality Bill 1996* [1997] 2 IR 321.

[36] *M D (A minor) v Ireland* [2012] IESC 10.

manner in which it similarly serves to minimise its inter-institutional impact. By contrast, the constraints considered in the next section are those that apply after the order actually invalidating the legislation has been issued.

Fitzgerald CJ explained the doctrine in *Maher v AG*[37] in the following terms:

> The application of the doctrine of severability or separability in the judicial review of legislation has the effect that if a particular provision is held to be unconstitutional, and that provision is independent of and severable from the rest, only the offending provision will be declared invalid … . It is essentially a matter of interpreting the intention of the legislature in the light of the relevant constitutional provisions, and it must be borne in mind in all cases that Article 15, s. 2, sub-s. 1, of the Constitution provides that 'the sole and exclusive power of making laws for the State is hereby vested in the Oireachtas: no other legislative authority has power to make laws for the State'. If, therefore, the Court were to sever part of a statutory provision as unconstitutional and seek to give validity to what is left so as to produce an effect at variance with legislative policy, the Court would be invading a domain exclusive to the legislature and thus exceeding the Court's competency. In other words, it would be seeking to correct one form of unconstitutionality by engaging in another.

Thus, as Hogan and Whyte point out, 'these partial deletions are only carried out when this can be done cleanly and without violence to the presumed legislative will'.[38] This is, once again, a doctrine which is characterized in its conception and execution by inter-branch respect and judicial restraint.

(vii) Conclusion Taken together, these principles might be thought to cumulatively echo Lord Steyn's extrajudicial observation that: 'A judge's task is to interpret not to interpolate. There is a Rubicon which judges may not cross: principles of institutional integrity forbid it.'[39] It is clear that the simple existence of a power to strike down legislation will not necessarily engender an undue eagerness to resort to the exercise of that power. The Irish jurisprudence demonstrates that procedural and substantive measures can be used to facilitate legitimate inter-institutional disagreement and significantly limit the scope for the exercise of a

---

[37] [1973] IR 140.

[38] Gerard Hogan and Gerry Whyte, *JM Kelly: The Irish Constitution* (4th edn, Bloomsbury Professional 2002) 885.

[39] Lord Steyn, 'Deference: A Tangled Story' [2005] PL 346, 347.

judicial override. The character and effects of these inter-branch dynamics are more complex and potentially varied than the equation of judicial supremacy with a power to annul would allow.

B. Posterior responses to judicial supremacy

Of course, the fact that constitutional adjudication operates differently across different systems and different legal cultures is not a novel insight. Critics might be expected to respond that – regardless of the reality of the judicial-political dynamics within an individual state – the mere potential for a judicial override is sufficient to support their concerns. The fact that a judiciary may be reluctant or even generally unwilling to strike down legislation does not mean that the remedy's residual presence is without effects. Whether for reasons of constitutional piety, institutional self-censorship or political calculation, the threat of an adverse ruling may be enough to dissuade the political organs from embarking on a course of action which they would otherwise have undertaken. From this point of view, the hypothetical presence of a 'final word' can create that unbalanced conception of constitutional rights and roles which produces 'the overlegalisation or judicialisation of principled public discourse and the legislative and popular debilitation that has long been identified as a major institutional cost of constitutionalisation'.[40]

It is correct to observe that the conferral of a rights jurisdiction upon the courts can (and often will) prompt litigation-averse behaviour on the part of the political branches. Indeed, part of the asserted advantages of the Commonwealth model is that it is argued to encourage rights-oriented reflection in respect of government planning. Whether such reflection reflects a positive spirit of rights-oriented concern or a more calculating desire to avoid an embarrassing or disruptive judicial ruling does not detract from the fact that it is almost certain to occur. In practice, therefore, the differences between the Commonwealth system and one in which the judiciary retains a limited right to invalidate legislation may be less stark than originally anticipated.

The potential for such putatively different systems to generate broadly similar behaviour on the part of political or judicial actors underlines the point that it is the claimed finality of the power to invalidate which is the core of the distinction between judicial supremacist and non-supremacist systems. There are strong reasons to contend, however, that the assumption that judicial rulings in such cases are final – on which this distinction and, arguably, the Commonwealth model as a whole rests – is

---

[40] Gardbaum, 'Reassessing the New Commonwealth Model' (n 7) 173.

inaccurate and overstated. Two, in particular, are highlighted here – one specific to Ireland, which is considered in the following section, and one of more general application, which is the subject of the discussion in Section C below.

Ireland: the referendum process In Ireland, the ruling of a court on a question of constitutionality can, and on occasions has, been overridden by a simple majority vote of the people in a referendum on that relevant issue. The process for amending the constitution is a relatively straightforward one, requiring the passing of a bill proposing an amendment by the Oireachtas and the approval of that bill by the people. There have been numerous occasions on which a referendum has been held to address the decisions or reasoning of the courts on questions of constitutional interpretation. Some have involved overturning the outcome of court proceedings.[41] Others have been held to address potential issues which were anticipated by courts in the course of their ruling.[42] Others still have amended, refined or otherwise addressed the policy issues arising from a decision of the courts on a narrower constitutional issue.[43]

That is not to suggest that the referendum process is not without potential difficulties. A referendum is, of course, a majoritarian tool which may be susceptible to abuse in certain circumstances. Doubts have also been expressed by some about the public's knowledge or understanding of the sometimes complex issues involved. The key point for the purposes of this argument, however, is the existence of such a relatively simple amendment mechanism undermines the claim that a power to invalidate legislation necessarily gives the judiciary the 'final word' on contestable political questions. As Gerry Whyte summarizes the Irish experience, 'the People (or, perhaps more accurately, the political elite) are quite prepared to take action to control judicial decision-making with which they do not agree'.[44]

This suggests that much of the international debate about 'finality' and 'judicial supremacy' is premised on an unconscious and misguided

---

[41] *Crotty v An Taoiseach* [1987] IR 713.

[42] As with adoption in *M v An Bord Uchtála* [1977] IR 287; and, arguably, concerns about abortion expressed following the recognition of a right to marital privacy in *McGee v AG* [1974] IR 284.

[43] See, for example, the referendum on various amendments relevant to the regulation of abortion following *AG v X* [1992] 1 IR 1; or the referendum on Cabinet confidentiality after *AG v Hamilton (No.1)* [1993] 2 IR 250.

[44] Gerry Whyte, 'The Role of the Supreme Court in our Democracy: A Response to Mr Justice Hardiman' (2006) 28 *DULJ* 1.

equation of 'American-style' judicial review with other unrelated features of the US constitutional system, like its cumbersome amendment procedures, and its sharp political and geographic polarization.

It might be countered that the vesting of a power in the people to override a court ruling does not avoid the problem of an imbalance of power between the judiciary and the legislature. Under such a system, the judiciary might not have an absolutist final word but they retain the final word *as against the legislature*. Given the likely practical infrequency of amending referenda, the system might still be fairly characterized as, in the main, one of judicial supremacy.

The first point to note in response to this is that it is not being suggested that Ireland offers the only model for combining strong judicial review powers with a non-supremacist system. The main point being made is the much smaller one that the vesting of such powers in the courts does not have to result in the judiciary wielding a 'final word' on contested questions of rights or values.

Secondly, if the objection is that Parliament ought to have the final word on such questions, then the argument is one which seems based not on constitutional balance but on residual notions of parliamentary supremacy. This plainly brings in much larger and familiar disputes about democratic legitimacy, electoral monism, popular sovereignty and judicial review. These will not be rehearsed here. It is sufficient to note that the model's recourse to notions of electoral supremacy means not only that it necessarily rests on substantially contestable grounds but also weakens assertions of intermediate balance.

The simple point illustrated by Ireland's system is that a concern for democracy does not necessarily require a constitutional structure which vests the final word on legal or constitutional issues in the legislature. In a system with a popularly-endorsed constitutional text, the courts are as entitled as the legislature to make a claim that they, by their actions, speak for and on behalf of the people.[45] This is particularly so in a system like Ireland's where there is a realistic possibility of popular amendment. As Whyte has noted, it is possible in such a system to see popular approval not only in a referendum result but also in the decision of the legislature not to pursue an amendment.

> The silence of the People in the face of judicial activism does not have to be interpreted as the silence of impotent rage – it could be regarded as the

---

[45] For a more detailed elaboration of this argument, see Eoin Carolan, 'Recovering the Republic? Democratic Representation and the Mixed Theory of Government' (2012) 47(2) *Irish Jurist* 173.

> approving silence of an electorate who are satisfied with the decisions of their judges, or, perhaps more accurately, the disinterested silence of an electorate (or their political representatives) who are not sufficiently antagonised by those decisions to wish to change them.[46]

As the recent rejection of a proposal to overturn a 2004 Supreme Court decision[47] about which the political classes had long complained re-confirmed, it is misguided to equate the views of elected representatives on constitutional policy with those of their electorate.

C. The illusion of the final word

The Irish example shows that there may other mechanisms for dealing with the aftermath of the courts' decision to annul a legislative provision. However, even in a system which lacks alternative institutional tie-breakers, there is a more basic and fundamental objection to the case for the Commonwealth model. A central claim is that this avoids the supremacist problem of allowing the judiciary to have the 'final word' by preserving the conclusive authority of Parliament in a more democratically appropriate manner. Weak-form review is praised for ensuring that courts 'do not necessarily or automatically have final authority on what the law of the land is'.[48] '[T]he whole point of an override clause is to ensure that the judges do not have the final word'.[49]

The difficulty with this, however, is that this decisional finality is almost always illusory. The image of the declamatory edict, by which a ruler simultaneously commands and secures compliance, has little relevance to the complex, multi-actor and multi-level character of contemporary government. By focusing to such an extent on a 'final word' problem, the Commonwealth model gives chase to a chimera.

The idea of government as a conflict between a limited number of super-institutions is, again, linked to wider theories of democracy, representation and the separation of powers. In particular, the familiar tripartite theory of the separation of powers supports and encourages this concept of government by focusing attention on the division of action and influence between these central institutions. Yet, as has previously

---

[46] Whyte (n 44).

[47] *Maguire v Ardagh* [2002] 1 IR 385.

[48] Gardbaum, *The New Commonwealth Model of Constitutionalism* (n 5) 26–7.

[49] Jeffrey Goldsworthy, *Parliamentary Sovereignty: Contemporary Debates* (CUP 2010) 217.

been pointed out,[50] this theory misses much of the reality of how power and influence is distributed across our post-Montesquian systems of government.

First of all, as new governance,[51] supranational, and network[52] scholars would point out, a substantial portion of governmental activity at levels above, below or outside the traditional three branches. To suggest that the legislature or the judiciary have the final word when their decisions may both be subject to either an amendment or an override at the supranational level, or a circumvention in the non-public sphere, is to ignore significant patterns of power distribution.

Secondly, even if the multilateral innovations of recent decades are left to one side, this idea of government as a holy trinity of centralized institutions remains descriptively inadequate and normatively incoherent. In a bureaucratic system, government is no longer – if it ever was – a matter of command and control. Rather, as scholars like Richardson[53] and Mashaw[54] have shown, administrative or regulatory bodies retain substantial discretionary powers in the interpretation, implementation and observance of the orders given to them – whether by the legislature, the executive or the courts.

Thirdly, even if it is accepted that our theories of government should primarily (if incompletely) concentrate on the relationship between the judicial and political branches, the concept of the 'final word' still appears highly suspect. This is because of differences in the character and associated consequences of the decision-making process conducted by these institutions. Although both the legislature and the courts[55] may articulate and act upon particular and sometimes varying views of social or constitutional policy, their conduct occurs in different contexts and takes different forms. The legislature, being tasked with the creation of general rules, may have regard to different considerations, may attach

---

[50] Eoin Carolan, *The New Separation of Powers: A Theory for the Modern State* (OUP 2009).

[51] See, for example, Gráinne de Búrca and Joanne Scott (eds), *Law and New Governance in the EU and the US* (Hart 2006); Stephen Osborne, *The New Public Governance?: Emerging Perspectives on the Theory and Practice of Public Governance* (Routledge 2009).

[52] Jerry L Mashaw, *Greed, Chaos and Governance: Using Public Choice to improve Public Law* (Yale UP 1997); HS Richardson, *Democratic Autonomy: Public Reasoning about the Ends of Policy* (OUP 2002).

[53] Richardson, ibid.

[54] Jerry L Mashaw, *Due Process in the Administrative State* (Yale UP 1985).

[55] The focus in this paragraph on their relationship reflects the focus on this in the Commonwealth or parliamentary model.

different weight to those considerations, and – most critically – will express itself in provisions of general application. The courts, on the other hand, while discussing principles in general terms, do so in the context of an adjudication upon the situation-specific rights of an individual or individuals. This means that the court's ruling – even if it extends to the striking down of legislation – is, strictly speaking, confined to the issue and the circumstances which were adduced in evidence before that court. Thus, contrary to the impression often conveyed in debates about judicial supremacy, the permanent effects of a declaration of unconstitutionality are, in fact, often quite narrow. Assertions of an enduring judicial 'final word' are further weakened by the residual entitlement of the legislature to proactively respond to an adverse result.

To use an example from Irish law, the objective of the litigants in the *Howard v Commissioners for Public Works* proceedings was to prevent the construction of a visitors' centre in an area of unusual geological features known as the Burren. The litigants succeeded before the High Court, which ruled in their favour on the basis that the decision to grant permission for the construction of the centre had been ultra vires the authority that made it.[56] The Oireachtas responded within a few days by passing an Act which conferred just such a power on the authority in question. The litigants then initiated fresh proceedings alleging that the Act was unconstitutional on the grounds that it contravened the separation of powers and interfered with their rights arising from the High Court decision in their favour. Lynch J confirmed that the Oireachtas was prohibited from interfering with original determination:

> The Oireachtas cannot alter or reverse that finding or the declaration and injunction made on foot of the same. To attempt to do so would contravene the constitutional separation of the powers of government given between the various organs of State established by the Constitution in that the legislature (the Oireachtas) would be trespassing on and into the judicial domain.[57]

However, he also emphasized that this prohibition was limited to the narrow basis upon which the original decision was decided.

> The basis of that finding and declaration, as I have said, is that the first defendant is a creature of statute, and was not given such powers by any

---

[56] *Howard v Commission for Public Works (No 1)* [1994] 1 IR 101.
[57] *Howard v Commission for Public Works (No 3)* [1994] 3 IR 394, 407.

> statute prior to the date of the judgment … . Why should it be impossible for the Oireachtas to do so now by the Act of 1993?[58]

Thus, there was no general entitlement to the benefits which the litigants had accrued – and indeed sought – from the litigation. The Oireachtas was perfectly entitled to authorize the activity which the court had impugned, provided it did so in a way that addressed the legal defect identified in that case.

Although the original decision in *Howard (No 1)* was concerned with a statutory rather than constitutional defect, the same point can be made in respect of constitutional litigation. Generally speaking, a decision to strike down a legislative provision on constitutional grounds will not mean that the legislative objective is, itself, unlawful. Nor does it necessarily mean that that objective may only be pursued by radically different means. In many situations – especially in the era of proportionality-based review – the problem identified is the way in which the means adopted has a disproportionate impact on a particular individual or groups of individuals. In those situations, it may often be possible to reintroduce broadly similar measures by ensuring that their impact on the groups in question is more carefully calibrated.

Thus, the tendency in debates to assume a binary choice can leads to 'pointless Punch-and-Judy posturing about legislative or judicial supremacy' that overlooks '[t]he reality … that decision making in the modern state is generally a contingent, multi-stage and ongoing process in which the notion of any institution having the "final word" is almost always meaningless'.[59]

In this regard, it is telling perhaps that even the ruling in *Roe v Wade* – which seems too many to represent the apotheosis of judicial supremacy in social matters – has not prevented many states from imposing often substantial restriction on the availability of abortion services.[60] This underscores the extent to which the political branches – whether by means of legislation or by executive measures – will almost always have available to them a range of options to, at worst, limit the impact of a judicial determination on their preferred policies.

---

[58] Ibid.

[59] Eoin Carolan, 'The Relationship between Judicial Remedies and the Separation of Powers: Collaborative Constitutionalism and the Suspended Declaration of Invalidity' (2011) 46 *Irish Jurist* 180.

[60] See, for example, Paul Harris, 'North Dakota's Last Abortion Clinic Fights On', *The Observer* (London, 11 May 2013) <http://www.guardian.co.uk/world/2013/may/11/abortion-north-dakota-under-siege> accessed 8 April 2015.

3.1.4 Collaborative Constitutionalism?

The analysis above suggests that the claims of the Commonwealth model may be overstated. That is not to say, of course, that the HRA, with its interpretive obligation and declaration of incompatibility, lacks comparative interest. What seems more questionable, however, are the somewhat Anglocentric claims of global novelty or institutional balance that may be made on its behalf. As the Irish experience – and that of other states discussed in this book – suggests, the common tendency (not limited to the literature on the Commonwealth model) to associate the 'strong-form'[61] judicial review with American constitutional structures may encourage a doctrinal clarity that belies the empirical diversity of domestic constitutional orders. If 'the model's great novelty is to decouple the power of judicial review from judicial supremacy or finality',[62] this may be less novel than first assumed.

On one analysis, the Commonwealth model might more properly be seen less as a bold innovation and more as an effort to preserve-by-adjustment a Diceyan model of parliamentary supremacy which was dangerously out of step with the currents of international, and even domestic,[63] constitutional doctrine.[64] From this perspective, the model represents not a middle ground between judicial and parliamentary supremacy but rather a limited upgrade on a parliamentary model which has now been withdrawn from sale.[65]

This suggests that there remains scope for the articulation of alternative conceptions of constitutional government which eschew the exaggerated images of institutional conflict that the language of judicial or parliamentary supremacy tends to evoke. The remainder of this chapter sketches a

---

61 Mark Tushnet, *Weak Courts, Strong Rights: Judicial Review and Social Welfare Rights in Comparative Constitutional Law* (Princeton UP 2009).

62 Gardbaum, 'Reassessing the New Commonwealth Model' (n 7) 170.

63 One interesting question is how the English courts' development of a common law doctrine of fundamental rights might have developed if the HRA 1998 had not been introduced. It might be argued that this may have produced a not dissimilar situation in which Parliament may have been obliged and entitled to respond to adverse judicial rulings on fundamental rights issues.

64 For a more recent and persuasive argument to this effect, see Stephen Gardbaum, 'Separation of Powers and the Growth of Judicial Review in Established Democracies (Or Why Has the Model of Legislative Supremacy Mostly Been Withdrawn from Sale?)'(2014) 62 *Am J Comp L* 613.

65 Mark Tushnet, 'New Forms of Judicial Review and the Persistence of Rights- and Democracy-based Worries' (2003) 38 *Wake Forest L Rev* 813.

model of collaborative constitutionalism which could be considered as one potential candidate to fulfil this role.[66]

This model of collaborative constitutionalism bears some resemblance to the familiar theories of 'dialogue or 'deference'. It is arguable, however, that these metaphors bring with them uncomfortable connotations of misplaced respect, 'servility, or perhaps gracious concession'.[67] It is not clear, for example, why the respective institutions should be obliged to take account of the position of the other if the issue is one on which the body has strong views. If a court, for example, finds a clear breach of a constitutional principle, should it alter its view simply because of a grudging legislative response? In constitutional terms, the contravention does not become any less objectionable by its legislative repetition.

> It is true that a court should be fully conscious of its limitations as a tribunal of fact, as well as of its shortcomings as a judge of the wisdom of public policy or of the merits of expert opinion. Reasons for humility and caution in the face of government perceptions of the public interest, however, do not dictate the surrender of judgment; nor should any claims of special knowledge or expertise go untested.[68]

As Allan's caveats intimate, there should be no suggestion that the courts should enjoy an infallible or unquestioned authority over constitutional affairs. Aileen Kavanagh has rightly pointed out that 'courts sometimes labour under conditions of uncertainty'.[69] This uncertainty can be tolerated, however, if it is accepted that judicial decisions which touch on constitutional values will often produce some form of reaction or response on the part of other institutions. This interaction is at the heart of dialogical justifications for judicial review. Richard Clayton has summarized this well in the Canadian context:

> To my mind, a great value of judicial review and this dialogue among the branches is that each of the branches is made somewhat more accountable to

---

[66] See also Carolan, 'The Relationship between Judicial Remedies' (n 59).

[67] *R (Pro-Life Alliance) v BBC* [2003] UKHL [23], [75] (Lord Hoffmann).

[68] TRS Allan, 'Human Rights and Judicial Review: A Critique of "Due Deference"' (2006) CLJ 671, 695.

[69] Aileen Kavanagh, 'Defending Deference in Public Law and Constitutional Theory' (2010) LQR 222, 235.

> the other … . This dialogue between and accountability of each of the branches have the effect of enhancing the democratic process, not denying it.[70]

However, it is argued here that the key benefit of this interaction is not dialogue but accountability. It is the ability of another institution to demand an explanation, on pain of sanction, for a particular act that brings with it the democratic benefits to which Clayton alludes – an independent check, alternative perspectives, public reasoning and deliberation, and so on. Particularly from the point of view of the court, the fact that its decision may produce a response which the court might then be asked to examine should be irrelevant. As Allan argues, the question for it is a legal one to be determined on the basis of the material before it on that occasion.

> Insofar as any question arising is understood as having, in principle, a correct legal answer, it raises a matter of law for the court to determine. Insofar as a question is capable of a range of different answers, depending on the views and judgments of Members of Parliament or government ministers, it is not a matter of law for judicial determination unless it is contended that an action or decision falls outside the permitted range of discretion.[71]

It should be emphasized that the model does not depend on an imprecise or arbitrary distinction between law and politics. Such function-oriented distinctions are especially problematic in the constitutional sphere. The point is that the collaborative model does not need to draw such distinctions. The recognition that no institution has the final word liberates theories of judicial review from the necessity to acknowledge, explain or delineate the supremacy of an institution over a particular area.[72] The model can instead concentrate on protecting the input of legitimate institutions to constitutional affairs. If we acknowledge the inherently provisional character of any attempt at resolving contested values, this should draw the sting from supremacist concerns. As argued elsewhere:

> An institutional decision is not the end of the process but is rather an opening position in an ongoing negotiation about governance. Exercising power is a

---

[70] Richard Clayton, 'Judicial Deference and "Democratic Dialogue": The Legitimacy of Judicial Intervention under the Human Rights Act 1998' [2004] PL 33, 44.

[71] Allan, 'Human Rights and Judicial Review' (n 68) 678.

[72] In this regard, an alternative description of the model might be as one based on contingent constitutionalism.

> collaborative and deliberative process in which each institution engages with the others' decisions on its own terms, subjecting them to its own internal scrutiny. This also crucially means that one institution's amendment of another's position is not decisive. The original institution will have the opportunity to respond to any such changes and to make any further amendments or refinements that it feels are appropriate.[73]

The legitimacy of such a diversity of institutional inputs is based on the claim that they bring valid alternative perspectives to shared problems of constitutional government. In many respects, the central challenge of a rights-based constitutional system is to strike a balance between the interests of the individual and those of society as a whole. Where an institution has a valid claim to contribute to that task – be it based on representation, expertise, its institutional procedures, or so on – the collaborative model recognizes its entitlement to form its own views on a specific issue but also the entitlement of others to set forth their views. Unlike the dialogue model, collaboration does not necessarily require deference or even engagement with alternative perspectives. The supremacy of a unilateral perspective is ousted at the systemic rather than the institutional level. Of course, the model's recognition of legitimate alternative inputs would mandate a degree of inter-institutional balance and respect. Respect should be owed, however, on the basis of the institution itself rather than on the decision made in a particular case. Respect does not demand institutional politesse in the face of an approach felt to be utterly wrong. It requires only that an institution recognize that the other body is entitled to express such views and to act upon them until another institution intervenes.

What Ireland demonstrates, therefore, is the potential for a rights-based constitutional system to be justified in a way which avoids both legislative and judicial supremacy. What is not suggested, however, is that the Irish system is one which can or should be copied in other systems. This collaborative model of constitutional interaction is a contextual one which is likely to be influenced by differences in constitutional text, institutional framework, political culture or legal tradition. However, this recognition of contextual flexibility is also likely to substantially complicate attempts to classify or compare constitutional systems. The move from a purely institutional analysis of rights-based review to one more sensitive to political realities does, however, seem necessary to more

---

[73] Carolan, *The New Separation of Powers* (n 50) 186.

accurately understand the power dynamics within a domestic system.[74] Classifications based on isolated institutional features can obscure as much as they explain. As Eamon de Valera put it in the same Dáil debate:

> I do not care whether we should fall into some category of States or not. It was not to fall into a category of States our people have fought through the centuries. Our people have fought for independence and the point about the republic was that it was in that form that our independence was crystallised in our time. That is the significance of the republic but it was not that we might be classed by some jurists as this type of State or not that we were worrying.[75]

[74] This move is also evident in Gardbaum's 2013 book (n 5). This provides a perceptive analysis of the contextual differences between the ways in which the model has operated in practice in various states. This raises a much larger question, however, about the purpose of models in comparative law and, specifically, whether it is helpful to describe a model that operates to such different effect as a 'model'.

[75] Eamon de Valera debating The Republic of Ireland Bill, 1948 (Dáil Éireann Debates 24 November 1948, vol 113).

3.2 A TALE OF TWO RIGHTS-BASED REVIEWS OR HOW THE EUROPEAN CONVENTION ON HUMAN RIGHTS ACT 2003 HAS IMPACTED ON THE IRISH MODEL OF REVIEW

Cliona Kelly

3.2.1 Introduction

The currently under threat[1] UK Human Rights Act 1998 (HRA or 1998 Act), which incorporated the European Convention on Human Rights 1950 (ECHR or Convention) into domestic law, was designed to balance judicial input into rights review with the 'virtually hallowed' status of parliamentary sovereignty.[2] Unlike the UK, Ireland has a written constitution – *Bunreacht na hÉireann* enacted in 1937 – which protects fundamental rights and empowers the superior courts to strike down legislation which is incompatible with the Constitution.[3] However, despite the fundamental differences between the UK and the Irish constitutional landscape, Ireland's European Convention on Human Rights Act 2003 (ECHR Act or 2003 Act) was modelled on the UK HRA.

This chapter shows how the incorporation of the ECHR in Ireland was not attributable to any strong desire for constitutional change per se but was primarily due to the need to adhere to State obligations under the

---

[1] See Kanstantsin Dzehtsiarou and Tobias Lock (eds), 'The Legal Implications of a Repeal of the Human Rights Act 1998 and Withdrawal from the European Convention on Human Rights' (14 May 2015) available at http://ssrn.com/abstract=2605487 accessed 3 June 2015.

[2] Francesca Klug and Amy Williams, 'The UK's 1998 Human Rights Act: Clarity and Confusion' in Suzanne Egan, Liam Thornton and Judy Walsh, *Ireland and the European Convention on Human Rights: 60 Years and Beyond* (Bloomsbury 2014) 92.

[3] Article 15.4.2° of *Bunreacht na hÉireann* states: 'Every law enacted by the Oireachtas which is in any respect repugnant to this Constitution or to any provision thereof, shall, but to the extent only of such repugnancy, be invalid.' Article 34.3.2° states:

> Save as otherwise provided by this Article, the jurisdiction of the High Court shall extend to the question of the validity of any law having regard to the provisions of this Constitution, and no such question shall be raised (whether by pleading, argument or otherwise) in any Court established under this or any other Article of this Constitution other than the High Court, Court of Appeal or the Supreme Court.

Belfast/Good Friday Agreement. A sub-constitutional approach was chosen to avoid the need for a constitutional referendum, and in that context the HRA provided a useable template. This resulted in a two-tier system of rights and judicial review – with constitutional rights, prima facie subject to 'strong' judicial review, enjoying a privileged status over Convention rights, which are subject to 'weak' judicial review, similar to that in the HRA. The Irish system is thus a hybrid, revealing traits of both legal constitutionalism and the new Commonwealth model. However, it is clear that it is also missing certain crucial aspects of Gardbaum's Commonwealth model, in particular a formalized version of parliamentary human rights review.[4]

This chapter examines the relationship between the ECHR Act and the Constitution, to show how this version of the Commonwealth model operates against the matrix of a written constitution with strong judicial review. It explores to what extent differences between the HRA and the ECHR Act can be attributed to the Constitution, and the approach the courts have taken in trying to reconcile two forms of judicial review of rights within the State. It will be shown that the Constitution is still the preferred source of rights within Ireland, and the mechanisms in the ECHR Act are very much of a measure of last resort, to be relied upon only in respect of those Convention rights which are not already protected by the Constitution. When you add to this mix the generally restrictive interpretation given to the ECHR Act by the courts, it is no surprise that the 2003 Act has had a limited impact in the Irish sphere. However, this does not mean that Convention rights are not given effect within Ireland. The stronger review powers of the judiciary regarding constitutional rights help secure the minimum standard of human rights protection originally sought by the drafters of the ECHR, and the jurisprudence of the European Court of Human Rights (ECtHR or Strasbourg Court) may be relevant when the courts interpret rights contained in the Constitution. Thus, Convention rights are often protected, albeit indirectly, by the Constitution itself, and there is often simply no need to rely on mechanism of the ECHR Act. Rights review in Ireland is thus multi-tiered and complex, with a continued emphasis on strong judicial review mechanisms despite the partial adoption of the Commonwealth model at the turn of the century.

---

[4] Stephen Gardbaum, *The New Commonwealth Model of Constitutionalism: Theory and Practice* (CUP 2013).

3.2.2 The Incorporation of the European Convention on Human Rights in Ireland

Although Ireland ratified the ECHR in 1953, by the turn of the century Ireland was the only member state of the Council of Europe which had not yet incorporated the ECHR into their domestic law. As Ireland is a dualist state,[5] the failure to introduce domestic legislation to incorporate the Convention into national law meant that the Convention could not be relied upon as a binding authority by an individual in an Irish court.[6] Thus, for example in *Re Ó Laighléis*,[7] the Supreme Court held that it was not possible for the applicant to argue that the Offences against the State (Amendment) Act 1940 was in violation of his Convention rights and thus invalid. The courts increasingly viewed the Convention as having persuasive effect, for example when considering the extent to which the Constitution implicitly protected a particular right, but there was no obligation on the courts to have regard to a decision of the ECtHR.[8] If an individual felt that their rights under the ECHR had been violated, and no alternative domestic remedy was available to them, such as an action based on a breach of their rights under the Constitution, the only option available to them was to bring an action against the State before the Strasbourg Court.

Despite the difficulties caused by this limit on the application of the Convention in the domestic sphere, there was a marked hesitancy to incorporate the Convention into national law. There was a perception that

---

[5] This dualist approach to international obligations is based on art 15.2.1° of the Constitution, which states that 'the sole and exclusive power of making laws for the State is hereby vested in the Oireachtas: no other legislative authority has power to make laws for the State', and art 29.6 of the Constitution, which provides that 'no international agreement shall be part of the domestic law of the State save as may be determined by the Oireachtas'.

[6] For a detailed review of the approach of the Irish courts to the ECHR before incorporation see Ronagh McQuigg, 'The European Convention on Human Rights Act 2003: Ten Years On' (2014) 3 International Human Rights Law Review 61, 62–72; Fiona de Londras and Cliona Kelly, *European Convention on Human Rights Act 2003: Operation, Impact and Analysis* (Round Hall 2010) 24–38.

[7] [1960] 1 IR 93.

[8] See, for example, *Norris v Attorney General* [1984] IR 36 in which the Supreme Court refused to have regard to the decision in *Dudgeon v United Kingdom* (1981) 4 EHRR 149.

the Constitution already adequately guaranteed the protection of fundamental rights in Ireland,[9] and that incorporation of the Convention was thus unnecessary. There was furthermore a fear, described as 'a psychological block',[10] that the Convention would undermine or replace the rights regime under the Constitution, and thus represent an encroachment upon national sovereignty.[11] There was therefore minimal internal political pressure or motivation to incorporate the Convention or to instigate any major constitutional reforms.

The most significant recommendations for reform of the Irish Constitution were probably that of the Constitution Review Group, established by the government in April 1995 and lead by Dr TK Whitaker. In its 1996 Report, this group recommended that the ECHR be incorporated into national law.[12] However, this call appears to have been somewhat preempted by various public statements from academics,[13] human rights organizations[14] and politicians[15] the previous year. This was often in the form of submissions to the Northern Ireland Forum for Peace and

---

9 See, for example, the comment of the Constitutional Review Group in 1996 that the Constitution had 'generally speaking, proved to be an effective method of safeguarding individual rights so that the overall impact of the courts on modern Irish life, in their handling of constitutional issues, has been beneficial, rational, progressive and fair'. See the Constitution Review Group Report of May 1996 (Stationery Office, Dublin, Pn 2632) 188, quoting Gerard Hogan and Gerry Whyte, *JM Kelly The Irish Constitution,* (3rd edn, Gill & Macmillan 1994) xcii. The Group did however admit that the list of rights protected by the Constitution is 'incomplete by modern standards' (Constitution Review Group Report, 188).

10 Donal O'Donnell 'A Comparison of Article 6 of the European Convention on Human Rights and the Due Process Requirements of the Constitution of Ireland' (2004) 4 *Judicial Studies Institute Journal* 37, 48.

11 Ray Murphy and Siobhan Wills 'The European Convention on Human Rights Bill 2001' (2001) 6(9) *Bar Review* 541.

12 Constitution Review Group Report (n 9) 193.

13 See, for example, Professor James Casey, 'Major constitutional overhaul unlikely', *The Irish Times* 21 April 1995; Gerald Quinn and Donncha O'Connell 'Symbolic day for European Law should prompt review of Irish rights', *The Irish Times* 30 June 1995.

14 For example, in the Northern Ireland Forum for Peace and Reconciliation in March 1995, the Irish Council for Civil Liberties took the view that both the Irish and UK Governments should take steps to incorporate the Convention into domestic law: 'ICCL welcomes abolition of State of Emergency' *The Irish Times* 1 April 1995.

15 See, for example, comments of Brian Lenihan TD at the Northern Ireland Forum for Peace and Reconciliation on 31 March 1995: 'Forum thanks group for its "list of horrors"', *The Irish Times* 12 April 1995.

Reconciliation,[16] and in the end it was the Northern Ireland peace process – rather than any internal political pressure or inherent desire for constitutional change – which acted as the catalyst for incorporation. As part of the 1998 Belfast/Good Friday Agreement, the Irish Government agreed to 'take steps to further strengthen the protection of human rights in its jurisdiction' and to 'ensure at least an equivalent level of protection of human rights as will pertain in Northern Ireland'.[17] The government did not expressly promise that the Convention would be incorporated; only that the issue would be 'further examined'. However, it soon became apparent that to ensure equivalence – or at least the perception of equivalence – between the human rights regimes in Northern Ireland, where the Convention had domestic effect,[18] and the Republic, where it did not, incorporation of the Convention was necessary. The decision to incorporate the Convention was made largely for symbolic and political reasons, rather than out of any concern that the existing method of judicial review was failing to protect human rights or otherwise in need of improvement, or that the existing system failed to adequately protect human rights per se:

> Incorporation … is important, since, in the context of the impending cross-border bodies and the North-South ministerial Council, it is important to have a neutral yardstick of fundamental rights protection. Irrespective of the legal virtues of the Constitution as compared with the ECHR, the latter provides a politically neutral template for sensitive cross-border dealings which the former could never hope to attain.[19]

The question that arose, then, was how the obligation to have equivalent human rights protection was to be fulfilled. Some options were more likely to be taken up than others – for example, as early as 1975, it was proposed that an all-Ireland court would be necessary to ensure that Convention rights would be equally protected across the entire island of

---

16 See n 14 and 15.

17 Belfast/Good Friday Agreement, 'Rights, Safeguards and Equality of Opportunity', s 6, para. 9.

18 The UK had been in the process of incorporating the Convention at the time of the Good Friday Agreement. See Home Office, *Rights Brought Home: The Human Rights Bill* (Cm 3782, 1997).

19 Gerard Hogan, 'The Belfast Agreement and the Future Incorporation of the European Convention of Human rights in the Republic of Ireland' (1999) 4(4) *Bar Review* 205, 210.

Ireland, but this was never likely to have been acted upon.[20] Similarly, the suggestion that the incorporation of the ECHR could be coupled with the creation of a new constitutional court was rejected.[21]

One pertinent issue was whether it would be possible to provide a mechanism of strong judicial rights review, similar to that already in existence with regard to constitutional rights, whereby any legislation incompatible with the Convention could be struck down by the courts. This would have the advantage of being a familiar mechanism which would reinforce the existing system of strong judicial review. Although open to criticism,[22] the prevailing view was that it would not be possible for a *legislative* provision to provide that all other legislation must be consistent with the ECHR in order for it to be valid and enforceable. The powers of review of the court are limited by Article 34.3.2° of the Constitution,[23] and a court cannot refuse to apply a statutory provision which is constitutional. Thus, during the debates on the European Convention on Human Rights Bill, it was stated that it would be 'impermissible for the Irish legislature to bring forward in Ireland an authoritative source of human rights which had the effect of invalidating Irish legislation or overriding the function of the courts under the Constitution to … apply it among the citizens'.[24]

If the courts were to have the power to invalidate legislation which was not in compliance with the Convention (thus making Convention rights subject to the same process of judicial review as rights in the Constitution), then it would have to involve a constitutional amendment by means of a referendum. This amendment could have replaced the existing fundamental rights provisions with the text of the Convention;[25] it could have retained the existing human rights provisions of the Constitution

---

20 See John Lynch debating in Dáil Eireann Debates 20 November 1975, vol 285, no 13, para. 1730 (Criminal Law (Jurisdiction) Bill, 1975, Seanad, Second Stage).

21 See Casey (n 13).

22 See, for example, the views of the Irish Human Rights Commission in Submission on the European Convention on Human Rights Bill to the Joint Oireachtas Committee on Justice, Equality, Defence and Women's Rights (June 2002) 7; de Londras and Kelly, *European Convention on Human Rights Act* (n 6) 10–11.

23 See n 3.

24 Michael McDowell, Select Committee on Justice Equality Defence and Women's Rights, February 18, 2003. See also Constitution Review Group Report (n 9) 191.

25 Constitution Review Group Report (n 9) 193. See also Casey (n 13).

with Convention rights as an 'add on';[26] or it could have taken the form of a general clause providing for the invalidity of any law inconsistent with the State's obligations under the Convention.[27] Why were these options not followed? Arguably, it would have been simpler to have one system of human rights protection within the State, with one method of judicial review. However, the first option was not viable as it could potentially lower the protection available in certain areas where the Constitution provides for a high level of rights protection, such as the right to a jury trial.[28] The second and third options were most likely rejected for political reasons, including the difficulties of obtaining a majority vote in what could potentially be a divisive referendum on the issue, particularly if the Irish stance on sensitive issues such as abortion was perceived to be under threat by the Strasbourg Court.[29] Thus, despite criticisms, the general political position was that strong judicial review of Convention rights whereby a court would be able to invalidate any legislation incompatible with the Convention was not an option.

Two main factors, then, resulted in the adoption of a form of indirect, sub-constitutional incorporation based on the UK HRA: (1) the desire for equivalence with the regime in Northern Ireland, and (2) the difficulties inherent in achieving the consensus necessary for constitutional reform. However, as we are about to see, the mechanisms used in the HRA could not simply be neatly transplanted into the Irish system, and the combination of 'structural factors'[30] such as the existence of a codified constitution and the established system of strong judicial review meant that the impact of the Convention was quite different in the two jurisdictions, thus bringing into question the sought after equivalence that was one of the goals of the ECHR Act.[31]

---

[26] This option was not considered by the Constitutional Review Group.

[27] Constitution Review Group Report (n 9) 193.

[28] Ibid., 190.

[29] See, for example, the comments of Michael McDowell, Select Committee on Justice Equality Defence and Women's Rights, February 18, 2003.

[30] Samantha Besson, 'The Reception Process in Ireland and the United Kingdom' in Helen Keller and Alec Stone Sweet (eds), *A Europe of Rights: The Impact of the ECHR on National Legal Systems* (OUP 2008) 32.

[31] See Fiona de Londras, 'Neither Herald nor Fanfare: The Limited Impact of the ECHR Act 2003 on Rights Infrastructure in Ireland' in Egan and others (n 2) 51–3.

3.2.3 Adapting the New Commonwealth Model of Rights Review to a Written Constitution

This section examines the extent to which the Irish ECHR Act conforms to Gardbaum's 'Commonwealth Constitutionalism model',[32] and the extent to which the legal transplant which occurred had to be adapted to take into account Ireland's constitutional structure.

Gardbaum's Commonwealth model involves the enactment of a bill of rights, and 'its enforcement through the twin mechanisms of judicial and political rights review of legislation, but with the legal power of the final word going to the politically accountable branch of government, rather than the courts'.[33] It thus 'decouples the power of judicial review of legislation from judicial supremacy or finality'.[34] However, this weak form of judicial review is only one component of this model: Gardbaum views it as an 'entire package'[35] which also includes 'mandatory pre-enactment political rights review'.[36] Gardbaum highlighted four essential features of this Commonwealth model: a legalized and codified charter or bill of rights; mandatory rights review of legislation by the political branches before enactment; some form of constitutional review of legislation by the courts; and a 'formal legislative power to have the final word on what the law of the land is by ordinary majority vote'.[37] Gardbaum has noted that this model only really works 'where there is no existing big-C constitution'.[38] It is thus no surprise that the Irish legal system 'reflects only partial rather than general adoption of the new model'.[39] However, the questions which arise are, first, to what extent is it in fact possible to model a system of rights review on a Commonwealth model such as the HRA when there is a written constitution in place, and, second, to what extent can this still be said to conform to the Commonwealth model?

A. Overview of the ECHR Act 2003

The ECHR Act does not provide for direct incorporation of the ECHR, but defines the means by which the Convention can be relied upon in the

---

32 Gardbaum (n 4).
33 Ibid., 2.
34 Ibid., 2. See also 26–7.
35 Ibid., 15.
36 Ibid., 15, 25.
37 Ibid., 30–31.
38 Ibid., 13.
39 Ibid., 11.

domestic setting. The 2003 Act provides for a relatively complex and multi-layered mechanism. It includes an interpretative obligation, whereby a court 'shall' interpret and apply any statutory provision or rule of law in a manner compatible with the State's obligations under the Convention 'in so far as is possible, subject to the rules of law relating to such interpretation and application'.[40] If it is not possible to interpret a statutory provision or rule of law in a Convention-compatible manner, and if no other legal remedy is available, then the High Court or Supreme Court may make a 'declaration of incompatibility'.[41] This is a declaration that the statutory provision or rule of law is incompatible with the State's obligations under the Convention. However, a declaration of incompatibility does not affect the 'validity, continuing operation or enforcement of the statutory provision or rule of law in respect of which it is made'.[42] The court has no power to strike down or refuse to apply the law; nor does the declaration bind the government to repeal or change the law in question. There is merely a requirement that declarations of incompatibility be laid before the Irish Parliament (Dáil).[43]

The ECHR Act also provides a remedy where Convention rights are breached because of the administrative actions of the State, as opposed to where the source of the incompatibility with Convention rights is a result of the legislative action of the State. The 2003 Act provides that every 'organ of the State' must perform its functions in a manner compatible with the State's obligations under the Convention. However, this is 'subject to any statutory provision', so that, where an organ of the State acts in accordance with legislation, then they will not be found liable under this provision.

At first glance, these provisions might seem similar to those found in the HRA, which includes an interpretative obligation to read legislation 'in a way which is compatible' with Convention rights,[44] the concept of a declaration of incompatibility,[45] and an obligation on public authorities to act compatibly with the Convention.[46] However, closer analysis reveals that these provisions underwent a transformation when translated into the Irish context and can operate quite differently – to the extent that the

40 ECHR Act 2003, s 2.
41 Ibid., s 5.
42 Ibid., s 5(2)(a).
43 Ibid., s 5(3).
44 Human Rights Act 1998, s 3.
45 Ibid., s 4.
46 Ibid., s 6.

ECHR Act has been described as a 'pale imitation' of the HRA.[47] Moreover, one needs to also be aware of what is missing from the ECHR Act – in particular there is no obligation equivalent to the obligation on a minister in charge of a bill in the UK to make a statement on whether the provisions of a bill are compatible with Convention rights.[48] Nor is there any comparable 'fast track' procedure whereby, if a minister considers there are 'compelling reasons' for using the procedure, he 'may by order make such amendments to the legislation as he considers necessary to remove the incompatibility'.[49] These omissions have ramifications for the effectiveness of the ECHR Act as a mechanism to protect Convention rights, and represent a significant deviation from Gardbaum's model.

B. The duty to interpret legislation consistently with protected rights

In Gardbaum's model, judicial review includes not only declaratory decisions, but may consist of a duty to interpret legislation consistently with protected rights.[50] In the Irish context, this duty already existed prior to the ECHR Act, by virtue of the 'double construction rule' whereby a statutory provision 'will not be declared invalid where it is possible to construe it in accordance with the Constitution'.[51] Thus

> if in respect of any provision or provisions of the Act two or more constructions are reasonably open, one of which is constitutional, and the other or others are unconstitutional, it must be presumed that the Oireachtas intended only the constitutional construction and a Court called upon to adjudicate upon the constitutionality of the statutory provision should uphold the constitutional construction.[52]

However, there are clear constitutional limits on the application of this rule: Article 15.2.1° of the Constitution provides that the 'sole and exclusive power of making laws for the State' is vested in the Oireachtas, and it is thus not possible for the courts to interpret a statutory provision in accordance with the Constitution where this would usurp the legislative function of the Oireachtas.

---

47 Jim O'Keefe, Select Committee on Justice Equality Defence and Women's Rights February 18, 2003.

48 Human Rights Act 1998, s 19.

49 Ibid., s 10.

50 Gardbaum (n 4) 30, 32.

51 *East Donegal Co-operative Ltd v A-G* [1970] IR 317, 341 (Walsh J).

52 *McDonald v Bord na gCon* [1965] IR 217, 239 (Walsh J).

This was the backdrop against which the new interpretative obligation in section 2 of the ECHR Act was introduced. Section 2, which appears at first glance to be inspired by section 3 of the HRA,[53] states:

> In interpreting and applying any statutory provision or rule of law, a court shall, in so far as is possible, subject to the rules of law relating to such interpretation and application, do in a manner compatible with the State's obligations under the Convention provisions.

It is clear that the section 2 obligation had to fit into the current constitutional framework. It is thus subject to the same constitutional limitations as the 'double construction rule', and it is not possible for the courts to interpret a statutory provision in a Convention-compatible manner where this would amount to an act of legislation rather than interpretation. As Fiona de Londras and I have argued elsewhere, presumably this is what is to be inferred from the phrase 'in so far as possible' in section 2, and this limitation was necessary to ensure the constitutionality of the provision.[54] However, the biggest difference between section 2 of the ECHR Act and section 3 of the HRA stems not from this constitutional limitation,[55] but rather from the inclusion of the phrase 'subject to the rules of law relating to such interpretation and application'. This additional limitation, which is noticeably absent from the HRA's interpretative obligation, is arguably not necessary to ensure the constitutionality of the provision (or at the very least is over inclusive), and it is difficult to see what the legislator was trying to achieve with its inclusion. It is somewhat bizarre to have a rule of interpretation which is 'subject to' existing rules relating to such interpretation – taken literally, it would mean that the courts cannot apply the interpretative obligation in section 2 where it would result in a different interpretation or application of the law than that which would be reached according to the rules of interpretation which would apply if section 2 did not exist. Such a minimalist approach would severely limit the force of the section to the point that it would have no effect. Unfortunately, to date, the Irish courts have for the most part[56] taken a narrow approach

[53] Section 3 of the HRA states: 'So far as it is possible to do so, primary legislation and subordinate legislation must be read and given effect in a way which is compatible with the Convention rights.'

[54] de Londras and Kelly (n 6) 79.

[55] This limitation would be, in any event, inherent in the UK's conception of separation of powers also: see, for example, the discussion in *Bellinger v Bellinger* [2003] 2 AC 467.

[56] The case of *S v Adoption Board* [2009] IEHC 429 is a notable exception.

and restricted the application of section 2 for reasons which are often unrelated to constitutional concerns regarding the separation of powers.[57] It is this difference in wording – rather than the constitutional context per se – which has reduced the significance of the UK approach to the interpretative obligation:

> The consequences of this difference ... are important, because it means that in this jurisdiction a Court, when attempting to construe a law in a Convention compatible way, is still bound by the rules of law which heretofore have governed such interpretation, whereas in the UK no such restriction is imposed by Parliament. The range of manoeuvre available to a U.K. court ... is not available to an Irish Court. The practical consequence of this is that, whereas in the U.K. it would appear that a Court can impose a Convention compatible meaning unless that meaning clearly conflicts with the express terms, or the necessary implication of such terms of the law in question, in this jurisdiction, a Court is required by the Oireachtas to adhere to existing rules of interpretation which means that the dominant rule of statutory construction must still prevail. ... In effect, the kind of creative interpretation permitted under s.3 (1) of the U.K. Act may not be permissible under s.2 of the Act of 2003 unless the creation [envisaged] could be said to have been intended by Parliament.[58]

Thus, although the ECHR Act ostensibly contains an interpretative obligation, it would be an exaggeration to suggest that it incorporates a mechanism of judicial review anything like that found in section 3 of the HRA. This, however, cannot be attributed to the Constitution, but to poor, arguably defensive, drafting on the part of the legislator, reinforced by a lack of activism on the part of the courts.[59]

C. The declaration of incompatibility

In the UK, the HRA creates a system of shared political and judicial responsibility for rights protection which represents a compromise between respect for parliamentary sovereignty and the desire to have

---

[57] See, for example, *Foy v An t-Ard Chláraitheoir* [2007] IEHC 470 where the Convention compliant interpretation was refused not on the basis of separation of powers, but on the basis that the non-Convention compliant interpretation was 'well established'.

[58] *Dublin City Council v Gallagher* Unreported, November 11, 2008 (O'Neill J).

[59] For a discussion of an alternative approach to section 2 see, Cliona Kelly, 'Maximising the Potential of the European Convention on Human Rights Act 2003: The Interpretative Obligation and the Importance of Framing' in Egan and others (n 2) 55.

increased judicial engagement with Convention rights. A central – and, at the time of its creation, unique – feature of this system is the declaration of incompatibility. The declaration of incompatibility allows for the commencement of a dialogue between the courts and Parliament. The courts may declare that a statutory provision is incompatible with the ECHR but may not strike down or refuse to apply primary legislation.[60] For its part, Parliament is on notice of the violation and can be expected to engage with the Convention violation, while retaining the power to decide what exactly, if anything, is to be done about it. Along with the interpretative obligation, the declaration of incompatibility forms part of the 'weak form judicial review' in the UK version of the Commonwealth constitutional model.

The ECHR Act borrows the concept of a declaration of incompatibility, yet its philosophical basis is different to that in the UK. If the declaration of incompatibility in the UK owes its origins to the supremacy of Parliament, in Ireland it can said to be due to the supremacy of the Constitution. As discussed above, it is generally (although not universally)[61] accepted that it is not permissible for the courts to refuse to apply a legislative provision which is constitutional; hence it was not possible for the ECHR Act to provide that the courts could declare invalid or refuse to apply a statute which, while constitutional, was incompatible with the ECHR. However, given the culture of judicial enforcement of rights, there was clearly a desire to include the courts in a discussion of Convention rights, and the device used by our closest neighbours satisfied this requirement, even if it was designed for an entirely different legal framework. The result is that we are left with a mechanism which, while being 'entirely appropriate for the constitutional superstructure for which it was designed'[62] nonetheless 'may seem alien within the Irish context of legally determinable, constitutionally entrenched rights'.[63] However, given the constitutional limitations in place, and the reluctance to hold a referendum to introduce constitutional change, it is difficult to see what could have taken its place, and it may be that was 'appropriate' for the UK is also 'appropriate' for Ireland, albeit for entirely different reasons.

---

[60] There is a limited power to strike down subordinate legislation in the HRA where the breach is not inevitable because of primary legislation: see ss 3(2)(c), 4(3), 4(4) and 21.

[61] See n 22.

[62] Fiona de Londras, 'Declarations of Incompatibility under the ECHR Act 2003: A Workable Transplant?' (2014) 35 *Stat LR* 50, 55.

[63] Ibid., 54.

There is now a dichotomy of rights within the Irish legal system – constitutional rights, which are subject to strong judicial review,[64] and Convention rights in regards to which the courts have declaratory powers only, with the political branch being left to determine whether any incompatibility with the Convention needs to be remedied, and if so, how. The declaration of incompatibility has been described as a 'pale shadow' of the declaration of unconstitutionality.[65] This difference in approach between a breach of constitutional rights and a breach of Convention rights extends to the payment of damages. While damages may be payable for a breach of one's constitutional rights,[66] there is no obligation on the State to pay any form of compensation to a party who has suffered an injury or loss as a result of the incompatibility with the Convention. On an application by a party to the proceedings, the government may, in its discretion, make an ex gratia payment of compensation to that party, but it is not required to do so.[67] The only mandated action subsequent to the declaration is found in section 5(3), which provides that the Taoiseach (Irish Prime Minister) 'shall cause a copy or any order containing a declaration of incompatibility to be laid before each House of the Oireachtas within the next 21 days'. There is no obligation however that the Taoiseach indicate what remedial action should be taken,[68] or that the issue is even debated in the Oireachtas, or that the statutory provision or rule of law in question is amended or repealed.

A declaration of incompatibility has, therefore, little or no legal effect. It merely acts 'to all intents and purposes as a warning to the State that Irish law was not in conformity with the Convention'.[69] The question which arises is whether this warning will be taken seriously and encourage debate and reform, or whether it will be viewed as insignificant when compared with the serious legal repercussions of a judicial declaration that a law is unconstitutional. A further factor to take into

---

[64] Although ultimately also subject to political review and referenda: See Eoin Carolan in Chapter 3.

[65] See Gerard Hogan, 'The Constitution and the Convention: Happily Married or a Loveless Co-existence?' in Egan and others (n 2) 85.

[66] *Meskell v Córas Iompair Éireann* [1972] IR 121; *Grant v Roche Products* [2008] IESC 84.

[67] ECHR Act 2003, s 5(4).

[68] See *Fennell v Dublin City Council* [2005] 1 IR 604, 619 (Kearns J).

[69] Suzanne Egan, 'The European Convention on Human Rights Act 2003: A Missed Opportunity for Domestic Human Rights Litigation' (2003) 10 *DULJ* 230, 247.

account is the source of the right – as discussed below, a declaration of incompatibility will only be made in relation to rights which are not already protected in the Constitution, and which are thus derived from a foreign rather than a domestic source. As de Londras states, 'whether or not one believes that a right *other than a constitutional right* being breached without there being any available remedy in law is serious, depends on whether one values those rights that derive from non-constitutional instruments, such as international human rights law'.[70]

The courts have indicated an expectation that a declaration of incompatibility will be given due consideration by the legislative branch. Charleton J has stated that where a declaration of incompatibility has been made by a court, 'it is to be inferred' that a 'political will may exist to alter relevant legislation in favour of compatibility'.[71] Similarly, in *Foy*, McKechnie J expressed the opinion that 'as such a declaration can only issue from a constitutional court, such a court can have a reasonable expectation that the other branches of government (Article 6 of the Constitution) would not ignore the importance or significance of the making of such a declaration'.[72]

However, the *Foy* case itself illustrates the apathy and snail-like pace of reform that can follow a declaration of incompatibility. In *Foy*, the applicant sought a declaration that the Civil Registration Act 2004 was incompatible with the Convention as it failed to offer transsexuals the right to rectify their birth certificates to reflect their true gender, contrary to Article 8 of the ECHR. The State attempted to distinguish *Goodwin v United Kingdom*,[73] and argued that Ireland's constitutional protection of marriage justified the application of a margin of appreciation in this situation. However, McKechnie J rejected this argument, noting that 'the legal regime in the United Kingdom at the relevant time was virtually identical, under all major headings, to what which still pertains in this jurisdiction'.[74] McKechnie J conceded that it was a matter for the Oireachtas to choose what approach they took in response to the decision in *Goodwin,*[75] but that the State's failure to deal with the issue was unacceptable:

---

[70] de Londras, 'Declarations of Incompatibility under the ECHR Act 2003' (n 62) 61–2.

[71] *Doherty v South Dublin County Council & Ors* [2007] IEHC 4.

[72] *Foy v An t-Ard Chláraitheoir & Ors* [2007] IEHC 470 [110].

[73] *Goodwin v United Kingdom* (2002) 35 EHRR 18.

[74] *Foy v An t-Ard Chláraitheoir* (n 72) [96].

[75] Ibid., [102], [115].

> This State, which is personally charged with the responsibility of appropriately responding to *Goodwin*, has failed or declined to produce evidence of any movement, even at an initiating, debating or investigative level, on the plight of transsexual persons in this country. Given the silence of the Government on this issue, an issue which it must have known would be legally critical on the Convention point, one can only conclude that it has taken no steps of any significance to redress the undoubted difficulties which continue to exist. Noting the absence of any express provision in the Civil Registration Act, 2004, a legislative vehicle most suitable for this purpose, it must be seriously questioned whether the State has deliberately refrained from adopting any remedial measures to address the ongoing problems.[76]

The High Court thus found that the State was in breach of its obligations under Article 8 of the ECHR and made a declaration of incompatibility regarding the relevant provisions of the Civil Registration Act 2004.[77] The declaration of incompatibility was made in October 2007, yet the General Scheme of the Gender Recognition Bill was not published until July 2013, more than five years later. After consideration by a Joint Oireachtas Committee,[78] a revised General Scheme for the Gender Recognition Bill was published in June 2014, but at the time of writing this was still working its way through the Oireachtas.[79] Thus, there is still no legislation on this issue nearly eight years later. This slow pace of reform can be contrasted with the situation in the UK. After the decision in *Bellinger*[80] in April 2003, in which a declaration was made that section 11(c) of the Matrimonial Causes Act 1973 was incompatible with the ECHR, the government acted relatively quickly with the Gender Recognition Act 2004 being enacted in just over a year.

The slow pace of reform after the declaration of incompatibility in *Foy* can also be contrasted with the speed with which the Irish legislature would have had to react if the Civil Registration Act 2004 had been declared unconstitutional. As de Londras points out, the 2004 Act would have been invalid, causing a gap in legal regulation which would have

---

[76] Ibid., [100]–[102].

[77] Ibid., [115].

[78] Joint Oireachtas Committee on Education and Social Protection, Report on the General Scheme of a Gender Recognition Bill 2013 (Stationery Office, 2014) <http://www.oireachtas.ie/parliament/media/committees/educationandsocialprotection/Report-on-Gender-Recognition-Bill.pdf> accessed 3 June 2015.

[79] For an analysis, see Tanya Ní Mhuirthile, 'Article 8 and the Realisation of the Right to Legal Gender Recognition' in Egan and others (n 2) 201.

[80] *Bellinger v Bellinger* [2003] UKHL 21.

had to have been quickly resolved, lest there be no requirement whatsoever to register births within the State.[81] The speed with which this can be achieved is remarkable. For example, on 10 March 2015, the Court of Appeal in *Bederev v Ireland and others* made an order declaring section 2(2) of the Misuse of Drugs Act 1977 unconstitutional on the ground that it contravened the principle of separation of powers in Article 15.2.1 of the Constitution.[82] This meant that section 2(2) and any executive orders made under it were invalid. The practical consequence of this was that the possession of certain drugs such as ecstasy and ketamine was no longer an offence. However, immediately after the judgment in *Bederev* the health minister confirmed that the government would rush through emergency legislation to deal with this lacuna in the law,[83] and the Misuse of Drugs (Amendment) Act 2015 came into force on 12 March 2015, a mere two days after the Court of Appeal decision. Similarly, in the aftermath of the Supreme Court decision in *CC v Ireland*[84] on 23 May 2006, in which it was held that certain provisions of the Criminal Law (Amendment) Act 1935 were unconstitutional, the lacuna left in the law on statutory rape was remedied quickly by the Criminal Law (Sexual Offences) Act 2006, which was signed into law on 2 June 2006.[85] Although arguably exceptional examples, given the potential health and societal implications of the long-term legalization of an array of drugs or the absence of an offence of statutory rape, it demonstrates the push for immediate change provided by constitutional invalidity,[86] as opposed to the much weaker nudge provided by a declaration of incompatibility.

There are signs, however, that the Oireachtas is beginning to take a finding of incompatibility more seriously. A significant area of litigation under the ECHR Act has been in relation to eviction procedures for public authority housing. Section 62 of the Housing Act 1966 provided that where a tenancy agreement between a housing authority and a tenant

---

81 de Londras, 'Declarations of Incompatibility under the ECHR Act 2003'(n 62) 63.

82 *Bederev v Ireland & Ors* [2015] IECA 38.

83 'Significant health risks spur emergency law on drugs', *The Irish Times* 10 March 2015.

84 [2006] 4 IR 1.

85 Although the speed with which this was enacted in itself causes issues, as there very little time for parliamentary engagement with the rights issues raised by the Bill, or for the Irish Human Rights Commission to be consulted: see de Londras and Kelly (n 6) 237.

86 Although, as Eoin Carolan points out, the change made is often minimalist, merely aiming to satisfy the technical requirements of the Constitution: see Eoin Carolan in Chapter 3.

has been terminated but the tenant refuses to give up possession of the dwelling, the housing authority can apply to the District Court for a warrant for possession. The District Court did not have any discretion to refuse the warrant or any jurisdiction to examine the merits of any application, but was obliged to issue the warrant for possession once the criteria in section 62 were met.[87] This was objected to on the basis that it meant that there was no obligation on the housing authority to give reasons for its decision and there was no independent review of the merits of the authority's case. Section 62 had been previously held to be constitutional,[88] but in 2012 in *Dublin City Council v Donegan*,[89] the Supreme Court made a declaration that it was incompatible with Article 8 of the ECHR. After some delay, section 62 of the Housing Act 1966 was repealed by the Housing (Miscellaneous Provisions) Act 2014,[90] which gives the District Court more discretion to independently review any proceedings for possession of a local authority dwelling.[91] Comments made during the Oireachtas debates indicate that the need to act on the Supreme Court's ruling was a decisive factor in the repeal of section 62. For example, Minister of State at the Department of the Environment, Community and Local Government, Jan O'Sullivan, stated that 'on the termination of local authority tenancies, we needed to respond to the court's decision that we needed to bring the legislation in line with the European Convention on Human Rights'.[92] Of course, technically speaking the Court did not decide that the Oireachtas 'needed to bring the legislation in line' with the Convention, but merely declared that the legislation was *not currently in line* with the Convention. Other comments made during debates on the 2014 Act similarly suggest that the Oireachtas was bound to act so that the law would be compatible with the ECHR Act,[93] even though State's obligations are international rather than domestic in nature, and it is moreover a nonsense to talk of the law being

---

[87] *Dublin Corporation v Hamilton* [1999] 2 IR 486; *Byrne v Scally*, Unreported, High Court, October 12, 2000.

[88] *The State (O'Rourke) v Kelly* [1983] IR 58.

[89] *Donegan v Dublin City Council and Others* [2008] IEHC 288.

[90] Housing (Miscellaneous Provisions) Act 2014, s 18(3).

[91] Ibid., s 12.

[92] Dáil Debates, 15 May 2014. (Housing (Miscellaneous Provisions) Bill 2014: Second Stage).

[93] See, for example, the comment of Deputy Jan O'Sullivan in the Seanad on 1 July 2014, when at the end of an otherwise accurate description of the law, she stated that: 'New legislation is, therefore, required in this area to provide for repossession procedures compatible with the European Convention on Human Rights Act.'

compatible with the ECHR Act, which merely sets out a mechanism to give effect to the ECHR in the national sphere.[94] Despite this technical confusion, the increased engagement of the Oireachtas with declarations of incompatibility by the court is to be welcomed.

D. Administrative actions of organs of the State

Although this chapter focuses on judicial review of legislative actions (or inaction), it is worth briefly noting the extent to which the Constitution has impacted on the availability of a remedy where the administrative actions of 'an organ of the State' are in breach of Convention rights. Section 3(1) of the ECHR Act provides that every 'organ of the State' must perform its functions in a manner compatible with the State's obligations under the ECHR.[95] Section 3(2) provides that the court may, if no other remedy in damages is available, award damages to a person who has suffered injury, loss or damage as a result of a breach of section 3(1) by an organ of the State.[96] However, this is 'subject to any statutory provision', so that where an organ of the State acts in accordance with legislation then they will not be found liable under this provision, even if that legislation is incompatible with the Convention. The appropriate remedy in that situation is a declaration of incompatibility under section 5, which, as discussed above, in no way affects the validity of the legislative provision in question. This is in keeping with the overall scheme of the 2003 Act, with its emphasis on weak judicial review and keeping the ultimate decision-making power with the Oireachtas. It ensures that, while providing a remedy where an organ of the State acts essentially ultra vires in a manner which is in breach of Convention rights, section 3 cannot be used as a means of achieving 'by … the back door'[97] the cessation of legislation which, while incompatible with the Convention, is otherwise constitutional and valid. The restriction also ensures that organs of the State will not be faced with a conflict between

---

[94] As discussed below, however, confusion as to the effect and impact of the ECHR Act has also been relatively common amongst litigants seeking to rely on the 2003 Act.

[95] For an analysis of s 3 of the 2003 Act, see de Londras and Kelly (n 6) ch 5.

[96] There is an issue regarding whether the remedy in section 3 is limited to damages, and it would seem that, at least in judicial review proceedings, an applicant may be entitled to an order of *certiorari* or an order of *mandamus* on the basis of a breach of s 3(1). See de Londras and Kelly (n 6) 115–27 and 211–17.

[97] *Pullen v Dublin City Council* [2009] 2 ILRM 484, 498. For criticisms of this case, see de Londras and Kelly (n 6) 212–17.

choosing between their obligations under section 3 and their obligations under other statutory provisions or, indeed, the Constitution.[98]

The definition of 'organ of the State' in the ECHR Act excludes the President, the Oireachtas and the courts. The first exclusion is largely uncontroversial, and most likely required by the Constitution.[99] The exclusion of the Oireachtas is in keeping with the overall scheme and sub-constitutional status of the 2003 Act. Although it has been argued that the Oireachtas should have more of a proactive role in relation to the Convention, within the current scope of the 2003 Act this could be done using measures such as ministerial declarations of compatibility and rights-based auditing of bills (see below) rather than by means of an extension of the obligation in section 3. Finally, the exclusion of the courts was justified on the basis that 'they are already under a duty to administer justice in accordance with the provisions of the law and the Constitution'.[100] On first impression the exclusion of the courts from the definition of organ of State appears to provide a lesser protection than that provided by section 6 of the HRA, which applies to the courts, albeit with some limitations.[101] However, despite this apparent difference, the obligation on the UK courts in the HRA and on the Irish courts in the ECHR Act is in fact quite similar, particularly when one takes into account the obligation on the courts in sections 2 and 4 of the ECHR Act.[102]

E. The absence of a political review mechanism

An essential pillar of Gardbaum's model is one which is glaringly missing from the Irish schema, namely a mandatory political review mechanism which 'transfers some of the responsibility for rights protection from the external and more indirect mechanism of judicial review to

---

[98] The obligation in s 3 is of course subject to the provisions of the Constitution. Hence, if there is a conflict between the obligation to perform functions according to constitutional principles and the obligation in s 3, the constitutional obligation will prevail.

[99] Article 13.8.1 states:

> The President shall not be answerable to either House of the Oireachtas or to any court for the exercise and performance of the powers and functions of his office or for any act done or purporting to be done by him in the exercise and performance of these powers and functions.

[100] Explanatory Memorandum to the European Convention on Human Rights Bill 2003, 3.

[101] See Human Rights Act 1998, s 9.

[102] See de Londras and Kelly (n 6) 113–14.

the legislature itself'.[103] The ECHR Act does not provide for any official process whereby Convention-related issues must be addressed within the Irish legislative process; nor is any such process found elsewhere in the Irish statute book or in the Constitution.[104] In contrast, Article 15.4.1° of the Constitution states that the 'Oireachtas shall not enact any law which is in any respect repugnant to this Constitution or any provision thereof'. Given the repercussions of a failure to ensure constitutionality of legislation – that is its invalidity[105] – there is a strong incentive for Parliament to ensure that all legislation complies with the Constitution, but there is no such incentive to assess compliance of legislation with the Convention. Indeed, before any bill is signed into law by the President, the President has the power under Article 26 of the Constitution to refer that bill to the Supreme Court to review its constitutionality; but there is no similar mechanism in place to review a bill for compliance with the Convention. The Irish Human Rights and Equality Commission has a mandate to consider human rights issues which may arise in proposed legislation, but it cannot direct the Oireachtas to act in a particular manner and, moreover, it does not always have sufficient time to undertake a full rights analysis.[106] As de Londras and I have pointed out, the speed with which legislation is passed and the 'guillotining' of the time for parliamentary debate is problematic. It has often meant that there is simply no time to have a meaningful deliberation of human rights issues raised in sometimes controversial bills.[107] The ECHR Act did nothing to combat this, focusing mainly on litigation rather than parliamentary processes and the creation of a culture of rights. That said, it appears that the Convention is de facto taken into account at different stages through the legislative process, and explanatory memoranda to bills frequently refer to the ECHR, albeit briefly. The difficulty is that review tends to be 'ad hoc, voluntary and unsystematic' rather than 'formalized, mandatory and deliberate',[108] meaning that it can be disregarded in the cases where arguably it matters most.

---

[103] Gardbaum (n 4) 25.

[104] See de Londras and Kelly (n 6) ch 9.

[105] Article 15.4.2° states: 'Every law enacted by the Oireachtas which is in any respect repugnant to this Constitution or to any provision thereof, shall, but to the extent only of such repugnancy, be invalid'.

[106] This function is currently found in section 10 of the Irish Human Rights and Equality Commission Act 2014.

[107] de Londras and Kelly (n 6) 233–44.

[108] Gardbaum (n 4) 25–6.

This can be contrasted with the position in the UK under the HRA which provides for a parliamentary system of rights scrutiny whereby the minister in charge of the bill must either make a statement to the effect that in his view the provisions of the bill are compatible with Convention rights, or make a statement to the effect that, although a statement of compatibility cannot be made, the government nonetheless wishes to proceed with the bill.[109] Although clearly this does not guarantee that legislation is in fact compatible with the Convention – and even if Parliament is of the view that legislation is compatible, it is open to the courts to disagree – it means that at the very least consideration of Convention rights is incorporated into the parliamentary process, encouraging a culture of rights-awareness and providing a layer of ex ante protection which is not reliant on litigation. This process is strengthened by the work of the Joint Committee on Human Rights, a select committee established by Parliament which scrutinizes legislation and considers its compliance with human rights standards. It is to be regretted that the ECHR Act did not introduce similar structures in the Irish context. Even a system of strong judicial review can benefit from parliamentary rights auditing of legislation. Moreover, the incentive to legislate in compliance with the Constitution afforded by strong judicial review in place only applies to constitutional rights and not to Convention rights, which require bolstering by a further mandatory system of political review.

3.2.4 The Evolution of the Relationship Between the ECHR Act and the Constitution

The section above discussed the extent to which Ireland's constitutional framework had an impact on the design of the ECHR Act. However, the relationship between the Constitution and the Convention/ECHR Act continued to evolve after the promulgation of the 2003 Act, and the precise interaction between the two sources of rights had to be clarified by the courts. The following sections focus on the issue of whether the courts should prioritize the constitutional review mechanisms or the system of review provided by the ECHR Act. It also discusses the difficulties litigants (or rather, their lawyers) have faced in moving from the familiar language and mechanism of constitutional rights to the rather more alien language and effects of the ECHR Act.

---

109 Human Rights Act 1998, s 19.

A. The doctrine of constitutional avoidance and the declaration of incompatibility

An initial difficulty was whether the courts, if faced with a claim of unconstitutionality and a claim of incompatibility in the same case, should deal with the constitutional claim or the Convention claim first. This issue is best understood in light of the doctrine of constitutional avoidance, which provides that the courts will seek to avoid considering the constitutionality of a measure unless it is not possible to resolve the dispute on the basis of the non-constitutionality arguments.[110] Taken literally, this would mean that the court should seek to resolve the dispute on the basis of the ECHR Act before resorting to the Constitution. However, this appeared to conflict with section 5 of the ECHR Act, which provides that a declaration of incompatibility can only be made 'where no other legal remedy is adequate and available'. The question which thus arises is whether, when both Convention and constitutional issues arise, the doctrine of constitutional avoidance requires the court to consider the Convention matter first, or whether section 5 of the ECHR Act requires the court to consider the constitutional issue first.[111]

In *Carmody*,[112] the Supreme Court held that the doctrine of constitutional avoidance did not apply when an applicant sought a declaration of incompatibility under the 2003 Act. The Court focused on the fact that a declaration of incompatibility could not provide a remedy which would resolve the issue before the parties. Thus, if an applicant claims both that a provision is repugnant to the Constitution and that it is incompatible with the ECHR, the issue of constitutionality is to be decided first. This means that if the Court finds that a provision is unconstitutional, it need not go further and determine whether or not it is also incompatible with the Convention. This reinforces the Convention's status as a supplementary source of rights, with the declaration of incompatibility in particular acting as a measure of last resort, to be relied upon only where no other legal remedy is 'adequate and available'. Moreover, when faced with a choice between two competing forms of rights review, the Supreme Court firmly asserted the Court's role in the enforcement of rights, for a sequencing which prioritizes constitutional issues implicitly endorses a system of strong judicial review. The judgment also means that in any case where a declaration of incompatibility is made, the statutory provision or rule of law is, by default, constitutional.

---

110 See *Murphy v Roche* [1987] IR 106.

111 See the discussion in de Londras and Kelly (n 6) 40–44.

112 *Carmody v Minister for Justice, Equality and Law Reform* [2009] IESC 71.

The approach taken by the Supreme Court is by no means an indication of an aversion towards the Convention. Given that a declaration of incompatibility is of no legal effect, it is surely better for the applicant that they can rely on their constitutional rights and secure a meaningful vindication of their rights. As Hogan J, writing extra-judicially, has pointed out, the ECHR was not originally intended as a form of substitute Constitution, but 'what was rather contemplated was that the ECHR would establish basic standards throughout the Council of Europe'.[113] Moreover, there is often an overlap between rights under the Constitution and rights under the Convention, with Convention jurisprudence being increasingly taken into account in the interpretation of constitutional rights, such that 'constitutional and ECHR law have cross-pollinated each other'.[114] This increased synergy could potentially be the greatest impact of incorporation, and a welcome one given that the Constitution has a better remedial scheme than that under the ECHR Act and is thus more effective at securing those basic standards. The learned judge expressed similar views in the case of *S v Minister for Justice, Equality and Law Reform:*

> [The] Oireachtas did not intend that the ECHR should operate as a form of parallel constitution which in some way supplanted the Constitution or vied for supremacy in the hierarchy of legal normal created by the Constitution. If that had been intended, then a constitutional amendment ... would have been necessary. In the absence of such a constitutional amendment, the Oireachtas must therefore be taken to have intended that recourse to the ECHR would operate at a sub-constitutional level as a form of supplementary protection in the – hopefully rare – event that the Constitution's protections fell short of the standards required by the ECHR itself.[115]

While academics, myself included, have suggested ways in which Convention rights can be better secured in the domestic sphere, whether by reforming the ECHR Act itself or by altering the way litigants and the courts approach and interpret the 2003 Act, it is important to clarify that this is not always synonymous with a suggestion that the Convention rights necessarily be prioritized over those in the Constitution, or that the mechanism in the ECHR Act be used or improved so that it is the primary means of enforcing those rights. Rather, those suggestions relate to the need for better and more effective protection of rights which are *not already* protected in the Constitution. Of course, one might prefer a

---

113 Hogan, 'The Constitution and the Convention' (n 65) 73, 80.

114 Ibid., 73.

115 *S v Minister for Justice, Equality and Law Reform* [2010] IEHC 31 [6].

system whereby rights are enjoyed not as a result of strong judicial review, but rather as a result of a dialogic mechanism such as that in the UK, but that is a separate issue which arguably relates more to separation of powers and the question of *who* decides on the issue of rights, rather than the question of how to maximize rights protection.

B. The interpretative obligation in the ECHR Act and the Constitution

The decision in *Carmody* related only to declarations of incompatibility and arguably does not apply where there is an alternative method which could resolve the issue between the parties. In theory at least, under section 2 of the ECHR Act, the courts can interpret a statutory provision or rule of law in a manner compatible with the State's obligations under the Convention, and thus provide a favourable resolution to the applicants without having regard to the Constitution. Although some applicants would wish to have the impugned provision declared invalid by reference to the Constitution, others may wish to have a provision interpreted by the court under section 2 so as to provide a solution to the problem at hand, particularly where the apparent incompatibility is due to an omission in the statutory provision or is a case of under-inclusiveness. However, the courts have taken a restrictive approach to section 2 so far, and it is has only produced results in a limited number of cases. This means that the constitutional argument is most likely still open to most litigants despite the theoretical remedy in section 2. In most cases, it will also be the more favourable path to success, provided of course that there is in fact a constitutional right on which to rely.

Moreover, where two different and mutually inconsistent interpretations of a statute are possible, one of which is in accordance with the Constitution and one of which is in accordance with the Convention, the constitutional interpretation will be preferred.[116] It is not, of course, inevitable that a constitutionally-compliant interpretation and Convention-compliant interpretation of a statute would be mutually inconsistent. For example, in *Makumbi v Minister for Justice, Equality and Law Reform*[117] Finlay Geoghegan J interpreted the Refugee Act 1996 (Section 22) Order 2003[118]

---

[116] This is in keeping with the presumption of constitutionality and the sub-constitutional status of the 2003 Act. As Murray CJ stated in *Carmody v Minister for Justice* [2010] 1 IR 635, 650: 'the provisions of the Act of 2003 cannot compromise in any way the interpretation or application of the Constitution …'.

[117] High Court, Finlay Geoghegan J, 15 November, 2005.

[118] SI No 423/2003.

in light of the right to life as guaranteed by Article 40.3.2 of the Constitution and Article 2 of the Convention. It was held that in accordance with the presumption of constitutionality, the powers of the minister under this Order were to be construed and carried out in accordance with the principles of constitutional justice, meaning the minister could not implement a transfer order where the life of the person to whom it applied was at risk. The Court then indicated that a similar result would have been achieved under section 2 of the ECHR Act, based on the State's obligations under Article 2 of the Convention. However, it is clear that the constitutional interpretation was prioritized in the judgment. Similarly, in the 2014 *Gormley*[119] decision, the Supreme Court interpreted the due process guarantee in Article 38.1 of the Constitution with reference to the ECtHR's Grand Chamber judgment in *Salduz v Turkey*,[120] although it held that on a proper interpretation of the Constitution the standard in *Salduz* was met, so it was unnecessary to consider the ECHR Act.

C. The need for litigants to recognize the new system of judicial review

At this stage – over ten years since the incorporation of the ECHR into Irish law – it should be clear that it is not enough for a litigant in an Irish court to rely on the Convention in broad or general terms; rather the exact basis for a claim based on the ECHR Act needs to be identified. It is thus essential that those seeking to rely on Convention rights fully appreciate that the 2003 Act has a different mechanism of judicial review to that found in the Constitution, and can clearly identify the most effective cause of action for a particular litigant. Although it is perhaps understandable that litigants in earlier cases failed to identify clearly the basis on which they were relying on the Convention in Irish courts,[121] and more recent cases have shown a greater and more nuanced understanding of the operation of the 2003 Act, it is somewhat alarming that as recently as 2012, and before the Supreme Court, an applicant's lawyers were seemingly incapable of correctly formulating a claim under the 2003 Act, falling back instead on the familiar language of constitutional rights.

In *MD (A Minor) v Ireland, Attorney General and Director of Public Prosecutions,*[122] the applicant sought a declaration that certain provisions

---

[119] *The People (Director of Public Prosecutions) v Gormley* [2014] IESC 17.

[120] *Salduz v Turkey* (2009) 49 EHRR 19.

[121] *McD v L and Anor* [2009] IESC 81; *Clifford v Minister for Education and Science and others* [2005] IEHC 288.

[122] [2012] 2 ILRM 305.

of the Criminal Law (Sexual Offences) Act 2006 were unconstitutional; a declaration which was denied by both the High Court and the Supreme Court. He also sought a declaration that the 2006 Act was 'in breach of art.8 of the European Convention on Human Rights in that it denies the appellant his right to respect for private life'[123] and 'in breach of art.6 and art. 14 of the European Convention on Human Rights in that it denies the appellant the right to a fair trial on grounds of gender'.[124] The difficulty here is that the applicant simply generically sought to rely on the Convention, as though the Convention had direct effect in Irish courts, and did not expressly seek, for example, a declaration under section 5 of the ECHR Act that the relevant provisions of the 2006 Act were incompatible with the State's obligations under the Convention.[125] Unsurprisingly, the Supreme Court rejected the applicant's claim:

> The claim, as pleaded, is simply that [the statutory provision] is 'in breach of' the Convention. That formulation is not acceptable. It treats the Convention as if it had direct effect and presumes that the court has the power to grant a declaration that a section is in breach of the Convention. It is clear from the judgments of this court in *McD v L* that the European Convention on Human Rights Act 2003 did not give direct effect in Irish law to the European Convention on Human Rights.[126]

This case confirms the status of the ECHR in a dualist state. If litigants want to rely on the Convention before the Irish courts, they have to clearly identify the basis of that claim under the ECHR Act. The 2003 Act will only be effective to protect Convention rights if it is used correctly. A good starting point would be for lawyers to recognize that there is a clear distinction between the type of judicial review and remedial mechanisms in the ECHR Act and the Constitution. It is not enough to simply transplant the language used in the context of constitutional rights to the context of the 2003 Act; in other words, it is not enough for lawyers who are familiar with the concept of seeking a declaration that a statutory provision is unconstitutional, to simply assume that the same mechanism applies in the context of the 2003 Act and seek a declaration that the statutory provision is 'in breach of' the Convention. The 2003 Act has a relatively complex mechanism that needs to be fully understood if a successful claim is to be made under it, and at a minimum it is essential that it is pleaded correctly.

---

123 Ibid., 309 [8].
124 Ibid.
125 Ibid., 324 [61].
126 Ibid., 324 [59] (citations omitted).

3.2.5 Conclusion

The Irish system of rights review is a tale of two sets of rights – constitutional rights, which are subject to 'strong' judicial review, reflecting a system of legal constitutionalism, and Convention rights, which are to be primarily enforced by the legislature, supported by a form of dialogic judicial review. Convention rights thus supplement rather than replace the constitutional regime. The incorporation of the ECHR in Ireland was not instigated by any dissatisfaction with the existing regime of strong judicial review of the Constitution, but rather by government commitments in the Belfast/Good Friday Agreement. The sense of collective ownership of the Constitution in Ireland remains strong, as is illustrated for example by the strong public engagement with the referendum on same sex marriage in May 2015.[127] The sub-constitutional scheme introduced by the ECHR Act was thus unlikely to represent a dramatic revolution in judicial rights review, or supplant the role of the Constitution in relation to rights review; nor was it ever likely that the courts would interpret it in such a manner. As Hogan J has stated,

> The reality is that constitutional courts/supreme courts already successfully functioning under a particular and entrenched judicial order are not going lightly to throw over their own constitutional tradition absent an express constitutional amendment which specifically mandates this course of action.[128]

That said, within the confines of this constitutional structure, there was arguably more that could have been done to ensure the protection of rights in Ireland. Certain restrictions both in the drafting of the ECHR Act and the courts' approach to the 2003 Act are not necessitated by the Constitution. Nor is there any ostensible reason why a mandatory political review mechanism such as that in the UK HRA could not have been introduced, thus encouraging a culture of rights awareness within parliamentary processes. The minimalist approach of the ECHR Act is thus apparent, and it is unlikely to represent a challenge to the dominant constitutional paradigm of strong judicial review.

---

[127] See the Thirty-fourth Amendment of the Constitution (Marriage Equality) Bill 2015. The constitutional amendment was passed by a referendum on 22 May 2015.

[128] Hogan, 'The Constitution and the Convention' (n 62) 78.

4. Australia

James Stellios and Matthew Zagor

4.1 AUSTRALIAN CONSTITUTIONALISM AND THE UK-STYLE DIALOGUE MODEL OF HUMAN RIGHTS PROTECTION

James Stellios*

4.1.1 Introduction

A key feature of the 'dialogue'[1] model of human rights protection enacted in the United Kingdom Human Rights Act 1998 (HRA or 1998 Act) was the experimental use of the judiciary to issue declarations of incompatibility if legislation could not be interpreted in a human rights consistent way. The use of the judiciary in this way has led to considerable debate about the scheme's compatibility with fundamental tenets of British constitutionalism. In particular, this innovative use of the judiciary for rights protection has posed a challenge to traditional conceptions of the judicial function and raised concerns about the abdication of legislative power threatening parliamentary sovereignty. While these debates are important, their impact has remained within the political sphere, the

* My thanks to Professor Peter Cane for his comments.

[1] There is considerable imprecision with the expression 'dialogue': see, for example, Leighton McDonald, 'New Directions in the Australian Bill of Rights Debate' [2004] PL 22. The High Court of Australia in *Momcilovic v The Queen* (2011) 245 CLR 1 took issue with the appropriateness of that description for a UK-style human rights scheme ([67]–[68] (French CJ); [84] (Gummow J); [207] (Crennan and Kiefel JJ). However, the expression is used in this chapter for convenience as a short-hand way of referring to a human rights scheme, based on the UK Human Rights Act 1998 (HRA), containing an interpretive rule and a judicial power to make a declaration of incompatibility.

highest claim being that this 'dialogue' model of rights protection should be repealed.[2]

The UK-dialogue experiment has attracted Australian interest – both at the federal and state levels. In a federal system reluctant to embrace enhanced opportunities for judicial involvement in the protection of rights, the dialogue model was seen as an opportunity to provide non-traditional mechanisms for rights protection. Unlike its ancestor in the United States, the Australian Constitution does not contain a judicially enforceable bill of rights, and the few provisions resembling constitutional limitations for rights protection have been given exceptionally narrow interpretations. The Australian States do not have entrenched constitutions at all, let alone judicially enforceable rights. Thus, within the Australian constitutional system, judicial involvement in rights protection has been limited almost entirely to the 'administration of common justice'[3] – that is, the resolution of disputes about legal rights and duties and the application to legislation of interpretive presumptions protective of rights.

The constitutional systems of the Australian States evolved to reflect British constitutional traditions, and the federal Constitution was drafted to adapt parliamentary sovereignty and responsible government to a federal system of government. These legal and political conditions, it was assumed by many, were capable of embracing the UK-style dialogue model, and two Australian jurisdictions have adopted legislative schemes closely modelled on the UK HRA.

However, the federal Constitution was also drafted to reflect the tripartite arrangement of government powers and institutions found in the US Constitution. The organization of powers and institutions into legislative, executive and judicial compartments has provided a foundation for the High Court of Australia to draw constitutional implications that place limitations on the federal Parliament's power to design government institutions. More controversially, this federal constitutional arrangement has been held by the High Court to place limitations on the ways in which State Parliaments design their judicial institutions. In *Momcilovic v The Queen*,[4] the High Court relied upon these structural limitations to frustrate the operation of dialogue models in Australia: whether enacted at the federal or state level. As a consequence, constitutionalism

---

2 For an analysis of rights-based review in the UK, see Chintan Chandrachud and Aileen Kavanagh in Chapter 2.

3 William Blackstone, *Commentaries on the Laws of England* (1765) book 1, ch 7, 259.

4 *Momcilovic* (n 1).

Australian-style – specifically, *separation of powers* implications – presents impenetrable obstacles to the effective operation of a UK-style dialogue model, and has locked in a limited role for the judiciary in the protection of rights, smouldering experimentation and elevating selective political theories of separation of powers to the level of constitutional entrenchment.

4.1.2 Australian Conditions for Judicial Review

A. Australian constitutionalism: a British/American hybrid

In 1901, by Act of the Imperial Parliament, the former British colonies of New South Wales, Victoria, South Australia, Queensland, Tasmania and Western Australia 'united in a Federal Commonwealth under the name of the Commonwealth of Australia'.[5] The Commonwealth Constitution,[6] which gave effect to this federal union, was drafted over the course of two Constitutional Conventions in the 1890s. Its drafting and enactment was largely encouraged, supported and facilitated by the Imperial Government.[7]

By the time of federation, the Australian colonies had been granted by the Imperial Parliament substantial autonomy and powers of self-government. Colonial constitutions, as Acts of the Imperial and colonial Parliaments, were flexible and largely unlimited instruments of government. The dominant constitutional norms that characterized their governance structures were responsible government and parliamentary supremacy. Within this legal and political tradition, the role of the courts was to administer the law by resolving legal disputes and, in the course of doing so, to give effect to the sovereign will of the Imperial and colonial Parliaments. This was constitutionalism in the Diceyan tradition of parliamentary sovereignty.[8] Judicial review to invalidate legislation was limited to striking down colonial legislation that was repugnant to Imperial law. Attempts by colonial judges to assert a broader power of judicial review were met with Imperial responses to restore the sovereign

---

[5] Preamble, Commonwealth of Australia Constitution Act 1900 (Imp).

[6] The Commonwealth Constitution was contained in s 9 of the 1900 Imperial Act.

[7] See, generally, Nicholas Aroney, *The Constitution of a Federal Commonwealth: The Making and Meaning of the Australian Constitution* (CUP 2009); J A La Nauze, *The Making of the Australian Constitution* (MUP 1974).

[8] Jeffrey Goldsworthy, *The Sovereignty of Parliament: History and Philosophy* (Clarendon Press 2009) 1.

power of colonial Parliaments and contain the judicial review power of the courts.[9]

It was these legal and political conditions with which the drafters of the Australian Constitution were most familiar when they set about their task of drafting a constitution to federate the Australian colonies. As will be further explored, the power of judicial review was certainly contemplated, but for the purpose of securing and protecting the terms of the federal compact. The legal and political conditions of Australian constitutionalism did not provide fertile ground for the judicial protection of rights against the democratic expression of legislative will. As Gleeson CJ, former Chief Justice of the High Court of Australia, said in *Roach v Electoral Commissioner*:[10]

> The Australian Constitution was not the product of a legal and political culture, or of historical circumstances, that created expectations of extensive limitations upon legislative power for the purpose of protecting the rights of individuals. It was not the outcome of a revolution, or a struggle against oppression. It was designed to give effect to an agreement for a federal union, under the Crown, of the peoples of formerly self-governing British colonies. Although it was drafted mainly in Australia, and in large measure … approved by a referendum process in the Australian colonies, and by the colonial Parliaments, it took effect as an Act of the Imperial Parliament. Most of the framers regarded themselves as British. They admired and respected British institutions, including parliamentary sovereignty.

However, the constitutional system was to be a *federal* one, and various existing federal models for constitutional governance were considered by the drafters over the course of Constitutional Conventions held in 1891 and 1897–98. When deciding upon a blueprint for Australian federalism, the US Constitution proved most influential. Andrew Inglis Clark, one of the key delegates to the 1891 Convention, had distributed a draft constitution to the other delegates prior to the commencement of that Convention. Inglis Clark's intimate familiarity with the American Constitution is well documented,[11] and the Australian Constitution bears many

---

[9] The Imperial Parliament enacted the Colonial Laws Validity Act 1865 (UK) to confirm the plenary power of colonial Parliaments, subject to repugnancy with Imperial laws. For an account of Australian events leading to the enactment of the Colonial Laws Validity Act, see John M Williams, 'Justice Boothby: A Disaster that Happened' in George Winterton (ed.), *State Constitutional Landmarks* (The Federation Press 2006) 21.

[10] (2007) 233 CLR 162, 172.

[11] See, for example, John M Williams, 'With Our Eyes Open: Andrew Inglis Clark and Our Republican Tradition' (1995) 23 *FL Rev* 149.

of the central *federal* constitutional features of the US Constitution.[12] For example, the federal legislature is given a set of defined powers, with the states retaining their broad powers. In the event of conflict, the federal laws are to prevail. And, importantly, the power of judicial review was anticipated as a mechanism for maintaining the federal compact.[13]

B. The allocation of federal power across the three arms of government

The US Constitution, however, provided further inspiration. When organizing the powers of the federal body politic, Inglis Clark followed the allocation set out in articles I, II and III of the US Constitution. Thus, Chapters I, II and III of the Australian Constitution identify, respectively, three categories of governmental power – legislative, executive and judicial – and allocate those powers to three arms of government, the federal Parliament, executive and judicature. Despite this textual allocation of powers, it is unclear what the framers intended to achieve by this constitutional arrangement. Was this simply intended 'as a draftsman's neat arrangement, without any hint of further significance',[14] or was the arrangement designed to reflect a commitment to a *separation* of powers and intended to give effect to a particular set of constitution values?

The historical record reveals very little to assist.[15] Unlike the detailed elaboration of the libertarian virtues of a separation of powers in the *Federalist Papers*,[16] that drew from the writings of Montesquieu,[17] the framers of the Australian Constitution did not debate such theories nor their underlying purposes or values. While it might be assumed that its

---

12 For an analysis of rights-based review in the US, see Michel Rosenfeld in Chapter 1.

13 See Brian Galligan, 'Judicial Review in the Australian Federal System: Its Origin and Function' (1979) 10 *FL Rev* 367; Helen Irving, '*Its First and Highest Function*: The Framers' Vision of the High Court as Interpreter of the Constitution' in Peter Cane (ed.), *Centenary Essays of the High Court of Australia* (LexisNexis Butterworths 2004) 17.

14 This was the view later expressed by Robert Garran, the Secretary to the Drafting Committee during the 1897–98 Convention: *Prosper the Commonwealth* (Angus & Robertson 1958) 194.

15 See J M Finnis, 'Separation of Powers in the Australian Constitution' (1968) 3 *Adel L Rev* 159; Fiona Wheeler, 'Original Intent and the Doctrine of Separation of Powers in Australia' (1996) 7 PLR 96.

16 *Federalist Papers* (1788) Nos 47, 51 (James Madison) and 78 (Alexander Hamilton).

17 Charles-Louis De Secondat, Baron De Montesquieu, *The Spirit of Laws* (1748) book XI, ch 6.

chief architect, Inglis Clark, was familiar with the American background, it cannot, with any confidence, be assumed that there was broader familiarity with such ideas among the Convention delegates. As one of Australia's leading constitutional commentators noted, '[t]here is no evidence that the Federal Fathers in general had the slightest desire to imitate the French theory of separation of powers, which was based upon a misrepresentation of English practice, nor the American theory which was based upon a misrepresentation of the French'.[18] Thus, it is unclear the extent to which any constitutional entrenchment of a separation of powers was thought by the drafters to provide content to the power to exercise judicial review. The legal and political context suggests that the role of the courts to control the sovereign will of Parliament in this respect was intended to be limited.

C. Constitutional protection for rights

This position is not entirely surprising. As already alluded to, the constitution was not widely seen by the delegates as an instrument to protect individuals from the exercise of government power.[19] In this respect, British constitutional tradition was dominant: individual rights would be protected by the common law and the English institutions of parliamentary supremacy and responsible government.[20] As Dawson J said in *Australian Capital Television Pty Ltd v Commonwealth*:[21]

> [t]hose responsible for the drafting of the Constitution saw constitutional guarantees of freedoms as exhibiting a distrust of the democratic process. They preferred to place their trust in Parliament to preserve the nature of our society and regarded as undemocratic guarantees which fettered its powers. Their model in this respect was, not the United States Constitution, but the British Parliament, the supremacy of which was by then settled constitutional doctrine.[22]

---

[18] Geoffrey Sawer, *Australian Federalism in the Courts* (MUP 1967) 152.

[19] See, for example, Haig Patapan, 'Competing Visions of Liberalism: Theoretical Underpinnings of the Bill of Rights Debate in Australia' (1997) 21 MULR 497, 505-08; Stephen Gageler, 'Foundations of Australian Federalism and the Role of Judicial Review' (1987) 17 *FL Rev* 162, 170–73.

[20] Jeffrey Goldsworthy, 'The Constitutional Protection of Rights in Australia' in Gregory Craven (ed.), *Australian Federation: Towards the Second Century* (MUP 1992) 151.

[21] (1992) 177 CLR 106, 186.

[22] See also the comments of Sir Owen Dixon when contrasting the US and Australian Constitutions to the American Bar Association, *Jesting Pilate* (Law Book 1965) 102:

Indeed, it was the desire to retain the power to discriminate on racial grounds that led to the rejection by the framers of due process and equal protection guarantees similar to those contained in the Fifth and Fourteenth Amendments of the US Constitution.[23]

There is the occasional section in the Australian Constitution that resembles an American-style bill of rights provision, the clearest of these being section 80[24] that requires jury trials for federal offences and section 116[25] that prevents Parliament from establishing or regulating religion. However, these provisions have been read in very limited ways by the High Court: Parliament can avoid a jury trial by prescribing a summary procedure[26] and section 116 can only be offended when Parliament legislates with a clear and exclusive purpose of affecting the religious interests reflected in the provision.[27] Indeed, given their history

---

> In [the United States] men have come to regard formal guarantees of life, liberty and property against invasion by government, as indispensable to a free constitution. Bred in this doctrine you may think it strange that in Australia, a democracy if ever there was one, the cherished American practice of placing in the fundamental law guarantees of personal liberty should prove unacceptable to our constitution makers. But so it was. The framers of the Australian Constitution were not prepared to place fetters upon legislative action, except and in so far as it might be necessary for the purpose of distributing between the States and the central government the full content of legislative power. The history of their country had not taught them the need of provisions directed to the control of the legislature itself.

23 La Nauze (n 7) 229–32.

24 Commonwealth of Australia Constitution Act 1900, s 80: 'The trial on indictment of any offence against any law of the Commonwealth shall be by jury …'.

25 Ibid., s 116: 'The Commonwealth shall not make any law for establishing any religion, or for imposing any religious observance, or for prohibiting the free exercise of any religion, and no religious test shall be required as a qualification for any offence or public trust under the Commonwealth'.

26 A view first accepted in *R v Archdall and Roskruge; Ex parte Corrigan and Brown* (1928) 41 CLR 128. For a detailed account of the way that the High Court has interpreted section 80, see James Stellios, 'The Constitutional Jury – "A Bulwark of Liberty"?' (2005) 27 *Syd LR* 113.

27 *A-G (Vic) (Ex rel Black) v Commonwealth* (1981) 146 CLR 559; *Kruger v The Commonwealth* (1997) 190 CLR 1. For a detailed account of the way that the High Court has interpreted s 116, see George Williams and David Hume, *Human Rights under the Australian Constitution* (2nd edn, OUP 2013) ch 7. There were proposals in 1988 to strengthen these constitutional 'rights' and extend them to apply to the States (see *First Report of the Constitutional*

and interpretation, the provisions perhaps may be better explained as forming part of the federal architecture.[28]

Beyond the text of the Constitution, there have been efforts to extract constitutional protections for rights as implications necessarily arising from the text and structure of the constitution. Most importantly for the purposes of this chapter, there have been some attempts to establish the tripartite allocation of powers as a basis for protecting rights. As will be explained further below, there are difficulties with this jurisprudence: first, it is not clear what theoretical basis or tradition for a separation of powers is being relied on when such attempts are made; and, secondly, the invocation of liberty protecting rationales of the separation of powers has had little meaningful impact when it matters most.

The High Court has also developed an implied constitutional protection for political communication from undue legislative and executive interference.[29] Although some initial formulations emphasized the liberty-enhancing purpose of such protection, the limitation has survived, despite considerable criticism,[30] on the basis that it is not a constitutional 'right', but a limitation necessary for the effective operation of the systems of representative and responsible government created by the text of the constitution.[31] This textual basis has opened the door for the protection of voting rights from undue legislative interference, although

---

Commission, vol 1, 1988, 25–6), but the referendum held for constitutional change was unsuccessful.

[28] Section 80 has been explained as a structural provision that facilitates the exercise of federal judicial power (see Stellios, 'The Constitutional Jury' n 26). As for s 116, the convention debates indicate that s 116 was designed to leave religious matters within State control (see Williams and Hume n 27).

[29] First recognized in *Nationwide News Pty Ltd v Wills* (1992) 177 CLR 1 and *Australian Capital Territory Pty Ltd v Commonwealth* (1992) 177 CLR 106.

[30] Most recently, in *Monis v The Queen* (2013) 249 CLR 92, Heydon J said at 184:

> Those who drafted the Constitution, those who secured legislative approval of it by each colonial legislature, and the people who approved it by their ballots would each say, if they could examine the authorities on the implied freedom of communication: '*Non haec in foedera veni*'. Yet in compacts other than constitutions, clearness and obviousness are common conditions precedent to the implication of terms. Close examination of the implied freedom of political communication would involve analysis of these issues. That examination may reveal that it is a noble and idealistic enterprise which has failed, is failing, and will go on failing.

[31] *Lange v Australian Broadcasting Corporation* (1997) 189 CLR 520, 567.

that too has been controversial.[32] The High Court has also toyed with the idea that the 'rule of law' is an assumption upon which the constitution is based.[33] However, to date, the idea has been primarily used to underpin statutory interpretive presumptions that, subject to a contrary intention, Parliament has not intended to abrogate fundamental rights,[34] and to highlight the entrenched role of the judiciary to check that the other arms of government are operating within constitutional and legislative power.[35]

Thus, the terms of the Australian Constitution, and their interpretation by the High Court, do not generally display a concern for limiting legislative power for the purpose of protecting individual liberty.[36] This can be explained by the legal and political context of the constitution's drafting, and the High Court's reluctance to stretch its power of judicial review beyond its clear constitutional mandate of maintaining the federal compact.

D. The framers' concern with judicial independence and impartiality

What the historical record does show is a concern by the drafters of the constitution for the protection of judicial independence and impartiality. The prevailing view during the debates was that the judiciary should be limited to the exercise of traditional judicial power to administer justice and that the conferral of non-judicial power would, potentially, threaten judicial independence and impartiality. For example, a proposal that the High Court be given power to give an advisory opinion, on the constitutional validity of federal legislation prior to a dispute arising, was resisted on the basis that such a function would unnecessarily embroil the

---

[32] *Roach v Electoral Commissioner* (2007) 233 CLR 162; *Rowe v Electoral Commissioner* (2010) 243 CLR 1. Although the limitation has been described by some judges as a 'right to vote', that has been a minority view. A majority of the Court has either justified the limitation as an institutional protection for representative and responsible government, or rejected the limitation entirely.

[33] In *Australian Communist Party v Commonwealth* (1951) 83 CLR 1, 193, Dixon J said that the constitution 'is an instrument framed in accordance with many traditional conceptions, to some of which it gives effect ... others of which are simply assumed. Among these I think that it may fairly be said that the rule of law forms an assumption'.

[34] See, for example, *Saeed v Minister for Immigration and Citizenship* (2010) 241 CLR 252, 259.

[35] *Plaintiff S157/2002 v Commonwealth* (2003) 211 CLR 476, 513–14.

[36] For a helpful overview and analysis of the rights jurisprudence of the High Court, see Adrienne Stone, 'Australia's Constitutional Rights and the Problem of Interpretive Disagreement' (2005) 27 *Syd LR* 29. For a more detailed account, see Williams and Hume (n 27).

court in political controversy and threaten its independence. Awaiting a dispute to arise would put some distance between the politics of the challenged legislation and the role of the court in determining validity. It would also assist in the efficient performance of the judicial function as the existence of a real dispute before the High Court would contextualize and highlight the implications and consequences of the court's decision.[37]

As to why independence and impartiality were considered essential judicial characteristics, the framers gravitated to two core reasons. First, independence and impartiality were required for the judiciary to police the federal system: protecting the states from an overreaching federal government and from each other. Secondly, the independent and impartial administration of justice would protect the liberties of the individual in their disputes amongst themselves and with their governments.[38]

E. Separation of judicial power principles

As already mentioned, the constitution allocates federal government power across the three institutions of federal government. Section 71 of the constitution vests federal judicial power in specified courts. The remaining provisions of Chapter III identify the circumstances in which federal judicial power will be exercised, and the scheme for how federal judicial power is invested in Australian courts. From this separate identification and vesting of federal judicial power, in contrast to federal legislative power (dealt with in Chapter I) and federal executive power (dealt with in Chapter II), the High Court has established two separation of judicial power principles: first, that federal judicial power can only be exercised by the courts referred to in section 71[39] and, secondly, that courts exercising federal jurisdiction can only exercise judicial power or non-judicial power incidental to the exercise of judicial power.[40] Central to the development of these principles has been the concern to protect the independence and impartiality of Australian courts.

There are three important points to emphasize about these rules for the purpose of this study. First, the High Court has accepted a fairly narrow conception of federal judicial power. For the High Court, federal judicial power involves the determination of a dispute about pre-existing legal

---

37 See James Stellios, *The Federal Judicature: Chapter III of the Constitution* (LexisNexis 2010) 73–9.

38 Ibid., 67–72.

39 *The Waterside Workers' Federation of Australia v J W Alexander Ltd* (1915) 20 CLR 54.

40 *R v Kirby; Ex parte Boilermakers' Society of Australia* (1956) 94 CLR 254 (Boilermakers case).

rights or duties. In other words, courts are limited to the 'administration of common justice'. Powers, the exercise of which have no consequences for the resolution of a dispute about pre-existing legal rights and duties, are generally not considered to be judicial in character. Thus, the separation principles above can be recast more precisely to require that, in federal jurisdiction, only the courts identified in section 71 can determine disputes about pre-existing rights and that such courts can only engage in the determination of disputes about pre-existing rights (and the exercise of incidental powers).[41]

Secondly, it is not clear why the exclusion of all non-judicial power (other than incidental non-judicial power) is necessary to maintain independence and impartiality of the judiciary. A lower threshold test, which asks whether the power is *incompatible with* the court's exercise of judicial power, has been suggested by judges and commentators alike as a less severe means of achieving the same objectives.[42] A test of incompatibility is perfectly capable of protecting judicial independence and impartiality without excluding exercises of 'largely innocuous'[43] non-judicial power. However, as will be seen below, the High Court has recently reaffirmed the stricter rule.

Thirdly, the High Court has not spoken clearly on the purpose to be served by an independent and impartial judiciary. Independence and impartiality are seen as functional characteristics, but there has been considerable variation in the explanations of the purpose to be achieved. The key judgments establishing the separation of judicial power principles echo the framers' intention for an independent and impartial judiciary to protect the *federal* system.[44] Other judgments, with allusions

---

41 There are various devices developed by the High Court to soften the application of such rigid rules: for example, the use of historical analogies to characterize a function as judicial and the recognition that some powers have no inherent character and may be exercised by different arms of government. It has also been recognized that judges can exercise non-judicial power in their personal capacity if certain conditions are satisfied. For a general explanation of these techniques, see Stellios, *The Federal Judicature* (n 37), 138–58; 389–94.

42 See, for example, James Stellios, *Zines's The High Court and the Constitution* (The Federation Press, 6th edn, 2015) 328–31; Sir Anthony Mason, 'A New Perspective on Separation of Powers' (1996) 82 *Canberra Bull Pub Admin* 1, 5-6.

43 To adopt an expression used by Crennan and Kiefel JJ in *Momcilovic* (n 1) 228.

44 Stellios, *The Federal Judicature* (n 37).

or references to Montesquieu or Blackstone,[45] emphasize the liberty-protecting purpose of a separation of powers.[46]

It is not always clear what separation of powers theory or tradition is being relied upon when such formulations are invoked. In fact, despite their periodic incantation, it is difficult to detect a real commitment to such liberty-protecting objectives in the case law. The High Court has certainly accepted, relying on the *Commentaries* of Blackstone, that the adjudgment and punishment of criminal guilt requires an exclusive exercise of judicial power according to the usual curial process,[47] and that any usurpation of that power by Parliament will breach separation of power principles. However, further appeals to Blackstone by a minority grouping of judges has not found favour with a majority of the High Court when the limits of the liberty-protecting value of separated judicial power have been put to the test. Thus, for example, over Blackstonian-inspired dissents, a majority of the court has consistently adopted an expansive view of the power of military tribunals to impose punishment, including imprisonment, outside the judicial framework.[48] The power of Parliament to order the incarceration of journalists for contempt of Parliament has been upheld;[49] so too has the legislative prescription of mandatory sentences, despite any disproportionality between the sentence and the level of criminality involved.[50] The indefinite detention of aliens[51] and the forced removal of indigenous children from their families have been considered to be consistent with separation of judicial power

---

45 *Victorian Stevedoring & General Contracting Co Pty Ltd v Dignan* (1931) 46 CLR 73, 89 (Dixon J); 114 (Evatt J); *A-G (Cth) v The Queen* (1957) 95 CLR 529, 540 (PC); *R v Davison* (1954) 90 CLR 353, 98 (Kitto J); *Harris v Caladine* (1991) 172 CLR 84, 161 (McHugh J); *Grollo Palmer* (1995) 184 CLR 348, 392 (Gummow J); *The Queen v Quinn; Ex parte Consolidated Food Corp* (1977) 138 CLR 1, 11 (Jacobs J).

46 This line of reasoning is best captured by the statement by five members of the Court in *Wilson v Minister for Aboriginal and Torres Strait Islander Affairs* (1996) 189 CLR 1, 11: 'The separation of the judicial function from the other functions of government advances two constitutional objectives: the guarantee of liberty and, to that end, the independence of judges' (Brennan CJ, Dawson, Toohey, McHugh and Gummow JJ).

47 *Chu Kheng Lim v Minister for Immigration* (1992) 176 CLR 1.

48 The string of cases accepting a broad view commenced with *Re Tracey; Ex parte Ryan* (1989) 166 CLR 518.

49 *R v Richards; Ex parte Fitzpatrick & Browne* (1955) 92 CLR 157.

50 *Magaming v The Queen* (2013) 252 CLR 381.

51 *Al Kateb v Godwin* (2004) 219 CLR 562.

principles.[52] Furthermore, despite strong dissenting judgments relying on Blackstone, a majority has permitted the imposition of retrospective criminal liability.[53]

Indeed, the indecision and uncertainty in the High Court runs much deeper. There is even doubt as to whether the core value of protecting liberty, and its deprivation, requires an exclusive exercise of judicial power. In the 1992 decision of *Chu Kheng Lim v Minister for Immigration*,[54] a majority of the High Court considered that, subject to limited qualification, 'the power to order that a citizen be involuntarily confined in custody is, under the doctrine of the separation of powers enshrined in our Constitution, part of the judicial power of the Commonwealth entrusted exclusively to Chapter III courts'.[55] So fundamental was this commitment to Blackstone's vision of a separation of judicial power that the majority was able to assert confidently that, leaving aside exceptional categories:[56]

> ... the citizens of this country enjoy, at least in times of peace ..., a constitutional immunity from being imprisoned by Commonwealth authority except pursuant to an order by a court in the exercise of the judicial power of the Commonwealth.[57]

However, this core position has now been thrown into doubt. In a series of cases in 2004,[58] the High Court was divided on the continuing force of this *Lim* proposition. On the one hand, it seemed to be rejected by at least three judges,[59] with McHugh J directly commenting that it 'cannot

---

[52] *Kruger v Commonwealth* (1997) 190 CLR 1.

[53] *Polyukhovich v Commonwealth* (1991) 172 CLR 501.

[54] (1992) 176 CLR 1.

[55] Ibid., [28] (Brennan, Deane and Dawson JJ; with Mason CJ agreeing in this respect in a separate judgment), drawing from Blackstone's *Commentaries* to the same effect.

[56] For example, arrest and detention pursuant to a warrant; Parliament's power to punish for contempt; military tribunals and detention in cases of mental illness and infectious disease.

[57] (1992) 176 CLR 1, 28–9.

[58] *Re Woolley; Ex parte Applicants M276/2000* (2004) 225 CLR 1; *Al Kateb* (n 49); *Behrooz v Secretary Department of Immigration and Multicultural and Indigenous Affairs* (2004) 219 CLR 486; *Minister for Immigration and Multicultural and Indigenous Affairs v Al Khafaji* (2004) 219 CLR 664; *Fardon v A-G (Qld)* (2004) 223 CLR 575.

[59] *Re Woolley* (n 58) 24 (McHugh J); *Al Kateb* (n 51) 649 (Hayne J, with Heydon J agreeing).

stand'.[60] For these judges, the deprivation of liberty was only required to be an exercise of judicial power if detention was intended to have a *punitive* purpose. On the other hand, Gummow and Kirby JJ strongly defended the position in *Lim*, with Gummow J reformulating the proposition 'in terms that, leaving the "exceptional cases" aside, the involuntary detention of the citizen in custody by the State is permissible only as a consequential step in the adjudication of criminal guilt of that citizen for past acts'.[61] Gummow J supported this defence by reference to the following statement by Scalia J in *Hamdi v Rumsfield*, made (as acknowledged by Gummow J) with reference to Blackstone and Alexander Hamilton, 'The very core of liberty secured by our Anglo-Saxon system of separated powers has been freedom from indefinite imprisonment at the will of the Executive'.[62]

In short, liberty-protecting values have been periodically invoked as an underlying justification for the separation of judicial power principles. However, it is not always clear which separation tradition is being relied upon. Furthermore, when pushed to its limits, liberty-protecting values readily crumble to accommodate other constitutional imperatives. Again, this is not surprising given the legal and political conditions that prevailed at the drafting of the constitution and which have characterized its interpretation.

A third rationale identified in separation of power cases is the need for judicial independence and impartiality for the performance of a checks and balances function, that is to keep the other arms of government within their constitutional and legislative power. As four judges said in *TCL Air Conditioner (Zhongshan) Co Ltd v The Judges of the Federal Court of Australia,*[63] '[t]he doctrine of the separation of powers is directed to ensuring an independent and impartial judicial branch of government to enforce lawful limits on the exercise of public power'. In other words, it is seen as a manifestation of the rule of law which, in this respect, encompasses a judicial review role for the courts to ensure that governments operate within constitutional constraints – whatever they may be.

With these legal and political conditions for judicial review in mind, the next section will outline the reception of the dialogue model of

---

[60] *Re Woolley* (n 58) 24.

[61] *Fardon* (n 58) 612.

[62] *Al Kateb* (n 51) 612, citing *Hamdi v Rumsfeld* (2004) 72 USLW 4607, 4621.

[63] (2013) 251 CLR 533, [104] (Hayne, Crennan, Kiefel and Bell JJ).

human rights protection into Australia and the constitutional obstacles to their adoption in Australian jurisdictions – both federal and state.

4.1.3 Australian 'Dialogue' Models of Human Rights Protection

The reception of a UK-style dialogue model of human rights protection into Australian jurisdictions has been documented in detail elsewhere.[64] The Australian Capital Territory Legislative Assembly was the first to introduce a statutory scheme for the protection of rights, with the enactment of the Human Rights Act 2004 (ACT). The Victorian Parliament followed with the enactment of the Charter of Human Rights and Responsibilities Act 2006 (Vic). Both Acts followed the design of the 'dialogue' model of human rights protection in the UK HRA:

- The Acts set out a range of human rights, derived largely from the International Covenant on Civil and Political Rights.[65]
- There are *five core features* of the statutory scheme. First, the executive government must assess whether a bill to be introduced into the legislature is consistent with human rights and present a statement recording that assessment to the legislature.[66] Secondly, a legislative committee considers the human rights issues that arise from a bill.[67] Thirdly, when an issue arises as to whether statutory provisions are consistent with human rights, the provisions must be interpreted in a way that is 'consistent'[68] or 'compatible'[69] with

64 See, for example, McDonald (n 1); Caroline Evans, 'Responsibility for Rights: the ACT Human Rights Act' (2004) 32 *FL Rev* 291; Simon Evans and Caroline Evans, 'Legal Redress under the Victorian Charter of Human Rights and Responsibilities' (2006) 17 *PLR* 264; George Williams, 'The Victorian Charter of Human Rights and Responsibilities: Origins and Scope' (2006) 30 *MULR* 880; James Allan, 'The Victorian Charter of Human Rights and Responsibilities: Exegesis and Criticism' (2006) 30 *MULR* 906.

65 Although, the ACT legislation has been amended to include a right to education drawn primarily from the International Covenant on Economic, Social and Cultural Rights (s 27A).

66 In the case of the ACT, the statement is presented to the Legislative Assembly by the Attorney-General (s 37); in Victoria, it is the minister proposing to introduce the bill (s 28).

67 Human Rights Act (ACT), s 38; Charter (Vic), s 30. In Victoria, the relevant committee also considers the compatibility of statutory rules with human rights.

68 Human Rights Act (ACT), s 30(1).

69 Charter (Vic), s 32(1).

human rights (for convenience, referred to as the 'interpretive rule'). Fourthly, if, in a proceeding before the Supreme Court of the ACT or Victoria, the court is of the view that a provision cannot be interpreted consistently with a human right, it may declare that the law is not consistent with the human right (again, for convenience, referred to as a 'declaration of inconsistency').[70] Finally, the Acts make it 'unlawful' for public authorities to act in a way that is 'inconsistent'[71] or 'incompatible'[72] with human rights or fail to give proper consideration to a relevant human right when making a decision, and set out the proceedings that may be brought for such 'unlawful' action.[73]

- Failure to comply with the legislative scrutiny provisions has no legal consequence. The Acts make it clear that such a failure has no effect on the 'validity, operation or enforcement' of the enacted provisions.[74]
- A declaration of inconsistency does not affect the 'validity, operation or enforcement' of the relevant provisions.[75] Nor does it affect 'the rights or obligations of anyone' (in the case of the Human Rights Act (ACT)) or 'create in any person any legal right or give rise to any civil cause of action' (in the case of the Victorian Charter).

It can be seen that the central design, particularly the five core features, of both legislative schemes are closely modelled on the UK HRA.[76]

---

[70] A 'declaration of incompatibility' in the ACT under section 32(2), and a 'declaration of inconsistent interpretation' in Victoria under section 36(2).

[71] Human Rights Act (ACT), s 40B(1).

[72] Charter (Vic), s 38(1).

[73] Human Rights Act (ACT), s 40C; Charter (Vic), s 39.

[74] Human Rights Act (ACT), s 39; Charter (Vic), s 29.

[75] Human Rights Act (ACT), s 32(3)(a); Charter (Vic), s 36(5)(a).

[76] Other Australian jurisdictions have contemplated the enactment of statutory human rights schemes. Most significantly, in 2008, the Commonwealth Government established a Human Rights Consultation Committee to inquire into human rights protection. Having conducted a national consultation process, the Consultation Committee recommended that the Commonwealth Parliament enact a Human Rights Act based on the 'dialogue' model of rights protection with the five core features set out above from the Human Rights Act (ACT) and the Victorian Charter (see *National Human Rights Consultation Report* (2009) recommendations 19, 20, 26–30). However, the recommended scheme was to be more ambitious, covering an expanded set of human rights from seven international human rights treaties. The Commonwealth Government rejected the

4.1.4 The Australian Constitutional Impediments to the Dialogue Model

Soon after the enactment of the Human Rights Act (ACT), concerns began to emerge about the compatibility of the dialogue model with the requirements of the Australian Constitution.[77] The UK HRA had been drafted for a unitary legal system without a constitutionally entrenched separation of powers and, in following that model in the Australian Capital Territory and Victoria, the Australian constitutional context had not been fully taken into account.

The concerns were debated at two levels: first, whether the separation of judicial power principles developed by the High Court would frustrate any future attempts by the federal Parliament to adopt a dialogue model. Specifically, whether the *federal* Parliament could require courts to give human rights consistent interpretations to federal legislation (that is to enact the interpretive rule) and, in the event that a court could not read legislation in a rights-consistent way, to authorize the court to make a declaration of inconsistency. As already explained, the High Court has developed principles which provide that the federal Parliament can only confer judicial powers on courts (and those which are incidental), and judicial power has been narrowed to the determination of the parties' rights and duties in dispute. There were two key concerns about the dialogue model: that a creative use of the interpretive rule might transform the judicial activity of *interpretation* applied in the course of resolving a dispute between the parties into a legislative function of *making law*; and that the making of a declaration of inconsistency – which has no legal impact on the rights and duties of the parties in

proposal, with the Attorney General expressing concern that its enactment would divide the community: see *Australia's Human Rights Framework* (2010), Foreword (Attorney General). However, the government decided to adopt the recommendations to create the front-end *executive* and *legislative* scrutiny mechanisms, and these mechanisms, along with the expanded set of human rights, have now been implemented with the enactment of the Human Rights (Parliamentary Scrutiny) Act 2011 (Cth). For an explanation of the enactment of this scheme, see James Stellios and Michael Palfrey, 'A New Federal Scheme for the Protection of Human Rights' (2012) 69 *AIAL Forum* 13.

[77] See James Stellios, 'Federal Dimensions to the ACT Human Rights Act' (2005) 47 *AIAL Forum* 33.

dispute – can be considered a judicial function. The academic commentary was evenly divided on these questions, with much of the dispute focusing on the more problematic power to make a declaration.[78]

The second level at which these debates took place was whether the Australian Constitution prevented *State* and *Territory* legislatures from enacting a dialogue model with the interpretive rule and the judicial power to make a declaration of inconsistency. For those unfamiliar with constitutional law on the Australian federal judicature, this requires some further elucidation. Although the US Constitution was closely followed when the Australian Constitution was drafted, there were two important departures from the US framework when it came to Chapter III – the Federal Judicature. While the US Constitution contemplated that an entire set of federal courts would be created to administer federal jurisdiction, the delegates to the Australian conventions agreed that state courts should be made available for the exercise of federal jurisdiction. This departure from the American model was largely for reasons of economy – concern having been expressed about the financial burden of creating a complete set of lower federal courts.[79] The second important departure from the American model was in the role contemplated for the High Court in its appellate jurisdiction: it was to operate as a general court of appeal from lower federal and state courts – whether the lower court was exercising federal or state judicial power.

These structural features of the federal judicature have had considerable 'integrating' impact on Australian judicial systems, two of which are of present significance. First, the federal Parliament has exclusive power

---

[78] See, for example, Geoffrey Lindell, 'The Statutory Protection of Rights and Parliamentary Sovereignty: Guidance from the United Kingdom?' (2006) 17 *PLR* 188; Jim South, 'The Campaign for a National Bill of Rights: Would "Declarations of Incompatibility" be Compatible with the Constitution' (2007) 10 *Con Law Pol Rev* 2; Dominique Dalla-Pozza and George Williams, 'The Constitutional Validity of Declarations of Incompatibility in Australian Charters of Human Rights' (2007) 12 *Deakin LR* 1; Stephanie Wilkins, 'Constitutional Limits on Bills of Rights Introduced by a State or Territory' (2007) 35 *FL Rev* 431; James Stellios, 'State/Territory Human Rights Legislation in a Federal Judicial System' (2008) 19 *PLR* 52; Michael McHugh, 'A Human Rights Act, the Courts and the Constitution' (2009) 11 *Con Law Pol Rev* 86; Advice provided by Solicitor-General to the National Human Rights Consultation, *National Human Rights Consultation Report* (2009), Appendix E; Helen Irving, 'The Dilemmas in Dialogue: A Constitutional Analysis of the NHRC's Proposed Human Rights Act' (2010) 33 *UNSWLJ* 60.

[79] K H Bailey, 'The Federal Jurisdiction of State Courts' (1939–1941) 2 *Res Jud* 109, 109.

to determine the law that applies when a state court is exercising *federal* judicial power. State laws – in particular those conferring powers or functions on state courts – cannot apply of their own force, but must be picked up as 'surrogate' federal laws.[80] When picking up these state laws, the federal Parliament must comply with the federal separation of judicial power principles and, consequently, cannot pick up state provisions which would otherwise confer powers on the state court which are neither judicial nor incidental thereto.

Secondly, although the federal separation of powers principles outlined earlier only apply to the *federal* Parliament, because state courts can exercise *federal* judicial power and all appeals from a state court can go to the High Court, principles have been developed to prevent state Parliaments from undermining this constitutional scheme. In particular, the High Court has held that state Parliament cannot confer powers on state courts which would be *incompatible with* an exercise by them of federal judicial power. This limitation applies whether state courts are exercising federal or state judicial power.[81]

Thus, in addition to the constitutional concerns expressed about the *federal* Parliament implementing in future a dialogue model with an interpretive rule and a power to make a declaration of incompatibility, concerns were expressed about the effectiveness of such dialogue models when adopted by the *States* and *Territories* of the federation. These concerns were realized to a large extent when the High Court handed down its decision in *Momcilovic v The Queen*.[82]

4.1.5 Momcilovic v The Queen

A. Background to the case

Momcilovic had inauspicious origins,[83] although they need only be set out briefly. The appellate had been found guilty by the Victorian County Court of the Victorian offence of trafficking in a drug of dependence. The Victorian criminal provisions provided that the unauthorized possession of a certain quantity of a controlled drug was prima facie evidence of

---

80 This is largely achieved in a global fashion by two provisions of the federal Judiciary Act 1903 (Cth), namely ss 68(1) and 79(1).

81 This limitation was first accepted in *Kable v Director of Public Prosecutions (NSW)* (1996) 189 CLR 51 (Kable case).

82 (2011) 245 CLR 1.

83 For a detailed discussion of the procedural history, see Will Bateman and James Stellios, 'Chapter III of the Constitution, Federal Jurisdiction and Dialogue Models of Human Rights' (2012) 26 *MULR* 1.

trafficking and deemed Ms Momcilovic to be in possession of drugs found in her apartment. The onus then shifted to Ms Momcilovic to show that the drugs were not in her possession. Despite disclaiming knowledge of the drugs, she was unable to persuade a jury of that fact. Before the Victorian Court of Appeal, Ms Momcilovic invoked the interpretive rule in the Victorian Charter. The jury, she argued, had been improperly instructed by the trial judge that the criminal provisions has shifted the *legal* onus of proof to her. Section 25(1) of the Charter protected her 'presumption of innocence' and, thus, she contended, the onus provision should only be read as shifting the *evidential* burden of proof – not the *legal* burden. The Victorian Court of Appeal held that the provision could only be interpreted as shifting the legal burden, and agreed that the consequence of reading the provision in that way was that it was inconsistent with the human right to be presumed innocent. A declaration of incompatibility was made to that effect.

On appeal to the High Court, various constitutional questions were raised concerning the validity of the Charter. Of central importance to the determination of the constitutional issues was the fact that, by the time the offence was prosecuted in the County Court of Victoria, Ms Momcilovic had moved to another Australian jurisdiction – Queensland. The prosecution consequently involved a dispute between the prosecuting authorities of Victoria and the resident of another state. The constitution identifies this as a case of federal jurisdiction[84] and, thus, when the County Court and the Victorian Court of Appeal were exercising their functions, they were exercising federal judicial power.

Consequently, there were two main issues to be determined by the High Court: first, whether the interpretive rule and power to make a declaration of inconsistency had conferred on the Victorian Court of Appeal functions which were *incompatible with an exercise of federal judicial power*; secondly, since the Court of Appeal had been exercising federal jurisdiction, could the Victorian Charter provisions be picked up and applied as 'surrogate' federal laws: the principles identified earlier tell us that the provisions cannot be picked up if they do not involve an exercise of judicial power or power incidental to the exercise of judicial power. The conclusions on this second question also would have significant implications for any future federal UK-style dialogue charter of rights constructed along similar lines.

---

[84] Section 75(iv) of the Constitution conferred on State courts by section 39(2) of the Judiciary Act 1903 (Cth).

B. Did the interpretive rule and declaration involve an exercise of judicial power or incidental non-judicial power?

The seven judges of the High Court delivered six judgments, and the spread of their conclusions on these and other issues complicates the analysis.[85] It is enough for present purposes to say that six judges (all but Heydon J) considered the interpretive rule in section 32(1) of the Charter to fall within the proper realm of judicial interpretation and had not crossed the line into law-making. Accordingly, the interpretive rule could be applied by the Victorian courts when exercising federal judicial power, and could form part of any future federal dialogue model for the protection of human rights.[86]

As for the making of a declaration, five judges (French CJ, Gummow, Hayne, Heydon and Bell JJ) considered its exercise to involve neither judicial power, nor incidental non-judicial power. As the statutory scheme makes clear,[87] the making of a declaration of incompatibility has no impact on legal rights and duties in dispute between the parties and, thus, according to the way in which the High Court has previously conceptualized judicial power, the declaration does not have the requisite core characteristic. Despite the fact that the power to make a declaration has been exercised by courts in the UK since 1998, the High Court could not classify the function as judicial on a historical or analogical basis.[88] Given this analytical disconnect from the dispute between the parties, these five judges were not persuaded that the making of a declaration would assist in any way with the resolution of the parties' dispute and, consequently, could not be seen as *incidental* to the exercise of judicial power.[89] The logical consequences of these conclusions were twofold: first, the Victorian Court of Appeal could not exercise the power to make a declaration when it was exercising federal judicial power (which it was

---

[85] For a detailed explanation of the various combinations and permutations, see Bateman and Stellios (n 83).

[86] These conclusions are complicated by the fact that the six judges were evenly divided on whether the 'justification' provision in s 7(2) of the Charter was to be applied as part of the interpretive exercise. See Bateman and Stellios (n 83) for a detailed explanation of this complication.

[87] Subsection 36(5) provides that a declaration does not 'affect in any way the validity, operation or enforcement of the statutory provision in respect of which the declaration was made'.

[88] (2011) 245 CLR 1, 65 (French CJ, with Bell J agreeing); 96–7 (Gummow J, with Hayne J agreeing).

[89] Ibid., [65]–[66] (French CJ, with Bell J agreeing); [96]–[97] (Gummow J, with Hayne J agreeing); [185] (Heydon J). The remaining two judges (Crennan and Kiefel JJ) considered it to be incidental to the resolution of the dispute [227].

in this case); and, secondly, a future federal charter could not include a judicial power to make a declaration.

C. Was the declaration power incompatible with an exercise of federal judicial power?

Because this was state legislation conferring functions on a state court, one of the central questions to be addressed by the High Court was whether the functions conferred were *incompatible with* an exercise of federal judicial power. As was explained earlier, because the constitution permits Parliament to commandeer state courts to exercise Commonwealth judicial power, and because the High Court operates as a general appellate court from all lower Australian courts (whether exercising federal or state judicial power), the High Court has said that state Parliaments cannot confer functions on state courts which are *incompatible with* an exercise of federal judicial power.[90] *Incompatibility* has been measured, in part, by judicial *independence* and *impartiality*. Assessed against those constitutional standards, declarations of incompatibility were held by a majority of the court to be valid. The dialogue model of human rights protection left it to Parliament to make decisions about human rights protection: the declaration was a mere mechanism to bring human rights issues to the attention of the executive and legislative arms of government. As such, it did not affect the independent and impartial exercise of judicial power by the court. The dissenting judgments of Gummow, Hayne and Heydon JJ considered that the court was being required to provide an advisory opinion to the other arms of government and, thus, was being co-opted to set in train a law reform process.

4.1.6 Australian Constitutionalism, the Separation of Powers and the Role of Courts in Protecting Rights

As can be seen, the High Court's decision in *Momcilovic* has disrupted the operation of the dialogue model of human rights protection in Australia. The federal Parliament could not put in place a scheme that empowered the judiciary to make a declaration of incompatibility. Indeed, there is some uncertainty as to the scope of an interpretive rule that might be adopted.[91] There are similar difficulties for the effective operation of the existing dialogue schemes in Victoria and the Australian

---

[90] This principle was first recognized by the High Court in the Kable case (n 81).

[91] For a detailed explanation of this point, see Bateman and Stellios (n 83) 11–17.

Capital Territory (or any other future state or territory dialogue scheme) when the Supreme Courts of the respective jurisdictions are exercising federal judicial power.

It would seem that Australian constitutionalism is locked into a narrow role for the judiciary in the protection of rights. As explained earlier, the dominant constitutional norms of responsible government and parliamentary sovereignty, as understood and accepted at the time of federation, resulted in few, if any, constitutional limitations for the protection of rights. The decision in *Momcilovic* prevents the Commonwealth Parliament from giving courts the power to make a declaration and imposes significant obstacles to the effective operation of declaration provisions in state and territory legislation. Thus, short of constitutional amendment, the role of the judiciary in Australia in the protection of rights is limited to the 'administration of common justice' in its traditional sense – that is the impartial and independent resolution of disputes about legal rights and duties. In the course of doing so, the courts can apply various presumptions about the legislature's intention to not intrude on fundamental common law rights, and statutory charters of rights can operate to expand the range of rights that benefit from the presumptions. But the judiciary's role in protecting rights is limited to a traditional model of adjudicating disputes about legal rights and duties.

Most arguments against a UK-style charter of human rights being adopted in Australia have been directed to the judicial declaration mechanism and are inspired by concerns for preserving parliamentary sovereignty.[92] Rights are said to be deeply contested, and the judiciary's voice on rights protection should not be permitted to have undue impact on the political compromises reached. However, the Australian constitutional position adds a further layer to the debate. Even if the parliamentary sovereignty objections can be met,[93] the constitutional separation of powers presents further obstacles.

However, should a constitutional separation of powers be seen as having this consequence for declarations of incompatibility? After all, the separation of powers is commonly heralded – including, as has been seen, by the High Court itself – for its liberty-protecting value. It might be suggested that there is irony in the invocation of separation principles in *Momcilovic* to undermine a central aspect of a scheme that seeks to protect human rights. However, such an argument requires closer analysis

---

[92] See, for example, Allan (n 64).

[93] See, for example, Jeffrey Goldsworthy, 'Judicial Review, Legislative Override and Democracy' in Tom Campbell, Jeffrey Goldsworthy and Adrienne Stone (eds), *Protecting Human Rights* (OUP 2003) 263, 268.

of separation of powers theories, if not consideration of underlying political theories of the relationship between the state and individuals,[94] before such assertions may be confidently made.

On closer analysis, different conceptions of separation of powers may in fact point in different directions.[95] There are certainly arguments that can be made that some conceptions of separated power are perfectly consistent with a judicial power to make a declaration. Classic separation arguments, that exercises of arbitrary power are minimized if governmental power is dispersed,[96] might support a role for the judiciary to point out the impact of legislation on statutorily defined rights. The checks and balances function of a mixed constitution, so closely associated with separation of powers theories,[97] might also present a basis for supporting a judicial role, beyond the traditional resolution of the dispute, to highlight human rights deficiencies arising from that dispute to the political arms of government.

Additionally, if separated powers is conceptualized along efficiency lines,[98] the judiciary might be particularly well placed and equipped to point out the impact of legislation on statutorily defined rights in a particular factual situation presented in a legal dispute. As Jeremy Webber has observed when defending statutory bills of rights:

> The procedures of legislatures are not adapted to the dissection of a particular set of events but rather to the exploration of broad social concerns in a manner that marshals an extensive spectrum of opinion. They are focused on the determination of social facts, not the parochial detail of adjudicative facts. Moreover, legislatures are not subject to the rationalistic controls on evidence and argument, designed to screen out prejudgment and prejudice, that are observed by courts. Legislatures to have their own rationalistic procedures – structured processes for formulating propositions, justifying those propositions, considering alternative formulations, criticising, amending, adopting – all in a manner that draws on the assembled wisdom of the chamber. But

---

[94] See N W Barber, 'Prelude to the Separation of Powers' (2001) 60 *CLJ* 59, 63, where it is suggested that the constitutional theory of a separation of powers 'must be prefaced by a political theory if it is to possess any normative force'.

[95] As Eoin Carolan has commented, '[t]he theory, in its various guises, is clearly capable of supporting diametrically opposite understandings of the state'. See Eoin Carolan, *The New Separation of Powers* (OUP 2009) 31.

[96] See Eric Barendt, 'Separation of Powers and Constitutional Government' [1995] PL 599; Philip Pettit, *Republicanism: A Theory of Freedom and Government* (Clarendon Press 1999) 180.

[97] See Lawrence Claus, 'Montesquieu's Mistakes and the True Meaning of Separation' (2005) 25 *OJLS* 419, 420.

[98] See Barber, 'Prelude to the Separation of Powers' (n 94) 64–6.

> these procedures are designed to refine and adopt general propositions, not to secure dependable outcomes in specific cases. Judicial procedures, on the other hand, are entirely focused on the analysis of the specific set of events.[99]

Perhaps the dialogue model of rights protection fits within Nicholas Barber's conception of a 'valuable division of moral labour': '[i]nstitutions may properly limit the range of factors they consider in making a decision because they know that another institution is on hand to weigh the considerations they have failed to assess'.[100] Thus, depending on what conception one has in mind, there are perfectly coherent arguments that can be made that a judicial declaration is consistent with a separation of powers.

Of course, there are other conceptions of separated power that may sit uncomfortably with the use of courts to make declarations. The Blackstonian conception of the judiciary resolving disputes in 'the administration of common justice' puts a premium on the independence of the judiciary from the other arms of government. The role of the judiciary within this conception extends to the determination of the dispute between parties and, in the context of UK-style dialogue charters, that process comes to an end with the application of the interpretive rule – that is, the application of the interpretive presumption that the legislature did not intend to intrude on an expanded set of human rights. The declaration function is extraneous to that conception of the judicial role and liable to be seen with some suspicion, and that suspicion may be justified if the declaration function threatens judicial independence.

Furthermore, the checks and balances function of keeping the other arms of government to account – *particularly in the context of an entrenched constitution* – necessarily requires the strictest insulation for the judiciary from the political arms of government. As Alexander Hamilton said in *Federalist Paper No 78* when defending the tenure protections for federal judges:

> If, then, the courts of justice are to be considered as the bulwarks of a limited Constitution against legislative encroachments, this consideration will afford a strong argument for the permanent tenure of judicial offices, since nothing will contribute so much as this to that independent spirit of judges which must be essential to the faithful performance of so arduous a duty.

---

[99] Jeremy Webber, 'A Modest (but Robust) Defence of Statutory Bills of Rights' in Tom Campbell, Jeffrey Goldsworthy and Adrienne Stone (eds), *Protecting Rights Without a Bill of Rights* (Ashgate 2006) 263, 276.

[100] N W Barber, 'Self-Defence for Institutions' (2013) 72 *CLJ* 558, 572.

Functions tending to threaten that insulation might, again, be viewed with some suspicion. So, which of these conceptions of separated power was at play in *Momcilovic*? As explained earlier, the High Court has vacillated in its explanation of the justifications for federal separation of judicial power principles. It is perhaps partly for that reason that the principles have been applied formulaically without an analysis that connects with the underlying justifications. Thus, in *Momcilovic*, we see that the separation of judicial power principles were applied without much interrogation, and certainly without any regard to liberty-protecting understandings. For the majority, declarations do not involve the determination of disputes about legal rights and obligations, and the separation of power analysis ended there.

Only Heydon J, who held the entire legislative scheme to be invalid, engaged with the underlying reasons for why the interpretive rule and, by extension, the declaration, breached separation of power principles. There were two main grounds for Heydon J's conclusions: first, that the interpretive provision authorized 'remedial' interpretations, that is, that the judiciary was authorized to amend the legislative provisions and, secondly, that the balancing process to be undertaken under the justification provision in section 7(2) was legislative in character. The first ground can be put to one side because no other judge considered that the provision should be read in that way. The second ground requires further consideration. For Heydon J, there were two related problems with the balancing process in section 7(2). The first was that the language used was 'highly general, indeterminate, lofty, aspirational and abstract[:] ... nebulous, turbid and cloudy'. The words 'reasonable', 'justified', 'demonstrably' justified, 'free and democratic society', and 'based on human dignity, equality and freedom' did not present objectively determinable criteria to be applied by a court. Secondly, the balancing process to be undertaken was not a matter for the judiciary. As Heydon J said:

> ... the nature of a right and various aspects of a limitation on it, the nature of a right and other rights, the nature of a right and 'all relevant factors', which could include many matters of practical expediency of which courts know nothing, social interests about which it is dangerous for courts to speculate and considerations of morality on which the opinions of the governed may sharply differ from those of the courts. It is for the legislatures to decide what is expedient in practice, what social norms must be accepted, and what moral outcomes are to be favoured.[101]

---

[101] *Momcilovic* (n 1) 171.

Heydon J concluded that 'fundamental disputes of this kind – turning on questions of expediency, social policy and morality – call for legislative resolution, not judicial'. In other words, courts are not equipped to perform these functions. This is a classic statement about the indeterminacy and contestability of rights. When packaged as arguments sourced in a concern about parliamentary sovereignty, persuasive responses can be advanced that the legislature retains the power to accept or reject the judiciary's view and, thereby, parliamentary sovereignty is preserved.[102] However, when packaged as a separation of powers argument, the view that judiciaries are ill-equipped to make these judgments presents a counterpoint to the efficiency argument presented earlier that courts are well placed to point out human rights issues arising from an application of the interpretive rule.

Three of the other judges (French CJ and Crennan and Kiefel JJ) may have been attracted to this analysis. The three judges took the view that section 7(2) had no role to play in the interpretive process leading to a declaration, with indications that the balancing process in that provision was a legislative function. For French CJ, 'the justification of limitations on human rights is a matter for the Parliament', and that understanding 'accords with the constitutional relationship between the Parliament and the judiciary'.[103] For Crennan and Kiefel JJ, 's 7(2) contains no method appropriate to the ascertainment of the meaning and effect of a statutory provision'.[104]

The three remaining judges clearly disagreed. For Gummow, Hayne and Bell JJ, the criteria presented in section 7(2) were 'of a kind that are readily capable of judicial evaluation',[105] although the compatibility of that function with the judicial method was not explored. But, as will be seen, for Gummow and Hayne JJ, there were other problems with the judiciary's suitability to exercise the power to make a declaration: the declaration was the first step in a law reform process.

Thus, there are competing perspectives on whether courts are equipped to perform the balancing function that might be required by the interpretive process before a declaration power could be exercised.

However, this was not the only way in which separation ideas were framed. When applying the *Kable* test of incompatibility, Gummow J (with Hayne J agreeing) considered that the declaration power 'attempt[ed] a significant change to the constitutional relationship

---

102 See Goldsworthy, 'Judicial Review' (n 93).
103 *Momcilovic* (n 1) 44.
104 Ibid., 219–20.
105 Ibid., 250 (Bell J).

between the arms of government with respect to the interpretation and application of statute law'.[106] The declaration provided 'formal advice to the Attorney-General': that is, 'the giving to the Executive of an advisory opinion upon a question of law'. Gummow J continued:

> In the division between judicial and legislative functions it is appropriately the responsibility of the legislature to decide whether the existing statute law should be altered or repealed. It is no part of the judicial power, in the exercise of a function sought to be conferred on the courts by statute, formally to set in train a process whereby the executive branch of government may or may not decide to engage legislative processes to change existing legislation.[107]

For Gummow J, the declaration translated into a breach of the state court's institutional integrity, but this analysis explains much about the judge's conception of a separation of judicial power and why declarations fell foul of the separation limitations. The passage might suggest that the judiciary is ill-equipped and, thus, ill-suited to exercise this function. However, for Gummow J, there was additional significance for refusing to accept the declaration function. To fully understand this point, it is important to recall the considerations of the framers when drafting the constitution and the central High Court decisions establishing the separation of judicial power principles in Australia. Of primary concern to the framers and in those judgments was the preservation of judicial independence to protect the federal system. As Gummow J said in *Momcilovic*:

> The system of federal government in Australia is constructed upon the recognition that there rests upon the judicature 'the ultimate responsibility for the maintenance and enforcement of the boundaries within which governmental power might be exercised'.[108]

This suggests that, for Gummow J, courts should be limited to the resolution of disputes about legal rights and obligations because any departure from that orthodox understanding of the judiciary's role to administer common justice might detrimentally impact upon judicial independence and impartiality to police the federal system. The framers were concerned with the impact on judicial independence of the judiciary

---

[106] Ibid., 95–6.
[107] Ibid., 96.
[108] Ibid., 89, quoting from the High Court's decision in the *Boilermakers* case (n 40) 276.

being given the power to give an advisory opinion on the constitutional validity of legislation.[109] The Privy Council in *Boilermakers* was also concerned with the possibility that, if permitted to exercise non-judicial power, a court might be called on to review its own non-judicial decisions, thereby threatening its independence.[110] And, in *Momcilovic*, Gummow J's concern appears to be that the making of a declaration will involve the court in initiating law reform, potentially embroiling it in political controversy. At the heart of each of these concerns is the independence and impartiality of the judiciary.[111]

Of course, a majority did not share that characterization of the declaration. For French CJ (with Bell J agreeing), the advisory nature of a declaration actually served to reinforce the separation of powers within the constitutional system. The UK dialogue scheme left it for the legislature 'ultimately to determine whether the laws it enacts will be consistent or inconsistent with human rights'.[112] It thus served to reinforce the institutional integrity of the state court.

Crennan and Kiefel JJ's characterization of the declaration was very different to that of Gummow J. For Crennan and Kiefel JJ, it merely constituted a conclusion about its interpretive function: 'a statement, made by the Supreme Court following upon its interpretation of a statutory provision in the context of the Charter, that an inconsistency between the two statutes is evident, and of which the Attorney-General is notified'.[113] For the judges, a declaration is not an 'advisory opinion':[114] 'the Court does not purport to advise on law reform'.[115] Although the declaration might trigger law reform, the law reform steps, if any, are left to be taken by the executive and legislature. In Crennan and Kiefel JJ's view, although the making of a declaration does not involve the 'administration of the law',[116] it is 'largely innocuous so far as concerns the Supreme Court'.[117] Indeed, it was considered by Crennan and Kiefel JJ to be incidental to the court's administration of the law, noting that '[i]t is not unknown for judges to incidentally pass comments upon conclusions

109 Stellios, *The Federal Judicature* (n 37).

110 *A-G (Cth) v The Queen* (1957) 95 CLR 529, 541.

111 This view may also have been shared by Heydon J, although his reasoning is unclear in this respect.

112 *Momcilovic* (n 1) 68.

113 Ibid., 222.

114 Ibid.

115 Ibid., 227.

116 Ibid., 223.

117 Ibid., 228.

they have reached about defects in legislation in the course of their reasons'.[118] On this view, one might venture to suggest that courts, along the lines of the efficiency argument identified earlier, are uniquely placed to suggest possible changes to the law following from the court's application of the interpretive rule to the legislation in the particular case.

This spread of views about the requirements of a separation of powers is certainly not unique to the High Court of Australia. Eoin Carolan has shown that a similar pattern of indecision and imprecision has emerged in the jurisprudence in the US and Ireland.[119] The Australian position certainly lends weight to Carolan's conclusion that:

> The contemporary curial treatment of the separation of powers theory is institutionally deficient in several significant respects. The separation of powers is, put simply, an institutional vision in search of an ideal.[120]

4.1.7 Concluding Observations

In his classic work on the separation of powers, Vile said:

> The 'doctrine of the separation of powers' is by no means a simple and immediately recognizable, unambiguous set of concepts. On the contrary it represents an idea of political thought in which there has been an extraordinary confusion in definition and use of terms.[121]

The High Court of Australia historically has struggled to present its separation principles in a coherent way, and we see in *Momcilovic* some confusion about the theoretical underpinnings of the principles. There was certainly a strong flavour of efficiency explanations of a separation of powers, although the efficiency arguments went both ways. While the application of the interpretive rule without the balancing exercise in section 7(2) was seen by the court as particularly attuned to the judicial method, the balancing exercise was seen by many of the judges as beyond judicial competence. The declaration was seen by some judges as a first step in law reform, whilst others saw it as an 'innocuous' statement of conclusion following the application of the interpretive rule.

However, much more thinking is needed before such conclusions can be confidently reached. The declaration sits somewhere in between

---

118 Ibid., 227.

119 Carolan (n 95) ch 2.

120 Ibid., 44.

121 M J C Vile, *Constitutionalism and the Separation of Powers* (OUP 1967) 2.

traditionally clear conceptions of judicial and legislative functions. It is a function that arises out of the 'triadic model' that best characterizes the conventional judicial process, but has clear implications 'that go beyond the parties appearing before the judge'.[122] As Nicholas Barber has said:[123]

> The court, and the judges, are strong when faced with issues that can be contained within the triadic model, they become weaker as this model is departed from. They are particularly well-placed to decide discrete disputes between parties that are regulated by pre-existing law. Their competence is placed under pressure as they move from this task towards the broader goal of setting social policy.

Declarations of incompatibility raise difficult questions because they sit somewhere in between.

On the other hand, Blackstonian understandings of the judiciary being limited to the administration of common justice, which places a premium on the independence of the judiciary, was also a strong idea pressed, at least, by Gummow J. This is consistent with Gummow J's previous expositions of the Blackstonian judicial tradition.

What is lacking in all of this is an explicit recognition of the separation of powers tradition that the judges were working within, and an appreciation that alternative traditions – like an efficiency or checks and balances explanation – might lead to different outcomes. What is also lacking is a recognition that the separation of powers – if indeed a constitutional imperative – sits alongside other constitutional principles like parliamentary sovereignty and responsible government in a constitutional framework for the advancement of the interests of the federal body politic.

Of most concern is the High Court's readiness to constitutionalize separations of powers theories without an express acknowledgment of the doctrinal tradition being preferenced. This has locked Australian constitutionalism into certain models of rights protection, limiting the judiciary's role to applying conventional interpretive assumptions about legislatures not intruding into rights, albeit in relation to an expanded set of statutorily defined human rights. Parliamentary sovereignty and responsible government were seen by the framers of the constitution as inconsistent with the inclusion of an entrenched bill of rights, and the separation of powers is seen by the High Court as preventing the

---

122 Barber, 'Self-Defence for Institutions' (n 100) 76.
123 Ibid., 79.

adoption of key judicial features of a UK-style dialogue model of rights protection. In the absence of constitutional amendment, the scope for innovation in judicial involvement for human rights protection is now considerably limited.

What *Momcilovic* really demonstrates clearly is that Australian separation of judicial power principles have lost sight of their justificatory foundations. For most judges, the principle that courts are limited to the determination of disputes about legal rights and duties was applied formulaically, without an assessment of what was offensive about judicial declarations within the UK-style dialogue model. The underlying policy reasons only emerged in most judgments because the High Court had to consider whether the exercise of such a function by state courts was *incompatible* with their exercise of federal judicial power. It was only then that most judges revealed their separation of power thinking. If one revisits the foundations for the separation principles, both during the Convention debates and in the key High Court judgments establishing the principles, one sees the objective as being the preservation of judicial independence and impartiality. While High Court judges have, at times, flirted with theoretical accounts of efficiency and the dispersion of power, Australian constitutionalism was intended to be much less ambitious.

It may be that restricting the judiciary to the 'administration of common justice' is the neatest or most manageable way to preserve its independence and impartiality. But, the overreach of the strict limitation does have the effect of suffocating innovation.[124]

The compatibility of declarations with Australian constitutionalism should have been assessed in *Momcilovic* against the standards of independence and impartiality. Of course, different judicial minds might disagree on what conclusions are reached. And, as is demonstrated by the different characterizations of, on the one hand, Gummow and Hayne JJ and, on the other hand, Crennan and Kiefel JJ, the assessment of the declaration power against that standard may depend upon whether the interpretive process leading to the declaration involves a balancing exercise. But, at least the appropriate constitutional standard would be applied in order to justify the constitutionalization of a limited role for the Australian judiciary in the protection of rights.

---

[124] Indeed, the federal Parliament, with the enactment of its new human rights scheme, has decided to steer clear of the interpretive rule and the judicial declaration power. In light of *Momcilovic*, the decision has proved to be a prudent one.

4.2 ADVENTURES IN THE GREY ZONE: CONSTITUTIONALISM, RIGHTS AND THE REVIEW OF EXECUTIVE POWER IN THE MIGRATION CONTEXT

Matthew Zagor*

4.2.1 Introduction

A. Thesis and themes

Australian refugee law is characterized by exclusion – exclusion from territory, from the 'migration zone', from the 'community', from the refugee determination regime, from the courts, the judicial process, and ultimately from the law itself. The physical and legal isolation of the refugee is a product of various legal strategies, from legislation mandating the indefinite detention of 'unlawful' non-citizens to the more recent experiments in 'excising' parts of the country from the operation of statute and the scrutiny of the courts. Australia's innovative use of legislation to carve out spaces within which an unencumbered executive power can expand has unsurprisingly seen commentators turn to cosmological metaphors to explain the phenomenon,[1] borrowing Lord Steyn's description of the US naval base at Guantanamo Bay as a 'legal black hole',[2] and Agamben's exploration of the 'camp' as existing in a state of exception.[3] This chapter builds upon David Dyzhenhaus' nuanced description of these spaces as 'grey holes' where the impression of

---

* Thanks to Associate Professor James Stellios, Dr Rayner Thwaites, Professor John Bell and Dr Marie-Luce Paris for their comments.

[1] The phenomenon is not new in Australian jurisprudence. As Robert French points out, even Sir Owen Dixon 'was not above cosmological metaphor'. French CJ, 'Litigating in a Statutory University' (Victorian Bar Association 2nd Annual CPD Conference, Melbourne, 18 February 2012).

[2] Johan Steyn, 'Guantanamo Bay: The Legal Black Hole' (Twenty-Seventh F A Mann Lecture, British Institute of International and Comparative Law, London, 25 November 2003).

[3] Illustrating the influence on the discipline of the scholarship of Arendt, Foucault and Agamben was the University of Oxford's Refugee Studies Centre seminar series 'Camp Life: Exception, Emergence and Spaces of Forced Migration'. See critique of some of these approaches in Carl Levy, 'Refugees, Europe, Camps/State of Exception: "Into The Zone", the European Union and Extraterritorial Processing of Migrants, Refugees, and Asylum-seekers (Theories and Practice)' (2010) 29 *Refugee Survey Quarterly* 92.

legality is created by legislative and judicial endorsement of strategies which exclude meaningful judicial review of executive conduct. It explores the curious attempt to use the law in order to suspend the law, the changeable role of the judiciary in both consolidating and piercing these legislatively crafted exclusionary zones, and the muscular anti-dialogic reassertion of legislative dominance that invariably accompanies perceived judicial interference.

The main subject matter of this chapter is thus the relatively well-trodden public law ground of the relationship between the executive and courts.[4] It first presents an overview of Australian constitutional rights and judicial method. Given the potential breadth of these topics and the inevitable brevity of its coverage here, this section is necessarily incomplete and anecdotal, designed to provide an overview of key themes rather than a discrete methodology, let alone a comprehensive review of the subject matter. It contrasts the notorious rights reluctance of the Australian political system and its culture of deference and trust in the executive with the impressive architecture of administrative justice that has developed over the past three decades, as well as the contentious role played by 'legalism' as both a shield and a sword in the juridical arsenal for scrutinizing executive conduct. Finally, in the spirit of comparative constitutionalism, it introduces the explanatory potential of the British debate between political and legal constitutionalists, and the analogous if somewhat incoherent constitutional narratives that co-exist in today's Australian political and legal discourse.

In order to explore these themes and the idiosyncratic approach taken by the Australian judiciary to executive power, the chapter presents five key cases in which the courts have considered the source, depth, breadth and control of executive power in a migration context. In each instance, the High Court or Federal Court was faced with arguments about either an unreviewable, expansive or quasi-quarantined form of power – often created by innovative statutory schemes – and a concomitant restriction of an alien's fundamental rights.[5] The rights at stake relate to liberty of person, access to justice, cruel and inhuman treatment or punishment,

---

[4] See James Stellios in Chapter 4.1 about Australian constitutionalism in general and how it can be compared with the UK-style dialogue model of human rights protection.

[5] The constitutional term 'alien' is now equated with 'non citizen'. See *Shaw v Minister for Immigration and Multicultural Affairs* (2003) 218 CLR 28 [2] (Gleeson CJ, Gummow and Hayne JJ) ('citizenship may be seen as the obverse of the status of alienage'). See also *Singh v The Commonwealth* (2004) 222 CLR 322. I use the terms interchangeably, depending upon context. For a

and the panoply of protections available under the 1951 Refugee Convention, not least the prohibition on refoulement. Government arguments were peppered with standard appeals to the deference owed to the political branches in matters relating to foreign affairs, migration and border control. The principal aim of the chapter is to examine the judicial response to such claims within the context of the trajectory of Australian public law.

B. Australian constitutional rights and judicial method: a very brief introduction

At the risk of repeating the mundane, Australia's Constitution is almost entirely devoid of any recognizable rights protections. Those explicit rights which the framers considered worthy of inclusion are either of minimal effect (for example, the right to a jury trial for indictable federal offences in section 80),[6] or have been read down by successive courts (for example, the 'establishment' clause in section 116).[7] The reasons for the failure to adopt stronger rights provisions, such as Inglis Clark's ill-fated equality clause, are well canvassed in the literature,[8] although there is often a divide in emphasis, one mirrored in the contemporary debate for the creation of a rights Charter. Rights sceptics focus upon the original and ongoing trust in political institutions to remedy rights-infringing conduct. This trust is traced to the relatively painless birth of the polity through democratic and parliamentary processes, and contrasts with the 'new values' which were required to shape the constitutional settlements in other common law countries. Responsible government, regular elections and the enforcement of common law rights by an independent judiciary are presented as adequate to the task of checking abuses of power without the anti-democratic judicialization that bills of rights import.[9] Indeed, some scholars argue that Australia has already

---

challenge to the current understanding, see Anthony Gray, 'The Meaning of an "Alien" in the Constitutional Universe' (2013) 20 *AJ Admin L* 89.

[6] See James Stellios 'The Constitutional Jury: "A Bulwark of Liberty" (2005) 27 *Syd LR* 113.

[7] Notably in *Attorney-General (Vict); Ex rel Black v The Commonwealth* (1981) 146 CLR 559; *Kruger v The Commonwealth* (1997) 190 CLR 1.

[8] See, for instance, George Williams, *Human Rights under the Australian Constitution* (OUP 2002) 25–68.

[9] See summary of the arguments in the National Human Rights Consultation in National Human Rights Consultation Report (30 September 2009), as reported in 'The case against a Human Rights Act' ch 13 <https://www.ag.gov.au/RightsAndProtections/HumanRights/TreatyBodyReporting/Pages/HumanRightsconsultationreport.aspx> accessed 29 April 2015.

experienced a 'rights revolution' that has been predominantly political and democratic, rather than judicial, reflecting Waldron rather than Dworkin in its orientation.[10]

By contrast, Charter proponents point to concerns expressed by the framers that constitutional rights would be enjoyed by the Crown's non-white subjects, hindering the viability of discriminatory laws and policies which pre-dated federation and were planned for the new Commonwealth.[11] Citizenship was similarly omitted from the text to preclude such an eventuality arising even indirectly.[12] As George Williams notes, this 'undermined any pretence that the framers were generally concerned to foster human rights or that they viewed responsible government as being appropriate because of its scope to protect minority rights. Their intention was in fact the opposite'.[13] The Constitution, according to this view, was specifically designed for control and exclusion, entrenching the central government's power to implement and counter any threats that might frustrate the experiment of building an Anglo-Saxon haven in the great South land. Powers with respect to race, aliens and migrants were drafted with this agenda in mind. Used to pass the legislation which was to implement the infamous White Australia Policy,[14] these powers have been interpreted broadly by courts to support exclusionary practices for the past 100 years, with significant rights ramifications. From this perspective, any rights revolution arising in the political sphere has either bypassed aliens and refugees, or is too fragile to provide them with meaningful rights protection.

---

[10] See, for instance, Brian Galligan and FL (Ted) Morton, 'Australian Exceptionalism: Rights Protection Without a Bill of Rights' in Tom Campbell and others, *Australian Exceptionalism: Rights Protection Without a Bill of Rights* (Ashgate 2006).

[11] Henry Higgins, later a member of the High Court, said of Inglis Clark's equal protection of the laws' amendment: 'It protects Chinamen too, I suppose, as well as negroes?' See Williams (n 8) 151.

[12] See Helen Irving, *To Constitute a Nation: A Cultural History of Australia's Constitution* (CUP 1999) ch 9.

[13] Williams (n 8) 151.

[14] Alfred Deakin, the first Commonwealth Attorney-General, famously opined on introducing the Immigration Restriction Bill in the first Parliament: 'At the very first instant of our national career we are as one for a white Australia.' (Commonwealth Parliamentary Debates, House of Representatives, 12 September 1901, vol 4 excerpts).

At the more extreme end of the interpretive spectrum are those who consider the white Australia policy to have an ongoing, spectre-like influence over contemporary political and legal discourse.[15]

While this narrative of an ingrained exclusionary ethic in the polity may have some explanatory value with respect to political strategies, it is difficult to discern in legal doctrine, judicial method, or current justifications for remaining a constitutional rights-free zone. Nonetheless, the constitutional control mechanism put at the disposal of the Commonwealth government over non-citizens, and the attitude of trust and deference towards the political limbs of government in the management of the borders and those non-citizens who cross them, retain their potency, not least in the area of judicial review of executive action which impacts on the rights of non-citizens – the subject matter of this chapter.

Often linked to the Australian reluctance to embrace judicially enforceable rights is the method of 'strict and complete legalism' which is purported to characterize the dominant judicial mindset and to provide Australian jurisprudence with its 'no nonsense', policy-free reputation. Yet apart from the notoriously obscure nature of Justice Dixon's phraseology,[16] it is far from clear that legalism, in the sense of adherence to traditional methods of interpreting texts, is in itself a cause for rights hesitancy. As recent cases on executive power demonstrate, contemporary legalism is playing its part in opening up executive conduct previously considered immune from judicial scrutiny. The court's newly discovered enthusiasm for couching its decisions in the language of statutory construction can be viewed in this light. It is legalism's oft-described tendency to provide cover for judicial policy predilections[17] that makes it

---

[15] Robert Manne 'Tragedy of Errors: Australia's Shipwrecked Refugee Policy' *The Monthly* (Australia, March 2013) <https://www.themonthly.com.au/australia-s-shipwrecked-refugee-policy-tragedy-errors-guest-7637> accessed 29 April 2015.

[16] Stephen Gageler, 'Beyond the Text: A Vision of the Structure and Function of the Constitution' (2009) 32 *Aust Bar Rev* 138, 144 ('[legalism is] an emphatic statement of the obscure').

[17] Leslie Zines, *The High Court and the Constitution* (5th edn, The Federation Press 2008) 606–7. Gageler (n 16) 143–4. That legalism is not incompatible with judicial policy choices is widely recognized. As Gageler notes: 'legalism is incapable of fulfilling its own agenda' (Stephen Gageler, 'Foundations of Australian Federalism and the Role of Judicial Review' (1987) 17 *FL Rev* 162, 178). See also judicial statements that 'policy cannot be excluded from the curial interpretive process' when interpreting and applying legislation designed to effect a policy in *Thomas v Mowbray* (2007) 233 CLR 307, 348–51 [80]–[91] (Gummow and Crennan JJ). More broadly, see critique of the ideology

such a useful tool for either rubber-stamping or upending legislatively imposed rights restrictions while retaining the perception of impartiality. This chapter will consider whether this is an appropriate, problematic or ultimately rights-regressive technique.

Legalism aside, even in the absence of express constitutional rights provisions, Australian judicial method retains considerable rights potentiality. The High Court's structural review of the Constitution has 'uncovered' implied freedoms in the text and structure, and procedural rights in the separation of judicial power arising in Chapter III on the Judicature. As in the UK, methods of statutory interpretation, including the presumption against interference with fundamental rights or the 'principle of legality', have been adopted by our current and immediate past Chief Justices as 'constitutional' principles.[18] Moreover, the judicial examination of executive power has been as vigorous, if not more so, than our British counterparts, and from earlier on.[19] Developments from the late 1970s opened up a wide array of executive decisions for judicial scrutiny, complemented in the 1990s by the expansion of grounds of review for 'jurisdictional error,' the consolidation of the 'jurisdictional fact' doctrine, and the constitutionalization of the writs available under the High Court's original jurisdiction.

Given its reach into the exercise of public power, and the relative absence of more orthodox rights remedies, it is unsurprising that human rights claims have found a home in administrative law.[20] This has frequently come in the context of decisions under the Migration Act 1958 (Cth) (hereafter Migration Act), not least in the reinvigoration of 'jurisdictional error' as administrative justice's unifying principle.[21]

---

of legalism in Judith N Shklar, *Legalism: Law, Morals and Political Trials* (Harvard UP 1986) 8.

[18] See, for instance, Robert French, 'The Courts and the Parliament' (2013) 87 *ALJ* 820.

[19] See DG Benjafield and Harry Whitmore, *Principles of Australian Administrative Law* (3rd edn, Law Book Co 1966) 33, cited by Robert French, 'Administrative Justice – Words in Search of Meaning' (Australian Institute of Administrative Law Annual Conference, National Administrative Law Forum 2010, Sydney, 22 July 2010).

[20] See Ben Saul, 'Australian Administrative Law: The Human Rights Dimension' in Matthew Groves and HP Lee (eds), *Australian Administrative Law: Fundamentals, Principles and Doctrines* (CUP 2007); Robin Creyke, 'The Performance of Administrative Law in Protecting Rights' in Campbell (n 10).

[21] Stephen Gageler, 'Impact of Migration Law on the Development of Australian Administrative Law' (2010) 17 *AJ Admin L* 92, 93. Similarly, see Naomi Sidebotham, 'Relevant and Irrelevant Considerations' in Groves and Lee

These developments have had a mixed reception. For John Macmillan, they represent 'an overt judicial strike' on assumptions of reviewability, a form of 'judicial activism' that has rewritten the executive/judicial relationship and undermined the constitutional imperative of judicial restraint, not least in the area of migration law.[22] By contrast, French CJ sees them as reflecting a nascent form of 'administrative justice'. In attempting to frame a unifying theory to accommodate the new administrative law, French CJ has identified 'normative standards of general application to administrative decision-making and review processes' by reference to a multiplicity of sources – 'the written constitution, representative democracy, the rule of law, formal or conventional separation of legislative, executive and judicial powers, and a milieu of recognized common law rights and freedoms' – as well as to international human rights norms. Taking his cue from Anthony Bradley's view of administrative justice as reflected in article 6 of the European Convention on Human Rights,[23] French CJ has gone so far as to surmise that 'many of the human rights guaranteed by the International Covenant on Civil and Political Rights will be met by the observance of minimum standards of legality, rationality, fairness, accessibility, affordability and efficiency'.[24] Such statements complement and extend the 'rule of law' rhetoric which has frequently accompanied administrative law jurisprudence.[25]

---

ibid., 186, who notes that 'constantly changing migration legislation has necessitated the evolution' of grounds including unreasonableness and irrationality (in *Re Minister for Immigration and Multicultural Affairs; Ex parte Applicant S20 /2002* (2003) 77 ALJR 1165), and relevancy as part of jurisdictional error (in *Minister for Immigration and Multicultural Affairs v Yusuf* (2001) 206 CLR 323).

[22] John McMillan, 'Who is in Charge? The Impact of Judicial Review on Ministerial Decision Making' (Fair and Open Decision Making: The 1991 Administrative Law Forum, Royal Australian Institute of Public Administration (ACT Division) and Australian Institute of Administrative Law, Canberra, 29-30 April 1991) 2, cited by French (n 19), 8–9. See also John McMillan, 'Judicial Restraint and Activism' (2002) *30 FL Rev* 335; Caron Beaton-Wells, 'Australian Administrative Law: The Asylum Seeker Legacy' [2005] PL 267.

[23] AW Bradley, 'Administrative Justice: A Developing Human Right?' (1995) 1 *EPL* 347, cited in French (n 19).

[24] French (n 19) 16.

[25] 'Rule of law' jurisprudence has a significant historical pedigree in Australia, not just in the administrative law context. See Ian Holloway, Simon Bronitt and John Williams, 'Rhetoric, Reason, and the Rule of Law in Early Colonial New South Wales' in Hamar Foster, Benjamin L Berger and AR Buck (eds), *The Grand Experiment: Law and Legal Culture in British Settler Societies* (UBC Press 2008) 78.

While the Chief Justice's observations may reflect a degree of rights-consciousness at the highest level of the judiciary, they also betray a somewhat limited and curial-centric view of what rights entail, reducing them to their procedural rather than substantive components. In practice, such principles have proved protective less of human dignity than of the court's inherent jurisdiction.[26]

C. Competing constitutionalisms

In light of the comparative nature of the current exercise, it is worth briefly addressing one final related theme: the virtual absence from Australian doctrinal and theoretical debates of the divide between political and legal constitutionalists which has so dominated judicial review scholarship in the UK, not least in the realm of rights protection.[27] The prima facie reasons for this are somewhat unsatisfactory. With a written constitution and a tradition of judicial review dating back to colonial times and considered 'axiomatic' under the Constitution,[28] it could be said that the division has little relevance in the Australian context. That would be too simplistic. Several core assumptions of political constitutionalism enjoy strong endorsement in Australia. This includes an albeit qualified doctrine of parliamentary sovereignty or 'legislative predominance' – recently confirmed as a 'basal assumption'[29] of the Constitution – and a robust commitment to responsible government as a check on executive power. This is complemented by a widespread conviction that our democratic institutions are not just 'in reasonably good working order' but are best placed to decide issues where there is 'substantial and good faith disagreement'.[30] Opponents of bills of rights make similar arguments when defending the status quo, drawing upon the political constitutionalism playbook if not its terminology.

---

[26] Note Saul's discussion on the 'convergence and divergence' of human rights and administrative law, and his discussion of proportionality and the principle of legality in Saul (n 20) 52–3.

[27] One notable exception in the field of rights review is the work of Stephen Gardbaum who views the new constitutional model of statutory bills of rights as merging the two constitutionalisms. It is arguable that such a merger already exists in the Australian constitutional model.

[28] *Australian Communist Party v Commonwealth* (1951) 83 CLR 1, 262–3 (Fullagar J) (Communist Party case).

[29] *Williams v Commonwealth of Australia* (2012) 248 CLR 156, 233 [136] (Gummow and Bell JJ) (School Chaplains case).

[30] Jeremy Waldron, 'The Core Case against Judicial Review' (2006) 115 *Yale LJ* 1346.

Moreover, our lawyers and judges are, for the most part, proud positivists. Legal realism has never held much sway in the Australian judicial fraternity, our judges more often sounding like their nineteenth century British predecessors in decrying the practice of judge-made law than their American cousins.[31] Our academics have traditionally been loathe to engage in the type of scrutiny of the judiciary that has pervaded the US literature for almost a century and has in the past 30 years so influenced the British academy. Serious judicial biography, for instance, is of recent pedigree;[32] and key tomes on the judiciary rarely engage in contextual critique, preferring analyses of doctrine, method and outcome.[33] There is no equivalent of the fiery polemic of Griffith, or the historical trajectory traced by Stevens.[34] Nor have our judges engaged in the type of public debate and lobbying that preceded the introduction of the UK Human Rights Act 1998, conduct which would be seen as breaching the constitutional convention to stay above the political hue and cry. The sacrosanct, if artificial, divide between the judicial and political functions, in other words, is jealously guarded.

This judicial culture is in turn reflected in the separation of powers jurisprudence developed by the High Court, not least its overriding concern (mitigated in recent years) with retaining 'public confidence' in the integrity of the institution. As a result, laws which authorize the court or judicial officers to undertake functions too closely aligned with the political branches of government will be struck down as incompatible with federal judicial office for undermining that confidence, or impairing

---

31 Justice Heydon's speech, reported in *Quadrant* (2003) and widely considered to be his application for a seat on the High Court, is perhaps the most notorious example of this tendency.

32 Sarah Burnside, 'Australian Judicial Biography: Past, Present and Future' (2011) 57 *Australian Journal of Politics and History* 221, similarly identifies the historical lack of interest in judicial biography as a manifestation of Australia's dominant (non realist) legal culture.

33 For instance, Enid Campbell and HP Lee, *The Australian Judiciary* (2nd edn, CUP 2012), which remains the core text on the institution, is devoid of any contextual analysis. Works that have looked at the court in context include those by Brian Galligan, *Politics of the High Court: A Study of the Judicial Branch of Government in Australia* (University of Queensland Press 1986); Jason L Pierce, *Inside the Mason Court Revolution: The High Court of Australia Transformed* (Carolina Academic Press 2006); and Haig Patapan, *Judging Democracy: The New Politics of the High Court of Australia* (CUP 2000). It is instructive that the latter two works concern the phenomenon of the Mason Court.

34 Robert Stevens, *The English Judges: Their Role in the Changing Constitution* (Hart 2002).

the court's 'institutional integrity'.[35] Although this doctrine would not necessarily preclude investing the court with the power to consider breaches of rights, it nonetheless reflects a deferential predisposition and court scepticism, even within the institution itself, analogous to that of the political constitutionalists.[36]

Additionally, the Australian federal Parliament has a habit of reacting strongly to perceptions of judicial overreach, engaging less in either dialogue or legislative capitulation than in the muscular reassertion of dominance.[37] The concern of republican political constitutionalists that judicial rights decisions have a chilling effect on legislative action and political deliberation[38] is not just absent in the Australian context, it is turned on its head: legislative responses to judicial setbacks are apt to be undertaken with bipartisan support, and minimal debate. Nor is there much evidence of a 'principle proposing dialogue' sought by legal constitutionalists.[39] In this respect, despite our entrenched legal constitutionalism, Australia has retained a republican-style rhetoric, not least

---

[35] *Grollo v Palmer* (1995) 184 CLR 348; *Wilson v Minister for Aboriginal and Torres Strait Islander Affairs* (1996) 189 CLR 1; *Kable v Director of Public Prosecutions (NSW)* (1996) 189 CLR 51. On the ambiguity of the test of 'public confidence', see Chief Justice Brennan in *Nicholas v The Queen* (1998) 193 CLR 173, 197; Elizabeth Handsley, 'Public Confidence in the Judiciary: A Red Herring for the Separation of Judicial Power' (1998) 20 *Syd LR* 183; *Moti v The Queen* (2012) 245 CLR 456, 494–6 [98]–[102] (Heydon J). As Handsley notes, 'public confidence' places security of the judiciary above considerations of separation of powers – or indeed of rights. Similarly, Robert Orr SC, has quipped that judges are 'more concerned with the reputation of the courts than the liberty of subjects' (Robert Orr, 'Kable v DPP: Taking Judicial Protection Too Far?' (1996) 11 *AIAL Forum* 11).

[36] This draws upon distinctions and assumptions identified in Paul Craig, 'Political Constitutionalism and Judicial Review' in Christopher Forsyth and others (eds) *Effective Judicial Review: A Cornerstone of Good Governance* (OUP 2010) 19, 20–21.

[37] Craig's description of legislative responses fails to capture the more common scenario in Australia in which the legislature will try to find its way around a curial setback, often tightening draconian statutes even when it 'wins' in court.

[38] See, for instance, Adam Tomkins, *Our Republican Constitution* (Hart 2005); Richard Bellamy, *Political Constitutionalism: A Republican Defence of the Constitutionality of Democracy* (CUP 2007). For the alleged tension between law and politics inherent in the criticism, see discussion in Martin Loughlin, *Sword and Scales* (Hart 2000).

[39] Tom Hickman, *Public Law after the Human Rights Act* (Hart 2010) 60.

when it comes to matters of rights, border control and the treatment of non-citizens.

The uncomfortable Australian marriage between the two forms of constitutionalism is not easy to theorize. One of the more recent (implicit) attempts is in an influential essay by Justice Stephen Gageler.[40] For Gageler, the starting point for any exercise of judicial power must be the 'essentially political' institutions of representative and responsible government by which the institutions of government are made politically accountable to the people of Australia. Under this model, judicial power ought to conform to the 'strengths and weaknesses of the ordinary constitutional means of constraining governmental power', and judicial review guided by the 'primacy of the political process'. Following these principles, judicial deference is appropriate 'where political accountability is inherently strong', whereas judicial vigilance is appropriate 'where political accountability is either inherently weak or endangered'.[41] For Gageler, these principles have already informed shifts in judicial reasoning where deference has given way to vigilance. While the examples he gives primarily relate to federal limitations, the theory is potentially adaptable to the rights of non-citizens, as we shall see.

4.2.2 Sovereignty, Deference and Executive Power

A. *Tampa* and its aftermath: the rise of the sovereign executive

The 2001 case of *Ruddock v Vadarlis*,[42] known colloquially as the *Tampa* decision after the Norwegian vessel that rescued 433 asylum seekers on the high seas, represents the high water mark of a judicially-endorsed unimpeded executive power. Its position as a 'moment' in constitutional history and its rapid rise to anti-canonical status in the pedagogy make it a useful analytical starting point, both for the judicial reasoning employed and the legislative response which was to follow in its wake.

The Tampa had been refused entry to Australia's territorial sea, the port of Christmas Island being closed on executive order – the first time such action had been taken outside wartime. Insisting upon his international obligation to disembark the rescuees, the captain took the vessel into Australian waters, and the ship was promptly boarded by the Special Air Service Regiment.[43] Facing an increased number of boatloads of

---

[40] Gageler (n 16).

[41] Ibid., 152.

[42] *Ruddock v Vadarlis* (2001) 110 FCR 491 (Tampa case).

[43] For the broader political context within which the incident took place, see David Marr and Marian Wilkinson, *Dark Victory* (Allen & Unwin 2003).

mostly Afghan and Iraqi asylum seekers, and trailing in the polls in the run up to the November elections, the government presented itself as exercising the exclusive sovereign right to determine entry to Australia, the Prime Minister John Howard famously declaring that '[w]e will decide who comes to this country and the circumstances in which they come'. This assertion of sovereignty was to morph into a ubiquitous campaign slogan, directed not just at people smugglers and their refugee clients, but at the opposition Labor Party who were depicted, successfully, as soft on border control. It was also, if only indirectly, a warning shot across the bow of the courts should they consider interfering.

Yet interfere is exactly what the court did. Despite being unable to access the asylum seekers, the Federal Court recognized the standing of Eric Vadarlis, a Melbourne-based solicitor, to apply for an order in the nature of *habeas corpus* to seek their release, relying upon the fundamental importance to the common law of the ability to challenge the legality of another's detention.[44] On 11 September 2001, Justice North ordered that the rescuees be released from detention on the mainland. Two weeks later, now operating in the shadow of the attacks in the US and a new political rhetoric that depicted the hapless Hazaras aboard the Tampa as potential terrorists, the original decision was reversed by majority in the full Federal Court, Justice French (as he then was) writing the lead judgment.

The Solicitor General's key argument was that the Commonwealth executive was acting pursuant to its prerogative power, embraced by section 61 of the Constitution which vests executive power in the Queen,[45] to exclude aliens, and to detain and expel them to achieve that purpose.[46] French J found the existence of such a power to be inherent in

---

[44] Standing to apply for other writs – notably an injunction and mandamus – was not so readily forthcoming, a result of the need to have a party directly affected before the court.

[45] Section 61 of the Constitution states: 'The executive power of the Commonwealth is vested in the Queen and is exercisable by the Governor-General as the Queen's representative, and extends to the execution and maintenance of this Constitution, and of the laws of the Commonwealth.'

[46] More accurately, French J described the power as one 'to authorise the barring of entry by preventing a vessel from docking at an Australian port and adopting the means necessary to achieve that result. Absent statutory authority, it would extend to a power to restrain a person or boat from proceeding into Australia or compelling it to leave'. See Tampa case (n 42) 544 [197].

the notion of sovereignty itself. Jettisoning the time-honoured technique of locating the prerogative in precedent, French J bluntly concluded:[47]

> The power to determine who may come into Australia is so central to its sovereignty that it is not to be supposed that the Government of the nation would lack under the power conferred upon it directly by the Constitution, the ability to prevent people not part of the Australia community, from entering.

Crucially, an analogous statutory power in the Migration Act was found not to have abrogated this inherent executive power, not least because of its significance to national sovereignty.[48] The result was that various protections available under the Migration Act, including access to a robust mechanism for determining refugee claims, were stripped from the detainees, as was any judicial examination of the executive's actions beyond identification of the source of the power to exclude. The exercise of power under section 61 of the Constitution, it seems, would be subject to the least intrusive form of constitutional review.

Sovereignty was thus to act as a double trump, providing both a sword for government action and a shield from robust scrutiny. It offered an avenue for the recognition of power long thought to have fallen into desuetude, and the justification for its primacy over what might otherwise have been considered to be comprehensive statutory abrogation; indeed, such a power had not been appealed to outside statute in either Britain or Australia for over 200 years, its last recorded use, according to Holdsworth, being to prevent the 'too frequent importation of vagrant and vagabond Jews' – a point not lost on Black CJ in his powerful dissent.[49] Since then, statute had governed almost every instance of exclusion and expulsion discernible on the historical record. Yet on this occasion, parliamentary sovereignty and the nuances available in the conflicting speeches in *De Keyser's Royal Hotel* gave way to a virtually un-codifiable executive sovereign power over border control, and a concomitant judicial attitude of deference towards its exercise. As French J asserted, with more than a hint of political constitutionalism, '[t]hese

---

[47] Tampa case (n 42) 543 [193] (French J). Similarly at 542 [191]: 'The scope of the executive power conferred by s 61 of the Constitution is to be measured by reference to Australia's status as a sovereign nation and by reference to the terms of the Constitution itself.'

[48] Tampa case (n 42) 540 [185] (French J).

[49] Black CJ relies on Holdsworth, who in turn referred to *The Calendar of Home Office Papers* 1770–1772, in which this quote appears.

powers may be exercised for good reasons or bad. That debate, however, is not one for this Court to enter'.[50]

Reliance on sovereignty as defined by an exclusionary ethic also enabled the court to discount historical sources from within both the English constitutional tradition as well as international legal jurisprudence that depict a more complex and qualified view of the concept. As Nafziger has persuasively argued, the depiction of sovereignty as somehow defined by an unfettered power to exclude represents a late nineteenth century British common law gloss on a more nuanced, less absolutist reading of the work of earlier domestic and international law jurists.[51] Endorsement of a blunt, undifferentiated reading of sovereignty added the perfect curial complement to John Howard's muscular campaigning on the issue of border control. This in turn operated to distract judicial attention from exploring more closely the meaning of 'sovereignty' in domestic and international legal theory, and from the nature of Australia's international legal obligations towards refugees. To borrow from Murray Hunt, sovereignty obstructed the proper articulation of what might be legitimate reasons for deference 'behind a vocabulary of spaces and boundaries which are asserted as if the underlying assumptions about the constitutional division of powers were not contentious'.[52] Although Hunt was describing parliamentary sovereignty, the same linguistic and structural mechanism is on display in assumptions regarding the executive's sovereign authority over 'border security'.[53]

---

[50] Tampa case (n 42) 542 [192] (French J).

[51] James Nafziger, 'The General Admission of Aliens Under International Law' (1983) 77 *AJIL* 804. See also Eve Lester, 'Myth-conceiving Sovereignty: The Legacy of the Nineteenth Century' in Fiona Jenkins, Mark Nolan and Kim Rubenstein (eds), *Allegiance and Identity in a Globalised World* (CUP 2014) 354–80.

[52] Murray Hunt, 'Sovereignty's Blight: Why Contemporary Public Law Needs the Concept of "Due Deference" in Nicholas Bamforth and Peter Leyland (eds), *Public Law in a Multi- Layered Constitution* (Hart 2003) 337, 339, cited in David Dyzenhaus, *The Constitution of Law: Legality in a Time of Emergency* (CUP 2006) 208. French J's arguments are more consistent with John Finnis' espousal of a 'nationality-differentiated risk-acceptability' constitutional principle. See John Finnis, 'Nationality, Alienage and Constitutional Principle' (2007) 123 *LQR* 417. For a response to Finnis, see Rayner Thwaites, *The Liberty of Non-citizens: Indefinite Detention in Commonwealth Countries* (Hart 2014).

[53] For an analogous study of 'unbending sovereignty' and executive discretion in British and American approaches to asylum-seekers, see Christian Joppke, 'Asylum and State Sovereignty: A Comparison of the United States, Germany

Finally, the legislative reaction to the *Tampa* litigation merits mention for its entrenchment at the level of statute of the court's endorsement of this constitutional model, and its creation of the new legal 'grey hole' within which refugee law and policy was to operate for the next decade. In addition to retroactively validating the actions of the government, the legislature passed several privative clauses to oust the jurisdiction of the court over migration matters generally, 'excised' areas of Australia from the migration zone to preclude the operation of the Migration Act where boats arrive, and gave power to the minister to take boat arrivals to third countries where their claims could be processed, again by members of the executive, but now extraterritorially. These issues of excision and extraterritoriality will be explored further below.

B. An 'open source' executive power and the rule of law

A decade on, the *Tampa* case retains its constitutional significance, the two sets of opposing judgments standing as hallmarks to conflicting perspectives on the source, nature and exercise of executive power, especially when used coercively to impact on people's rights.[54] There remains particular disquiet amongst constitutional law scholars that the ascendancy of an ahistorical approach to identifying executive power has undermined established constitutional theory which evolved alongside parliamentary sovereignty to limit the abuse of arbitrary power. Commenting upon this trend, George Winterton expressed concern at the 'vague and politically-charged criterion' for establishing the content of the power:[55]

> An interpretation of Ch II [on the Executive Government] which ignores British and Australian constitutional history by taking its words at face value

---

and Britain' in Christian Joppke (ed.), *Challenge to the Nation State: Immigration in Western Europe and the United States* (OUP 1999); also Matthew Gibney, *The Ethics and Politics of Asylum Liberal Democracy and the Response to Refugees* (CUP 2004).

[54] For commentary on the case, see Peter Gerangelos 'Parliament, the Executive, the Governor-General and the Republic: The George Winterton Thesis' in HP Lee and Peter A Gerangelos (eds) *Constitutional Advancement in a Frozen Continent: Essays in Honour of George Winterton* (The Federation Press 2009); The Hon JJ Spigelman AC, 'Public Law and the Executive' (2010) 34 *Aust Bar Rev* 10; Duncan Kerr SC 'Executive Power and the Theory of its Limits: Still Evolving or Finally Settled?' (2011 Constitutional Law Conference, UNSW Gilbert and Tobin Centre of Public Law, 18 February 2011).

[55] George Winterton, 'The Relationship Between Commonwealth Legislative and Executive Power' (2004) 25 *Adel L Rev* 21, 34–5.

is not 'post-colonial', but rather one which judges the constitutional architecture merely by its façade. Furthermore, it is potentially dangerous, for it could lead to grossly exaggerated views of the Governor-General's independent powers … .

Some of French J's judicial peers expressed similar consternation at what was considered to be a dangerous decoupling of executive power from its constitutional bearings. As former NSW Supreme Court Chief Justice James Spigelman noted extrajudicially in 2010:[56]

> The extent of the executive power of the Commonwealth appears to have been cut free from the traditional conception of prerogative powers in a manner which means that there is now no source of guidance as to the boundaries of executive power.

For those steeped in British constitutional law, there is another quirk in the majority's approach to the source of executive power. It is a fundamental precept of British constitutional legal theory that no new prerogatives could be created after the 1688 constitutional settlement. As Diplock LJ famously said in *BBC v Johns* in 1965, 'it is 350 years and a civil war too late for the Queen's courts to broaden the prerogative'.[57] This rather unwieldy principle, which was intended to stand as a check on the extension of executive power absent legislation, has similarly fared poorly in the deferential hands of UK judges, as Adam Tomkins points out.[58] As with *ex parte Northumbria Police Authority*, commentators might have been left wondering post-*Tampa* whether the Australian courts are similarly 'prepared to grant to the Crown such elastic and ill-defined powers, and to subject their exercise to such modest – even superficial – review'.[59]

A deep disquiet with an executive able to define the limits of its own powers has been an underlying trope in Australian case law and commentary on executive power and rights, from the seminal *Communist Party* case onwards.[60] Indeed, the key principle in that case – that a stream

---

[56] Spigelman (n 54).

[57] *British Broadcasting Corporation v Jones* [1965] Ch 32, 79 (Diplock LJ), cited by Black CJ in Tampa case (n 42) 501 [30].

[58] Adam Tomkins, *Public Law* (Clarendon Press 2003) 83, noting the outcome in *R v Secretary of State for the Home Department, ex parte Northumbria Police Authority* [1989] 1 QB 26. Tomkins has also linked the two cases in Tomkins, *Our Republican Constitution* (n 38) 60.

[59] Tomkins, *Our Republican Constitution* (n 38).

[60] Communist Party case (n 28).

cannot rise above its source,[61] and that this reflects an assumption of the 'rule of law' in accordance with which the Constitution was framed[62] – is cited in talismanic fashion by those seeking to challenge both statutory grants of executive power and reliance upon inherent executive power under section 61.[63]

Yet, the High Court has proven adept at finding ways around such limitations, not least in cases seeking judicial imprimatur to restraints on liberty in the name of security or border control.[64] More recently, we have learned that the Commonwealth executive is able to act where it has found there to be a 'crisis', defined, it seems, by the national government itself, although open to limited constitutional review. The *Pape* decision – which did not directly concern rights and so will not be explored here – confirmed the worst fears of those who bemoaned setting free section 61 from the historical prerogative.[65] Summarizing these concerns, Heydon J noted:[66]

> The great maxim of governments seeking to widen their constitutional powers would be: 'Never allow a crisis to go to waste.' … It would be regrettable if

---

[61] Ibid. Fullaghar J on:

> The validity of a law or of an administrative act done under a law cannot be made to depend on the opinion of the law-maker, or the person who is to do the act, that the law or the consequence of the act is within the constitutional power upon which the law in question itself depends for its validity.

[62] Ibid., 193 (Dixon J).

[63] See, for instance, *Plaintiff S157/2002 v The Commonwealth* (2003) 211 CLR 476, 492 [31] (Gleeson CJ); 513 [103] (Gaudron, McHugh, Gummow, Kirby and Hayne JJ). More recently, it was argued unsuccessfully in *Plaintiff M47/2012 v Director-General of Security* [2012] HCA 46 [356]–[363] (Heydon J); more successfully in *South Australia v Totani* (2010) 242 CLR 1, 90–93 [232]–[237] (Hayne J); and partly successfully in *Pape v Federal Commissioner of Taxation* (2009) 238 CLR 1 (Pape case), 24 [10] (French CJ); 170 [496] and 193 [552] (Heydon J).

[64] See, for instance, *Thomas v Mowbray* (2007) 233 CLR 307 (on preventative 'control orders' in anti-terrorism legislation), and *Al-Kateb v Godwin* (2004) 219 CLR 562 (Al-Kateb case) (on mandatory, indefinite immigration detention, discussed below). The intra-curial debate between Kirby and Callinan JJ about the correctness of the decision in the Communist Party case in *Thomas v Mowbray* is illuminating, raising 'questions of value and policy preference that are not readily resolved by resort to legal argument'. See Hernan Pinto-Lopez and George Williams, '"Enemies Foreign and Domestic" *Thomas v Mowbray* and the New Scope of the Defence Power' (2008) 28 *U Tas LR* 84, 108.

[65] Pape case (n 63).

[66] Ibid., 193 [551] (Heydon J).

> the field were one in which the courts deferred to, and declined to substitute their judgment for, the opinion of the Executive or the legislature. That would be to give an 'unexaminable' power to the Executive, and history has shown, as Dixon J said, that it is often the Executive which engages in the unconstitutional supersession of democratic institutions. On the other hand, if the courts do not defer to the Executive or the legislature, it would be difficult for the courts to assess what is within and what is beyond power.

In some respects, *Tampa* and *Pape* bookend a period of high judicial deference, supported by a controversial and poorly theorized jurisprudence. The constitutional dilemma evident in *Tampa* and, more explicitly, *Pape* was identified by Duncan Kerr, former Attorney-General and now a judge on the Federal Court:[67]

> *Vadarlis* and *Pape* present a conundrum. In order to undertake the task of defining the limits of the executive power conferred by s 61, Australian courts have to make judgments requiring policy or political choices, thereby straying close to, or over, the boundary of the separation of powers imposed by Chapter III. On the other hand, to decline to undertake that task is unthinkable.

For Kerr, *Pape* may have confirmed the High Court's commitment to 'an autochthonous rationale for the source of Australian executive power,' but it also illustrated in both the majority and dissenting judgments 'that the court has begun to grapple with some of the complex underlying issues exposed by *Tampa*'.[68] This grappling was to reach maturation in *Williams v Commonwealth*,[69] in which the court limited the executive's capacity to enter into contracts and spend money absent legislative authority by reference to the principles of federalism and, crucially, the political oversight of the executive required by responsible government – a decision that is implicitly consistent with Stephen Gageler's principles of where deference must give way to vigilance. As I hope to show below, this shift in judicial attitudes towards the exercise of an unfettered

[67] Duncan Kerr, 'The High Court and the Executive: Emerging Challenges to the Underlying Doctrines of Responsible Government and the Rule of Law' (2009) 28 *U Tas LR* 145, 176.

[68] Ibid., 146.

[69] School Chaplains case (n 29). See Gabrielle Appleby and Stephen McDonald, 'Looking at the Executive Power through the High Court's New Spectacles' (2013) 35 *Syd LR* 253. The decision was further reinforced in *Williams (No 2)* (2014) 252 CLR 416.

executive power may also be reflected in more recent decisions of the court on executive control of non-citizens where fundamental rights are at stake.

Between *Tampa* and *Pape*, however, lie two important cases concerning statutory sources of broad executive power over detainees which illustrate contrasting judicial approaches towards the problem.

C. *Al-Kateb*: legalism, deference and the Australian anti-canon

Deference undoubtedly reached its rights-unfriendly nadir in a set of decisions which rubber stamped the constitutionality of legislation granting the executive the authority to detain non-citizens indefinitely for the purpose of excluding them from entering the 'Australian community'. As Gummow J suggested in dissent in *Al-Kateb*, 'exclusion' from such a legally ambiguous entity is an Orwellian euphemism, not least when it is being used to deny the basic right to personal liberty, potentially for life. Relying again on the *Communist Party* case, Gummow J noted:[70]

> The continued viability of the purpose of deportation or expulsion cannot be treated by the legislature as a matter purely for the opinion of the executive government. The reason is that it cannot be for the executive government to determine the placing from time to time of that boundary line which marks off a category of deprivation of liberty from the reach of Ch III [on the Judicature].

The validity of detention appeared in part to depend upon an executive expectation of eventual release. In Mr Al-Kateb's case, this was expressed by the Solicitor General, somewhat perversely, as an ongoing 'hope' that Palestine would eventually become a state, thereby allowing for his removal – an argument which Hayne J apparently found persuasive.[71] Relying upon such broad executive aspirations to support the protective purpose (and thus constitutionality) of detention, the majority found the legislation was (implicitly) unambiguous and thus incapable of being read against the presumptions against abrogation of fundamental rights or international obligations. That the House of Lords was almost simultaneously declaring the indefinite administrative detention of suspected international terrorists to be incompatible with both common law

[70] Al-Kateb case (n 64) 613 [140] (Gummow J).

[71] Ibid., 639 [230] (Hayne J).

and statutory human rights norms highlights the isolation within which Australia's highest court was operating at this time.[72]

To add to the legalist flavour of the decision, the court found that in characterizing the purpose of legislation, the *impact* of detention on vulnerable detainees was an irrelevancy. This reasoning reached its logical if perverse conclusion n *Re Woolley* in which the evidence of serious and long-term harm to children of indefinite administrative detention was found to have no bearing on whether the detention was punitive, the only benchmark considered by the court being that of statutory purpose.[73] The impact of detention and the statute's purposes were thus hermetically segregated despite the affective nature of the 'punishment' and the repeated conclusions by international bodies that Australia's regime amounted to arbitrary detention and cruel, inhuman and degrading treatment.[74]

It may be trite to reproach legalism for acting as a masking ideology for judicial policy predilections.[75] Nonetheless, the accusation here is apt. Despite the cold legal reasoning and their use of dry, inaccessible legal idiom, the language of the majority judges exhibits a palpable ethic of blame. The detainees are depicted as somehow responsible for their own fate, having taken a known risk when they came to Australia by boat that they would be indefinitely detained. Moreover, the speeches are mired in the discourse of illegality, not least when consequentialist reasoning is employed. Thus concern is expressed by Hayne J about not awarding an advantage to those who 'illegally … penetrate' our borders, and by McHugh J about protecting the operation of the Migration Act from those who would thwart it by their unlawful entry.

As these displays of policy preferences indicate, with deference comes judgment. A similar criticism can be levelled at Beaumont J's concurring speech in the *Tampa* case in which he intimated that standing might have

---

[72] See analysis in Matthew Zagor 'Judicial Rhetoric and Constitutional Identity' (2008) 19 *PLR* 271.

[73] *Re Woolley; Ex parte Applicants M276/2003* (2004) 225 CLR 1.

[74] See, for example, *A v Australia*, UN Human Rights Committee, UNHCR Communication No 560/1993, CCPR/C/59/D/560/1993, 3 April 1997; and more recently, *FKAG et al v Australia*, Communication No 2094/2011, CCPR/C/108/D/2094/2011, 26 July 2013; and *MMM et al v Australia*, Communication No 2136/2012, CCPR/C/108/D/2136/2012, 20 August 2013.

[75] See discussion of legalism as a 'noble lie' in Robert Woods, 'Rights Review in the High Court and the Cultural Limits of Judicial Power' 41 *FL Rev* 585, 605. For a detailed overview of legalism in Australian constitutional law, see Zines (n 17) 596–618; Cheryl Saunders, *The Constitution of Australia: A Contextual Analysis* (Hart 2011) 90–95.

been denied on the basis that 'it is wrong that a person should rely on his or her own unlawful act to secure an advantage which could not have been obtained if the person had acted lawfully'.[76] Judges, it seems, are not immune from internalizing the political trope that the 'genuine' refugee is one who does not jump the 'queue' in coming by boat.

The continuing mandatory detention of boat arrivals, and the failure of the courts to prevent the 'tragic' outcomes of indefinite detentions[77] remain key arguments wielded by proponents of a federal bill of rights.[78] As with *Tampa*, *Al-Kateb* rapidly took on the mantle of a 'moment' for the discipline, an anti-canonical 'inflection point'[79] that confirms the worst suspicions about the Australian constitutional regime and the misplaced trust it places in the executive on matters of aliens and rights; as Jamal Greene said about *Dred Scott*, 'we hate it because it abided constitutional evil'.[80] That the courts retain a limited oversight over detention is hardly reassuring. As Aronson and Groves have pointed out, 'Australian legislation has tended to undermine the writ [of habeas corpus] by legalizing draconian detention powers, rather than by direct attacks on the writ itself'.[81] The availability of habeas may thus be constitutionally protected, but it provides little if any protection against arbitrary yet statutorily supported administrative detention.[82]

The result is what David Dyzenhaus has described as a judicially sanctioned grey rather than black hole, where the executive can cast those

---

[76] Tampa case (n 42) 518 [107] (Beaumont J). Beaumont J displayed a similar attitude in costs proceedings: *Ruddock v Vadarlis (No 2)* (2001) 115 FCR 229, 247 [56] (Beaumont J: 'the real object of the litigation is not to uphold the liberty of the subject, but to bring non-citizens into Australia').

[77] Al-Kateb case (n 64) 580 [31] (McHugh J); *Al Khafaji* (2004) 219 CLR 664, 668 [4] (McHugh J).

[78] See the submissions to the Brennan committee, and the frequent references to the Al-Kateb case as a rallying point.

[79] Terminology borrowed from Robert Ashman, 'Australia's Dred Scott' (2013) [paper with author].

[80] Jamal Greene, 'The Anticanon' (2011) 125 *Harv L Rev* 379, 411. Kirby J made the analogy with *Dred Scott* and *Korematsu,* suggesting that the decision would eventually be viewed 'with a mixture of curiosity and embarrassment'. See Al-Kateb case (n 64) 629 [190] (Kirby J).

[81] See Mark Aronson and Matthew Groves, *Judicial Review of Administrative Action* (5th edn, Thomson Reuters 2013) 840.

[82] The High Court struck down a provision that would have deprived it of the power to review the legality of detention of non-citizens in *Chu Kheng Lim v Minister for Immigration, Local Government and Ethnic Affairs* (1992) 176 CLR 1.

it wishes to exclude without fear of meaningful judicial review.[83] Such grey holes are 'in substance black but ... in effect worse because they give to official lawlessness the façade of legality', thereby undermining what he calls the 'rule of law project'.[84] The retention of habeas and judicial endorsement of the statutory regime of mandatory indefinite detention provide such a veneer. To take the cosmological analogy a step further, the 'grey hole' is designed to operate as a black hole, acting as an 'event horizon' whereby conduct which occurs in its vicinity has no effect on the legal system itself.

This analysis begs the question of judicial deference. Dyzenhaus again is instructive, adopting (and adapting) Murray Hunt's explanatory model of contemporary forms of deference. Hunt argues that judges and commentators tend to flip arbitrarily between the narratives of democratic (or political) positivism and liberal constitutionalism, employing the former when deferring to the 'sovereign' power of Parliament. As the above cases demonstrate, such deference has historically characterized matters touching on national security and immigration. For our purposes, a narrative of political or constitutional positivism arguably characterizes the deferential approaches of the majorities in *Tampa* and *Al-Kateb*. By contrast, liberal constitutionalism and 'rule of law' rhetoric have triumphed when the court's jurisdiction has been threatened, as illustrated in the next case to be considered – that is *Plaintiff S157*.

D. Rejecting a self-defined jurisdictional space: *Plaintiff S157/2002*

The Gleeson High Court (1998–2008) was both condemned and praised for its return to so-called 'strict legalism'.[85] Yet when it came to legislation that attempted to oust the court's original jurisdiction to judicially review executive decisions, the court found the amorphous principles of the 'rule of law' more appealing, and its tolerance for rights-limiting executive power overly strained.

As noted above, the post-*Tampa* package of legislative reforms included a privative (or ouster) clause designed, according to the government, to expand the jurisdiction conferred on administrative decision-makers in migration cases in such a way that excess of jurisdiction would only occur in the event of a decision not made in *good faith*[86] – a variety

---

83 See Dyzenhaus (n 52) 3.

84 Ibid., 59, 207.

85 See Zines (n 17) 606.

86 The government relied upon a similar argument of 'good faith' in executive decisions in *Plaintiff M70* (2011) 244 CLR 144 (Plaintiff M70 case). Consistent with the 'trust' model of government, it seems that courts can only

of the 'trust us' deferential attitude which has characterized all such rights-limiting provisions implemented in the public interest. As drafted, the provision (which is still on the books) precludes any type of judicial review or the issuing of any type of judicial remedy or writ.[87] Although its express policy objective was to protect an overburdened judicial system from unmeritorious litigation, the legislative amendments were accompanied by the political rhetoric that 'determination of protection matters should lie with the executive and with elected politicians, rather than with the unelected judiciary'.[88] In legal terms, as the Solicitor General put it, 'where one is dealing with immigration there is no reason why Parliament cannot delegate to the executive branch the power to exercise a totally open-ended discretion as to what aliens can and what aliens cannot come to and stay in Australia'.[89]

The privative clause, it was argued, achieved this end by implicitly extending the lawful authority of the decision maker.[90] Again, the spatial metaphor seems apt: a legislatively crafted provision was to operate by expanding the jurisdictional space within which executive errors could be made.[91] The legal fiction was thus maintained that the judicial review jurisdiction of the court was not being restricted or ousted; errors that went to jurisdiction could still be remedied.

Consistent with the approach he would later take in his dissent in *Al-Kateb*, Gleeson CJ read the provision in light of the constitutional 'assumption' of the rule of law, recognized by Dixon J in the *Communist Party* case and entrenched in the judicial review jurisdiction of the court.[92] More specifically, the court was concerned that the provision purported to provide the executive with a capacity to define the limits of its own jurisdiction. This would have amounted to an exercise of judicial

---

intervene when this 'faith' has been breached. Otherwise, they should not intervene at all.

[87] Migration Act 1958 (Cth) s 474.

[88] Mary Crock, 'Judging Refugees: The Clash of Power and Institutions in the Development of Australian Refugee Law' (2004) 26 *Syd LR* 72.

[89] DMJ Bennett QC in Plaintiff S157 of 2002 v The Commonwealth of Australia S157/2002 [2002] HCATrans 420 (3 September 2002).

[90] This argument was based on the principle developed by Dixon J in *R v Hickman; Ex parte Fox* (1945) 70 CLR 598. See discussion in Nicholas Gouliaditis, 'Privative Clauses: Epic Fail' (2010) 34 *MULR* 870, 872–4.

[91] By analogy, the 'margin of appreciation' developed by the European Court of Human Rights employs a similar metaphor of fungible 'space' within which a degree of discretion is judicially recognized. See discussion in Hickman (n 39) 124.

[92] Commonwealth of Australia Constitution Act 1900, s 75(v).

power, and thus be unconstitutional for breach of the separation of powers doctrine.[93] Again, for Gleeson CJ, this conflicted with his constitutionalism. He quoted from Denning LJ that '[i]f tribunals were to be at liberty to exceed their jurisdiction without any check by the courts the rule of law would be at an end'.[94]

To avoid such an outcome, the provision was read in such a way as not to protect 'decisions' made in error of jurisdiction, including where there had been a failure to accord a person procedural fairness. Such 'decisions' were void, and not 'privative clause decisions' at all, and therefore not protected from review by the clause. The result is that the provision does little if any work, but remains constitutional – an outcome, as Groves and Lee point out, that is 'a curious mix of deference and assertion'.[95] The decision thereby retains its legalist character by cloaking its policy rationale in the impartiality of statutory construction, a process which Thomas Poole described as 'legalistic alchemy' or 'active formalism'.[96]

Plaintiff S157/2002 may have represented a blow to the new rights-restrictive migration regime, but was explicable by reference to the jealousness with which the High Court protects its own jurisdiction, and the entrenchment of the constitutional writs. A more substantive legal vacuum, however, was created by way of those legislative provisions which made up what became known as the 'Pacific Solution'. This was to be unpacked by a differently constituted court in *Plaintiff M61* and *Plaintiff M70*.

---

93 See *Plaintiff S157/2002 v The Commonwealth* (2003) 211 CLR 476, 484 [9] (Gleeson CJ); 505 [73] (Gaudron, McHugh, Gummow, Kirby and Hayne JJ).

> 'It is beyond the capacity of the Parliament to confer upon an administrative tribunal the power to make an authoritative and conclusive decision as to the limits of its own jurisdiction, because that would involve an exercise of judicial power.'

94 Ibid., 483 [8] (Gleeson CJ) quoting Denning LJ in *R v Medical Appeal Tribunal; Ex parte Gilmore* [1957] 1 QB 574, 586.

95 Groves and Lee (n 20) 363.

96 Thomas Poole, 'Common Law of Judicial Review or Juridical Archipelago? (On the Future of Administrative Law, Comparative Administrative Law Conference, Yale Law School, 7–9 May 2009). See also Duncan Kerr and George Williams, 'Review of Executive Action and the Rule of Law Under the Australian Constitution' (2003) 14 *PLR* 219, 222 ('intriguing blend of pragmatism and principle').

4.2.3 *Plaintiff M61* and *Plaintiff M70*: Discerning New Shades of Grey

A. Excision and extraterritoriality: setting the scene

The post-*Tampa* refugee regime consisted of two key mechanisms, both designed to implement a policy of legal and physical exclusion, and both essentially still on foot. The first, known as excision, involves removing those areas of Australia most frequently reached by unauthorized boats from the operation of key provisions of the Migration Act. Specifically, those without visas who arrive by sea in an 'excised offshore place' become 'offshore entry persons'[97] who, as a result of that status, are precluded from making valid visa applications.[98] This effectively resolved the dilemma of the Tampa, consolidating legislatively what the court had allowed to occur using section 61 of the Constitution. The fate of those who arrived post-*Tampa* would now be resolved by a second mechanism whereby the minister was empowered to 'take' an offshore entry person to a declared country for processing.[99]

Two broad ministerial discretions still accompany this basic statutory architecture. Under sections 46A and 195A of the Migration Act the minister can 'lift the bar' on an unauthorized arrival, allowing them to apply for a visa or be granted a visa respectively where the minister 'thinks it is in the public interest' – words traditionally considered impervious to judicial second-guessing. This power can only be exercised by the minister personally, and, the minister is under 'no duty to consider whether to exercise the power' – otherwise known as a 'no consideration' clause.[100] The second discretion (since replaced) concerned the minister's power to declare a country as one to which offshore entry persons could be taken. In the weeks following the arrival of the Tampa, both Nauru and Papua New Guinea were so declared by the minister, and asylum-seekers taken there for processing.[101]

---

[97] Section 5 of the Migration Act 1958 (Cth) was amended in May 2013, the term 'offshore entry person' being replaced with 'unauthorised maritime arrival', defined in s 5AA.

[98] Migration Act 1958 (Cth), s 46A.

[99] Ibid., s 198A, now replaced with s 198AD.

[100] For a history of no consideration clauses and the innovative approach of the Court to their interpretation in *Plaintiff M61/2010E v Commonwealth* (2010) 243 CLR 319 (Plaintiff M61 case), see Christopher Tran, 'The "Fatal Conundrum" of "No-Consideration" Clauses after *Plaintiff M61*' (2011) 39 *FL Rev* 303.

[101] The then Minister for Immigration made a declaration under s 198A(3)(a) of the Migration Act 1958 (Cth) relating to the Republic of Nauru on 2 October 2001, and relating to Papua New Guinea on 12 October 2001.

This Pacific Solution, with its unique mechanisms of excision and extraterritorial processing, thereby saw the spatial metaphor reach full maturity. Refugee scholars turned in particular to Agamben, whose work on the camp (inspired by Hannah Arendt) seemed particularly apposite for appreciating the new liminality within which asylum seekers were being held; the Australian refugee camps on Christmas Island and in third countries were posited, justifiably if somewhat inaccurately, as existing in a 'state of exception', carved out of the law by executive and legislative decree, and susceptible neither to Australian judicial oversight and remedy nor media scrutiny or political accountability. For Hyndman and Mountz, this respatialization of asylum[102] was the result of its recharacterization as a security issue which in turn involved a moving of the legal into the political, a 'neutralizing' of the rule of law in the name of security, where 'sovereignty is exercised in the act of suspension, and also in the self-allocation of the legal prerogative'.[103] Similarly, Crock and Ghezelbash described the post-*Tampa* legislative regime as designed 'to match the physical isolation of asylum seekers with their metaphysical isolation from the rule of law in Australia'.[104] The cosmological metaphor employed by Lord Steyn to describe Guantanamo as a 'legal black hole' now seemed particularly apt, and was unsurprisingly adopted as part of the critical discourse.

With the election of the Labor Government in 2007, the camps in Nauru and Manus Island were shut down. Adopting the language of its detractors, the Pacific Solution was depicted by the incoming government as inhumane, unfair, ineffective, wasteful, punitive and a 'stain on Australia's international reputation', as well as an 'outsourcing' of Australia's obligations under the Convention.[105] Yet the legislative machinery of the Pacific Solution remained on the books, and when the

---

102 See Jennifer Hyndman and Alison Mountz, 'Another Brick in the Wall? Neo-Refoulement and the Externalization of Asylum by Australia and Europe' (2008) 43 *Government and Opposition* 249.

103 Ibid., 251.

104 Mary Crock and Daniel Ghezelbash, 'Due Process and Rule of Law as Human Rights: The High Court and the "Offshore" Processing of Asylum Seekers' (2011) 18 *AJ Admin L* 101, 103.

105 See, for instance, Senator Chris Evans, Minister for Immigration, 'Refugee Policy Under The Rudd Government – The First Year' (Address to the Refugee Council of Australia, 17 November 2008). The government had also ended temporary protection visas for similar reasons, and announced a new, more humane approach to immigration detention, while retaining the mandatory detention provisions in the 1958 Act.

number of boat arrivals rose again in late 2007,[106] it became apparent that the government would utilize excision in a new way.

The first approach was to set up a separate processing regime for so-called 'Irregular Maritime Arrivals'. In a key public statement released on 29 July 2008, the government announced that in the future all claims for asylum by offshore entry persons would be processed on the remote territory of Christmas Island. This would be achieved through a purportedly non-statutory refugee determination process during which time offshore entry persons would be held, indefinitely, in a newly enlarged detention centre. As had occurred in 2001, the government insisted that it would still act consistently with its obligations under the 1951 Refugee Convention. This was to be achieved by ensuring that in each case that a person screened in as a 'genuine' Convention refugee would be considered by the Minister for Immigration under his non-compellable discretion to 'lift the bar' on visa applications and grants under section 46A or section 195A of the Migration Act.

The examination by the courts of these two provisions provided the first significant challenge to the new respatialised asylum model, and an opportunity for the court to indicate a change in judicial attitudes towards executive detention and over-reliance on the inherent executive power in section 61 of the Constitution.

B. *Plaintiff M61* (the *Offshore Processing* case): the imperative of detention and international obligations

Plaintiff M61/M69 concerned two Sri Lankan boat arrivals who challenged findings that they were not refugees under the new purportedly non-statutory regime.[107] As the High Court noted, the government's submissions were that:

> the assessments and review had been undertaken in exercise of non-statutory executive power under s 61 of the Constitution. It followed, so they submitted, that there was no obligation to afford procedural fairness in the conduct of those assessments and reviews, *and that it mattered not whether those who undertook the inquiries had misunderstood or misapplied the law.*[108]

From the government's perspective, the combination of excision and the bar on making visa applications had carved out a space within which a

---

[106] For a consolidation of the numbers since 2001, see Refugee Council of Australia, 'Statistics on Asylum Seekers Arriving in Australia' <http://www.refugeecouncil.org.au/r/stat-as.php> accessed 30 April 2015.

[107] Plaintiff M61 case (n 100).

[108] Ibid., 336 [15] (emphasis added).

full discretionary non-statutory executive power could be utilized to consider a non-citizen's refugee claim, free from judicial interference or even, it seems, the obligation to adhere to established legal principles and norms. Unlimited discretion provided the government with a *choice*, but not an *obligation*, to act consistently with legal principle or precedent. This went beyond the 'extension of jurisdiction' argument made in *Plaintiff S157/2002*: decision-makers could now err with impunity; not even a 'good faith' limitation to their discretion existed.

A key issue before the court was whether the offshore processing regime was, in fact, non-statutory. To answer that question, the court needed to consider those post-*Tampa* provisions which created the Pacific Solution, including those that precluded non-citizens from applying for visas and provided for their removal to offshore countries for processing. Referring to ministerial statements and procedural documents which had accompanied the introduction of the Pacific Solution in 2001, the court found that the provisions which carved out the excised space were part of an express scheme to implement the 1951 Refugee Convention.[109] As a result, the Migration Act was now to be read as reflecting Parliament's intention to fulfil Australia's international obligations.[110]

It was an unintentionally ironic finding. For most international law scholars, the 2001 changes which brought in excision and offshore processing were tantamount at best to a breach of the obligation to perform treaties in 'good faith', at worst to a repudiation of the 1951 Refugee Convention.[111] Yet here the High Court concluded that the very mechanism by which Australia had limited its obligations through legislation had in fact provided those obligations with a statutory basis, transforming the Migration Act from the 'facultative' machinery legislation French J had identified in *Tampa* to the detriment of the rescuees, to one with a rights-protective purpose at its core, against which all other provisions were now to be read.

The character of the Migration Act as implementing an international human rights treaty provided the necessary but not sufficient context for interpreting the 'no consideration' clause and concluding that the decision-making power was, in fact, statutory. The more specific rights imperative against which the clause was to be construed arose instead courtesy of a controversial but ingenuous decision of Deborah Mortimer SC, appearing for Plaintiff M61, to concede the legality of detention. At

---

[109] Ibid., 341 [34].

[110] Ibid., 339 [27]: 'the text and structure of the Act proceed on the footing that the Act provides power to respond to Australia's international obligations'.

[111] Vienna Convention on the Law of Treaties 1969, arts 26 and 60.

first blush, this seemed a missed opportunity to reargue *Al-Kateb* before a potentially more sympathetic court.[112] However, the legality of detention was to be an essential component of a sophisticated argument that the assessment and review scheme were, in fact, statutory.

As the court noted[113]

> how could continued detention under the Migration Act be lawful if what prolongs the detention (the Department making inquiries) has no statutory footing? ... It is not readily to be supposed that a statutory power to detain a person permits continuation of that detention at the unconstrained discretion of the Executive. Yet a proposition of that kind lay at the heart of the submissions advanced on behalf of the Commonwealth and the Minister.

This perspective on the exercise of a statutory power thus had crucial ramifications for the legality of detention. As the court reiterated, detention was valid for the purposes of granting a visa, deportation or removal.[114] That the minister was considering whether to allow a valid application to be made *in each instance* ensured the detention remained valid.[115] Otherwise, such detention would not be authorized by the Migration Act.

The court also relied upon the principle that where a statute confers a power upon which a right, interest or legitimate expectation depends, then natural justice governs the exercise of that power.[116] Here the requirements of procedural fairness were attached to the minister's decision to consider whether to exercise the power to 'lift the bar' because that decision directly affected the claimant's liberty by prolonging the detention of that person for so long as the assessment took to complete.[117] Once again, the right of liberty of person played a crucial role in construing the Migration Act and ensuring judicial oversight.

The result of this rather convoluted but compelling reasoning was twofold. At the practical level, the process for determining refugee claims of those who were statutorily barred from applying for visas was found to have a statutory basis, and thus be subject to the rules of procedural fairness and the precedents set by the courts in the area of administrative

---

112 In the six years that had passed since the Al-Kateb case was handed down, only two of the majority judges remained on the bench – Hayne and Heydon JJ.

113 Plaintiff M61 case (n 100) 348 [63]–[64].

114 Ibid., 337–8 [21]–[22].

115 Ibid., 351 [71].

116 Ibid., 352 [74], citing *Annetts v McCann* (1990) 170 CLR 596, 598.

117 Ibid., 353 [77].

law and interpretation of the 1951 Refugee Convention. Furthermore, review by the courts of all these matters remained on foot – even when conducted by private entities.

C. *Plaintiff M61*: legalism and the challenge of rights

Plaintiff M61 marked a significant if largely unheralded shift for the judicial protection of non-citizen rights from arbitrary executive abrogation. The decision was rightly hailed as a vindication of the rule of law, holding the government legally accountable and minimizing the application of broad, unreviewable discretions. However, the move away from deference to the executive in its exercise of non-statutory power in border security, and the new willingness to see the Migration Act as implementing human rights treaty obligations, has been less commented upon.[118] This may, in part, have to do with the judicial language employed. For such a seminal case, the speeches are unusually devoid of rule of law rhetoric (the phrase appears nowhere) or flowery appeals to the fundamental right of liberty (Blackstone goes unmentioned). Neither constitutional imperatives nor common law principles of legality were front and centre, even if their relevance was discernible. Rather, the court did something that has increasingly characterized its approach to political matters in recent years: it presented its decision as one of statutory construction.

It may be that this is a deliberate strategy, a way of avoiding more controversial forms of rights-based review and insulating judicial decisions from political attack. That it is part of a legitimacy-building exercise whereby legalism will transition in the coming years into rights-protective judicial review with a more explicit political content is, however, more uncertain:[119] the methodology still remains too internally convoluted and case-specific, the High Court's concern with public confidence too sensitive. Moreover, as Woods points out, legalistic methodology undercuts the Court's capacity to 'move into more elevated and openly political forms of rights review'.[120] It does not resolve the tension between the competing constitutionalisms, or assist in predicting judicial direction in the future.

---

[118] An exception to this is the treatment by Thwaites (n 52). See also Crock and Ghezelbash (n 104) 108, who note that an implicit reliance upon international human rights law underpinned the decision.

[119] The strategy of building legitimacy is discussed in Woods (n 75).

[120] Ibid.

D. *Plaintiff M70* and the legislative reassertion of executive power

Plaintiff M61 caused a minor political stir, although primarily as a convenient stick to be wielded by the opposition against a government depicted as having lost control of the nation's borders.[121] Its legal importance, and the extent to which it may have reflected a fundamental shift of sentiment and method on the bench, seemed to be lost on the political class. The government's loss the following year in *Plaintiff M70,*[122] however, was to have more sustained political and legal consequences.

Plaintiff M70 concerned the so-called 'Malaysian Solution'. In July 2011, the government announced that it had signed an agreement with Malaysia to send 800 offshore entry persons to that country in return for 4000 recognized refugees in Malaysian camps – a deal aimed both at alleviating the burden on Malaysia while acting as a disincentive to those who might be tempted to jump the mythical refugee queue. On 25 July 2011, Malaysia was declared under the Migration Act as a country to which unauthorized arrivals could be taken for processing. Shortly thereafter, the first planeload of asylum-seekers was chosen for removal. On 31 August 2011, the High Court found that the minister's declaration was made without power and was invalid.

At face value, the decision again revolved around statutory construction. Indeed, the point was made repeatedly by refugee law commentators in the days after the handing down of the decision, perhaps in an understandable attempt to allay what rapidly became a bi-partisan attack on the court's credentials to make such a politically significant decision.[123] Yet to characterize *Plaintiff M70* as 'simply' or 'purely' about

---

[121] See, for instance, 'Offshore Processing to Continue, despite High Court Ruling, says Gillard Government' *Sydney Morning Herald* (Sydney, 11 November 2010), which reports the opposition foreign affairs spokesperson, Julie Bishop, saying 'this represents a total failure on Labor's part on protecting Australia's borders'.

[122] Plaintiff M70 case (n 86).

[123] Michelle Foster on ABC Radio National's Law Report on 6 September 2011 ('It was simply a case of interpreting the relevant provisions of the Migration Act'); George Williams in *The Australian* ('The High Court simply found that Malaysia didn't satisfy those criteria. ... They're written very clearly in the act'; Joe Kelly, 'Bench ruling on Malaysian Solution slammed as narrow' 2 September 2011); Jane McAdam on ABC's PM on 31 August 2011 ('it was a decision focused purely on a particular section of the Migration Act ...'). Contrast Foster's subsequent view of the case's significance in 'The Implications of the Failed "Malaysian Solution": The Australian High Court and Refugee Responsibility Sharing at International Law' (2012) 13 *Melbourne Journal of*

statutory construction is disingenuous, just as distinguishing it from the constitutionally-centered *Tampa* decision, with its emphasis on non-statutory executive power, misses revealing lines of comparison.

At one level, the main argument was relatively straightforward. Section 198A(3) of the Migration Act authorized the minister to declare that a specified country provides certain forms of protection to asylum seekers and refugees, meets relevant human rights standards in providing that protection, and provides access to an effective procedure for assessing their need for protection. The plaintiffs submitted that these were objective jurisdictional facts,[124] and thus, consistent with the 'rule of law', reviewable by the court, with limited scope for the notion of 'judicial deference'.

In response, the government presented several arguments that ultimately called for judicial restraint in scrutinizing executive decision-making. Its primary position was that section 198A of the Migration Act at most required the minister to act in 'good faith' in making a declaration, regardless of the 'truth of the content of that declaration'.[125] Declarations, in other words, were to be assessed on the basis of trust rather than accuracy or truth.

Yet the government's preliminary argument was more far reaching. According to the Solicitor General, the government could rely on removal under section 198 of the Migration Act, the broad power to remove non-citizens 'as soon as reasonably practicable'. This provision has no express criteria for its exercise, and was thus potentially quarantined from judicial scrutiny for any alleged absence of jurisdictional facts preconditioning its exercise, or jurisdictional error in its construction. Section 198, in other words, was presented as the government's *Tampa*-like trump card, a broad executive power to remove in order to exclude.

None of these arguments – neither the 'trust us' attitude towards section 198A of the Migration Act nor the unconditional sovereign power purportedly available under section 198 – found favour with the majority. Consistent with its earlier characterization of the Migration Act in *Plaintiff M61* as implementing Australia's international obligations, the majority found that to read section 198 as providing a power to remove a

---

International Law 395, 398 ('valuable contribution to international refugee law jurisprudence').

[124] Five judges reached this conclusion. French CJ, consistent with his earlier decisions on the Federal Court, relied instead on plain jurisdictional error. Heydon J dissented.

[125] Plaintiff M70 case (n 86) 194 [108] (Gummow, Hayne, Crennan and Bell JJ). See also 178 [56] and 180 [58].

refugee claimant to any country would deny the legislative intention evident from the Migration Act as a whole to facilitate compliance with treaty obligations.[126] The broad discretion to remove, in other words, could not be used to deport a *potential* refugee towards whom Australia might have protection obligations. Only section 198A, with its Convention-derived protections, could do that job. Once a person's claim to be a refugee was finalized, then section 198 could come into play.

Attention therefore focused upon the various factors in section 198A of the Migration Act which formed part of the minister's declaration. Although the provision listed very clear elements, it was far from clear that the declaration itself was judicially reviewable or, if it were, that they were objective let alone jurisdictional facts. Indeed, the provision had been drafted to avoid exactly such judicial scrutiny by a government which, it should be remembered, had only recently before its passage argued the 'act of state' doctrine with respect of the Tampa rescuees.

Again drawing upon in *Plaintiff M61*, the court found that references in section 198A of the Migration Act to access to procedures and provision of protections 'are to be understood as a reflex of Australia's obligations'.[127] As a result, '[t]he access and protections to which those sub-paragraphs refer must be provided as a matter of legal obligation'.[128] As Malaysia had no such obligations in domestic or international law, the declaration was found to be invalidly made.

It is not unforeseeable that an earlier bench would have agreed with Heydon J that these were matters touching upon international comity best assessed by the executive.[129] The key to such an understanding, as Heydon J suggested, lay in the *Tampa*-esque notion of an absolute ('entirely free') executive discretion with respect to the entry of 'foreigners'.[130] That, by 2011, Heydon J was a lone voice in making such

---

[126] Ibid.

[127] Ibid., 195 [116] and 196–7 [119] (Gummow, Hayne, Crennan and Bell JJ).

[128] Ibid. Plus French CJ, ibid 182 [66]:

> The questions the Minister must ask himself, about whether the relevant 'access' and 'protection' are provided and 'human rights standards' are met, are questions which cannot be answered without reference to the domestic laws of the specified country, including its Constitution and statute laws, and the international legal obligations to which it has bound itself. The use of the terms 'provides access … to effective procedures', 'protection' and 'relevant human rights standards' are all indicative of enduring legal frameworks.

[129] Plaintiff M70 case (n 86) 211 [166] (Heydon J).

[130] Heydon J opened his decision with a direct accusation of hypocrisy leveled against the Human Rights Commissioner and former Federal Court

deferential appeals to sovereignty cannot be explained solely by reference to the statutory text and the common law tools for its examination.

E. Responding to *Plaintiff M70* and beyond

The Prime Minister's response to *Plaintiff M70* was immediate and personal. She took specific aim at the Chief Justice for inconsistency, and accused the court, tellingly if bizarrely, of having missed an opportunity to 'send a message' to asylum seekers.[131] There followed extraordinary scenes in the Parliament over the next few months as the government tried to pass legislation to overcome the decision so that the executive's power to take asylum seekers offshore without judicial interference could be restored. This it eventually did in August 2012 by way of scrapping section 198A of the Migration Act and replacing it with a provision that no longer contains any obvious objective facts. The new declaration power in section 198AB is premised upon only one condition – that the minister 'thinks that it is in the national interest to designate the country to be a regional processing country'.[132]

With the election of the Abbott Government in September 2013, the resurrection of exclusive executive control over refugees continued apace, from the militarization of border control to the proposed repeal of complementary protection criteria and their replacement with non-reviewable, non-compellable ministerial powers.[133] By 2015, this extension of absolute ministerial discretion had been further codified in legislative amendments deliberately aimed at purging *Plaintiff M61* and its legacy from the jurisprudence.[134]

Justice, Catherine Branson, and continued with an indirect attack on the Chief Justice by citing his earlier decisions while on the Federal Court (notably *P1/2003 v MIMA* [2003] FCA 1029) as direct authority. Specifically, he noted earlier cases which cited with approval Lord Mustill's statement in *T v Immigration Officer* [1996] AC 742, 754 that [this country] 'is entirely free to decide, as a matter of executive discretion, what foreigners it allows to remain within its boundaries'.

131 Matthew Franklin 'Julia Gillard versus the High Court as the PM takes aim at Chief Justice Robert French' *The Australian* (2 September 2011).

132 Migration Act 1958 (Cth), s 198AB. In considering the 'national interest', the Minister must have regard to the assurances given by the country as to whether it will adhere to the non-refoulement norm and make or allow to be made an assessment of refugee status.

133 Migration Amendment (Regaining Control over Australia's Protection Obligations) Bill 2013.

134 Migration and Maritime Powers Legislation Amendment (Resolving the Asylum Legacy Caseload) Act 2014, sch 5.

While the decisions in *Plaintiff M61* and *Plaintiff M70* were largely greeted with praise within the legal profession,[135] accusations of judicial activism, judicial hegemony, and a creeping judicialization of politics were also to be found among constitutional law commentators. Thus Ron Sackville, a prominent social justice advocate and former Federal Court judge, derided the agenda of administrative justice and the rise of 'jurisdictional error' as heralding a 'new age of judicial hegemony'.[136] The court, however, continues to give mixed signals. At one level, there are indications it recognizes the limits of its power play with Parliament, rejecting challenges to the recent changes to the Migration Act, once again courtesy of the rules of statutory construction. Thus after two days of argument, a six-member bench of the High Court held unanimously – and with unprecedented brevity – that that the new 'regional processing' provisions were within the Constitution, curtly rejecting a proportionality test[137] which would have required consideration of the practical operation of the manifestly rights-infringing offshore detention regime. By focusing exclusively upon a broad *Al-Kateb*-esque reading of the constitutional purpose of removal, the court skillfully avoided any rights-based inquiry, and another run-in with an already riled legislature. The court similarly limited its inquiry into the validity of the designation of Papua New Guinea as a 'regional processing country',[138] noting that 'what is in the national interest is largely a political question', and rejecting the argument that the minister was required to take into account other considerations, including Australia and Papua New Guinea's international human rights obligations, and Papua New Guinea's capacity to implement these obligations. The brevity of the decision appeared to reflect an unwillingness to test too far the limits of its nascent rights-protective stance. Yet within six months, the court was revisiting executive detention in a decision which many scholars consider to reflect a move away from the

---

[135] This praise extended beyond refugee lawyers, relying primarily upon the decisions' broad 'rule of law' characteristic. See, for instance, Peter Johnston, Simon Young, Richard Hooker and Tom Pontre, 'Probing the Frontiers of Administrative Law' (2011) 67 *AIAL Forum* 1, 28 ('[Plaintiff M70 case] contributes significantly to the meaningful solidification of the "rule of law" ideal'.)

[136] Ronald Sackville, 'An Age of Judicial Hegemony', *The Australian Financial Review*, 13 November, 2012.

[137] See *Plaintiff S156-2013 v Minister for Immigration and Border Protection* [2014] HCA 22 (18 June 2014) [22]–[38]) (French CJ, Hayne, Crennan, Kiefel, Bell and Keane JJ).

[138] Ibid [40].

cold constitutional reasoning in *Al-Kateb*.[139] Again, the decision displays little in the way of rights-rhetoric, saying much by saying little at all. The façade of apolitical legalism in both cases ensures commentators must read between the lines to ascertain the existence of shifting judicial attitudes.

4.2.4 Conclusion: Legalism and Judicial Penetration of the Grey Zone

The experiments in excision, exclusion and extraterritoriality which have characterized Australian refugee policy for the past decade were accompanied by assertions of executive power that presented new challenges to the usually deferential court. The *Tampa* case represents the high point of judicial endorsement of an unmoored power, the reasoning relying upon a muscular and undifferentiated notion of sovereignty that was to be used by successive governments to justify everything from executive detention to removal of non-citizens without due process. Yet the legislative creation of such spaces of legal exception within which executive power expands and rights protection diminishes was always going to test the judiciary's 'rule of law' mettle.

First, the High Court has confirmed a general retreat from the 'open source' approach to an executive power cut free from its historical and structural constitutional moorings.[140] *Plaintiff M61* and *Plaintiff M70* indicate that this greater caution extends to the traditional deference in the control of non-citizens. Sovereignty is no longer a trump card behind which assumptions about the roles of the limbs of government can be shielded before the court. Connectedly, we seem to be witnessing a gradual re-assertion of an Australian variety of legal constitutionalism encroaching upon what might be considered sacrosanct ground for the political constitution: border control and migration.

Although Australian judges are reticent in providing clues to their motivations, there are several potential causes for this shift. A concern to limit rights breaches has discernibly, if quietly, provided a judicial goal. Liberty of the person in particular played an essential role in *Plaintiff M61*. It may also be that we are seeing a reaction to the anti-canonical

---

[139] *Plaintiff S4-2014 v Minister for Immigration and Border Protection* [2014] HCA 34 (11 September 2014). See Joyce Chia, 'High Court Verdict Spells the End for Australian Immigration Detention as We Know It' *The Guardian* (London, 11 September 2014) <http://www.theguardian.com/commentisfree/2014/sep/11/high-court-verdict-spells-the-end-for-australian-immigration-detention-as-we-know-it> accessed 30 April 2015.

[140] School Chaplains case (n 29).

status which *Al Kateb*, *Re Woolley*, and *Tampa* have achieved domestically and internationally. It cannot have escaped judicial attention how out of line Australian courts are with their common law cousins: the High Court's well-known exceptionalism is increasingly in tension with their place in a rights-conscious global judiciary.

That the judicial branch now sees 'administrative justice' as part of a legitimate judicial agenda may also have influenced its new direction. This is probably as much an institutional as an ideological factor. Given the jurisprudence, it is inevitable that the consolidation of the doctrines of 'jurisdictional error' and 'jurisdictional fact', and the constitutionalization of the prerogative writs in section 75(v) of the Constitution, would have an influence on judicial dispositions towards executive conduct more broadly, and a greater propensity to use this constitutionally entrenched power of judicial review as a rights-corrective mechanism.

In this sense, it seems unlikely that we are merely witnessing a 'correction' to legislative overreach represented in the post-*Tampa* package. It may be true that the legislature went too far in its attempt to use legislation to hive off parts of Australia from the operation of the law and the scrutiny of the courts. As with the all-embracing, all-excluding privative clause, such tactics are anathema to any theory of law outside an emergency (and even, for many, within one). In this sense, the High Court in both *Plaintiff S157* and the twinned cases of *Plaintiff M61* and *Plaintiff M70* discarded the fiction that a 'legal black hole' could be legislatively crafted, and dealt a blow to Australia's unique experiment of externalizing the 'other' internally.

Nonetheless, Dyzenhaus' more subtle theory of 'grey holes', penned in the wake of *Al-Kateb* (and influenced by Schmitt), is still potentially apposite, not least given the legalist methodology judges continue to employ to open up these excluded zones to judicial scrutiny.[141] This is evident in the court's reluctance to couch decisions in terms of rights, married with an insistence upon the function of the judiciary, outside constitutional review, as merely enforcing the boundaries of statutory power. I tend to agree with Woods who has observed that legalism undercuts the court's capacity to 'move into more elevated and openly political forms of rights review'.[142] Moreover, falling back on legalism's narrative fails to resolve the tension between competing constitutionalisms, or assist in predicting judicial direction. Just as Australian legalism

---

[141] For a discussion of such theories of formal legality, see Hickman (n 39) 64–6.

[142] Woods (n 75) 605.

operates as a legitimating discourse in creating grey zones, so does it provide an easy route for legislatures to override judicial decisions. As evident in the reaction to almost every set back, the political response is not so much engagement with judicial reasoning on the nature and impact of executive power as reassertion of institutional dominance, to the detriment of rights. It seems we have a long way to go before genuine, informed and respectful dialogue becomes the norm on the subject of the legal rights of non-citizens.

5. Finland

Intermediate constitutional review in Finland: promising in theory, problematic in practice

Juha Lavapuro, Tuomas Ojanen and Martin Scheinin

5.1 NEW COMMONWEALTH CONSTITUTIONALISM GOES TO FINLAND?

The current state of Finnish constitutionalism can be understood as an interplay between constitutional history emphasizing legalism and legislative supremacy, on the one hand, and a shift towards directly applicable individual rights and commitment to internationalism, on the other hand.

The transformative turn towards rights-based constitutionalism and international commitment is of relative recent origin as it is essentially a product of a 25-year-long process involving the breakthrough of fundamental and human rights in the early 1990s, the accession to the European Union (EU) in 1995, as well as several constitutional reforms between 1995 and 2011.[1]

This development has resulted in a shift from centralized and legislative-sovereignty-based constitutionalism to a paradigm that is institutionally pluralist and predominantly rights-based.[2] Together with

[1] Tuomas Ojanen, 'From Constitutional Periphery Toward the Center-Transformation of Judicial Review in Finland' (2009) *Nordisk tidsskrift for menneskerettigheter* 194. For an early account, see Martin Scheinin, Ihmisoikeudet Suomen oikeudessa (Human Rights in Finnish Law) (Jyväskylä: Suomalainen Lakimiesyhdistys 1991).

[2] See in detail, Juha Lavapuro, Tuomas Ojanen and Martin Scheinin, 'Rights-Based Constitutionalism in Finland and the Development of Pluralist Constitutional Review' (2011) 9 *Intl J Cons* L 505; See also J Lavapuro, Uusi

institutional reforms that purported to retain the old trust in democratic legitimacy and legislative sovereignty while also providing an effective system for the protection of individual rights by the judiciary, the contemporary Finnish constitutionalism seems to share largely, if not exclusively, all essential features of such intermediate, 'third', forms of constitutional review[3] of which various models of new Commonwealth constitutionalism is the paradigmatic case.[4]

However, there have been several remarkable difficulties in transplanting this model into workable practice. These difficulties, stemming mostly from Finnish legal tradition, suggest a specific set of problems involved with 'third' models of constitutional review. Interestingly enough, these difficulties have not resulted in the degeneration of intermediate constitutional review back to a traditional legislative sovereignty model or in moving further to a system of a fully-fledged judicial review. Instead, the results have been institutional confusion and tensions, as the main constitutional actors do not seem to have a clear conception about their constitutional roles. On a more general level, these problems also originate in difficulties in stepping from the 'culture of authority' to the 'culture of justification'.[5] This applies in particular to the Constitutional Law Committee of Parliament (*Perustuslakivaliokunta*), which is not only responsible for the politically organized but legally authorized abstract ex ante review of the constitutionality of legislation, but is also traditionally regarded as being the main authority of constitutional interpretation.

---

perustuslakikontrolli (New Constitutional Review) (Suomalainen Lakimiesyhdistys 2010) 301; K Tuori, *Ratio and Voluntas* (Ashgate 2013) 366.

3 See for instance, Mark Tushnet, *Weak Courts, Strong Rights: Judicial Review and Social Welfare Rights in Comparative Constitutional Law* (Princeton UP 2008); Rosalind Dixon, 'Creating Dialogue About Socioeconomic Rights: Strong-Form Versus Weak-Form Judicial Review Revisited' (2007) 5 *Intl J Cons L* 391; Jane L Hiebert, 'Parliamentary Bills of Rights: an Alternative Model?' (2006) 69 MLR 7; Aileen Kavanagh, *Constitutional Review Under the UK Human Rights Act* (CUP 2009).

4 A central contribution was provided by Stephen Gardbaum in Stephen Gardbaum, 'The New Commonwealth Model of Constitutionalism' (2001) 49 *Am J Comp L* 707. See also, Peter Hogg and Alison Bushell, 'The Charter Dialogue Between Courts and Legislatures (or Perhaps the Charter of Rights Isn't a Bad Thing After All)' (1997) *Osgoode Hall LJ* 75.

5 RA Edwards, 'Judicial Deference Under the Human Rights Act' (2002) 65 *MLR* 859.

5.2 BETWEEN TRADITION AND REFORM

Finnish constitutionalism has traditionally been based on a mix of legalism (strict legal positivism) and an equally rigid understanding about valid law as an expression of the democratic will of the people.[6] Although these premises usually appear unproblematic at the level of ordinary legal practices, in the constitutional setting they have resulted in peculiar outcomes. As the eminent Finnish constitutional scholar, Paavo Kastari once described, Finnish constitutionalism was essentially 'rigid but flexible'.[7] While the constitutional system historically was characterized by its focus on rigid formalities and procedural matters, it was simultaneously always substantively vulnerable to various exceptions deemed necessary in various political and societal conditions.

This 'rigid flexibility' has been expressed in various institutional choices that define the foundations of the Finnish constitutional system. To begin with, although the Constitution Act of 1919 already included a catalogue of constitutional rights in its Chapter II, these rights were understood as being addressed primarily to the legislature, not to the courts or the executive, until the late 1980s.[8] Hence, it was essentially for the legislature alone to decide what the abstract provisions of the constitution actually meant. Conversely, the courts and authorities were supposed to protect rights mainly through the application of ordinary legislation.

At the same time, the material significance of the constitution was rather dubious due to the institution of so-called exceptive enactments, allowing the adoption of legislation that in substance derogated from the constitution without amending the text thereof, subject to the proviso that such legislation was approved in the procedure applicable for constitutional amendments. As the qualified procedure was de facto easily attainable under broad coalition governments, the protection of constitutional rights became procedural in nature, essentially dealing with the

---

[6] For a general description of Finnish constitutional law, see, for example, Jaakko Husa, *The Constitution of Finland* (Bloomsbury 2010) 272. For a comparative account that includes also an assessment of Finnish constitutionalism, *see* especially Maartje de Visser, *Constitutional Review in Europe: A Comparative Analysis* (Hart 2013) 528.

[7] Paavo Kastari, Valtiojärjestyksemme oikeudelliset oerusteet (The Legal Foundations of Our System of Government) (WS 1969) 86.

[8] See Scheinin (n 1) 197–215.

appropriate parliamentary procedure.[9] Between 1919 and 2000, 888 exceptive enactments were adopted with the outcome that some constitutional provisions actually featured as empty shells undermined by numerous exceptive enactments.[10] Since the reform of the domestic system for the protection of fundamental rights in 1995, the importance of the institution of exceptive enactments has radically decreased as the constitutional doctrine has been that exceptive enactments should only be used for the incorporation of those international treaties that conflict with the Constitution. Conversely, exceptive enactments are avoided in the context of domestic legislation. As a consequence, the use of exceptive enactments has drastically diminished since the late 1990s. In addition, the Constitution of 2000 introduced a material limit for exceptive enactments by requiring that the derogation from of the constitution must remain 'limited'. Nevertheless, the possibility to adopt exceptive enactments still exists.[11]

Moreover, unlike most constitutional democracies where the courts act as guardians of the constitution, in Finland this task was fairly early given to one of the permanent committees of Parliament, the Constitutional Law Committee. As a result, constitutional review of legislation was organized in a purely preventative fashion, exercised in abstracto as an integral part of the legislative process of Parliament by a political body consisting of members of Parliament (MPs). In essence, the crucial task of the committee was to decide whether a government bill could be adopted by a simple majority vote as an ordinary Act of Parliament or whether the Act should be enacted as an exceptional enactment through a qualified majority, analogously to constitutional amendments.

Finally, the constitutional doctrine emphasizing the role of Parliament in constitutional matters was supplemented with an equally rigid doctrine prohibiting the courts from reviewing the constitutionality of ordinary legislation. In practice, the prohibition of judicial review resulted in de

---

9 Martin Scheinin, *Welfare State and Constitutionalism: Nordic Perspectives* (Copenhagen: Nordic Council of Ministers 2001).

10 See the Report of the Working Group on Constitution 2000. [Perustuslaki 2000 työryhmän mietintö] Reports and Guidelines of the Ministry of Justice 8/1995, 99. According to the established constitutional doctrine, exceptive enactments remain in force notwithstanding the amendments to the constitution.

11 See Tuomas Ojanen, 'Constitutional Amendement in Finland' in Xenophon Contiades (ed.), *Engineering Constitutional Change: A Comparative Perspective on Europe, Canada and the USA* (Routledge 2013) 106.

facto inapplicability of constitutional and human rights in ordinary court proceedings.[12]

From the late 1980s onwards, these fundamental characteristics of Finnish constitutionalism started gradually changing due to the following three distinct, yet closely interconnected factors: a rights revolution, the Europeanization of the domestic legal order, and certain constitutional reforms.

The most crucial single source of constitutional dynamics was perhaps Finland's joining of the Council of Europe and the European Convention on Human Rights (the ECHR) in 1989–90.[13] The main novelty brought by the ECHR was the introduction of an effective and binding international judicial monitoring mechanism that allowed individuals to bring their cases to an international court if they had not succeeded on the domestic level. Moreover, the ECHR was implemented into the domestic legal order in 1990 through the method of incorporation that, according to the Constitutional Law Committee, warrants direct applicability of the ECHR provisions by courts and authorities. The committee also established that while Parliament still retained authority to enact legislation conflicting with the ECHR, domestic courts and authorities should nevertheless interpret, as far as possible, domestic legislation in conformity with the ECHR (human rights friendly interpretation approach).[14] Finnish courts increasingly began to apply not only the provisions of the ECHR but also other international human rights treaties that had earlier been incorporated into Finnish legal order.

The next phase of constitutional transformation was constituted by Finland joining the EU in 1995. The immediate result of accession was judicial empowerment of all Finnish courts to review national law, including the constitution, for its compatibility with EU law. Yet, courts were still prohibited from examining the constitutionality of Acts of Parliament.

The final tide of constitutional change came in the form of two comprehensive constitutional reforms. On the one hand, Chapter II of the Constitution Act of 1919 pertaining to constitutional rights was thoroughly revised in 1995 with the outcome that the constitution came to include a broad and modern catalogue of fundamental rights which were designed to lend themselves to direct application by courts and authorities. The latter purpose was warranted by section 22 providing that: 'The

[12] See Ojanen (n 1) 202–6, Scheinin (n 1) 212.
[13] See Lavapuro, Ojanen and Scheinin (n 2) 512–13.
[14] See Constitutional Law Committee Opinion 2/1990 (18 April 1990).

public authorities shall guarantee the observance of basic rights and liberties and human rights.' Hence, section 22 made it clear that this constitutional obligation applied to all public authorities alike and not just the legislator. Moreover, the Constitutional Law Committee reiterated the interpretive obligation of courts and authorities to interpret legislation in harmony with fundamental and human rights so as avoid conflicts between existing legislation and fundamental and human rights, as well as to promote these rights in a best way possible. However, the prohibition of judicial review still remained intact.

The new Finnish Constitution entered into force on 1 March 2000. As a part of this reform, the prohibition of judicial review was replaced by section 106 of the constitution providing for the primacy of the constitution in cases where the court finds the application of an Act of Parliament to be in *evident* conflict with the constitution. However, while the primacy clause ended the prohibition of judicial review, it purported to reconcile the new power of courts with the traditional constitutional authority of the Constitutional Law Committee of Parliament by acknowledging only a limited role for judicial review. Indeed, the *travaux préparatoires* of section 106 explicitly acknowledge that the primary review mechanism is still intended to be the abstract ex ante review by the Constitutional Law Committee whereas section 106 may only be applied by courts in concrete cases involving an evident conflict so that courts may only give primacy to the constitution instead of invalidating the conflicting Act of Parliament. Hence, the legislature still possesses the final responsibility for complying with the constitution.

5.3 THE FINNISH MODEL AS A PECULIAR EXAMPLE OF INTERMEDIATE CONSTITUTIONALISM

The developments described above have transformed the Finnish constitutional system from one based on traditional legislative sovereignty to one where both individual rights and courts enforcing these rights have a significant role. However, instead of becoming a fully-fledged system of judicial review, the current system is characterized by a tension between old doctrines and institutions emphasizing the legislative supremacy of Parliament, and a new paradigm underlining both the importance of rights and judicial safeguards and the role of courts in general. In this new setting, both the democratically elected legislature and the independent courts, as well as such public authorities as the Parliamentary Ombudsman, share distinct, yet complementary and partly overlapping duties to protect fundamental and human rights. Hence, the current constitutional model can be termed as intermediate, in clear contrast with the earlier one.

Analogies for the current form of Finnish constitutionalism cannot be found in the Nordic or German legal cultures that are otherwise closest to the Finnish legal system. Instead, the nearest family resemblance is in such institutional solutions that have emerged in Commonwealth countries during the last decades.[15] This becomes apparent if one compares the central features of current Finnish constitutionalism with central elements of Stephen Gardbaum's presentation of new Commonwealth constitutionalism.[16]

Essential in Gardbaum's model is the simultaneous presence of both mandatory pre-enactment political rights review and weak-form judicial review. More precisely, these two essential postulates can be broken down into the following four institutional features:

1) codified bill or catalogue of rights;
2) mandatory rights-based ex ante review of legislation by the political branches before the enactment of legislative instruments;
3) some form of constitutional review of legislation by the courts; and
4) formal legislative power to have the final word on the content of the legal order, notwithstanding constitutional review by the judiciary.

For Gardbaum, these aspects differentiate the new Commonwealth model of constitutionalism from both traditional parliamentary sovereignty models and judicial supremacy models. In Gardbaum's framework, the combination of the first and the third feature distinguishes the model from models based on parliamentary sovereignty whereas the second and fourth feature coalesces to separate the Commonwealth model from constitutional systems based on judicial supremacy.

Although Gardbaum's analysis is mainly geared towards the Commonwealth countries, it is also fruitful for analysing other constitutional systems. In light of this model, the traditional Finnish constitutional

---

[15] See also Lavapuro, Ojanen and Scheinin (n 2).

[16] See Stephen Gardbaum, *The New Commonwealth Model of Constitutionalism: Theory and Practice* (CUP 2013) 30–31. We have chosen to use Gardbaum's model as the basis for the analysis of the intermediate nature of Finnish constitutionalism mainly because it seems to provide the most generalizable account on the third forms of constitutionalism. To be sure, there are other ways of analyzing similar types of constitutional design and theory. However, they are often presented in a more country-specific context. See for instance Hogg and Bushell (n 4).

system was clearly based on parliamentary sovereignty principles with the legislator also having the ultimate word as regards the content of the legal order. The fundamental rights catalogue in the Constitution Act of 1919 did not alter this overall appearance as these rights were understood to be binding primarily on the legislature that could also override them with a qualified majority due to the possibility of exceptive enactments.

With regard to constitutional changes after 1980s, Gardbaum's analysis is even more applicable as the contemporary Finnish model provides yet another interesting variation of such intermediate form of constitutionalism that does not fit into the old dichotomy between legislative sovereignty and judicial supremacy. These features are discussed in more detail below.

5.3.1 The System of Codified Rights

To begin with, there exists a *system of codified and enforceable rights* that includes not only fundamental rights guaranteed in Chapter II of the constitution but also international human rights treaties incorporated through Acts of Parliament into the domestic legal order. Section 22 of the 2000 Finnish Constitution obliges all authorities to guarantee the observance of fundamental and human rights. Moreover, the system of rights is legalized as courts are actively invoking these rights. The case law of the Supreme Court provides a neat illustration. Prior to 1990, there was a total lack of references by the Supreme Court to human rights treaties, and only one single decision referred to fundamental rights.[17] In 2014, 28 decisions out of 104 precedents included a reference to human rights and/or fundamental rights. Usually, the main argumentation is based on the ECHR, as interpreted by the European Court of Human Rights (ECtHR), but other human rights treaties and constitutional provisions are also cited by the Supreme Court. As a result, there truly exists a directly enforceable system of rights based on both the constitution and international human rights norms.

5.3.2 Abstract Ex Ante Constitutional Review of Legislation

Mandatory rights review of legislation by the political branches before enactment has traditionally been an essential part of constitutional review mechanisms in Finland as the preceding presentation of the role of the Constitutional Law Committee of Parliament has revealed. Currently, the

[17] See Scheinin (n 1).

constitutional mandate of the committee is prescribed by Section 74 of the Constitution as follows: 'The Constitutional Law Committee shall issue statements on the constitutionality of legislative proposals and other matters brought for its consideration, as well as on their relation to international human rights treaties.'

As a political body, the Constitutional Law Committee is composed of 17 MPs. There are no other formal competence requirements and they do not have to be lawyers by education. Instead, legal expertise is provided by three parliamentary officials who draft the committee's opinions, as well as by experts in constitutional law and international human rights law, usually constitutional law professors, that are regularly heard as a de facto permanent part of the committee's proceedings. As an eminent Finnish constitutional expert, Professor Emeritus Antero Jyränki, has described, the committee is essentially a *Doppelgänger* – Dr Jekyll/Mr Hyde – in the centre of the constitutional machinery.[18] It is inherently a political organ consisting of democratically elected politicians working as an integral part of the parliamentary system but simultaneously entrusted with a legal task to supervise the constitutionality of the legislative proposals and other matters pending before Parliament.

The opinions issued by the Constitutional Law Committee serve two important functions: they provide authoritative interpretations of the constitution and determine the proper legislative procedure, that is whether the government bill may be adopted as an ordinary law through a single majority or whether it has to be enacted through a qualified procedure for constitutional enactments due to its conflict with the constitution. However, as the doctrine is nowadays to avoid the use of exceptional enactments and the aim is also otherwise to guarantee the appropriate protection of rights, the committee is currently in the habit of demanding amendments to the government bill so as to achieve harmony with the constitution and human rights obligations binding upon Finland.[19]

The threshold of sending a matter to the Constitutional Law Committee is quite low as is also the threshold of finding constitutional problems in matters brought to the committee. For instance, in 2014 the committee gave 75 opinions out of 367 government bills, and demanded changes in 24 opinions for the purpose of achieving harmony with the constitution and/or human rights treaties. From a purely quantitative perspective,

---

[18] See A Jyränki, *Valta ja vapaus (Power and Freedom)* (Talentum 2003) 393–5.

[19] See Husa (n 6) 230–32.

therefore, political pre-enactment review of rights by the committee does have a real impact on legislative proceedings.[20] However, this does not necessarily imply constitutional activism by the committee.[21] As will be discussed below, the opinions of the committee are usually strikingly dogmatic and apolitical, as well as unanimous without involving any genuine discussion and reflection of moral principles, political values or party lines.

5.3.3 Weak Judicial Review

Current Finnish constitutionalism also recognizes *such forms of constitutional review of legislation by the courts* that can be categorized within a weak form model of judicial review. The essential components of this particular weak form of judicial review are constituted by the obligation of courts to interpret legislation in a fundamental and human rights friendly manner in accordance with Section 22 of the Constitution and by a limited scope of judicial review under section 106. Both in terms of general doctrines and actual practice, the interpretive obligation is clearly the primary method of guaranteeing the observance of the constitution and Finland's international human rights obligations. Section 106 of the constitution, in turn, is a secondary device, and as a weak version of judicial review it is not designed to replace the primacy of the abstract ex ante constitutional review by the Constitutional Law Committee. Instead, judicial review is only supposed to address omissions left by the Constitutional Law Committee's review, inasmuch as unforeseen constitutional problems could arise in the courts' application of the law in particular cases. The requirement of an 'evident conflict' also functions to channel the constitutional interpretations and arguments applied at legislative stage by the Constitutional Law Committee into the concrete legal argumentation of the judiciary because, as a rule, a court should not regard the conflict as evident within the meaning of section 106 if the Constitutional Law Committee has already considered the relevant Act of Parliament to be in harmony with the constitution. In Finland, as in other Nordic countries, the preparatory works of legislation, including the

---

[20] See also V-P Viljanen 'Onko Eduskunnan asema lainsäädäntövallan käyttäjänä muuttunut?' (Has the Legislative Power of the Parliament Changed?) (2005) *Lakimies* 1050, 1062.

[21] See especially Juha Lavapuro 'Valtiosääntöinen managerialismi ja perusoikeudet' (Constitutional Managerialism and Fundamental Rights) (2010) *Oikeus* 6.

government bill and any committee reports from the Parliament's consideration, are regarded as informative sources of law that assist courts in the interpretation and application of laws passed by Parliament.

Overall, the weak form constitutional review by Finnish courts has resulted in a remarkable asymmetry between the judicial protection of constitutional rights, on the one hand, and the protection of similar rights under international human rights treaties and EU law, on the other.[22] While judicial review under Section 106 of the Constitution is greatly restricted in various ways, duly incorporated international human rights treaties, let alone EU law, presuppose an unlimited mandate for courts to set aside conflicting domestic laws. Hence, the tendency has not only been towards more effective judicial protection of human rights and EU law than of constitutional rights. The outcome has also been an asymmetrical relationship between the constitution, international human rights treaties and EU law in Finnish courts so that the constitution with its fundamental rights provisions has been rendered a secondary system of safeguards for rights. Consequently, several major aims of the reform of the domestic system for the protection of constitutional rights in 1995, such as strengthening the direct applicability of constitutional rights by courts and making the domestic system the primary system of rights protection, have not materialized. Although international human rights obligations binding on Finland were originally supposed to provide only the minimum standard of protection, they have actually become the highest yardstick of judicial scrutiny.[23]

5.3.4 Parliament's Ultimate Power to Legislate

The final parallel with Gardbaum's new Commonwealth model is based on those fundamental choices that ultimately leave the *Finnish Parliament with the final word on what the law of the land is.* Judicial review by courts is in many ways limited, including by precluding any judicial

---

[22] See Ojanen (n 1).

[23] In its precedent KKO 2012:11, the Supreme Court gave, in plenum composition, a primacy to section 10 of the constitution on the basis that a provision of an Act was in conflict with article 8 (right to private and family life) of the ECHR as interpreted in the light of the case law of the ECtHR, which in turn was to be understood as establishing also the minimum content of section 10 (right to private life) of the constitution. Therefore, the provision of the act was in manifest conflict with the Constitution in the meaning of section 106 of the constitution and the court gave primacy to the provision in the constitution. See http://korkeinoikeus.fi/fi/index/ennakkopaatokset/pohjoismaiseteu-jaihmisoikeus liitynnaisetratkaisut/2008/kko200893inenglish.html.

power to declare Acts of Parliament unconstitutional and invalid. Instead, the supreme constitutional authority is still clearly situated in Parliament in general and in the hands of the Constitutional Law Committee in particular. Furthermore, Parliament still has, at least in principle, the power to adopt substantively unconstitutional laws due to the availability of the institution of exceptive enactments under Section 73 of the Constitution. Although this possibility is no longer actively used, it nevertheless still belongs to constitutional reserve, ready to be used if the situation so requires.

Of course, parliamentary sovereignty has been greatly relativized by EU law and Finland's international obligations. As will be discussed in more detail below, however, the Constitutional Law Committee has continued to emphasize both the ultimate role of the constitution and Finland's sovereignty in general by emphasizing the primacy of the domestic system of rights protection over EU law and by requiring that *Kompetenz-Kompetenz* should remain in the hands of Finland together with other EU Member States.[24]

5.4 FINNISH INTERMEDIATE CONSTITUTIONALISM IN PRACTICE

In order for intermediate constitutionalism to present a genuine third alternative to traditional legislative sovereignty and judicial supremacy models, there must exist some kind of real constitutional dialogue and interaction between the courts and the legislature. In essence, there should be such a rational constitutional discourse in which difficult constitutional issues are not decided on the basis of authority, hierarchy and supremacy but on the basis of open, reasoned and rational argumentation. As such, hardly anything in the design of the intermediate constitutionalism actually guarantees that key constitutional actors act in this manner. As pointed out by Mark Tushnet, the theory is actually bland in this respect as the new model may easily degenerate into either one of the two polar opposites to which it was offered as an alternative.[25] For instance, intermediate systems may degenerate back into legislative sovereignty if the courts try to get the legislature to respond to their constitutional interpretations, but the legislature in fact ignores them or just overrides what the courts have decided. And vice versa, a system

---

[24] Tuomas Ojanen, 'EU Law and the Response of the Constitutional Law Committee of the Finnish Parliament' (2007) *Scandinavian Studies in Law* 203.

[25] See Tushnet (n 3) 43–7.

where courts ignore the legislature's constitutional interpretations or where legislature consistently amends legislation to comply with the judiciary's constitutional interpretation, cannot genuinely be described as examples of intermediate constitutionalism.

Interestingly, the Finnish model appears to have fallen into both of the possible routes of degeneration by regressing into judicial supremacy in some respects and into legislative sovereignty in some other. The explanation seems to be because of the difficulty of maintaining an appropriate system of rights review by a politically constituted body, on the one hand, and the difficulty of engaging in a substantive and principled constitutional dialogue in a legal environment where the tradition has been far from dialogic or constitutional in any substantive-normative sense, on the other. These problems emerge especially in hard cases of constitutional law which either are particularly value sensitive, or where either the constitution or Finland's international obligations seem to require fundamental changes to existing constitutional doctrine, legislation or legal practice.

5.4.1 Disoriented Ex Ante Review

According to Gardbaum, political rights review ought to consist in 'political and moral deliberation' so that it could bring about 'freer perspectives of principle' than is typical of judicial reasoning.[26] Hence, the rights review exercised by a political body should represent a genuine alternative to judicial review of legislation.[27]

However, the essential characteristics of ex ante abstract constitutional review by the Constitutional Law Committee – the committee is inherently political and its review takes place during the legislative process and before the final adoption of the Act – appear to fall short of achieving Gardbaum's ideas. The Constitutional Law Committee does not exercise political rights review in the sense of being 'political'. In

---

[26] See Gardbaum (n 4) 80.

[27] This requirement of 'alternative' and 'non-legalistic' approach to constitutional review is also crucial in terms of answering the challenge imposed by the well-known critique of judicial review that emphasizes both the undemocratic nature of judicial review and the level of disagreement about rights. Accordingly, if rights disagreements are mostly not issues of interpretation in a narrow legalistic sense, it becomes quite logical to argue that this power should be left to the democratic institutions – provided they function appropriately and take rights seriously. See Jeremy Waldron, 'The Core of the Case Against Judicial Review' (2005) 115 *Yale LJ* 1346; See also Gardbaum (n 4) 51–61.

fact, the opposite is true. The committee is a political body that produces extraordinarily formal legal opinions. It is also de facto crucially dependant upon the legal expertise provided by regularly heard experts in constitutional law.

In practice, the committee's argumentation does not usually reflect different political views about the meaning of various constitutional rights and their relevance in terms of other important governmental interests. Instead, the argumentation tends to be thoroughly dogmatic, often just paraphrasing the wording of the constitution, its preparatory works and a set of interpretive rules, which the committee has constructed in its earlier opinions.

Furthermore, although the review by the committee seems to be effective in quantitative terms, in practice it overwhelmingly focuses on various formalities and technicalities of constitutional law, at the expense of substantive issues. Although the permissible limitations test for interferences with rights includes steps that purport to make sure that the government bill serves a legitimate aim, that it is proportionate and that it does not violate the essence of any fundamental right, the committee hardly ever finds the government bill unconstitutional on these grounds. Instead, its findings on unconstitutionality usually stem from the ambiguous and imprecise formulation of legislative provisions. For instance, the committee has frequently required amendments to proposed legislation simply on the ground that the right of one public authority to receive personal data from other public authorities would be based on a 'need' in relation to fulfilling some legitimate task of the authority, instead of 'necessity' in relation to fulfilling that task. In these cases, the mere replacing of the word 'need' with 'necessity' has sufficed to achieve compliance with the constitution.[28]

In fact, one the most remarkable features of the Finnish ex ante constitutional review is that its outcomes are actually strikingly exempt from such political and moral deliberations that would certainly give rise to arguments about correct moral principles in constitutional courts and other constitutional systems. To provide a comparative example: Opinions 10/2005 and 23/2005 by the Constitutional Law Committee concern Government Bill 187/2004 amending the Act on Executive Assistance to the Police by the Defence Forces. The bill as such was a part of a series of anti-terrorism legislation enacted in Finland after the terrorist attacks in New York on 11 September 2001. The purpose of Bill 187/2004 was to authorize the defence forces to provide assistance to the

[28] See Lavapuro (n 21).

police in counter-terrorism situations. The terrorist attacks in New York are specifically mentioned in the bill as an example of a situation that would require assistance from defence forces. Essentially, the Finnish Bill was an analogous but more abstract version of the Air-transport Security Act (*Luftsicherheitsgesetz*) which was adopted by the German Bundestag in 2004 and later struck down by the German Constitutional Court on the ground that the Act violated human dignity.[29] Although the proposed Finnish Act did not include explicit provisions that would have empowered the police and defence forces to shoot down a civilian aircraft in extreme situation of terrorism prevention, this possibility was implied. The Constitutional Law Committee found the bill unconstitutional not because it violated human dignity or some other important human rights but because its formulation was too ambiguous. Accordingly, the committee held that Bill 187/2004 could be adopted if it only were amended with provisions that would guarantee that force would be used proportionately and only as a last resort.

Another illustrative example is provided by cases concerning the equal status of sexual minorities. In 2001 the committee gave its opinion[30] about a Government Bill on Registered Partnership.[31] In terms of equality and prohibition of discrimination, Bill 200/2000 was a clear step forward, which was also noted by the Constitutional Law Committee. After referring to the equality and privacy provisions of the constitution, the committee pointed out that notwithstanding the general aim of the bill to advance equality, some elements of sexual orientation based segregation remained: registered partners were not entitled together to adopt a child or individually to adopt the child of their partner; nor were they entitled to take a common family name. In principle, this amounted to differential treatment that was prohibited by Section 6(2) of the Constitution.

However, according to committee's unanimous view, such differential treatment was justified. In four short paragraphs, the committee stated first, that the constitutional principle of equality does not provide for strict limitations upon the legislator's discretion;[32] secondly, that the bill

---

[29] See Bundesverfassungsgericht (BVerfG), 59 NJW 751 (2006). See also O Lepsius, 'Human Dignity and the Downing of Aircraft: The German Federal Constitutional Court Strikes Down a Prominent Anti-terrorism Provision in the New Air-Transport Security Act' (2006) 7 *German Law Journal* 761.

[30] See Constitutional Law Committee Opinion 15/2001 (30.3.2001).

[31] Government Bill 200/2000 (*Hallituksen esitys laiksi virallistetusta parisuhteesta*).

[32] This doctrine was originally articulated in the context of deregulation of rental control in the areas where there were no longer discrepancies between

concerned a new type of legislation in a matter which was also undergoing a change at international level; and thirdly, that marriage legislation required decisions about the future and values of the society which justified the special treatment of marriage as a relationship between a man and a woman. No substantive reasons or different interpretations about the constitutional meaning of equality, privacy or marriage were provided. For that purpose the final opinion is often cleansed from all traces of disagreement.

5.4.2 Defective Constitutional Dialogue Between Domestic Key Actors

One key component of intermediate constitutionalism is constitutional dialogue or some other meaningful form of interaction between main constitutional actors. Otherwise the system would only represent constitutional departmentalism with different institutions having completely unconnected and separate constitutional tasks.

However, there is still a lack of genuine constitutional dialogue between major constitutional actors. The interpretive practice of the Constitutional Law Committee is still based on rather formal, isolated and monologous opinions with only sporadic references to case law by domestic courts. Even in cases involving interpretive tensions between the committee and the courts, the committee has been prone to disregard judicial interpretations.

The practice of the courts also leaves a lot to be desired. The two highest courts, the Supreme Court and the Supreme Administrative Court, have usually been uninterested in taking judicial notice of the interpretive practice of the Constitutional Law Committee, and even when making references to it, judicial practice appears to be selective, as well as being usually confined to cases only involving the application of section 106 of the constitution. Moreover, even when some constitutional actors occasionally plunge into dialogic mode, others typically fail to follow suit.

A series of cases pertaining to the principle of *ne bis in idem* (that is the right not to be tried or punished twice) provides a telling example of these defects. The problem with *ne bis in idem* principle stems from the fact that the Finnish court system is divided into two main branches – ordinary courts dealing with civil suits and criminal cases, and administrative courts reviewing the decisions of executive authorities. The system does not prevent a situation were the same conduct can be assessed on

---

supply and demand. See Constitutional Law Committee Opinion 12/1990 (26.10.1990).

both judicial tracks which follow different procedural norms. In particular, the imposition of tax surcharges has not been considered a criminal sanction but an administrative sanction to be reviewed by administrative courts. The principle of *lis pendens* has been strictly followed within criminal proceedings but not between criminal and administrative procedures. As a result, administrative sanctions have not traditionally prevented the bringing of criminal charges for the same conduct in ordinary courts, and vice versa. This system became problematic after the ECtHR held in cases *Jussila v Finland*[33] and *Ruotsalainen v Finland*[34] that tax surcharges were criminal sanctions for purposes of the ECHR and fell within the scope of Article 4 of Protocol No 7 to the ECHR on the principle of *ne bis in idem*.

In a series of decisions delivered in 2010 and 2011, both the Supreme Court[35] and Supreme Administrative Court[36] followed the ECtHR's rulings in *Jussila v Finland*; *Ruotsalainen v Finland* and especially the landmark judgment in *Zolotukhin v Russia*,[37] and held that the principle of *ne bis in idem* applies in criminal cases as well as in cases that concern administrative sanctions. However, both courts also held that *ne bis in idem* did not apply to a situation in which two sets of proceedings concerning the same matter were pending at the same time.

The Constitutional Law Committee was silent about the issue until its Opinion 9/2012 on a Government Bill amending the Aliens Act and the Employment Contract Act. The latter Act included provisions about the possibility to impose penalty payments to employers for actions that were also covered by criminal sanctions. The committee pointed out that the principle of *ne bis in idem* may be applied in these situations. However, in contrast with the established jurisprudence of the two Supreme Courts, the committee emphasized that the principle does not apply only to consecutive proceedings, but also to proceedings that were simultaneously pending (*lis pendens*). Therefore, as a final decision in one set of proceedings would prohibit both the initiation and continuation of proceedings in the other set of proceedings if the matter was the same,[38] the committee effectively overruled a consistent line of argumentation by

---

33 *Jussila v Finland* App no 73053/01 (ECHR, 23 November 2006).

34 *Ruotsalainen v Finland* App no 13079/03 (ECHR, 16 June 2009).

35 See Supreme Court precedents KKO 2010:45 and KKO 2010:46. See also Supreme Court Precedents KKO 2010:82, KKO 2011.35, KKO 2011:80, KKO 2011:93 and KKO 2011:111.

36 See Supreme Administrative Court's precedent KHO 2011:41.

37 *Sergey Zolotukhin v Russia* App no 47940/99 (ECHR, 10 February 2009).

38 See Constitutional Law Committee Opinion 9/2012 (26.04.2012) 4.

both Supreme Courts without saying anything at all about it. As a matter of fact, the Constitutional Law Committee did not even cite the case law of the courts – it simply ignored them.

The committee's 9/2012 Opinion was heavily criticized, especially by Supreme Court's President Pauliine Koskelo who – according to news outlets – approached the Chair of the Constitutional Law Committee with an informal letter.[39] However, the committee reaffirmed its position in Opinion 17/2013 on the Government Bill for an Act on Tax Surcharges and Customs Duty Surcharges Imposed by a Separate Decision.[40] As a way of responding to the criticism towards it earlier decision, the Committee emphasized that its earlier interpretation about the scope of *ne bis in idem* was connected to a specific government bill so that it could not be used as a direct source of constitutional interpretation of existing legislation. Accordingly, the very institution, which had otherwise underlined its supreme role as the most authoritative interpreter of the constitution, now suggested that its interpretation was only relevant in the context of the government bill at issue.

The Supreme Court responded rapidly. In its judgment delivered in July 2013 – little over a month after the Constitutional Law Committee's last opinion on the matter[41] – the court overruled its own earlier line of precedents by adopting the view of the Constitutional Law Committee on the scope of application of the *ne bis in idem* principle. As a justification for this change, the Supreme Court referred to the constitutionally mandated status of the Constitutional Law Committee and underlined the importance of the committee's interpretations in the application of the law.

Interestingly, in passing the Supreme Court rejected the Constitutional Law Committee's view that the committee's interpretations would only be confined to a specific government bill with the impossibility of making any conclusions about the constitutionality of existing law on the basis of them. After emphasizing that it must decide the case in accordance with the law, the court emphasized that the *ne bis in idem* principle concerns the interpretation legal safeguards that are protected by the constitution.

---

39 See for instance <http://www.mtv.fi/uutiset/rikos/artikkeli/tulkintakiista-uhkaa-lopettaa-satojen-talousrikosjuttujen-oikeuskasittelyn/2048020> accessed 31 July 2015.

40 Constitutional Law Committee Opinion 17/2013 (31.05.2013).

41 See Supreme Court precedent 2013:59.

> On this issue, the Constitutional Law Committee has expressed its clear position, which excludes the possibility to limit the application of ne bis in idem solely to successive procedures. With respect to these factors, the Supreme Court takes the view that the effects of the Constitutional Law Committee's interpretations cannot be limited only to the interpretation of the provisions that the Committee has specifically considered. Instead, the main principles and objectives of the Committee's interpretations should be taken into account in the interpretation of existing law. This is also supported by the fact that they are presented in a context in which the scope of application of the ne bis in idem principle has been specifically reviewed. Ultimately, the right to equality before the law as provided by Section 6 of the Constitution requires the Court to take into account the positions of the Committee when it must provide legal answers to similar questions.[42]

In contrast to the Supreme Court, the Supreme Administrative Court refused to approve the wide interpretation adopted by the Constitutional Law Committee. Instead, it deferred to the level of protection provided by the ECtHR's case law and especially its judgments in cases *Nykänen v Finland*;[43] *Glantz v Finland*;[44] and *Häkkä v Finland*.[45] In particular, the Supreme Administrative Court emphasized that the Constitutional Law Committee did not specifically require retroactive changes to the existing law. Moreover, the Supreme Administrative Court deferred to the Constitutional Law Committee's understanding about the limited scope of application of its opinions.

The *ne bis in idem* cases bring to surface a set of more general problems. To begin with, the main constitutional actor, the Constitutional Law Committee appears to be uncertain about its constitutional role. If its argument about the strictly contextual nature of the committee's opinions were to be accepted as such, the significance of the constitution would be radically relativized. While there might exist a system of review of legislation, it could not be used as a precedent nor could it arguably be based on any objective legal ground that would transcend the particular instances of the constitution's application.

There was also a total absence of constitutional dialogue with national courts by the committee even though the two highest courts had already on numerous occasions dealt with the same issue in several precedents. Moreover, the Supreme Administrative Court severely compromised the views of the Supreme Court and the Constitutional Law Committee by

---

42 Ibid.
43 *Nykänen v Finland* App no 11828/11 (ECHR, 20 May 2014).
44 *Glantz v Finland* App no 37394/11 (ECHR, 20 May 2014).
45 *Häkkä v Finland* App no 758/11 (ECHR, 20 May 2014).

strictly deferring to the ECtHR's jurisprudence. From the perspective of intermediate constitutional review, the Supreme Administrative Court's decision provides an example of degeneration into strong-form judicial review with ECtHR at its apex in a context where there clearly existed other constitutional options offering higher standards of protection to individuals.

On a positive note, the Supreme Court acted as the model presupposes. Its argumentation was in dialogic relationship with the ECtHR, the Constitutional Law Committee and its own previous precedents. The Supreme Court did not passively defer to the Constitutional Law Committee's opinion but provided substantive legal reasons for this judicial deference. Moreover, the Supreme Court refused to accept the committee's view that the latter's interpretations would be of case-specific relevance only as this would have considerably weakened not only the committee's interpretive authority but ultimately the normative binding nature and the relevance of the constitution.

5.4.3 Habitual Avoidance of Conflicts and Genuine Constitutional Dialogue with the EU

As in other member states, EU membership has entailed both a *vertical* transfer of domestic legislative and judicial powers to the supranational level and a *horizontal* shift of competences from the legislature to the judiciary especially by empowering all domestic courts to review *all* domestic law, including Acts of Parliament and even the constitution itself, for compatibility with EU law. Hence, the primacy of EU law actually proved to be the final straw for the abolition of the total prohibition of judicial review through enacting section 106 of the Constitution in 2000 in a manner already discussed above.

In principle, the constitutional changes brought by EU membership have occurred quite painlessly. Case law of the Court of Justice of the European Union (CJEU) is currently routinely invoked by Finnish courts. The two highest courts, the Supreme Court and the Supreme Administrative Court, especially are in the habit of not only making detailed references to the judgments of the CJEU but also analysing the CJEU's case law meticulously.[46] After the entry into force of the Lisbon Treaty

---

[46] See, for example, Judgment of 2012:55 by the Supreme Administrative Court in which it ruled that a public university was obliged to deliver data on professorial salaries to a newspaper, which had requested the data to be used for editorial purposes, provided that the newspaper granted the university with appropriate commitments and other adequate guarantees concerning the security

on 1 December 2009, judicial references to the EU Charter of Fundamental Rights have also begun to emerge in domestic case law.[47]

Similarly, the Constitutional Law Committee of Parliament has adopted the practice of taking notice of EU law, including the EU Charter of Fundamental Rights and the case law of the CJEU. In European comparison, it is significant to note that the committee has actually systematically referred to the EU Charter of Fundamental Rights since the parliamentary session of 2001, on occasions in which the committee has reviewed either proposals for EU legislation or domestic implementing enactments of EU law for their compatibility with the constitution and international human rights obligations binding upon Finland.[48] The Constitutional Law Committee usually invokes constitutional provisions, the ECHR and the EU Charter of Fundamental Rights, including the case law of the European courts, on fundamental and human rights in tandem.

Nevertheless, underneath this practice, there also exists a clear and wide tendency to avoid, as far as possible, all tensions between domestic law and EU law. The supreme constitutional authority, the Constitutional Law Committee of Parliament would be well suited to actively and – if necessary – also critically supervise conformity of proposals for EU legislation or their domestic implementing enactments with domestic constitutional standards. However, as the committee fails to qualify as a court or a tribunal within the meaning of EU law, it is incapable of making a reference for a preliminary ruling by the CJEU in the

---

of the data. The reasoning of the Court discusses at length the impact of the Data Protection Directive, as well as CJEU judgments in Case C-73/07, *Satakunnan Markkinapörssi and Satamedia*, 16 December 2008, Joined Cases C-465/00, C-138/01, C-139/01, *Österreichischer Rundfunk and others*, 18 October 2007, and Joined Cases C-92/09 and C-93/09, *Volker and others*, 9 November 2010.

[47] For an overview of Finnish court practice regarding the case law of the ECtHR and the CJEU, see Tuomas Ojanen, 'Eurooppatuomioistuimet ja suomalaiset tuomioistuimet' ('European Courts and Finnish Courts') (2005) 103 *Lakimies* 1210.

[48] The first reference by the Committee to the EU Charter can be found in its very first opinion of the parliamentary session of 2001, Opinion 1/2001 (9.02.2001). See also Opinion 18/2012 (11.10.2012) by the Constitutional Law Committee on the Bill amending the Act on the Processing of Personal Data by the Police and the Act on the Processing of Personal Data by the Border Guard. The committee explicitly referred to article 8 of the Charter, article 8 of the ECHR, including the judgment by the ECtHR in the case of *Rotaru v Romania*, as well as the Council of Europe's Convention for the Protection of Individuals with regard to Automatic Processing of Personal Data, as premises of constitutional review.

interpretation of EU law or the validity of EU legislation. This does not only inhibit the committee from engaging the CJEU in a direct constitutional dialogue but also seriously hampers the constitutional review of EU-related measures by the committee as the appropriate exercise of such review often requires sufficient understanding of the correct meaning of EU law.

Moreover, the Committee tends to avoid making clear declarations of incompatibility between EU law and the constitution.[49] The committee has typically settled for making some general observations on the question of standards of rights protection in the domestic implementation of EU legislation by observing, for instance, that the domestic implementation of EU legislation must not weaken the domestic standard of rights protection. Accordingly, the committee has a few times required such changes to domestic acts implementing EU legislation that do not openly run in conflict with EU law but only compromise the 'maximal' implementation of it. For instance, the committee introduced changes to Acts implementing such EU measures as Council Framework Decision 2002/584/JHA of 13 June 2002 on the European Arrest Warrant and the Surrender Procedures between Member States and Council Framework Decision 2002/475/JHA of 13 June 2002 on Combating Terrorism. However, these exceptional cases prove the rule, that is, the avoidance of any open conflicts between the Constitution and EU obligations.

Opinion 18/2014 by the Constitutional Law Committee provides another example of the impact of EU law on constitutional review by the committee. In its opinion, the committee discussed at length the judgment by the CJEU in *Digital Rights Ireland and Seitlinger and Others* when reviewing the constitutionality of the Bill on the Information Society Code, particularly to the extent that the bill included provisions

---

[49] For a detailed analysis see: J Salminen, *Yhä läheisempään liittoon?: Tutkielma valtiosäännön integraationormin sisällöstä ja vaikutuksista (Toward ever closer union? Essay on the content and effects of the Constitution's integration norm)* (Turun yliopisto 2015) 446. Perhaps the most open constitutional critique of EU legislation is presented in Constitutional Law Committee's opinions 25/2005 (15.06.2005) and 4/2008 (28.02.2008) where the committee held that the Act implementing Council Regulation (EC) No 1782/2003 of 29 September 2003 establishing common rules for direct support schemes under the common agricultural policy violated the right to private property as provided by section 15 of the constitution. The committee required that the implementing Act was amended with a short transitional provisions that would guarantee the protected expectations of the lessor in cases where the lease agreement was concluded before the revisions to the common agricultural support scheme.

on data retention.[50] Because of the CJEU's judgment, the Constitutional Law Committee found it necessary to reconsider the domestic constitutional doctrine regarding the constitutional protection of 'metadata' of electronic communications (information about the parties and about a message being sent and delivered between them). Earlier, the established constitutional doctrine had been that the processing of metadata was invariably seen as falling within such 'peripheral areas' of privacy where relatively wide-ranging limitations were permissible because the legislator was understood as enjoying a wide margin of discretion. By contrast, the content of electronic communications was seen as falling within the 'core' of privacy with strong constitutional safeguards.[51]

Now, however, the committee took the view in light of the CJEU's judgment that a rigid distinction between the content of the electronic communications and metadata cannot any longer be treated as a determining factor for the assessment of the level of intrusions into privacy and data protection. As a combination of various forms of metadata can reveal a lot of confidential and sensitive personal information on the individual and sensitive personal relationships, particularly when combined with information obtained from other sources, constitutional attention should be given to the details of a particular situation as a whole. For this reason, it was important to analyse what types of metadata are at issue and what is their combined effect upon the right to privacy and data protection. As a result, domestic legislation on data retention, and constitutional doctrine regarding the level of intrusions by metadata into privacy and data protection, were significantly revised. However, in contrast to constitutional courts in several other member states where the courts had questioned the constitutionality of data retention directive

[50] In *Digital Rights Ireland*, the CJEU essentially ruled that the Data Retention Directive was invalid ex tunc because the EU legislature had 'exceeded the limits imposed by compliance with the principle of proportionality in the light of Articles 7, 8 and 52(1) of the Fundamental Rights Charter'. See Joined cases C-293/12, C-594/12 *Digital Rights Ireland and Seitlinger and Others*, para 69. For a comment, see, for example, Tuomas Ojanen, 'Privacy Is More Than Just a Seven-Letter Word: The Court of Justice of the European Union Sets Constitutional Limits on Mass Surveillance Court of Justice of the European Union, Decision of 8 April 2014 in Joined Cases C-293/12 and C-594/12, *Digital Rights Ireland and Seitlinger and Others*' (2014) *EuConst* 528.

[51] For this constitutional doctrine, see, for example, Constitutional Law Committee Opinions 6/2012 (20 April 2012); 67/2010 (8.3.2011); 66/2010 (8.3.2011); 62/2010 3.3.2011; 29/2008 (13.11.2008); and 23/2006 (8.6.2006).

earlier, in Finland the development followed a reverse track: the Constitutional Law Committee was ready to seriously question the constitutionality of the Implementation Act of the Data Retention Directive but only after the CJEU had already done the same thing. And even when doing so the committee, at best, did it at half measure.

Finnish courts, in turn, have typically found Finnish law to be by and large in harmony with EU legislation, which in turn may suggest that the legislature has been willing to comply with EU law and – as a side effect – to restrain the tendency towards the growing role of the judiciary. Moreover, while Finnish courts have embraced such fundamental qualities of EU law as direct effect, indirect effect and primacy without any sign of at least overt resistance, courts seem to have exercised their powers under EU law against a backdrop of judicial self-restraint. In particular, the cases in which Finnish courts have given primacy to EU law over conflicting national legislation have remained relatively few in number. Instead, the traditional constitutional doctrine emphasizing the subordination of the courts to the democratically elected legislature has impelled courts to interpret, as far as possible, national legislation in harmony with EU law so as to avoid any open conflict.[52]

In fact, the Finnish courts have so far declined from passing any judicial views on such constitutional aspects of EU membership as the relationship between legislative sovereignty of Parliament and EU obligations or the relationship between the domestic system for the protection of fundamental and human rights and EU law. Again, there may have been a bit of a shunning or judicial self-restraint towards EU law as Finnish courts made only 91 references for a preliminary ruling by the CJEU in the years 1995–2014, the Supreme Administrative Court of Finland being at the forefront as it alone made 45 references.[53] Yet, Finnish courts nowadays decide hundreds, if not thousands of cases involving an EU-law element annually. What is also of significance is that all references by Finnish courts for a preliminary ruling by the CJEU have so far concerned the interpretation of EU law. By contrast, any reference by a Finnish court on the validity of EU legislation, including in light of fundamental rights, is yet to emerge.

Indeed, case law by Finnish courts is conspicuous by the absence of constitutional issues involving EU law. Perhaps the most significant

---

[52] For the domestic reception of direct effect, primacy and other fundamental doctrines of EU law in Finland, see, for example, Ojanen (n 1) 198–201.

[53] The Court of Justice of the European Union, Annual Report 2014, p. 119.

constitutional case has so far been the case of *Satakunnan Markkinapörssi* in which a reference by the Supreme Administrative Court for a preliminary ruling by the CJEU came to have an impact on the evolution of EU law in the field of privacy and data protection. In the case, the reference necessitated the CJEU striking a balance between the right to privacy and the protection of personal data, on the one hand, and freedom of expression and the right to information, on the other, as well as defining the notion of journalism in the age of electronic communications.[54]

5.5 CONCLUSION: THE DIFFICULTY OF HAVING ONE'S CAKE AND EATING IT TOO

The transformation of Finnish constitutionalism away from the strict legislative sovereignty paradigm and towards an intermediate, 'third', form of constitutionalism begun 25 years ago with the incorporation of the ECHR in 1990. As such, there certainly exists a constitutional family resemblance between post-1990 Finland and new Commonwealth constitutionalism, especially that of the post-1998 UK (that is after the incorporation of the ECHR by the Human Rights Act). However, unlike the UK and Commonwealth countries more generally, the legal culture of Finland is based on the civil law system. It shares a tradition where the ideal type of a judicial decision is concise, follows the wording of a statute, makes only limited references to previous precedents, and typically avoids in-depth analysis of substantive reasons and other justifications.

This mode of legal thinking has applied to constitutional decision-making, too. Together with a set of other constitutional idiosyncrasies, it has amplified the risks involved in the general design of the 'third' form constitutionalism. In contrast to typical constitutional courts of civil law systems, the legitimacy of the decisions by the Constitutional Law Committee of Parliament has not required explication of substantive reasons in the similar manner and thoroughness that is to be expected in constitutional adjudication. The committee has not been forced to fill the gap between the abstract language of the constitution and its different interpretations with better reasons because this gap has already been filled by direct democratic authorization. Combined with the abstract

---

[54] Case C-73/07 *Satakunnan Markkinapörssi and Satamedia* [2008] ECR I-9831.

nature of the committee's review more generally, the practice of the committee is still characterized by legal formalism which does not necessarily provide the most fruitful ground for in-depth constitutional dialogue about the meaning of constitutional principles. In regard to EU law, the committee with its ex ante review of legislative proposals and incapability of making requests for preliminary rulings by the CJEU is also in a danger of getting side-tracked of the essential mechanisms of constitutional dialogue in Europe.

Finnish courts, especially the Supreme Court, have more or less been able to adjust to the changed constitutional circumstances in terms of the growing importance of supranational legal practice and the wider applicability of constitutional provisions. However, several challenges still remain. The Constitutional Law Committee of Parliament is not able to provide opinions that would provide adequately clear guidance to courts – especially compared to the jurisprudence of the ECtHR which is regularly cited by Finnish courts. In fact, the Supreme Court has started to use the jurisprudence of the ECtHR as the main source for establishing the minimum level of protection of *constitutional rights*. Courts are also in the habit of putting so much emphasis on the ECHR that this has resulted in a marginal significance of other human rights treaties binding upon Finland.

Above all, there is an absence of a substantive and principled constitutional dialogue between major domestic constitutional actors. This problem is particularly serious in hard cases of constitutional law which either are particularly value sensitive, or where either the constitution or Finland's international obligations seem to require fundamental changes to existing constitutional doctrine, legislation or legal practice.

ACKNOWLEDGEMENT

The chapter on Finland is derived from an article: Juha Lavapuro, Tuomas Ojanen and Martin Scheinin, 'Rights-based constitutionalism in Finland and the development of pluralist constitutional review' *Int J Constitutional Law* (2011) 9 (2): 505–31.

PART II

Constitutional courts and constitutional reforms: specific European experiences towards an evolution of the Kelsenian model

6. Italy

The Italian system of constitutional review: a Kelsenian model moving towards a decentralized model?

Paolo Passaglia*

6.1 INTRODUCTION

The Italian system of constitutional adjudication is one of the oldest examples of the so-called European model, which has been largely influenced by Kelsen's theory. Indeed, many of its key features are similar to those that characterize most European systems, such as the choice for a centralized model, with a constitutional court conceived especially as a means to protect fundamental rights.

Although it took part in the European cultural and legal climate that, after World War II, supported the establishment of bodies having the purpose of preventing abuses by political bodies, the Italian system possesses some peculiar features that distinguish it from other European constitutional courts. Most of these peculiarities date back to the period when the Italian Constitutional Court was conceived and established: in particular, a crucial part was played by the choices of the Constituent Assembly concerning the ways in which cases and questions could be submitted to the court such as, for example, the absence of an avenue for direct appeal to the court by individuals – a strongly distinctive feature of the Italian system.

The evolution of constitutional case law, together with major changes in the legal system as a whole, progressively reshaped the functions of the Constitutional Court, that has undergone a considerable evolution over the decades and especially in the last 20 years. Indeed, today, the

* The author wishes to thank Sarah Pasetto for her comments and suggestions.

members of the Constituent Assembly would hardly recognize the current court as the body that they had in mind when they introduced, in the Italian legal order, a form of judicial protection of fundamental rights and the supremacy of the Constitution vis-à-vis the Parliament and government. Precisely because of the major changes undergone by the court over the years, a careful consideration of history appears to be the most effective approach to briefly outline the key features of the Italian system of constitutional adjudication. Therefore, to better appreciate the evolution of the Constitutional Court, the first part of this chapter deals with the history of the protection of rights before the adoption of the 1947 Republican Constitution. In the second part, an overview of the choices relating to the establishment of the Constitutional Court and of the model that was adopted are discussed, and the peculiarities of the system are highlighted. The third part takes into account the evolution of the Italian system of constitutional adjudication, having regard to the relationships between the court and the main political bodies, on the one hand, and the ordinary courts, on the other hand. Particular attention is paid to the effects on the court of the major changes occurring in relation to European integration and to the consolidation of the Constitution as the supreme law of the land. As will be seen in the fourth part of this chapter, the way in which the Constitution has progressively penetrated society and legal culture has changed the role of the Constitutional Court to such an extent that Italian scholars are examining new issues, essentially regarding the need to grant new competences to the court.

6.2 EVOLUTION OF THE MODEL OF CONSTITUTIONAL REVIEW

6.2.1 General Constitutional Setup

The Italian tradition of constitutionalism dates back to the nineteenth century, although its fundamental principles were fully established only in the aftermath of World War II. With regard to the nineteenth century, it is essential to draw a clear distinction between theory and practice. As far as theory is concerned, Italian culture had been very much influenced by the ideals of the French Revolution and contractarian theories, at least since Napoleon's campaigns. In practice, however, during the European Restoration, reference to constitutionalism was the key element in the struggle to achieve a limited government, a struggle which produced however only ephemeral political victories or, at most, compromises between traditional and constitutional points of view. These compromises formed the basis of the unitary state, as demonstrated by the fact that the first King of Italy was designated, in 1861, 'by the grace of God and the will of the Nation' and that the first Italian constitution – in fact granted by King Charles Albert to Sardinian subjects in 1848 and extended to all Italians 13 years later – was named 'statute' precisely to avoid the name 'constitution', which the Savoyard establishment considered too liberal.[1] Indeed, the notion of the 'revolutionary' nuance of the term was deeply entrenched in Italian liberal culture, as demonstrated by the definition of constitution given by Pellegrino Rossi, one of the most important figures of Italian liberalism; in his lectures on constitutional law in Paris during the 1930s, he stated that the constitution was 'the law of free states, those which escaped the rule of privileges'.[2]

The first decades of the Italian unitary state were characterized by a confrontation between tradition and liberalism, in which the main issue to address was that of legitimacy: despite the traditional legitimacy supporting the Crown, the growing importance of the principle of democracy led to the establishment of the principle of parliamentary accountability. However, it would not be accurate to equate this development with the formation of a Westminster system of parliamentary democracy, both because the Crown retained essential prerogatives on foreign and military affairs, thereby also influencing the government as a whole, and because parliamentary accountability was sometimes 'sterilized' by the practice of dissolving the Chamber of Deputies and closing legislative sessions for the purpose of freeing the government from control and censures.

The concept of constitutionalism was thus limited to an affirmation of the idea of a balance of powers. Limited government was still far from being an issue, for several reasons. First, the constitution (the so-called Albertine Statute) did not bind the legislature, so that effectively, Acts of Parliament (that had received the royal assent) could not be subjected to review for consistency with any higher law. Second, human rights were not conceived as a limit on government, since their recognition was not due to an adoption of an Anglo-Saxon meaning of the rule of law but

---

[1] On Italian constitutional history, see, among others, Carlo Ghisalberti, *Storia costituzionale d'Italia (1848–1948)* (Laterza 2000); Roberto Martucci, *Storia costituzionale italiana. Dallo Statuto albertino alla Repubblica (1848–2001)* (Carocci 2002); Giuseppe Volpe, *Storia costituzionale degli italiani.* I. *L'Italietta (1861–1915)* (Carocci 2009).

[2] Pellegrino Rossi, *Cours de Droit constitutionnel professé à la Faculté de Paris, recueilli par M A Porée* (Librairie du Guillaumin 1866), vol 1, 8 [the lectures collected were delivered in 1835–1836 and in 1836–1837].

was, rather, inspired by the German concept of *Rechtsstaat*: rights did not limit government simply because their existence derived from the recognition granted to them by the government and Parliament. In this context, it was hard to even conceive of judicial review of legislation, although the judicial branch did sometimes attempt to introduce judicial review of parliamentary procedure at least. In any case, this weak form of judicial review was swept away during the Fascist dictatorship (1922–43).[3]

The weakness of Italian democracy meant that it did not succeed in dealing with the troubles that stemmed from World War I, and the parliamentary regime soon gave way to a dictatorship, as happened in several other European countries where democracy was too young and fragile to resist the onslaught of populism. In Italy, the rejection of constitutionalism and, more generally, of liberal democracy (labeled 'plutocracies' by Benito Mussolini) lasted over two decades and eventually resulted in the moral disgrace of anti-Semitic laws and in the tragedy of World War II. After the war, the legal and political reconstruction began with the popular choice in favor of a republican system and with the election of a Constituent Assembly, that drafted the new Constitution and adopted it at the end of 1947. Italian constitutionalism thus entered a brand new phase, marked by the establishment of a human-rights oriented system and in which a new wave of case law inspired by natural law imposed limits on the government and even on the legislature, which were now bound by a Constitution conceived as the supreme law of the land. In this connection, two features of the new Constitution must be highlighted.

On the one hand, for the first time, a genuine bill of rights was adopted to protect human rights from all kinds of infringement, by any type of authority: the only way to avoid the obligations enshrined in the Constitution was supposed to be through adopting constitutional amendments, for which it was necessary to follow a complex procedure that was practically guaranteed either to generate parliamentary opposition or to afford the people with the chance to block the majority's illiberal initiatives. Unfortunately, another way would be discovered very soon:

---

[3] Concerning attempts to establish a form of judicial review of legislation before the Fascist dictatorship, see Francesco Racioppi, 'Il sindacato giudiziario sulla costituzionalità delle leggi' (1905) La legge 705; Alessandro Pizzorusso, 'Garanzie costituzionali' – Article 134 in Giuseppe Branca (ed.), *Commentario della Costituzione* (Zanichelli-Il Foro italiano 1981) 43; Francesco Roselli, 'Giudici e limiti al potere legislativo vigente lo Statuto albertino' (1986) Rivista trimestrale di diritto e procedura civile 476; Jörg Luther, *Idee e storie di giustizia costituzionale nell'Ottocento* (Giappichelli 1990) 190.

delaying the implementation of constitutional provisions. The use and abuse of this 'instrument' (a kind of 'majority filibustering')[4] paralyzed the concrete protection of many constitutional rights, especially social rights and rights to equality, for a long time, so that several constitutional provisions were implemented only in the 1970s.

On the other hand, for the first time, a mechanism for constitutional review was set up, to provide the system with an effective means of reacting against infringements of the supreme law. This aim was pursued by Articles 134–137 of the Constitution, which contained the provisions on the Constitutional Court. Oddly enough, but perhaps not surprisingly, these articles too were subjected to majority filibustering, since the court began its functions only in 1956, that is over eight years from the Constitution's entry into force. However, constitutional review preceded the Constitutional Court thanks to Clause 2 of the VII Transitional and Final Provision of the Constitution, which allowed ordinary courts to decide the controversies that would ordinarily have been referred to the Constitutional Court.[5]

6.2.2 Original Model of Constitutional Review

The choice in favor of a special court, endowed with the power to decide several constitutional controversies and, above all, to strike down legislation that was inconsistent with the Constitution did not translate, however, into a straightforward adoption of the Kelsenian model. In fact, a hybrid system was established. In Italy, the Constitutional Court wields two kinds of power: the power to decide special constitutional controversies and the power to perform constitutional review of legislation.

---

[4] See Piero Calamandrei, 'L'ostruzionismo di maggioranza' (1953) Il ponte 129, 274, 433.

[5] Cf Pasquale Costanzo, 'Disposizioni transitorie e finali I-XVIII. Leggi costituzionali e di revisione costituzionale (1948–1993) – Disp. trans. VII' in Giuseppe Branca and Alessandro Pizzorusso (eds), *Commentario della Costituzione* (Zanichelli-Il Foro italiano 1995) 143.; Marco Bignami, *Costituzione flessibile, Costituzione rigida e controllo di costituzionalità in Italia (1848-1956)* (Giuffrè 1997); Andrea Simoncini, 'L'avvio della Corte costituzionale e gli strumenti per la definizione del suo ruolo: un problema storico aperto' (2004) Giurisprudenza costituzionale 3065; Ugo De Siervo, 'L'istituzione della Corte costituzionale: dall'Assemblea costituente ai primi anni di attività della Corte' in Paolo Carnevale and Carlo Colapietro (eds), *La giustizia costituzionale fra memoria e prospettive: a cinquant'anni dalla pubblicazione della prima sentenza della Corte costituzionale* (Giappichelli 2008) 55.

The special controversies are those that arise from the distribution of power among the supreme bodies of the State, or between the central State and the Regions (Article 134(2) of the Constitution). The Constitutional Court also has the power to decide whether a referendum can be held, depending on whether its object falls within the domain determined by Article 75 of the Constitution. Finally, the court decides on charges of high treason or attempts to subvert the constitutional order brought against the President of the Republic (Article 90 of the Constitution; before 1989, the same power was also wielded in relation to ministers). From a comparative point of view, it could be noted that the Italian Court was not endowed with many 'accessory' competences: for instance, the court – unlike many other European constitutional courts – does not have any say as far as elections are concerned.

As for review of legislation, both abstract and concrete forms were established. Abstract review addresses either appeals from the national government against a regional legislative act or appeals lodged by a Region against a national legislative act. Complaints must be filed within 60 days following the publication of the challenged act(s). In these cases, the Constitutional Court decides – in principle – without referring at all to the concrete implementation of legislative provisions, even though the submission of a complaint does not paralyze the implementation of questioned provisions, so that these may have already produced effects when the court reviews them.[6] In these cases, the constitutional proceedings are designed to resolve disputes on the limits of the central State's and Regions' respective powers; the court therefore either protects the autonomy of the Regions from encroachment by the central government, or protects the State's legislative power against misuse of power by regional legislatures.[7]

---

[6] This statement is true for complaints that fall under the 2001 constitutional reform. Previously, the review of provisions already in force was conceivable only for national primary legislation, since regional legislation was challenged before the promulgation of the President of the Region, such that the law-making process was suspended and the Act could enter into force only after the Constitutional Court had decided on its consistency with the constitution. On this subject, see Carlo Padula, *L'asimmetria nel giudizio in via principale. La posizione dello Stato e delle Regioni davanti alla Corte costituzionale* (Cedam 2006); in French, see Massimo Luciani and Paolo Passaglia, 'Autonomie régionale et locale et Constitutions – Rapport italien' (2006) Annuaire international de justice constitutionnelle 229.

[7] As a matter of fact, the national government can censure any kind of breach of the constitution; thus, its claim is not necessarily related to the aim of protecting the State's legislative power.

In Italy, unlike what Kelsenian orthodoxy would suggest,[8] constitutional review can also be concrete. The Constituent Assembly rejected the idea of giving individuals the power to appeal to the court directly: the protection of individual rights – and, more generally, the constitutionality of legislative acts – must be invoked through the activity of ordinary courts, that are empowered to refer a question to the Constitutional Court when there are doubts as to the constitutionality of a legislative provision that should be applied in proceedings before them. Thus, the Constitutional Court reviews the constitutionality of the provisions on the basis of the case in which the issue arose, such that the concrete implementation of the provision is one of the elements that should be germane to the court's judgment.[9]

This two-step procedure creates a hybrid system, in the sense that it is both decentralized and centralized. It is decentralized with regard to its first stage, because any ordinary court, from the lowest court to the Court of Cassation (the Italian Supreme Court), can raise a question on the constitutionality of a legislative provision; without these initiatives, the Constitutional Court could not operate, since it has no power to initiate the constitutional review of legal provisions. Ordinary courts are thus the 'gatekeepers' of constitutional review proceedings (this definition was suggested by Piero Calamandrei,[10] a legal scholar who had been a member of the Constituent Assembly): their task is to decide whether a question of constitutionality, that can be raised either by the parties to the proceedings or by the court itself, should be submitted to the Constitutional Court. Submission requires two conditions to be met: first, the court must consider that to decide the case, it will have to apply the legislative provision in question (the condition of '*rilevanza*', that is of influence on the decision); second, the court must have doubts as to the

---

8 See Kelsen's criticism of the Austrian constitutional reform of 1929 that introduced the instrument of judicial reference to the Constitutional Court: Hans Kelsen, 'Judicial Review of Legislation. A Comparative Study of the Austrian and the American Constitution' (1942) 4 *Journal of Politics* 183.

9 Due to the sheer number of contributions, it is impossible to compile a complete bibliography on the judicial reference procedure. Among the most recent ones, see Silvia Bagni, *La questione incidentale nel controllo di costituzionalità. I sistemi italiano e spagnolo a confronto nel quadro dei modelli elaborati dalla dottrina* (Clueb 2007); Lorenzo Delli Priscoli and Paolo Giovanni Demarchi, *L'eccezione di incostituzionalità: profili processuali* (Zanichelli 2008); Nicola Pignatelli, *Le 'interazioni' tra processo amministrativo e processo costituzionale in via incidentale* (Giappichellì 2008).

10 Piero Calamandrei, *La illegittimità costituzionale delle leggi nel processo civile* (Cedam 1950) XII.

consistency of the legislative provision with the Constitution. In other words, the court need not be confident of the provision's unconstitutionality, but simply lack certainty as to its consistency with the Constitution (the condition of '*non manifesta infondatezza*'; the referring court cannot be certain that the Constitutional Court would reject the question).[11]

In the second stage, the procedure is characterized by a strictly concentrated model: the Constitutional Court itself affirmed the principle of the unity of constitutional justice, which means that only one court can issue judgments on the constitutionality of legislation.[12] More precisely, the Constitutional Court is the only authority empowered to strike down legislation: indeed, any ordinary court takes a stand on the constitutionality of a legislative provision, when it decides whether the conditions for submitting a question to the Constitutional Court have been met; the Constitutional Court, however, far exceeds this operation, since it has the power to declare a provision unconstitutional, such that the provision is withdrawn and expelled from the legal system. The withdrawal is effective on the day after the judgment is published and has retrospective effect, because once the court has issued a declaration of unconstitutionality the provision can no longer be applied, neither to facts that may happen in the future, nor to facts that have already taken place but on which final judgment has not yet been entered.

The power to strike down legislation is clear evidence that the Kelsenian conception of constitutional courts as 'negative legislators', which do not make law but only strike down legislation that is inconsistent with a higher law, was adopted.[13]

---

[11] On the conditions required for submitting a question of constitutionality to the Court, see Mauro Cappelletti, *La pregiudizialità costituzionale nel processo civile* (Giuffrè 1957); Franco Pizzetti and Gustavo Zagrebelsky, '*"Non manifesta infondatezza" e "rilevanza" nell'instaurazione incidentale del giudizio sulle leggi* (Giuffrè 1974); Nicolò Trocker, 'La pregiudizialità costituzionale' (1988) Rivista trimestrale di diritto e procedura civile 796; Francesco Dal Canto, 'La rilevanza e il valore del fatto nel giudizio di costituzionalità delle leggi in via incidentale' in Elena Malfatti, Roberto Romboli and Emanuele Rossi (eds), *Il giudizio sulle leggi e la sua 'diffusione'* (Giappichelli 2001) 145; Gian Paolo Dolso, *Giudici e Corte alle soglie del giudizio di costituzionalità* (Giuffrè 2003); Luisa Azzena, *La rilevanza nel sindacato di costituzionalità dalle origini alla dimensione europea* (Jovene 2012).

[12] See Antonio Agrò, Augusto Cerri and Franco Modugno (eds), *Il principio di unità del controllo sulle leggi nella giurisprudenza della Corte costituzionale* (5th edn, Giappichelli 2008).

[13] As a matter of fact, currently such a definition could be confirmed with difficulty, if anything because the Constitutional Court has granted itself the

The principle of the unity of constitutional justice, and its corollaries, is limited to primary legislation. The Constitutional Court is empowered to review all legislative acts, both national and regional, and governmental decrees that have the same force as parliamentary legislation either by virtue of a delegation of power from the Parliament to the executive (art 76 of the Constitution) or because an emergency that requires immediately effective provisions has arisen (art 77 of the Constitution). When it comes to subordinate legislation, however, the Constitutional Court does not exercise any competence: the consistency of this category of measures with (the constitution and) primary legislation is ascertained by ordinary courts; these have the power to refuse to apply inconsistent measures, while administrative courts may also strike them down, and thus achieve general effects for their declarations.

6.2.3 Transformation of Model

The provisions regulating the Italian system of constitutional review have not been fundamentally amended since the 1950s. Nevertheless, there are some exceptions that should be mentioned. The first is the restriction of the criminal cases that can be brought before the Constitutional Court (since the constitutional reform of 1989, ministers are no longer subject to the court's jurisdiction). The second is the change introduced in 2001 regarding abstract review of regional law; whereas previously this review occurred a priori, now it takes place a posteriori.

Despite rather steady legislative and constitutional regulation, the role and activity of the Constitutional Court have changed significantly over the years. Several factors have contributed to this; most are not directly related to constitutional justice, but have nevertheless – and unsurprisingly – had major effects.

First, the political and social context in which the Constitutional Court operates has changed over the decades. In the 1950s, when the court was established, and in the 1960s, a major issue was the implementation of many constitutional provisions. This failure to implement meant that old legislative provisions, most of which were adopted during the Fascist dictatorship, were still in force, although being in many cases seriously

---

power not only to strike down provisions, but also individual words or expressions in the text of a provision. In this case, by erasing part of the text but not the provision itself, the court changes the contents of the provision. The distance from the idea of 'negative legislator' is even greater when the court declares a legislative provision to be unconstitutional for what it fails to contain, and thus adds a part to its contents to make the provision consistent with the constitution.

inconsistent with the Constitution. Thus, the court's main task was to strike down the provisions that were too obviously and seriously unconstitutional to be tolerated any longer. The court then acted as a substitute for Parliament, in the sense that it remedied the omissions in the implementation of the new Constitution.[14] Thanks to this activity, the court gained legitimacy among lawyers, politicians and citizens. Indeed, the court was in a very comfortable position: it was perceived as the guardian of the Constitution without necessarily being an anti-majoritarian institution,[15] since no political party could expressly uphold Fascist legislation against the Constitution.

Eventually, the old legislation was progressively eliminated entirely, either by the court's declarations of unconstitutionality or by legislative repeal. In the 1970s and 1980s, the Constitution was at last (more or less) implemented. The court's main task then became the review of republican legislation: the situation was thus changing, because most of the judgments concerned legislative provisions that had resulted from a political choice of the current parliamentary majority. Nevertheless, the court could still hardly be defined as an anti-majoritarian institution, simply because the type of democracy that characterized Italy was a 'consensus democracy' as defined by Arend Lijphart.[16]

A brand new political situation emerged in the 1990s, when the electoral law was changed to set up a mixed plurality-proportional system, which transformed Italian democracy into a basically majoritarian one,[17] with strong confrontations between the centre-left and centre-right coalitions. The enduring clash between the two coalitions put the court in a far less comfortable position, because its judgments very often began to be interpreted as either disapproval or approval of the majority's political choices.[18] Moreover, the transition to a majoritarian democracy

---

[14] For an analysis of the interactions between the Constitutional Court and the legislature, see, in French, Paolo Passaglia, *Le Juge constitutionnel et le Législateur: L'expérience italienne* (Éditions Universitaires Européennes 2011).

[15] On the 'countermajoritarian difficulty', see A M Bickel, *The Least Dangerous Branch: The Supreme Court at the Bar of Politics* (Bobbs-Merrill 1962) 16.

[16] See Arend Lijphart, *Patterns of Democracy: Government Forms and Performance in Thirty-Six Countries* (Yale UP 1999).

[17] See, again, Lijphart's definition of patterns of democracy (ibid).

[18] Concerning the impact of the Constitutional Court on the political context, and its evolution through the decades, see Paolo Barile, Enzo Cheli and Stefano Grassi (eds), *Corte costituzionale e sviluppo della forma di governo italiana* (il Mulino 1982); Carlo Mezzanotte, *Corte costituzionale e legittimazione politica* (Tipografia Veneziana 1984); Alessandro Pizzorusso, Roberto Romboli and

marked a turning point also as regards the public perception of the constitution. From the 1948 to the 1994 parliamentary elections, almost all the parties in the Chambers of Parliament had been part of the constitution-making process and the vast majority of them had approved the Constitution; they therefore recognized its values as the foundation of both the legal system and of society as a whole. On the contrary, since the 1994 parliamentary elections, new parties took a seat in the Chambers, parties that had not participated in the constitution-making process and that, in some cases, did not perceive the Constitution as the fundamental benchmark for all political choices. The Constitution began to be called into question and gradually, the need for reforms arose;[19] the fact that most of the reforms proposed were not adopted (and have remained as yet unadopted) contributed to diminish the Constitution's legitimacy among the political branch and in public opinion. As a result, the legitimacy of the Constitutional Court too was called into question, since the Constitution is 'the branch in which the Court is situated'.[20]

Among the reforms adopted, that on the development of regional authorities is certainly the most important. This achievement has had extremely significant consequences for the Constitutional Court. At the beginning of the Republic's history, only five of the 20 Regions of Italy (the five that enjoyed special autonomy) were functioning; all Regions were fully set up only in the 1970s. The increasing number of entities and their expanding powers were the main factors in the multiplication of direct complaints to the Constitutional Court, which acted as an arbiter in disputes between the central State and Regions, both in abstract constitutional review of legislation and in disputes arising from the adoption of administrative acts and judicial decisions. The 2001 constitutional reform reshaped and strengthened regional authorities and their relations with the State. Unfortunately, the new constitutional provisions were so unclear that much uncertainty concerning the boundaries of the powers of

---

Emanuele. Rossi, *Il contributo della giurisprudenza costituzionale alla determinazione della forma di governo italiana* (Giappichelli 1997); Enzo Cheli, *Il giudice delle leggi. La Corte costituzionale nella dinamica dei poteri* (2nd edn, il Mulino 1999); Antonio Ruggeri and Gaetano Silvestri (eds), *Corte costituzionale e parlamento. Profili problematici e ricostruttivi* (Giuffrè 2000); Francesco Dal Canto and Emanuele Rossi (eds), *Corte costituzionale e sistema istituzionale* (Giappichelli 2011).

[19] Actually, constitutional reforms were proposed even before, in the 1980s, by the Socialist Party; it was however in the next decade that the subject became a key-topic of political debate.

[20] This expression was used by Gaetano Silvestri, 'Referendum elettorali: la corte evita un labirinto e si smarrisce in un altro' (1991) Il Foro italiano I-1349.

the different levels of government arose, thus bringing about a massive increase in the number of controversies that were referred to the Constitutional Court. As a result, the role of the latter within the constitutional system changed significantly, because its traditional main function as protector of individual rights lost its absolute dominance and now faced competition from the function of arbitration, which was once no more than marginal.

Disputes arise not only between the central State and the Regions. The last two decades have seen increasing conflicts between the political branch and the judiciary. As a matter of fact, one of the main causes of the transition to a new system of government, at the beginning of the 1990s, was the discovery of, and judicial reaction to, a vast system of corruption. Criminal prosecutions against many political leaders, especially those of the Christian Democrat Party and the Socialist Party, the two main parties of the majority, led to a dramatic turnover in Parliament. The turnover did not however end the conflicts, since several new political leaders either deeply disapproved of what they called a 'revolution by judiciary' that had taken place or were prosecuted themselves (for crimes that were not always related to political activity). The Constitutional Court was often asked to settle this type of disputes, which often concerned the immunity enjoyed by members of Parliament in relation to their prerogative of free speech, which was frequently used (and sometimes abused) as a shield against criminal prosecutions.

As far as protection of rights is concerned, another major change occurred especially at the end of the twentieth century, in connection with European integration. On the one hand, over the years the European Court of Human Rights (ECtHR) had developed a body of case law concerning fundamental rights that created the conditions for it to compete with the Constitutional Court. Nevertheless, the possibility of invoking Strasbourg's adjudication requires all internal remedies to be exhausted first: because of this limitation, the Constitutional Court can easily intervene before the ECtHR, so that problems can arise at most in relation to the influence of European case law over constitutional case law. In other words, the Constitutional Court can be influenced by the ECtHR only insofar as the interpretation of constitutional provisions is concerned. Thus, the competition between the two courts relates to the kind of protection granted to a fundamental right and the settlement of conflicts between opposing rights, but does not imply an actual alternative between the protection granted at the national level and that granted by the ECtHR.

Instead, the real 'rival' of the Constitutional Court appears to be the Court of Justice of the European Union (CJEU), that has been taking advantage of the expansion of the Union's competences, especially of the enforcement of the European Union Charter of Fundamental Rights. The latter allows the CJEU to develop a case law on rights that has the potential to become a genuine alternative to that issued by the Constitutional Court, for the simple reason that the preliminary ruling mechanism is very similar to the internal system for referring cases to the Constitutional Court: indeed, judges can often choose between the two, to determine which – the constitutional or the European one – is more convenient to pursue. The dialogue between national courts and the CJEU has much intensified, so that the Constitutional Court no longer enjoys a 'monopoly' in interacting with ordinary courts. In other words, the protection of rights is ensured at both national and European levels. In Italy, to date, no safeguard for the Constitutional Court's role in the legal system has been established, unlike the *Question Prioritaire de Constitutionnalité* that was introduced in 2008 in France (the notion of 'priority' referring to the ordinary courts' obligation to raise a question of unconstitutionality *before* proceeding to a review for compatibility with supranational law).[21]

The Constitutional Court's role as a protector of rights has also been changing, in relation to the type of interaction established with ordinary courts. One of the reasons that led to the establishment of the Constitutional Court was that ordinary courts were not considered sufficiently responsive to the new constitutional values. Since the entry into force of the Constitution, the situation has changed significantly: the Constitution has been recognized as the foundation of the legal system; constitutional provisions have proven to be effective in shaping a new civil society; and legal education has considered constitutional law to be a key field of study. All these factors have resulted in judges adopting a different approach to the Constitution: they have increasingly chosen to apply it directly, considering a law and not only a political document that requires legislative implementation.

One of the most powerful demonstrations of the cooperation established between the Constitutional Court and ordinary courts over the years concerns legislative interpretation. The time when conflicts between the Constitutional Court and the Court of Cassation as to which of the two authorities had the final word over legislative interpretation is long past. In the 1960s, those conflicts had led to the so-called 'war between the Courts' that eventually ended with the courts mutually recognizing their respective responsibilities. Today, the Constitutional

---

[21] See Marie-Luce Paris in Chapter 8.

Court is acknowledged as the supreme interpreter of the Constitution, and the Court of Cassation as the supreme interpreter of legislation.[22] Since then, the Constitutional Court has deferred to the Cassation's interpretation of laws, claiming only the power to strike down legislation or, at most, proposing its own interpretation of primary legislation when there is no consolidated interpretation. This is the 'living law' doctrine, an expression that may recall Roscoe Pound's distinction between 'the law in books' and 'the law in action',[23] the latter being – in the Italian adaptation – the law as it 'lives', that is, the law resulting from the way in which a text (the legal provision) is interpreted. By accepting this doctrine, the Constitutional Court bound itself to accepting the consolidated interpretation of a provision; thus, the court cannot override an interpretation that is generally adopted by ordinary courts.

The emphasis on the importance of judges is certainly related to the growing awareness of the complexity of contemporary societies. This complexity sets a new balance in the relations between enacted law and case law: indeed, the idea that it is possible to meet any social need through legislation, as the most appropriate way to ensure equality and justice, is no longer defendable. Contemporary societies' complexity, in fact, requires specific regulations rather than general rules, since every case appears to be different. In other words, the best solution for a case is that which enables consideration of the individual situation in as much detail and as precisely as possible. If every case is different, there is no general rule that can aspire to take all possible variables into account without creating the risk of hyper-regulation, which would have the consequence of requiring judges to apply provisions that may be logical in theory, but, once applied to a specific case, could lead to a situation where the '*summum jus*' is equivalent to '*summa iniuria*'. These considerations formed the basis for a new conception of enacted law; although this was never recognized as an 'official' doctrine, it nevertheless greatly influenced legislation and case law in practice.

Pursuant to this doctrine, enacted law must be 'flexible', in the sense that it should be limited to the expression of principles and general rules. As a result, also the judiciary's role should change, since it should be for the judge to apply those principles and general rules and deliver a

---

[22] On this subject, see Giuseppe Campanelli, *Incontri e scontri tra Corte suprema e Corte costituzionale in Italia e in Spagna* (Giappichelli 2005) 217.

[23] Roscoe Pound, 'Law in Books and Law in Action' (1910) 44 *Am L Rev* 12.

decision that takes all the elements of individual cases into account, to reach a solution that matches justice as much as possible.[24]

The increasing consideration for the role played by ordinary courts formed the basis for a new type of dialogue between the Constitutional Court and ordinary courts, the latter having been authorized to set aside the duty to refer to the former. As will be seen below, the constitutional case law of the last two decades has strengthened ordinary courts' powers, reserving for the Constitutional Court only those matters that cannot be solved by ordinary judicial interpretation. The ultimate consequence is the creation of a new balance in the protection afforded to fundamental rights, in which the role of ordinary courts has been enhanced at the expense of the Constitutional Court.

Combining the increasing number of conflicts that the Constitutional Court is called upon to settle and its diminishing activity on the protection of rights, the statement of a former President of the Court, Professor Valerio Onida, does not appear to be wrong: in his view, the institution, originally conceived as '(the) Court of rights', is turning into '(a) Court of conflicts;' in other words, the tasks that were once secondary are becoming ever more essential, in the ordinary activity of the Court.[25]

The ability to hear references from ordinary courts has always been by far – at least until the last few years – the Constitutional Court's most important competence, because, on the one hand, the vast majority of judgments issued defines this type of procedure and, on the other hand, most of the major constitutional case law had been decided pursuant to such references. Until ten years ago, references were the source of over 80 per cent of judgments and in some years were accountable for over 90 percent.[26] The court delivers on average 400–500 judgments every year, which means that at least 300 judgments (but often more than 400) would reach the court through references, while the other competences of the

---

[24] The doctrine was expressed, in the 1990s, by Gustavo Zagrebelsky, and thus it probably influenced the Constitutional Court's case law while Zagrebelsky was a member of the court (as well as in the aftermath of his mandate). See Gustavo Zagrebelsky, *Il diritto mite. Leggi, diritto, giustizia* (Einaudi 1992).

[25] Cf Valerio Onida, 'La giustizia costituzionale nel 2004. Introduzione del Presidente' (Palazzo della Consulta, 20 January 2005) <http://www.cortecostituzionale.it/documenti/relazioni_annuali/Relazione%20breve%20_Onida_.pdf> accessed 9 October 2014, 19.

[26] See Paolo Passaglia, 'Les âges du contrôle de la constitutionnalité des lois par voie d'exception en Italie' in Laurence Gay (ed.), *La Question Prioritaire de Constitutionnalité. Approche de Droit Comparé* (Bruylant 2014) 573 ff and statistical reports at 699 ff.

court have not exceeded, altogether, 100 judgments per year. These data justify the definition of the court as the court of rights. In principle, references from an ordinary court seek to ascertain the compatibility of legislative provisions with the parties' constitutional rights. On the contrary, the other forms of review are all more or less related to conflicts that have arisen either between the central State and Regions (in relation to a legislative act, in abstract review of constitutionality, or other kind of acts, in conflicts concerning the division of other powers), or between bodies and institutions of the State (that is conflicts between the supreme bodies of the State).

In the early 2000s, the situation changed dramatically. References decreased, along with the judgments to which they gave rise, whereas conflicts increased, especially between the central State and the Regions. In 2012, for the first time in the Constitutional Court's history, the judgments originating from references accounted for less than half of the total amount, not even reaching 45 per cent: concrete review had been overtaken by abstract review.[27] Only a few years ago, these results would have been simply inconceivable.

Analysis of the recent evolution is, of course, crucial when dealing with the transformation of the model of Italian constitutional justice. And once the increasing number of conflicts has been explained, the core question is to understand the reason why judicial references have been decreasing. Some of the factors mentioned so far can give part of the answer. The others require a consideration of recent constitutional case law. This is the main aim of the next paragraphs.

6.3 PRACTICE AND ENDURANCE OF CONSTITUTIONAL REVIEW

6.3.1 Constitutional Law and Supranational Law: Impact on Judicial Review of Legislation

The growing influence of supranational law on the Italian legal system and the Constitutional Court's role has been seen above. Now we will analyze the impact of the development of supranational law (and supranational courts) on constitutional case law.[28] To this end, the

---

27 Ibid., 592 ff and statistical report at 712.

28 On this subject, see, among others, Paolo Falzea, Antonio Spadaro and Luigi Ventura (eds), *La Corte costituzionale e le Corti d'Europa* (Giappichelli 2003); Antonio D'Atena and Paolo Grossi (eds), *Tutela dei diritti fondamentali e*

Constitutional Court's approach to EU law must be clearly distinguished from that adopted towards to the European Convention on Human Rights (ECHR).

The interaction between EU law and Italian law had been a very controversial subject for several years, until the Constitutional Court accepted, in 1984, the principle of primacy of what was then called 'Community' law over national law. Since then, the situation has changed little, even though the 2001 reform of Article 117 of the Constitution recognized the primacy of EU law over national legislation through the new Clause 1, according to which: '[l]egislative powers shall be vested in the State and the Regions in compliance with the Constitution and with the constraints deriving from European Union law and international obligations'.

In Judgment No 170 of 1984, the Constitutional Court allowed ordinary courts to decide conflicts between Community law having direct effect and national legislation, in the sense that the latter cannot be applied if it is inconsistent with the former. To avoid derogating from the principle of the unity of constitutional justice, however, the Constitutional Court recognized EU law's primacy only pragmatically, rather than theoretically: the decision on whether to apply national law was not to be considered as resulting from an illegitimacy, but simply as the consequence of judicial choice in favor of the special provision (the EU one)

---

costituzionalismo multilivello (Giuffrè 2004); Paola Bilancia and Eugenio De Marco (eds), *La tutela multilivello dei diritti* (Giuffrè 2004); Nicolò Zanon (ed.), *Le Corti dell'integrazione europea e la Corte costituzionale italiana* (Edizioni Scientifiche Italiane 2006); Vincenzo Sciarabba, *Tra Fonti e Corti. Diritti e principi fondamentali in Europa: profili costituzionali e comparati degli sviluppi sovranazionali* (Cedam 2008); Pietro Perlingieri, *Leale collaborazione tra Corte costituzionale e Corti europee* (Esi 2008); Daniele Butturini, *La tutela dei diritti fondamentali nell'ordinamento costituzionale italiano ed europeo* (Esi 2009); Tommaso Giovannetti, *L'Europa dei giudici. La funzione giurisdizionale nell'integrazione comunitaria* (Giappichelli 2009); Giuseppe Martinico, *L'integrazione silente. La funzione interpretativa della Corte di giustizia e il diritto costituzionale europeo* (Jovene 2009); Giuseppe De Vergottini, *Oltre il dialogo tra le Corti. Giudici, diritto straniero, comparazione* (il Mulino 2010); Giancarlo Rolla (ed.), *Il sistema europeo di protezione dei diritti fondamentali e i rapporti tra le giurisdizioni* (Giuffrè 2010). In English, see Giuseppe Martinico and Oreste Pollicino, *The Interaction between Europe's Legal Systems. Judicial Dialogue and the Creation of Supranational Laws* (Edward Elgar Publishing 2012). In French, see Massimo Luciani and others, 'Justice constitutionnelle, justice ordinaire, justice supranationale: à qui revient la protection des droits fondamentaux en Europe? – Rapport italien' (2004) Annuaire international de justice constitutionnelle 251.

over the general provision (the national one); the national provision thus still remained in force, because only EU acts prevented it from being applied. Thus, the Constitutional Court de facto granted immediate operation to the primacy of EU law, as the CJEU had ordered in the *Simmenthal* Judgment of 9 March 1978; but the price to pay was the elimination of the Constitutional Court's power to review the compatibility of national legislation with EU law. Previously, this was conceived as a matter of constitutionality, since a breach of EU law meant that the legislation (also) infringed the constitutional provision that obliges Italian legislatures (at both national and regional levels) to act in conformity with EU law. Before 2001, the fundamental constitutional provision was Article 11, according to which 'Italy agrees, on conditions of equality with other States, to the limitations of sovereignty that may be necessary to a world order ensuring peace and justice among the Nations' (European integration being perceived as establishing organizations that pursue such an objective); however, as mentioned above, after 2001, the relevant constitutional provision is Article 117(1).

For the Constitutional Court, Judgment No 170 of 1984 marked the beginning of the trend of self-exclusion from EU matters that led to the longstanding refusal to engage in any dialogue with the CJEU. Indeed, the Constitutional Court 'exiled' itself from the interaction between European and national law. This became plain when, in the 1990s, the Constitutional Court ordered ordinary courts to refer to it only once the interaction between EU and national law had been settled: if the compatibility between the two was at issue, ordinary courts were supposed to first submit the question to the CJEU through a reference for a preliminary ruling; only once the Court of Justice had decided, could the Constitutional Court be called upon to settle the constitutional issue.[29]

The only power that the Constitutional Court reserved for itself – by virtue of the so-called 'counter-limits' doctrine or the '*dottrina dei controlimiti*' – was that of reviewing the compatibility of EU law with the supreme principles of the Italian legal order and inalienable individual rights,[30] thereby expressing a position that is not too different from that adopted by the German Federal Constitutional Court with the '*Solange I*' doctrine. Unlike the evolution experienced by German case law, however, in Italy the doctrine has not changed, so far. Still, it was

---

[29] See, in particular, Judgment No 536 of 1995, which has been repeatedly followed so far.

[30] The 'counter-limits doctrine' was first affirmed in Judgment No 98 of 1965 and was confirmed in several others, such as Nos 173 of 1973, 170 of 1984 and 232 of 1989.

merely a theoretical reservation, since it is difficult to imagine the Italian Constitutional Court declaring an EU act to be inconsistent with inalienable rights. Indeed, since the counter-limits doctrine was established, the court has never applied it in practice.

The refusal to participate in European judicial integration was confirmed for a long time by the attitude towards references for preliminary rulings. The Constitutional Court considered itself to not be in the position to make such references, since it could not be conceived as a 'judge' in the sense envisaged by the EC Treaty. The idea was that if a conflict between EU and national law existed, it was not for the Constitutional Court to request the Court of Justice to settle it: the doctrine imposing an obligation on ordinary courts to settle the question *before* submitting a constitutional reference released the Constitutional Court from having to defer to the Luxembourg Court. This reasoning held as long as the Constitutional Court had to decide a judicial reference, but the problem persisted in cases of abstract review, because there was no judge (and thus no institution empowered to refer questions to the Court of Justice for a preliminary ruling) that could take part in the proceedings, and the Constitutional Court's self-exclusion could not be remedied by other courts.

Taking these problems into consideration, the Constitutional Court eventually changed its attitude with Judgments Nos 102 and 103 of 2008, at least as far as abstract constitutional review is concerned. The court accepted defining itself as a 'judge' in the sense envisaged by the Treaty on European Union, so that it is empowered (or rather, obliged – with the exception carved out by the '*acte clair*' doctrine – since it is the only jurisdiction that can take part in the proceedings) to submit a reference for a preliminary ruling. This is a very important step towards a more cooperative attitude in European matters, and the best indication yet that the Constitutional Court has finally agreed to engage in dialogue with the CJEU and transcended its traditional conception of the separation of the EU and national legal orders. The new attitude was confirmed even in judicial reference procedure, when the Constitutional Court, in Order No 207 of 2013, overruled its previous judgments on the point and accepted to make a reference for preliminary ruling.

As far as interaction with the ECHR (and the ECtHR) is concerned, the Constitutional Court has always considered the ECHR to be an ordinary international treaty, with only one notable exception: in Judgment No 10 of 1993, it emphasized the ECHR's peculiarities to prevent primary legislation from derogating from or repealing it, on the basis of the fact that it must be conceived as a direct implementation of Article 2 of the Constitution, that recognizes and guarantees inalienable human rights.

Judgment No 10 of 1993 was, however, an exception to a rather consistent body of case law. That judgment adopted a remarkably different approach: since, within national legal orders, dualism leads to international treaties acquiring the force of the national measure that incorporates them, the ECHR was classified as having legislative force because an Ordinary Law No 848 of 1955 authorized its ratification and ordered its incorporation into the Italian legal system. The effects of such definition has changed pursuant to the 2001 constitutional reform. Under Article 117(1) of the Constitution, as amended, national and regional legislatures must act 'in compliance ... with the constraints deriving from ... international obligations'; thus, the ECHR, being an 'international obligation', now prevails over national legislative acts. The constitutional provisions do not provide further details. Therefore, it was for the Constitutional Court to specify how and to what extent this primacy could be affirmed. In theory, the approach could have been the same one adopted in relation to EU law, and in fact some ordinary courts, after 2001, decided on the compatibility of national legislative acts with the ECHR themselves, just as they were empowered to do in relation to EU law. However, in Judgments Nos 348 and 349 of 2007, the Constitutional Court opted for a different approach that minimized the impact of the constitutional reform from at least two points of view. First, there was little doubt that the ECHR's primacy referred to legislation and not to the Constitution (whereas for EU law, the question is yet to be settled); in any case, the court dissolved any doubts still lingering, by recognizing the ECHR's primacy only vis-à-vis legislation. Due to the Convention's intermediate position, infringements result in breaches of the hierarchy of the sources of law. This breach amounts, ultimately, to an inconsistency with the constitutional provision that established the ECHR's primacy. In other words, breach of the Convention's provisions is an indirect infringement of Article 117(1) of the Constitution.

The remaining issue concerns the form with which such an infringement should be declared. It is precisely on this subject that the second important element of the Constitutional Court's approach emerges. Once the court has established that the contrast between the ECHR and national legislation has led to an (indirect) violation of the Constitution, the solution adopted in relation to EU law could not be applied here, due to the principle of the unity of constitutional justice: only the Constitutional Court can decide upon the unconstitutionality of legislative acts. Thus, conflicts cannot be settled with a declaration from an ordinary court; the constitutional review of legislation performed by the Constitutional Court becomes essential. As a result, it is the Constitutional Court that ensures the compatibility of the Italian legal order with the ECHR provisions, either by deciding judicial references or appeals seeking abstract review.

Once the authority empowered to review legislation has been determined, the next issue to be addressed concerns the ECHR's actual contents. In this regard, constitutional case law is unanimous in recognizing the authority of the ECtHR to – as Chief Justice Hughes had stated, with reference to the US Constitution – state 'what the Convention is'. As a result, the ECtHR's case law is considered the 'voice' of the ECHR, and the interpretations issued therein bind all national courts, including the Constitutional Court.

In practice, settling a conflict between the ECHR and national law requires the Constitutional Court to compare the two, not only to declare their compatibility or their incompatibility, but also to establish which law best protects fundamental rights. The comparison can lead to different outcomes, that were analyzed in Judgments Nos 311 and 317 of 2009. The simplest case is when compatibility is affirmed: no problems arise, and the national legislative provision is applied, since it is consistent with both the Constitution and the ECHR.

When the comparison leads to the recognition that the national legal system, combining constitutional and legislative provisions, offers better protection for the right at issue, the only possible consequence is that the national provisions must be applied since applying the ECHR would result in lesser protection for the right, this choice would be inconsistent with the Constitution. After all, the ECHR itself accepts this consequence, since under Article 53 states that '[n]othing in [the] Convention shall be construed as limiting or derogating any of the human rights and fundamental freedoms which may be ensured under the laws of any High Contracting Party or under any other agreement to which it is a party'.

The thorniest problems, however, arise in the opposite case, when the protection available under the national legal system is lacking compared to the ECHR. To deal with this situation, the Constitutional Court departed from a rigorous implementation of the principle of hierarchy and rather opted for a substantive approach, aiming to protect rights and freedoms to the utmost, 'even by developing the potentialities of the constitutional provisions' as declared in Judgment No 317 of 2009. In other words, the ECHR can influence constitutional interpretation, insofar as a legislative provision that would be consistent with the Constitution is subject to a declaration of unconstitutionality, because of the absence of protection that emerges from its comparison with the ECHR.

One question remains: what criteria are to be used in this comparison? Prima facie, the object of the comparison could clearly not be anything other than the right or freedom at issue. In fact, the Constitutional Court adopted a more comprehensive approach, requiring a comparison to be made between the right at issue and other relevant interests protected by the Constitution (for example, freedom of speech cannot be analyzed individually but must be considered in conjunction with the protection of other subjects' privacy, honor, etc.): thus, the comparison cannot refer to a single right, but rather to a specific situation and its regulation by the legal system as a whole. This appears to be the choice that the Constitutional Court has made to give effect to the power, recognized by the ECtHR to national authorities, to consider overriding reasons in the public interest, and thus adapt the legal framework of rights protection to national peculiarities.

6.3.2 Constitutional Review and Legislative Interpretation

Over the years, the Constitutional Court became the forerunner of a new role for ordinary courts in the context of constitutional review, by encouraging a new approach to legislative provisions, based on the expansion of judicial means of interpretation. In Judgment No 356 of 1996, the court expressed the new approach with words that would later be repeated continuously: '[i]n principle, legislative acts are not declared unconstitutional because it is possible to interpret them so as to render them unconstitutional (and there are courts willing to apply such an interpretation), but because it is impossible to interpret them so as to render them constitutional'. This led to constitutional case law that required ordinary courts to refrain from submitting a reference to the Constitutional Court until they had examined – and excluded – the possibility of interpreting the provision at issue so as to render it constitutional.[31] A third condition for the submission of a judicial reference to the Constitutional Court was thus introduced by means of case law: in addition to '*rilevanza*' and '*non manifesta infondatezza*', established, respectively, by Article 1 of Constitutional Law No 1 of 1948 and Article 23 of Ordinary Law No 87 of 1953, now ordinary courts must first examine the possibility of making the legislative provision consistent

---

[31] On this subject, see Giusi Sorrenti, *L'interpretazione conforme a Costituzione* (Giuffrè 2006); Pasquale Femia (ed.), *Interpretazione a fini applicativi e legittimità costituzionale* (Edizioni Scientifiche Italiane 2006); Marilisa D'Amico and Barbara Randazzo (eds), *Interpretazione conforme e tecniche argomentative* (Giappichelli 2009); Corte costituzionale, *Corte costituzionale, giudici comuni e interpretazioni adeguatrici* (Giuffrè 2010); Elisabetta Lamarque, *Corte costituzionale e giudici nell'Italia repubblicana* (Laterza 2012).

with the Constitution by means of interpretation.[32] Indeed, it is a well-established doctrine that the Constitutional Court will not decide on the merits of a case unless the referring court has documented the need for the reference due to the inefficiency of interpretation alone.

From a comparative point of view, the new condition may call to mind the UK Human Rights Act 1998, in particular its section 3(1) on the interpretation of legislation. This could be redrafted as follows to adapt it to the Italian situation: '[s]o far as it is possible to do so, primary legislation ... must be read and given effect in a way which is compatible with the [Constitution]'. To continue the comparison between the UK system and judicial reference in Italy, section 4(2) of the Human Rights Act could be redrafted as follows: '[i]f the court is satisfied that the provision is incompatible with [the Constitution], it may make a declaration of that incompatibility'. However, the similarities with the UK end here, since a British declaration of incompatibility leads (or at least should lead) to political decisions to amend the legislation in question, whereas Italian declarations give rise to a review for constitutionality. To sum up, while in a weak form of judicial review, as that established in the UK, a declaration of incompatibility is a substitute for a decision of unconstitutionality, in a strong form of judicial review, such as that in Italy, declarations of incompatibility are the prerequisite for a decision of unconstitutionality.[33]

This conclusion should not be limited to judicial references and concrete review of legislation. As a matter of fact, in abstract review too, the idea that a decision of unconstitutionality is the last resort is well-entrenched. This is demonstrated by the rather high number of 'interpretative dismissals' issued by the court, that are decisions in which the Constitutional Court does not declare a provision unconstitutional but rather offers an interpretation itself, one that makes the provision compatible with the Constitution. These decisions prove that in abstract review of legislation, the same body is entitled to experiment with interpretations to achieve consistency with the Constitution; then, should

---

[32] The question should arise on the compatibility of the new condition and the '*non manifesta infondatezza*', since when the Constitutional Court requires ordinary courts to state that it is impossible to interprete the provision in conformity with the Constitution, it can hardly be maintained that to the condition for submitting a question to constitutional review is only a lack of certainty as to the provision's consistency with the Constitution.

[33] For the opposition between weak and strong forms of judicial review, see Mark Tushnet, *Weak Courts, Strong Rights: Judicial Review and Social Welfare Rights in Comparative Constitutional Law* (Princeton UP 2009).

the experiment fail, to decide whether there are grounds for a declaration of unconstitutionality. Reference to a Latin maxim warns against extremity in dealing with the validity of legal acts: *utile per inutile non vitiatur*, meaning that 'the useful must not be vitiated by the useless'. This reference helps remarkably in understanding the approach adopted by the Constitutional Court.

6.3.3 The Constitutional Court's Impact on Other Powers

The Constitutional Court has played a key role within the Italian legal system. This is true as regards the first decades of its functioning, and remains so even for more recent times characterized by important changes in the political situation. The transition to a majoritarian democracy, as seen above, was characterized by a high degree of discord, both between left-wing and right-wing coalitions and between the political branch and the judiciary. The Constitutional Court has arbitrated most of these disputes, especially those between the political branch and the judiciary. As far as conflicts between political coalitions are concerned, the court has had greater difficulties, due to the absence of power for the opposition to directly contest the majority's decisions. Notwithstanding this problem, the court has fulfilled its function thanks to both judicial references and direct complaints submitted by the Regions. Actually, after the constitutional reform of 2001, the Regions opened a third field of conflicts, concerning the distribution of legislative and administrative powers between the central State and the Regions. Naturally, the Constitutional Court was asked to decide on these controversies. Moreover, while adjudicating, the court was effectively also asked to implement the new constitutional provisions, due to the absence of organic legislation to substantiate the remarkable innovations introduced.

The social and economic crises of recent years have exacerbated many conflicts, especially in relation to the policy choices made to deal with the crisis and manage decreasing funds. From time to time, the Constitutional Court was called upon to settle some of these conflicts, and always succeeded in ensuring the protection of the basic principles of the legal system. This is no small achievement, considering that difficulties can enhance the importance of finding solutions, to the point that even law can be neglected to a certain extent: in his classification of social systems, Ugo Mattei identifies a category of systems based on the 'rule of politics' where the pursuit of a political objective (for example, economic development or self-sufficiency) prevails (or can prevail) over compliance with legal rules. Taking these risks into account, the Constitutional Court's role can be described as protecting the 'rule of law' in times of crisis, vis-à-vis the danger of slipping into a 'rule of politics'. In the 1980s, Louis Favoreu stated that the French Constitutional Council led 'politics to be captured by law'[34] in a country where, in 1981, a member of Parliament could still boldly reply to critiques moved by the opposition by saying 'you are legally wrong because you are a political minority';[35] in the last two decades, the Italian Constitutional Court has ensured that politics, that had already been captured by law, remained submissive to the law even when this submission could not be taken for granted. To accomplish this task, the court had only one instrument: referring to the Constitution and emphasizing its binding effects over all decisions and policies; in other words, by reasserting the conception of the Constitution as the supreme law.

As a matter of fact, even the new approach to judicial legislative interpretation mentioned above is connected to the rising awareness that a constitution is above all a source of law, no matter how peculiar it may be and no matter how important its political dimension. Also, a constitution conceived as a source of law must be treated as a source of law, just like any other. After all, this is nothing more than an application of Chief Justice Marshall's legacy, which was to see 'the very essence of judicial duty' in deciding on the operation of each of the conflicting laws, the Constitution being one of them: 'if both the law and the Constitution apply to a particular case, so that the Court must either decide that case conformably to the law, disregarding the Constitution, or conformably to the Constitution, disregarding the law, the Court must determine which of these conflicting rules governs the case'.[36]

Thus, the interplay between the Constitutional Court and ordinary courts is also influenced by the growing need to make the constitution the cornerstone of the entire legal system. Paradoxically, the way to pursue this objective requires a diminution of the factual importance precisely of the first guardian of the constitution: the more the constitution is perceived as a law that differs from others only because of its supremacy, the less is the Constitutional Court needed to assess this supremacy; the more widely is the constitution applied (especially to influence legislative interpretation), the less must the Constitutional Court apply it (especially to react to infringements by legislative acts).

---

[34] See Louis Favoreu, *La politique saisie par le droit: Alternances, cohabitation et Conseil constitutionnel* (Economica 1988).

[35] The statement was expressed by a Socialist member of the National Assembly on 13 October 1981, during a debate concerning a law regulating the nationalization of factories.

[36] *Marbury v Madison* 5 US 137 (1803) 178.

On the basis of these statements, it is not surprising that the evolving concept and strength of the Constitution have produced changes in the system of constitutional justice, and it is reasonable to expect further transformations in the near future.

6.4 FINAL REMARKS

As previously said, in recent years a dramatic fall in judicial references is characterizing the activity of the Constitutional Court.This fall can be easily explained by the concurrence of supranational courts and, above all, by the new approach to legislative interpretation. The problem does not lie in the numbers, but rather in the type of cases that are submitted to the Constitutional Court. On the one hand, the court must often deal with minor issues, in which the constitutional matter remains in the background; thus, the number of judicial references could, and probably should, decrease even further. On the other hand, by giving ordinary courts the power to conform legislation through interpretation, the Constitutional Court has accepted the risk that it would not be called upon to decide pivotal constitutional matters, since the condition for avoiding a reference to the Constitutional Court is to argue that the legislation *can* be interpreted consistently with the Constitution. One could surely ask whether it is acceptable that the Constitutional Court, the supreme interpreter of the Constitution, did not take part on high-profile debates on constitutional matters.

Avoiding the Constitutional Court is not only due to the choices made by ordinary courts. There is longstanding debate on whether the court's impossibility to intervene on certain important issues is due to the presence of certain immunities (for example, the court cannot review Parliamentary election proceedings because of Article 66 of the Constitution, according to which the Houses of Parliament are the only judges of their own elections): in other words, there are some off-limits zones for constitutional justice. Moreover, some legislative acts are not supposed to be applied in proceedings before ordinary courts, since it is difficult to meet the conditions for submitting a judicial reference (in particular, that of '*rilevanza*'): for this reason, it is very unlikely that the Constitutional Court will have its say, since the system of constitutional justice lacks efficient alternatives for access to the court.[37]

---

[37] As far as problems in acceding the Constitutional Court are concerned, see Renato Balduzzi and Pasquale Costanzo (eds), *Le zone d'ombra della giustizia costituzionale. I giudizi sulle leggi* (Giappichelli 2007); Roberto Pinardi (ed.), *Le*

All these arguments lead to the recognition that the Constitutional Court's marginalization on important constitutional issues may be the result of two factors, which are entirely independent of each other: the first has to do with constitutional case law, and the second with the system's framework. As far as systemic problems are concerned, the main solution is to reform either the Constitution or the legislative provisions on the Constitutional Court, to allow other subjects, entities or authorities, to submit questions through new forms of proceedings or appeals. From time to time, the introduction of a remedy to give standing to individuals seeking to protect their constitutional rights was suggested.[38] Such a reform would certainly enable the Constitutional Court to afford better protection to rights and to intervene in cases where judicial references would be impossible or highly unlikely. Nevertheless, the cost of these benefits would not be insignificant, because endowing individuals with standing for constitutional review leads to a massive increase in the cases to be decided. Ultimately, the alternative would be to accept either the protracting of constitutional proceedings and the consequent delay in decisions, or selectivity in deciding cases. The first option does not appear very attractive: the Italian Constitutional Court experienced a backlog in the 1980s, and the reduction in the time required to decide a case that was achieved at the end of that decade was considered an important result for the protection of rights, since the principle that 'justice delayed is justice denied' is unanimously shared. The second option is therefore almost necessary, but case selection in civil law countries is not as 'normal' and 'acceptable' as it may be in common law countries, where the practice plays an important part in the efficient operation of courts (the example of the US Supreme Court speaks for itself). On the contrary, the tradition in civil law countries tends to require courts to decide (all the) cases brought before them: the

zone d'ombra della giustizia costituzionale. I giudizi sui conflitti di attribuzione e sull'ammissibilità del referendum abrogativo (Giappichelli 2007).

[38] On these propositions, see Roberto Romboli, *La riforma dell'*amparo *costituzionale in Spagna e l'introduzione di un ricorso individuale diretto in Italia*, in *Scritti in onore di Lorenza Carlassare* (Jovene 2009) 1555; Paolo Passaglia, *Sull'inopportunità di introdurre il ricorso diretto individuale: il dibattito italiano*, in Rolando Tarchi (ed.), *Patrimonio costituzionale europeo e tutela dei diritti fondamentali. Il ricorso diretto di costituzionalità* (Giappichelli 2012) 323.

French concept of '*déni de justice*' (denial of justice),[39] as an infringement of the fundamental right to justice, illustrates the Continental approach to the issue quite paradigmatically. If it is difficult to accept the introduction of individual constitutional appeal together with a procedure of case selection, then the only alternative could be to accept a de facto selection (for example, by deciding minor cases by summary judgment), that could however lead to problems of excessive judicial subjectivity.

Other types of remedies would create fewer problems, and would ensure constitutional review in fields that currently appear off limits. For example, reforms could focus on constitutional review of parliamentary elections, or could grant the parliamentary opposition the power to submit questions of constitutionality, so that legislative acts that would be difficult to refer to the Constitutional Court could be brought before it, thanks to the dissenting minority of Parliament. These reforms, associated with others, would create 'a more perfect' system, thus empowering the guardian of the Constitution to accomplish its tasks even in areas where currently a lack of protection can be observed.

New competences would strengthen the court's role without changing its essence. This would not be the case, however, with regard to certain changes in constitutional case law. As described above, the development of 'constitutionally oriented' legislative interpretation reduced the number of judicial references to the Constitutional Court. It is worth asking whether this process has gone too far, whether the court designed for itself a role that is now becoming excessively marginal. In other words, the question is whether a centralized system of constitutional review can tolerate the importance that the Constitutional Court has granted to ordinary courts.[40] A negative answer would lead to calls for an overruling in constitutional case law, to force ordinary courts to submit constitutional questions as soon as a doubt of constitutionality arises: this would mean reverting to the original distribution of responsibilities between the Constitutional Court and ordinary courts, the distribution suggested by the constitutional and legislative provisions that regulate constitutional justice through the condition of '*non manifesta infondatezza*'.

However, ultimately, this point of view would amount to nothing more than turning back time. Thus, the question is whether the Constitutional

---

[39] Article 4 of the French Civil Code of 1804 states that '[a] judge who refuses to give judgment on the pretext of legislation being silent, obscure or insufficient, may be prosecuted for being guilty of a denial of justice'.

[40] For the analysis of the evolution towards a decentralized model, see Ana Maria Nico, *L'accentramento e la diffusione nel giudizio sulle leggi* (Giappichelli 2007).

Court and the legal system as a whole can ignore the fact that Constitution has deeply penetrated society and the courtrooms, to the point that the system of constitutional justice as conceived many decades ago no longer suits present needs. Indeed, such a change in the conception of the Constitution has occurred that perhaps the Constitutional Court's guidance in implementing the Constitution is no longer needed; or rather, is needed only infrequently, and not constantly, as it had been in the past. As a result, instead of trying to revitalize judicial references to the Constitutional Court, the core of the problem could be addressed by accepting the fact that since constitutional consciousness has grown up, the reference proceeding has begun to grow old. Maybe, the time has come to think of the Italian system of constitutional review from a different point of view.

7. Spain

The Spanish experience of rights-based review or how constitutional case law has been more principled than legislation in defence of fundamental rights

Agustín Ruiz Robledo

The power granted to the American courts to rule on the unconstitutionality of laws still forms one of the most powerful barriers that has ever been raised against the tyranny of political assemblies.

Alexis de Tocqueville, *Democracy in America*, 1835

7.1 INTRODUCTION

The Constitution of 1978 designed, for the first time in Spanish history, a powerful Constitutional Court with three main functions: to ensure the normative force of the Constitution, to resolve conflicts between territorial powers of the autonomous State, and to guarantee the fundamental rights of citizens. This chapter presents a brief exposition of the Constitutional Court and its functions analyzing its normative configuration but also dealing with the practice both of the composition of the court and its judgments. It concludes with a personal assessment of its position and usefulness in the Spanish political-legal system.

7.2 EVOLUTION OF THE SPANISH MODEL OF CONSTITUTIONAL REVIEW

7.2.1 Historical Context

Spanish constitutional history dates back to 1812 when Parliament, known as Las Cortes, approved the first constitution in Cadiz, a city at that time besieged by the French invaders. Troubled Spanish history gave birth to another five constitutions during the nineteenth century (in 1834, 1837, 1845, 1869 and 1876), some progressive and others conservative, but all heirs, to a greater or lesser degree, to the suspicion of judges held by the Cadiz Constituent Assembly. Therefore, the Constitution reserved the interpretation of the laws to Parliament and ordered the courts to refer to Parliament any question on the 'interpretation of any law' that might arise in its application. Without going to that extreme, for more than 100 years, the Spanish legal system was based solely on the principle of legality, which all judges and courts were subject to, without being able not to enforce a law deemed unconstitutional, in contrast with the courts in the United States for example. The Constitution was considered just a 'programmatic law' whose effectiveness depended on the development of the legislation that Parliament would give to it.

In 1931, the Second Republic was proclaimed and established several new Spanish institutions, one of which was the creation of a Court of Constitutional Guarantees, whose function was precisely to ensure the submission of laws to the Constitution, as the Czechoslovak and Austrian Constitutions had done a few years before, in 1920. However, the fear of what was then called the 'dictatorship of the robes' meant that the court's composition was completely inadequate, with most of its members elected by municipal councillors, as a kind of territorial second chamber of Parliament. The subsequent operation of this court was unlucky – everything bad that could happen did, in an unfortunate Republic that disappeared with the coup d'état of General Franco in 1936 and his subsequent dictatorship, which logically offered no room for a constitutional court since there was not even room for a constitution worthy of the name.[1]

7.2.2 Original Model of Constitutional Review: Constitutional Jurisdiction in the 1978 Constitution

Nearly 50 years and a few wars after 1931, the parliamentary representatives elected in the democratic elections of June 1977 saw constitutional justice in a very different light from that of the Second Republic. Constitutional justice was then thought to be very useful for three objectives: first, to guarantee the normative force of the constitution; second, to protect the rights of citizens; and third, to resolve the

---

1 See Martin Bassols Coma, *El Tribunal de Garantías Constitucionales de la II República: la primera experiencia de justicia constitucional en España* (Boletín Oficial del Estado 2010).

inevitable conflicts of competence that would occur in the autonomous State.[2] As had happened before in other European countries, which had suffered dictatorships in the twentieth century with Germany in the lead, the Spanish people were quick to establish the basis of constitutional justice convinced – as was, a century earlier, Alexis de Tocqueville – that the judicial control of constitutionality is 'one of the most powerful barriers that has ever been raised against the tyranny of political assemblies'.[3]

The disjunction between the diffuse model of constitutional justice of the US and the Kelsenian concentrated type was rapidly resolved by the Constituent Assembly in favour of the latter. This was both for the theoretical reason that the Assembly considered the function of the control of constitutionality as a distinct function of the judiciary to apply the law to the specific case, and for the practical reason of not putting the interpretation of the Constitution in the hands of a judiciary appointed during Franco's time. Thus, the 1978 Constitution established a Constitutional Court with so wide a range of competences, that sometimes it is said to be one that has the most powers in the world.[4] The appointment process is different from the one used for selecting judges, in which the political parties have a major role. That kind of election comes, largely, from the conception of the constitution as a pact between the main political and social forces of the country that are, therefore, entitled to reserve the designation of the body that ultimately controls compliance of the constitutional text. The current Constitutional Court is arguably a countermajoritarian organ in the sense that its main function is to ensure that the majority does not break the constitutional pact to the prejudice of the minority.

7.2.3 Transformation of the Model

Spanish lawmakers were so convinced of the need for constitutional justice that within a year of the 1978 Constitution entering into force, they enacted Organic Law 2/1979 of 3 October 1979 on the Constitutional Court (LOTC). In the following months, longstanding jurists were

---

[2] See Agustín Ruiz Robledo, *Constitutional Law in Spain* (Wolters Kluwer 2012) 132–3.

[3] Alexis de Tocqueville, *Democracy in America* (first published 1835, trans and eds, Harvey C Mansfield and Delba Winthrop, University of Chicago Press 2000) 103–4.

[4] See Eduardo García de Enterría, *La Constitución como norma y el Tribunal Constitucional* (3rd edn, Civitas 1991).

elected to serve on the court, so that, far from the precedents of the Second Republic, their prestige could endorse the decisions of the new constitutional body. Their first judgment is dated 26 January 1981. It has only been 34 years since then, a relatively short time for an institution, and even more so in this case, considering that not a comma of Title IX of the Constitution, exclusively reserved to the Constitutional Court, has been amended.

However, the model that was created in 1979 has changed considerably because many of its elements have been modified in the eight reforms of the LOCT. Indeed new competences have been added (defence of local and *foral* autonomy), others removed (prior appeals against laws), the requirements to access the court modified (protection of rights and conflict of jurisdiction) and the internal operation of the court reorganized (distribution of cases between the Plenary and Chambers). To explain this pattern in the practice and endurance of Spanish constitutional review, I shall first detail the composition of the Constitutional Court and then address its competences, noting in both cases the normative regulation and practices derived from it, highlighting especially its role in rights-based litigation as defender of fundamental rights.

7.3 PRACTICE AND ENDURANCE OF CONSTITUTIONAL REVIEW

7.3.1 The Composition of the Constitutional Court

The Constitution regulates in great detail both the composition, and the status and functions of the Constitutional Court. It highlights its central role which is more important than the role of the other organs of constitutional relevance, which the Constitution merely mentions, remitting their regulation to law, as is the case for the Supreme Court. Article 159 of the Constitution states that the Constitutional Court is composed of 12 members appointed by the King, four of whom shall be nominated by Congress with a three-fifths majority, four by the Senate with an identical majority, two at the proposal of the government of the nation and two by the General Council of Judicial Power. Members of the Constitutional Court are appointed from among Spanish citizens who are judges, prosecutors, university professors, civil servants and lawyers, all of whom must be jurists of recognized competence with at least 15 years of professional experience. Tradition indicates that, at the least, the two members chosen by the General Council of Judicial Power shall be judges, although that number is usually higher. At present, there are seven such judges, a number that had not been achieved until now. Moreover, historically, the Spanish Constitutional Court has been, like the European Court of Human Rights (ECtHR), a court of professors, which has proved controversial. While to some, professors are better prepared to understand the problems that their decisions may create in the political system, and judges are too attentive to the legal interpretation of the text, to others, professors tend to take their dogmatic categories to their judgments, without worrying too much if these match the text of the Constitution, while judges are supposed to adhere both to the letter and spirit of the Constitution.[5]

Organic Law 6/2007 of 24 May 2007 amended the LOTC so that, among other issues, it laid down that the four judges chosen by the Senate had to be among the candidates presented by the legislative assemblies of the Autonomous Communities in the terms established by the standing orders of the chamber, so that each chamber must propose two candidates.[6] The Popular Party presented two appeals of unconstitutionality against the new draft of the LOTC and the Senate's standing orders as limiting the upper chamber's power of decision, a power not subject to such a condition under Article 159 of the Constitution. The Constitutional Court dismissed both appeals: the first because the aim of permitting the participation of the Autonomous Communities in the initial phase of the selection of judges held by the Senate was not contrary to its configuration as an organ of territorial representation;[7] the second appeal, which claimed that the draft LOTC was contrary to the Senate's standing orders, was also rejected, although the court came up with an interpretation in accord with Article 184.7 of the Constitution on the standing orders. Under this provision, if the majority of three-fifths needed to choose the four judges from among the candidates proposed by the autonomous assemblies was not obtained in the upper chamber, the Senate could freely vote for other jurists to fill the vacant places.[8] The judges' appointment is for a period of nine years and the Constitutional Court is renewed by one-third every three years – obliging them to be chosen by lot on the first two occasions that the court had to be renewed

---

[5] See Roberto Blanco Valdés, '¿Para qué sirve el tribunal constitucional?' (2012) No 225 *Claves de razón práctica* 86–97.

[6] About this major reform of the LOTC, often referred to in this Chapter, see Pablo Pérez Tremps (ed.), *La Reforma del Tribunal Constitucional: actas del V Congreso de la Asociación de Constitucionalistas de España* (Tirant lo Blanch 2008).

[7] STC 49/2008, 9 April, Case *Article 16 LOTC*.

[8] STC 101/2008, 24 July, Case *184.7 del Reglamento del Senado*.

in 1983 and 1986. This periodic renewal permits the composition of the principal interpreter of the Constitution to adapt to the changes that, by virtue of the democratic process, are produced in the constitutional organs in charge of designating them.

In practice, and to date, the quorum of three-fifths of the Congress and Senate – 210 votes and 158 votes, respectively – has been obtained only if PSOE (the Socialist Party) and PP (the Conservative Party) agree. This has resulted in delays and procrastination on a number of occasions. In recent years, these delays have continued to accumulate for about three years for the Senate and one and a half years for Congress, so that the entire Constitutional Court has been renewed in less than three years: in January 2011, four judges were renewed by the Senate; in July 2012, four by the Congress; and in June 2013, the two selected by the government and the two selected by the General Council of Judiciary Power were renewed. The outgoing President of the Constitutional Court, Pascual Sala, described in his farewell speech how this accumulation of renewals was a 'serious anomaly' that harmed 'the proper functioning of the Court'.[9] In that same speech, Sala criticized another recent anomaly: Organic Law 8/2010 of 4 November 2010 has amended the LOTC to provide that 'if there is delay in the renewal by third of judges, the new appointed ones shall subtract from their time of service the delay in the renewal'. Since this provision clashes with Article 159.3 of the Constitution as a mandate for judges of nine years, I think Sala has every reason to describe it as 'nonsense' and to demand that it be changed urgently before it causes an institutional problem when, in 2017, the legal time limit for judges appointed by the Senate expires, despite being constitutionally entitled to three more years in the post.

Concerning these two anomalies pointed out by the former president of the Constitutional Court, I would dare to point out yet another anomaly in the appointment of constitutional judges. The quorum of three-fifths majority in the Congress and the Senate was established in the Constitution in order to seek consensus, namely that deputies and senators would agree on the personalities of who should be appointed. This was done on the occasion of the first election of the members of the Constitutional Court. However, the system has evolved, if not degenerated, into a quota system, or *lottizzazione*, in the words of Italian journalist Alberto Ronchey expressed in 1977 – an expression later adopted in the Spain

---

[9] See Pascual Sala's speech at <http://www.tribunalconstitucional.es/es/actividades/Documents/DISCURSO%20RENOVACI%C3%93N-2012.pdf> accessed 2 May 2015.

context.[10] Now, when Parliament has to discuss the appointment of members of the Constitutional Court, or any other institution, the discussion between the political parties is solely to agree on how many members each will appoint, but once the right 'batch' has been agreed on, nobody dares ask about the suitability of the individuals who have been elected.

Therefore, the hearings of the nominees in the appointment committees of the Congress and the Senate, required under the 2007 amended LOTC, were made in a few hours and were mostly about praise and congratulations among the majority political parties and blame from most of the smaller parties for having been excluded from the pact – this was nothing like the tough hearings that take place in the US Senate, for example, on the suitability of the proposed candidates. Although obviously, it is not sensible to copy a foreign institution if the political culture of the host country (with its rigid party discipline) is very different from the original (separation of powers and independence of senators).[11] Without questioning the quality of the judges being elected by this system, it is worth commenting on one of its perverse effects: as noted above, the LOTC was amended in 2007 so that the four members to be appointed by the Senate have now to be chosen from nominations submitted by the legislatures of the Autonomous Communities, as a response to the criticism made by peripheral nationalists who believed that they were not represented in the Constitutional Court whose role is to resolve disputes between the Autonomous Communities and the State. When, in 2011, the Senate first used the new method of appointment, only one of the four members chosen (two by PSOE as their share, two by PP) was a specialist in autonomous law and not one of them received the backing of the nationalist parties. The contempt of the major parties for the Senate, with its territorial function given by the Constitution, went so far that the people who negotiated the agreement about the candidates were the spokespersons for PSOE and PP in Congress.

From this, one can infer that the seemingly elaborated system of appointment of the members of the Constitutional Court – as regards the number of authorities involved in the appointment process, the range of profiles allowed for membership, the periodical renewal of membership,

---

[10] Alberto Ronchey, *Accadde in Italia: 1968–1977* (Garzanti Libri 1977).

[11] About the difficulties of importing a particular US institution to a different political system, see the interesting and ironic reflections of Nicolás Ramiro Rico, 'Breves apuntes críticos para un programa moderadamente hetetodoxo del "derecho poltico" y de su muy azorante enseñanza' in *El animal ladino y otros estudios políticos* (Alianza 1980) 114–15.

and representation of the Autonomous Communities since 2007 – has evolved into an imperfect system largely because of anomalies revealed in practice by a highly politically divisive context. For all these reasons, we may conclude that although the Constitution has created an elaborate appointment system, involving a number of constitutional organs and demanding great technical skills of its members, the use that the parties have made of it so far is far from being the most appropriate in order to strengthen the prestige and authority of the court.

7.3.2 The Competences of the Constitutional Court

The Spanish Constitutional Court has several competences to ensure the normative force of the Constitution, resolve conflicts between territorial powers of the autonomous State and guarantee the fundamental rights of citizens. Although every competence can serve these three functions, the most specific to ensure fundamental rights is the appeal for constitutional protection and the defence of rights.

A. The control of the constitutionality of laws and norms with the force of law, either of the State or the Autonomous Communities

In Kelsen's theoretical design of constitutional justice at the beginning of the twentieth century, the appeal of unconstitutionality against laws was the typical competence of the 'guardian of the constitution'. It was recognized as the primary competence of the Spanish Constitutional Court by Article 161 of the Constitution. However, Kelsen's scheme, in which this review is only initiated at the instance of political organs, was modified in Austria in 1929 to permit the ordinary and constitutional courts to collaborate – a tendency which has been maintained in most European constitutions, including Spain.[12] Ordinary courts have the capacity to refer questions on unconstitutionality when they have to apply a norm with the force of law which they consider to be contrary to the constitution. This specific control of laws so deeply displeased Kelsen that he considered the function of ensuring the supremacy of the constitution must be made by the constitutional court in abstract judgments of norms, in which the appellants did not have, in principle, any another objective than to maintain the supremacy of the constitution

12 See Pedro Cruz Villalón, *La formación del sistema europeo de control de constitucionalidad* (CEC 1987).

acting as a 'negative legislator'.[13] However, they should not intervene where the interests at stake were those of specific people; moreover the intervention of the supreme interpreter of the fundamental law was dependent on the opinions of ordinary courts and not on the major constitutional actors.

The Spanish experience has confirmed Kelsen's idea of a collaboration between the ordinary courts and the Constitutional Court assigning to the ordinary courts a role in guaranteeing the constitutionality of the laws, as in the diffuse US system. However, the essential feature of a concentrated control has not entirely disappeared: the monopoly to declare that a norm is within the law lies exclusively in an organ not integrated into the judicial power, namely the Constitutional Court. Far from being counterproductive, this collaboration between the ordinary courts and the Constitutional Court is proving to be the best way to 'purify' the legal system and expel unconstitutional norms. And this occurs without indicating that in many such cases of judicial review of unconstitutionality, which in Spain are very frequent, the appellants' interest in asserting their arguments – or political interests – without being genuinely concerned to ensure the supremacy of the Constitution, as is sometimes demonstrated by their immense cynicism: it is enough that a party that filed a constitutional complaint against a law, allegedly regarded as an 'attack' on the Constitution, wins the election so that the urgency of changing the law is lost.

The LOTC details the norms that can be subject to constitutional review, either by way of an individual appeal or by way of referral of a question by a judge.[14] Judgments pronounced in proceedings for unconstitutionality take effect from the moment of their publication in the Official State Gazette. The Constitutional Court can declare the unconstitutionality of the principles challenged based not only on the provisions cited in the proceedings, but also any others it deems violated. This is much more so if they are from other normative texts, whose most evident

---

[13] See Hans Kelsen, *General Theory of Law and State* (first published 1945, Clark 2007) 268 ff.

[14] Six categories of such norms can be distinguished and they are as follows: (i) Statutes of autonomy and other organic laws; (ii) Other provisions with the force of law, without prejudice, in the case of legislative-decrees, to the control that the laws of delegation themselves may stipulate in favour of the courts, although in practice no law has ever established such control; (iii) International treaties; (iv) Standing orders of the Chambers and Parliament; (v) Laws, acts and normative provisions with force of law of the Autonomous Communities; (vi) Standing orders of the legislative assemblies of the Autonomous Communities.

and paradoxical effect occurred in the STC 31/2010 case where the Constitutional Court declared unconstitutional various articles of the Catalan Autonomous Statute of 2006, without having been able to do the same with other similar articles in other autonomous statutes, such as that of Andalusia of 2007.[15]

A special feature of the Spanish constitutional system must be pointed out at this stage: in federal states where the supreme interpreter of the Constitution has to say if a law – whether federal or state law – respects the division of powers, it only has to compare this law with the Constitution. However, the Spanish Constitutional Court also has to refer to the Statute of Autonomy of the Autonomous Community involved and other laws that may affect the delimitation of competences, such as the Organic Law of Judicial Power, the Law on Financing of the Autonomous Communities, etc. This set of laws has the doctrinal name of 'constitutionality block'. The arguing of these constitutional cases is made difficult in practice because, given the large number of norms to be taken into account by the constitutional judge in order to determine who has the disputed competence, the parties always find something on which to base their position and the Constitutional Court has to argue at length as to why it chooses one norm over another.

After setting out the general characteristics of the control of unconstitutionality, the specific characteristics of the appeal and question of unconstitutionality must be explained. First, the Constitution establishes, under Article 162, that the appeal of unconstitutionality can be lodged, first, by the President of the Government, then the Ombudsman, or 50 deputies, 50 senators, the executive bodies and the legislative assemblies of the Autonomous Communities. The LOTC has restricted the authority of these two autonomous bodies – executive and legislative – to lodge appeals against laws, provisions or acts with the force of law to those that may affect their own sphere of autonomy. The Constitutional Court has accepted the constitutionality of that restriction even though, at first, it interpreted it strictly as a defence of its own competences; from the decision in STC 199/1987 of 16 December 1987 dealing with the case of

---

[15] The specialists also have different opinions abouts this judgement. See Enrique Álvarez Conde, Cecilia Rosado Villaverde and Francisco SanJuan Andrés (eds), *Estudios sobre la Sentencia 31/2010, de 28 de junio, del Tribunal Constitucional sobre el Estatuto de Autonomía de Cataluña* (Universidad Rey Juan Carlos 2011). See my opinion in Agustín Ruiz Robledo, 'El preámbulo del Estatuto catalán como manifestación del Estado neoautonómico' (2011) No 13 Revista General de Derecho Constitucional (extraordinario dedicado al Estatuto de Autonomía de Cataluña después de la STC 31/2010) 1–15.

the *Ley Antiterrorista II*,[16] the court has given it a much wider interpretation considering that as the appeal on grounds of unconstitutionality is designed to purify the legal system and not for the preservation of the scope of competences, a 'point of material connection between state law and the autonomous community sphere of competences' is enough,[17] so that the court has practically admitted all challenges made by the autonomous bodies. As this 'point of connection' is very easy to establish, the doctrine has come to view this as a tacit derogation of the requisites demanded by the LOTC for autonomous bodies to be able to appeal against state laws.

The appeal of unconstitutionality is lodged by way of petition addressed to the Constitutional Court within the period of three months from the publication of the norm with the status of law. The petition must set out the articles of the contested norm as well as the constitutional provisions that are alleged to have been violated. Once declared admissible, the petition – which does not generally suspend the validity of the impugned norm – is sent by the Constitutional Court to the Congress and the Senate, to the government and, when appropriate, to the executive and legislative organs of the Autonomous Communities. All these organs may be officially represented and make representations. To try to lessen the litigation between the State and the Autonomous Communities, Organic Law 1/2000 of 7 January 2000 amended the LOTC to enable the head of the government, and where relevant, the executive and legislative bodies of the Autonomous Communities, to lodge this appeal within a period of nine months, provided always that both parties agree to open negotiations to resolve the discrepancies caused by the new norm. The experience so far has shown that it is reasonably efficient at solving conflicts between the State and an Autonomous Community when both are of the same political colour, but much less so when they are of different political persuasions.

Secondly, as regards the question of unconstitutionality, this constitutional remedy enables Spanish judges and courts to ask the Constitutional Court about the adaptation of a law to the fundamental norm, when, in particular proceedings, they consider that a law applicable to the case and on whose validity the judgment depends, is unconstitutional. The judge or the court referring the question may not limit herself or itself to expounding her or its doubts or to transmitting the opinions of the

---

16 STC 199/1987, 16 December, Case *Ley Antiterrorista II*.

17 STC 194/2004, 4 November, Case *Gestión conjunta de los parques nacionales*.

parties, but must give an opinion grounding the unconstitutionality of the norm and explaining its importance for the resolution of the case at hand. This question is presented, as required by the LOTC, once the action has been concluded and before the expiry of the period for giving judgment and after hearing the parties and the Department of Public Prosecutions. In practice, the constitutional remedy of the question of unconstitutionality was rarely used in the early stages of its existence because judges, trained in the principle of legality, would routinely compare the law that they had to implement with the provisions of the Constitution. However, with the passing of time – and with the entry of new members into the judiciary – judges have accepted that the Constitution is a norm which limits Parliament's power and the question of unconstitutionality has become the most important way to judge the constitutionality of laws, rather than by appeals, questions having the advantage over appeals of being much more objective and often with less political baggage.[18] Thus, for example, in 2011, 51 questions were presented against 31 appeals; in 2012, 42 compared to 38, and in 2013, 106 against 76.

The individual courts making up the Constitutional Court itself, or where relevant, the sections, may present a question of unconstitutionality to the Plenary if they consider that an appeal of unconstitutionality should be granted because the applicable law violates a fundamental right. As with a question referred by the ordinary courts, the internal question is presented before judgment is given, and the time limit to give the judgment is suspended until the Plenary has given its decision. This procedure was set out in the reform made by Organic Law 6/2007 of 24 May 2007, since the original wording of Article 55.2 of the LOTC stipulated that the self-question should be submitted after judgment was passed. However, this could cause a disagreement between the opinion of a formation of the Constitutional Court and the Plenary. This has been criticized by a majority of constitutional academics, and this criticism was, for once, taken into account by the legislator.[19]

B. The conflicts of jurisdiction and the government's challenge to the provisions and rulings of the Autonomous Communities

In the context of a decentralized state, positive and negative conflicts of jurisdiction may be distinguished. First, the government of the nation and

---

[18] See Juan Manuel López Ulla, 'La cuestión de inconstitucionalidad tras la reforma de la Ley Orgánica 6/2007 del Tribunal Constitucional' in Pérez Tremps (n 6) 177–216.

[19] See Manuel Aragón Reyes, 'La reforma de la Ley Orgánica del Tribunal Constitucional' (2009) No 29 *Revista Española de Derecho Constitucional* 22.

the governing councils of the autonomous legislatures may lodge appeals alleging positive conflict of jurisdiction within two months against the provisions, rulings and acts emanating from State organs or from the Autonomous Communities when they consider that they do not respect the 'block of constitutionality'. The great majority of these conflicts are between the State and one or more Autonomous Communities and only very exceptionally between the Communities inter se. The most relevant role of the Constitutional Court in relation to the autonomous State – whether by this way of conflict or the appeal of unconstitutionality – is that both the central organs of the State and those of the Autonomous Communities have appealed to it with great frequency, something that has not happened at all in Germany, for example, which was the principal model borne in mind when designing Spanish constitutional justice. This has led the Constitutional Court to pronounce a great number of rulings profiling the system of competences to the point that we can speak of a 'jurisprudential autonomous State' since the court's decisions have a central role in forming the State.[20]

Secondly, as regards negative conflicts, private individuals may lodge allegations of negative conflicts of competences when none of the bodies – State or Autonomous Communities – to which they have made a request, considers itself competent to resolve any claim. These types of conflict have been rare in the more than 30 years of existence of constitutional remedies; the Constitutional Court has only given three judgments of this type and 20 judgments of inadmissiblity based on various grounds. Curiously, in all three judgments, the Constitutional Court denied that the conflict was in fact negative and so directed the appellants to the ordinary jurisdiction. And completely unknown, at least until now, is the possibility of a negative conflict presented by the State claiming that a specific competence is that of an Autonomous Community which it refuses to exercise under Article 71 of the LOTC. The reverse possibility – that of the Autonomous Communities lodging a

---

[20] See, for example, STC 76/1983, 5 August, Case *LOAPA* (the Constitutional Court declared the bulk of Organic Law on Harmonization of the Autonomous Process unconstitutional); STC 164/2001, 11 July, Case *Ley del Suelo de 1998* (the Constitutional Court ruled that the town planning competences belonged to the greater extent to the Autonomous Communities hereby extraordinarily limiting the State's capacity to regulate land as well as its capacity to pass supplementary legislation); and STC 31/2010, 28 June, Case *Estatuto de Autonomía de Cataluña* (the Constitutional Court declared 14 stipulations of the Statute of Catalonia 2006 unconstitutional and reinterpreted many others).

negative conflict – does not exist, this, however, would be useful, given that, at present, there is no judicial remedy to resolve disagreements between the State and an Autonomous Community on questions of transfers of services and civil servants.

Article 161.2 of the Constitution allows the government to challenge before the Constitutional Court the provisions and rulings adopted by the organs of the Autonomous Communities with the effect of suspending the provision appealed. The LOTC has developed this constitutional remedy as a residual instrument in relation to appeals and conflicts, so that an illegal act that supposedly breaches the Constitution may be appealed when, due to its political content, it is more appropriate for constitutional rather than ordinary jurisdiction to review it. This residual power has given rise to a very low number of proceedings – by December 2012, only six judgments had been made. However, Article 161.2 of the Constitution is much more important in the autonomous State than could be deduced from the number of cases because Articles 30 and 62 of the LOTC permit the government to lodge appeals of unconstitutionality and conflicts of competences, having the effect of suspending the operation of the norm or the application of the act complained of, although the Constitutional Court must ratify or lift the measure within five months. All the governments that Spain has had since the enactment of the 1978 Constitution, without distinction of political party, have systematically used this power.

Recently, the government has used the capacity assigned to it under Article 161.2 of the Constitution to appeal a decision of great political and social significance, namely the Resolution of the Parliament of Catalonia of 23 January 2013, which adopted the Declaration of sovereignty and the right to self-determination by the people of Catalonia. The legal problem raised by this Resolution – and on which there is great division among scholars – is whether it can be challenged. Indeed, for some, the Resolution has no legal effect, which would make it just a manifestation of will (which could even be protected as freedom of thought), but not in a legal 'provision'. The Constitutional Court unanimously held that the Resolution was unconstitutional because sovereignty is vested in the whole Spanish people, and not only in the people of Catalonia.[21]

---

[21] STC 42/2014, 25 March, Case *Declaración de soberanía de Cataluña.*

C. The conflict of power between constitutional bodies of the State

The LOTC creates a procedure to resolve conflicts between government and the Congress, the Senate or the General Council of Judicial Power, or between any of these organs inter se. The procedure commences with an application to the plenary of the organ that considers its sphere of powers prejudiced, after previously requesting, in vain, that the encroaching organ modify its action or to remedy its inaction. As in the cases of conflicts of competences, the Constitutional Court must determine the disputed power, using not only what is set out in the Constitution, but also what is set out in the organic laws that assign competences to constitutional bodies.

In one such instance, the General Council of Judicial Power claimed that the competence to elect 12 of its members did not belong to Parliament as the Organic Law 6/1985 on Judicial Power of 1 July 1985 so stipulated; to this, the Constitutional Court argued that a hypothetical invasion of the authority of a constitutional body like this caused by a law must be challenged by way of appeal on the grounds of unconstitutionality and not by this conflict-based remedy.[22] The second case in this type of procedure was a conflict initiated by the government against the Senate, in which the Constitutional Court gave judgment in favour of the government that had claimed that its constitutional capacity to declare certain bills as urgent had been invaded.[23] Behind that institutional confrontation was a political confrontation: in November 1995, the Socialist Government was a minority in the Senate, so that a majority articulated by the Popular Party reduced to 20 days the discussion on the decriminalization of abortion, a goal that the Constitutional Court could not avoid in a judgment five years later.

D. Conflicts in defence of local self-government

The 1978 Constitution, faithful to the design of classic constitutional justice, failed to provide any procedure to allow local bodies to challenge laws that they considered contrary to their local autonomy. However, in subsequent years, the idea grew that it would be desirable to grant this, above all after the adoption of the European Charter of Local Autonomy

---

22 STC 45/1986, 17 April 17, Case *LOPJ-I*. See Ángel José Gómez Montoro, *El conflicto entre órganos constitucionales* (Centro de Estudios Constitucionales 1992).

23 STC 234/2000, 3 October, Case *Tramitación urgente del Proyecto de Ley Orgánica sobre regulación de la interrupción voluntaria del embarazo*. See David Delgado Ramos, 'De la separación de Poderes al conflicto entre órganos constitucionales' (2009) No 7 *Revista de las Cortes Generales* 143–84.

in 1985, which established that local bodies must have a way of legal appeal available for the defence of their competences. This proposal, well adapted to the Constitution, materialised in the reform of Article 162 to allow municipal and provincial governments to have the right, under certain conditions, to lodge an appeal of unconstitutionality. However, because in Spain political parties are reluctant to amend the Constitution, what was used on this occasion, was the open clause of Article 161.1.d of the Constitution in order to revise the LOTC which resulted in a complex constitutional procedure now established under Organic Law 7/1999 of 21 April 1999.

The conflict in defence of local autonomy allows local bodies (whose number vary according to the scope of application of the contested norm) to appeal the laws and norms with force of law of the State and of the Autonomous Communities that challenge local autonomy. This procedure has the exclusive aim of determining whether or not that autonomy has been damaged or breached. If the decision is provisional, then the Plenary of the Constitutional Court will refer an internal question of unconstitutionality that will give rise to a new judgment, in which it can now be declared whether the State or autonomous norm appealed is contrary to the Constitution. In spite of the strength with which local representatives demanded this legal instrument, it has not been much used.[24] Only two judgments have been passed on these conflicts under this procedure by the Constitutional Court so far, although seven are currently pending.

E. Prior control of treaties

Treaties may be subject to an appeal or a question of unconstitutionality, in accordance with the principle of supremacy of the Constitution and the specific mandate of Article 85.1 which requires an amendment to the Constitution for the conclusion of treaties that contain provisions conflicting with constitutional provisions. Therefore, Article 27 of the LOTC includes treaties among the norms that can be appealed and/or made the subject of questions of constitutionality. However, Spanish authorities cannot modify treaties with the same freedom as they can amend a law, as recognized under Article 96 of the Constitution: 'Their provisions may

---

[24] See Enric Fossas Espadaler, 'El conflicto en defensa de la autonomía local: un experimento constitucional fallido', in Pérez Tremps (n 6) 903–24. See my opinion: Agustín Ruiz Robledo, 'El conflicto en defensa de la autonomía local' in Federico A Castillo Blanco (ed.), *Modificaciones y panorama actual del Régimen Local Español* (CEMCI 2000) 113–49.

be repealed, amended or suspended in the manner provided in the treaties themselves or in accordance with the general rules of international law.'

Because of this special feature of treaties, as agreements between two or more States, the Constitution expressly provides for a request on the constitutionality of international treaties, giving the possibility to consult the Constitutional Court before ratification with a view to examining the compatibility of a particular treaty with the Constitution. This is in order to prevent, as far as possible, a treaty already in force, valid and fully binding on Spain under international law, being declared unconstitutional – a hypothesis that has, fortunately, never happened. However, the Constitution puts strict limits on the standing requirements required to initiate this review: only the government, the Congress or the Senate (all of these three are in practice the same: the ruling party) may request the Constitutional Court to declare whether the text of a treaty signed ad referendum is consistent with the Constitution and therefore can be ratified by the competent constitutional body – the government or Parliament, whichever is the case under Article 94 of the Constitution, although it is likely to be Parliament. The opinion issued by the Plenary of the Constitutional Court in this process is not a non-binding opinion or report, but rather a 'Declaration'. The effect of this Declaration is fully binding on State powers, so that if the Constitutional Court considers that there is a contradiction between the Constitution and the treaty intended to be ratified, the only alternative would be either to amend the Constitution or not to give the final consent to the treaty.

To date, the government has used this method of control of treaties in only two cases. In the first case – that of the Declaration 1/1992 of 1 July of 1992 – the Constitutional Court unanimously declared that the ratification of the Maastricht Treaty would require amendment of Article 13.2 of the Constitution in order to allow citizens of other States of the European Union to be candidates in local elections. In the second case – that of Declaration 1/2004 of 13 December of 2004 – the Constitutional Court decided by a majority that there was no need to amend the Constitution to incorporate the Treaty establishing a Constitution for Europe. This decision bears, to a certain extent, a particular significance as far as the relationships between constitutional law and EU law regarding fundamental rights protection is concerned. Some commentators analysed Declaration 1/2004 as a change of mind to previous statements of the Constitutional Court which had only admitted the supremacy of EU law over sub-constitutional legislation and matters in which it had been given competences, but did not support the displacement of the Constitution in the field of fundamental rights. In contrast,

Declaration 1/2004 holds the principle that primacy of EU law over the Spanish Constitution is also allowed.[25]

To be exhaustive on this issue of constitutional review of treaties, one final comment relates to treaties in force and ratified by Spain, none of which has, so far, been appealed before the Constitutional Court. However, there has been one case in which the validity of a treaty was involved which is the constitutional challenge against the Decree-Law 14/1998 of 9 October of 1998 for the accession of Spain to various agreements of the International Monetary Fund. The appeal on the constitutional challenge to this set of agreements was upheld as the Constitutional Court did not accept that the Decree-Law met the financial treaty ratification requirements that Article 94 of the Constitution reserves to Parliament; however, that Decree-Law was not annulled in the end in order 'to avoid damage that might in another case accrue to the IMF and other States'.[26]

7.3.3 The Role of Constitutional Review in Enforcing Rights: Appeal for Constitutional Protection and the Defence of Rights

In principle, the jurisdictional protection of fundamental rights is the duty of ordinary courts in all types of proceedings. In addition, Article 53.2 of the Constitution stipulates that the rights recognized in Article 14 and Section I of the Second Chapter (Fundamental Rights) are protected before the ordinary courts by a procedure based on the principles of preference, or priority, and speed. This same Article 53.2 provides the legal basis for a constitutional remedy, namely the appeal for constitutional protection to the Constitutional Court for the defence of those rights. The subsidiary character of the appeal for constitutional protection with regards to appeals to the ordinary jurisdiction is at the basis of Article 123 of the Spanish Constitution. The provision states that the Supreme Court is the highest judicial organ in all 'orders, except in matters concerning constitutional guarantees', which logically are matters for the Constitutional Court, bearing in mind that decisions of the Supreme Court and Constitutional Court can be challenged before the ECtHR provided the conditions set out in the European Convention on Human Rights (ECHR) are met.

---

[25] See Antonio López Castillo, Alejandro Sáiz Arnaiz and Víctor Ferreres Comella, *Constitución Española y Constitución Europea: análisis de la Declaración del Tribunal Constitucional (DTC 1/2004, de 13 de diciembre)* (Centro de Estudios Constitucionales 2005).

[26] STC 155/2005, 9 June, Case *Decreto-ley sobre FMI.*

In practice, the use of appeal for constitutional protection started sporadically, until it became so widespread that it threatened to affect the functioning of the Constitutional Court. In order to prevent this, Organic Law 6/2007 of 6 May 2007 tightened the requirements of the appeal for constitutional protection such that the long periods before appeals were resolved – which in some cases had reached ten years – have now shortened to within one or two years.[27] Another problem that has arisen in the practice of appeal for constitutional protection has been produced by the frictions and conflicts between the Constitutional Court and the Supreme Court. These tensions have had three moments of maximum public expression as briefly presented here. First, in February 1994, a majority of the judges of the First Court of the Supreme Court, disagreeing with a decision of the Constitutional Court,[28] which had overruled one of the Supreme Court's decisions, agreed to ask the King to exercise his role of moderator between institutions. After the wave of criticism that this provoked, both ordinary and constitutional judges must have had second thoughts because the petition was never formalized. Secondly, on 23 January 2004, the Court of the Civil Jurisdiction of the Supreme Court condemned 11 judges of the Constitutional Court for serious negligence in the exercise of their function, which led to a tough accord in the Plenary of the Constitutional Court on 3 February 2004 concluding with the invasion of constitutional jurisdiction. However, although the constitutional judges paid the fine, they subsequently filed an appeal for constitutional protection, this was recently decided by the constitutional Court on 5 June 2013 – none of the 11 condemned constitutional judges were part of the court formation on this occasion: the Constitutional Court considered that the conviction by the Supreme Court was a violation of the fundamental right to effective judicial protection because constitutional resolutions 'are not subject to appeal or judicial review by any court', not even by the Supreme Court. Thirdly, in the case on *Interrupción de la prescripción de los delitos*,[29] the Constitutional Court held that the case law relating to the statute of limitations on crimes of Article 132 of the Criminal Code, then being conducted by the Criminal Chamber of the Supreme Court, was contrary to the right to effective judicial protection. The Supreme Court responded with a non-jurisdictional agreement of the Plenum of 25 April 2006 in which it

---

[27] See Francisco Fernández Segado, *La reforma del régimen jurídico-procesal del recurso de amparo: (reflexiones en torno a la Ley Orgánica 6/2007, de reforma de la Ley Orgánica del Tribunal Constitucional* (Dykinson 2007).

[28] STC 7/1994, 17 January.

[29] STC 63/2005, 14 March.

declared that it would 'maintain the existing case law on the interruption of prescription despite the Constitutional Court's decision', later quoted in several judgments. The Constitutional Court reaffirmed its doctrine.[30]

To prevent these clashes – so unedifying to the public – several measures were taken under Organic Law 6/2007 of 6 May 2007 among which was that Constitutional Court's judgments cannot be subject to any legal proceedings in any State court. Subsequently, Organic Law 5/2010 of 22 June 2010 amended the Criminal Code to clarify the case of interruption of the statute of limitations on crimes, thus avoiding the discrepancy in interpretation between the two highest courts.[31] Despite this, the delay with which the domestic judiciary operates has resulted in several judgments of the Constitutional Court annulling sentences of the ordinary courts in applying the doctrine of the Supreme Court on prescription and not that of the Constitution Court – thus implying a 'manifest disregard of the duty of compliance with the doctrine of the Constitutional Court, which is a patent failure of the mandate set out in Article 5.1 Organic Law of Judicial Power from which derives the consequent injury to the applicant's right to effective judicial protection enshrined in Art. 24.1 SC'.[32]

Violations of those fundamental rights enshrined in Articles 14–29 of the Constitution have to originate in provisions, legal acts or unlawful conduct of the powers of the State, the Autonomous Communities and other public bodies, and their officials and agents. On that basis, the Constitutional Court has rejected actions initiated against foreign governments or against the institutions of the European Union.[33] On the other hand, the Constitutional Court has found a way to allow violations of the fundamental rights committed by individuals to be constitutionally reviewed: when a case before it in which the basic cause is the action of an individual (for example, a redundancy with an alleged violation of a fundamental right), then the Constitutional Court has indirectly analyzed this action on the basis that the ordinary court has violated the right to an effective remedy since the ordinary court has not resolved the violation of another constitutional right.[34]

---

[30] See STC 29/2008, 20 February, Case *Kio*.

[31] See Rosario Serra Cristóbal, 'Nuevos tiempos en las relaciones entre el Tribunal Supremo y el Tribunal Constitucional en España: ¿De las desavenencias a una relación dialogada?' (2014) No 18 *Anuario Iberoamericano de Justicia Constitucional* 371–99.

[32] STC 32/2013, 11 February, Case *Studios Viales*.

[33] STC 64/1991, 22 March, Case *APESCO*.

[34] STC 18/1984, 7 February, Case *Caja de Ahorros de Asturias*.

The right to bring such an appeal for constitutional protection is very wide, and every natural or legal person with a legitimate interest may do so, as can the Ombudsman and the Ministry of Public Prosecutions. The time limit is, however, peremptory as the appeal must be lodged within 30 working days of the notification of the final judicial ruling, a period that is extended to three months from the decision becoming final when the appeal is made against a parliamentary act without the force of law. The Ministry of Public Prosecutions may intervene at all stages of the appeal on these grounds to defend legality, citizens' rights and the public interest protected by law. Exceptionally, public administrations can also appeal in the few cases where they hold rights to which this form of appeal is applicable (such as that of effective guardianship).[35]

The procedure for admitting the appeal for hearing, which in other constitutional matters is almost automatic, is difficult to overcome in these cases and much more so since the 2007 reform of the LOTC. The 2007 reform amended the requirements of the appeal for constitutional protection in order to reduce the Constitutional Court's overwhelming caseload, which had resulted in some decisions being delayed by ten years. While until 2007, the appeal only had to set out the facts and legal grounds about an alleged fundamental rights violation, after the 2007 reform, the requirement of an alleged breach was no longer in itself enough and it now has to be justified by the special constitutional importance of the appeal. The Constitutional Court will now allow an appeal to be lodged only if it is of special importance, all others being rejected ad limine. Article 50 of the LOTC lays down three criteria in this regard: 'its importance for the interpretation of the Constitution, for its application or for its general efficiency and for the determination of its content and the scope of fundamental rights'. The Plenary of the Constitutional Court set out in 2009 its criteria in a catalogue of seven suppositions, although confirming that this was an approach that could be changed in the future.[36] These criteria are as follows:

(1) that the appeal poses a problem on a fundamental right where there is no existing doctrine of the Constitutional Court;
(2) that the appeal gives the Constitutional Court the opportunity to clarify or change its doctrine;

[35] The LOTC regulates this meticulously under different procedures according to whether the act appealed against is administrative (art 43 LOTC), judicial (art 44 LOTC) or parliamentary without the force of law (art 42 LOTC).

[36] STC 155/2009, 25 June, Case *Vallejo Marchal.*

(3) when the alleged violation of a fundamental right appealed against originates from the law;
(4) if the alleged breach of the fundamental right results in a repeated jurisprudential interpretation of the law that the Constitutional Court considers as damaging the fundamental right in question;
(5) when the doctrine of the Constitutional Court on the fundamental right referred to in the appeal is repeatedly ignored by the ordinary jurisdiction;
(6) in the case that a judicial organ shows a manifest intention not to respect the doctrine of the Constitutional Court; and
(7) when the matter raised goes beyond the case at hand because it poses an important legal question with general social or economic repercussions, or has general political consequences.

Once the leave for appeal has been granted, the Constitutional Court may suspend the operation of the act appealed against to ensure the effectiveness of the appeal. Decisions granting the appeal must set out three statements, which are normally cumulative, namely a declaration of the nullity of the act appealed, a recognition of the right asserted, and the restoration of the appellant's full integrity of her/his right.

7.4 CONCLUSION

The Spanish Constitution of 1978 designed a Constitutional Court with sufficient powers to ensure the superiority of the founding text, the effective exercise of fundamental rights and adjudication of jurisdictional disputes in the autonomous State – the three major functions of constitutional justice. The Constitutional Court's birth occurred in 1980 with great anticipation and was surrounded by the utmost prestige, given the high level of jurists chosen to create it. The first judgments of the Constitutional Court confirmed all expectations, with significant decisions such as those which delimited Church-State relations that had been intertwined in the Franco era,[37] purified ancient laws to ensure their conformity with the new Constitution,[38] limited democratic legislative power to maintain the supremacy of the founding law,[39] or guaranteed direct effect of fundamental constitutional rights (although there was no a

[37] STC 1/1981, 26 January, Case *Ejecución de sentencia de tribunal eclesiástico.*

[38] STC 4/1981, 2 February, Case *Ley de Bases de Régimen Local de 1953.*

[39] STC 5/1981, 13 February, Case *Estatuto de Centros de 1980.*

specific law developing this right).[40] The Constitutional Court was right even in the writing of its decisions, with a style that, while using technical language, managed to be clear and well-argued. Tocqueville would smile to see how Spain was fulfilling his sharp statement on the role of constitutional justice.

For about 20 years, the *auctoritas* of the Constitutional Court was huge and its jurisprudence more than satisfactorily carried out its function of supreme interpreter of the 1978 Constitution. Especially it managed, thanks mostly to the appeal for constitutional protection, to project fundamental rights throughout the legal system and in the activity of the judges, who came to apply the Constitution daily, far from the idea of a programmatic text without application by the courts, subject only to the rule of law. Admittedly, the Constitution was a law that was often interpreted in a formal and very mechanical way, leading to such disproportionate results as, for example, to reject a claim because the lawyer's signature was missing, although the lawyer in the proceedings in question appeared to be perfectly identified. The Constitutional Court was forced to abandon these practices, imposing the most suitable interpretation for the effectiveness of fundamental rights.

However, at the end of the twentieth century, the Constitutional Court's reputation began, for various reasons, to suffer. These included the failure to make periodic renewals of the court, and the fact that the new election of judges was not based on the consensus of the parties to find the best unbiased judges, but rather on obtaining a share of the quota – besides which, those responsible for the appointment did not always strive to find the 'best sword' of the legal world. In any case, all this conveyed the image of a politicized court with its members labeled 'conservative' or 'progressive' depending on who was designated. Moreover, the Constitutional Court began to accumulate a backlog of cases causing delay, giving judgments ten years after the start of the proceedings. The flood of appeals for constitutional protection was the main cause of the delay, compounded by the frequent use of the other appeals by individual parties.

Criticism of constitutional jurisprudence has thereafter become increasingly common, up to the point where the main nationalist parties in Catalonia, the Basque Country and Galicia disqualified all its jurisprudence on the distribution of powers in the Barcelona Declaration of 1998, accusing the Constitutional Court of adopting a centralist stance. In subsequent years, came other controversial decisions such as the 2004

---

[40] STC 11/1981, 8 April, Case *Decreto-ley de Huelga*.

judgment of the Supreme Court against its members, or the appeal against the Statute of Catalonia which, instigated in 2006, was not resolved until 2010, and in a way that, in Catalonia, was thought of as an attack. Simultaneously, the political parties were unable to agree on the renewal of the members of the Constitutional Court. Finally, other judgments with great media coverage in which the Constitutional Court decided in favour of the government of the day, and in contradiction with its precedents, have contributed to give many jurists and citizens the impression that the Constitutional Court is politicized. For example, as above mentioned, its Declaration 1/2004 established that it was not necessary to amend the Constitution to ratify the Treaty establishing a Constitution for Europe thus going against its own doctrine set out in the previous Declaration 1/1992. Another example is Judgment 62/2011 of 5 May 2011 in which the court overturned the earlier decision of the Supreme Court that prevented the coalition BILDU (a Basque nationalist party thought to be linked to the terrorist organization of ETA) from standing in the elections – a judgment that the Constitutional Court adopted by six votes against five and separating itself from its own doctrine on the reviewing role of judicial decisions.

Therefore, it is not surprising that many scholars have made proposals for constitutional reform including, in the most extreme, the one of the very demise of the Constitutional Court. In my opinion, we should start from what has already been resolved, or find ways of doing so. Thus, the 2007 amendment of the LOTC has been quite effective to discharge the appeals for constitutional protection, since the Constitutional Court has managed to rule on more cases than those lodged.[41] Also, in the legislative area, conflicts of competences are reasonably regulated with the possibility of opening a negotiation process between the parties. However, the survival of the appeal of unconstitutionality does seem very questionable, leading, as it does, to multiple political clashes between both the main parties of the State and between the central and autonomous governments.

This leads, precisely, to the heart of the problem, which is not so much legal as political, or rather related to political culture: Spanish politicians seem to have internalized Clausewitz who could be paraphrased as regards the appeal for constitutional protection as being the continuation of politics by legal means. First, politicians would try to control it as best

---

[41] In 2012, 7205 appeals for constitutional protection were lodged and 7515 resolved, compared with 10 792 lodged appeals and 15 693 resolved appeals in 2009.

as they can and then use it as often as they can to justify their argument. And here is a paradox that perhaps may have its psychological explanation: Spanish politicians in the government (be it national, regional or local) often act as if the Constitution is only there to regulate the electoral process, so that when they win an election, they consider they have a democratic mandate to act without any limits, beyond their personal commitment to the common good; but opposition politicians have a completely different view and believe that the Constitution is a 'cookbook full of recipes' that would allow them to take measures that restrict extraordinarily the will of the winning party. Needless to say that some politicians move easily from one to the other view, depending only on the post they occupy in Parliament or in the country.

This last point is especially complicated since some ruling parties in the Autonomous Communities have claimed that their Communities should not be limited by the Constitution, or that they have right to do 'constitutional engineering' to the effect that the Constitution does not interfere with their will, especially if it has been endorsed directly by the citizens, as in the Statute of Catalonia of 2006. In this case, the Constitutional Court was faced like Ulysses and the classics with the complicated dilemma of navigating between Scylla and Charybdis: if it was to accept the appeal, the Constitutional Court would end by crashing against the Scylla of the almost complete unconstitutionality of the Statute, with serious damage being directed at the integration of Catalan's aspirations to self-government espoused by most political parties and with the bonus of legitimacy having been endorsed by the citizens. But, if to avoid that risk, the Constitutional Court followed the thesis of the defenders of the Statute, the court would have accepted it completely, which would have meant that the legal logic of Charybdis would have swallowed it with great prejudice, in this case, to the supremacy of the Constitution since many statutory articles clearly contradicted it. The Constitutional Court tried a brokered way denying that Catalonia could be defined as a 'nation', therefore eliminating some articles and reinterpreting many others of the 2006 Statute. In my opinion, this was a commendable attempt to find a middle way. However, other opinions were different: the Catalan party, that supported the view that the judgment on the Statute was an attack on Catalonia, organized a mass demonstration in Barcelona on 10 July 2010; from the opposite side, some press media of great social weight felt that the judgment had been a great concession to the nationalists, a view shared by many Spanish nationals. Bridging the gap, we could say that the *third Spain* of the Second Republic, which believed in a compromise between opposing views, turned out to be a minority.

Technically, these issues can be tempered by, for example, removing the appeal of unconstitutionality and extending the prior declaration of treaties to the statutes of autonomy, as indeed the LOTC expected to do in its original law in 1981, which was later repealed. Perhaps we should insist that the real solution is not so much technical as a matter of political culture, meaning that political parties should internalize constitutional mandates and act with *constitutional loyalty*. It would generally mean fewer unconstitutional laws, and then specifically, in relation to the Constitutional Court, it would mean both seeking the election of its members by consensus and appealing to the court only in cases where there are sufficient arguments to defend the unconstitutionality of the norm. We are hopeful that one day something like this will happen.

8. France

The French system of rights-based review: from exceptionalism to parochial constitutionalism

Marie-Luce Paris*

Le respect de la Constitution est non un risque mais un devoir.[1]

8.1 INTRODUCTION

France is generally categorized in the European continental model of constitutional review of legislation operated by a specialized court. Yet, the French system, based on a tradition of *légicentrisme* and a fear of 'government by judges', has very much stood apart in this regard. There has been, as for other things, an '*exception française*' featuring a system with originally no proper constitutional court and, until a 2008 reform, a limited form of constitutional review. Before then, rights were protected by a mechanism combining ex ante abstract constitutional review of legislation operated by the French Constitutional Council (FCC or Council) against the provisions of the 1958 Constitution, and a form of conventionality review performed by ordinary judges against rights

* Part of the research for this chapter was developed during a fellowship at the Australian National University Centre for European Studies, Canberra, Australia. The author would like to thank the ANUCES for their sponsorship in allowing presentation of earlier findings. I also express my gratitude to Matthew Zagor and James Stellios, colleagues in the ANU College of Law. My thanks also go to John Bell and Marc Verdussen for their helpful comments.

[1] 'Respecting the Constitution does not represent a risk but is a duty' by Pierre Mazeaud (former President of the Constitutional Council) replying to Pascal Clément, Minister for Justice, in the context of legislation on electroning tagging (Press release, 27 September 2005).

contained in international conventions, in the European Convention on Human Rights (ECHR) in particular. This has changed with the introduction of ex post concrete constitutional review in 2008. The *Question Prioritaire de Constitutionnalité* (QPC) or Priority Preliminary Ruling on the Issue of Constitutionality is a new constitutional remedy which allows individuals to challenge before ordinary courts laws already in force that infringe their constitutional rights and freedoms. Subject to a filtering mechanism involving the two highest courts (namely the Council of State, the supreme administrative court, and the Court of Cassation, the supreme judicial court), the issue of constitutionality is decided by the FCC under Article 61-1 of the Constitution:

> If, during proceedings in progress before a court of law, it is claimed that a legislative provision infringes the rights and freedoms guaranteed by the Constitution, the matter may be referred by the Conseil d'État or by the Cour de Cassation to the Constitutional Council which shall rule within a determined period.[2]

With nearly 500 QPC decisions rendered by the Council since its entry into force in 2010, the new review has solidly and rapidly established itself in domestic constitutional law.[3] In addition to being a 'French legal success story'[4] from a quantitative perspective, the QPC has also been a qualitative advance which has affected all areas of law, most prominently criminal law, tax law, procedural law, environmental law and public health law. Significant rulings have provoked changes in the legislation on, for example, police custody, involuntary confinement and sexual harassment.[5] The introduction of ex post review certainly represents a landmark in the development of constitutionalism in the French context, bringing the now more complete system of rights-based review in line with the dominant European model of constitutional review. Yet, the QPC

---

[2] All translations are from the Council's website unless otherwise stated. See <http://www.conseil-constitutionnel.fr/conseil-constitutionnel/english/homepage.14.html> accessed 19 June 2015.

[3] As of 1st March 2015. For figures on the QPC, see the Council's website, 'Découvrir la QPC' <http://www.conseil-constitutionnel.fr/conseil-constitutionnel/francais/la-question-prioritaire-de-constitutionnalite/decouvrir-la-qpc/decouvrir-la-question-prioritaire-de-constitutionnalite-qpc.47106.html> accessed 19 June 2015.

[4] Olivier Dutheillet de Lamothe, 'A French Legal Success Story: The 'Question Prioritaire De Constitutionnalité' (14 September 2012) <http://www.conseil-constitutionnel.fr/conseil-constitutionnel/root/bank_mm/discours_interventions/2012/dutheillet-sept2012.pdf> accessed 19 June 2015.

[5] QPC decisions are available on the Council's website; some are translated into English.

had to 'fit in' an already settled and complex domestic courts system featuring, as outlined above, a singular scheme of rights adjudication involving review of constitutionality and review of conventionality. Various issues arose at drafting stage and in the first years of operation of the QPC, posing interesting challenges in terms of constitutional justice and governance. In the course of the analysis below, the argument will be made that this seemingly convergence does not mean that all exceptionalism has disappeared. Rather, issues of constitutional design and adjudication affecting the drafting and operation of ex post review have been marked by a great deal of parochialism. The primary concern for setting up the QPC was to restore the 'competitiveness' of the domestic constitutional remedy, as against the remedy based on the review of conventionality. The technique of the QPC was crafted with almost only domestic considerations in mind allowing a very limited comparative insight (except maybe vis-à-vis the Belgian system deemed to be the closest in this regard). In other words, if the French system of rights-based review has utterly changed from an internal perspective, it is still rooted in a very peculiar approach to constitutionalism.

This chapter is divided into two main parts. The first part, about the evolution of the model of constitutional review, aims at explaining the original form of constitutional review and its subsequent development with emphasis on the QPC. The second part examines the practice and endurance of the new form of review through the analysis of specific issues raised by the introduction of the QPC from an institutional perspective, in particular the changing role of the FCC and its dialogue with other courts – ordinary and European – as well as with the legislative power.

8.2 EVOLUTION OF THE MODEL OF CONSTITUTIONAL REVIEW

Before the introduction of the QPC, French constitutionalism was an exception in the European context.[6] This was best embodied by the paradox that the Constitution, as benchmark for review, was theoretically at the top of the pyramid of norms, but judicially impotent. Constitutional provisions, which originally did not feature the equivalent of a bill of rights, could not be invoked by French citizens to challenge legislation

---

[6] Guillaume Tusseau, 'La Fin D'Une Exception Française?' (2011) 137 *Pouvoirs* 5. See also 'In Honor of the Late Louis Favoreu: France's Exceptionalism in Constitutional Review' (2007) *Intl J Cons L* Special Issue.

applicable to their case which had allegedly infringed their rights and freedoms. Constitutional justice featured a limited model of ex ante abstract constitutional review[7] whereby, upon referral by politicians, the FCC would review statutes after their adoption by Parliament and before promulgation by the President of the Republic. This original form of constitutional review has evolved beyond expectations.

8.2.1 General Constitutional Setup

France presents one of the oldest constitutionalisms of the world with over 15 fundamental texts since 1789.[8] However, the experience of a series of constitutions is misleading since most constitutional texts were either not applied or misapplied, with, in any case, no conclusive experience of constitutional review.[9] Regarded as political devices for guaranteeing the existence and operation of political institutions and the separation of powers, constitutions merely followed the fate of the political regimes to which they were attached.

As a reaction to the Third and Fourth Republics, the Fifth Republic marks a departure from this limited approach to constitutionalism. In particular, deliberate changes were made to the institutional balance in order to remedy the defects of previously unstable parliamentary regimes. The main concern was to establish a more 'rationalized' (ie strictly organized) parliamentary system which resulted in innovative features: first, the weakening of the position of Parliament was translated into several key constitutional provisions, including the delimitation of the legislative domaine under Article 34, and the right for the government to legislate in certain areas on delegation from the legislature under Article

---

[7] This type of constitutional judicial review is also called a priori review. For the typology of constitutional reviews, see, for example, Juliane Kokott and Martine Kaspar 'Ensuring Constitutional Efficacy' in Michel Rosenfeld and Andras Sajó (eds), *The Oxford Handbook on Comparative Constitutional Law* (OUP 2012) 806.

[8] The 1958 Constitution is the 15th fundamental text since 1789, or 22nd if non-applied texts are included.

[9] On French constitutional law, see, among others, Louis Favoreu and others (eds), *Droit Constitutionnel* (14th edn, Dalloz 2012); Pierre Pactet and Ferdinand Melin-Soucramanien, *Droit Constitutionnel* (31st edn, Dalloz Sirey 2012); Bernard Chantebout, *Droit Constitutionnel* (29th edn, Dalloz Sirey 2012); Guillaume Drago, *Contentieux Constitutionnel Français* (3rd edn, PUF 2011). In English, see John Bell, *French Constitutional Law* (OUP 1992); G A Bermann and Etienne Picard (eds), *Introduction to French Law* (Kluwer 2008), Sophie Boyron, *The Constitution of France: A Contextual Analysis* (Hart 2012).

37; secondly, the establishment of the FCC was envisaged as a means to regulate the relationships between the government and Parliament, and ensure that the latter would not encroach on the powers of the former.[10] For that purpose, the FCC was endowed with the exercise of a limited form of constitutional review.

8.2.2 Original Model of Constitutional Review

The main basis for constitutional review is provided for under Article 61(2) of the Constitution:[11]

> Acts of Parliament may be referred to the Constitutional Council, before their promulgation, by the President of the Republic, the Prime Minister, the President of the National Assembly, the President of the Senate, sixty Members of the National Assembly or sixty Senators.

This provides for a limited form of ex ante abstract constitutional review upon referral by members of the executive and legislative branches of government. This is complemented by Article 54 of the Constitution which allows the FCC to review the compatibility of treaties and international conventions with the Constitution before they are ratified, which may require an amendment of the Constitution if unconstitutionality is found. The review under Article 54 of the Constitution has generated an important body of case law as shown by the bulk of decisions on the EC/EU Treaties (namely Maastricht, Amsterdam, Schengen, Treaty establishing a Constitution for Europe, and Lisbon), but also on other agreements such as the Treaty of Rome establishing the International Criminal Court.

The French arrangement has been exceptional as much because of the peculiarity of the FCC – which has eventually become akin to a constitutional court – as because it provides *only* ex ante constitutional review. Both features are in fact linked since this type of review was

---

[10] The other novel feature concerned the powers of the President of the Republic who shall, under Article 5 of the Constitution, ensure the respect of the Constitution and act as an arbiter to secure the proper functioning of public powers. The Fifth Republic is described as a mixed or hybrid regime, that is at root parliamentary but in part presidential because of the strong autonomous powers afforded to the President.

[11] In addition to review of ordinary laws, Article 61(1) provides for a mandatory review of organic laws before promulgation, legislative proposals made under Article 11 before their submission to referendum, and rules of procedures of parliamentary assemblies before their entry into force.

originally envisaged as a form of strengthened version of advisory opinions on legislation being delivered by special bodies close to the executive.[12] The FCC originally fulfilled the role of 'watchdog of the executive' (although delivering binding judgments and not opinions) and was not established as a proper constitutional court similar to those created after the Second World War in Germany and Italy, for example. Staffed with nine members appointed for nine years by political authorities – three appointed by the President of the Republic, three by the President of the National Assembly and three by the President of the Senate – the Council was very much a vassal of the executive power.[13] Despite a significant evolution, the FCC still stands apart from most other comparable constitutional courts in Western democracies.[14] As for the singularity of ex ante review, it is a form of review which has developed after the ex post form of review, in legal systems with a duality of jurisdictions in particular, and appears to be the least widespread form of review from a comparative perspective. While France has been isolated, it was not the only country, before 2008, to ban ex post review of laws. The Dutch legal system now remains 'one of the last bulwarks to maintain a prohibition on constitutional review by the judiciary',[15] as well as, to an extent, the Finnish system.[16]

---

[12] This is the case of Councils of State which deliver opinions in a number of other jurisdictions. In Ireland, for example, the Council of State (*an gComhairle Stáit*) has to be consulted by the President of the Republic who decides to refer a bill to the Supreme Court for a decision on the question of its compatibility with the Constitution before signing it into law under Article 26.1.1° of the 1937 Constitution.

[13] The FCC also includes former Presidents of the Republic who are members by law.

[14] The FCC can nevertheless be compared with such constitutional courts for its additional competence as an electoral court regarding parliamentary and presidential elections, as well as referendum proceedings. Apart from its judicial role, the Council acts as a formal constitutional authority and delivers opinions (for example, on the fulfilment of Article 16 conditions on emergency powers) and gives decisions (for example, on the incapacity of the President of the Republic under Article 7) accordingly.

[15] Article 120 of the Dutch Constitution states that '[c]ourts shall not review the constitutionality of acts of Parliament and treaties [as opposed to other acts of public authorities]'. See Gerhard Van der Schyff and Anne Meuwese, 'Dutch Constitutional Law in a Globalizing World' (2013) 9 *Utrecht Law Review* 1; Leonard Besselink, 'Constitutional Adjudication in the Era of Globalization: The Netherlands in Comparative Perspective' (2012) 18 *EPL* 231.

[16] See Juha Lavapuro, Tuomas Ojanen, and Martin Scheinin in Chapter 5 of this collection.

The limited form of constitutional review thus followed the orthodoxy of French *légicentrisme.* Besides, unsatisfactory previous domestic attempts at introducing a stronger form of review, as well as unconvincing foreign experiences, also explain the overall reluctance towards constitutional review. As a matter of fact, the history of judicial review of legislation in France has been full of paradoxes and failures.[17] Despite early provisions in the 1789 Declaration of the Rights of Man and of the Citizen (1789 Declaration) which posed the principle of constitutional justice[18] and attested of the limits of the law,[19] France had come to 'sacralise' the law. Inherited from Rousseau's legal theory, an idealized conception of the law, as 'the expression of the general will', started to emerge. The law was perceived as the best way to reconcile the exercise of power with the protection of citizens' liberties by limiting the action of the executive. A shift towards Parliament ensued, which, as the national representation enacting the general will, was regarded as the repository of sovereignty. The law was regarded as illimited (ie no restriction on its scope), indivisible (ie no delegation of the power to make law) and unquestionable (ie judicial immunity as judges were supposed to 'serve' the law and not sanction it). *Légicentrisme* combined with an historical hostility towards judges[20] made it difficult to envisage judicial review of legislation.[21] The *loi-écran* doctrine, whereby the administrative judge

---

[17] David Lévy, 'La Question Prioritaire De Constitutionnalité: De La Culture De La Loi A La Culture De La Constitution' in *Conseil Constitutionnel Et QPC : Une Révolution ?* (2011) 368 *La Documentation Française* 20, 21.

[18] Preamble:

> … to the end that the acts of the legislative power and those of the executive power, since they may be continually compared with the aim of every political institution, may thereby be the more respected; to the end that *the demands of the citizens, founded henceforth on simple and incontestable principles*, may always be directed toward the maintenance of the Constitution and the happiness of all' (emphasis added).

[19] Article 5 reads: 'The law has the right to forbid only those actions that are injurious to society. Nothing that is not forbidden by law may be hindered, and no one may be compelled to do what the law does not ordain'. Article 8 reads: 'The law must prescribe only the punishments that are strictly and evidently necessary; and no one may be punished except by virtue of a law drawn up and promulgated before the offense is committed, and legally applied'.

[20] The hostility towards judicial power stemmed from the *Ancien Régime* when deeply conservative judges in the courts (then called Parliaments) opposed royal measures aimed at reforming the regime.

[21] Proposals to introduce judicial review of legislation were periodically put forward though. The most cited examples include, under revolutionary times, a

refused to review the compatibility of an administrative act with the Constitution if the act in question was the exact transposition of a law, appeared as the contemporary illustration of the cautionary approach vis-à-vis the law.[22]

The Fifth Republic breaks from these tenets as '[d] esacralisation of the law towards the recognition of the political and judicial authority of the Constitution [emerged] thanks to constitutionalism and rationalization of parliamentary regime'.[23] The excesses of previous governments led to unstable regimes where the legislative would dominate the executive and result into totalitarian practices, most notably in the case of other European jurisdictions. The acknowledgment that the law was unable to fulfil its role in securing individual and collective rights and freedoms, and in providing for political stability, led to a shift in favour of the supreme norm envisaged as a more solid bulwark against these risks. In France, the sovereignty of the law was challenged by curtailing the sovereignty of Parliament. So, from the standpoint of constitutional law, it was more at an institutional and political level, rather than judicial level, that the law as such was challenged. The weakening of the law resulted, first, from the delimitation of its scope under Article 34 of the Constitution; secondly, from the constraint of international law under Article 55; and, thirdly, from the first expression of constitutional review – albeit in a limited form until 2008 – under ex post review. From then on, the law was no longer supreme and had to give way to other (conflicting) norms of expressly superior rank.

8.2.3 Transformation of the Model

The transformation of the French system of constitutional review is synonymous with the expansion of the role of the FCC through case law and political reforms. This transformation has been qualified as a

---

proposal by Sieyès, and under the Third Republic, a proposal by Carré de Malberg.

[22] See *Paulin* case (Cass Crim of 11 May 1833, S. 1833, 1, p. 357) and *Arrighi* case (CE of 6 November 1936 *Sieur Arrighi* Rec p. 966; D. 1938. 3. p. 1) as recently confirmed by the Council of State in CE of 5 January 2005 *Deprez and Baillard* about the impossibility for the administrative judge to review the constitutionality of a law in force; See F L Morton, 'Judicial Review in France: A Comparative Analysis' (1988) 36 *Am J Comp L* 89.

[23] Lévy (n 17) 25 (translation is mine).

'juridical coup d'état'.[24] The departure from the sovereignty of the law has consisted of a double transformation involving the full acceptance of the principle of judicial review of legislation as well as the recognition of the normative force of the Constitution.

A. Transformations before 2008: a few revolutions

The progressive transformation of the FCC, from an ancillary institution with a circumscribed role into a judicial body akin to a constitutional court, is well known.[25] Originally established to control Parliament from encroaching on the prerogatives of the executive, the Council has come to develop an elaborated system of rights-based review, generating 'its own general theory of rights and freedoms' and becoming 'the guardian of rights and civil liberties'.[26] This stands as a significant example – though not the only one[27] – of incremental institutional evolution.

The 1971 Decision on Freedom of Association is the landmark of the judicial empowerment of the FCC.[28] This is the first decision which struck down a law for breach of fundamental rights. The law in question had instituted a prior form of administrative review imposed on the instigators of an association before the association could be legally established. This was regarded as an infringement of the right to freely constitute an association. The 'discovery' of the principle of freedom of association represents the novelty in constitutional adjudication. Instead of relying on the bare Constitution, which did not contain any such principle, the FCC decided to encompass the text of the Constitution's Preamble as basis for its review. As the Preamble contained references to the 1789 Declaration and Preamble to the 1946 Constitution, the FCC decided to integrate the principles contained thereof into the constitutional norms of reference (known as '*bloc de constitutionnalité*'). Deriving a specific freedom from the general provision on freedom and from the general principles of the 1946 Preamble, the FCC could then count freedom of association as one of the French constitutional principles. Bearing significant legal and political implications, the 1971 Decision arguably represents the 'first sign of the emergence of a culture of the

---

[24] Alec Stone Sweet, 'The Politics of Constitutional Review in France and Europe' (2007) 5 *Intl J Cons L* 69, 80.

[25] John Bell, Sophie Boyron and Simon Whittaker, *Principles of French Law* (OUP 1998) 147–66. See also Louis Favoreu, *La Politique Saisie Par Le Droit* (Economica 1988).

[26] Bell (n 25) 156.

[27] Compare with the evolution of the French Council of State.

[28] FCC Decision 71-44 DC of 16 July 1971 (*Liberté D'Association*).

Constitution'[29] transforming it from an instrument primarily concerned with the institutional structure of government to one providing for substantial protection of fundamental rights. In what had become the hallmark of its constitutional review role vis-à-vis the law, the FCC later declared that 'the law expresses the general will within the limits of the Constitution'.[30]

The 1974 constitutional revision, expanding the referral to 60 deputies or 60 senators – de facto to the opposition in Parliament – is another turning point.[31] The reform significantly increased the activity of the FCC and raised its profile in the political landscape. Via this referral, the FCC has tested the constitutionality of many laws touching upon some of the most significant political and societal issues of modern France such as the termination of pregnancy, immigration, bioethics, civil partnership, headscarf ban, decentralization, nationalizations and privatizations, and the participation of France to the European integration. The FCC has not become the 'third chamber' of Parliament though and has managed, as key to the acquisition of its independence from political power, to handle conflicts between the majority and the opposition on the legal terrain. This is thanks to a subtle use of politico-legal arguments – the best example being the case law on nationalizations and privatizations in the 1980s.[32]

This description would be incomplete without including the 1975 Decision on The Voluntary Interruption of Pregnancy (IVG)[33] which gave rise to a competing – or complementary[34] – form of rights-based review. In the IVG case, the FCC refused to review the conformity of laws with

[29] Lévy (n 17) 26.

[30] FCC Decision 85-197 DC of 23 August 1985 (*Loi Relative A L'Evolution De La Nouvelle Calédonie*) pt 27.

[31] Law No 74-904 of 29 October 1974 (*Révision De L'Article 61 De La Constitution*). The same reform was put in place concerning referral of international agreements. See Law No 92-554 of 25 June 1992 (*Ajoutant A La Constitution Un Titre: Des Communautés Européennes Et De L'Union Européenne*).

[32] FCC Decision 81-132 DC of 16 January 1982 (*Loi De Nationalisation*) and FCC Decision 86-207 DC of 26 June 1986 (*Loi Autorisant Le Gouvernement A Prendre Diverses Mesures D'Ordre Economique Et Social*).

[33] FCC Decision 74-54 DC of 15 January 1975 (*Loi Relative A L'Interruption Volontaire De Grossesse dite Loi IVG*).

[34] See, for example, Olivier Dutheillet de Lamothe, 'Contrôle De Constitutionnalité Et Contrôle De Conventionnalité' in *Mélanges En L'Honneur De Daniel Labetoulle: Juger L'Administration, Administrer La Justice* (Dalloz 2007) 315.

international treaties and decided to put the onus on the different organs of the State, including the courts, to give effect to the provisions of these instruments within the limits of their competences. The Council regarded the review of the conformity of laws with the provisions of the Constitution (review of constitutionality or *contrôle de constitutionnalité*), as being of preventive and abstract nature. It was therefore of a different type from the review of the conformity of laws with the provisions of treaties (review of conventionality or *contrôle ce conventionnalité*) which is of curative and concrete nature, and is to be performed by the ordinary judges. The expansion of this parallel form of review by civil and administrative judges – with an important harmonizing role by the Council of State and the Court of Cassation in respect of each judicial order – has arguably been regarded as the most interesting development concerning the relationship between the different orders of jurisdictions in the context of fundamental rights protection.[35] While unable to strike it down, ordinary judges have empowered themselves with a 'critical review' of legislation by setting aside, on many occasions, domestic provisions found incompatible with international agreements, mostly as regards the ECHR. The 1975 IVG Decision is still good law and the FCC has reaffirmed its position, including after the entry into force of the QPC.[36]

Another significant enhancement is the development by the FCC of a tailor-made constitutional review as regards secondary EU legislation. In a series of 2004 and 2006 decisions, the Council declared that it was competent to review the constitutionality of laws transposing EU directives since the transposition of these directives was a 'constitutional duty' under Article 88-1 on France's participation to the EU. The obligation to transpose directives into domestic law can only be exceptionally thwarted by an 'expressly'[37] contrary provision of the Constitution – in other words, when the provisions of the law purpoting to transpose the directive conflict with 'French constitutional identity'. One typical example would be the principle of *laïcité* (State secularism). In 2004, the

---

[35] See Marie-Luce Paris, 'Europeanization and Constitutionalization: The Challenging Impact of a Double Transformative Process on French Law' (2010) 29 *YEL* 21, 47.

[36] See, for example, FCC Decision 2010-605 DC of 12 May 2010 (*Loi Relative A L'Ouverture A La Concurrence Et A La Régulation Du Secteur Des Jeux D'Argent Et De Hasard En Ligne*) pt 16.

[37] FCC Decision 2004-496 DC of 10 June 2004 (*Loi Pour La Confiance Dans L'Economie Numérique*) pt 7 and FCC Decision 2004-498 DC of 29 July 2004 (*Loi Relative A La Bioéthique*) pt 4.

FCC justified this exception under the provisions of the (failed) Treaty establishing a Constitution for Europe which contained the obligation of the EU to respect the constitutional identity of the member states.[38] In 2006, the Council took this line of reasoning to its logical conclusion and struck down a legislative provision as being 'manifestly incompatible' with the directive it purpoted to implement.[39] The net effect of this case law has been the introduction of a limited form of review of conventionality in the hands of the FCC.[40]

So, contrary to what is usually presented, the FCC has been cautious in expanding its role. On two occasions, the Council chose to limit the scope of its review and handed over its competence to the ordinary courts: first, in 1975 (IVG ruling) by declaring itself incompetent to review the conformity of a domestic statute with an international or European treaty, the Council handed over to the national courts the task of ensuring observance of Article 55 on primacy of international law, and of setting aside French laws incompatible with international treaties; secondly, in 2004 (e-commerce ruling) – following the same logic – the Council handed over the responsibility of protecting fundamental rights to the Court of Justice of the European Union (CJEU) by refusing to review the constitutionality of a law transposing an EU directive, unless it conflicts with French constitutional identity.

Ex post constitutional review was to be introduced into this rather settled and complex framework of existing rights-based reviews.[41] Aimed

---

[38] FCC Decision 2004-505 DC of 19 November 2004 (*Traité Etablissant Une Constitution Pour L'Europe*) pt 12.

[39] FCC Decision 2006-540 DC of 27 July 2006 (*Loi Relative Aux Droits D'Auteur Et Aux Droits Voisins Dans La Société De L'Information dite Loi DADVSI*). See, for an example of uphold legislative provision, FCC Decision 2006-543 DC of 30 November 2006 (*Loi Relative Au Secteur De L'Energie*).

[40] See also FCC Decision 1998-400 DC of 20 May 1998 (*Loi Organique Déterminant Les Conditions D'Application De L'Article 88-3 De La Constitution*) pt 4. The extension to full review of conventionality in the hands of the Council was wished by its President, Jean-Michel Debré, but rejected in the 2008 reform. For the opposite solution (that is a form of deconcentrated constitutional review in the hands of ordinary courts), see Denys de Béchillon, 'Plaidoyer Pour L'Attribution Aux Juges Ordinaires Du Pouvoir De Contrôler La Constitutionnalité Des Lois Et La Transformation Du Conseil Constitutionnel En Cour Suprême' *Renouveau Du Droit Constitutionnel : Mélanges En L'Honneur De Louis Favoreu* (Dalloz 2007) 116–17.

[41] Marie-Luce Paris 'Taking the Constitution Seriously: A Question of Priority under the New French Constitutional Review' (Society of Legal Scholars Annual Conference, Southampton, September 2010).

at improving matters, the QPC had to 'fit in'. Even though the remedy was long overdue,[42] it was hoped that it would help clarify the ordering of the different types of review.[43] In the discussion leading up to the reform, the advantages and defects of the existing review mechanism were thoroughly questioned. Suffice is to mention here two standpoints. One was to discredit ex ante review because of its restictive access and the reduced scrutiny it involves. Activated upon referral by politicians, abstract constitutional review under Article 61(2) means indeed that the review is not systematic (although most legislation was referred to by the opposition from 1974); also, it can happen that, for whatever reason, politicians agree not to refer a law to the FCC, thus leaving 'constitutional manholes' in the form of unchecked legislative provisions which can prove problematic when later applied by ordinary courts. In terms of scope and level of scrutiny, the concern was that the FCC can only strike down a law when 'conceived', and not when actually applied, thereby rendering it immune from any future constitutional challenge. There is always the risk that this type of ex ante 'legal audit', disconnected as it is from the concretness of the application of the impugned law, 'may ignore significant problems that only become visible when law meets reality'.[44] Also, the level of scrutiny is quite superficial since, for practical reasons, the FCC has only a limited timespan for review – one month, which can be reduced to eight days at the request of the government in the case of urgency.

Another standpoint was that, on the contrary, ex ante review was enough. Introducing ex post review would have been redundant in view of the relatively complete system of review combining ex ante abstract constitutional review performed by a specialized constitutional court upon request by political authorities, and concrete review (of conventionality) performed by ordinary courts upon request by citizens. Conventionality review could indeed be assimilated to a form of 'constitutional' review in the sense that '[i]n not ensuring itself the primacy of a treaty over a *loi*, but leaving it to the ordinary courts to ensure this supremacy, the Constitutional Council has opened for these courts a new form of

---

[42] See the analogy with the infamous French military plane rafale, 'superb on plan, but too late in its realization'. See Joseph Pini 'La Lumière Des Expériences Etrangères' in Robert Badinter and others (eds), *Le Contrôle De Constitutionnalité Par Voie Préjudicielle En France: Quelles Pratiques?* (PUAM 2009) 149.

[43] Joël Rideau, 'Contrôle De Constitutionnalité Et Contrôle De Conventionnalité: Les Orphelins De La Pyramide' (2009) 3 *Revue Du Droit Public* 601, 629.

[44] Kokott and Kaspar (n 7) 806.

constitutional review'.[45] This assertion can arguably be regarded as yet another sign of the well advanced constitutionalization of the French legal order, rooting a transcendental culture of the Constitution within the competences of the judiciary via a form of decentralized review. However, the lack of equivalence between rights protected under the Constitution and rights protected under the ECHR made it difficult to equate satisfactorily constitutionality review with conventionality review.[46] In other words, the so-called complementarity of both types of review was never really accepted. Conventionality review will actually prove to be a bone of contention with regard the establishment of the QPC to which we now turn.

B. The 2008 reform: a constitutional momentum

The QPC was part of a major constitutional reform aimed at modernizing the institutions of the Fifth Republic.[47] Adopted on 23 July 2008, the constitutional revision stands as the twenty-fourth, and last revision to date, of the 1958 Constitution, and as its most important amendment quantitatively and qualitatively speaking.[48] Quantitatively, roughly more than one-third of the constitutional provisions (39 articles out of 89) were changed and nine entirely new provisions were introduced. Qualitatively, a renewal of the institutional balance between the different branches of power aimed at adapting French political institutions to modern democracy and in particular to correct the defects of a regime which had become too 'presidential' and executive-driven. The objective was threefold, namely to give more control over the executive power, to reinforce

---

45 Olivier Dutheillet de Lamothe, former member of the Council (2001-2010), cited in John Bell, 'French Constitutional Council and European Law' (2005) 54 ICLQ 735, 737.

46 The principle of equality, the right to strike, the principle of *laïcité* (State secularism), the principle of continuity of public services, the principle of independence of academic professors, for example, are not protected as such under the ECHR.

47 Law No 2008-724 of 23 July 2008 (*Modernisation Des Institutions De La Vème République*).

48 Although of major importance, the constitutional amendment was not submitted to the popular vote and was adopted by a narrow majority by the Congress (ie the formation of Parliament competent to vote on constitutional revisions). Referendums are seldom used in France, even for significant constitutional reforms. See Marie-Luce Paris, 'Popular Sovereignty and the Use of the Referendum: Comparative Perspectives with reference to France' in Eoin Carolan (ed.), *The Constitution of Ireland: Perspectives and Prospects* (Bloomsbury 2012) 279.

the powers of Parliament, and to grant new rights to citizens. This significant overhaul certainly created a constitutional momentum. Yet, the rebalancing of power between the executive and legislative fell short of expectations because of intrinsic flaws. The tenets of the reform in this respect were based on the old paradigm of the separation of powers between the government and Parliament while this paradigm was not necessarily as relevant as it used to be. The focus arguably needed to shift on the more decisive concern about the relation between the majority and the opposition.[49]

By contrast, the QPC part of the reform has been able to sustain this constitutional momentum precisely because of its potential to shift the paradigm. In addition to purging the legal order of unconstitutional laws, the primary aim of the QPC reform was to confer a new right to the individual. The reform had also the significant function of reintroducing the prevalence of the constitutional norm in two respects: first, by outing the Constitution from the universities and throwing it into courts, proponents of the reform argued that the Constitution should no longer appear as this 'neglected text',[50] but should be part of the scheme of constitutional remedies available to citizens; secondly, by making the Constitution a ground for a constitutional claim, the reform would contribute, to some extent, 'to re-nationalize judicial proceedings'[51] relating to the protection of fundamental rights, therefore avoiding the recourse to international texts to the detriment of the Constitution. The introduction of the QPC was also the result of good political timing in the context of a more consensual political debate. As outlined above, there were previous attempts at introducing ex post review of legislation, and the 2008 reform was the third one.[52]

---

[49] Pascale Ducoulombier, 'Rebalancing the Power between the Executive and Parliament: The Experience of French Constitutional Reform' (2010) PL 688, 708.

[50] Dominique Rousseau (ed.), *La Question Prioritaire De Constitutionnalité – Guide Pratique* (2nd edn, Gazette du Palais/Lextenso 2010) 3.

[51] Denis Simon, 'Conventionnalité et Constitutionnalité' (2011) 137 *Pouvoirs* 19, 20. This movement of 'repatriation' from the European to the domestic arena finds some analogy with what happened in the UK on the occasion of the incorporation of the ECHR into domestic law which started with the aptly named White Paper 'Rights Brought Home: The Human Rights Bill' (HMSO, 1997, Cm 3782).

[52] See Constitutional Revision Bill No 1203 of 30 March 1990 (Badinter Proposal) and Constitutional Revision Bill No 231 of 10 March 1993 (Vedel Proposal). See Michel Verpeaux, 'La QPC : La Troisième Fois Est La Bonne' in

In terms of its technique,[53] only a few points will be mentioned about the QPC. The QPC was never intended to replace the existing ex ante review. Rather it was envisaged to reinforce the overall mechanism of constitutional review. The idea was that the existing review, of political nature under Article 61 would be complemented by the new judicially-based review under Article 61-1 involving the interaction between the constitutional judge and the ordinary judge.

A QPC is, first, raised before a first instance court, an appeal court or one of the supreme courts; secondly, it is filtered by one of the supreme courts (that is the Council of State or the Court of Cassation) if coming from lower instances; and eventually, it is decided upon by the FCC. The Council will conclude to either an unconstitutionality – total or partial – or constitutionality, with possibly reserves of interpretation, or else decide that the question is without object. Although decided in a concrete case, the review is an abstract ruling on the law in question. This brings to the fore the specificity of the new constitutional remedy which is subjective in terms of its aim but objective in terms of its procedure. As a new remedy for the citizen's benefit, its aim is to protect individual rights. To that effect, the QPC is designed to be easily accessible. The QPC can be raised by any party before any court, at any time during court proceedings. The remedy stands as a party-instigated procedure mediated by the judge who cannot raise it ex officio. In that sense, the QPC is not a direct remedy at the disposal of the citizen, nor an autonomous action in the hands of the judge.[54] The QPC is to be referred

---

Conseil Constitutionnel Et QPC: Une Révolution? (2011) 368 *La Documentation Française* 8.

[53] The main texts applicable to the QPC are Article 61-1 of the Constitution, Organic Law No 2009-1523 of 10 December 2009 (*Application De L'Article 61-1 De La Constitution*), FCC Decision 2009-595 DC of 3 December 2009 (*Loi Organique Relative A L'Application De L'Article 61-1 De La Constitution*). Several detailed works have been published on the QPC. See, among others, Rousseau *La Question Prioritaire De Constitutionnalité* (n 50), Bertrand Mathieu, *Question Prioritaire De Constitutionalité: La Jurisprudence* (Lexis-Nexis 2013), Jacques-Henri Stahl and Christine Mangué, *La Question Prioritaire De Constitutionalité* (2nd edn, Dalloz 2012).

[54] The QPC is not an exception of unconstitutionality, despite the expression being mistakenly used by the media and other non-experts at drafting stage. Some have tried to advocate the transposition of the German model but as 'a wishful thinking'. See Francois-Xavier Millet, L'Exception D'Inconstitutionnalité En France Ou L'Impossibilité Du Souhaitable?' (2008) 5 *Revue Du Droit Public* 1305. It is not technically speaking a 'preliminary reference' either on the model of the Preliminary Reference Procedure under Article 267 TFEU.

to the sole FCC as a result of a tripartite cooperation between parties to the proceedings, the ordinary judge and the constitutional judge. The accessibility of the procedure and the intervention of different levels of judicial cooperation means that the individual may not in fact be the one at the centre of the QPC proceedings. Rather, what is the focal point in QPC proceedings is the allegedly unconstitutional law ; this is confirmed by several procedural features such as, for example, the fact that a QPC can proceed whatever the issue of the main ordinary proceedings, which might elapse or be discontinued for some reason, is; or the fact that QPC rulings, including those upholding the constitutionality of the disputed law, have an erga omnes effect.

A QPC is declared admissible, by a first instance or appeal judge, under four conditions: if (i) the allegedly unconstitutional provision is of legislative nature; (ii) its application is necessary for the outcome of the case; (iii) it has not been previously declared compatible with the Constitution by the FCC (except for a change of circumstances of fact or law); and (iv) the issue of constitutionality presents a 'serious character'.[55] If declared admissible, the ordinary judge will then suspend the proceedings until a decision is reached by the FCC. In the eventuality of an issue of conventionality (that is compatibility of the challenged law with the ECHR) raised during the same proceedings, the QPC should be dealt with *by priority*, with the reserve of the *Melki* case law.[56] The priority rule is a rule of procedure here, aimed at sequencing the different forms of review – review of constitutionality, on the one hand, and review of conventionality, on the other hand. This is how the Council explained it in its decision on the 2009 Organic Law implementing the QPC:

> [W]hen requiring that arguments of unconstitutionality be examined in priority to those based on the failure of a statutory provision to comply with international commitments entered into by France, Parliament, when enacting the Organic Law, intended to ensure compliance with the Constitution and reiterate the place of the latter at the apex of the national legal system. This priority *merely results in specifying the order* in which the arguments raised before the court to which the matter is referred be examined. It does not restrict the jurisdiction of said court, once the provisions pertaining to the

[55] The admissibility criteria are the same when the QPC is raised before one of the supreme courts, except for the last one: the issue must be 'new' or 'present a serious character'; it means that the law in question must not have been previously examined by the Council (either ex ante or ex post) and been declared constitutional in the motivations and operative part of the Council's decision.

[56] See below.

priority preliminary ruling on the issue of constitutionality have been complied with, to ensure the superiority over national laws of legally ratified or approved treaties or agreements and norms of the European Union. (emphasis added).[57]

In the interest of procedural efficiency, the ordinary court is required to refer 'without delay' to the relevant supreme court which, in turn, has three months to refer, or not, to the FCC. If the issue has not been expressly decided within this time-limit, it is automatically referred to the FCC. The Council has a further three months to rule on a QPC.[58]

There is also a number of substantive requirements which concern the parties to the proceedings, the courts, the 'legislative provision [infringing] the rights and freedoms guaranteed by the Constitution' and the 'rights and freedoms guaranteed by the Constitution'. Regarding the parties, these can be natural[59] as well as legal persons.[60] Apart from the ordinary parties to the dispute, third parties intervening in the proceedings can also raise a QPC in the interest of the good administration of justice. These peripheral actors include the Public Prosecutor (*ministère public*),[61] as well as the highest political authorities, namely the President of the Republic, the Prime Minister, and the Presidents of each House of Parliament – the same authorities which appoint the members of the FCC.[62] The possibility to consult both the Public Prosecutor (via an opinion) and the representatives of the legislative and executive powers (via observations) arguably contributes to assist the FCC in making an informed and legitimate decision, especially when it concludes to an unconstitutionality. As far as courts are concerned, a

---

[57] FCC Decision 2009-595 DC (n 53) pt 14.

[58] Another important procedural requirement relates to the form in which a QPC must be presented. The party and his/her counsel must make address their claim in a separate writing which states the grounds for their claim, even in the case of criminal proceedings which are usually mainly oral.

[59] Natural persons can be adults or minors, French nationals or non-nationals, whether legally or illegally residing on the French territory.

[60] The notion of legal persons is as generous and includes private (ie companies, charities, associations, societies, foundations, trade-unions, interest groups) as well as public entities (ie local authorities).

[61] Which representative can raise a QPC in criminal proceedings, for example since s/he is a party to these proceedings. Things are different regarding civil judicial proceedings in which the Public Prosecutor is not a party. Practice has revealed that the Public Prosecutor has embraced this role with caution, acting more as an observer than an actor of the procedure.

[62] The QPC is susceptible to challenge a piece of legislation that they might have once proposed or adopted, or applied for some years.

QPC can be raised 'during proceedings in progress before a court of law',[63] and the expression is broad enough to allow for only a few exceptions, most notably regarding criminal courts.[64]

Another illustration of the broadness and flexibility of the procedure is that, although not of *ordre public*, the QPC can be raised at any stage of the proceedings provided these are pending. In other words, there is no need to exhaust other judicial remedies before forming a QPC claim. The only condition is that no judicial decision must have yet intervened on the substantive claim as this original claims is the legal 'justification' of the QPC.[65] An overview of the meaning of 'a legislative provision [infringing] the rights and freedoms guaranteed by the Constitution' is given here in order to understand the rationale of the procedure. Again, the notion of 'legislative provision' calls for a broad approach encompassing either one '*disposition législative*' or several ones, related or not,[66] contained in one particular law or in different ones, whether the law is still in force when the QPC is raised or not. The only requirement is that the legislative provision(s) must be contained in a written norm, thus excluding those found in general principles of law. However, the FCC has accepted that the consistent judicial interpretation of a norm, and not necessarily the norm per se, could be the object of a QPC. This is only logical given that the challenge is againt the 'living norm' as

---

[63] Parties must be represented by counsel in QPC proceedings whenever this representation is mandatory to appear in court. A court of law is understood as a body which, performing its functions under the public service of justice, renders judgements, according to the rule of law, in the name of the state over legal disputes put before it and which decisions are legally binding. In the French system, these courts are those whose decisions are susceptible of appeal before one or the other supreme court of their relevant order, namely the Council of State or the Court of Cassation.

[64] A QPC cannot be invoked before the Court of Assizes, the competent criminal court for the most serious criminal offences, due to the special procedure and composition of this court which includes a jury (the suspension of proceedings, often for several months, would be difficult to manage when convening and then re-convening a jury). This is mitigated by the fact that a QPC can be raised at other stages of the criminal procedure.

[65] A QPC can be raised at appeal or cassation level, even for the first time.

[66] See, for example, FCC Decision 2010-92 QPC of 28 January 2011 (*Mme Corinne C Et Autres* or Prohibition of marriage between person of the same sex) which involves the combined interpretation of Articles 75 and 144 of the Code Civil which allowed the Council to conclude, at the time, that marriage, in French law, is defined as the union of a man and a woman.

applied concretely by the ordinary judge. As regards the other requirements about the legislative provision(s), there are no temporal, substantive or formal limitations to the notion of '*disposition législative*'.[67]

The case of EU primary and secondary law requires explanations. Under the principle of constitutional immunity of international treaties under Article 55 of the Constitution read together with the *Pacta sunt servanda* rule (deduced from the Preamble to the 1946 Constitution), laws authorizing the ratification or approval of an international agreement, including the EU Treaties, cannot form the object of a QPC as this would amount to an indirect challenge to the provisions of the international agreement itself; besides, these laws, which sole purpose is authorizing ratification, cannot alter the rights and freedoms of the individual.[68] Since the FCC cannot review the compatibility of external norms with the Constitution, whether under ex ante or ex post review, a QPC cannot concern legislative provisions which purport to exactly transpose into domestic law the 'sufficiently precise and unconditional' provisions of an EU directive, for the very same reason indicated above. However, building on its previous case law,[69] the FCC is entitled to review those legislative provisions which reflect the exercise of a certain margin of appreciation by the domestic legislature in its choice of form and means in the implementation of the directive – even though annulling the challenged law could impede the actual transposition of the directive. The only exception to the absence of constitutional review of laws transposing directives relates to the infringement by the directive and implementing law of 'a rule or principle inherent to the constitutional identity of France' (unless the constituent power has agreed to such infringement); in the case of a QPC, this constitutional derogation would

---

[67] The litigant can challenge any legislative provision whenever it was adopted or entered into force, either before or after the 2008 reform, and also before or after the entry into force of the constitutional norm invoked (for instance, it could include legislative provisions adopted under the Fourth Republic). The requirement is that the norm be capable of conferring rights on an individual and being applied to that individual in judicial proceedings. Exceptions include constitutional laws, referendum laws and institutional laws which cannot form the object of a QPC. In comparative terms, this is remarkable in the case of constitutional laws since the Italian and German constitutional judge, for example, would review such laws.

[68] Both the Court of Cassation and the Council of State arrived at the same conclusion albeit via slightly different reasoning. See Cass Crim No 10-82938 of 17 May 2011 and CE No 312305 of 14 May 2010 (*Rujovic*).

[69] See above.

have to concern 'a right or freedom guaranteed by the Constitution' which cannot find an equivalent under EU law.

Last, the requirement of 'rights and freedoms guaranteed by the Constitution' is, again, broadly defined. Whatever its denomination or source, any constitutional norm conferring rights and freedoms can be invoked in support of a QPC. A contrario, rights and freedoms protected under international and European texts, mainly the ECHR and EU law including the EU Charter of Fundamental Rights, cannot form the basis of a QPC.[70] Rights and freedoms do not need to be qualified as 'fundamental' but, whatever their level of protection, they are those 'guaranteed under the Constitution' as interpreted by the FCC. '[R]ights and freedoms guaranteed by the Constitution' do not equate constitutional norms of the *bloc de constitutionnalité*; only those which confer rights and freedoms are included.[71] A brief enumeration includes rights and freedoms under the 1789 Declaration,[72] the Preamble to the 1946 Constitution such as the Fundamental Principles Recognized by the Laws of the Republic,[73] and Political, Economic and Social Principles Particularly Necessary to Modern Life.[74] Rights and freedoms contained in the

---

[70] FCC Decision 2010-4/17 QPC of 22 July 2010 (*M. Alain C Et Autres*) pt 11. The only exception in the case of EU law seems to be the right to vote and stand in local elections for EU citizens residing in France. This right, derived from the Maastricht Treaty, was 'constitutionalized' under Article 88-3 of the Constitution. In contrast, the 'constitutional duty' of transposition of directives into domestic law derived from the interpretation of Article 88-1 has been excluded.

[71] Constitutional duties and principles, as well as objectives of constitutional value, are further categories of constitutional norms under French law. These are not enunciated in terms of 'rights and freedoms'. Subtle distinctions have to be made for these to be considered as falling into the remit of the QPC procedure.

[72] For example, freedom as diversely declined in the case law of the Council includes individual freedom, itself interpreted in its multifarious aspects such as freedom of movement, freedom to marry, respect of private life, inviolability of private and professional dwelling; right to secrecy of correspondence. It is also freedom of opinion. Taken in its economic aspects, it includes freedom to undertake business, freedom to enter into a contract, and the right to property. In the area of criminal law, it comprises the principle of legality, the personalization of sentences, the principle of non-retroactivity of stringer sentences, presumption of innocence and procedural rights.

[73] *Principes Fondamentaux Reconnus Par Les Lois De La République*. These principles are referred to, but not enumerated, in the 1946 Preamble. They are the result of a jurisprudential construction of the Council drawing on principles developed by the Council of State. Examples include freedom of association, freedom of conscience, the right to education (declined into the right

2004 Charter of the Environment are also included and have indeed been invoked in support of QPCs, such as the right to live in a balanced and healthy environment, the right to access information relating to the environment held by public authorities and to participate in the taking of public decisions that have an impact on the environment.[75]

8.3 PRACTICE AND ENDURANCE OF CONSTITUTIONAL REVIEW

The new form of constitutional review has occupied central stage since its entry into force in 2010. The success of the QPC is due to the efficiency of the procedure (such as the radical remedy of unconstitutionality, the priority rule, and the broadness of referral requirements) addressing a real need (that is the need for constitutional justice), complemented by an unprecedented campaign of information and training programme carried out by the FCC, the Council of State and the Court of Cassation. This resulted in an 'appropriation [of the reform] by its actors' – judges, counsels and academics – who understood its efficiency right away.[76] While the practice of the QPC has certainly

---

to higher education, the independence of university professors and researchers), the rights of the defence, the principle of independence of the administrative courts etc.

[74] *Principes Politiques, Economiques Et Sociaux Particulièrement Nécessaires A Notre Temps*. They are generally fomulated in the 1946 Preamble. Examples include the right to claim asylum, the protection of human dignity, the right to health, the principle of continuity of the public service, and work-related rights such as the right to join (and not join) a trade-union, the right to strike, the principle of participation of employees in the management of a company.

[75] See, for example, FCC Decision 2011-116 QPC of 8 April 2011 (*M Michel Z Et Autre* or *Neighbourhood nuisance and environment*) pt 5; FCC Decision 2011-182 QPC of 14 October 2011 (*M Pierre T* or *Administrative right of way and development for the purpose of fire prevention*) pt 2.

[76] Emmanuel Piwnica, 'L'Appropriation De La Question Prioritaire De Constitutionnalité Par Ses Acteurs', (2011) 137 *Pouvoirs* 169. The marketing of the QPC was as much at the initiative of the institutions (foremost the Council) as it was as at the instigation of the 'constitutional law lobby', law professoriate in particular '[acting] as a kind of specialised interest group promoting its own legal agenda'. See Arthur Dyèvre, 'The Melki Way: The Melki Case and Everything You Always Wanted to Know About French Judicial Politics (But Were Afraid to Ask)' (2011) available at SSRN: http://ssrn.com/abstract=1929807 accessed 19 June 2015. There was also the creation of an expert journal (*Constitutions. Revue De Droit Constitutionnel Appliqué*) and the rebranding of

revived the debate on constitutionalism, the new review has also revealed the few challenges coming with it. The endurance of the QPC very much depends indeed on a further transformation of the FCC, as well as on a proper dialogue with domestic and European courts, and the legislative power.

8.3.1 The Coming of Age of the Constitutional Council

Constitutional protection of rights before the QPC had become marginalized by the parallel use of a 'Europeanized' protection of rights via the more accessible conventionality review before the ordinary courts. Deemed a redundant and doomed institution,[77] the FCC has seemingly experienced a 'third birth'[78] with the QPC reform. The Council's judicial role now extends to the review of constitutionality of legislation (that is ex ante under Article 61, and ex post under Article 61-1), the review of constitutionality of international agreements under Article 54, as well as the review of legislative proposals made by the governement (and its obligation to submit impact studies alongside the bills under Article 39).

The focus of the 2008 reform was judicial in nature in that it afforded a new remedy to the citizens. There was thus little modification concerning the FCC as an institution. Apart from an amendment concerning the appointment procedure, no changes were made regarding its name or the composition and qualifications of its members.[79] The mode of designation and absence of qualification requirement have been criticized for a long time. Nevertheless, it seems that, in this instance, incremental change has resulted in a satisfactory practice. Regarding the mode of designation, the nomination by political authorities – and the absolute

the main constitutional law journal (*Les Nouveaux Cahiers Du Conseil Constitutionnel*).

[77] Dominique Rousseau and Eric Spitz, 'Le Crépuscule Du Conseil Constitutionnel' *Le Monde* (Paris, 6 December 2001).

[78] Quoted in Jean-Claude Colliard, 'Un Nouveau Conseil Constitutionnel?' (2011) 137 *Pouvoirs* 155, 156. The first birth is its creation and the second, the enhancement of its role in 1974.

[79] Suggested by current Senator and former President of the Council, Robert Badinter, the change of name into *Cour Constitutionnelle* was rejected during parliamentary debates on the ground that the Council was (still) an 'original institution endowed with a crucial role in the balance of constitutional powers', hence standing apart from equivalent courts in other jurisdictions. See Debates in Senate, 24 June 2008, Minister of Justice.

freedom in their choice[80] – has appeared as an oddity contrasting, internally, with the status of the *fonction publique* for top civil servants (which requires a retirement age), and, externally, with the mode of designation in most other European constitutional courts (which impose qualifications and retirement age among other requirements, as well as an appointment procedure associating at least two political authorities). Yet, the mode of designation has not led to extreme politization of the FCC. The choice of an appointment procedure is one thing, the status awarded to members is another. The Council has arguably managed to remain independent of the political power thanks to such rules as the non-renewable term of appointment, a strict regime of ineligibilities, and the secrecy of its deliberations. Still, the 2008 reform introduced a degree of parliamentary scrutiny in the nomination process.[81]

A similar positive evolution can be observed regarding professional qualifications. Most of the members of the FCC have been politicians and a few of them experienced lawyers. This trait has been rectified in practice and, today, all members are qualified lawyers, with nominating authorities having generally favoured competence over political loyalty. It is expected that this habit will become rooted in the nomination process as the QPC procedure (and indeed ex ante referrals) calls for an increasingly technical legal analysis. It is unlikely then that formal changes will be made in the near future in this respect and one can rather expect informal developments stemming from the changing role of the constitutional judges and the parliamentary scrutiny of their nomination.[82] Overall, there is no ideal solution in respect of appointment procedures of constitutional court's members. Every system tends to mix

---

[80] Jean-Pierre Camby, 'La Nomination Des Membres Du Conseil Constitutionnel, Ou La Liberté Absolue De Choisir' (1999) 6 *Revue Du Droit Public* 1573.

[81] Under amended Articles 56 and 13 of the Constitution, nominations proposed by the President of the Republic can be opposed by the standing committees of both Houses of Parliament.

[82] The ex officio nomination of former Presidents of the Republic is still controversial though. All former Presidents have decided to sit on the Council, although some have not done it in practice. The historical justification for this life membership relates to the need to ensure the social and material standard of living of former Presidents, as part of the broader issue of their political and legal status. However, offering them a political fit within the Council is certainly no longer justified. One proposal was to make them life senators but this was rejected because of the judicial immunity that would be granted to them.

political and judicial considerations. In short, the French system has compared quite favourably with others.[83]

Similarly, no changes were required as to the form of the QPC decisions. Paradoxically, QPC decisions are not much longer and more thoroughly motivated than those 'DC' (*décisions de conformité*) decisions in the context of ex ante review. As Baranger argues, the QPC procedure 'has not … induced the court to significantly alter the way in which its cases are drafted. The court's style has remained essentially the same'.[84] The judicial style of the FCC can be described as 'hyperformalist' meaning that legal problems can be solved exclusively through deduction of a particular conclusion in a given case from abstract or general premises, as opposed to the policy argument model of reasoning.[85] This can again be regarded as one area where the FCC stands apart from other constitutional courts' practices which, supported by contemporary political philosophy, have put the emphasis on the duty to give reasons. However, this style has no reason to change in terms of French judicial reasoning, since the FCC sees it as more acceptable to defer to the other branches of government in order to avoid being embroiled in policy arguments, hereby leaving the last word to Parliament as expressing a weak form of review.

Still, the FCC has taken responsibility for other adjustments to its judicial making process in a further move towards its juridictionalization. As a contentious procedure, the QPC deals with the concrete application of a law to a case in which the subjective rights of the individual are at stake. The procedure is therefore subject to the requirements of a fair trial

---

83 See Agustín Ruiz Robledo in Chapter 7 for the difficulties regarding the Spanish Constitutional Court.

84 Denis Baranger, 'Constitutional Justice and Constitutional Politics in France: Policy Arguments in the Case Law of the Constitutional Council' available at SSRN <http://ssrn.com/abstract=2181913> accessed 19 June 2015.

85 Ibid. One can then understand the form and content of the Council's decisions in which the choice of constitutional norms of reference is not necessarily justified (as epitomized by the 1971 Decision) nor the deduction process clearly used. The link between the constitutional norm referred to (or 'the "major" premise') and the legislative provision under scrutiny or the norm deriving from an international convention (or 'the "minor" premise') is tenuous, if non existent. The secrecy of deliberations, the principle of unanimity in decision-making with no separate or dissenting opinions, the judicial syllogism in the method of reasoning and drafting are factors which shape this particular mode of reasoning.

under Article 6 of the ECHR.[86] To this aim, the FCC has adopted specific rules of procedure aimed at securing transparency, due process of law and impartiality.[87] Parties are involved at each stage of the proceedings, from the referral by a supreme court, the instruction stage, to the public hearing and the ruling. Counsels (whose role is without object under the ex ante review of abstract nature) are now fully associated to the QPC proceedings and are notified of all acts of the case. Impartiality and transparency are guaranteed by the orality and publicity of judicial hearings and by a system of abstention and recusation of members of the FCC.[88] What has really been defining in terms of judicial transformation – and will continue to play a significant role in the success of the QPC – is the relationship that the FCC has developed with other courts, national and European.

8.3.2 Judicial Interplay with Domestic and European Courts

Five courts – namely the FCC, the Court of Cassation, the Council of State, the CJEU and the European Court of Human Rights (ECtHR) – now share the power of reviewing French law 'in a sovereign capacity'.[89] This can be interpreted as 'a source of major disorder' but also 'as a source of precious enrichment both for the rule of law and the very functioning of society'.[90] It can only be so if these courts interact properly for the benefits of the citizens. The operation of ex post concrete constitutional review has certainly enhanced the 'dialogue of judges'[91]

---

[86] See ECtHR Series A 262 of 23 June 1993 *Ruiz-Mateos v Spain* (1993) 16 EHRR 505.

[87] Rules of procedure of 4 February 2010 relating to proceedings before the Council on applications for a priority preliminary ruling on the issue of constitutionality.

[88] Physical transformation of the Council's building (Montpensier wing of the Palais Royal) was also necessary with the creation of a room for counsels and one for the public.

[89] Denys de Béchillon, 'Cinq Cours Suprêmes ? Apologie (Mesurée) Du Désordre' (2011) 137 *Pouvoirs* 33.

[90] Ibid., 34.

[91] The expression is attributed to Bruno Genevois, supreme administrative judge, who first coined it in the case CE Ass. No 11604 of 22 December 1978 *Ministère De l'Intérieur c. Cohn Bendit* (Rec. p. 524, Dalloz 1979, 155). He declared, in the context of the relationships between the European Community judge and the domestic judge: 'At the level of the European Community, there should not be a government of judges nor a war of judges. There must be place for a dialogue of judges' (translation is mine).

thanks to the key role played by the FCC. The Council has been acting as a sort of 'judicial hub' where rights-based substantive and procedural constitutional issues have converged. As much as the domestic courts have empowered themselves via European law (in particular via the preliminary reference procedure vis-à-vis EU law and conventionality review vis-à-vis ECHR law), the Council has definitely been empowered by the QPC. The procedure has helped dissolve many of the complexes that have hampered, at times, the development of constructive relationships with other courts in the context of a pluralist legal order. Below is an outline of how this constitutional dialogue has developed so far, first vis-à-vis domestic courts, and second, vis-à-vis European courts.

A. A difficult relationship with the Court of Cassation

The introduction of the QPC has shaken the French judicial landscape due to the enhanced role conferred upon the FCC.[92] The FCC is now organically linked to the Court of Cassation and the Council of State through the filter-referral mechanism. Each kind of proceedings – constitutional and ordinary – has lost its autonomy. Whereas their relationship was based on 'civility and mutual understanding' before, the courts are now 'legally obliged to each other'.[93] Also, the FCC has the last word on the issue on constitutionality albeit within the very strict limits of the issue raised – not like the kind of strong form of review observed in the US system. Under Article 62(2), its decisions are binding on all public authorities and courts, even though no actual enforcement procedure exists for that purpose; in addition, FCC rulings are not subject to appeal or other form of review. Even though its judicial profile was gaining in importance under ex ante review, the FCC stood in the realm of politics.

---

[92] The same kind of observations – that the Council was disturbing an orderly court system – were made when the Council was first established. In the words of Dean Vedel

> the Constitutional Council was introduced in a developed legal system, one of the most sophisticated of the civilized world, based on a conceptual matrix, a tradition of logics, and a complex though orderly court system. Then arrives a new (constitutional) judge who, in the hierarchy, seems to, at least in theory, place itself above all other judges. It is because of this disruptive effect that the Council was regarded as so disturbing …

adapted from a quote cited in Nicolas Molfessis, 'La Résistance Immédiate De La Cour De Cassation A La QPC' (2011) 137 *Pouvoirs* 83, 93.

[93] Dominique Rousseau, 'Le Conseil Constitutionnel, Cour Suprême?' in *Conseil Constitutionnel Et QPC : Une Révolution ?* (2011) 368 *La Documentation Française* 38.

Things are now different under the QPC which has rooted the judicial activity of the FCC into the French court system by making the constitutional judge a full actor of the judiciary.

Overall, ordinary courts have used the referral mechanism in a reasonable fashion thus marking their willingness to embrace the new review. The FCC has not been inundated with referrals nor has it been sidelined with too few.[94] This has reinforced the 'hyperspecialization' of courts whereby the ordinary judge examines issues of conventionality, and the constitutional judge retains its monopoly over issues of constitutionality. In other words, there is no question of reversing the IVG precedent.[95] Each category of judge will keep their own private preserve in a model of concentrated constitutional review of legislation whereby the FCC, thanks to the filtering system and having the last word on the issue of constitutionality, would be the court at the top. By its mechanics, the QPC has indeed put the FCC in a position to become a supreme (constitutional) court. This potential development has generated tensions since there are already two well-established supreme courts.[96] The courts have developed their respective review competence based on the paradigm of the hierarchy of *norms*; the ordinary courts are dealing with the law and treaties, while they can enforce the primacy of constitutional provisions at the top of the pyramid. The conundrum stems from the fact that the QPC has introduced the possibility of a rivalry of *courts* by placing the FCC at the heart of the judicial procedure.

While the Council of State has embraced the QPC quite well, the reform has been more disruptive for the Court of Cassation.[97] This Court

---

[94] As of 1 March 2015, the Council has received 465 QPCs, in quasi equal proportion from the Court of Cassation (258) and Council of State (207). This is out of the more than 10 000 QPCs posed by citizens before ordinary courts since 2010; more than 2 300 of them have been referred to the supreme courts, hence giving a proportion of around 23 per cent of referral rate.

[95] The Council reaffirmed its position after the entry into force of the QPC. See FCC Decision 2010-605 DC of 12 May 2010 (*Loi Relative A L'Ouverture A La Concurrence Et A La Régulation Du Secteur Des Jeux D'Argent Et De Hasard En Ligne*) pt 11. Similarly, ordinary courts have not changed their position regarding their refusal to examine the constitutionality of laws ; see, for example, Cass Com No. 08-17541 of 7 July 2009.

[96] Although this is technically wrong to assert that there are two 'supreme' courts. There can be, by definition, only *one* supreme court and to say that two exist is to say that none exist. Nevertheless, this is how the tension rising from the enhanced role of the Council has been formulated.

[97] According to the First President of the Court of Cassation, the QPC is a '(judicial) cultural revolution' which [has] deeply affect[ed] the role of the judge

has disputed the QPC procedure via two angles: first, by challenging its priority feature, and secondly, by making a controversial use of the filter mechanism. First, in the *Melki* case, the Court of Cassation sought to undermine the new review in its quintessential feature of priority. The *Melki* saga, which involved the Court of Cassation,[98] FCC,[99] Council of State[100] and CJEU[101] over the space of a few months between April and June 2010, epitomizes the judicial dialogue between national and European courts.[102] Suffice it to say here that the Court of Cassation showed resistance at both ends of the litigation. The court started by making a preliminary reference to the CJEU instead of following the course of the QPC procedure initiated at domestic level.[103] In essence, the Court of Cassation argued that the binding effect of the decisions of the FCC would deprive the ordinary judge of the possibility to make a reference to the CJEU (or set aside a legislative measure in the case it viewed it as contrary to EU law) before a ruling was available from the FCC – and that was not acceptable to the Court. At the other end of the litigation –

---

and the relations between sources of law, namely the relation between statute law and case law (Parliamentary debates on the Institutional Law, Vincent Lamanda, 1 September 2010, Rapport, AN, 2838).

[98] Cass No 10-40.002 QPC of 16 April 2010 (concl. Domingo, *Gazette du Palais*, 23–27 May 2010, 8-16). The case involved the arrest, detention and deportation of two Algerian nationals, who illegally entered France but whose identity had been checked by French forces at the frontier between France and Belgium. They claimed that several provisions of the Code of Criminal Procedure, which were the ground for the action of the border police, were contrary to the free movement of persons, hence a classic issue of conventionality. They also grounded their claim in constitutional terms: because French obligations under the TFEU have a constitutional value according to art 88-1, the challenged criminal law provisions were also contrary to the Constitution.

[99] FCC Decision 2010-605 DC (n 36).

[100] CE No 312305 of 14 May 2010 (*Rujovic*) pt 1. The Council of State confirmed that the priority rule was procedural and could be departed from in order to preserve the effectiveness of EU law. It was up to the administrative judge, as primary EU law judge and referral judge of the QPC, to decide which procedure to prioritize in the particular case at hand.

[101] CJEU (GC) Cases C-188/10 and C-189/10 of 22 June 2010 (*Aziz Melki and Sélim Abdeli*). See below.

[102] See Daniel Sarmiento, 'L'Affaire Melki: Esquisse D'un Dialogue Des Juges Constitutionnels Et Européens Sur Toile De Fond Française' (2010) *Revue Trimestrielle De Droit Européen* 588 ; François-Xavier Millet, 'Le Dialogue Des Juges A L'Epreuve De La QPC' (2010) *Revue Du Droit Public* 1729.

[103] The first instance judge, who had to rule on the criminal measures regarding the two litigants, had referred a QPC to the Court of Cassation.

and despite the conciliatory ruling of the CJEU in the case – the Court of Cassation failed to fully enter the 'game of loyal cooperation',[104] by deciding on the basis of EU law *only*, without examining if the conditions for a QPC referral were met in that particular case. By refusing to consider the conditions for a constitutional referral, the Court instructed the first instance judge to set aside, *as contrary to EU law*, the legislative provisions of criminal procedure. By this attitude, the Court of Cassation certainly ostracized itself. Its stance was criticized with vigour at the time.[105]

Secondly, a certain degree of 'pre-judgment' on the issue of constitutionality, or 'soft constitutionality review', is part of the procedure since ordinary courts assess referral requirements – in particular that the issue on constitutionality is new or presents a 'serious character'. By refusing to refer a question to the FCC when they regard the issue as lacking seriousness, ordinary courts exercise a kind of indirect constitutional review, hereby developing a form of decentralized review. The problem comes when ordinary courts make an overtly strategic use of their filtering role.[106] In this regard, the Court of Cassation refused to refer on several occasions whether the refusal concerned specific texts or was motivated by considerations of principles. The Court refused to refer, for example, the *Loi Gayssot* on the prohibition of the Holocaust denial.[107]

---

[104] Marc Bossuyt and Willem Verrijdt, 'The Full Effect of EU Law and Constitutional Review in Belgium and France after the Melki Judgment' (2011) 7 *EUConst* 355, 379.

[105] See the strong titles in the doctrine and press in the midst of the *Melki* saga in, for example, Guy Carcassonne and Nicolas Molfessis, 'La Cour De Cassation A L'Assaut De La Question Prioritaire De Constitutionnalité' *Le Monde* (Paris, 22 April 2010), Dominique Rousseau and Daniel Lévy, 'La Cour De Cassation Et La Question Prioritaire De Constitutionnalité: Pourquoi Tant De Méfiance ?' *Gazette Du Palais*, 25–27 April 2010, Anne Levade, 'Renvoi Préjudiciel Versus Question Prioritaire De Constitutionnalité: La Cour De Cassation Cherche Le Conflit !'(2010) 20 *Recueil Dalloz* 1254.

[106] Similarly, the Council can use its power of appreciation to judge about a change of circumstances leading to reconsideration of legislative provisions already examined. This was the case in the decision on the police custody regime. Noting a sharp increase in the number of people in custody, the Council considered this as a valid change of factual circumstances justifiying ex post review of the legislation in the area. See FCC Decision 2010-14/22 QPC of 30 July 2010 (*M Daniel W Et Autres*) pts 15–18.

[107] Cass No 09-80774 QPC of 7 May 2010 (*Mme X Et Alii v Fédération Nationale Des Déportés Et Internés, Résistants Et Patriotes Et Autres*) and Law No 90-615 of 13 July 1990 (*Tendant A Réprimer Tout Acte Raciste, Antisémite Ou Xénophobe*).

The Court controversially based its appreciation of the lack of serious character on an interpretation of the law which had the effect of rendering it constitutionally compatible. However, it was well acknowledged that the constitutionality of the *Gayssot* law was doubtful, especially as regard freedom of expression.[108]

There are interesting reasons for this hostility of the Court of Cassation. One is that the QPC has revealed the still conservative penchant of the Court vis-à-vis review of legislation and its reluctance to further depart from *légicentrisme*. Another reason may lie in the unease towards a reform which was, after all, imposed by the political power, rather than judicially developed like conventionality review. What is striking though was the political reaction to this hostility. Not only were several changes brought about in order to discipline the Court of Cassation, but also the Court was threatened with further curtailement if it maintained its negative attitude. For example, in the midst of the *Melki* saga, Parliament decided to abolish the special formation of the Court of Cassation competent to decide on referrals to the FCC, hereby depriving the Court of a forum to exercise its discretion.[109] In order to prevent further attempts by the Court to pre-judge on the issue of constitutionality, there were also proposals to suppress the requirement of 'seriousness', thereby depriving the ordinary courts of their interpretative power in this respect, and the possibility of an appeal of the refusal to refer to the FCC.[110] These proposals did not prosper, but if they had, the FCC would have been endowed with the power to decide on its own competence since it would have been able to decide on referrals in lieu of the supreme ordinary judges. This line of reactions is remarkable from the point of view of the separation of powers (ie the legislator instructing the judiciary) and from the point of view of the historical origins of review of legislation. Judicial review of legislation was originally conceived as

---

[108] The constitutionality of the *Gayssot* law was tested at national and international level. At national level, it was at odds with a similar legislation – the 2012 law on the Armenian Genocide Denial – which was declared unconstitutional because it violated the freedom of speech. At international level, if the Human Rights Committee upheld the condemnation of a French litigant under the provisions of the International Covenant on Civil and Political Rights, the Committee nevertheless indicated that the scope of the *Gayssot* law could be interpreted as being too broad.

[109] Organic Law No 2010-830 of 22 July 2010 (*Relative A L'Application De L'Article 65 De La Constitution*).

[110] Senator Hyest's proposal (to appeal the refusal to refer before the Council) and Deputy Warsmann's proposal (the Council can instruct the supreme courts to reconsider the conditions for referral) cited in Molfessis (n 92) 96–7.

against Parliament in order to review the legislature's action – it turns out that the QPC has been considered as the 'daughter of Parliament'[111] having been promoted and defended by it!

Tensions have now appeased with the Court of Cassation. It is unlikely that the FCC will soon rise to become *the* supreme court, either by official consecration or by incremental metamorphosis.[112] However, the FCC still faces potential tension, especially as regards conventionality review. Any litigant can now simultaneously challenge a law against the provisions of the Constitution and against the provisions of European law (that is EU law or the law of the ECHR) hereby increasing the possibility of rivalry between courts.[113] Yet, signs of a healthy dialogue exist regarding the Council's relationships with European courts.

B. From indirect to direct dialogue with the Court of Justice of the European Union

Having generally accepted the implications of Europeanization of the French legal order, the FCC does not challenge the role and competence of the European courts and has made reference to their decisions on several occasions.[114] Still, the Council has refused to include international law and European law in its norms of reference.[115] Rights-based review in France is still split between review of constitutionality and review of conventionality. The rapprochement between the FCC and the CJEU occurred when two issues came to the fore: the first was about the compatiblity of the new review with EU law, as previously discussed, and the second was about the possibility for the FCC to make a preliminary reference to the CJEU.

The first issue was about the sequencing between the QPC referral and the preliminary ruling referral under Article 267 TFEU. The end result

---

[111] Guy Carcassonne, 'Le Parlement Et La QPC' (2011) 137 *Pouvoirs* 73, 75.

[112] Even before the 2008 reform, the Council was resisting being a supreme court. See Bertrand Mathieu and others, *Les Grandes Délibérations Du Conseil Constitutionnel* (Dalloz 2009) 345.

[113] This was the case, for instance, as regards its decision on the police custody regime. The Court of Cassation, which had previously referred a QPC, decided that the provisions declared constitutional by the Council, were nevertheless incompatible with the rights protected under the ECHR and set them aside. See Cass Crim No 10-82902, No 10-82306, No 10-82051 of 19 October 2010.

[114] For example, in the case of the CJEU, see FCC Decision 2004-496 DC (n 37) pt 7.

[115] Contrary to the Belgium Constitutional Court for example. See Marc Verdussen in Chapter 9.

was that the CJEU held the QPC 'EU-compatible', but under conditions. In the *Melki* case, the CJEU declared that:

> Article 267 TFEU does not preclude such national legislation [which establishes an interlocutory procedure for the review of the constitutionality of national laws], in so far as the other national courts or tribunals remain free:
>
> – to refer to the Court of Justice for a preliminary ruling, at whatever stage of the proceedings they consider appropriate, even at the end of the interlocutory procedure for the review of constitutionality, any question which they consider necessary,
> – to adopt any measure necessary to ensure provisional judicial protection of the rights conferred under the European Union legal order, and
> – to disapply, at the end of such an interlocutory procedure, the national legislative provision at issue if they consider it to be contrary to EU law.[116]

This conditional acceptance is typical of the dialogic mode between the domestic courts and European courts, both concerned with the articulation of their systems of rights protection.[117] It is reminiscent of the position of the German Federal Constitutional Court towards a potential conflict between EU provisions and fundamental provisions protected under German Basic Law in the *Solange* litigation, or of the solution adopted by the ECtHR which establishes a presumption of equivalence of protection between EU law and the ECHR protection of fundamental rights in the *Bosphorus* case. After the '*Solange* technique' and '*Bosphorus* test', the '*Melki* way'[118] now sees the CJEU reconciling EU law with a constitutional mechanism of rights protection. Although the CJEU left to the referring judge the task of finding an EU conform interpretation, the Court implicitely grounded its reasoning on the FCC's interpretation which it took almost word by word. The dynamic of dialogue works by cross-fertilization. The issue was also raised as regards the

---

[116] See above. CJEU (GC) Cases C-188/10 and C-189/10 (n 101) paras 51–57. Another condition derives from the exclusive jurisdiction of the CJEU to rule on the validity of secondary EU provisions. This commands that the priority rule may not apply to legislative provisions exactly transposing EU directives since the abrogation of such norms by the Council would impede the appreciation of their validity by the CJEU.

[117] See Asteris Pliakos, 'Le Contrôle De Constitutionnalité Et Le Droit De l'Union Européenne: La Réaffirmation Du Principe De Primauté' (2010) 3 *Cahiers De Droit Européen* 487; Jacqueline Dutheil De La Rochère, 'La Question Prioritaire De Constitutionnalité Et Le Droit Européen – La Porte Etroite' (2010) 46 (3) *Revue Trimestrielle De Droit Européen* 577.

[118] Dyèvre (n 76).

priority rule under Belgian constitutional law. Although the *Chartry* case before the CJEU failed on admissibility,[119] an analogy could arguably be drawn between the two mechanisms (even if they are not exactly similar) making the solution adopted in *Melki* transposable to the Belgium situation.[120] If this first issue is now settled, some argue that further tensions might arise between the French legal order and EU law.[121]

For reasons of strict time-limits, the FCC has considered, until recently, as impracticable to refer a preliminary ruling to the CJEU. The breakthrough came when the Council made its first ever preliminary reference on an issue relating to the European Arrest Warrant (EAW) in the *Jeremy Forrest* case,[122] certainly encouraged by the outcome of the *Melki* case. The issue was the following one: among the several loopholes left by the French legislation transposing the EAW provisions,[123] was the lack of the possibility to appeal a decision extending the effects of the EAW – which was the issue raised by the plaintiff before the Court of Cassation, claiming this was contrary to the principle of equality before the law and the right to an effective judicial remedy. According to the Court of Cassation, the admissibility of the appeal was dependent on

---

[119] See CJEU Case C-457/09 of 1 Mars 2011 (*Chartry*). The issue raised in this case fell outside the scope of EU law.

[120] See Marc Verdussen in Chapter 9.

[121] Denis Simon, 'Conventionnalité Et Constitutionnalité' (2011) 137 *Pouvoirs* 19, 29–30.

[122] FCC Decision 2013-314P QPC of 4 April 2013 (*Jeremy F*). The case arose when an EAW was issued against a British teacher who had flown to France with one of his pupils. His detention and transfer from French to British authorities caused problems as the offence he was interrogated for (sexual intercourse with a minor) was different from the offence under which he was initially prosecuted when the EAW was issued (child abduction). The British authorities had asked the French criminal court to extend the effects of the EAW to the second offence which it did. The plaintiff, who had agreed to the first offence but did not accept the second qualification, raised the issue of the absence of appeal against the decision of the French court. The plaintiff was eventually sentenced to five years' imprisonment by a British Crown Court in June 2013.

[123] Council Framework Decision 2002/584/JHA of 13 June 2002 on the European Arrest Warrant and the surrender procedures between Member States (OJ L 190, 18 July 2002), as amended by Framework Decision 2009/299/JHA (OJ L 81, 27 March 2009). The Framework decision imposed a short period of 30 days for a decision on the extension of the effects of the EAW, but left a margin of appreciation to the member states regarding the remedies against decisions on transfers and extension of the effects of the EAW. France's transposition was arguably hasty in this regard.

the conformity of the challenged legislative provision with Articles 6 and 16 of the 1789 Declaration on equality before the law and observance of the law, respectively. In 'an anti-Melki reaction',[124] the Court of Cassation then suspended the criminal proceedings and referred a QPC to the Council about the provisions of Article 88-2 of the Constitution which constitutionalized the EAW.[125]

This very 'political' choice of the FCC shows, first, that the preliminary reference is a significant move towards a further judicialization of the FCC. Secondly, it is a landmark as regards the role of the Council in a multilevel European legal order and in its relationships with the CJEU in particular. This can be interpreted in two ways. In one way, it shows that the FCC considers itself like any other European constitutional court, most of which already take part in this dialogue and have referred questions to the CJEU.[126] In another way, it can be interpreted as if the Council was considering itself like any other French ordinary court entitled to refer to the CJEU.[127] While some have argued that this amounts to the exercise of conventionality review by the Council (ie review of the compatibility of the Constitution with EU law), it might be better to interpret it as a necessity imposed in the context of its constitutional review role calling for a merger of the two types of review (constitutionality and conventionality) with regard the specific case of EU law. In any event, the frontiers between reviews and between the different

---

[124] Henri Labayle, 'Never Say Never Again: Quand Le Mandat D'Arrêt Européen Conduit Le Conseil Constitutionnel A Poser Sa Première Question Préjudicielle A La Cour De Justice' 7 April 2013 accessed at <http://www.gdr-elsj.eu/2013/04/07/cooperation-judiciaire-penale/never-say-never-again-quand-le-mandat-darret-europeen-conduit-le-conseil-constitutionnel-a-poser-sa-premiere-question-prejudicielle-a-la-cour-de-justice> accessed 19 June 2015.

[125] Article 88-2 reads: 'Statutes shall determine the rules relating to the European arrest warrant pursuant to acts adopted by the institutions on the European Union.'

[126] For example, CJEU Case C-399/11 of 26 February 2013 (*Stefano Melloni v Ministerio Fiscal*) from the Spanish Constitutional Court which asked the Court of Justice whether the Framework Decision allowed the Spanish courts to make the surrender of Mr Melloni subject to the possibility of judicial review of his conviction, as required by the case law of the Spanish Constitutional Court.

[127] This ability to refer a preliminary ruling to the CJEU is limited however, as it is only possible in the context of a QPC. Making a preliminary ruling to the Court of Justice is still impossible in the context of ex ante review because of the time limit of three months and because of the impossibility to ask for a procedure of urgency.

roles of the courts have been blurred further remodelling the French system of rights-based review.

C. Harmonious relationship with the European Court of Human Rights

At first glance, the QPC is in conformity with the subsidiary character of the ECHR system: the remedy ensures that litigants will seek protection of their rights and freedoms at domestic level. Besides, by taking into account the case law of the ECtHR, the FCC confirms its harmonious relationship with the ECHR system – and this has no reason to change.[128] The ECHR does not entail the establishment of constitutional review. However, when it exists, in whatever form, access to it must not be hindered according to the right of access to court and the right to obtain a determination of the dispute by the competent court.[129] The QPC is an additional constitutional remedy granted to the citizens. Under Article 35 of the ECHR, all available domestic remedies must have been exhausted before an application is made to the ECtHR. An applicant is obliged to seek a domestic remedy only if it is considered 'effective' by the Strasbourg Court.[130] The right to an effective remedy requires either the prevention of a human rights violation or an adequate redress.[131] The question then arises whether the QPC is effective – in other words, whether the national institution (in this case the FCC) has the opportunity to prevent, or redress, human rights violations before a case is taken to the ECtHR.

An interesting analogy can be made here with the declaration of incompatibility under the British and Irish acts of incorporation of the ECHR which equates a rights-based review at domestic level.[132] The nexus of their efficiency lies in the possibility of obtaining such a declaration, and that this declaration is being followed by governmental remedial action. The ECtHR does not assess the effectiveness of a

---

128 The Council has cited the ECHR and ECtHR's case law on several occasions. See, for example, FCC Decision 2004-505 DC of 19 November 2004 (*Traité Etablissant Une Constitution Pour L'Europe*).

129 ECtHR *James and others v United Kindgom* Series A 98 of 21 February 1986 (1986) 8 EHRR 123.

130 ECtHR *Akdivar v Turkey* of 16 September 1996 (1997) 23 EHRR143, ECHR 1996-IV paras 66–9.

131 ECtHR *Kudla v Poland* of 26 October 2000 (2000) 35 EHRR198, ECHR 2000-XI paras 155–8.

132 See Aileen Kavanagh and Chintan Chandrachud in Chapter 2, and Cliona Kelly in Chapter 3.

remedy in abstracto and the example of the position of the Court vis-à-vis the declaration of incompatibility under the HRA 1998 in the UK and the ECHR Act 2003 in Ireland is relevant in this regard. In *Burden v UK*,[133] the ECtHR accepted that a declaration of incompatibility under the British HRA 1998 could be regarded as an effective remedy, hence putting the litigant under the obligation to pursue it (although the obligation to wait for the remedial action is not clear).[134] Comparatively, the situation is not as clear in the case of the Irish ECHR Act 2003 where declarations of incompatiblity have not proven to effectively lead to steps amending the offending legislative provisions.[135]

Under the French QPC, the nexus of effectiveness lies in the reasonable use of the filter mechanism by the supreme courts (that is, the litigant must have a reasonable chance to reach the constitutional stage) and the possibility to obtain effects in the particular case (that is, the litigant must benefit from a provision being struck down for unconstitutionality). On the face of it, it is unlikely that a QPC could be regarded as an effective remedy: only a proportion of around one-fifth of the issues of constitutionality are referred to the FCC; besides, there is always the risk of resistance by the Court of Cassation in its referral 'policy' leaving the litigant with little prospect of a constitutional claim; most of all, the QPC

---

[133] ECtHR (GC) *Burden v United Kingdom* of 29 April 2008 (2007) 47 EHRR 38.

[134] The ECtHR suggested that 'it cannot be excluded that at some time in the future the practice of giving effect to the national courts' declarations of incompatibility by amendment of the legislation is so certain as to indicate that s 4 of the Human Rights Act is to be interpreted as imposing a binding obligation' (*Burden v United Kingdom* para. 43).

[135] In *A, B and C v Ireland*, the Court did not consider that an application under the ECHR 2003 for a declaration of incompatibility of the relevant legislative provisions and for an associated *ex gratia* award of damages, could be regarded as an effective remedy which had to be exhausted. It stated so for several reasons:

> The rights guaranteed by the 2003 Act would not prevail over the provisions of the Constitution. In any event, a declaration of incompatibility would place no legal obligation on the State to amend domestic law and, since it would not be binding on the parties to the relevant proceedings, it could not form the basis of an obligatory award of monetary compensation. In such circumstances, and given the relatively small number of declarations to date only one of which has recently become final, a request for such a declaration and for an *ex gratia* award of damages would not have provided an effective remedy to the first and second applicants.

(ECtHR (GC) *A, B and C v Ireland* of 16 December 2010 para. 150).

ruling is abstract in nature and does not entail the payment of compensation, for example; also, the postponement of the effects of unconstitutionality deprive the litigant of any satisfaction, which has been the case for significant pieces of legislation such as the police custody and sexual harrassment legislations. However, when the FCC rules on a QPC, it strives to respect the subjective rights of the individual as well. Indeed, the procedure must have an *effet utile* for the party invoking the unconstitutionality, as well as for all parties whose case on the same issue is pending. The FCC has done so on many occasions and postonment of the effects of the abrogation have been exceptional, justified on public order or legal certainty grounds.[136]

8.3.3 Impact on Parliament

The FCC has a sort of 'love-hate' relationship with Parliament. As a counter-power, the Council curbs the exercise of power by the other branches of government by ruling independently on their decisions.[137] Whereas originally set up to regulate the exercise of powers between the government and Parliament, the Council has morphed into being the guarantor of constitutional rights and freedoms and 'protector of the rule of law' – a dual dimension aptly expressed in Article 16 of the 1789 Declaration which refers to the separation of powers and the guarantee of rights. In that context, an optimistic view of the relationships between the FCC and Parliament – that is one not based on constraint and negative terms, but expressed in terms of dialogue and collaboration – is to be expected.[138] The idea of a shared constitutional responsibility in the task of protecting rights and freedoms has been developed in the case of other

---

[136] See FCC Decision 2009-595 DC (n 53) pt 17, and numerous others since the first QPC decision such as, for example, FCC Decision 2010-1 QPC of 28 May 2010 (*Mr and Mrs L*) pt 12. Exceptionally, the Council postponed the effects of the abrogation of the police custody legislation in order to allow Parliament to enact a new law. See FCC Decision 2010-14/22 QPC of 30 July 2010 (*M Daniel W Et Autres*) pt 30.

[137] 'Le Juge Constitutionnel Est-Il Un Contre-Pouvoir?', Table Ronde Du Centre Français de Droit Comparé, Paris, 21 June 2010, (2010) 3 *Revue Internationale De Droit Comparé* 788.

[138] On this idea, see, for example, George Bergougnous, 'Le Conseil Constitutionnel Et Le Législateur' (2013) 38 *Les Nouveaux Cahiers Du Conseil Constitutionnel* 7 ; Olivier Dord, 'La QPC Et Le Parlement : Une Bienveillance Réciproque' (2013) 38 *Les Nouveaux Cahiers Du Conseil Constitutionnel* 24.

jurisdictions.[139] Even though the Council censures or abrogates the work of Parliament, the FCC will do it with deference, ensuring that the line between the political decision and the judicial decision is not crossed.

This is already the case in the context of ex ante review which, under Article 61, is embedded in the elaboration of the law. While abrogating significant pieces of legislation,[140] the FCC has been acting as an essential interlocutor of Parliament, offering guidance, sort of guarding Parliament against its own fault. The censure of unclear[141] or excessively convoluted[142] pieces of legislation, or of those which do not have any normative substance,[143] are a good illustration of this. At a time of legislative inflation degrading the quality of laws, the FCC has been adamant to impose the respect of certain principles in the drafting process, such as the principle of legal certainty and the principle of clarity of the law. However, the FCC has made sure to respect the private preserve of Parliament and has consistently held that the Council does not have the same power of appreciation as that of the legislature.[144] The object of constitutional review is not for the FCC to substitute its own interpretation to that of the legislature's.[145] It is not to hinder nor delay

---

[139] See in particular Aileen Kavanagh and Chintan Chandrachud in Chapter 2, and Eoin Carolan in Chapter 3.

[140] The Council has censored a few symbolic political commitments. See, for example, FCC Decision 2009-580 DC of 10 June 2009 (*Loi HADOPI*) on the diffusion and protection of creation on the Internet, and FCC Decision 2009-599 DC of 29 December 2009 (*Loi De Finances Pour 2010*) on carbon tax, the latter being analysed as a direct confrontation between the executive power, instigator of this emblematic environmental measure, and the constitutional judge.

[141] FCC Decision 2001-455 DC of 12 January 2002 (*Loi De Modernisation Sociale*) pt 9.

[142] FCC Decision 2003-473 DC of 26 June 2003 (*Loi Habilitant Le Gouvernement A Simplifier Le Droit*) pt 5.

[143] FCC Decision 2004-500 DC of 29 July 2004 (*Loi Organique Relative A L'Autonomie Financière Des Collectivités Territoriales*) pt 12.

[144] FCC Decision 74-54 DC of 15 January 1975 (*Interruption Volontaire De Grossesse*) pt 1, reaffirmed under the QPC in, for example, FCC Decision 2010-2 QPC of 11 June 2010 (*Mme Vivianne L*) pt 4: 'Article 61-1 of the Constitution, like Article 61, *does not vest the Constitutional Council with any general power of appraisal and decision- making similar to that vested in Parliament.* This Article merely vests the Council with jurisdiction to rule on the conformity of a statutory provision with rights and freedoms guaranteed by the Constitution' (emphasis added).

[145] FCC Decision 80-127 DC of 20 January 1981 (*Loi Renforçant La Sécurité Et Protégeant La Liberté Des Personnes*) pt 13.

the exercise of its power by the legislature, but to ensure it respects the Constitution.[146]

Things are different under Article 61-1 since ex post review is detached from the legislative process in time and initiative. The QPC is part of the implementation of the law, and not part of its elaboration, and parliamentarians are excluded from the constitutional litigation because they cannot raise a QPC. Yet, the FCC has been mindful of its role and has resorted to the techniques of interpretation already in use under ex post review such as 'reserves of interpretation' in order to save a law from abrogation.[147] The Council has also used techniques specific to ex post review such as the postponment of the effects of the abrogation under Article 62(2).[148] Lastly, self-restraint has been expressed when the FCC has left a margin of appreciation to Parliament in areas involving public policy choices or the assessment of scientific and technological data which parliamentarians are more entitled to decide upon. This is the case with societal choices which, by nature, are to be decided by democratically elected representatives. A topical illustration is the litigation on same sex marriage which the FCC 'handed over' to Parliament which eventually adopted the same sex marriage legislation in 2013, after one of the most virulent demonstrations of public opinion in years. In this litigation, the FCC ruled – before the 2013 law was enacted – that it was not for the constitutional court:

> to substitute its judgment for that of the legislator regarding the consideration of [the] difference of situation [between couples of the same sex and those composed of a man and a woman], and that consequently the grievance relating to the violation of Article 6 of the Declaration of 1789 on equality before the law was not operative.[149]

---

[146] FCC Decision 85-197 DC of 23 August 1985 (*Loi Relative A L'Evolution De La Nouvelle Calédonie*) pt 27.

[147] FCC Decision 2010-8 QPC of 18 June 2010 (*Epoux L*) pt 18.

[148] The most emblematic decision in this regard is the case of 30 July 2010 on Police custody legislation. In order to avoid the disturbing effect of an immediate abrogation of the whole legislation on Police custody (only the provisions on custody for acts of terrorism were regarded as unconstitutional) and to maintain this important means of policing and temporary deprivation of liberty aimed at preventing disruption of public order, the FCC decided to postpone the abrogation up until one year after its decision, hence leaving sufficient time for the legislature to pass a new law. See FCC Decision QPC 2010-14/22 of 30 July 2010 (n 136) setting the dealine of 1 July 2011, and Law No 2011-392 of 14 April 2011 (*Relative A La Garde A Vue*).

[149] FCC Decision 2010-92 QPC (n 66) pt 9. See also Law No 2013-404 of 17 May 2013 (*Ouvrant Le Mariage Aux Couples De Personnes De Même Sexe*)

This shows that decisions on unconstitutionality imply a form of processual dialogue between the legislative power and the constitutional judge when the FCC 'hands over' to Parliament.

The position of Parliament vis-à-vis the FCC is more ambiguous. The legislature has never been too keen on accepting a too direct link with the FCC. Parliament has interpreted its own role as one consisting of drafting and voting the law, while internalizing the constitutional constraint,[150] but certainly not as one committed to its 'constitutional' defence which is left to the Secretary General of the Governement whatever the origin of the text (government bill or private members's bill).[151] Still, Parliament has defended the introduction of the QPC by reuniting all the conditions for its success; it has kept it in the hands of the Council in order to avoid a decentralized review available to ordinary judges; it has prioritized the issue of constitutionality through the priority rule; and it has imposed short time-limits to constrain ordinary judges to refer in good time

8.4 CONCLUSION

Talking about 'changing lanscape' regarding rights-based constitutional review in France is talking about a revolution as much as about an evolution. The introduction of ex post concrete review is revolutionary because of its radical effects (that is the abrogation of the law in force) and its transcendental reach (such as the indifference to the traditional public/private law divide, and the separation between the administrative and civil legal orders since both judicial orders are involved, or the formal link created between the FCC and the CJEU). The QPC has certainly prompted a new era of constitutionalism in that it has touched upon every aspect of it: first, the *norm* as embodied in the Constitution; secondly, the *judiciary* with an impact on how the courts perceive their

---

which was declared constitutional ex ante in Decision 2013-669 DC of 17 May 2013 (*Loi Ouvrant Le Mariage Aux Couples De Personnes De Même Sexe*).

[150] The same is true for the government. See, for example, the *Circulaire* of 25 May 1988 on The Working Methods in Government issued by a left-wing Prime Minister which urged members of the executive to respect the rule of law and avoid risks of unconstitutionality when drafting bills and proposing amendments.

[151] The 2009 Organic Law on the application of Article 61-1 provides for the possibility for the President of the National Assembly and the President of the Senate (like for the other constitutional authorities, President of the Republic and Prime Minister) to present observations before the Council. It is significant that this has seldom been used by them (not at all by the President of the Senate).

role in the protection of the Constitution and the ensuing shift of powers within the courts system; thirdly, *constitutional politics* with a control over the exercise of the governing power; and lastly, *society* with the 'popularization' of the social pact. On this last point, the Constitution is now 'the citizens' business', and the FCC is the 'new face [of democracy]'.[152] The QPC has contributed to modify the relationship of the French people with their Constitution since the Constitution is now invocable and enforceable against state authorities. For all these reasons, the QPC has purpotedly put an end to the French peculiarity in the field.[153] The domestic system of rights-based constitutional review is heading towards completeness and arguably converge with the dominant European model of constitutional review. The Constitution is no longer limited to an institutional one merely dealing with the organization and separation of powers ('Constitution-separation of powers'), but is conforted in its role as a 'Constitution-protection of rights' and living instrument, therefore rekindling with the kind of common values first set out in 1789.[154]

This is also an evolutionary process since the FCC pursues what it has been doing before, that is 'redefining the constitutional landscape' by refining its review framework for the protection of rights as well as 'redefining the working of the institutions, their inter-relationships and the role of the state itself'.[155] Through its new role, not only does the FCC continue its work on the judicial protection of individual rights, but it is also very much bringing the general interest, hence the idea of the state, to the fore.[156] In fact, several processes are at work as regards the development of rights-based constitutional review. These processes which

---

[152] Patrick Roger, 'Au "Non" De La Loi' *Le Monde* (Paris, 2 March 2013).

[153] Interview with Jean-Michel Debré, 'Un Progrès Pour L'Etat De Droit Dans Notre Pays' *Le Figaro* (Paris, 25 May 2010).

[154] Lévy (n 17) 32–3. See also Marie-Luce Paris, 'New Constitutional Review in France: How does the French Constitution finally speak to its People – or does it?' (Public Lecture, ANU Centre for European Studies and Centre for International and Public Law, Canberra, April 2011). Some are more wary of the beneficial impact on citizens's rights. See, for example, Guillaume Tusseau, 'La Fin D'Une Exception Française ?' (2011) 137 *Pouvoirs* 5; Myriam Hunter-Henin, 'Constitutional Developments and Human Rights in France: One Step Forward, Two Steps Back', (2011) 60 *ICLQ* 167. For a more balanced view, see Olivier Duhamel, 'La QPC Et Les Citoyens' (2011) 137 *Pouvoirs* 183.

[155] Bell and others (n 25) 156.

[156] Baranger (n 84) 14.

have been theorized under the concepts of juridification of law (understood as an increase in rules and individual rights nationally, and inter- and supranationally, and as a reallocation of powers to autonomous institutions such as courts),[157] judicialization of politics, constitutionalization, and Europeanization of constitutional review, are given a new relevance under the QPC practice.

In this context, French constitutionalism has changed, albeit on its own terms. It boasts peculiarities which further soften traditional distinctions. Strict descriptions relating to its centralized nature, or to the divide between courts dealing with constitutional review and those dealing with conventionality reviews, are blurred. Constitutional review is still centralized and abstract in nature (even in the case of ex post review, the FCC does not deal with the case at hand), but has become decentralized in part: ordinary courts which exercise conventionality review, are now empowered to exercise a 'soft constitutional review' when they decide, as filters, whether an issue of constitutionality is new or sufficiently serious. On the other hand, the FCC exercises a marginal review of conventionality as regards EU law. The Council has now all the attributes of a constitutional court, but also some of a supreme court. All this reinforces the impression of a parochial evolution – a converging system of review, but not quite embracing completely a judicially-based constitutionalism.

In such context, what is needed is a continuing acceptance by the FCC, and indeed other courts, of pluralism and dialogue – pluralism in the sense that there is no hierarchy of norms anymore; and dialogue in the sense that there is no hierarchy of courts either. We agree that 'the concept of pre-ordained hierarchy is replaced by that of a network of legal rules and principles which are related to each other operationally when key decisions have to be made in individual situations',[158] although the pre-eminence of the Constitution is reinforced at domestic level by the case law of the FCC, even more so under the QPC practice. The collaborative dimension, which is typical of other systems of constitutional review from a comparative perspective, is deeply relevant. The FCC, but also domestic and European courts, acknowledge the diversity of solutions between differents courts and the fact that this 'judicial

[157] Anne-Mette Magnussen and Ana Banasiak, 'Juridification: Disrupting the Relationship between Law and Politics?' (2013) 19 *ELJ* 326.

[158] Bell (n 45) 735, 743.

diplomacy'[159] can indeed lead to a positive form of competition whereby one court supercedes another in its effort to increase the efficiency of rights protection.[160]

[159] Jean-Paul Costa, *La Cour Européenne Des Droits De L'Homme: Des Juges Pour La Liberté* (Dalloz 2013) 224.

[160] A topical example in this regard is again the custodial regime. The Council first censured the standard custodial regime, with the exception of the special regime relating to terrorism offences. The latter regime was, a few weeks later, denounced by the Court of Cassation via a conventionality review on the basis of its incompatibility with the ECHR. The effect of both rulings (the one by the Council and the one by the Court of Cassation) on the flaws of the different kinds of custodial regimes led to the postponment of their effects so as to give time to the government to propose a new coherent piece of legislation to Parliament.

9. Belgium

The Belgian experience of rights-based review: has the Constitutional Court become a body subordinated to the European Court of Human Rights?

Marc Verdussen

9.1 INTRODUCTION

The aim of this chapter is to describe, explain and evaluate the way the Belgian Constitutional Court protects the fundamental rights by which I mean rights recognized by both constitutional law and international law. Belgium is party to a range of international treaties relating to fundamental rights, such as the European Convention on Human Rights (ECHR) and, within the framework of the European Union (EU), the Charter of Fundamental Rights of the EU. The influence of these international treaties has been strong and has contributed to improving many aspects pertaining to the protection of fundamental rights. Gradually, ensuring respect for these fundamental rights has become a significant part of the work of the Constitutional Court. But it has not always been so. The original model of constitutional review in Belgium has undergone a significant evolution from a review concerned with division of powers rendered necessary by the imperatives of a newly established federalism towards a system geared towards fundamental rights protection under the increasing influence of European legal systems and norms. Such an evolution of the practice of constitutional review has arguably created a link of quasi-subordination between the Constitutional Court and the European Court of Human Rights (ECtHR) as far as rights-based litigation of Belgian individuals is concerned.

9.2 EVOLUTION OF THE MODEL OF CONSTITUTIONAL REVIEW

First, it is important to put Belgian constitutional review in its general constitutional context to emphasize its main institutional and historical features, starting with federalism.

9.2.1 General Constitutional Setup: Belgian Federalism

Despite being an old State with an old Constitution, Belgium has had a Constitutional Court for only about 30 years. Belgium gained its independence in 1830 and adopted a Constitution in 1831. Under the influence of the French Revolution of 1789, Belgium was pervaded by a culture of the supremacy of the law (*'légicentrisme'*): 'How could such a genuine incarnation of the national will, as Parliament was viewed, violate the supreme law of the land which emanates from this very national will?'.[1] That is the reason why, for a long time, the Constitution remained silent on the possibility of reviewing the laws.[2] And the ordinary courts and tribunal have never been authorized to strike down unconstitutional laws.

The establishment of the Constitutional Court derives from the Constitution of 1980 for reasons explained below. Article 142 of the Constitution provides: 'There is for the whole of Belgium one Constitutional Court, the composition, competence and functioning of which are determined by statute.' This constitutional provision was implemented by the Act of 28 March 1983 and afterwards by the Special Act of 6 January 1989, which was amended on numerous occasions. Officially inaugurated in 1984, in the centre of Brussels, the Constitutional Court delivered its first judgment in 1985. Since then, it is beyond doubt that 'the law expresses the general will only insofar as it respects the Constitution', according to the formula expressed by the French Constitutional Council.[3] In most European States, the constitutional court was created after a period of dictatorship, at a moment of democratic revival. Change has come in this way in States such as Germany, Italy, Spain, Portugal, and Central European countries. In Belgium, the Constitutional Court was not

---

[1] Rusen Ergec, 'The Emergence of Constitutional Justice in Belgium' in Eivind Smith (ed.), *Constitutional Justice under Old Constitutions* (Kluwer Law International 1995) 148–9.

[2] By 'laws', we mean rules enacted by Parliament.

[3] Michel Troper, 'The Logic of Justification of Judicial Review' (2003) 1 *Intl J Cons L* 120.

created in order to protect fundamental rights. Its raison d'être lies in the transformation of the system of government from a unitary to a federal State.

Belgium has always been a constitutional monarchy, a democratic State, and subject to the rule of law. Belgium has always been a decentralized State, with provinces and municipalities. However, Belgium has not always been a federal State. Unlike most traditionally federal States, Belgium is an example of federalization by disaggregation which is the result of the gradual metamorphosis of an initially unitary structure. It took shape following a top-down process, namely the disintegration of a sovereign State under the pressure of 'an increasing centrifugal logic'.[4] Moreover, the formation of the federal structure took place gradually since it is founded on a multinational federalism which itself is the product of a long historical evolution. The history of Belgium 'has been a complex mixture of peaceful co-existence, political tension and cultural affirmation which has gradually been translated into political claims for increased autonomy by the different language groups'.[5] The watershed towards federalism began in 1970 and was progressive, occurring in steps. At that time, Belgium was 'an exotic hybrid of a political system which is neither truly federalist nor as ferociously unitarist as before'.[6] Gradually, it has become a real federal State, with a high degree of devolution of powers and competences. In this respect, Professor Kris Deschouwer emphasized that 'the gradual evolution towards a federal state was thus reached in the classical Belgian way, by letting the tension build up and then finally opting for compromise'.[7] Consequently, 'the process of change has been erratic rather than deliberately aimed at a federal outcome', so much so that federalism in Belgium is 'the result not of a deliberate choice but of incremental conflict management'.[8]

---

[4] Ferran Requejo, 'The Case of Minority Nations' in Michael Burgess and Alain-G Gagnon (eds), *Federal Democracies* (Routledge 2010) 290.

[5] Johanne Poirier, 'Formal Mechanisms of Intergovernmental Relations in Belgium' (2002) 12 *Regional & Federal Studies* 25.

[6] JA Dunn, 'The Revision of the Constitution in Belgium: A Study in the Institutionalization of Ethnic Conflict' (1974) 27 *The Western Political Quarterly* 163.

[7] Kris Deschouwer, 'And the Peace Goes On? Consociational Democracy and Belgian Politics in the Twenty-First Century' (2006) 29 *West European Politics* 903.

[8] Kris Deschouwer, 'Kingdom of Belgium', Forum of Federations/ International Association of Centers for Federal Studies, p. 2 <http://www.forumfed.org/libdocs/Global_Dialogue/Book_1/BK1-C02-be-Deschouwer-en.pdfin> accessed 12 June 2015.

Belgium has two kinds of federated entities: the regions and the communities. All regions and communities are vested with a distinct legal personality and are placed on an equal footing. Article 1 of the Constitution provides: 'Belgium is a Federal State which consists of communities and regions.' There are three regions: the Flemish Region, the Walloon Region and the Brussels-Capital Region. These sub-entities have a territorial basis. There are three communities: the Flemish Community, the French Community and the German-speaking Community. The communities are superimposed to the regions. This factor, which 'sets Belgium apart from other federations where the territorial nature of the subunits is unambiguous',[9] contributes towards the complexity of a system that can be perceived as rather bewildering. But 'it is hardly surprising that such complexity exists in all contemporary societies where the State is answerable for the various needs and expectations of citizens'.[10] Each of the communities and regions is self-governing and possesses its own Parliament (legislative assembly) and its own government (executive organ). Each community and each region have the power to enact legislation with the same hierarchic rank and binding power as federal law. The regions have legislative competences in areas such as natural environment, housing, economic affairs, energy policy, and transport. The communities are responsible for culture, education and 'personalised' matters such as health policy (sanitary education and preventive medicine), assistance to individuals (aid to families, to the disabled, to the elderly, to the minors, to the immigrants) and, pertaining to social security policy, child benefits.

Although characterized by a three-tier governmental structure and composed of several federate groups, the Belgian federal State features a deep and long-standing language cleavage between its French-speaking population and its Dutch-speaking population, this one having 'embarked upon a project of nation-building which puts it in the same category as

---

[9] Wilfried Swenden and Theo Jans, '"Will It Stay or Will It Go?" Federalism and the Sustainability of Belgium' (2006) 29 *West European Politics* 881.

[10] R Anderson, 'Administrative Law' in Hubert Bocken and Walter De Bondt (eds), *Introduction to Belgian Law* (Kluwer Law International/Bruylant 2000) 81. The institutional framework of the regions and the communities is laid down by the Constitution and by several laws, among which are the Special Institutional Reform Act of 8 August of 1980, providing for the structures and powers of the Flemish Region, the Walloon Region, the Flemish Community and the French Community; the Institutional Reform Act for the German-speaking Community, providing for the structures and powers of the German-speaking Community; and the Special Brussels Institutions Act of 12 January 1989, providing for the structures and powers of the Brussels-Capital Region.

stateless nations such as Catalonia, Scotland or the Basque Country'.[11] This dichotomy 'reveals itself as the main catalyst for understanding Belgium's federal dynamics'[12] and is 'probably the most striking feature of the Belgian federation'.[13] Besides, the cleavage 'has been embedded into a federal structure of mind-boggling complexity that both reflects and reinforces the organization of political, social, and cultural life on the basis of language'.[14] To a very great extent, the survival of the State will depend on the partners' readiness to uphold – in the words of Michael Walzer – a 'mutual tolerance'.[15] The challenge is tricky because 'the radically different profiles' of the two component units mean that they 'are constantly being compared with each other'.[16]

Over time, the constituent power had come to realize that the federal State was in need of an arbiter in charge of supervising the observance of the constitutional division of powers between the federal legislator and the legislators of the regions and communities. Indeed, since 'there [was] no hierarchy of legislative instruments enacted by the various entities of the Belgian State, and this [might have caused] conflicts of competence between the communities/regions and the federal state', it was felt that, to resolve such conflicts, 'a constitutional court was needed, since leaving this task to the parliaments would make Belgium ungovernable'.[17] Hence the origin of the Constitutional Court, created because of the transformation of Belgium from a unitary State into a federal State, and not to primarily address concerns about the protection of fundamental rights.

---

[11] Wielfried Swenden, Marleen Brans and Lieven De Winter, 'The Politics of Belgium: Institutions and Policy under Bipolar and Centrifugal Federalism' (2006) 29 *West European Politics* 869.

[12] Wilfried Swenden, 'Asymmetric Federalism and Coalition-Making in Belgium' (2002) 32 *Publius – The Journal of Federalism* 69.

[13] Kris Deschouwer, 'Belgium: Ambiguity and Disagreement' in Raoul Blindenbacher and Abigail Ostien (eds), *Dialogues on Constitutional Origins, Structure, and Change in Federal Countries* vol. 1 (McGill-Queen's University Press, Forum of Federations/International Association of Centers for Federal Studies 2005) 11.

[14] Robert Mnookin and Alain Verbeke, 'Persistent Nonviolent Conflict with no Reconciliation: The Flemish and Walloons in Belgium' (2009) 72 *Law and Contemporary Problems* 153.

[15] Michael Walzer, *On Toleration* (Yale UP 1997).

[16] Herman Van Goethem, *Belgium and the Monarchy: From National Independence to National Disintegration* (University Press Antwerp 2010) 271.

[17] Maurice Adams, 'Disabling Constitutionalism. Can the Politics of the Belgian Constitution Be Explained?' (2014) 12 *Intl J Cons L* 286.

9.2.2 The Original Model of Constitutional Review: The Constitutional Court and its Powers of Review

The Constitutional Court is conceived as a specialized judicial body, independent of the legislative, executive and judiciary powers and whose status and composition are adapted to the review of laws.[18] It is a Kelsenian organ, comparable to the Federal Constitutional Court of Germany or the Constitutional Courts in Italy and Spain, for example.[19] The Constitutional Court has a monopoly in reviewing the constitutionality of laws (rules having force of law). That is the reason why the review performed by the Constitutional Court is called 'constitutional review' and not 'judicial review', which is more suited to reviews performed by all ordinary courts, in the US or in Canada, for example. Constitutional review is widely used throughout European countries with civil law systems.

The Constitutional Court is composed of 12 judges. Strict legal requirements are laid down for both linguistic and socio-professional balances in the membership of the Constitutional Court. Six of the judges must belong to the Dutch language group and six of the judges to the French language group. Six judges must have at least five years' experience as members of Parliament – without necessarily having a legal training – and six judges must have a legal background as university professor of law at a Belgian university, judge at the Court of Cassation (which is the highest ordinary court) or Council of State (which is the

---

[18] Legislation governing the Constitutional Court is the Special Constitutional Court Act of 6 January 1989 which is divided into seven titles on, respectively, the jurisdiction of the Constitutional Court, the organization of the Constitutional Court, the operation of the Constitutional Court, the use of languages before and in the services of the Constitutional Court, the procedure before the Constitutional Court, together with final and transitional provisions.

[19] Gerhard Dannemann, 'Constitutional Complaints: The European Perspective' (1994) 43 *ICLQ* 143; Victor Ferreres Comella, 'The European Model of Constitutional Review of Legislation: Toward Decentralization?' (2014) 2 *Intl J Cons L* 462; Lech Garlicki, 'Constitutional Courts versus Supreme Courts' (2007) 5 *Intl J Cons L* 64; Andrew Harding, Peter Leyland and Tania Groppi, 'Constitutional Courts: Forms, Functions and Practice in Comparative Perspective' (2008) 3 *Journal of Comparative Law* 10; Martin Shapiro and Alec Stone Sweet, 'The New Constitutional Politics of Europe' (1994) 26 *Comparative Politics Studies* 402; Alec Stone Sweet, 'Why Europe Rejected American Judicial Review. And Why It May Not Matter' (2003) 101 *Mich L Rev* 2745; Alec Stone Sweet, *Governing with Judges: Constitutional Politics in Europe* (OUP 2000) 31.

highest administrative court), or legal secretary with the Constitutional Court. At least one of the judges with a legal background must have proved an adequate knowledge of the German language. On 4 April 2014, the Special Act on Constitutional Court was amended in order to provide that the Constitutional Court shall consist of at least one-third of judges of each gender, but this new requirement will not enter into force immediately. The constitutional judges are appointed by the federal executive power from a list of two candidates, drawn up alternately by the House of Representatives and by the Senate. The list of candidates must be adopted by a two-thirds majority vote of the members present. The judges are appointed by law – 'for life' – although this actually means until the age of 70. There are strict rules of incompatibility with other offices, posts and professional activities. More generally, the Constitutional Court is a judicial body and, as such, is required to comply with the general legal principle relating to the subjective and objective impartiality of judges.[20]

The Constitutional Court makes decisions either in benches of seven judges or, as is more frequent, in plenary sittings. Proceedings before the court are written, the parties being invited to address written submissions to the court. Rules of procedure before the Constitutional Court comply with international rules on a fair trial since proceedings are contradictory, hearings are open to the public, judgments contain the grounds for the decision and arc pronounced within a reasonable time and in open court. It must be pointed out that it is not compulsory for the parties to be assisted or represented by an advocate, and parties can appear personally. As to the judges, they deliberate in a collegial way and in secret, with no possibility of dissenting opinions. The judgments are final and conclusive and not open to appeal, except for a complaint to the ECtHR. Originally, the Constitutional Court – whose name was 'Court of Arbitration' ('*Cour d'arbitrage*'), which was 'clearly inadequate, it being a term used both in national and international law to denote a judicial form of settlement of conflicts by adjudicators freely chosen by the parties'[21] – was given very restricted powers. The court was only in charge of the jurisdictional conflicts of laws enacted by legislators of the regions and the communities themselves or between the latter and the federal legislator. In

---

[20] It should also be mentioned that the Dutch-speaking and French-speaking judges of the Constitutional Court elect a Dutch-speaking and a French-speaking president from their respective language groups. The presidency of the Constitutional Court is assumed for a one-year term on a rotational basis. This term commences on 1 September each year.

[21] LP Suetens, 'Judicial Review in Belgium' in Smith (n 1) 319.

other words, the jurisdiction of the Constitutional Court was restricted to the constitutional rules allocating powers to the different legislators. At that time, the Constitutional Court was seen as 'a kind of constitutional court with limited powers'.[22]

Unlike the French Constitutional Council, for instance, the Belgian Constitutional Court does not act a priori. It has the power to annul or declare unconstitutional, in whole or in part, a law infringing the Constitution (the constitutional rules allocating powers to the different legislators) as follows. First, the Constitutional Court has the power to rule on an action for annulment (constitutional complaint) brought before it within six months – reduced to 60 days in case of a law concerned with the ratification of a treaty – of the publication of the law in the *Moniteur belge*. When the Constitutional Court annuls a law, such annulment operates *erga omnes* and has retroactive effect, which means that the annulled provision must be deemed to have never existed. Nevertheless, when necessary, the Constitutional Court may specify, by a general ruling, which effects of the nullified provision are to be considered maintained or to be provisionally maintained for the period determined by the Constitutional Court. The purpose of such ruling is to prevent the grave hardship that would flow from the pure and simple annulment of the provision. The action for annulment is instituted by a political organ – the federal government, or the government of a region or a community, or the president of a legislative assembly at the request of two-thirds of their members – or by a natural or legal person with a legitimate interest. Popular actions are not admissible and neither moral reprobation of a law, nor the desire to ensure compliance with the law in all circumstances, constitutes a sufficient legitimate interest.[23] Only persons whose situation might be directly and adversely affected by the law can establish an interest. The interest of a natural person is individual. The interest of a legal person, such as an association or a company, is collective.

When an action for annulment has been submitted to the Constitutional Court, the constitutional judges rule on an abstract case that is not related to actual proceedings pending before a court or tribunal. Two relevant examples of such action are the following ones. The first case concerns the modalities of publication of laws; laws become binding only when they have been published in the *Moniteur belge*. Up until the end of

[22] Patrick Peeters, 'Federalism: A Comparative Perspective. Belgium Transforms from a Unitary to a Federal State' in Bertus De Villiers (ed.), *Evaluating Federal Systems* (Martinus Nijhoff 1994) 196.

[23] Constitutional Court, 14 October 1999, Case n°110/1999.

2002, a paper version of the *Moniteur belge* was published daily. For economic reasons, an Act of 24 December 2002 decided that the *Moniteur belge* would not be published in hard copy anymore, but only on the *Moniteur belge*'s website. An action for annulment was brought before the Constitutional Court, alleging breach of the constitutional principle of equality and non-discrimination under Articles 10 and 11 of the Constitution: it was argued that the contested provision would discriminate between citizens on the basis of their financial and social position, since only the rich and the skilled would have access to the *Moniteur belge*'s website. For these reasons, the Constitutional Court annulled the contested law, by highlighting that Internet access to official texts might be quicker and easier for some people, but many others would be left with no effective access, particularly if no related measures were taken to make consultation possible.[24] Conversely, in another example in a different field, the Constitutional Court rejected, at the end of 2012, an action for annulment of a law banning the wearing of clothing that covers the face, or a large part of it, in a public space. In its judgment, the Constitutional Court decided that the law, better known as the 'anti-burqa law', does not violate fundamental rights including personal freedom, freedom of expression, freedom of religion, the right to privacy, the right to lead a life that is in keeping with human dignity, and the principle of equality and non-discrimination.[25]

Second, the Constitutional Court has the power to declare unconstitutional a law, without annulling it. This may happen when a preliminary question is raised by a court or a tribunal during an ordinary lawsuit if that court or tribunal has a doubt as to the constitutionality of a law that should be applied by the judge.[26] The nature of the review exercised by the Constitutional Court on a preliminary question is concrete since it is directly related to actual proceedings pending before the trial judge. The decision has no general effect and the provision declared unconstitutional is not removed from the legal system, but merely held inapplicable in the

---

24 Constitutional Court, 16 June 2004, Case n° 106/2004.

25 Constitutional Court, 6 December 2012, Case n° 145/2012. See Saïla Ouald Chaib and Eva Brems, 'Doing Minority Justice Through Procedural Fairness: Face Veils Bans in Europe' (2013) 2 *Journal of Muslims in Europe* 1–26.

26 Since 2003, a preliminary question can no longer be referred to the Constitutional Court when the question is about the constitutionality of a law assenting a treaty establishing the EU or the ECHR or an additional protocol to the ECHR. This exclusion is justified by the necessity to guarantee the stability of Belgium's international relations.

instant case. This kind of review has proven more and more concrete as shown in the following example. In that case, a Crown counsel had applied to a tribunal seeking the annulment of a marriage between a father-in-law and a daughter-in-law since there was an absolute impediment to this marriage under Article 161 of the Civil Code, which provides that '[i]n direct line, marriage shall be prohibited between all ascendants and descendants and relatives by marriage in the same line'. Under Article 163 of the same Code, marriage between an uncle and a niece, or a nephew, or between an aunt and a niece, or a nephew, remains prohibited, but Article 164 provides that this prohibition can be lifted by royal order where there are 'serious grounds' for doing so. In connection with these proceedings the tribunal decided to question the Constitutional Court first as to whether Article 164 of the Civil Code was compatible with the constitutional rules of equality and non-discrimination under Articles 10 and 11 of the Constitution, taken together with Article 12 of the ECHR, in that it made it possible for restrictions on marriage to be lifted by royal order only in the cases set out in Article 163 of the Civil Code, whereas an absolute prohibition existed in other comparable situations, such as marriage between a parent-in-law and a child-in-law after the death of the spouse who created the relationship by marriage. The court noted that, whereas the impediment to marriage between ascendants and descendants and relatives by marriage in the same line had its basis in the incest taboo, the impediment to marriage between relatives by marriage in direct line with no biological ties was based on moral and social reasons, not on physiological or eugenic criteria. The legislator thereby sought to safeguard the sanctity of the family and to guarantee the place of each generation within the family. The court held that the difference in treatment resulting from the existence or lack of an impediment to marriage between, first, a parent-in-law and a child-in-law and, secondly, relatives in a collateral line, was founded on an objective criterion, namely the nature and degree of the relationship between the persons concerned. In view of the closer link between a parent-in-law and a child-in-law, the court deemed this criterion appropriate to achieve the aim pursued by the legislator. The court nonetheless held that, on account of its absolute nature, the measure had disproportionate effects, since it entirely prohibited marriage between a parent-in-law and a child-in-law after the death of the spouse who created the relationship by marriage. In the operative provisions, the court ruled that since Article 161 of the Civil Code, where taken in conjunction with Articles 163 and 164, absolutely prohibited marriage between a parent-in-law and a child-in-law after the death of the spouse who created the relationship by marriage, it violated Articles 10 and 11 of the Constitution, taken together with Article 12 of the ECHR.

In accordance with the Special Act on the Constitutional Court, the court or tribunal which refers a preliminary question, and any other court or tribunal passing judgment in the same case, must comply with the ruling of the Constitutional Court in the settlement of the dispute on the main proceedings. From time to time, the Constitutional Court, in answering a preliminary question, finds a law as construed by the court or tribunal to be unconstitutional, but may also advise on another interpretation in keeping with the Constitution. If the court or tribunal accepts this 'salutary' interpretation proposed by constitutional judges, the court or tribunal may apply the law, as interpreted by the Constitutional Court, to the pending case. This judicial method is widely used in constitutional litigation in Europe.

When the Constitutional Court in ruling on a preliminary question has found a law unconstitutional, the Special Act on the Constitutional Court provides that an action can be brought by persons who have an interest, and by certain authorities, for the annulment of the provision in question, thereby linking the two constitutional remedies available under the Belgian model of constitutional review.

9.2.3 Transformation of the Original Model of Constitutional Review: The Protection of Fundamental Rights by the Constitutional Court

Today, the Constitutional Court has to be regarded as a fully-fledged constitutional court. However, this review does not yet encompass the whole text of the Constitution, even if in 2003, the scope of the constitutional review performed by the Constitutional Court was widened to include fundamental rights as guaranteed under the Constitution. Indeed, the Constitutional Court has exclusive jurisdiction to review regulations having force of law – 'only in exceptional cases is the review restricted to regulations having force of law, as in Belgium', because 'usually other acts are also reviewed by the constitutional courts'[27] – for compliance with the rules governing the division of powers of the federal

---

[27] André Alen and Michel Melchior, 'The Relations Between the Constitutional Courts and the Other National Courts, Including the Interference in this Area of the Action of the European Courts', XIIth Conference of European Courts, Brussels, 14–16 May 2002, (2002) 23 *HRLJ* 307.

State, the regions and the communities,[28] and with the fundamental rights recognized under the Constitution. Fundamental rights provisions and the rules governing the division of powers are sometimes linked. In this respect, the transformation from a unitary to a federal State has raised the problem of which levels of power are competent to protect fundamental rights, both in the way such rights are formulated and in the way they are enforced. On an entirely different point, we note that in the context of the Sixth Reform of the State, a constitutional amendment, adopted on 6 January 2014, extended the jurisdiction of the Constitutional Court to an a priori review of regional referendums and the review of decisions of the House of Representatives or its bodies concerning the election expenditure for the election of that legislative assembly.[29]

In any event, if we take the Constitutional Court's docket into account, fundamental rights-related litigation has turned out to be the main role for the Constitutional Court. But it must be stressed that the jurisdiction of the Constitutional Court is limited to the rights enumerated under the Belgian Constitution, which enshrines a corpus of common rights. These rights are those enumerated in Articles 8 to 32 (common rights), Articles 170 and 172 (fundamental rights in fiscal matters), and Article 191 of the Constitution (extension of fundamental rights to foreigners). Most of these rights were recognized in 1831, when the Belgian Constitution was framed. These rights are civil and political rights, known as the first generation of fundamental rights, and include the principle of equality and non-discrimination, personal freedom, the right to own property, freedom of expression, freedom of religion, freedom of the press, freedom of assembly, and freedom of association. On the whole, these rights have remained unchanged. One exception concerns freedom of education which was enhanced in 1988 by adding some guarantees in order to ensure the enjoyment of this constitutional freedom.

Over the years, a few more rights were added, such as the right to privacy, the right to administrative transparency, as well as several economic, social and cultural rights, such as the right to work, the right to social security, the right to decent housing, the right to a protection of a healthy environment, the right to cultural and social fulfilment, which are based on the right to lead a life that is in keeping with human dignity.

---

[28] On the case law of the Constitutional Court regarding the allocation of powers, see Steph Feyen, *Beyond Federal Dogmatics: The Influence of EU Law on Belgian Constitutional Case Law Regarding Federalism* (Leuven UP 2013) 87–183.

[29] Those new provisions were implemented by two special Acts of 6 January 2014 amending the Special Act on the Constitutional Court.

Currently, the federal Parliament is discussing the adoption of new provisions on fundamental rights dedicated to the disabled. All these economic, social and cultural rights, which pertain to the second generation of fundamental rights, imply the active intervention of public authorities, through positive measures aimed at progressively enforcing these rights, within the context of the welfare state rationale.

Constitutional review operated by the Constitutional Court, by way of action for annulment or by way of declaration of unconstitutionality, is thus limited to the above-mentioned rights and the competence of the Constitutional Court does not extend to fundamental rights recognized under international conventions such as the ECHR. This assertion has to be explained and nuanced as far as the practice of Belgian constitutional review is concerned. In this respect, rights-based litigation has undergone a distinctive evolution displaying a dichotomy between constitutional fundamental rights protected by the Constitutional Court, on the one hand, and fundamental rights protected under international (and European) treaties by any domestic court or tribunal, on the other hand. The argument is made that this development has led to a certain prominence of European, notably ECHR-based, rights giving the impression that the Constitutional Court has become subordinated to the ECtHR.

9.3 PRACTICE AND ENDURANCE OF CONSTITUTIONAL REVIEW

The Court of Cassation, in its famous 'Eurocentric'[30] 1971 judgment in the *Fromagerie Franco-Suisse 'Le Ski'* case, ruled that any judge must refuse to apply all laws violating directly applicable international law, including the laws enacted after the coming into force of the international law.[31] According to the Court of Cassation, this obligation derived from the nature itself of treaty-based international law. The court argued that it

[30] Arthur Dyèvre, 'European Integration and National Courts: Defending Sovereignty under Institutional Constraints?' (2013) 9 *EUConst* 150.

[31] Cour de Cassation, 27 mai 1971, *Pasicrisie*, 1971, I, 887, concl. W-J Ganshof van der Meersch. See Paul Craig, 'The EJC, National Courts and the Supremacy of Community Law' in Ingolf Pernice and Roberto Miccù (eds), *The European Constitution in the Making* (Nomos 2003) 36–7; University of Oxford, Law Faculty, Oxford Pro Bono Publico, *Reconciling Domestic Superior Courts with the ECHR and the ECtHR: A Comparative Perspective*, Submission to the Commission on a Bill of Rights, 24 November 2011, 16–21 <http://www.law.ox.ac.uk/denning-archive/news/events_files/OPBP_Submission_to_The_Bill_of_Rights_Commission-_Nov_2011.pdf> accessed 12 June 2015.

is 'the very nature of the international law as determined by the treaty that leads to this primacy'. In this case, the judges were faced with a conflict between a provision of the European Economic Community Treaty and a domestic provision enacted after the Belgian ratification of the EEC treaty. As Professor Patricia Popelier observed, the judgment of the Court of Cassation 'was a milestone, as it reversed its attitude towards international law and put an end to the former inviolability of parliamentary legislation'.[32] Does this mean that the Constitutional Court never refers to international treaties when it reviews a law? It certainly does not.

9.3.1 Specific Judicial Methods of Review

Having some leeway on this point, the Constitutional Court has framed two specific judicial methods in order to incorporate international treaties in its rationale and to overcome constitutional isolation, following the arguably natural inclination among judges to expand the scope of their authority. Quite obviously, in this particular case, it is entirely to the advantage of the individual. These methods are the combination method and the reconciliation method.

A. The combination method

The principle of equality and non-discrimination is laid down in Articles 10 and 11 of the Constitution. According to Article 10 '[n]o class distinctions exist in the State. Belgians are equal before the law; they alone are eligible for civil and military service, but for the exceptions that can be created by a law for particular cases. Equality between women and men is guaranteed'. According to Article 11, 'enjoyment of the rights and freedoms recognized for Belgians must be provided without discrimination'.

From the outset, the Constitutional Court has asserted that the constitutional principle of equality and non-discrimination 'does not preclude a difference in treatment from being established in respect of certain categories of persons, provided that there are objective and reasonable grounds for the criterion for differentiation'. It explains that 'the existence of such grounds must be assessed by reference to the aim and the effects of the rule under consideration; the principle of equality is violated where it is shown that there is no reasonable relationship of

[32] Patricia Popelier, 'Report on Belgium' in Giuseppe Martinico and Oreste Pollicino (eds), *The National Judicial Treatment of the ECHR and EU Laws: A Comparative Constitutional Perspective* (Europa Law Publishing 2010) 87.

proportionality between the means employed and the aim pursued'. The Constitutional Court has used the constitutional principle of equality and non-discrimination to its fullest potential, notably to extend its own jurisdiction to any fundamental right recognized under an international treaty, self-executing or not. The court may do so only if a link can be established between the principle of equality and non-discrimination and the international right, which is quite easy to demonstrate. The court now holds as a general rule that 'the violation of a fundamental right is ipso facto a breach of the principle of equality and non-discrimination'.[33]

The Constitutional Court's reasoning is combinatorial: it combines the banning of discrimination – which is a domestic constitutional principle – with one fundamental right recognized by an international treaty. Through a 'creative interpretation method',[34] the Constitutional Court considers that 'rights and freedoms' mentioned in Article 11 of the Constitution include those arising out of provisions of international conventions binding Belgium which are made applicable in the domestic legal system by an act of assent. In other words, the Constitutional Court considers that it must have cognizance of the violation of such a fundamental right if this violation creates a difference in treatment between two categories of persons which is discriminatory and thus inconsistent with the principle of equality and non-discrimination. This reasoning is now recurrent in the case law of the Constitutional Court. In a way, the court has used the principle of equality and non-discrimination as an 'access road' towards international law.

This 'access road' is crucial in that it allows expansion of a limited and arguably poor list of domestic constitutionally protected rights. Consequently, this judicial method is especially useful in order, via the vehicle of the constitutional principle of equality and non-discrimination, to include in the constitutional review several rights missing under domestic law, such as the guarantees to a fair trial of Article 6 of the ECHR. In this way, the Constitutional Court has contributed to the modernization of the constitutional rights catalogue. One illustration is provided by a case on labour law. The Companies Act provided that the dismissal of protected workers (trade union representatives) for economic

---

33 Constitutional Court, 27 July 2004, Case n° 136/2004.

34 Dean Spielmann, 'Jurisprudence of the European Court of Human Rights and the Constitutional Systems of Europe' in Michel Rosenfeld and András Sajó (eds), *The Oxford Handbook of Comparative Constitutional Law* (OUP 2012) 1242.

or technical reasons was subject to the authorization of an equi-representative body made up of representatives of employers and workers, which must make a unanimous decision within two months. If the said body had not made its decision by the statutory deadline, employers and protected workers could take the matter to the industrial tribunal. If the said body had made its decision by the statutory deadline, no legal remedy was provided for. The Constitutional Court decided that there was a discriminatory infringement of the right, guaranteed to everyone under Article 6 of the ECHR, to have a decision determining his civil rights brought before a court.[35]

When referring to the ECHR in using this judicial method, the Constitutional Court has unsurprisingly taken the Strasbourg case law into consideration. One relevant example relates to labour law and concerns a teacher who had been sentenced to five years' imprisonment. Under Article 7 of the Electoral Code, the sentence automatically suspended his right to vote and stand for election. This provision was challenged before the Constitutional Court through a preliminary question. In its judgment, the court pointed out that the right to vote and the right to stand for election, which stem in particular from Article 3 of the Protocol 1 of the ECHR, must, under Article 14 of the ECHR and Articles 10 and 11 of the Belgian Constitution, be secured without discrimination.[36] According to the Constitutional Court, while these are rights that are fundamental to democracy and the rule of law, they are not absolute and may be restricted. However, any restrictions may not impair the very essence of these rights and deprive them of their effectiveness; they must be imposed in pursuit of a legitimate aim, and the means employed must not be disproportionate. Even though Article 7 of the Electoral Code continues to be in keeping with the legitimate objective pursued when enacted in 1894, it has disproportionate consequences, according to the Constitutional Court, in that it deprives sentenced persons of their right to vote and stand for election for a period that may be much longer than the period for which they serve their sentence. In its reasoning, the Constitutional Court took into consideration the judgment of the ECtHR in the *Hirst* case.[37]

Furthermore, the Constitutional Court has used the same judicial method with primary EU law and even with secondary EU law. Should

---

[35] Constitutional Court, 8 July 1993, Case n° 57/93.

[36] Constitutional Court, 14 December 2005, Case n° 187/2005.

[37] ECtHR, Grand Chamber, *Hirst v United Kingdom (No 2)*, 6 October 2005.

the case occur, if the Constitutional Court is doubtful about the interpretation to be given to the EU law, it will raise a preliminary question to the Court of Justice of the European Union (CJEU or Court of Justice). This is common.[38] In one particular case for example, the Constitutional Court raised no less than 12 preliminary questions.[39]

B. The reconciliation method

Whereas the combination method is attractive for fundamental rights which are not recognized under the Constitution, the reconciliation method is worthwhile in the case of constitutionally-based fundamental rights. When there is an analogy between a fundamental right laid down in the Constitution, on the one hand, and a fundamental right laid down by an international provision, on the other hand, the Constitutional Court holds that the first one has to be interpreted in light of the second one. The two rights are regarded as forming an 'inextricable unity' ('*ensemble indissociable*'):[40] the guarantees established by the international provision form an inseparable whole with the constitutional guarantees. The court has repeatedly uttered the same sentence, namely that 'where a treaty provision that binds Belgium is similar in scope to one or more of the constitutional provisions, the guarantees established by that treaty

[38] See, inter alia, Constitutional Court, 21 January 2009, Case n° 11/2009, B.2.1-B.10.3. On this judgment, see Peter Van Elsuwege and Stanislas Adam, 'The Limits of Constitutional Dialogue for the Prevention of Reverse Discrimination. Constitutional Court, Judgment 11/2009 of 21 January 2009' (2009) 5 *EuConst* 327–39.

[39] Constitutional Court, 6 April 2011, Case n° 50/2011. The CJEU has jurisdiction to give preliminary rulings concerning the interpretation of the EU treaties and of acts of the institutions, bodies, offices or agencies of the Union. According to Article 267-3 of the Treaty on the functioning of the EU, 'where any such question is raised in a case pending before a court or tribunal of a Member State against whose decisions there is no judicial remedy under national law, that court or tribunal shall bring the matter before the Court'. However, according to the Court of Justice, such a court or tribunal has not to comply with its obligation to bring the matter before the Court of Justice if 'it has established that the question raised is irrelevant or that the Community provision in question has already been interpreted by the Court of Justice or that the correct application of Community law is so obvious as to leave no scope for any reasonable doubt' (see EU Court of Justice, 6 October 1982, Case 283/81, *SRL Cilfit v. Italian Ministry of Health*).

[40] Constitutional Court, 27 July 2004, Case n° 136/2004.

provision form an inseparable whole with the constitutional guarantees'.[41] For example, Article 22 of the Constitution provides that 'everyone has the right to the respect of his private and family life, except in the case and conditions determined by the law'. Relying on Article 8 of the ECHR, the Constitutional Court has considered that the link between Article 22 of the Constitution and Article 8 of the ECHR allows the court to decide that any infringement by the authorities of the right to respect for one's private and family life must be provided for by legislation that is sufficiently precise and necessary to the pursuit of a legitimate aim, which entails in particular that there must be a reasonable balance between the measure's consequences for the person concerned and the interests of society.[42]

Formally, that does not mean that the Constitutional Court can directly examine if the international provision has been violated, because, as said before, the only formal reference used by the Constitutional Court remains constitutional rights. In other words, international human rights instruments are not theoretically included in the '*bloc de constitutionnalité*'. However, in practice, the distinction between a direct and an indirect reference to an international provision is not always clear-cut. It is hardly surprising, therefore, that the parties before the Constitutional Court often rely on both constitutional rights as well as internationally recognized rights, without distinguishing between them two.

The Constitutional Court has referred to a number of internationally recognized rights so far contained in, for example, the International Covenant on Civil and Political Rights or the International Covenant on Economic, Social and Cultural Rights. Furthermore, more than once, the court has relied on group-specific international treaties, such as the European Social Charter or the International Covenant on the Rights of the Child. For example, in 2013, the Constitutional Court decided that 'the legislature, when devising legal regulations in the field of filiation, must allow the competent authorities to weigh up the interests of the different individuals concerned in actual cases, otherwise it risks adopting a measure disproportionate to the legitimate aims pursued'. When weighing up these interests, those of the child take on special importance. Both Article 22bis-4 of the Constitution and Article 3-1 of the Convention on the Rights of the Child require the courts to attach overriding

---

41 Ibid.

42 Constitutional Court, 18 March 2010, Case n° 29/2010.

importance to the interests of the child in all actions concerning them, and this includes procedures for establishing filiation.[43]

However, as is the case in other European jurisdictions, the most commonly referred rights are those contained in the ECHR. In this case, when referring to European rights, the Constitutional Court refers to the material standards established by the ECHR and accordingly takes into consideration the Strasbourg case law, without necessarily drawing conclusions.[44] For example, as above mentioned, the Constitutional Court stated in 2012 that the law banning the wearing of clothing that covers the face in public space does not violate the fundamental right of freedom of religion and referred in its ruling to the ECtHR judgment in the *Leyla Sahin* case.[45] However, the ECtHR judgment is not properly analysed in the Constitutional Court's judgment, which 'reflects a lack of balancing of the interests at stake', the 'arguments made by the legislator [being] easily accepted without a thorough proportionality analysis'.[46]

The right(s) taken into account by the Constitutional Court may also be located in primary EU law and especially in the Charter of Fundamental Rights of the EU. In that case, if the court is doubtful about the interpretation to be given to the EU right, it will frequently refer a preliminary question to the CJEU. Incidentally, preliminary questions referred through the combination method and the reconciliation method are questions of interpretation. In other cases, the Constitutional Court has also raised preliminary questions on validity issues, after changing a

---

[43] Constitutional Court, 7 March 2013, Case n° 30/2013.

[44] See Luc Lavrysen and Jan Theunis, 'The Belgian Constitutional Court: A Satellite of the ECtHR?' in *Liberae cogitationes: Liber amicorum Marc Bossuyt* (Intersentia 2013) 331–54.

[45] ECtHR, *Leyla Sahin v Turkey*, 10 November 2005, para. 108:

> Pluralism, tolerance and broadmindedness are hallmarks of a 'democratic society'. Although individual interests must on occasion be subordinated to those of a group, democracy does not simply mean that the views of a majority must always prevail: a balance must be achieved which ensures the fair and proper treatment of people from minorities and avoids any abuse of a dominant position. ... Pluralism and democracy must also be based on dialogue and a spirit of compromise necessarily entailing various concessions on the part of individuals or groups of individuals which are justified in order to maintain and promote the ideals and values of a democratic society.

[46] Saïla Ouald Chaib, 'Belgian Constitutional Court says Ban on Face Coverings does not violate Human Rights', *Strasbourg Observers*, 14 December 2012 <http://strasbourgobservers.com/2012/12/14/belgian-constitutional-court-ban-on-face-coverings-does-not-violate-human-rights/> accessed 12 June 2015.

constitutional issue into an EU issue.[47] Undoubtedly, the Belgian Constitutional Court is, in Europe, the one which has raised the largest number of preliminary questions to the Court of Justice so far. From 2003 to present, the court has raised 79 preliminary questions to the CJEU.[48] Examples of the most recent questions relate to value added tax regarding services provided by lawyers,[49] universal service relating to electronic communications networks services,[50] and benefits for disabled people.[51] As can be seen here again, Belgian constitutional judges display a real openness of mind towards international law, anxious as they are to be in accordance with the increasingly international character of our contemporary environment. One example in this area concerns the medical students case. Facing a considerable rise in the number of higher education students, many of them coming from France, a law was adopted with measures concerning the initial enrolment of students on certain courses of study at a college or university, particularly courses in the medical field which are mainly publicly funded courses. The law made a distinction between 'resident' applicants, who have their main residence in Belgium, and 'non-resident' applicants. By adopting this law, the legislator stated that this situation might well impose an excessive burden on public finances and jeopardize the quality of the education provided. Some non-resident applicants lodged an application for annulment before the Constitutional Court. One of the arguments raised by the applicants was based on a violation of the constitutional principle of equality and non-discrimination, taken in conjunction with several provisions of the EU Treaty, especially the provision on the prohibition of any distinction based on nationality. The court found that, although the criterion used to distinguish between the two categories of potential students was not nationality, the law was likely to have more effect on citizens of the EU who did not have Belgian nationality than on those who did, since it would be more difficult for the former to be classified as resident students. The court decided to refer a preliminary issue to the Court of Justice asking whether the applicable provisions of the EU Treaty prevented a member state from taking such measures as

---

47 See Thomas Vandamme, 'Prochain Arrêt: La Belgique ! Explaining Recent Preliminary References of the Belgian Constitutional Court' (2008) 4 *EuConst* 127–48.

48 See <http://www.const-court.be/> accessed 12 June 2015 ('Preliminary rulings from the Court of Justice').

49 Constitutional Court, 13 November 2014, Case n° 165/2014.

50 Constitutional Court, 19 December 2013, Case n° 172/2013.

51 Constitutional Court, 26 September 2013, Case n° 124/2013.

those contained in the law, when this State faces an influx of students from a neighbouring member state into several training courses in the medical field as a result of a restrictive policy pursued in that neighbouring state. The CJEU gave its ruling on 13 April 2010 showing that it is ready to take into account national policy concerns seriously while at the same time not accepting too many restrictions on the freedom of students to study abroad.[52]

When there is a conflict between the wording of the same fundamental right, laid down both at national and international levels, the Constitutional Court is reluctant to adopt a hierarchical approach, preferring to develop an integrative and flexible doctrine which allows it to freely

---

[52] EU Court of Justice, 13 April 2010, Case 73/08, *Nicolas Bressol e.a. et Céline Chaverot e.a. c. Gouvernement de la Communauté française*. See Sacha Garben, 'Case Law' (2010) 47 *CML Rev* 1493–510. See Summary of the judgment:

> With regard to the reasons put forward by the Belgian authorities to justify the discrimination in question, considering the system of financing of higher education in Belgium, the Court rejects as unfounded the justification of the excessive burden on public finances caused by the influx of foreign students. Regarding the risk that the quality of education would be jeopardised and the quality of the public health system in the French Community would be put at risk, the Court does not pronounce directly and definitively on the merits of the justifications in question. Whilst accepting that in principle national legislation which is indirectly discriminatory may be justified by requirements of this nature, the Court considers that it is ultimately for the national court, which has sole jurisdiction to assess the facts and interpret the national legislation, to determine whether and to what extent such legislation satisfies the requirements in question. The Court therefore confines itself to giving guidance to the Belgian Constitutional Court to assist it in its assessment. In particular, that Court will have to ascertain – on the basis of an objective, detailed analysis and solid, consistent data provided by the Belgian authorities – that there are genuine risks to public health. It must then assess, in the light of the evidence provided by the competent authorities, whether the legislation at issue can be regarded as appropriate for attaining the objective of protecting public health and in particular whether a limitation of the number of non-resident students can really bring about an increase in the number of graduates ready to ensure the future availability of public health services within the French Community. Finally, the Constitutional Court will have to ascertain whether the objective in the public interest relied upon could not be attained by less restrictive measures which aim to encourage students who undertake their studies in the French Community to establish themselves there at the end of their studies or which aim to encourage professionals educated outside the French Community to establish themselves within it.

(http://ec.europa.eu/dgs/legal_service/arrets/08c073_en.pdf).

reconcile constitutional and international norms in concreto.[53] Unfortunately, things are not that simple, especially when considering that most constitutional courts operate, at domestic level, in a complex court-system involving other (supreme) courts. Professor and Judge Lech Garlicki writes:

> Once a distinct constitutional court coexists with one or more supreme courts, this cannot but produce problems in mutual relations. Hence … the presence of tensions among the highest courts is systemic in nature. In other words, it would be erroneous to regard such tensions as an aberration that should not exist in the judicial system of a democracy. A state of persistent or endemic tension seems to be as natural for the developed democracies as for the post-communist new comers.[54]

What does a judge have to do in the following situation? In order to decide a case, a court or a tribunal has to apply a law which could infringe a fundamental right laid down both by the Constitution and by an international treaty? This situation is called '*concours de droits fondamentaux*' ('coincidence of fundamental rights'). A priori, two solutions are workable. On the one hand, the court or tribunal can favour the right recognized under the international treaty and, consequently, in accordance with the *Le Ski* precedent, refuse to apply the law violating the treaty. On the other hand, the court or tribunal can also give pre-eminence to the constitutional right and so raise a preliminary question to the Constitutional Court. Until 2004, the second solution was generally chosen by the ordinary judges, who relied on the subsidiarity nature of the constitutional protection towards the international protection.

However, in 2004, two decisions of the Court of Cassation caused a great stir.[55] In these, after concluding that a law did not violate the ECHR, the Court of Cassation refused to refer to the Constitutional Court a question as to the constitutionality of the provision in question. These decisions have been highly debated and harshly criticized. In affirming that the constitutional rights did not provide for a larger protection than the ECHR, the Court of Cassation encroached on the competence of the Constitutional Court, undermined its authority and eventually reduced to

---

[53] Nicolas Bonbled, 'Conflicts of Fundamental Rights Before the Constitutional Court of Belgium: The Case of Freedom of Expression' in Eva Brems (ed.), *Conflicts Between Fundamental Rights* (Intersentia 2008) 344.

[54] Garlicki (n 19) 63.

[55] Cour de Cassation, 9 November 2004, *Pasicrisie*, 2004, p. 1745; 16 November 2004, ibid., 2004, p. 1802.

nothing the centralized constitutional review established by Article 142 of the Constitution. In 2005, a symposium was held between the Constitutional Court, the Court of Cassation and the Council of State – the three highest courts in Belgium – in collaboration with the law faculties and the bar associations. Those taking part in the discussion came to an agreement which was then submitted as a bill to Parliament. Four years later, on 12 July 2009, and after much discussion, a new paragraph was inserted in Article 26 of the Special Act on the Constitutional Court as follows:

> Where it is invoked before a court of law that a statute, decree or rule referred to in Article 134 of the Constitution infringes a fundamental right which is guaranteed in an entirely or partly similar manner by a provision of Title II of the Constitution and by a provision of European or international law, the said court of law shall first refer the question of compatibility with the provision of Title II of the Constitution to the Constitutional Court for a preliminary ruling.
>
> Notwithstanding the first paragraph, the obligation to refer a preliminary question to the Constitutional Court shall not apply:
>
> 1 in the cases referred to in paragraphs 2 and 3;
> 2 if the court of law finds that the provision of Title II of the Constitution has manifestly not been infringed;
> 3 if the court of law finds that it appears from a judgment delivered by an international court of law that the provision of European or international law has manifestly been infringed;
> 4 if the court of law finds that it appears from a judgment delivered by the Constitutional Court that the provision of Title II of the Constitution has manifestly been infringed.

The new paragraph establishes a priority rule in favour of the centralized review exercised by the Constitutional Court while providing for four exceptions to the priority rule, notably when a judgment by an international court has already decided that there was a manifest violation of the international treaty. All exceptions are justified by the need to avoid needless proceedings. If a court or a tribunal invokes one of these exceptions and, as a result, refuses to refer a preliminary ruling, this refusal has to be duly motivated.

Taking into account this new paragraph, two scenarios have to be contemplated. First, the Constitutional Court can conclude that the law violates the Constitution. In that case, the court or tribunal must refuse to apply the law, without reviewing if this provision is in accordance with the international treaty. Such a review would be pointless. Secondly, the Constitutional Court can also rule that the law does not violate the

Constitution. In that case, the court or tribunal remains competent for reviewing the law against the international treaty and, in case of violation, may refuse to apply the law on that basis.

In that respect, has the above established priority rule settled the tension triggered by the Court of Cassation's case law? It would have been too good to be true. Although it was designed to sort out a mere internal conflict between two courts, namely the Constitutional Court and the Court of Cassation, the priority rule established in 2009 posed a tricky problem as regards EU law. In the famous case *Simmenthal*, the CJEU decided that:

> every national court must, in a case within its jurisdiction, apply Community law in its entirety and protect rights which the latter confers on individuals and must accordingly set aside any provision of national law which may conflict with it, whether prior or subsequent to the Community rule,

so that:

> any provision of a national legal system and any legislative, administrative or judicial practice which might impair the effectiveness of Community law by withholding from the national court having jurisdiction to apply such law the power to do everything necessary at the moment of its application to set aside national legislative provisions which might prevent Community rules from having full force and effect are incompatible with those requirements which are the very essence of Community law.[56]

In the case *Mecanarte*, the Court of Justice decided that 'a national court which in a case concerning Community law declares a provision of national law unconstitutional does not lose the right or escape the obligation under Article 177 of the EEC Treaty to refer questions to the Court of Justice on the interpretation or validity of Community law by reason of the fact that such a declaration is subject to a mandatory reference to the constitutional court'.[57]

Consequently, after the modification of Article 26 in 2009, three domestic tribunals decided to refer preliminary questions to the CJEU about the compatibility of the Belgian priority rule with EU law. Unfortunately, but beyond dispute, in the *Chartry* case, the Court of Justice deemed that the case – about a tax rule – did not possess a link with the scope of application of EU law and thus decided it was

---

[56] EU Court of Justice, 9 March 1978, Case 106/77, *Simmenthal,* paras 21–22.

[57] EU Court of Justice, 27 June 1991, Case C-348/89, *Mecanarte*, para. 46.

inadmissible.[58] However, the answer came from another jurisdiction which had established, at around the same time, a similar priority rule about the sequence of reviews, constitutional and conventional. The French legislator adopted a similar priority rule by enacting the a posteriori review called the '*Question Prioritaire De Constitutionnalité*', and the French Court of Cassation had raised a preliminary question about the compatibility of the French rule with EU law.[59] In the *Melki* case, the Court of Justice answered the question as follows:[60]

> Accordingly, the reply to the first question referred is that Article 267 TFEU precludes Member State legislation which establishes an interlocutory procedure for the review of the constitutionality of national laws, in so far as the priority nature of that procedure prevents – both before the submission of a question on constitutionality to the national court responsible for reviewing the constitutionality of laws and, as the case may be, after the decision of that court on that question – all the other national courts or tribunals from exercising their right or fulfilling their obligation to refer questions to the Court of Justice for a preliminary ruling. On the other hand, Article 267 TFEU does not preclude such national legislation, in so far as the other national courts or tribunals remain free:
>
> - to refer to the Court of Justice for a preliminary ruling, at whatever stage of the proceedings they consider appropriate, even at the end of the interlocutory procedure for the review of constitutionality, any question which they consider necessary,
> - to adopt any measure necessary to ensure provisional judicial protection of the rights conferred under the European Union legal order, and
> - to disapply, at the end of such an interlocutory procedure, the national legislative provision at issue if they consider it to be contrary to EU law.

In the light of this judgment, we may conclude that, in our view, the Belgian priority rule meets the requirements of the *Melki* judgment, especially because 'the priority rule only obliges the judge to refrain from conducting his EU review until the constitutional review has been finalized', but 'it does not forbid him to prepare this later review by

---

[58] EU Court of Justice, 1 March 2011, Case C-457/09, *Chartry*. See also EU Court of Justice, 22 September 2011, Case C-538/10, *Lebrun et Howet* and Case C-314/10, *Pagnoul*.

[59] See Marie-Luce Paris in Chapter 8.

[60] EU Court of Justice, 22 June 2010, Cases C-188/10 and C-189/10, *Aziz Melki and SélimAbdeli*, para. 57. See W T Eijsboutset and J-H Reestman, 'The Dance of Justice' (2013) 9 *EuConst* 1–6.

sending a preliminary question to Luxembourg'.[61] Nevertheless, as a cautionary measure, the Special Act on the Constitutional Court was amended on 4 April 2014, by adding the following sentence: 'These obligations shall not prejudice the right of the court of law, at the same time or at a later date, to refer a question to the Court of Justice of the European Union for a preliminary ruling'. The purpose of this amendment is to ensure that the Belgian priority rule is fully aligned with the requirements set out by the CJEU.

9.3.2 Prospects of Transformed Model and Practice

As a final word, one may say that the *Melki* case highlights a tricky question that lies at the heart of fundamental rights litigation: in a multi-layered system of fundamental rights, does anybody have the power of the last word? One might well doubt it. We are not sure it is necessarily a bad thing. At the very least, it reflects the emergence of new paradigms in the field of fundamental rights.

However, it remains no less true that, in the case of Belgium, the very marked influence of the Strasbourg case law on Belgian constitutional judges and their decisions raises the question of the survival of a national catalogue of fundamental rights, and might question the endurance of the dichotomy-based model of review – constitutional, on one hand, and conventional, on the other hand. A voluminous publication edited in 2011, written by a group of more than 70 authors, explored the case law of the highest national courts – namely the Constitutional Court, the Council of State and the Court of Cassation – in matters of fundamental rights.[62] The findings show that the distinctive feature of the Belgian catalogue of constitutional rights and the interpretation of these rights is less and less significant. As far as ordinary courts and tribunals are concerned, they favour an interpretation in conformity with the standards enshrined in international law, particularly the ECHR, which does not

---

[61] Marc Bossuyt and Willem Verrijdt, 'The Full Effect of EU Law and Constitutional Review in Belgium and France after the *Melki* Judgment' (2011) 7 *EuConst* 381. See also Jan Velaers, 'The Protection of Fundamental Rights by the Belgian Constitutional Court and the *Melki-Abdeli* Judgment of the European Court of Justice' in Monica Claes and others (eds), *Constitutional Conversations in Europe* (Intersentia 2012) 333–4.

[62] Marc Verdussen and Nicolas Bonbled (eds), *Les droits constitutionnels en Belgique: Les enseignements jurisprudentiels de la Cour constitutionnelle, du Conseil d'Etat et de la Cour de cassation* (Bruylant 2011) 1898 (in two volumes).

mean that they do not also refer to other international human rights instruments. In any case, the subsidiarity principle consequently plays only a limited role in the protection of fundamental rights. Indeed, the principle according to which fundamental rights should be better protected at local/national level than by the ECHR and the ECtHR has rather lost its significance in the Belgian context since domestic courts, especially the Constitutional Court, are more inclined to refer to European standards than to national standards as set out in the constitutional catalogue of rights. Moreover, 'the Constitutional Court is even willing to reduce the protection provided by the Belgian Constitution in the light of the ECHR'.[63] It is through its own action that the Constitutional Court has become 'a satellite of the ECtHR'.[64] Some reasons explain the 'Europe-friendly position' of the Constitutional Court. Among these is certainly the fact that 'the inclusion of international and EU law in its set of norms of control helped the Constitutional Court with limited competences, to obtain its position as a fully-fledged constitutional court'.[65] Clearly, the willingness of emancipation of the Constitutional Court has been an important factor of its progressive subordination to the ECtHR.

In our opinion, another reason why the Constitutional Court has been so open-minded and deferential to the ECtHR is the gradual dismantling of the federal State. The fact that the Constitutional Court relies systematically on the case law of the ECtHR, with the tacit approval of the constituent power, is indicative of a kind of resignation: Title II of the Constitution, which comprises a set of provisions designed to guarantee the enjoyment of fundamental rights, has become insufficient in view of the ECHR and there is no real desire to changes things in the political arena. The point at issue is the survival of a national catalogue of constitutional rights in a country that is intersected by a deep division between the French-speaking community and the Dutch-speaking community and where the common feeling of national identity has become

---

[63] Patricia Popelier, 'Judicial Conversations in Multilevel Constitutionalism. The Belgian Case' in Monica Claes and others (n 61) 90. See, among others, Constitutional Court, 21 December 2004, Case n° 202/2004.

[64] Lavrysen and Theunis (n 44) 354.

[65] Popelier (n 63) 89. See also Vandamme (n 47) 147–8:

> The Constitutional Court ... interpreted and applied the few powers it did have in its early days with eagerness and audacity. Especially the wide use of Articles 10 and 11 of the Belgian Constitution as portals has been ground breaking. This has allowed the Court to include EC and EU law (and other sources of public international law) in its set of norms of control.

blurred. Are there still some elements holding Belgium together? If so, fundamental rights should be an integral part of them. On this point, as in others, Belgium is standing at a crossroads.

10. Hungary

The illusion of a constitution in Europe: the Hungarian Constitutional Court after the Fifth Amendment of the Fundamental Law

Renáta Uitz*

10.1 INTRODUCTION

Constitutional courts were introduced in post-communist Central and Eastern Europe as tokens of transition to democracy. They were tasked not only with the peaceful dismantling of an old regime, but also with overseeing the creation of a new constitutional architecture meeting the standards of such elite clubs of European democracies as the Council of Europe and eventually, the European Union. By the time of the EU enlargement of 2004, post-communist constitutional courts had become skilled contributors to the European constitutional dialogue.[1] Continued engagement with European and foreign constitutional jurisprudence was as important to building their credentials on the European plain, as to reinforcing their legitimacy before domestic constitutional audiences.

In the post-communist club the Hungarian Constitutional Court was praised for two decades for its impressive transitional justice jurisprudence, its much revered fundamental rights jurisprudence building on

* All translations from the Hungarian are mine, unless otherwise noted. All websites were last visited on 20 August 2015.

[1] Wojciech Sadurski, *Constitutionalism and the Enlargement of Europe* (OUP 2012).

comparative arguments[2] and its standing against political players in the name of the rule of law and constitutionalism.[3] When in the 2010 general election a Conservative-Christian coalition lead by Viktor Orbán and his party, FIDESz won a constitution-making two-third majority in Parliament,[4] the Constitutional Court somewhat unexpectedly became a subject of constitutional engineering. The court was refashioned through numerous constitutional amendments to the old (1949/1989) Constitution,[5] and then through the new constitution adopted in 2011 (the Fundamental Law[6]) and its subsequent amendments.[7] Until the reelected FIDESz government lost its constitution-making majority in Parliament in February 2015, decisions of the Constitutional Court had been regularly overruled by constitutional amendment, and the court's guidance was also disregarded in subsequent parliamentary action on numerous issues.[8]

The frequency of constitutional amendments overriding the Constitutional Court fits into a broader pattern of refashioning Hungary as an illiberal democracy. In the words of Prime Minister Orbán's much discussed speech of July 2014:

---

[2] For a more recent analysis see Zoltán Szente, 'Hungary: Unsystematic and Incoherent Borrowing of Law. The Use of Foreign Judicial Precedents in the Jurisprudence of the Constitutional Court, 1999–2010' in Tania Groppi and Marie-Claire Ponthoreau (eds) *The Use of Foreign Precedents by Constitutional Judges* (Hart 2013), 253–72, arguing that the Hungarian Constitutional Court has never developed a comprehensive theory of constitutional borrowing.

[3] On the early jurisprudence of the Court see László Sólyom and Georg Brunner, *Constitutional Judiciary in a New Democracy: The Hungarian Constitutional Court* (Michigan 2000).

[4] The old Hungarian Constitution could be amended by a single two-third majority vote in Parliament (art 24(3)). This rule was retained by the Fundamental Law as well (art S(2)).

[5] Act no XX of 1949, available in English translation with the archives of Parliament at http://www-archiv.parlament.hu/angol/act_xx_of_1949.pdf.

[6] Original title: *Magyarország Alaptörvénye* [Fundamental Law of Hungary], the consolidated text of the Fundamental Law available in English translation at http://www.mfa.gov.hu/NR/rdonlyres/8204FB28-BF22-481A-9426-D2761D10EC7C/0/FUNDAMENTALLAWOFHUNGARYmostrecentversion01102013.pdf.

[7] The last amendment of the Fundamental Law (the Fifth Amendment) was adopted on September 26, 2015. Article 6 of this Amendment affected the Constitutional Court.

[8] Generally see Attila Vincze, 'Wrestling with Constitutionalism: The Supermajority and the Hungarian Constitutional Court' (2014) 8 *Vienna Journal of International Constitutional Law* 86.

> [the] Hungarian nation is not a simple sum of individuals, but a community that needs to be organized, strengthened and developed, and in this sense, the new state that we are building is an illiberal state, a non-liberal state. It does not deny foundational values of liberalism, as freedom, etc … But it does not make this ideology a central element of state organization, but applies a specific, national, particular approach in its stead.[9]

In the same speech the Prime Minister also declared that '[w]e are searching for (and we are doing our best to find, ways of parting with Western European dogmas, making ourselves independent from them) the form of organizing a community, that is capable of making us competitive in this great world-race'. Indeed, in the past five years Hungary's constitutional transformation has made all the major European constitutional actors uneasy, including the Venice Commission,[10] the European Court of Human Rights (ECtHR),[11] the EU's Parliament,[12] the Commission,[13] the Court of Justice of the European Union (CJEU),[14] and most recently, the European Council.[15]

---

[9] Speech at Baile Tusnad of July 26, 2014, as available in English translation at http://budapestbeacon.com/public-policy/full-text-of-viktor-orbans-speech-at-baile-tusnad-tusnadfurdo-of-26-july-2014/10592.

[10] For opinions on constitutional developments in Hungary see http://www.venice.coe.int/webforms/documents/?country=17&year=all.

On constitutional amendments overriding the Constitutional Court see esp. Opinion no 720/2013, *Opinion on the Fourth Amendment to the Fundamental Law of Hungary* 17 June 2013 at para. 80. Available in English at http://www.venice.coe.int/webforms/documents/?pdf=CDL-AD%282013%29012-e.

[11] Judgments with a domestic constitutional dimension include *N K M v Hungary* App no 666529/11 (ECHR, 14 May 2013) (98 per cent of special tax on civil service severance payments), *Magyar Keresztény Mennonita Egyház and others v Hungary* App nos 70945/11, 23611/12, 26998/12, 41150/12, 41155/12, 41463/12, 41553/12, 54977/12 and 56581/12 (ECHR, 8 April 2014) (finding Hungary's new church re-registration regime resulting in loss of legal personality for hundreds of religious communities to violate the Convention); *Baka v Hungary*, App no 20261/12 (ECHR, 27 May 2014) (removal of the chief justice of the Supreme Court through constitutional reform violates the Convention, pending before Grand Chamber).

[12] P7_TA(2013)0315 *European Parliament resolution of 3 July 2013 on the situation of fundamental rights: standards and practices in Hungary* (pursuant to the European Parliament resolution of 16 February 2012) (2012/2130(INI)).

[13] Communication from the Commission to the European Parliament and Council, *A new EU Framework to Strengthen the Rule of Law,* COM(2014) 158 final/2, 19 March 2014, as available at: http://ec.europa.eu/justice/effective-justice/files/com_2014_158_en.pdf.

With constitutional amendments used to discipline the Constitutional Court on multiple occasions,[16] the notion that the constitution establishes constraints on the exercise of political powers and that the Constitutional Court is meant to enforce these constraints may sound somewhat illusory. Nonetheless, the Hungarian Constitutional Court has confirmed these ideals in its recent case law.[17] In the face of direct political attacks on its institutional integrity and jurisprudence, and despite the changes affecting its make up and jurisdiction, the Constitutional Court has continued to remind the government of the constitutional and external constraints that (would and should) apply to its daily operations in the European constitutional space.[18] Somewhat ironically, the leading judgment which confirmed the existence of constitutional minimum standards defined in line with international obligations and the jurisprudence of the ECtHR concerned the constitutionality of constitutional amendments curbing the jurisdiction of the Constitutional Court and altering the manner of

---

[14] Cases with a domestic constitutional dimension are: Case C-286/12 *Commission v Hungary* [2012] OJ C 214/17 (early retirement of judges); Case C-288/12, *Commission v Hungary* [2012] OJ C 227/15 (early dismissal of the data protection commissioner through constitutional reform).

[15] See *Conclusions of the Council of the European Union and the member states meeting within the Council on ensuring respect for the rule of law*, General Affairs Council meeting, Brussels, 16 December 2014.

For an analysis of the Council's response to the Commission's monitoring plan see Dmitry Kochenov and Laurent Pech, 'Upholding the Rule of Law in the EU: On the Commission's 'Pre-Article 7 Procedure' as a Timid Step in the Right Direction' [2015] European Issue no 356, at http://www.robert-schuman.eu/en/european-issues/0356-upholding-the-rule-of-law-in-the-eu-on-the-commission-s-pre-article-7-procedure-as-a-timid-step.

[16] For an English language analysis of recent constitutional developments in this vein see Pál Sonnevend, András Jakab and Lóránt Csink, 'The Constitution as an Instrument of Everyday Party Politics: The Basic Law of Hungary' in Armin von Bogdandy and Pál Sonnevend (eds) *Constitutional Crisis in the European Constitutional Area: Theory, Law and Politics in Hungary and Romania* (Hart 2015), 33–109. For insightful analysis on the making of the Fundamental Law see Attila Gábor Tóth (ed.) *Constitution for a Disunited Nation: On Hungary's 2011* (CEU Press 2012).

[17] See the judgment on the constitutionality of the Fourth Amendment of the Fundamental Law, 12/2013 (V 24) AB decision, para. 37.

[18] On the relationship of the Hungarian Constitutional Court and the ECtHR most recently see Eszter Polgári, 'Hungary: Gains and Losses – Changing the Relationship with the European Court of Human Rights'. Manuscript of a chapter for the book project: Koen Lemmens, Patricia Popelier and Sarah Lambrecht (eds) *Shifting the Convention System: Counter-Dynamics at the National Level*, on file with author.

appointments to the court.[19] In this judgment which was rendered under the old Constitution after the new Fundamental Law had already been passed, referring to the relevant provisions of both constitutions the court said that it is obliged to follow the jurisprudence of the ECtHR in fundamental rights cases even when it would not follow the minimum standard in its own case law.[20]

The Constitutional Court is certainly not unanimous in its attempts to reinforce minimum standards of rights protection corresponding to international and European obligations: some justices are eager to depart from the old ways of the court as they seek to develop a novel, non-individualistic approach to fundamental rights[21] and a deferential form of constitutional adjudication befitting the new Fundamental Law. In calls for giving proper effect to the Fundamental Law in the face of European and international obligations the national particularities of the new Hungarian constitution are often presented in terms of national and popular sovereignty.[22] It is most likely that this battle of grand principles will not be settled due to the force of arguments, but will rather be resolved through natural changes to the composition of the Constitutional Court over time.[23]

While debates about the legal force or significance of European case law for constitutional interpretation are not unprecedented in constitutional courts,[24] the current Hungarian exchange takes place in a political

---

[19] 61/2011 (VII 13) AB decision, discussed below.

[20] 61/2011 (VII 13) AB decision, ABK 696, 711.

[21] Note that Justice Béla Pokol, who is the intellectual force behind challenges against an individualistic theory of constitutional rights, had already started advocating a community-based approach to constitutional rights under the old Constitution. See for example, his dissent in 174/2011 (XII 29) AB decision (on data protection in the health care context). In his understanding for an individual living in a community the survival of the community shall prevail over individualistic concerns (ABH 2011, 602, 612–613).

[22] In its most developed form the objection against the adoption of international and European standards is formulated by Justice Pokol in terms of the need to put a halt to global constitutional oligarchy in order to protect nation sovereignty. See for example, his dissent to 34/2013 (XI 22) AB decision at para 85.

[23] This is not to suggest that more recently appointed constitutional justices are not familiar with ECtHR case law or are not able to skillfully apply it.

[24] For a disagreement on the significance of ECtHR jurisprudence under the old Hungarian Constitution see for example, 166/2011 (XII 20) AB, where the majority integrated ECtHR jurisprudence into its interpretation of constitutional guarantees (paras 557–64), while concurring, Justice Bragyova insisted on

climate where the government is frequently seen to engage in anti-European rhetoric domestically as well as in Europe. The government routinely claims that the judgments of the ECtHR are not binding beyond the payment obligations they impose. In responding to the government's anti-EU rhetoric, in June 2015 the European Parliament noted with regret that the public consultation launched by the Hungarian Government on migration 'casts blame on the EU institutions and their policies without also acknowledging the responsibility of the Member States in these areas; recalls that the Member States are fully involved in the EU legislative process'.[25]

This chapter will first map Hungary's constitutional transformation until the Fifth Amendment of the new Fundamental Law from the perspective of the Constitutional Court. Thereafter the chapter will reflect on the recent jurisprudence of the Constitutional Court, focusing on the attempts by the court to reinforce constitutional constraints on the exercise of political powers under the new Fundamental Law. A close analysis of jurisprudence in its domestic and European constitutional and political context will provide insight into the operations of a constitutional regime wherein the mere existence of constitutional constraints has been questioned not only by the government but also by some justices of the Constitutional Court. The chapter will show how the contestation between the Hungarian Constitutional Court and the government cannot be presented as an instance of intense constitutional dialogue between a court and its political adversaries. As the Constitutional Court has pointed out, the government was found to adopt unconstitutional measures *after* the applicable constitutional standard had been clarified by the court, in light of international obligations.[26] Indeed, the prevailing rhetoric of the government has been that of defiance of European standards in the name of national values or national sovereignty, and not that of compliance

---

keeping international and constitutional obligations separate and attributed only persuasive force to ECtHR case law (paras 586–7).

[25] P8_TA-PROV(2015)0227, *Situation in Hungary, European Parliament resolution of 10 June 2015 on the situation in Hungary* (2015/2700(RSP)), at http://www.europarl.europa.eu/sides/getDoc.do?type=TA&language=EN&reference=P8-TA-2015-0227, para. 6.

[26] Most famously in the case of the assignment of trial courts in individual cases; the case which set the standards in meticulous detail is 166/2011 (XII 20) AB decision. The case where the Court expressed its disappointment with Parliament's refusal to follow its guidance is 36/2013 (XII 5) AB decision.

with European obligations.[27] Thus, the recent trials of the Hungarian Constitutional Court in the course of Hungary's constitutional transformation may serve as important lessons on not only on the vulnerability of constitutional courts, but also on the malleability of limits on constitution-making powers within the European constitutional space.

10.2 THE EVOLUTION OF CONSTITUTIONAL REVIEW IN HUNGARY

Although the Hungarian Constitutional Court was known to stand up to the political branches, and has had its tense moments with them over the years, it was not until after the elections of 2010 that the Constitution, and the Constitutional Court with it, became a subject – or rather an object – of pure political power demonstration through constitutional amendment. Until the end of 2013 the Constitutional Court's composition and jurisdiction had been affected by major constitutional and statutory amendments. These amendments complemented measures passed in response to the decisions of the Constitutional Court finding several governmental initiatives unconstitutional.

Despite these frontal attacks the Constitutional Court, to the best of its abilities, insisted on safeguarding the core of the Constitution against political whims. From its early responses to the government's display of its might the Constitutional Court attempted to establish some minimum standards which the constitution-making forces, Parliament and ultimately the government were meant to observe.

10.2.1 The Early Years of Constitutional Review in Hungary

1989 marked a new era of Hungarian constitutionalism: this was the year when the 1949 (Stalinist) Constitution was fundamentally transformed by the outgoing Communist Parliament as a result of the Round Table Talks. Further amendments were introduced after the elections of 1990, with the understanding that these amendments would be followed eventually by a complete constitutional overhaul. The Hungarian Constitutional Court established in 1989 thus commenced its operation with interpreting a temporary or transitional constitution, waiting for the final constitution

---

[27] On this point more broadly see my 'Can You Tell When an Illiberal Democracy is in the Making? An Appeal to Comparative Constitutional Scholarship from Hungary' (2015) 13(1) *Intl J of Cons L* 279–300.

promised in the preamble of the 1989 document. It was against this background that then President of the Constitutional Court, László Sólyom introduced the well-known and much-criticized concept of the 'invisible constitution'.[28] Although several attempts were made at drafting a new Hungarian constitution over the ensuing two decades,[29] before 2011 these attempts had not come to fruition due to a lack of political consensus, and constitution-making efforts did not interfere much with the operations of the Constitutional Court.

The Constitutional Court did not have an institutional antecedent in Hungary. The new court was largely seen at the time as the symbol of Hungary's fresh start as a constitutional democracy. At the time of its establishment it was clear to the drafters of the Constitution that the Constitutional Court would serve as a check on the political branches: it is not an accident that even in the initial design it had unusually broad jurisdiction and welcoming standing rules.[30] The power to invalidate legislative projects was given to the Constitutional Court after considerable debate, as initially some preferred to preserve the supremacy of Parliament (similarly to the early Polish model).[31] In the end, however, the court itself was given the power to overrule statutes before as well as after promulgation. Also, in the original design (literally) anyone could request the review of legislation. This form of *actio popularis* was imbedded in the old Constitution itself (Article 32/A(3)). Thus, there can be little doubt that the Constitutional Court was meant to serve as a mighty check on the political branches, including on the Parliament which has always had the power to pass constitutional amendments with qualified (two-third) majority under the old Constitution (Article 24(3)).

10.2.2 Towards the New Fundamental Law

The first in the series of amendments to the old Constitution, adopted on 5 July 2010 with immediate effect altered the manner of election of

---

[28] See Chief Justice Sólyom's concurring opinion in the death penalty case (23/1990 (X 31) AB decision), available in English translation at http://www.mkab.hu/letoltesek/en_0023_1990.pdf.

[29] The opinion of the Venice Commission on the 1995 regulatory concept of the Hungarian Constitution is available in English at http://www.venice.coe.int/webforms/documents/?pdf=CDL-INF%281996%29002-bil.

[30] See István Kukorelli (ed.) *Alkotmánytan* [Constitutional Studies] (Osiris 1995), 321.

[31] Explanatory note to art 17 of Act no XXXI of 1989.

constitutional justices.[32] The old rule required a parity-based committee to nominate candidates, in which all parliamentary parties had one vote. Such nominations had to be confirmed by a qualified (two-third) majority vote in Parliament.[33] Predictably, this rule was meant to foster consensus-building in Parliament, to ensure that the opposition of the day had a say on the shape of the most important check on majority politics. After the elections of 2010 the parity-based parliamentary committee was replaced by one based on proportional representation.[34] As a result of the amendment, the newly installed coalition government could easily overpower its opposition in the nomination committee.[35] By the end of July 2010 two new constitutional justices were elected by Parliament under the new rules.

The next constitutional amendment affecting the Constitutional Court was passed in November 2010.[36] It curbed the jurisdiction of the Constitutional Court to review the budget and its enforcement and legislation on taxes and tariffs and local taxes, unless such rules violated the right to life and human dignity or freedom of religion or belief. The constitutional amendment was prompted by a decision of the Constitutional Court invalidating a 98 per cent retroactive special income tax imposed, inter alia, on the severance payments of civil servants in late October 2010.[37]

The judgment of the Constitutional Court must have come as a surprise to the government not only because the newly appointed constitutional justices joined the majority, but also, because the law on the retroactive special income tax was duly preceded by a constitutional amendment adopted on 11 August 2010 authorizing various forms of additional taxes like the one challenged before the court.[38] Although this constitutional amendment was meant to prevent the Constitutional Court's finding the 98 per cent retroactive income tax unconstitutional, the court ruled that Parliament had imposed the special tax in an ultra vires manner, as

[32] President László Sólyom vetoed the constitutional amendment, his veto was overridden by Parliament.

[33] Article 36/A(4), old Constitution.

[34] Constitutional Amendment of 5 July 2010, art 1.

[35] Without the amendment the governing coalition of two parties would have faced three opposition parties (Jobbik, LMP and the Socialists) in a parity-based committee.

[36] Act no CXIX of 2010, art 2, amending art 32/A(2) of the old Constitution.

[37] 184/2010 (X 28) AB decision.

[38] The amendment added art 70/I(2) to the old Constitution.

the tax was punitive in nature and as such was not covered by the amendment carefully introduced in August 2010. In response to the decision of the Constitutional Court, Parliament re-enacted the law with the 98 per cent special retroactive income tax with slightly altered terms.[39] In its second decision on the matter the Constitutional Court found the special tax unconstitutional again, this time as a violation of the right to human dignity.[40] The rule limiting the jurisdiction of the Constitutional Court on economic legislation was retained in the new Fundamental Law (Article 37).[41] At the same time it is worth noting that the ECtHR has found that the 98 per cent retroactive income tax was confiscatory and as such violated the right to property under the European Convention on Human Rights (ECHR).[42]

The last amendment to the old Constitution affecting the Constitutional Court was passed by Parliament in June 2011, after the adoption of the new Fundamental Law. The new Fundamental Law raised the number of seats on the court from 11 to 15. In order to ensure a smooth transition to the new constitutional regime of the Fundamental Law, the old Constitution was amended to the same effect, adding four more constitutional justices to the bench with immediate effect in June 2011,[43] that is half a year before the entry into force of the new Fundamental Law. Ironically, with raising the number of constitutional justices to 15 the makers of the new Fundamental Law returned to the much-despised design of the 1989 Constitution. The original plan for the Constitutional Court had 15 justices. The transitional provisions of the 1989 Constitution[44] required five constitutional justices to be elected by the Parliament elected in 1985 (that is the outgoing Communist Parliament), another five justices to be elected by the Parliament elected in 1990 with the remaining five seats to be filled within five years. It was in 1994 when the number of seats on the Constitutional Court was reduced to 11.[45] Thus, somewhat ironically,

---

39 Act no 124 of 2010.

40 37/2011 (V 10) AB decision.

41 The prohibition is conditioned on the health of public finances: it only applies until public debt exceeds half of the GDP (art 37(4), Fundamental Law). With the Fourth Amendment, the temporal dimension of this limitation was extended: the limitation applies to all such economic legislation which entered into force in a period when public debt used to exceed half of the GDP, irrespective of the level of public debt at the time when the matter is brought to court.

42 *N K M v Hungary* App no 666529/11 (ECHR, 14 May 2013).

43 Act no LXI of 2011.

44 Act no XXXII of 1989.

45 Act no LXXIV of 1994.

the Fundamental Law returned to a model adopted initially by its much-despised antecedent.

When the constitutionality of the November 2010 constitutional amendments was challenged before the Constitutional Court, the court was critical of the use of constitutional amendments for political ends. Yet, in its July 2011 judgment the Constitutional Court refused to examine or invalidate the constitutional amendments directly affecting its manner of selection and jurisdiction.[46] The court clearly declined expanding its jurisdiction to review constitutional amendments, emphasizing that the Constitution lacked an express authorization to this effect. At the same time, it noted that it is the task of the court to *signal* to the constitution maker if it violated fundamental rights or the rule of law.[47] The court found it necessary to add that it did not have jurisdiction to assess whether Hungarian law violated EU law.[48] As mentioned in the introduction, although the court rejected the invitation to review constitutional amendments, this judgment remains the leading case on ensuring that the standards of fundamental rights protection under the Fundamental Law are not reduced below previously existing levels and do not fall below standards stemming from international law and European jurisprudence. The court reached this conclusion in response to argument from petitioners suggesting that the old Constitution might have had an unalterable core which could have been be used to test the constitutionality of constitutional amendments. Therefore, it is crucial to note that in the jurisprudence of the Hungarian Constitutional Court the notion of an unalterable constitutional core and the suggestion that the constitution-making power of Parliament is constrained is deeply intertwined with conceptions of limits drawn from international obligations and European human rights jurisprudence.

The architecture of the Constitutional Court reached its final form in December 2013, following the Fifth Amendment of the Fundamental Law. Initially, the Act on the Constitutional Court set an automatic retirement age of 70 for constitutional justices,[49] which shortened the otherwise 12-year judicial term.[50] The law putting the Fifth Amendment into effect amended the Act on the Constitutional Court to remove this retirement age.[51] The amendment was made to apply to all serving

46 61/2011 (VII 13) AB decision, ABK 696, 709.
47 Ibid., 712.
48 Ibid., 713.
49 Act no CLI of 2011, art 15(1)(a).
50 Ibid., art 6(3). The term is not renewable.
51 Act no CCVII of 2013, art 41(2).

constitutional court justices.[52] The five justices affected by this amendment were all appointed after the 2010 general elections.

10.3 THE PRACTICE AND ENDURANCE OF CONSTITUTIONAL REVIEW

Despite continued disciplining from the government through constitutional engineering the Hungarian Constitutional Court retains a broad jurisdiction under the new Fundamental Law. With the abolition of *actio popularis* and the introduction of proper constitutional complaint, the types of cases which can be brought before the Constitutional Court have somewhat changed. As a result of the institutional realignment, the Ombudsman (formally: the Commissioner for Fundamental Rights), ordinary courts, and the President of the Republic became active and important constitutional actors. In practice in many cases these constitutional actors do not solely act on their own initiative but are approached by private persons and civil society organizations which had lost their direct access to the Constitutional Court.

Under the Fundamental Law the Constitutional Court continues to have bitter struggles to reinforce previously existing constitutional safeguards. The court continues to rely extensively on its previous case law developed under the old Constitution, while it continues to engage in a conversation about the constitutional significance of international and European obligations. These exchanges take place in a climate where the government is clearly hostile to constraints on its powers to carry out its political aspirations despite losing its constitution-making majority in Parliament in February 2015. Repeated reminders from European constitutional actors on the constraints of constitutional engineering are routinely disregarded or even ridiculed by domestic political actors in the name of national sovereignty, a reaction which is clearly welcomed by some justices of the Constitutional Court.

10.3.1 The New Architecture of Constitutional Review under the Fundamental Law

When the 1989 Constitution was adopted the Hungarian Constitutional Court was meant to have broad jurisdiction. The right of anyone to approach the Constitutional Court (*actio popularis*) was entrenched in the

[52] Ibid., art 41(1).

Constitution itself.[53] In addition, the court had the power of abstract constitutional interpretation, preliminary review of legislation, abstract review power, the power to hear judicial referral and the power to hear constitutional complaints, the court also heard appeals in election matters and reviewed the constitutionality of referenda.

Although under the 1989 Constitution the Constitutional Court used to have broad powers, in sheer quantitative terms the overwhelming majority of petitions tended to reach the Constitutional Court through *actio popularis*. Still, the most strident cases were often filed by the President of the Republic as requests for preliminary abstract review of legislation. Although the legal rules of the Constitutional Court did not impose any deadline on the justices, the Constitutional Court tended to respond to the President relatively rapidly. Since the presidency of Ferenc Mádl it has been customary for the President of the Republic to post the full text of petitions to the Constitutional Court on its website, therefore, these procedures were at least slightly more transparent than the ones based on *actio popularis*.[54]

The jurisdiction of the Constitutional Court to hear disputes over referenda have become particularly sensitive since the autumn of 2006, as this time the then parliamentary opposition lead by FIDESz and its enthusiastic followers decided to pursue highly contentious political matters outside Parliament in the form of referendum initiatives. As a result, the Constitutional Court was literally flooded with referendum complaints – a development which had not been foreseen by the engineers of the constitutional institutional make-up of the Court. These referenda initiatives concerned the basic constitutional architecture of the old Constitution, such as a string of attempts concerning the possibility to dissolve parliament by popular demand.[55]

---

[53] *Actio popularis* is based on art 32/A(3) of the Constitution. For further rules see art 21(2) of the Act on the Constitutional Court (Act no XXXII of 1989).

[54] Until the judgment of the ECtHR in *Társaság a Szabadságjogokért v Hungary* App no 37374/05 (ECHR, 14 April 2009), the Constitutional Court treated *actio popularis* complaints as private data of the complainants, and did not permit access to these complaints in the name of the public interest. The ECtHR found a violation of art 10 in the case.

[55] On these decisions see my chapter 'Hungary: High Hopes Revisited' in Leonardo Morlino and Wojciech Sadurski (eds) *Democratization and the European Union, Comparing Central and Eastern European Post-Communist Countries* (Routledge 2010), 45–69.

Unlike its predecessor, the new Fundamental Law contains detailed rules on the jurisdiction of the Constitutional Court (especially under Article 24). The Constitutional Court has jurisdiction:

- to review the procedural validity of the Fundamental Law or its subsequent amendment before its promulgation upon the request of the President of the Republic;[56]
- to review the procedural validity of the Fundamental Law or its subsequent amendment within 30 days after its promulgation upon the request of one-quarter of the MPs, the government, the chief justice of the curia, the prosecutor general or the ombudsman;[57]
- to review legislation before its promulgation upon the request of the government, the speaker of the House or the President (preliminary review);[58]
- to review promulgated legal norms for their conformity with the Fundamental Law upon the request of the government, one-quarter of MPs, the ombudsman, the president of the *Kúria* (supreme court) or the prosecutor general (abstract review);[59]
- to review promulgated legal norms which is to be applied in a pending case upon the request of a trial court or judge (judicial referral);
- to accept a constitutional complaint for the violation of fundamental rights (1) against a promulgated legal norm applied in a particular case,[60] (2) against a particular judicial decision[61] or (3) directly against a promulgated legal norm in exceptional cases[62] (constitutional complaint);
- to review the compatibility of legal norms with international obligations ex officio or upon the request of one-quarter of the

---

56 Fundamental Law, added by the Fourth Amendment, art 24(5)(a).

57 Ibid., art 24(5)(b).

58 Fundamental Law, art 24(2)(a) and Act on the Constitutional Court, art 23. Act no CLI of 2011 on the Constitutional Court is available in English translation with the website of the Constitutional Court at http://www.mkab.hu/rules/act-on-the-cc.

59 The President of the Supreme Court and the Prosecutor General were added among the potential applicants by the Fourth Amendment.

60 Fundamental Law, art 24(2)(c) and Act on the Constitutional Court, art 26(1).

61 Fundamental Law, art 24(2)(d) and Act on the Constitutional Court, art 27.

62 Fundamental Law, art 24(2)(c) and Act on the Constitutional Court, art 26(2).

MPs, the government, the chief justice of the curia, the prosecutor general or the ombudsman;[63]
- to decide any other matter defined by Fundamental Law or an Act of Parliament.[64]

The Act on the Constitutional Court, for instance, provides the court with power to provide abstract constitutional interpretation upon the request of Parliament or its standing committee, the President of the Republic, the government or the ombudsman (Article 38(1)).[65] The court has 30 days to decide on the formal validity of constitutional amendments (Article 24(6)),[66] the preliminary review request (Article 6(6)), Fundamental Law), while it has 90 days to process a judicial referral (Article 24(2)(b)).[67] An additional limitation imposed on the court is that it can only extend its review power to legal rules not expressly challenged in the petition, if those are closely related in substance to the challenged provisions (Article 24(4)).

The list of the powers of the Constitutional Court suggests a formidable constitutional review forum. The most surprising of these powers, the power to test the formal (procedural) validity of constitutional amendments was added to the list by the Fourth Amendment. It is best read as an attempt to curb the increasing interest of the court after it came close to reviewing the constitutionality of constitutional amendments in late 2012, when the constitutionality of the Transitional Provisions of the Fundamental Law were challenged before it.

The new Fundamental Law, enacted in the spring of 2011, was meant to enter into force on 1 January 2012. In December 2011, Parliament passed – in addition to measures and cardinal laws enacted before – a set of Transitional Provisions to pave the way for the new Fundamental Law's entry into force. The legal norm entitled Transitional Provisions opened with a lengthy section entitled 'On Transition from Communist Dictatorship to Democracy' and the included some 31 numbered articles. While some of these were transitional in nature, others included additional rules to further elaborate on the provisions of the Fundamental Law. Although the Transitional Provisions were enacted pursuant to the

---

[63] Fundamental Law, art 24(2)(f) and Act on the Constitutional Court, art 32.

[64] Fundamental Law, art 24(5)(g).

[65] See for example, X/704/2013 AB decision upon the request of the Minister of Justice.

[66] Inserted by the Fourth Amendment.

[67] As amended by the Fifth Amendment, art 6(2).

procedure required for constitutional amendment, it was at least ambiguous whether these articles titled Transitional Provisions formed part of the new Fundamental Law. When the ombudsman challenged the constitutionality of the Transitional Provisions, Parliament hastily passed the First Amendment to incorporate the Transitional Provisions into the Fundamental Law.

Despite this noble last minute effort, the Constitutional Court found the Transitional Provisions unconstitutional.[68] The decision of the Constitutional Court relied heavily on the very nature of the new Fundamental Law which is expressed in its (unnumbered) postamble. In this segment the Fundamental Law proclaims itself to be the first 'unified Fundamental Law of Hungary'.[69] Relying on this provision on the Constitutional Court found that:

> [a]t the time of adopting the Fundamental Law including the rules of amending it and the postamble declaring the unity of the Fundamental Law, the constituent power deferred intentionally from its former practice – deteriorating constitutional legality – of amending the Constitution (formerly) in force several times after a very short debate on the initiative of individual members of Parliament (ten times in 13 months). … This is the reason why the Constitutional Court attributes key importance to the protection of the unity of the Fundamental Law (the will of the constituent expressed in it).[70]

The impatience of the Constitutional Court with the new parliamentary practice of routine constitutional amendments is as tangible in the language of this decision as is a credible search for constitutional normalcy under the new Fundamental Law. In response to the decision of the Constitutional Court, in early February 2013 the Bill for the Fourth Amendment of the Fundamental Law was tabled in Parliament.[71] The bill sought to restore the invalidated Transitional Provisions and other legal

---

[68] 45/2012 (XII 29) AB decision, available in English translation with the website of the Constitutional Court at http://mkab.hu/letoltesek/en_0045_2012.pdf.

[69] The articles reads: 'We, the Members of the Parliament elected on 25 April 2010, being aware of our responsibility before God and man and in exercise of our constitutional power, hereby adopt this to be the first unified Fundamental Law of Hungary.' (English translation as available with the website of the Hungarian Parliament at: http://www.kormany.hu/download/4/c3/30000/THE%20FUNDAMENTAL%20LAW%20OF%20HUNGARY.pdf).

[70] Internal quotations omitted.

[71] Bill no T/9929.

measures[72] into the core text of the Fundamental Law. Importantly, the new Fourth Amendment included further adjustments to the procedure and power of constitutional review. It granted the power to the Constitutional Court to review the procedural propriety of constitutional amendments[73] – ensuring that the court would not review the substance of such provisions. It also brought a prohibition on interpreting the articles of the Fundamental Law with reference to the decisions of the Constitutional Court under the previous Constitution, thus, hoping to remove 20 years of constitutional jurisprudence from the record of Hungarian constitutionalism.

When using its new jurisdiction to review the constitutionality of the Fourth Amendment itself, at the request of the ombudsman, the Constitutional Court upheld its provisions.[74] The Constitutional Court noted that its review extends only to such procedural requirements as are clearly defined in the Fundamental Law.[75] In its judgment the Constitutional Court noted that the criteria of assessment of the formal validity of constitutional amendments under the new provisions inserted by the Fourth Amendment are *narrower* than used previously by the court.[76] In this case this meant that although the right of opposition MPs to participate in the making of the Fourth Amendment in Parliament was curbed (in compliance with the House Rules), this procedure could not be challenged before the Constitutional Court.

Because of the sheer breadth of its powers few objections can be raised at first sight to the scope of the court's jurisdiction. The court retained preliminary and *a posteriori* review functions, it can review all types of legal norms (and not only Acts of Parliament), including constitutional amendments, and a large group of actors (including private individuals) may approach it. It is worth noting, however, that currently it is not that easy to challenge the government or Parliament before the Constitutional Court: at the moment no parliamentary faction controls one quarter of the votes in Parliament alone, so the powers of the opposition can only be exercised after some (unlikely) consensus-building. Lacking such agreement one needs to look for a source of dissent around the President, the ombudsman, ordinary courts (through judicial referral) or individuals who can launch a constitutional complaint.

---

[72] See the decisions of the Constitutional Court on elections, the law on families, etc.

[73] Fundamental Law, art 24(5).

[74] 12/2013 (V 24) AB decision.

[75] Ibid., para. 30.

[76] Ibid.

While the introduction of proper constitutional complaint in Hungary is a welcome development, the early jurisprudence of the Constitutional Court suggests that it is not an easy avenue of access. Although constitutional complaint against allegedly unconstitutional legal rules had already been available under the old Constitution, its relative lack of success and popularity is best explained by the much more convenient access to the court through *actio popularis*. Thus, the real novelty the new regulation of constitutional complaint brings is the opportunity to challenge the unconstitutional judicial application of otherwise constitutional legal rules. Attempts to extend the review power of the Constitutional Court to the jurisprudence of ordinary courts had not been very successful in Hungary before, as they generated much conflict and critique in the legal profession. The Constitutional Court took into account the practice of ordinary courts when it reviewed legal norms as they were applied in practice (the so-called 'living law' concept), but for the most part avoided regular confrontation with ordinary courts over the constitutionality of their jurisprudence.

From early on the Constitutional Court has been mindful of the differences between a constitutional complaint and an *actio popularis* application.[77] It was due to key differences that the court required access to legal assistance for petitioners of constitutional complaints.[78]

Although the constitutional complaint procedure in principle permits cases to be brought directly to the Constitutional Court without the exhaustion of judicial remedies, this route is not overused. Although it was feared that this exceptional direct access would replace the abolished *actio popularis*, so far it seems that the court is very cautious about taking a complaint through this route. In order to permit standing to applicants in such cases, the Constitutional Court requires the showing of a clear personal connection to the challenged norm.[79]

---

77 For early analysis of the impact of the removal of *actio popularis* in English see Katalin Kelemen, 'Access to Constitutional Justice in the New Hungarian Constitutional Framework: Life after the Actio Popularis?', in Antonia Geisler, Michael Hein and Siri Hummel (eds) *Law, Politics, and the Constitution. New Perspectives from Legal and Political Theory* (Peter Lang 2014), 63–78.

78 42/2012 (XII 20) AB decision. The significance of the difference is outlined at para. 30 et seq.

79 For example, 3110/2013 (VI 4) AB ruling. Cf. 3033/2014 (III 3) AB ruling: complaint referring to possible future membership in a union was ruled to be hypothetical.

While *actio popularis* could be filed for any type of unconstitutionality by anyone, the constitutional complaint is meant to remedy the violation of fundamental rights only, in individual cases.[80] As a result the court regularly rejects constitutional complaints which seek to enforce constitutional provisions without a direct connection to fundamental rights.[81] The Constitutional Court, however, accepts constitutional complaints challenging violations of the rule of law (Fundamental Law, Article B(1)) as an exception, in instances where the complaint concerns the prohibition of retroactive legislation or lack of adequate time to prepare for the entry into force of a new legal rule.[82] Similarly, constitutional complaints concerning the violation of judicial independence are also accepted.[83]

Although a constitutional complaint may only be filed against a final judgment of ordinary courts on the merits,[84] lately the court has accepted complaints against such interim procedural rulings which could not be challenged by an appeal against the final judgment.[85] This is certainly a welcome development, as the lack of constitutional complaint against interim judicial rulings means, for instance, that while petitioners challenging the terms of their pretrial detention could not reach the Constitutional Court, they could turn to the ECtHR.[86]

The Constitutional Court is filtering constitutional complaints rather carefully, and at times in a somewhat unpredicatble manner. The most important barrier remains the assessment of what amounts to a constitutional law issue 'of fundamental importance' foreseen by the Act on the Constitutional Court (Article 29). The assessment of the fundamental nature of the claim is essentially a discretionary decision of the court and

---

80 See for example, 3367/2012 (XII 15) AB ruling, para. 28 ('the aim of the constitutional complaint is the protection of individual subjective rights'). Also 25/2013 (X 4) AB decision (the Constituional Court is entrusted with enforcing fundamental rights in practice).

81 See for example, 3142/2014 (V 9) AB ruling: art VI(3) of the Fundamental Law requires the establishment of an independent data protection authority, yet, it does not provide a fundamental right.

82 See for example, 3003/2014 (I 31) AB ruling, para. 19; 3064/2014 (III 26) AB ruling, para. 11.

83 For example, 4/2014 (I 30) AB decision.

84 Act on the Constitutional Court, art 27.

85 3057/2015 (III 31) AB decision (on the suspension of cases of debtors of FOREX consumer loans).

86 3002/2014 (I 24) AB ruling, see concurring opinion of Judge Miklós Lévay at para. 24 and also the dissenting opinion of Judge András Bragyova, noting that the Fundamental Law contains detailed rules on pretrial detention.

the rejection of a constitutional complaint (for lack of fundamental importance) is not subject to appeal or review.

So far the Constitutional Court has been very cautious in its filtering of constitutional complaint applications. When screening petitions a mighty tool in the hands of the court (in addition to formal deficiencies, deadlines, non-exhaustion of remedies and lack of a personal interest[87]) is selecting cases that do not raise a novel constitutional issue. While this requirement reads as a variation on the *res iudicata* effect of constitutional court judgments, one needs to keep in mind that the text of the Fundamental Law is not identical to the text of the old Constitution. The *res iudicata* effect of previous Constitutional Court judgments has been an issue of contention in the case involving the constitutionality of the criminalization of the display of the red star under the Fundamental Law in 2013.[88] The Constitutional Court upheld the constitutionality of the provision in 2000,[89] yet, in the meantime the ECtHR had found in several cases that Hungarian ordinary courts applied the provision in a manner which violated Article 10 of the Convention.[90] The Constitutional Court agreed to accept the ECtHR judgment as a new circumstance (Act on the Constitutional Court, Article 31(1)) and found the contested provision unconstitutional.

With the abolition of *actio popularis* the President of the Republic and the ombudsman have become key constitutional actors in defence of fundamental rights. The President has brought a number of important cases to the court under the Fundamental Law,[91] yet, he is certainly not (and not meant to be) a human rights activist in the classic sense of the word.[92] Indeed, the ombudsman is the most likely actor to raise key constitutional challenges with the court in the current regime, and both holders of the office have lived up to this expectation so far. The enlarged role of the ombudsman is also illustrated by the fact that he requested the

---

[87] Note that an ordinary (that is, not direct) constitutional complaint may also be brought by the prosecutor general. Act on the Constitutional Court, art 26(3).

[88] 4/2013 (II 21) AB decision.

[89] 14/2000 (V 12) AB decision.

[90] The leading case is *Vajnai v Hungary* App no 33629/06 (ECHR, 8 July 2008).

[91] For example, the mandatory prior registration of voters was succesfully challenged by the President in 1/2013 (I 7) AB decision.

[92] The President signed the Fourth Amendment of the Fundamental Law, despite pressure from civil society organizations to veto it. Most recently the President refused to veto an amendment which made access to information more burdensome.

review of the Fourth Amendment from the Constitutional Court after the President refused to do so. The ombudsman described his petition as a constitutional make-up assignment, as other persons were not in the position to bring such a challenge of unconstitutionality before the Constitutional Court.[93]

10.3.2 The Fate of the Constitutional Court's Jurisprudence under the Old Constitution

The relationship between the new Fundamental Law and the Constitutional Court's settled case law has been increasingly complicated and contentious. As already mentioned, the Constitutional Court has been insisting that neither amendments to the old Constitution nor the new Fundamental Law can reduce the previously established minimum constitutional guarantees as these were familiar from the jurisprudence of the Constitutional Court. The court held that such constraints are derived from international and European obligations.

In the early days of making the new Constitution the government regularly offered assurances that the new Constitution would codify the settled jurisprudence of the Constitutional Court. Indeed, the government itself has not always been hostile towards the 'old' jurisprudence of the court being applied under the new Fundamental Law. In a request for abstract constitutional interpretation of the Fundamental Law's Europe clause (Article E) the government in its petition itself relied extensively on the old jurisprudence of the Constitutional Court.[94]

As a matter of practical legal reasoning this is certainly not surprising since the new Fundamental Law was adopted in compliance with the rules of the old Constitution. The sense or potential for discontinuity between the two Constitutions was initially fuelled by symbolic statements in the preamble of the new Fundamental Law (formally known as the National Avowal) concerning the origins of the new constitutional regime. These passages contain strong anti-communist statements such as:

> We date the restoration of the self-determination of our State, lost on the nineteenth day of March 1944, from the second day of May 1990, when the first freely elected popular representation was formed. We shall consider this date to be the beginning of our country's new democracy and constitutional order.

---

[93] 12/2013 (V 24) AB decision, para. 2.

[94] 22/2012 (V 11) AB decision.

Technically this declaration is difficult to square with another line in the National Avowal which proclaims that, 'We do not recognise the communist constitution of 1949, since it was the basis of a tyrannical rule; therefore we proclaim it to be invalid' – as the 1949 Constitution continued to be in effect (with major revisions) until the new Fundamental Law entered into force on 1 January 2012.

It is against this backdrop that one has to consider the insistence of the Constitutional Court to reinforce the premises of its old jurisprudence. In the words of the court:

> The Constitutional Court's duty is the protection of the Fundamental Law. The Constitutional Court can apply in the new cases the arguments connected to the questions of constitutional law judged upon in the past and contained in its decisions adopted before the Fundamental Law was put into force, provided that it is possible on the basis of the concrete provisions – having the same or similar content as that of the previous Constitution – and of the rules of interpretation of the Fundamental Law.[95]

Ever since this formative decision, it has been the standard practice of the Constitutional Court to refer to its 'old' case law where the text of the new Fundamental Law is not significantly different from that of the old Constitution.[96] Furthermore, in its decision on the 2011 church law[97] that Constitutional Court emphasized that the differences between the relevant provisions of the old Constitutional and the new Fundamental Law were due to the fact that the new text reflects the jurisprudence of the court under the old Constitution.[98] The court also followed its previous jurisprudence in a case where the Fundamental Law includes a provision which the old Constitution lacked: the court found that although the old Constitution did not have a general equality clause the case law has developed a general requirement of equal treatment, deriving from equality and dignity.[99]

In time, references to old case law came to be seen as the force leading the court to invalidate the government's major initiatives and ultimately,

---

[95] Decision 22/2012 (V 11) AB decision, para. 40, available at the website of the Constitutional Court in English at http://www.mkab.hu/letoltesek/en_0022_2012.pdf.

[96] See, for example, 34/2012 (VII 17) AB decision, para. 33; 35/2012 (VII 17) AB decision, para. 25; 3301/2012 (XI 12) AB decision, para. 20.

[97] 6/2013 (III 1) AB decision.

[98] Ibid., paras 128–9.

[99] 42/2012 (XII 20) AB decision, position reaffirmed in 1/2013 (I 7) AB decision, para. 88.

the force undermining the project of constitutional transformation introduced by the Fundamental Law. As a reaction, the Fourth Amendment expressly repealed two decades of constitutional jurisprudence.[100] There is little doubt that this provision was meant to put an end to the court's practice wherein the justices relied on premises of previous jurisprudence before they turned to finding key pieces of legislation unconstitutional.

The Constitutional Court's response to the Fourth Amendment has been rather laconic. In a decision of April 2013 the Constitutional Court said that it will continue to rely on arguments, principles and constitutional consequences stemming from its previous case law in cases where the provision of the Fundamental Law is essentially similar to the article of the old Constitution, if the two contexts are similar, and the rules of interpretation of the Fundamental Law permit it in the concrete case, and the reasoning needs to be incorporated in the justification of the new decision.[101] Subsequently the Constitutional Court linked its reliance on its old case law to the requirement of giving reasons for its judgments.[102] In this logic old case law is simply a record of arguments, and includes tried and proven justifications for particular positions. In this perspective the Fourth Amendment's notorious clause is seen by the Constitutional Court as setting a somewhat higher threshold of justification, but clearly not as a prohibition on judicial reasoning.

Initially the government explained the invalidation of the old jurisprudence of the court to the Venice Commission with the need to free the court from the confines of its old jurisprudence.[103] This justification is at least surprising, considering the earlier justification of various provisions in the new Fundamental Law with saying that the new rules simply codify existing constitutional jurisprudence.

Taking note of the Constitutional Court's defiance of the Fourth Amendment, the government responded to Venice Commission as well as to the European Parliament's LIBE Committee[104] that the invalidation of the old jurisprudence of the court is not problematic, as apparently it does

---

[100] Fundamental Law, Closing provisions, cl 5: Constitutional Court rulings given prior to the entry into force of the Fundamental Law are hereby repealed. This provision is without prejudice to the legal effect produced by those rulings.

[101] 13/2013 (VI 17) AB decision, para. 32; also 21/2012 (IV 21) AB decision. More recently, in 17/2013 (VI 26) AB decision, para. 7.

[102] 36/2013 (XII 5) AB decision.

[103] Opinion on the Fourth Amendment, para. 89.

[104] The LIBE committee is a standing committee of the European Parliament on Civil Liberties, Justice and Home Affairs responsible for protecting civil liberties and human rights.

not prevent the court from relying on its 'old jurisprudence'. In response to the government's arguments, the Venice Commission stated:

> 96. The Venice Commission therefore cannot support the Hungarian authorities' argument that the Constitutional Court should be more free to decide. As shown, there was no justification to declare the Constitutional Court's former case-law void in order to enable the Constitutional Court to renew its jurisdiction in cases where it is necessary. It is inherent in a Constitutional Court's approach to interpret a constitution on the basis of its provisions and the principles contained in it. These principles transcend the constitution itself and directly relate to the basic principles of the Council of Europe: democracy, the protection of human rights and the rule of law. It is these principles which are reflected in the case law of the Constitutional Court since its establishment.

Note that the Constitutional Court takes the context-sensitive application of old jurisprudence seriously when the provisions of the Fundamental Law differ from those of the old Constitution. For instance, unlike the old Constitution the Fundamental Law expressly refers to the protection of human dignity as a source of limitation on freedom of expression (Article IX(4)). The Constitutional Court decided to follow its old jurisprudence after reminding that protection of human dignity has been part of the case law of the court under the old Constitution.[105] The court also pointed out that its old jurisprudence followed the premises of the case law of the ECtHR in this respect.[106] Similarly, in a more recent case the Constitutional Court noted that although unlike the new Fundamental Law, the old Constitution did not mention expressly the requirement of concluding judicial processes within a reasonable time (Article 57(5)), the case law of the court under the old Constitution complied with applicable international standards in this respect.[107]

The practice of relying on old jurisprudence has its critics in the Constitutional Court. Justice Béla Pokol went as far as to say that only a new majority will be able to depart from the premises of the old case law.[108]

---

105 76/2014 (III 7) AB decision, para. 24.
106 Ibid., paras 25–44.
107 3057/2015 (III 31) AB decision.
108 Justice Béla Pokol, dissenting in 2/2014 (I 21) AB decision, para. 75.

10.3.3 References to International Obligations and European Standards: Solid Foundations or a Source of Escalating Tension?

The discussion so far has demonstrated that the Hungarian Constitutional Court is attempting to impose constraints on a mighty government under a Constitution that until recently used to be rather changeable. The Constitutional Court sought to ground its jurisprudence with reference to its longstanding case law, developed under the old Constitution. The court under the old Constitution, however, was known to develop the principles and standards of its case law with reference to foreign examples, as well as international and European standards.

The Constitutional Court in its leading case from 2011 explained that although the old Hungarian Constitution does not have an unalterable core defined by the constitution-making power, there are several resources which amount to fundamental standards in guaranteeing constitutional rights. These resources include *ius cogens*, generally accepted legal principles as well as international treaties promulgated in Hungary. According to the court these principles are applicable due to the force of *ius cogens*, and not as a result of the constitution-making power agreeing to them.[109] As mentioned earlier, the Constitutional Court insisted on following the minimum standards of rights protection as developed in the jurisprudence of the ECtHR. Subsequently the Constitutional Court went one step further and concluded that it has to do so due to the principle of *pacta sun servanda* enshrined in the Fundamental Law (Article Q) even where a particular conclusion would not follow from its own case law.[110] The Constitutional Court has to follow judgments rendered in cases against other countries as doing otherwise would result in condemnation of Hungary before the ECtHR in a similar case.

The most powerful critic of the Constitutional Court's reliance on ECtHR jurisprudence is undoubtedly Justice Béla Pokol. He insists on a sovereignty-friendly interpretation of Article Q, in order to halt the spread of global constitutional oligarchy.[111] According to him, Hungarian judges are bound by the European Convention on Human Rights, but not by the case law of the ECtHR. Hungarian judges should take the ECtHR case law as merely useful background information on what may follow from the Convention for their own decisions. According to Justice Pokol,

---

[109] 61/2011 (VII 13) AB decision, ABK, 710–11.

[110] 36/2013 (XII 5) AB decision, para. 26. For a similar stance see 7/2014 (III 7) AB decision, para. 25 and 16/2014 (V 22) AB decision, para. 23.

[111] 34/2012 (XI 22) AB decision, Justice Pokol dissenting, para. 85.

doing otherwise would transfer control over the legal system to an international actor.[112] Similarly, adhering to ECtHR jurisprudence in constitutional cases would amount to an admission that the ECtHR is entitled to extend international obligations without the participation of the member states.[113] For Justice Pokol it is important to resist the ever-expanding jurisprudence of the ECtHR.[114] Justice Mária Szívós expressed a similar view, arguing that the case law of the ECtHR should be considered as a helpful reference at best, since the ECtHR may alter its jurisprudence any time.[115]

Justice Pokol is equally suspicious of compliance with EU obligations, and urges the Constitutional Court to give effect to those provisions of the preamble of the Fundamental Law (National Avowal) which would prevent the melding of Hungary within the EU.[116] He expressed a similar vision of the withering of the Hungarian nation due to the imposition of European minimum standards for fundamental rights.[117] It is worth pointing out that the reservations of Justice Pokol about following ECtHR jurisprudence in constitutional cases echo concerns of leading Hungarian political actors who wish to defend Hungary's distinctive identity in the face of European pressure and criticism.

The sovereignty-based objection to following ECtHR jurisprudence has several intensities and variations. Milder accounts tend to accept that with ratifying an international treaty the sovereign constrains itself to some extent. The differentiation between treaty obligations and the case law of the ECtHR are rooted in this milder sovereignty narrative. While the Constitutional Court has referred several times to the self-constraint imposed by the sovereign on itself by ratifying international treaties, the court has used another argument which capitalized on the sovereignty narrative much more successfully in order to bring the ECtHR case law home. In a few cases the Constitutional Court argued that it is bound by ECtHR jurisprudence because Hungary submitted itself to the jurisdiction of the ECtHR.[118] Interestingly, there were no dissenting opinions on these points in these judgments.

---

[112] 34/2012 (XI 22) AB decision, Justice Pokol dissenting, para. 86.
[113] 7/2014 (III 7) AB decision, Justice Pokol dissenting, para. 113.
[114] 3025/2014 (II 17) AB decision, Justice Pokol dissenting, para. 90.
[115] 4/2013 (II 21) AB decision, Justice Szívós dissenting, para. 144.
[116] 32/2014 (VII 4) AB decision, Justice Pokol dissenting, para. 86.
[117] 4/2013 (II 21) AB decision, Justice Pokol concurring, para. 117.
[118] 13/2013 (IV 18) AB decision, para. 33; 25/2013 (X. 14.) AB decision, para. 27.

The consequences of giving effect to ECtHR judgments are far from settled. As mentioned, in its second decision finding the criminalization of the red star as a totalitarian symbol unconstitutional, the Constitutional Court acted upon the judgment of the ECtHR in the *Vajnai* case and its progeny.[119] Although the Constitutional Court decided to invalidate the challenged provision of the Criminal Code, concurring Justice Kiss wrote that it would have been sufficient to set a condition of constitution-conform interpretation instead of invalidating the law,[120] while Chief Justice Paczolay argued that the provision should have been invalidate *ex tunc*, and not *pro futuro*.[121] More recently, in a case where a trial judge requested the Constitutional Court to give effect to the judgment of the ECtHR in the church registration case[122] which found Hungary in violation of Articles 9 and 14 of the Convention, the Constitutional Court suspended the application of the challenged rules in the case pending before the trial judge and requested Parliament to remedy the inconsistency in the legal rules by setting a date, the Constitutional Court did not, however, invalidate the challenged rules.[123]

In addition to the debate on the binding force of international obligations and ECtHR jurisprudence in particular, there is a noteworthy conversation in constitutional cases on which constitutional actor is bound by international and European obligations. The Constitutional Court does not shy away from reminding Parliament of its duties to ensure compliance with positive obligations such as in a case concerning procedural and institutional guarantees of concluding court procedures within a reasonable time.[124] In early 2014 the Constitutional Court said that ensuring the compliance of international law and domestic law is not exclusively the task of the legislative.[125] Dissenting in another case Justice Dienes-Ohm, however, was of the view that the judgments of the ECtHR were binding on Parliament and not on the Constitutional Court,

---

119 4/2013 (II 21) AB decision. For a detailed discussion see text at note 143, below.

120 4/2013 (II 21) AB decision, Justice Kiss concurring, para. 110.

121 4/2013 (II 21) AB decision, Chief Justice Paczolay concurring, para. 140.

122 *Magyar Keresztény Mennonita Egyház and others v Hungary* App nos. 70945/11, 23611/12, 26998/12, 41150/12, 41155/12, 41463/12, 41553/12, 54977/12 and 56581/12 (ECHR, 8 April 2014). The ECtHR cited the earlier judgment of the Constitutional Court throughout the case in the affirmative.

123 23/2015 (VII 7) AB decision.

124 3057/2015 (III 31) AB decision, para. 33.

125 6/2014 (II 26) AB decision, para. 39.

as the court cannot attribute higher significance to the judgments of the ECtHR than to its own case law.[126]

This debate gains a new dimension when ordinary courts face the question of giving effect to ECtHR judgments rendered in similar cases. Whether such cases reach the Constitutional Court via judicial referral, or ultimately through constitutional complaints matters little: the potential for the Constitutional Court and the Supreme Court clashing over the application of European case law is equally possible. The Constitutional Court is very likely to address this problem in the near future in a case concerning a measure that is dear to the government.

Life imprisonment without parole has been a favoured criminal justice measure of the current government in its efforts to enhance security and fight crime.[127] Accordingly, life imprisonment is mentioned expressly in the Fundamental Law (Article IV(2)).[128] A trial judge brought a judicial referral before the Constitutional Court, challenging legal rules which permitted the trial court to exclude parole altogether when prescribing life imprisonment with reference to the ECtHR's judgment in *Vinter v the United Kingdom*.[129] In *Vinte*r the ECtHR said, inter alia, that:

> in the sense of a review which allows the domestic authorities to consider whether any changes in the life prisoner are so significant, and such progress towards rehabilitation has been made in the course of the sentence, as to mean that continued detention can no longer be justified on legitimate penological grounds.[130]

The Constitutional Court discontinued the procedure[131] after Parliament amended rules on life imprisonment.[132] Under the new rules prisoners

---

[126] 36/2013 (XII 5) AB decision, Justice Dienes-Ohm dissenting, para. 60.

[127] It was also in this spirit that Prime Minister Orbán engaged in public thought experiments concerning the re-introduction of capital punishment in Hungary. His statements were instantly condemned by the European Parliament in rather strong terms. See P8_TA-PROV(2015)0227, *Situation in Hungary, European Parliament resolution of* 10 June 2015 on the situation in Hungary (2015/2700(RSP)).

[128] Article IV(2): Life imprisonment without parole may only be imposed for the commission of a willful and violent criminal offence.

[129] *Vinter and others v the United Kingdom* App nos. 66069/09, 130/10 and 3896/10 (ECHR, 9 July 9 2013).

[130] Ibid., para. 119.

[131] 3013/2015 (I 27) AB ruling.

[132] Act no LXXII of 2014, art 109.

sentenced to life imprisonment without parole are entitled to an automatic pardon procedure 40 years after their imprisonment.[133] Despite the Constitutional Court's silence, it is safe to assume that the new Hungarian rule which permits the first review of a life sentence 40 years after incarceration is meant to enable *de facto* life imprisonment without parole, as the aims of the review prescribed by the ECtHR in *Vinter* can barely be achieved in a meaningful fashion.

Shortly after the ruling of the Constitutional Court, the Hungarian Supreme Court issued a resolution for legal harmonization (*jogegységi határozat*)[134] finding that life imprisonment without parole is part of the Hungarian constitutional regime and the imposition of this sanction is not prohibited by an international treaty. It is the task of courts to insert the judgments of the ECtHR under the Convention into the Hungarian legal system through the application of Hungarian law. This line of reasoning is not in line with the jurisprudence of the Constitutional Court on how the case law of the ECtHR should be taken into account in the course of the application of national law. In response, in July 2015 the Minister of Justice requested the Constitutional Court to clarify whether a trial court is required to make a referral to the Constitutional Court when it is meant to apply a legal norm which may violate an international treaty.[135]

10.4 DIALOGUE OR DEFIANCE? EUROPEAN STANDARDS IN PERSPECTIVE

Since 2010 constitutional amendments were used on several occasions to overrule the Constitutional Court to prevent its interference in a matter of political significance for the government. The Venice Commission found it particularly problematic that the Fourth Amendment was heavy with provisions that were meant to overrule the decisions of the Constitutional Court.[136] Although the Hungarian Government claimed that it had adopted the Fourth Amendment in order to comply with the decision of the Constitutional Court on the Transitional Provisions,[137] the Venice

[133] Art 46/B(1) of Act no. CCXL of 2013 on the enforcement of criminal sanctions, as amended by Act no LXXII of 2014.

[134] 3/2015 BJE.

[135] X/02129/2015 (pending application before the Constitutional Court).

[136] See Opinion no 720/2013, para. 80.

[137] Opinion no.720/2013, para. 78 (summarizing the government's argument), also the government's response to the Tavares report.

Commission recalled that the Constitutional Court 'did not oblige Parliament to readopt the annulled provisions as part of the Fundamental law'.[138]

In response to the Venice Commission's draft opinion of the Fourth Amendment, the government argued that its practice is best understood as 'revisiting' Constitutional Court judgments, and not overruling them.[139] In some cases, wherein the amendment clearly responds to the court's case law the government argued that the Constitutional Court decided solely on formal grounds, while in other cases the government argued that the new, constitutional-level regulation covered a different scope of matters than the invalidated one.[140] In its response the Venice Commission reiterated that the Hungarian Parliament retains its sovereign decision to adopt and amend the Constitution:

> In itself, the possibility of constitutional amendments is an important counterweight to a constitutional court's power over legislation in a constitutional democracy, as well as an important element in the delicate system of checks and balances which defines a constitutional democracy. Nevertheless, this approach can only be justified in particular cases, based on thorough preparatory work, wide public debate and large political consensus as in general is necessary for constitutional amendments.[141]

Indeed, the government's willingness to stand up not only against the Constitutional Court but also against European pressure gained a novel formulation in the Fourth Amendment. The idea was most likely in the making for several months and was triggered by the ECtHR's more recent reaffirmation of its finding in the 2008 *Vajnai* case where it concluded that the application of Hungary's application of its criminal prohibition of the display of the red star in public[142] violates Article 10.[143] In response, the Ministry of Justice and Public Administration announced in Parliament that Hungary will not comply with the

---

138 Ibid., para. 79.

139 Comments of the Government of Hungary on the Draft Opinion on the Fourth Amendment to the Fundamental Law of Hungary, para. 47, http://www.kormany.hu/download/d/5c/e0000/HUresponse_VenCom_DraftOp_20130611%28FINALfin%29.pdf.

140 *Comments of the Government*, para. 48.

141 *Opinion on the Fourth Amendment,* para. 84.

142 Article 269/B of the Criminal Code prohibits, inter alia, the public display of 'a swastika, an SS-badge, an arrow-cross, a symbol of the sickle and hammer or a red star, or a symbol depicting any of them'.

143 *Vajnai v Hungary* App no 33629/06 (ECHR, 8 July 2008). Affirmed in *Fratanoló v Hungary* App no 29459/10 (ECHR, 3 November 2011). Several

ECtHR's words and refuses to pay up. While over a dozen human rights organizations urged the government to comply with the judgment of the ECtHR, the Secretary of State for the Ministry submitted in Parliament that '[w]e believe that as a part of Hungary's sovereignty it can decide what triggers fear, what triggers terror in Hungarian citizens'.[144] Supporting the position of the government, the chair of the parliamentary committee for human rights submitted that it was the task of Parliament to defend a Hungarian court against the ECtHR.[145] In the end Parliament passed a resolution finding that payment obligations stemming from ECtHR judgments on account of this criminal ban should be paid from the funds reserved in the central budget for supporting political parties.[146] Thus, the discretion of the sovereign was again invoked to justify an apparent violation of fundamental rights.

Thereafter, among the rules introduced by the Fourth Amendment, a rather curious one on public payment obligations stood out. According to Article 37(6) of the Fundamental Law so long as the level of public debt exceeds half of the GDP, if funds allocated for such purpose are not sufficient, any public payment obligation which is triggered by the judgment of the Constitutional Court, the CJEU or any other court will be met by a special tax imposed for this particular purpose (Article 37(6)). This constitutional amendment, in essence introducing a special tax on human rights litigation, was removed ultimately by the Fifth Amendment, with the government arguing in the written reasons attached to the bill that unexpected fiscal obligations may be met adequately without a constitutional provision to this effect.

10.5 CONCLUSION: DISPELLING AN ILLUSION

The Hungarian Constitutional Court used to be among the most internationally respected courts for the quality of its jurisprudence and for its contributions to transition to democracy in the post-communist club. Currently it is best known as the victim of perpetual constitutional amendments. While the Hungarian Court had engaged in continuing

---

ECtHR judgments since then stand as evidence that at least some Hungarian criminal courts refuse to alter their practice to bring it in line with ECtHR case law.

[144] Journal of Parliament, 11 June 2012, Day no 200, Speech no 324 (in Hungarian).

[145] Ibid., Speech no 328 (in Hungarian).

[146] 58/2012 (VII 10) OGY resolution, point 3.

dialogue with the political branches, under the Fundamental Law it was in a rather unusual situation when its judgments would be over-constitutionalized literally overnight. The Constitutional Court so far has maintained the illusion that the constitution (that is, the Fundamental Law) is meant to constrain the exercise of governmental powers and that the Constitutional Court is meant to safeguard the constitution against being driven below the established European constitutional minimum. In doing so the Constitutional Court continues to consistently refer to its established jurisprudence, international obligations and European standards.

On the surface, under its new Fundamental Law Hungary appears to have a well-functioning constitutional regime. There is a lively debate among the justices on what constitutes international obligations, what it means to be bound by these obligations and what follows from submitting to these minimum standards for the case law of the court and also for other constitutional actors. Despite the change in the architecture of the Constitutional Court, its jurisdiction remains broad and the avenues for receiving meaningful constitutional cases are still open. Ordinary courts, the ombudsman, the President of the Republic and tireless private petitioners bring cases before the Constitutional Court. All these petitioners refer to the established jurisprudence of the court as much as to international and European standards and principles. The plight of the Constitutional Court and its judgments becomes apparent from the opinions and contributions of European constitutional actors, which regularly condemn the government for refusing to adhere to these carefully crafted constraints and play by shared European rules. It is from the perspective of external constitutional actors that the cautionary tale of an ever-defiant government and a battered Constitutional Court shed light on the highly illusory nature of the constitutional regime under the new Hungarian Fundamental Law.

PART III

Conclusion

11. Comparative law and fundamental rights

John Bell

Gardbaum[1] suggests that constitutional rights jurisprudence is subject to two main kinds of contradictory influences. On the one hand, 'structural similarities or convergences among constitutional systems may perhaps be best explained as a form of practical near-necessity within the dominant form of liberal-democratic constitutionalism'. On the other hand, substantive differences in constitutional rights within the general parameters set by these structural principles may be best explained by a combination of contextual factors, including differences in political and legal culture, expressive values and the age and content of the constitutional text'.[2] So his vision is that there is a common enterprise of constitutional liberalism which makes use of the institution of rights to advance democracy, but that, within the enterprise, there are distinctive, contextual features which lead to divergence. The authors in this collection have broadly endorsed the convergence hypothesis that Gardbaum sets out. They do see that liberalism these days requires the protection through the courts of fundamental rights. Even the Australian chapters argue for greater judicial activism in this area. But, at the same time, the chapters in this collection reveal a great diversity not only in institutional mechanisms (especially judicial review of legislation), but even in the rights protected.

The argument of this chapter is that this tension between general movements of ideas and values and local issues permeates the comparison of different systems of public law. Saunders suggests that '[c]onstitutional culture may be defined to include the assumptions that underlie a

[1] Stephen Gardbaum, 'The Structure and Scope of Constitutional Rights' in Tom Ginsburg and Rosalind Dixon (eds), *Comparative Constitutional Law* (Edward Elgar Publishing 2011) ch 21.

[2] Ibid., 403.

Constitution and the attitudes that affect its operation in practice'.[3] Such a definition includes the idea that there is a specific approach in each country to this tension between the transnational search to protect rights and the local understandings and practices that achieve such protection. All the same, it would be wrong to consider that there is a fixed constitutional culture in a particular country. First, the idea of a 'particular country' is problematic, since many countries have changing boundaries and populations. Countries like Germany have changed radically in the last 200 years. Populations are also changing thanks to European free movement rights and to general patterns of migration across the world. Albeit often slowly, the countries are re-inventing themselves and, with that, their constitutional culture. Secondly, it would be wrong to think that there is a fixed pattern of local responses to constitutional problems that constitutes a national 'constitutional culture'. Responses are often more pragmatic and changeable. Specific problems are met with specific responses at one time, but there may be no systematic approach. Boyron suggests[4] that the French constitutional tradition is made up of a series of experiments which are adopted, continued or rejected from time to time: 'French constitutional history may have lacked continuity but it is partly explained by the need to experiment with new mechanisms and new solutions in a bid to uncover a system that would bring political stability.'[5] From time to time, there have been different kinds of head of state, different ways of electing the Parliament, different balances of legislative power between the executive and the Parliament. Even in countries which have had a definite 'constitutional moment' such as Italy or Spain, the protection of fundamental rights moves on.

The combination of a changing society (and often populations) with experimentalism in constitutional practice gives rise to an essential provisionality and flexibility in constitutional practice. Some values and rules will be the same across countries or even within the same country over time, and there may be a kind of path dependency from one established way of resolving constitutional problems to the way in which a new problem is resolved. But experimentalism is a fundamental dynamic. Solutions to new problems will sometimes be found in terms of changing values and, more often in terms of institutions.

---

[3] Cheryl Saunders, 'A Constitutional Culture in Tradition' in Miroslaw Wyrzykowski (ed.), *Constitutional Cultures* (Institute of Public Affairs 2000) 37.

[4] Sophie Boyron, *The Constitution of France: A Contextual Analysis* (Hart 2013) 23–5.

[5] Ibid., 25.

This chapter argues that, from a comparative perspective, this problem of provisionality and experimentalism in the handling of the tension between the transnational nature of rights and local practice needs to be seen in two perspectives. First, it is necessary to focus on the state official who has to implement rights, not just the court which has the final word in interpreting them. Fundamental rights instruments are directed to the state and its officials who have the duty of realising them. We therefore need to pay attention not only to the norms (which may look quite similar between systems), but also to the institutions and processes by which rights are applied and enforced within specific, local legal systems (which may well differ one from another). In this perspective, rights are not so much constraints on a political majority, but rather standards of good government. Secondly, constitutions are work in progress documents (or groups of documents). The distinctiveness of legal systems results from their specific places in a conversation involving their specific constitutional past, their current specific local social needs, as well as more transnational external reference points, such as supranational instruments and courts protecting fundamental rights.

1. FUNDAMENTAL RIGHTS, CONSTITUTIONAL REVIEW AND THE PLACE OF OFFICIALS

Flexibility and experimentation are tied up with the nature of the constitution and the role of different actors within it. If, in liberal societies, constitutional provisions are meant to embody points of reference in a journey of self-government, then they need to adapt in order to reflect the way in which reference points change. For many chapters in this collection, constitutional judicial review plays an important part in guiding the community on this journey. The Irish and Australian chapters argue that common law jurisdictions are typically more reticent about the place of the courts than civil law systems.[6] My suggestion would be that the British constitutional experience from which the common law countries derive their background gives greater prominence to officials and trusts them more than many European civil law countries which have undergone dictatorship or invasion in the twentieth century.

Chen and Maduro suggest that constitutional review may perform one of three roles. It may fill gaps in constitutional norms, it may set the agenda for political institutions to fill those gaps, or it may have a more

[6] See Chapters 3 and 4 in this volume.

specific mission, involving 'a particular normative goal that ought to guide them in interpreting and applying the constitution'.[7] A focus on protecting fundamental rights is such a vision perspective. It involves prioritising the protection of rights, because, as Dworkin argues, that confers a particular legitimacy on a judicial institution within the organs of a democracy.[8] I will argue that a court-centred approach to fundamental rights and their determination fails to focus on the central case of respect for rights: their implementation by public officials. If rights are a central part of a democratic political order, then it is important that they become part of the routine of public life. An obvious example is the 'public sector equality duty' under the English and Welsh Equality Act 2010.[9] As Hepple notes in his study of this duty, the purpose of introducing this idea was to achieve a change in culture such that the promotion of equality became seen as part of the core business of the public sector, not just an additional burden.[10] Public bodies have the responsibility to define and enforce the requirements of equality in their areas. They produce regulations and codes which ensure that this duty to promote equality in relation to gender, race, disability, and so on is realized in the routine activities of making contracts, commissioning works, employment and offering services to the public. To adapt the language of private law, the primary (or compliance) obligation to respect rights like equality lies on the public official. The secondary (or remedial) obligation is for that body to provide a remedy when the primary obligation has not been complied with, but such a secondary obligation may sometimes not come into effect until there has been a judicial decision. In other words, secondary obligations can be of two kinds. On the one hand, there are autonomous remedial obligations by which the public official is required to provide a remedy himself, such as the duty to withdraw an invalid decision.[11] There are also enforced secondary obligations, by which a court orders an official to provide a remedy, or provides the substitute remedy itself. If we adopt the perspective of the official or the public sector body, we gain a better perspective on how the constitutional protection of fundamental rights by

---

[7] Albert HY Chen and Miguel Poiares Maduro, 'The Judiciary and Constitutional Review' in Mark Tushnet, Thomas Fleiner and Cheryl Saunders (eds), *Routledge Handbook of Constitutional Law* (Routledge 2013) 104–6.

[8] Ronald M Dworkin, *Law's Empire* (Fontana Press 1986) 397–9.

[9] Bob Hepple, *Equality: The New Legal Framework* (Hart 2011) 134 ff.

[10] Ibid., 134.

[11] See CE Ass. 3 February 1989, *Cie Alitalia*, AJDA 1989, 387 note Fouquet; CE Sect. 10 January 1930, *Despujol*, Leb.30.

the law operates in different legal systems. Compliance by an official is the primary situation to which the law is addressed.

So where do courts fit in? Perspectives on fundamental rights differ. The American tradition has always been to focus on the decisions of courts – a right is anything that a court has declared to be a right. Many of the chapters in this collection have concentrated on that kind of definition as a paradigm (only to distinguish the common law countries studied here from that approach). They do so for a purpose. Constitutional texts are incomplete, so it is natural that the articulation of rights is the product of judicial decisions. Judicial decision-making becomes a primary site for debate about what rights should be. The Belgian chapter makes clear, for example, that the updating which the Belgian Constitutional Court undertakes concerns not only the content of fundamental rights, but also the place of fundamental rights within the Constitution. Similar significance attaches to the decisions of constitutional courts in France and Italy.[12] The constitutional court has often become the authoritative interpreter of the constitution and the place where important debates on the constitution are held. Its decisions become a reference point, but they need to be translated into actions for the administration.

But there is a problem with a court-focused definition of rights. Such a definition encourages the view that a right is something that you can enforce in a court of law. The purpose of the law, however, is not to enable people to win the pathological cases which end up in court. Rather, the function of a right is to impose a duty on a public official which he or she must respect in the ordinary routine decisions and which can be enforced by the beneficiary in a number of ways, both judicial and non-judicial. Looked at from that perspective, the right needs to be clear, because the official needs to know what to do in order to comply. If the right needs to be vague, then it really only serves as a principle of action, a point of orientation in discretionary decision-making, rather than a binary rule which either applies or does not apply.

If we adopt the point of view of the official, then the comparison of the constitutional protection of fundamental rights has three aspects: the norms, the institutions and the processes.

[12] See Paolo Passaglia, in Chapter 6, talking about the transformation of the Italian courts into 'the Court of rights'. See also Marc Verdussen, in Chapter 9.

1.1 Norms

If an activity is to be central to the work of public officials, it needs to be laid down clearly. Expectations need to be stated, then communicated and enforced. Norms therefore take three forms: as enacted standards to be followed, as communicated expectations, and as disciplinary standards. My focus here is on the enacted standards, even if it is normal that intermediate communication and incentive structures to ensure compliance are significant in practice in instructing officials in what they must do. (Officials will rarely read the original statutes, but will receive the essentials mediated through digests, circulars and instructions.)

By and large, constitutions or specific bodies of norms like the 2010 Equality Act referred to above set out standards at a high level of abstraction. They are full of vague generalities, such as 'a right to education' or 'a right to association'. To the official on the ground, they are statements of values, points of orientation, rather than specific tasks to be undertaken. They convey approaches to be adopted in their daily work, but not specific instructions of what to do. If the public official is meant to be a guardian of the constitution and its fundamental rights, then such standard-setting norms serve as a reference point and legitimation. This function can be seen by the statement of a former head of the civil service, Lord Wilson, in the UK:

> If [civil servants] think the Minister is behaving in an unconstitutional manner, it is their job to make very clear what they believe the constitutional position is .... If ... they do not get an answer that they think is the proper answer or that is defensible, it is their job to go to the head of the civil service, who would take it up with the Prime Minister if necessary ... . If a Minister, in the end, rejects the advice, and if the Prime Minister rejects the advice and insists on going ahead, then in grey areas it is the job of Ministers to decide where the line should be, and there is a limit to how far the civil service can enforce the constitution, except in the ultimate, nuclear deterrent of resigning.[13]

On this account, a constitutional requirement, such as a fundamental right, becomes a trigger for some enforcement action within the public service, as well as in relation to the particular individual whose right is at issue. The constitutional standard legitimates the actions taken with regard to the minister. If the civil servant is meant to ensure rights are

---

[13] House of Lords, Constitution Committee, Sixth Report 2012: Accountability of Civil Servants, para. 46 <http://www.publications.parliament.uk/pa/ld201213/ldselect/ldconst/61/6102.htm> accessed 14 July 2015.

respected in his or her own sphere of action, then these standards provide reference points, values by which conduct is designed and judged. It is in this second area that more specific statements of what is required are often needed. It is here that communication standards are required. Within public organizations, the requirements of constitutional standards will be translated into more focused and operational statements. Thus, in the field of equality, the public service duty is then translated into codes – guidance for particular sectors, for example, schools or health, and internal codes of practice.[14] There may be circulars around the civil service as a whole.[15] So, for an official, it matters less what the legal status of a rule is than that a standard of conduct is required of her.

At whatever level of specificity rights are stated, problems of identification and interpretation arise.

1.1.1 Identifying rights

The description of legal systems as subject to multilevel governance is well-known. We know that there are rights recognized at different levels. Some people prefer to conceptualize the situation in terms of a hierarchy which locates the international norms within the national legal hierarchy of norms. Others prefer to see the situation as one of pluralism in which there is no absolute sovereign.[16] Whether we conceive this in hierarchical terms or not, there is a problem of integration. On MacCormick's model, legal systems are not necessarily integrated hierarchically.[17] But the decision-maker (our national official) is faced with rights from different sources. There are rights identified textually, either in the national constitution or more specifically in national legislation. Such rights might be the right of asylum, human dignity or the right of the free exercise of religious belief. There may be supranational declarations of rights that are directly applicable. In Europe, these are typically the EU Charter of fundamental rights and the European Convention on Human Rights (ECHR). As a result, rights to administrative fairness, to free movement of the person or to freedom from torture, to a fair trial or to family life

---

[14] Equality and Human Rights Commission, Public Sector Equality Duty <http://www.equalityhumanrights.com/advice-and-guidance/public-sector-duties> accessed 14 July 2015.

[15] See, for example, the French 'Circulaire du 19 janvier 2006 relative au respect des articles 34 et 37 de la Constitution', JORF n°18 of 21 January 2006, p. 1002.

[16] See Neil MacCormick, 'Beyond the Sovereign State' (1993) 56 *MLR* 1.

[17] Ibid., 9–11; Neil MacCormick, *Rhetoric and the Rule of Law* (OUP 2005) 208–9.

may be added to what is specifically in the national texts. On top, there are international law norms. So these might add the rights of a child, or social and economic rights. For the most part, the duty of the official is not to identify the rights themselves (the texts are fairly clear), but to establish a relationship between the different texts, to integrate them into a coherent practice. The official is not simply a messenger boy, sent to obey a series of instructions from different bosses in a random way. Rather, the official has a responsibility that his or her part of the government system operates effectively and that usually means coherently. Of course, coherence may be an ideal, rather than something which is always achieved. But it does entail that the official has to see different rights commitments as an integrated package. This means making the rights fit together in perhaps an original way. MacCormick is right that coherence and consistency are regulative ideals within both legal and administrative reasoning.

1.1.2 Interpreting rights

Interpretation is a major task in relation to rights. The very general terms in which rights are stated requires further specification. Choices have to be made about the scope of rights and their application as well as about the considerations which may override them. As I have stated elsewhere,[18] the function of legal interpretation is to find a norm that is applicable to a present situation, rather than just to discover the original intention of the drafter of a constitution (if that is, in fact, possible). As I have noted, the Belgian Constitution of 1831 is described as interpreted 'in the light of the European Convention on Human Rights', which entered into force in 1953. The constitutional text is interpreted in the light of the various commitments which a country has undertaken over time, and in the light of the current situation with which it is faced. Often the problems are new. For example, the problem of the rights of transsexuals arose both from new medical techniques and new social opinions.[19] In essence, we are asking the question how these words and ideas can be translated into a contemporary context. It is by placing herself in the appropriate context that the interpreter is able to produce an interpretation which is appropriate to the new question or the new

---

[18] John Bell, 'Interpreting Statutes Over Time', in François Ost and Mark Van Hoecke, *Time and Law: Is it the Nature of Law to Last?* (Bruylant 1998) 31–53.

[19] See ECHR 25 March 1992, D. 1993, 101 note Margénaud and Cass. Ass. Plén. 11 December 1992, *René X*, JCP 1993.II.21991 conclusions Jéol, note Memeteau.

situation in which society finds itself. The approach of the European Court of Human Rights (ECtHR) is typical in treating a statement of rights as a 'living instrument', to adapt to changed circumstances and additional rights commitments.

The vision of interpretation which I have just presented accepts that statements of the meaning of legal texts are going inevitably to be provisional and incomplete. They are provisional because new situations and social understandings will arise in which the interpretations of the past will need to be revisited. They are provisional also because a state may make new commitments to fundamental rights and these will have an impact on the way existing rights instruments are interpreted. Because the reconciliation of different norms and their interpretation in application arises in relation to specific problems, any statement will be incomplete. There is not a moment of restatement in a systematic way. The life of the law in this area is one of complexity and provisionality. As a result, it would be fair to say that legal *uncertainty* is a significant reality of any protection of fundamental rights. The contested nature of many of the rights makes the role of courts significant, but makes the job of the official harder. Even if the norms are supposed to be transnational, if not universal, the problem of interpretation may lead to diversity. This diversity is compounded by the structures within which the decision-making of officials is set in each national system.

1.2 Institutions

The previous section has argued that it is necessary for legal norms to be integrated and set out and interpreted in order for them to be effective. From the point of view of the official, there needs to be some authoritative guidance about how this task is to be performed. It is in this context that the importance of institutions emerges. Institutions provide a mechanism for reducing the inevitable uncertainty that surrounds the statement and practice of fundamental rights within a legal system.

Besselink has argued that legal systems differ in the degree of integration that they provide.[20] The common law systems with strict ideas of judicial precedent favour the approach of hierarchical integration at an institutional level: the decision of a supreme court prevails over any other court and its decisions provide a common reference point within the legal system. A system of reference procedures, such as those developing in

---

20 Leonard Besselink, 'The Proliferation of Constitutional Law and Constitutional Adjudication or How American Judicial Review Came to Europe After All' (2013) 9 *Utrecht Law Review* 19.

France, Spain and Italy, establishes a specialised supreme court focused on constitutional law matters to which other courts refer issues. Such a court establishes rulings on the meaning of the constitution which the other courts are expected to follow. In this way, a different institutional form of normative integration is achieved. In both types of system, the ideal of the integration of constitutional norms on fundamental rights becomes at least partly realized by institutional mechanisms. Within this perspective, order and legal certainty are dominant values in the application of fundamental rights. On the other hand, there are systems which do not offer this degree of formal integration. The French have been used to a number of supreme courts, each supreme within their sphere. Each institution produces decisions setting out its own view of fundamental rights, as they apply to criminal law, administrative law or constitutional law. Co-ordination is not secured institutionally, and there can be periods of significant divergence of opinion. On this view, correctness is the dominant value on fundamental rights (and often in relation to law in general). Paris, in her chapter, explains how there has been a move in France towards the first model through the *Question Prioritaire de Constitutionnalité*, but that it is not as systematic as the German system.[21]

Besselink worries about the proliferation of courts which make determinations on constitutional rights matters. There is a real danger that the same problem can be litigated through a number of different procedural mechanisms. For example, the rights of prisoners might arise through a challenge to an individual decision of the judge overseeing the implementation of the sentence (the *juge de l'application des peines*) or it may come in a challenge to a decision of a governor before the administrative courts.[22] There is a clear problem if the determination of the rights of a prisoner, for example in relation to strip searches, is different depending on the procedure adopted. This complexity is compounded if the same issue is subjected to a decision by the ECtHR in Strasbourg, perhaps in relation to another country. The prison governors and the prison officers are then very confused on how they should respect the rights of a prisoner. Interestingly, the solution adopted to the question of strip searches was to have authoritative statements from a non-judicial body.[23]

The problem of pluralism in institutions compounds the problem of normative complexity. This is particular significant where the different

---

21 See Marie-Luce Paris in Chapter 8.

22 See John Bell, 'Disciplining Prisoners' (2014) 20 *EPL* 15.

23 Ibid.

levels of norms are not considered to be hierarchically integrated and the institutions determining rights are also not hierarchically integrated. The official is then faced not only with a set of texts which he has to fit together, but also with a set of authoritative decisions on the meaning of those texts produced by a range of different institutions. There are the supranational institutions, such as the ECtHR and the Court of Justice of the European Union (CJEU). There may be a constitutional court as well as private law and public law supreme courts. Each is ruling definitively and authoritatively on the rights the official must respect in his dealings with citizens. But they may not be speaking with one voice. So, both substantively and institutionally, the situation of the official is, unhelpfully, complex.

1.3 Process of Rights Protection

Legal systems diverge in relation to the process by which rights are protected. Some systems like Germany (and copying it, Spain) have special procedures, such as references or petitions to a constitutional court, whereas the British-inspired common law systems use the ordinary judicial procedure. Processes are closely connected with institutions. A special legal institution for resolving constitutional issues, among which fundamental rights might figure prominently, tends to give rise to distinct procedures. Where there is a common institution, procedural distinctiveness is much less necessary. But there is a further issue and that concerns the specificity of constitutional questions. If such questions are identified by reference to a specific 'constitutional' text, then that formal legal basis may generate a distinctive kind of litigation or complaint. But where it is much more difficult to identify such a distinctive formal legal basis, then it may be hard to consider that there is, indeed a distinctive 'constitutional' process by which rights are protected.[24] This becomes obvious when we examine substantive issues and whether these are 'constitutional' or not. In particular, fundamental rights will appear in a wide variety of areas. They serve sometimes as peremptory norms, sometimes as standards governing administrative discretion and sometimes as principles of interpretation in relation to relationships between private individuals. As a result, focusing substantively on particular fundamental rights, then the problem can occur in any branch of the legal system and so the process to be followed will diverge from one system to another.

---

[24] See David Feldman, 'The Nature and Significance of "Constitutional" Legislation' (2013) 129 *LQR* 343.

The discussion in Zagor's chapter of the treatment of migrants[25] shows how hard it can be to have an issue recognized as fundamentally 'constitutional' or about 'fundamental rights'. That chapter and those on Ireland[26] within this collection demonstrate clearly that the process to be followed to enforce fundamental rights within administrative law is different from one system to another.

To come back to the official, it may be that judicial processes are actually very remote and have little influence on conduct. If a legal challenge to a decision is defended by a ministry as a whole, the impact on the individual official who took the decision may be very limited. He or she might have to provide some further information, but then the papers will be taken over by a litigation unit and that may be the last he or she hears of them. By the time the legal challenge has been decided, the official may have moved on and may well never know whether the case was won or lost by the claimant. An internal complaint system might have more direct repercussions on the individual. More significantly, disciplinary proceedings will have a very direct impact on the individual and influence future conduct. Appearance before a city council or parliamentary committee to answer questions might also have a very direct influence. My point is that process matters. If you want to have an influence on officials and how they take decisions, then you need to think about the process by which the decision is challenged and how far the official who made the decision is being called to account. Any presentation of the protection of fundamental rights needs to pay attention not only to the rights that individuals have, but also to the process by which redress is offered. Such processes are not just about the clarification of the content of rights (which is often the essential work of a constitutional court), but also the remedy of grievances. In Germany and Spain, the constitutional court is the recipient of complaints about the breach of fundamental rights (the *Verfassungsbeschwerde* and the *amparo*). In other countries, the complaints go elsewhere. A most obvious location in Britain and France is the ombudsman. Here, the investigatory process and its cheapness stand in stark contrast to the expense of court litigation.

1.4 Summary

So, any account of constitutional protection in a system needs to explain not only by what criteria norms relating to fundamental rights are

---

25 See Matthew Zagor in Chapter 4.
26 See Eoin Carolan and Cliona Kelly in Chapters 3.1 and 3.2 respectively.

identified and interpreted (if you like, the rules of recognition), but also the institutions through which fundamental rights are safeguarded and enforced, and the processes (legal or otherwise) by which this happens. The official needs to know not only 'what must I do?', but also 'to whom am I accountable for my performance?' and 'in what way will I be held to account?' Much of the writing on fundamental rights focuses on the first question, and it establishes the normative criteria for conduct. But that literature does not always explain the mechanisms for enforcing rights. Institutions and processes are likely to be specific to a legal system. So, even if the normative standards defining fundamental rights are similar between legal systems, the system of protection as a whole will not be the same. Flexibility and experimentation are inevitable if we have constitutional cultures which are on the move, even in the area of fundamental rights.

2. CONSTITUTIONS AS WORK IN PROGRESS DOCUMENTS

The second perspective of analysis on constitutions is to see them as bodies of norms and procedures that are produced in conversation with a country's constitutional past, with contemporary social problems and with external standards. These different dimensions help us to understand the peculiarities of different legal systems and the reasons why they may be in constant evolution. They are 'work in progress' documents, rather than foundational monuments. The need to adjust to social change may seem to be an essentially political imperative – a need to build support or legitimacy for the regime. At first sight, this may not appear to be a legal (normative) issue: legal rules would remain binding, even if it were considered politically illegitimate. But, as Smith noted,[27] the constitution exists to operate effectively in a political world. So it is part of the inherent dynamic of a constitution to be subject to pressures of a legal kind, and to achieve change in both the legal and the political spheres. Constitutional texts are adopted at very specific times for specific purposes. They are dealing with problems that have presented themselves in the immediate past or the challenges of the immediate future. To that extent, 'transplants' from other systems are problematic because the institutions or rules of one legal system were designed for a different

---

[27] Eivind Smith (ed.), *The Constitution as an Instrument of Change* (SNS Förlag 2003) 11, 15.

time and context. If something is transplanted, it will quickly be adapted.[28] It is more likely that one country will look at other countries that it sees as closer to its ideals on particular topics and seek inspiration from them. But the importing country has its own problems to solve and needs to ensure that the results are appropriate to its circumstances. So, 'inspiration and adaptation' are more likely than 'transplants'.[29]

The best way to understand the provisional character of constitutional instruments, including declarations of fundamental rights, is to pay attention to the constitutional reference points: conversations with the constitutional past, with contemporary needs and with external reference points.

2.1 Conversation with the Past

Most of the authors in this volume feel the need to start their explanation of their system with history. This illustrates that a constitution is the product of past practice and experience. A constitution may be a way of providing for a new start, but you do not begin with a *tabula rasa*. A country knows what has worked in the past and what has not. So the principle of judicial independence in the English Constitution was set out in the Act of Settlement of 1701. The relevant provisions were drafted with the recent experience of the attempts by James II to secure a compliant judiciary.[30] These principles were restated in a very different context in 2005, when the Constitutional Reform Act sought to establish a clearer separation of powers to conform to the Human Rights Act 1998 and to deal with the abolition of the office of the Lord Chancellor.[31] A further example is the way in which the German Basic Law of 1949 begins with protections of fundamental rights, whereas the Weimar Constitution of 1919 did not. The experience of the Nazi period made the Constituent Assembly wish to mark out a new departure.

The conversation with the past can make the list of constitutional provisions in any one country idiosyncratic. The choice of items to make

---

[28] See, for example, Catherine Dupré, *Importing the Law in Post-Communist Transitions* (Hart 2003) 153–4; David Nelken, 'Towards a Sociology of Legal Adaptation' in David Nelken and Johannes Feest, *Adapting Legal Cultures* (Hart 2001) 13–15.

[29] See John Bell, *French Legal Cultures* (Butterworths 2001) ch 1.

[30] Simon Shetreet and Sophie Turenne, *Judges on Trial* (2nd edn, CUP 2013) 22–31.

[31] Ibid., 7–11.

'constitutional' reflects the heritage of the past. Boyron[32] argues that the French Constitution of 1958 has to be understood in terms of its history, as a merger of different traditions that have developed since the Revolution. She notes that it is impossible to contemplate a unicameral Parliament after the experience of the Convention and the Second Republic, which ended in dictatorships. Likewise, the symbolic importance of the 1789 Declaration of the Rights of Man and of the Citizen is such that it could not be replaced by a contemporary restatement of rights.[33] Constitutional history would explain why English law did not have a right of association or a right of assembly before the Human Rights Act 1998. Instead, the topics were covered under the heading of 'Police Powers': how *the police* could lawfully stop people doing something, rather than what *people* were entitled to do. Associations of particular kinds had a defence to a claim that they were unlawful conspiracies, and, as a consequence, they were lawful. As Charles J put it in 1888, there is no right of public meeting, but people may do such an act lawfully.[34]

The presence of particular provisions says more about the context of constitution-making than about what is inherently 'constitutional'. Later interpreters of the constitution have to determine how to make sense of the provisions which happen to be included. They may conclude that the exclusion of a particular right was an anomaly or was merely circumstantial. An example of an anomaly was the exclusion of the right of association from the Preamble to the French Constitution of 1946. It was not a right recognized in the 1789 Declaration because associations were seen too much as potentially subversive or anti-social groupings, such as those prohibited in the *loi Le Chapelier* of 1791.[35] But by 1901, the reluctance to accept associations had waned. Accordingly, the decision by the French Constitutional Council in 1971 to accord constitutional status to the right of association reflected accepted standards, even if these were not explicit in the texts that made up the Constitution.[36] The Belgian

---

32 Boyron (n 4) ch 1.

33 Ibid., 26–7.

34 *R v Cunningham Graham and Burns* (1888) 16 Cox 420, 429 (Charles J). See generally David Feldman, 'Civil Liberties' in Vernon Bogdanor, *The British Constitution in the Twentieth Century* (British Academy 2003) 401–2, 408.

35 See John Bell, *French Constitutional Law* (OUP 1992) 149–51.

36 Ibid., 151–2, 272–3: CC Decision no. 71-44 DC of 16 July 1971. See also the right to education specifically excluded in 1946, but 'discovered' by the Constitutional Council in 1977: Ibid., 152, 319–20.

chapter shows clearly how the presence or absence of constitutional rights can be the product of political lobbying.[37]

At the same time, history is not determinative and the interpretation of the provision may be revised substantially. For example, Article 21(2) of the 1949 German Basic Law banned political parties that had as an aim the subversion of the basic democratic order. In the early years of the Federal Republic, this was used to ban a neo-Nazi party and the Communist Party and the Constitutional Court upheld this. But as the worries of the early years subsided, successor organizations were allowed to operate and, in 2003, an attempt to use the provision against a far right party failed.[38] This example shows that there can be revision of views even on fundamental rights.

History provides countries with a learning experience of what works and what does not. It also explains the current state of a country, its social divisions and its institutions. We do not start with a *tabula rasa*, we build on past experience, and the past is a reference point.

2.2 Conversation with Contemporary Problems

The German cases just discussed illustrate the way in which views about fundamental rights may change over time. The reason is that the rights do not just continue values from the past, but relate to the contemporary situation. In that case, the threat posed by minor political parties to the stability of democracy was seen as much less important beyond ten years after the Basic Law had come into force compared with the early days of the Federal Republic. A constitution or a declaration of fundamental rights is about what should happen now, not about what was thought to be good in the past. The document is a living instrument, which has to adapt in order to regulate the sort of situation which is now current. The constitutional court may be concerned to give a proper interpretation in the light of the wording of the constitution inherited from the past, but it also needs a solution which relates to the needs of the present. Although there may be great socio-economic similarity amongst the countries in this volume, there are also differences which make it appropriate for constitutions to do different things.

To begin with, some countries have special social issues, which affects what may be treated as a fundamental right. Belgium is an example in

[37] See Marc Verdussen in Chapter 9.

[38] See BVerfG 18 March 2003, *NPD*, 2 BvB 1/01; and DP Currie, *The Constitution of the Federal Republic of Germany* (University of Chicago Press 1994) 215–21.

that it is divided socially into linguistic communities in radical ways which need to be reflected in the Belgian Constitution. The emphasis on federalism in the Belgian chapter, but also (differently) in the Spanish chapter show that context is very important.[39] The fundamental rights of linguistic communities resident in a region run by the other linguistic community becomes a matter of great significance, since they define both the regions and the communities. At the same time, Article 30 of the Belgian Constitution protects the freedom of the individual: 'The use of languages common in Belgium is optional; it may only be regulated by statute and only in relation to acts of public power and for judicial matters.' By contrast, the French have sought to entrench the use of the French language through the Constitution through a 1992 revision to Article 2 of the Constitution.[40]

Every country professes the need for racial equality, but the interpretation can be very different. Whereas the British have enacted a duty to maintain statistics as part of a public sector equality duty, other countries, such as France and Germany, would refuse this idea on the ground that it contradicts equality. The French see people as French and then it is not possible to distinguish between them.[41] There is necessarily an attempt to manage social values such as language in Belgium, church and state in Ireland. These values affect the contemporary society and are not just historical.

2.3 Conversation with External Standards

In his chapter, Carolan shows the way in which the Irish Constitution was shaped by external models.[42] Similarly, at various times, French constitutional deliberation was shaped by reflection on the US, for example by de Toqueville, then by Lambert and finally by de Gaulle. It was also influenced by Austrian and German experiences. Foreign references are common when current domestic constitutional arrangements reach a crisis and thought turns to new ways of running the country. This is not to say that a country will slavishly copy another system. For example, Lambert used a careful study of the US Supreme Court to reject the idea of constitutional review for France.[43] When constitution-making is happening, then external standards are more likely to be used, especially in

[39] See Marc Verdussen in Chapter 9, and Agustín Robledo in Chapter 7.
[40] See CC Decision No 94-345 DC of 29 July 1994 (*Loi Toubon*).
[41] See John Bell, *European Judicial Cultures* (CUP 2006).
[42] See Eoin Carolan in Chapter 3.
[43] See Bell, *French Constitutional Law* (n 35) 27.

the area of fundamental rights. For example, Spain, emerging from a period of dictatorship, took particular note of the constitutions of two countries – Italy and Germany – which had successfully managed the transition from fascism to democracy.

Countries in Europe are geographically small and are inter-connected. They cannot just look inward to what they might adopt from their own experience. Indeed, from what was said earlier about the shifting territorial boundaries and populations of European states, then there is probably a range of experiences of constitutions even within a single European state. In such a context, other countries are a natural reference point for deciding what are the objectives which a country ought to realize – are they doing the right thing?

External standards may act as a source of inspiration. More controversially, they may serve as a guide to interpretation.[44] In this last area, it is a matter of the foreign law being a reference point for the correctness of a common provision. Where one has one's own constitutional provisions and is interpreting those, then it is less common that an external reference will be appropriate. To my mind, the most important combination is the way in which the argument from a foreign legal system adds lustre to an argument already available in the host legal system. This is because I believe the mechanism by which a foreign legal idea takes root in the host legal system is essentially by means of the mechanism of 'cross-fertilization'.[45] Through this form of influence, there remains an indigenous reason for a decision that integrates well within the host legal order. The foreign legal arguments may shape the debate and cast some possible solutions in a better light. But typically there is no wholesale direct transplanting of the solution from another system, unless it also integrates with a local solution.

In the case of supranational norms and their interpretative organs, these are not, in one sense, 'external'. They are a different part of the internal normative system. On the other hand, the voice of courts in Strasbourg – the ECtHR – and Luxembourg – the CJEU – are often felt to be disruptive of the national dialogue, but on the other hand, it provides a common reference point. Walker has pointed to the reflexive character of the relationship between national and EU levels, especially courts.[46] The

---

44 See John Bell, 'The Relevance of Foreign Arguments to Legal Development' (2011) 21 *Duke J Comp & Int'l L* 431.

45 Ibid., 450.

46 Neil Walker, 'The Migration of Constitutional Ideas and the Migration of *the* Constitutional Idea: The Case of the EU' in Sujit Choudhry (ed.), *The Migration of Constitutional Ideas* (CUP 2006) ch 12.

shared enterprise of protecting fundamental rights provides a reference point external to the simple national debate. The extent to which one national system is responsive to these norms is a concern.

The Italian author in this collection accepts the idea of a 'dialogue' between courts as the process through which a decision is reached on the meaning of fundamental rights.[47] This is not so much a formal process by which one institution defers to the views of another. Rather there is a process of alignment which arises from interactions over time. My own view would be that we should view the process not as a dialogue between a national court and a supranational court, for example the ECtHR. Rather, there is a 'conversation' in which a number of courts at national and supranational level participate, often in relation to a number of cases. The conversation is about a problem and the individual cases are instances which cause reflection to occur. The idea of a conversation, like that of dialogue, conveys a sense that the process is open-ended and there is not necessarily a definitive voice which closes the conversation with a decision. If we recognize the imperfection of human understanding, as well as the imperfection of the way in which principles are expressed, then we have to accept provisionality of decisions and uncertainty for all concerned. Each court is striving to develop the best understanding that it can of what rights involve. But they will not always succeed in getting it right first time. So there are reversals of decisions, conflicts between courts at national and supranational level. The Belgian chapter talks of the 'combination' and the 'reconciliation' of rights at national and supranational level. This model is not one of chaos, but of structured deliberation in circumstances of limited time and limited capacity to deliberate. Unlike in the hierarchical model, there is no authoritative figure to end discussion with a ruling. The image of a conversation reflects long-standing views in management that innovation requires flexibility and speed, so the model of the large-scale integrated organization needs to give way to the model of an entrepreneurial organization which gives priority to the opportunity to try innovative ideas (including the opportunity to fail).[48] To some extent this is inevitable if we move away from a model under which a single court takes the final decision on what must be done (either by hierarchical appeal or by reference) and move towards a decentralized and (loosely) coordinated system. Under the latter, it is the job of all public institutions to do their best to give

---

47 See Paolo Passaglia in Chapter 6.

48 Tom Peters, *Thriving on Chaos* (Pan Books 1987) 27.

effect to fundamental rights, and there may therefore be diversity in the solutions adopted.

3. CONCLUSION

Comparison between constitutions and their protection of fundamental rights leads us to expect that rights are not fixed, but are part of a moving picture of the constitutional life of a country. Statements of fundamental rights have to articulate both social aspirations and a baseline of minimum standards. For example, statements of welfare rights, which are positive duties on the state, are more aspirational in that they do not come with immediately obvious consequences. Thus, the right to education implies a duty on the part of the state to make provision, but this cannot be open-ended. It cannot mean that the state must pay for whatever parents want.[49] By contrast, classical liberal fundamental rights in relation to bodily integrity (for example, freedom from torture, arrest or imprisonment) are much more a matter of a social baseline below which it would be unacceptable to fall, especially as these involve mainly negative duties on the state.

The chapters in this collection offer illustrations of the way understandings and applications of fundamental rights are likely to change over time. What we understand as inappropriate detention changes in a climate of the fear of international terrorism. The right to employment becomes very different in the era of austerity than in an era of fairly full employment.

From the point of view of the official who has to realize fundamental rights in her daily routine, this flexibility and experimental nature of rights poses problems. Respect for rights is an obligation to do your best, rather than to achieve a result. It is a duty to be guided by certain values in the conduct of the ordinary routine of work. The official might consider such a requirement daunting and potentially difficult to comply with. But the context makes the duty more manageable. That duty is situated first within institutions and processes. There are organs of the state which provide guidance about what, in reality, needs to be done. Among those organs, the courts play a role as interpreter and as an authoritative guide to the current state of fundamental rights. There are

---

[49] See Gregorio Camara Villar, 'Constitucion y Educacion' in Gumersindo Trujillo, Luis Lopez Guerra, and Paolo Gonzales-Trevijano, *La Experiencia Constitutucional (1975–2000)* (Centro de Estudios Politicos y Constitucionales 2000) 265, 275–6.

established processes designed to ensure that fundamental rights are respected. But these institutions and processes are likely to differ from one country to the next, even if the normative duties on the officials are likely to share similarities. The second context is the constitutional culture of conversation between the current people applying the fundamental rights and the past and present needs of that society, with an eye towards external benchmarks and inspirations. The conversation shapes the perspectives of the official and those seeking to guide her. She is not left to work it all out for herself. Whereas there may seem to be many normative challenges involved in the application of fundamental rights, there may be, in practice, fewer problems because of the institutional setting and constitutional culture within which the official operates. But the constitutional culture of conversation differs from country to country. Even if some of the external reference points are the same (as they frequently are when countries share a commitment to a supranational legal order), the different experiences from the past and the distinctive problems of a particular society will make its expression and emphasis within fundamental rights distinctive.

The perspective of the official helps us to understand why constitutional traditions of fundamental rights protection may differ from one country to another. That perspective makes us pay particular attention to institutions and processes, as well as to the constitutional past and societal needs as features which may make one legal system different from another. On the other hand, the normative standards and the external reference points (also typically normative) may well be common and create a momentum for convergence. It is in the balance of these different features of a legal system that the tension identified by Gardbaum is lived out in the practice of a particular legal community. Comparative law in this context serves not to identify 'best' answers or 'best' practice, but to make us aware of the specific features of our own constitutional traditions, both why they work and what might be the specific constraints which we take for granted.

Index